"How is it that some biblical texts *justify* God's role in the Babylonian destruction of Judah, while others *protest* God's actions, and others cast *doubt* on God's justice in light of these events? If you want a compelling treatment that is careful to let the diverse biblical texts speak for themselves, look no further than *Voices from the Ruins*. Rather than viewing the diversity of biblical perspectives as problematic, Dalit Rom-Shiloni's careful analysis surprisingly reveals that diverse theological pluralism is an essential characteristic of biblical texts as God's people struggled to hold together their conceptions of divine justice, human responsibility, and divine mercy. Students and scholars alike stand to benefit from a careful reading of this insightful treatment of the biblical texts."

— Paul S. Evans
McMaster Divinity College

"Dalit Rom-Shiloni, in *Voices from the Ruins*, makes a significant contribution to the field of biblical theology. With a close and probing examination of texts in Jeremiah, Ezekiel, Psalms, and Lamentations, she focuses on how ancient Judeans grappled with the questions of divine power, presence, and fidelity, in relation to the destruction of Jerusalem in 587/586 BCE. Is G-d powerful, present, and trustworthy? These texts attempt to answer in the affirmative even as they recognize that G-d had failed to protect Jerusalem and Judah as promised. Her study is relevant for understanding divine presence, power, and fidelity in the present, too, as we moderns come to grips with questions raised by the Shoah (Holocaust), as well as justice and righteousness in our own contemporary world."

— Marvin A. Sweeney
Claremont School of Theology at Willamette University

"Dalit Rom-Shiloni meticulously analyzes the texts created by Israelite thinkers in the late sixth century as they reflected on the moral defensibility of YHWH's use of mass deportations and destruction. She shows these texts to be deeply interrelated, and in doing so reframes discussion not only of the relationship between theodicy and protest but of the nature of Hebrew Bible theology itself."

— Mark W. Hamilton
Abilene Christian University

"This rich, penetrating analysis should become a starting point for anyone interested in describing how the ancient Israelites thought about their God. It moves theology out of the realm of the ideal and into that of history by showing how the Israelites foregrounded the themes of 'justification, doubt, and protest' in their representations of God, especially in response to the upheavals of the sixth century BCE. Rom-Shiloni has made a major contribution with this new way of doing biblical theology."

— DAVID LAMBERT
University of North Carolina

VOICES FROM THE RUINS

*Theodicy and the Fall of Jerusalem
in the Hebrew Bible*

DALIT ROM-SHILONI

WILLIAM B. EERDMANS PUBLISHING COMPANY
GRAND RAPIDS, MICHIGAN

Wm. B. Eerdmans Publishing Co.
4035 Park East Court SE, Grand Rapids, Michigan 49546
www.eerdmans.com

27 26 25 24 23 22 21   1 2 3 4 5 6 7

ISBN 978-0-8028-7860-1

Library of Congress Cataloging-in-Publication Data

Names: Rom-Shiloni, Dalit, author.
Title: Voices from the ruins : theodicy and the fall of Jerusalem in the
     Hebrew Bible / Dalit Rom-Shiloni.
Description: Grand Rapids, Michigan : William B. Eerdmans Publish-
     ing Company, 2021. | Includes bibliographical references and index. |
     Summary: "An examination of the Hebrew Bible's theological discourse
     in the face of the catastrophic events of the Neo-Babylonian exiles and
     the destruction of the Jerusalem temple"—Provided by publisher.
Identifiers: LCCN 2020046889 | ISBN 9780802878601 (hardcover)
Subjects: LCSH: Theodicy—Biblical teaching. | Bible. Old Testament—
     Theology. | God—Biblical teaching. | Providence and government of
     God—Judaism. | Temple of Jerusalem (Jerusalem)
Classification: LCC BS1199.T44 R67 2021 | DDC 231/.8—dc23
LC record available at https://lccn.loc.gov/2020046889

To the blessed memory of Talia Abramovitz-Zwebner,
wishing strength to her loving family and friends

Contents

PREFACE

This study grows out of many years spent in the company of the biblical writings from the time of the destruction and exiles, during which time I was able to elucidate a number of the complex issues at stake for this corpus.[1] This process clarified for me in a stronger way the need within the discipline for a programmatic discussion of a non-Christian/non-Jewish Hebrew Bible theology—as a descriptive enterprise, one that has as its goal the articulation of what the Hebrew Bible speakers have to say in and for their own times, rather than the construction of a usable theology for modern faithful readers. The present context allows me to further develop the more general methodological contours of such a non-faith-driven, descriptive Hebrew Bible theology.[2]

My previous work suggested that an ideal first target for the development of such a methodological approach would be precisely the literature of the critical sixth century BCE. My continuing focus on this period offered the advantage of a demarcated body of sources for such a descriptive project. The most significant development suggested in this book is my advancement of "theodicy as discourse" as the rubric by which we may seek to understand the interplay of ideas in the sixth century.

This book is divided into two parts. Part I establishes the methodological foreground of the entire project, addressing four major tasks.

Chapter 1 presents the overall theological theme of theodicy as discourse. The modern definition of theodicy as justification of God, commonly accepted by both Jews and Christians, is shown to be less than satisfactory for an understanding of the Hebrew Bible on its own terms. Instead, the

---

1. See Rom-Shiloni, *God in Times of Destruction*; "Facing Destruction"; and "Psalm 44."
2. See also Rom-Shiloni, "Hebrew Bible Theology."

chapter articulates a notion of theodical discourse as the framework that best suits the interplay of voices with shared and diverging viewpoints.

Chapter 2 lays the foundation for the broader discussion of Hebrew Bible theology and builds the framework for a descriptive theological study. In search of methodological principles for studying the theologies of the Hebrew Bible, this chapter reveals a controversy between Christian and Jewish scholars (and theologians), as well as among Jewish scholars of Hebrew Bible theology as to what constitutes the proper aim, principles, and content of Hebrew Bible theology.

Chapter 3 describes the multiplicity of voices and the diversity of thought within the target corpora. Each section of this chapter outlines common scholarly approaches to the sources, challenges them, and sets out an alternative approach. An overarching methodological question is whether conceptualizing these sources as reflective of social or cultural dichotomies of different sorts—official and unofficial voices, orthodox and nonorthodox stances, or core and peripheral attitudes—is the most helpful approach to the description of the theological polemics seen in these sources. I suggest that theodical discourse is a more fruitful way to understand the polysemy of theological perspectives that form a discourse among equals. The presentation of the biblical sources allows me to further challenge traditional literary-historical approaches and to suggest an alternative, more complex methodology that takes into consideration both literary approaches and trauma studies. Such a methodology allows both synchronic and diachronic dimensions into the study of these theological reactions to the catastrophe.

Chapter 4 summarizes the previous methodological discussions and consolidates a proposition for a Tanakh/Hebrew Bible theology based on the shared conception of God as king.

Part II of this book goes to the texts themselves, to delve into the theological deliberations of the sixth century BCE in both Judah and Babylon. In chapter 5, I develop the argument that these deliberations are structured through the metaphor and the conception of God as king. Anthropomorphism emerges as the root metaphor that structures the different conceptions of God as king, through the related images of God as warrior for and judge of his people that permeate the texts. The subsequent chapters trace these two major roles of God: chapters 6–9 discuss conceptions of God as warrior, and chapters 10–12 focus on God as judge. Each chapter sets out the conceptual grounds that constitute the shared theological heritage and points of departure for the internal polemics concerning God's role in the catastrophes of the sixth century. Closer study of our sources reveals the plurality of sixth-century religious thought and enables a careful look into the interrelationships between the antagonists. The analysis of each complex of images concerning God's roles as king rotates through the three modes of the theodical discourse: justification, doubt, and protest.

The closing chapter (13) brings into view the entire theological map emerging from our sources, articulating the lines of agreement and disagreement, of innovative and traditional thoughts, expressed by historiographers, prophets, poets, and laypeople. Chapters 5–12 illustrate that beyond the things that kept them apart, all these voices shared basic conceptions of God, and they all struggled within a framework of theodical discourse to reconcile the disastrous reality with their sincerely pious conceptions of God as lord of his people.

English Bible translations are mainly from NJPS, frequently supplemented with my own translations. Verse numbers are given according to NJPS.

Bibliographic items are cited in the footnotes in shortened format, using author's surname + short title + page number. Full bibliographic data may be found in the bibliography.

ACKNOWLEDGMENTS

The search for a proper critical-descriptive methodology for Hebrew Bible theology motivated the writing of this book. My search in turn was spurred by the realization that the biblical sources that reflect on the Babylonian destruction of Jerusalem and Judah through the sixth century BCE (the Neo-Babylonian and early Persian periods) share a passionate concern with the problem of theodicy. They struggle over how to understand God's role in the events of destruction and exile. All the biblical speakers recorded in these sources are motivated by this question, whether they tried to justify God or are moved to expressions of doubt or even direct protest against him.

The ideas in this book were shaped through presentations and discussions in a number of contexts, and I owe a tremendous debt of appreciation to several diverse scholarly communities. I want to thank colleagues from the Society of Biblical Literature's Theology of Hebrew Scriptures Section and the International Society of Biblical Literature's Biblical Theology Section for our collegial and ongoing dialogue and for encouraging me to bring this study to fruition. I thank my colleagues Adele Berlin, Georg Fischer, Christian Frevel, and Konrad Schmid for long and intriguing talks and, not least, for our continual and respectful disagreements. I greatly appreciate the comments suggested by David Lambert and Marvin Sweeney over the last stage of the manuscript. Needless to say, any remaining imperfections may be laid at my own door. Thanks are due also to my colleagues and students in the Department of Biblical Studies of Tel Aviv University for intriguing me with their questions and perspectives.

The book gained its final shape in the summer of 2014 in Amsterdam, in Israel during 2015, in Oxford and in Zürich on a sabbatical leave in 2016, and finally back home in Jerusalem throughout 2017 to 2020. I thank Athalya Brenner for allowing me the privilege of writing in unique surroundings in Amsterdam; and likewise Jan Willem van Henten of the University of Amsterdam for his warm hospitality in Amsterdam over that summer. I extend my thanks to Martin Goodman, the president of the Oxford Centre for Hebrew and Jewish Studies in the University of Oxford, together with Jan Joosten, Hindy Najman, Alison Salvesen, and Sarah Pearce for their inspiring support over 2016, and to Konrad Schmid at the Theological Faculty of the University of Zürich.

This study was completed thanks to the generous help of the Israel Science Foundation, which funded the English editing (ISF grant 1860/11). This tremendous work was done by Dr. Ruth Clements, who for now well over a decade has been my first reader and my very meticulous critic. I greatly appreciate all she contributed to crystalizing my words and thoughts. The Chaim Rosenberg School of Jewish Studies and Archaeology and Yoran-Sznycer Endowment Fund in Memory of Their Parents Hannah and Shmuel supported the last phase of preparing the manuscript, and I am grateful to my student, Itai Argeman, for his work on the bibliography.

The book gained its last form and editorial shaping by the dedicated and professional team at Eerdmans Publishing. I am grateful to Andrew Knapp, the development editor, for his initial interest in the manuscript and his support; to the project editor, Jenny Hoffman, for handling the entire production; to the copyeditor, David Aiken, for his unbelievably tremendous and meticulous work; to the director of marketing and publicity, Laura Bardolph Hubers; and to many others who remained behind the scenes.

My loving family, my partner and husband Amnon, and our now grown-up children, Eshel and Moran, along with Jonathan and Aria; Carmel and Avidan, along with Hallel-Ya'eli, Ya'ir-Ya'akov, and Gefen-Yehudit; and Elad and Danny, have been the source of support I needed throughout this project. Both Elad and Danny assisted me with the graphics of this volume with great patience.

On a personal note, this book is dedicated to the blessed memory of Talia Abramovitz-Zwebner, a delightful, bright young lady and the best sister-friend of my Carmel. Talia fought cancer and unfortunately succumbed at the age of 27 (Jerusalem, April 15, 2015; Nisan 27). I hope that the discussions that follow here may allow Talia's loving family to gain strength and courage not only to search for justification, but also to cry in protest and still not to lose hope.

DALIT ROM-SHILONI
Jerusalem, Israel

ABBREVIATIONS

Dtr1	Deuteronomistic preexilic (Josian) editorial strand of Kings
Dtr2	Deuteronomistic exilic editorial strand of Kings
DtrJ	Deuteronomist-Jeremiah
LXX	Septuagint
MT	Masoretic Text
NJPS	*The Tanakh: The Holy Scriptures: The New JPS Translation according to the Traditional Hebrew Text* (Philadelphia: Jewish Publication Society, 1985)
PAN	prophecies against the nations

"Voices from the Ruins" is more than a catchy title. This book explores theological deliberations during one of the most critical periods in the history of Judah. The destruction of the temple, the fall of Jerusalem, and the capture of King Zedekiah in 586 BCE sealed the crushing defeat of the kingdom of Judah at the hands of the forces of the Babylonian king, Nebuchadnezzar II (605–562). These events followed approximately twenty years of subjugation to the Neo-Babylonian Empire, including several waves of deportations to Babylon; the Davidic dynasty came to an end when this last king of Judah was imprisoned and taken to Riblah and then to Babylon, where his sons were slaughtered before his eyes (2 Kgs 25:6–7).[1]

My interest in these theological deliberations arose from considering four major characteristics of Hebrew Bible compositions that reflect on the destruction and dislocation of the sixth century and are unique among surrounding cultures.

First, the Hebrew Bible preserves the voices of those who are defeated by and subjugated under the Babylonian Empire. This unique quality of the Hebrew Bible has long been recognized in reference to the earlier subjugation of Northern Israel to the Assyrian Empire in the eighth and seventh centuries. While thousands of written sources from the Neo-Assyrian Empire attest to its royal ideologies and international control, the Hebrew

---

1. Detailed accounts of the destruction and waves of deportation are found in 2 Kgs 24:8–25:30; Jer 39, 52. Other historical passages in Jeremiah attest to the circumstances of the final siege (21:1–10; 32:1–15; 34:8–22; chaps. 37–38). 2 Chr 36 features an abbreviated description of the period of the last kings of Judah. For the historical background see Malamat, "Last Kings of Judah" and "Twilight of Judah"; and Lipschits, *Fall and Rise of Jerusalem*, 1–133.

Bible supplies the other side of the coin, that of the peoples under imperial subjugation.[2]

The current study focuses on the Neo-Babylonian destruction of Judah and the deportations of its people. Whereas many other peoples of the ancient Near East suffered similar fates, only Hebrew Bible authors left us with abundant written literary compositions reflecting that time, created throughout that era and into the early Persian period. For my purposes, the corpus is restricted to Hebrew Bible sources that are explicitly and directly contextualized by those catastrophic events: the historiographical book of Kings, the prophetic books of Jeremiah and Ezekiel, and laments within Psalms and Lamentations. These sources, of diverse genres and perspectives, are narratively set within shared chronological and geographical boundaries.[3] Their chronological framework belongs to the Neo-Babylonian period, starting roughly with Josiah's death (609) and with Jerusalem's political subjugation to Babylon (604) following Nebuchadnezzar II's victory at Carchemish (605).[4] The narrative time frame culminates in the depressing era following the destruction (circa 560); thus, the restoration period is not included in this time frame, and the later boundary is drawn prior to 538.[5] The geographical precincts include

2. This unique perspective is pointed out by Tadmor, "Ahaz and Tiglath-Pileser"; Machinist, "Assyria and Its Image"; Cogan, *Imperialism and Religion*; McKay, *Religion in Judah*; and Morrow, "Tribute from Judah." The Neo-Babylonian records give much less information on the political and international aspects of the control over the empire; see Vanderhooft, *Neo-Babylonian Empire*.

3. The literary history of each of those compositions is of course more complex and stretches over a longer period. I adopt the position that most of those sources are composed during the course of the entire sixth century and thus down to the early Persian period; I further recognize that only relatively few passages within those compositions should be dated beyond this time frame (see §3.4).

4. The list of literary compositions written within this time frame and in the two geographical centers may indeed be much longer; but many of those not considered here constitute, at the most, only indirect sources for these traumatic national events. This is one substantial arena in which the present study (chaps. 5–7) differs from Carr's book on *indirect* reflections of the national trauma; see *Holy Resilience*, 7–8, 74–76.

5. Compare Middlemas (*Troubles of Templeless Judah*, 1–23), who takes the "templeless" period to include 587–515 and chooses to focus on evidence within Judah for ongoing cultic worship over this period; in *Templeless Age*, Middlemas traces several theological responses over time from "immediate responses to disaster, weal and woe, and visions of renewal and restoration" (137); thus she includes in her discussions Second Isaiah, Haggai and Zechariah (1–8), and the Holiness Code.

Judah (Egypt) and Babylon, the major regions in which Judeans are settled as of the Jehoiachin exile (598) and in the course of the sixth century.[6]

Second, more than anything else, these Hebrew Bible sources provide theologically oriented accounts of the historical events that took place in Judah and its environs. God is portrayed as actively involved in specific events and directly responsible for the fate of Jerusalem and its inhabitants. These explicit conceptions of God found among Judean communities in Judah and in Babylon in light of the historical catastrophe are at the heart of the present investigation.

The leading question I posed as I read the sources was: What did they (i.e., prophets, kings, historiographers, poets, and the people) say about God?—about God's role in the destruction and the exiles, about divine justice, and about the implications of this national catastrophe for the relationship between God and his people—both for their own times and for generations to come. An answer, or more precisely answers, to this multifaceted question emerges in the course of the current investigation through the mapping of the diverse theological deliberations with their manifold distinctions and interconnections.

The Hebrew Bible texts discussed here express theological conceptions, religious emotions, and thoughts concerning the God of Israel and other gods. The texts expose the people's national-religious identity and their connections to their land.[7] They attest to a wide spectrum of theological conceptions that required revision, reexamination, or even deeper transformation in the wake of the events that led to the destruction of Jerusalem, God's temple, and the kingdom of Judah by the Babylonians (586), as well as the crises that arose in their aftermath.

Third, this rich interplay of theological deliberations manifests one formative and shared theological conception and one primary shared theo-

---

6. Although Egypt represents another Judean settlement, the Hebrew Bible corpus of the sixth–fifth centuries seems to stem from either Judah or Babylon. See Rom-Shiloni, *Exclusive Inclusivity*, 1–8.

7. The only exceptions are Neo-Hittite and Aramean royal inscriptions of the ninth and eighth centuries BCE (Kilamuwa, Zakkir, and Bar-Rakib inscriptions), in which the kings refer to their status as Assyrian vassals, each in his own way. But these inscriptions hardly refer to theological issues (an exception is Zakir, lines 2–4, 11–17; see Gibson, *Textbook of Syrian Semitic Inscriptions*, 2.6–17); they certainly do not address their gods with questions such as those reflected in the Hebrew Bible. On the other side of the coin one may note the Mesha Inscription (Ahituv, *Echoes from the Past*, 389–418), which indeed testifies to a theology of war, to the distress to Israel caused by subjugation, and to the release from that time of distress (see §9.1.5).

logical framework. The major formative conception of God found through-out this collection of sources is an overarching concept of God as king, as ruler of Israel and controller of its history, including the events of the present crises. This conception is illustrated via the root metaphor of God as an anthropomorphic king, which is expressed through the related im-ages of God's roles as warrior, as judge, and as sovereign of his people.

The shared theological framework that embraces all these sources and their God-talk is one of "theodicy as discourse." The term "theod-icy" generally denotes the struggle to come to terms with the actions of a God deemed to be just, in the face of unbearable suffering; the notion of "discourse" recognizes that the theological ideas expressed in the sources are shaped in and by the cultural milieu—the religious thought and the national traditions—shared by all the speakers in interaction with one an-other. Employing a descriptive theological methodology, I argue that the wide-ranging theological deliberations evidenced by the sources—from vindications of God's actions to expressions of doubt in or protest against him—are motivated by the shared wish to justify God in the face of the national catastrophe. Hence, I develop a notion of theodicy as the basis for the theological discourse, or "theodical discourse."[8]

Fourth, this theodical discourse comprises a multifaceted "discourse among equals," of great diversity, at times in explicitly polemical tones (even involving physical violence). The theological topics are discussed in depth and with courage, albeit with pain, by mostly anonymous speakers, through the diverse genres of historiography, prophecy, and poetry. They reflect the passionate struggles of the various sixth-century players to com-prehend the meaning of the disaster for their relationship with God.[9]

8. My use of "theodical discourse" follows that of Brueggemann ("Some Aspects of Theodicy"), who articulates a distinction between a mode of "theodic settlement," used in situations when there is no theological difficulty in reconciling reality with the divine attributes, and one of "theodic crisis," invoked in situations that profoundly upset all traditional conceptions and inspire "theodic appeal" and "theodic protest," addressed directly to God. My treatment of theodicy as discourse enters into this discussion by elaborating even more on the aspect of protest, highlighting its theodical motivation.

9. I presented the notion of "theodical discourse" as the frame for the theological discussion in Tel Aviv in March 2014 and at the 2014 International Society of Biblical Literature meeting in Vienna under the title "Theodicy and Protest—Can They Walk Together? Hebrew Bible Texts versus Christian Biblical Theology." I am grateful to Hanne Loeland Levinson for her important comments on a previous draft of that paper and to Georg Fischer for his encouragement to address this issue within the Biblical Theology Section.

This monograph, then, pursues two intertwined tasks. The first task is to conduct a theological-phenomenological study of the conceptions evidenced by selected Hebrew Bible compositions during this dramatic era of destruction and dislocation. The second task is to construct a descriptive Hebrew Bible theology, focused on the theodical discourse discernable in the sixth-century sources.

PART 1

Questions of Method

Justification, Doubt, and Protest in Sixth-Century Biblical Literature

Bringing justification, doubt, and protest together under the unifying rubric of "theodicy as discourse" requires a discussion of each of these terms individually and a study of the ways they operate in relation to one another in Hebrew Bible texts. I begin by assessing some classical scholarly definitions of theodicy that shaped the way that the biblical evidence is traditionally understood, and I adapt Ronald Green's conceptual model of the "problem of theodicy" to map the biblical deliberations. The individual phenomena of justification, doubt, and protest are viewed through the analysis of two biblical examples, Jer 21:1–7 and Lam 2. Both texts have something to teach us about the limits of current definitions of theodicy for understanding these texts and the world that produced them; both texts demonstrate the need to expand or revise prevailing scholarly conceptions about theological reflections in Hebrew Bible texts. There are, however, risks inherent in superimposing alien categories onto the biblical thought-world and suggesting theodicy as discourse as an alternative framework for Hebrew Bible theology.[1]

1.1. Theodicy: Justification of a Just God

1.1.1. Scholarly Definitions and Their Legacies

The foundations of modern discussions of theodicy in the Hebrew Bible were laid by Gottfried Wilhelm Leibniz, who coined the term in 1710; in

---

1. A shorter version of the following discussion was published as Rom-Shiloni, "Theodical Discourse."

so doing, he opened the door to two quite different understandings of its meaning.[2] The construction, which brings together θεός and δίκη, may stand simply for "God's justice."[3] For Leibniz, theodicy appears to constitute the argument that God rules his world with justice, that he is a just judge, particularly in the face of human suffering.[4] But theodicy may also stand for "the justification of God" in all God's roles and actions, limited neither to the single role as a judge nor to the sole arena of justice.[5] Philosophical and theological discussions since Leibniz draw on both meanings, although Hebrew Bible texts allow us to distinguish between them.

Walter Brueggemann writes: "'Theodicy' is the ultimate, inescapable problem of the Old Testament (even though the term is never used)."[6] Indeed, within the thought-world of the Hebrew Bible, theodicy may be seen as a framework for the reformulation of religious thought in times of crisis; it seeks to account for the existence of evil and human suffering in a world that the believer assumes is conducted by God, the lord of history, according to just principles.

Theodicy assumes a place in biblical scholarship in several distinctive ways. James Crenshaw recognizes that "theodicy is the attempt to defend divine justice in the face of aberrant phenomena that appear to indicate the deity's indifference or hostility toward virtuous people."[7] According to Crenshaw, the defense and protection of the deity's honor appears as the major goal of theodicy in the Hebrew Bible; this process often advances the

2. Leibniz, *Theodicy*.

3. Theodicy is translated "divine justice" by Crenshaw ("Theodicy," 444) and used in that way by, e.g., Balentine ("Prayers for Justice"); and Laato and de Moor, *Theodicy in the World of the Bible*, vii–liv at viii.

4. Leibniz uses the word "theodicy" in the title of his book, but never explains this coinage in his writings. See Sarot ("Theodicy and Modernity"), who argues on this basis that "from the beginning [the term] did not have a clearly circumscribed meaning" (2, 20). Leibniz is said to have been influenced by Rom 3:4–5, where θεοῦ δικαιοσύνην means "acknowledging God to be in the right, acknowledging His justice"; see Cranfield, *Romans*, 1.183n1. According to Liddell, Scott, and Jones, *Greek-English Lexicon*, 202–3, δίκη serves as a noun meaning "judgment." It appears in Homer with the meaning "righteous lawsuit(s)"; but in verbal phrases it also designates punishment, as in δίκην/δίκα διδόναι ("suffer punishment"); the verb δικαιόω can mean "do a person right or justice," and in the New Testament it serves as "deem righteous, justify."

5. Green ("Theodicy"), for instance, broadens Leibniz's definition to include diverse divine roles beyond God's role as judge. His accentuation of the human "effort" to justify God goes well with this latter use of justification of God.

6. Brueggemann, "Some Aspects of Theodicy," 253.

7. Crenshaw, "Theodicy," 444.

defense of the divine honor at the expense of human suffering.[8] Crenshaw defines theodicy even more broadly as the human search for meaning in the face of the tensions between religious claims and experienced reality.[9]

Scholarship on *biblical* theodicy is devoted almost exclusively to sapiential works in which the central concern is the suffering of the individual, particularly Job and Ecclesiastes. Influenced by Greek philosophy (specifically, Platonic-Stoic thought), Walter Eichrodt sees theodicy as a central component within the conception of divine providence, which he understands to be a personal providence.[10] Gerhard von Rad discusses theodicy in the context of the suffering of the individual[11] and notes only in passing that theodicy is also found in some psalms of national complaint[12] as well as in passages proclaiming divine threats of retribution presented in Deuteronomistic historiosophy.[13]

A sociological (anthropological) approach to theodicy is presented by Klaus Koch and Brueggemann.[14] Koch approaches the issue by analyzing retribution conceptions, arguing that in wisdom literature (and Proverbs in particular), in preexilic and postexilic prophets (especially Hosea), in Psalms, and in sagas and historical traditions, the retribution conceptions are governed by human or national actions (good or wicked ones) and their "built-in consequence." Thus, in the national sphere, "the *actions of the nation bring unavoidable consequences* back on their own heads."[15] For Koch, theodicy is regulated in biblical literature through this sequence of action and built-in consequences. In both individual and national spheres, outcomes are determined by the human actions, which means that God is actively involved only in setting those consequences in motion.[16] Brueg-

---

8. Crenshaw, "Introduction," 1–9.

9. Crenshaw, "Popular Questioning," 380–82. Note Crenshaw's acknowledgment ("Theodicy," 446) of Kaufmann's influence on this definition of theodicy.

10. Eichrodt, "Faith in Providence and Theodicy," 27.

11. Von Rad, *Old Testament Theology*, 1.383–418. The suffering of the individual is also the main focus of comparative studies on theodicy in biblical compositions and ancient Near Eastern writings. See the informative articles by Loprieno, "Theodicy in Ancient Egyptian Texts"; Toorn, "Theodicy in Akkadian Literature"; Hoffner, "Theodicy in Hittite Texts"; and Moor, "Theodicy in the Texts of Ugarit."

12. Von Rad, *Old Testament Theology*, 1.357–58.

13. Von Rad, *Old Testament Theology*, 1.412n60.

14. Koch, "Is There a Doctrine?"; and Brueggemann, "Theodicy in a Social Dimension," 5.

15. Koch, "Is There a Doctrine?," 64, 65 (emphasis original).

16. Koch, "Is There a Doctrine?," 66, 74.

gemann defines theodicy as a critique of social systems, which act or fail to act in a humane fashion, and of gods who are responsible for the social order and who sponsor these systems and ensure their continuity. Brueggemann intentionally blurs the boundaries between the social sphere and that of divine justice, since in his view the matter of divine justice cannot be addressed outside the reality of social experience. In their sociological approaches, neither Koch nor Brueggemann addresses the position of theodicy within national-communal life.

Far less attention is paid to theodicy in national-communal contexts, as a response to military defeat and destruction. In the prophetic, poetic, and historiographic writings of the Hebrew Bible, theodical explanations are associated with the two major traumas of the national experience—the destruction of the kingdom of Israel and, even more, the destruction of Judah. Yehezkel Kaufmann claims that "all of biblical historiosophy is theodical."[17] He points out eighth-century prophets who seek to justify God and identifies the intention of justifying God as a leading theme in Lamentations.[18] In Paul Hanson's opinion, the historiographic text 2 Kgs 17 preserves a theodical perspective that takes shape in the aftermath of the destruction of Samaria.[19] Charles Whitley views Jeremiah as a pioneer in the creation of biblical theodicy, Walter Eichrodt points to Ezekiel, and Thomas Raitt designates both prophets as formulators of theodical perspectives.[20] Robert Carroll explains the extensive concern with theodicy as arising from the pressing needs of the exiles in Babylon, a concern that leaves its mark on the literature of both the sixth and fifth centuries.[21]

My investigations of these biblical texts focus on reactions to the national catastrophe, attentive also to contemporary, post-Shoah discussions of theodicy in the Hebrew Bible, in ancient Near Eastern texts, and in postbiblical Jewish sources. From this standpoint, the most intriguing and potentially helpful definition of the problem of theodicy is that of Ronald Green:

---

17. Kaufmann, *Toldot Ha-'Emunah*, 3.550n80.

18. Kaufmann, *Toldot Ha-'Emunah*, 3.595–97. On theodicy in biblical historiography, see Hoffman, "Creativity of Theodicy."

19. Hanson, "Israelite Religion."

20. Whitley, *Exilic Age*, 55; Eichrodt, *Ezekiel*, 237; and Raitt, *Theology of Exile*, 83–105.

21. Carroll, *From Chaos to Covenant*, 66–73.

The "problem of theodicy" arises when the experienced reality of suffering is juxtaposed with two sets of beliefs traditionally associated with ethical monotheism. One is the belief that God is absolutely good and compassionate. The other is the belief that he controls all events in history, that he is both all-powerful (omnipotent) and all-knowing (omniscient). When combined . . . these various ideas seem contradictory. They appear to form a logical "trilemma," in the sense that, while any two of these sets of ideas can be accepted, the addition of the third renders the whole logically inconsistent. . . . Theodicy may be thought of as the effort to resist the conclusion that such a logical trilemma exists. It aims to show that traditional claims about God's power and goodness are compatible with the fact of suffering.[22]

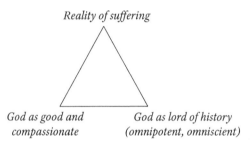

Fig. 1.1. Green's trilemma of theodicy

The primary importance of Green's definition is his recognition of "the *effort* to resist the conclusion that such a logical trilemma exists."[23] This effort is amply recorded in the biblical literature written before and after the destruction of Jerusalem. Indeed, the opposing theological positions

22. Green, "Theodicy," 431. For an extensive introductory discussion of the various definitions of theodicy and its manifestations, see Laato and de Moor, *Theodicy in the World of the Bible*, xx–liv.

23. Green, "Theodicy," 431 (emphasis added). The Epicurean trilemma, as described by Lactantius, contrasts God's goodness, God's power, and the existence of evil (*On the Anger of God* 13.7): "God, he [Epicurus] says, either wishes to take away evils, and is unable; or He is able, and is unwilling; or He is neither willing nor able, or He is both willing and able. If He is willing and is unable, He is feeble, which is not in accordance with the character of God; if He is able and unwilling, He is envious, which is equally at variance with God; if He is neither willing nor able, He is both envious and feeble, and therefore not God; if He is both willing and able, which alone is suitable to God, from what source then are evils? Or why does He not remove them?" (translation from Sarot, "Theodicy and Modernity," 7).

articulated in this literature seem to illustrate the problem of theodicy as a struggle to suppress one or another of the three points of this triangle (see fig. 1.1). Green's trilemma proves particularly helpful in describing Jeremiah's attempt to justify God.

1.1.2. "I Myself Will Battle against You" (Jeremiah 21:1–7)

Jeremiah 21:1–7 portrays a confrontation between the prophet and two officials sent to him by Zedekiah during the final Babylonian siege against Jerusalem.[24] They piously request divine help (21:2):

Please inquire of YHWH on our behalf, for King Nebuchadrezzar of Babylon is attacking us. Perhaps YHWH will act for our sake in accordance with all His wonders, so that [Nebuchadrezzar] will withdraw from us.	דרש־נא בעדנו את־יהוה כי נבוכדראצר מלך־בבל נלחם עלינו אולי יעשה יהוה אותנו ככל־נפלאתיו ויעלה מעלינו.

The officials use a well-known phrase drawn from the exodus tradition—עשה נפלאות ("perform wonders," see Exod 3:20)—to implicitly express their wish for an experience of divine salvation like that of this earlier deliverance.[25] God, they argue, has the ability to act now just as he acted long ago, to save his people even in this current crisis as they face the

---

24. The discussion here is restricted to theological issues; I deal with questions of authorship in Rom-Shiloni, "Facing Destruction," 192–94. While I do consider this passage to be Jeremianic, and thus well situated among early-sixth-century theological deliberations, the argument here should be taken into account even if this passage be treated as redactional and somewhat later.

25. The phrase עשה נפלאות is used to refer to divine wonders that took place from the time of the exodus until that of the settlement in the land: the plagues against Egypt (Exod 3:20), the exodus itself (Judg 6:13; Mic 7:15; Ps 106:22), the victory at the sea (Exod 15:11), the giving of the land (Exod 34:10; Josh 3:5), and all these events taken together (Neh 9:17; Pss 78:4, 11, 32; 107:8, 15, 21, 31). Ps 136 extends the sequence still further, all the way back to the creation. When the term alludes to the exodus, נפלאות on its own becomes the object of verbs of praise; e.g., סיפר נפלאות (Judg 6:13; Ps 107:8, 15, 21, 31). Without explicit reference to exodus traditions, עשה נפלאות appears in Pss 40:6; 72:18; 86:10; Job 5:9; 9:10; 37:5, 14; נפלאות alone appears in Ps 119:18; Job 37:14; 42:3. Only once, in Ps 131:1, does the term appear with a human subject, and there it is used disparagingly: that is, the humble human being does not produce or meditate on נפלאות, which are too "high" for him. The recitation of YHWH's wondrous works (generally conceived) becomes part of the liturgy as well. Note the phrases "I will tell all Your wonders" (Ps 9:2; cf. 26:7; 75:2; 86:3), "that I may study Your wondrous acts"

king of Babylon. Jeremiah's response to the officials shows that the prophet fully understands this plea, but is determined to show them that their plea is in vain (Jer 21:3–7):

> ³Jeremiah answered them, "Thus shall you say to Zedekiah: ⁴Thus said YHWH, the God of Israel: I am going to turn around the weapons in your hands with which you are battling outside the wall against those who are besieging you—the king of Babylon and the Chaldeans—and I will take them into the midst of this city; ⁵<u>and I Myself will battle against you with an outstretched hand and with mighty arm</u> [ונלחמתי אני אתכם ביד נטויה ובזרוע חזקה], with anger and rage and great wrath. ⁶I will strike the inhabitants of this city, man and beast: they shall die by a terrible pestilence. ⁷And then—declares YHWH—I will deliver King Zedekiah of Judah and his courtiers and the people—those in this city who survive the pestilence, the sword, and the famine—into the hands of King Nebuchadrezzar of Babylon, into the hands of their enemies, into the hands of those who seek their lives. He will put them to the sword; he shall not pity them; he shall have no compassion, have no mercy.²⁶

Playing upon the well-known Deuteronomic phrase that describes God's role in the deliverance from Egypt (ביד חזקה ובזרוע נטויה), the prophet establishes God himself as Jerusalem's primary foe: ונלחמתי אני אתכם ביד נטויה ובזרוע חזקה ("and I Myself will battle against you with outstretched hand and with mighty arm," Jer 21:5; see Deut 26:8; also 5:15; 11:2; Ps 136:12). The change of order, pairing יד with נטויה and זרוע with חזקה, inverts the language of God's battles against Israel's enemies. At the same time, it echoes the formulaic refrain developed earlier by Isaiah son of Amoz to describe God's justifiable wrath against his own people: על־כן חרה אף־יהוה בעמו ויט ידו עליו ויכהו ("that is why YHWH's anger was roused against His people, why He stretched out His hand against it and struck it," Isa 5:25; see 9:11, 16, 20; 10:4; 14:26).²⁷ This explicit portrayal

---

(119:27), "and Your wondrous acts I will recite" (105:2; 145:5; cf. 111:4). Even more, the lack of belief in YHWH's wondrous works is a sin (78:32).

26. Compare NJPS: "He will put them to the sword without pity, without compassion, without mercy." In my translation I try to reflect the active role played by the Babylonian king. See also Lundbom, *Jeremiah 21–36*, 93.

27. The inverted phrasing in Jer 21:5 is unique and seems to belong with other unique Jeremianic phrases (see §3.4.4.1). Other variations on the Deuteronomic phrase may be seen in 27:5 and 32:17, in which "great might" (בכחי הגדול) precedes the phrase

of God as the enemy is further established through verbal phrases in the first-person that illustrate God's actions as a warrior in Jer 21:4–7:

[4] I am going to turn around the weapons . . . and I will take them . . . ; [5] and I Myself will battle against you. . . . [6] I will strike. . . . [7] And then . . . I will deliver King Zedekiah of Judah . . . into the hands of King Nebuchadrezzar of Babylon.	[4] הנני מסב . . . ואספתי אותם . . . [5] ונלחמתי אני אתכם . . . [6] והכיתי את . . . [7] ואחרי־כן . . . אתן את־ צדקיהו מלך־יהודה . . . ביד נבוכדראצר מלך־בבל.

God is a fierce warrior who concedes only a minor role to the Babylonian emperor in bringing complete annihilation upon his own people (21:7).

Remarkably, this prophetic passage says nothing about justice. There is complete silence on the subject of any possible human sins that might justify such harsh divine punishment; the prophet seems to have no interest in explaining God's ferocity here. Moreover, the prophet's refutation concludes with the triad: לא־יחוס עליהם ולא יחמל ולא ירחם ("he shall not pity them; he shall have no compassion, have no mercy"). This cluster occurs as a description of God's activity in Jer 13:14 as well as in Ezekiel (e.g., 5:11).[28] In Jer 21:7 the syntax points to the Babylonian king as the agent of these verbs, yet God is clearly active behind the scenes; he summons the human enemy and gives the remnant of the people into his hands, to be executed without mercy (21:7a).

Does Jer 21:1–7, then, belong in a discussion of theodicy? I argue that it does. Green's model of the "trilemma of theodicy" may help us to situate this passage. Jeremiah 21:1–7 operates along two sides of Green's triangle (see fig. 1.2). Jeremiah is explaining the current reality of the Babylonian siege and the catastrophe that it portends as a clear illustration of God's omnipotence and omniscience as lord of history. But Jeremiah completely ignores the third pole, the expectation (as voiced by the officials who originally came to the prophet) that God should be "good and compassionate." Or perhaps I should say that the prophet implicitly *denies* that aspect of

---

זרוע נטויה, possibly due to the reference to God as creator; the "strong hand" occurs in 32:21 in the usual context of evoking the exodus.

28. For compassion (רחמים) as a divine mode of action, note the construct with חון and ריחם in Exod 33:19; 2 Kgs 13:23; Isa 27:11; 30:18; Ps 102:14; and also the use of ריחם alone in Deut 13:18; 30:3; 1 Kgs 8:50. See §12.3.

divine activity (21:7b). Jeremiah's insistence that only these two elements are active in the present scenario justifies the current situation as God's proper and legitimate sovereign role; Jeremiah simply suppresses the third pole of the triangle, the conviction of God's benevolence that is at the root of the officials' bewilderment.[29]

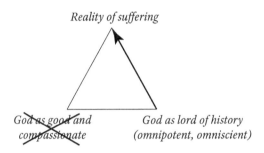

Fig. 1.2. Jeremiah 21:1–7 and the trilemma of theodicy

While Jer 21:1–7 has nothing explicit to say about the expectation that God should act compassionately, it does take a strong stand on God's absolute control of events as the lord of history: specifically, God's own intention and might power the Babylonian victory and Judah's subjugation and defeat. This construal of Jeremiah's argument may be validated by placing the polemical interchange between the prophet and the king's officials in our passage into its wider theological context.

This passage illustrates the prophetic refutation of two fundamental assumptions that underlie the officials' request—assumptions that at face value seem to be theologically contradictory: on the one hand, the expectation of divine deliverance, as in the past, based on traditional assumptions about God's sovereignty, that is, his covenantal connection with Israel, on his role as a saving warrior, and on his qualities as good and compassionate judge; and on the other hand, the (growing) fear that God must be either indifferent, impotent, or absent, since things have come to such a desperate pass. Both conceptions are common among Judahites of the early sixth

---

29. Another common tactic used to avoid this trilemma is to put the blame for God's punitive actions on the people's behavior: they sin against God, who justly acts against them. My discussion of Jer 21:1–7 points out that such a tactic is not a mandatory, explicit component of theodicy.

century, and the multivocal deliberations over each of them constituted substantial threats to belief in the God of Israel—threats to which neither prophets nor historiographers could remain unresponsive.[30]

Thus, Jeremiah's response goes beyond the specific questions asked by the king's officials to refute these more widely expressed theological challenges. The prophet minimizes the human power of the Babylonian emperor in the face of the much harsher threat of the omnipotent God himself, who here acts as the (sole) warrior against his people (Jer 21:7; see §9.1). Far from being impotent or indifferent, God himself continues to exercise against his people those same powers once employed against Egypt for the people's deliverance; and far from having abandoned his people, God is actually fighting against them (21:3–7). What Jeremiah could say about Chemosh and the defeat of the Babylonian gods (compare 48:7, 13; 51:44, 47), he would not dare to say about YHWH.[31] Rather, from the prophetic perspectives, it is God who strikes his own people with all his might; God is the ultimate foe of Jerusalem (or alternatively, he intentionally delivers his people into the hands of human foes).[32] This theological explanation is clearly the lesser of two evils from the prophet's point of view: accepting a notion of God's impotence, indifference, or absence courts risky results. Jeremiah's refutation presents a virtuosic justification

30. For expectations of divine deliverance, see, for instance, Jer 8:19–22; for fears about both God's seeming absence and his potential inability to deliver the people, see 14:7–9. Jer 8:19–22 illustrates both the hope for deliverance and the desperate perception that salvation is not forthcoming, to the point that protest challenges the very idea that God is present. Jer 14:7–9 addresses both the seeming absence of God and the issue of God's power to save (see §7.2).

31. In ancient Near Eastern texts, political defeat is characteristically portrayed as the result either of the god's/gods' impotence or of their abandonment of the city and kingdom of the defeated people. The gods' statues may at times be captured and taken away by the conquerors (see Cogan, *Imperialism and Religion*, 22–41). On those (and other) theological conceptions of war as implementing the power of the Assyrian god(s), see Oded, *War, Peace, and Empire*, 9–28, 151–54, 185–88; and on looting temples, as also restoring them, see 132–35. Sixth-century biblical prophecy reflects these features in prophecies against the nations (e.g., Jer 48:7, 13): the capture of the gods of Egypt (43:12), God's struggle against Babylon's gods (51:44), and the city's hope for destruction resulting from the abolition of its gods (51:47).

32. This line of thought is also shared by the historiography, which portrays God as the one who delivers his people into the hands of the human foe (e.g., 2 Kgs 24:2, 20). The image occurs frequently in Jeremiah (e.g., 4:5–9) and in poetry (e.g., Ps 44:10–12). This theological line of argumentation also governs prophecies in Ezekiel (see §9.1.1).

of God who is not expected to deliver his people, but on the contrary turns out to be his people's primary, omnipotent, and fully present foe.

An understanding of theodicy as "justification of God" (without reference to his role as a just judge, good and compassionate) broadens the scope of deliberation and allows us to take into account the diverse roles God is perceived to play in events of national defeat and destruction. Both Jeremiah and his interlocutors are grappling with a threat of impending disaster. The king's messengers express in the same breath their hopes for a traditional salvation and their fears that God is abandoning them. Jeremiah turns the tables: the God who saved Israel in the past is actively engaged in empowering the present catastrophe.

The "trilemma of theodicy" framework brings to light the multiplicity of engaged perspectives in one prophetic work on the meaning of the events leading up to the destruction. But Jeremiah's brand of justification does not necessarily carry the day; the communal laments give a different and equally vocal response to the trilemma of theodicy.

1.2. PROTEST AND DOUBT: ESSENTIAL COMPONENTS OF THE THEOLOGICAL DISCOURSE

1.2.1. Scholarly Perspectives on Doubt and Protest

Until the early 1980s, "doubt" and "protest" were not terms commonly used in Hebrew Bible scholarship on Psalms or Lamentations. Robert Davidson includes protest, questioning, and doubt in what he defines as "religious experience."[33] He uses the term "doubt" "in the widest sense to indicate any questioning of, or protest against the adequacy of inherited faith."[34] Richard M. Davidson adds that communal and individual laments in Psalms "contain within themselves a dialogue between doubt and faith,

---

33. Davidson, *Courage to Doubt*, 209. Davidson makes explicit his concern with Christian piety in the introduction to his book: "What is offered here is a study in a particular aspect of Old Testament spirituality, an aspect which may have more than a passing relevance today, when many, even within the believing community, find themselves forced to question and doubt, and often do so with an unnecessarily guilty conscience" (xi; also 213). Davidson and others connect doubt and protest to "skepticism."

34. Davidson, *Courage to Doubt*, 12.

scepticism and certainty, the baffling ambiguities of the present and the clear witness of tradition."[35]

Further progress on bringing to the fore doubt and protest as aspects of the religious experience is made by Claus Westermann, particularly through a discussion entitled "The Lament and Its Significance" in his commentary on Lamentations, where he makes the following observations:

> Consciously or unconsciously, for many interpreters the very word "lament" carries a negative connotation. For many, it is not quite proper to lament; for many, it is better to learn to suffer without lamenting. This especially holds true in the area of one's relationship to God. In this domain the lament supposedly has no place at all; lamentation is widely thought to be without authentic theological significance. Such a stance is rooted in the history of prayer—more precisely, in the absence of lamentation in prayer as traditionally practiced in the Christian church. In the Bible, however, lamentation has genuine integrity; in the Bible, lamentation reflects the very nature of human existence. . . . Lamentation is the language of suffering. . . .
>
> To a modern person [i.e., a modern *Christian* person], terms such as "lament" or "lamentation" designate thoroughly secular or profane realities; they no longer have anything to do with one's relationship to God. The Old Testament laments . . . , however, are all addressed to God. . . . In the Old Testament, it is seen as only natural, as normal, that a lament is directed toward God.[36]

Westermann's distinctions between the religious Christian attitude toward lament and its use within the Hebrew Bible (Old Testament, for Westermann) are intriguing. The Christian theological reservations against the

35. Davidson, "Some Aspects," 44.

36. Westermann, *Lamentations*, 89–91; and *Praise and Lament*, 206–13, 259–80. But then, even Westermann seems to be committed to a conception of "divine mercy," commenting: "For those who lament in the Old Testament, God is the One who can take away suffering. That sufferers have been given the opportunity to pour out their hearts before God, precisely in the language of the lament, is seen in the Old Testament as itself an expression of divine mercy. . . . In the Bible, then, the liberating possibility is opened up for sufferers to bewail their suffering directly to God. In the Bible, sufferers are allowed to voice their laments directly to their Lord" (*Lamentations*, 91). I challenge Westermann's observation by asking: is every lament in the Hebrew Bible indeed written as "an expression of divine mercy"? See also Linafelt's appreciation and criticism of Westermann in *Surviving Lamentations*, 13–16.

lament rest on the specific characteristics of doubt and protest, on the direct address to God, and on its governing theological stances, which question or even bluntly accuse God for the current distress. The pious Christian, however, according to Westermann, "learn[s] to suffer without lamenting" or, rather, opts for the justification of God in the face of suffering.

Walter Brueggemann wrote a paper entitled "The Costly Loss of Lament" in "the church" (i.e., the Christian community of faith).[37] Brueggemann is attentive to what he considers a regrettable tendency of contemporary Christianity not only to fail to appreciate lament as a "form of speech and faith," but rather, even intentionally, to silence and eliminate such speech forms.[38] For Brueggemann, this attitude toward the biblical laments (he focuses on Psalms) results in two significant losses. The first is "the loss *of genuine covenant interaction* because the second party to the covenant (the petitioner) has become voiceless or has a voice that is permitted to speak only praise and doxology. Where lament is absent, covenant comes into being only as a celebration of joy and well-being. . . . Covenant minus lament is finally a practice of denial, cover-up, and pretense, which sanctions social control."[39]

The second loss is the "stifling of the question of theodicy," which for Brueggemann is social in nature. Brueggemann suggests that "lament occurs when the dysfunction reaches an unacceptable level, when the injustice is intolerable and change is insisted upon."[40] He distinguishes between two lines of lament/complaint, one "addressed to God against neighbor" (e.g., Ps 109) and the other "addressed to God against God" (e.g., Ps 88). The latter is clearly the more dangerous one, as the petitioner complains to God against God's "own injustice," against God's dysfunction.[41] Nevertheless, Brueggemann emphasizes the necessity of lament and argues that "where the lament is absent, *the normal mode of the theodicy question is forfeited.*"[42] The crucial consequence of the loss of lament that Brueggemann points out is that of religious despair:

---

37. Brueggemann dedicates much attention to the topic of lament and protest; see, for instance, his *Unsettling God*.

38. Brueggemann, "Costly Loss of Lament," 59–60.

39. Brueggemann, "Costly Loss of Lament," 60 (emphasis original).

40. Brueggemann, "Costly Loss of Lament," 62.

41. Brueggemann, "Costly Loss of Lament," 63. Not least important is Brueggemann's recognition that in both types of complaint "the petitioner accepts no guilt or responsibility for the dysfunction, but holds the other party responsible."

42. Brueggemann, "Costly Loss of Lament," 63 (emphasis original).

A community of faith which negates laments soon concludes that the hard issues of justice are improper questions to pose at the throne, because the throne seems to be only a place of praise. I believe it thus follows that if justice questions are improper questions at the throne (which is a conclusion drawn through liturgic use), they soon appear to be improper questions in public places, in schools, in hospitals, with the government, and eventually even in the courts. Justice questions disappear into civility and docility. The order of the day comes to seem absolute, beyond question, and we are left with only grim obedience and eventually despair. The point of access for serious change has been forfeited when the propriety of this speech form is denied.[43]

Therefore, since the mid-1980s, Brueggemann joins Westermann and others in the call for a reevaluation of this biblical corpus among the prayers of the church.[44]

William Morrow also discusses the absence of lament from Christian liturgy.[45] Morrow points out several possible explanations for this and describes the scholarly change of attitude toward "recovering the lament tradition for the Christian church" and for the Western world in general, including the Jewish tradition.[46] In his illuminating research, Morrow traces the transformations and the waning of direct complaint and protest to Second Temple literature.[47]

Suggestions vary as to what might have stood behind this decline, which may be traced back to the penitential prayers in late biblical literature and which subsequently captured major place in Second Temple literature.[48]

---

43. Brueggemann, "Costly Loss of Lament," 64.

44. See Boda, "Priceless Gain of Penitence"; Mandolfo, *God in the Dock*; and Janowski, *Theological Anthropology*, 36–45, with a focus on the individual laments in Psalms.

45. Morrow, *Protest against God*, 210–18.

46. Morrow, *Protest against God*, 211, 215–18.

47. Morrow, *Protest against God*, 147–77.

48. On the decline of lament (and thus, silencing doubt and protest) for the sake of justification, see Balentine, *Prayer in the Hebrew Bible*. Clear Deuteronomistic (as also Priestly) phraseological and thematic influences on the penitential prayers are presented by Boda, *Praying the Tradition*; and Bautch, *Developments in Genre*. Focusing on Second Temple literature, see Werline, *Penitential Prayer*; and Boda, Falk, and Werline's valuable trilogy *Seeking the Favor of God*.

Scholars further emphasize the rise of the Christian conception of suffering in which God shares in the actual suffering and is less of an antagonist.[49]

One common observation seems to emerge fairly clearly out of these different discussions—the need to recognize a clear distinction between the Hebrew Bible compositions down to the end of the sixth century on the one hand, and later Persian period and Hellenistic extrabiblical literatures, down to both Jewish and Christian religious traditions of the common era.[50]

Later Jewish tradition also downgrades doubt and protest, but still retains it in both liturgy and individual prayer. Eliezer Schweid argues that "faith at its outset is an answer to theodicy" and that the writings of the Hebrew Bible are united by their constant struggle with the central question of divine justice.[51] For Schweid, the question of theodicy is genuinely historical, yet it is always active, in both the personal and the national spheres. From the depth of a new crisis, every period, every speaker, challenges the principles of divine justice and reevaluates earlier solutions, with the sense that previous resolutions are no longer satisfactory.[52]

It is in considering the character and function of the Hebrew Bible lament that we arrive at the supposed conflict between the terms "theodicy/justification" and "protest." One of my goals is to articulate the specific features of both protest and doubt (see chap. 8). An essential formal feature of protest is direct speech to God in the second-person; it is found mainly in contexts of lament, where God is held responsible for either the present disaster and/or long-term suffering. Nevertheless, protest also has a place within laments addressed at God that explicitly end with a plea for his deliverance.

While the definition of doubt seems to be somewhat evasive, it captures an intermediate position in this theological spectrum, side by side with protest. Doubt is characterized formally by interrogative sentences (simple questions or rhetorical ones). In classical scholarship, doubt is understood to result from the clash between two opposite conceptions or to represent the state of indecision between two antithetical perceptions.[53]

---

49. See Lane, "Arguing with God," 2549–51.

50. On the transition from lament to penitence as situated within the sixth century, see Rom-Shiloni, "Socio-Ideological Setting."

51. Schweid, *To Declare That God Is Upright*, 7–46 at 7.

52. Schweid, *To Declare That God Is Upright*, 21–24.

53. Etymologically, doubt is designated as coming from the Old Latin *dubo* ("two"),

Geddes MacGregor discusses doubt in religious context as inseparable from belief. He uses the imagery of the human body—the arteries and the veins—arguing that doubt is the component that sustains belief and that "faith descends on doubt . . . it rises beyond the doubt that is at the same time its necessary presupposition."[54]

The cluster of doubtful questions, protests against God, and pleas for salvation within biblical laments designates the religious experience reflected in Hebrew Bible texts. Part II of this book (chaps. 5–13) examines the Hebrew Bible evidence for indications of justification, doubt, and protest expressed by those directly affected by the upheavals of the Babylonian conquest. I follow MacGregor's understanding of the necessity of all three of these elements (justification, doubt, and protest) as components of the religious discourse.

Lamentations 2 problematizes the presumed dichotomy between justification and protest and illustrates the pious or believing stance from which such protest may come.

1.2.2. Communal Laments as the Cradle of Protest (Lamentations 2)

Lamentations 2 presents the most painful protest within the book of Lamentations.[55] The lament is stunning: it dares to accuse God, not only of orchestrating events, but of direct participation *in* the destruction occurring within Jerusalem. The poem portrays God as a tough warrior (e.g., 2:4–5), acting entirely out of raging anger (2:2b, 3a, 6c, 22b), yet in accord with long-held intentions (2:8a–b, 17a), and without compassion (2:2a, 17b, 21c).

To illustrate the author's overall conception of God and to draw the contours of his deep and painful protest, I point out several literary and conceptual characteristics of this lament.

a. Formal devices

1. *The use of* inclusio *focuses attention on divine wrath.* God's wrath is mentioned in both the opening and the close of the composition: איכה

---

that is, "doubt" is to hold to two minds, "stand at the crossroads of the mind"; as also the Greek διάζω ("I doubt"). Along this line is German *Zweifel*, with *Zwiefelgeist* standing for "skepticism, the spirit of doubt." Doubt is discussed in §7.2.

54. See MacGregor, "Doubt and Belief," 2424.

55. Westermann (*Lamentations*, 159) designates Lam 2 as "a unique testimony to how, in the Old Testament, one can speak to God."

יְעִיב בְּאַפּוֹ אֲדֹנָי אֶת־בַּת־צִיּוֹן . . . וְלֹא־זָכַר הֲדֹם־רַגְלָיו בְּיוֹם אַפּוֹ ("alas, the Lord in His wrath has shamed *bat* Zion . . . He did not remember His footstool on His day of wrath," 2:1) opposes הָרַגְתָּ בְּיוֹם אַפֶּךָ ("You slew them on Your day of wrath," 2:21c) and וְלֹא הָיָה בְּיוֹם אַף־יְהוָה פָּלִיט וְשָׂרִיד ("on the day of the wrath of the Lord, none survived or escaped," 2:22b). Lamentations 2 (as well as 1:12; 3:1, 43, 66; 4:11) does not present God's wrath as the motivation for his warlike actions against his people (contrast Deut 11:17; Jer 12:13; Ezek 22:24). Rather, God's wrath is a powerful weapon in the divine war described in Lam 2:1–9a: הָרַס בְּעֶבְרָתוֹ ("He has razed by His anger," 2:2b), גָּדַע בָּחֳרִי־אָף ("by blazing anger He has cut down," 2:3a), שָׁפַךְ כָּאֵשׁ חֲמָתוֹ ("He poured out His wrath like fire," 2:4c), and וַיִּנְאַץ בְּזַעַם־אַפּוֹ ("by His raging anger He has spurned," 2:6c) (see §9.1.5).

2. *Structurally, the listing of divine actions alternates with the recounting of their disastrous consequences.* First, (A1) God's warlike actions against royal public buildings, the temple, and known institutions (2:1–9a) lead to (B1) devastating results for the population (2:9b–12). Then, (A2) there is no one to heal Jerusalem since the warfare itself is planned and executed by God (2:13–17), and this results in (B2) further affliction visited upon Jerusalem's citizens, which again is attributed to God (2:18–19). Finally, the poem reaches its climax (2:20–22), in which God's warlike actions and their consequences are presented together (A+B) and God is directly accused. It is God the Warrior who causes the extensive deaths of maidens and youth (בְּתוּלֹתַי וּבַחוּרַי, 2:21b) and likewise of young children, as hinted in the last clause: אֲשֶׁר־טִפַּחְתִּי וְרִבִּיתִי (2:22, following עֹלְלֵי טִפֻּחִים, 2:20).[56]

3. *The theme "God as warrior" is developed in two primary ways.* First, the poet enumerates God's warlike actions through thirty-one verbal phrases that use exclusively human imagery (most are in the third-person singular, but 2:20–22 uses the second-person). Metaphorically, these phrases depict God as a human warrior who follows known human war maneuvers: God conquers the city in war (דָּרַךְ קַשְׁתּוֹ נִצָּב יְמִינוֹ, 2:4a),[57]

---

56. Compare other quite different suggestions as to how to divide this lament; see Hillers, *Lamentations*, 102–3; Westermann, *Lamentations*, 148; Gerstenberger, *Psalms, Part 2*, 485–91; Berlin, *Lamentations*, 67–68; and Dobbs-Allsopp, *Lamentations*, 78–79.

57. Compare Ps 7:12–13, where phrases describing the divine warrior (דָּרַךְ קַשְׁתּוֹ [see Lam 3:12] and also לָטַשׁ חֶרֶב) illustrate the epithet as אֵל זֹעֵם "a resentful God" (compare NJPS: "God pronounces doom each day"). In contradistinction to Lam 2, these phrases in Ps 7 occur side by side with language denoting YHWH's role as a just judge.

burns it with fire (שפך כאש, 2:3c; ויבער ביעקב כאש להבה אכלה סביב, חמתו, 2:4c), and destroys fortresses in Judah and in the walls of Jerusalem (הרס בעברתו, 2:2b). Contrary to other descriptions of God's role in the destruction, Lam 2 does not mention the cosmic or natural forces that are usually seen as weapons in divine warfare (compare סערת יהוה, Jer 23:19; the רוח משחית aroused against Babylon in Jer 51:1, 11; or natural afflictions like pestilence or beasts from the wilderness in Jer 5:6; Ezek 5:17; 14:15).

Second, explicit accusations are made against God. In three different phrases (Lam 2:4–5), the poem suggests that in his actions God had become or acted like a foe: דרך קשתו כאויב ("He bent His bow like an enemy," 2:4a), נצב ימינו כצר ("He poised His right hand like a foe," 2:4a), and היה אדני כאויב בלע ישראל ("the Lord has acted like a foe, He has laid waste Israel," 2:5a).[58] The author of Lam 2 knows that human enemies are involved in the destruction, and he does not fully ignore them. Yet he restricts their actions to speech and to cries of delight (2:16). In only three phrases does he hint at the warlike actions of the enemies themselves (2:3b, 7b, 17c). The enemies are summoned and empowered by the God of Israel to defeat his own people. Yet, in comparison to the magnitude of God's actions, the human forces play but a minor role. It is God who is Jerusalem's primary (and perhaps only) foe. Along these lines, איבי כלם in the final verse (2:22c) likely refers to God as the hidden subject who brings calamity upon his people.[59]

---

58. Lam 2:4–5 repeats the construction כאויבי כצר, which is translated as a simile by the Septuagint and the Targum. Renkema (*Lamentations*, 229) highlights this metaphorical use of *kaf* as suggesting "a certain hesitance on the poets' part to actually call him [God] 'the enemy.'" Dobbs-Allsopp (*Lamentations*, 84–85) notes that although explicitly expressed in these verses, the metaphor of God as an enemy is not further developed. Berlin (*Lamentations*, 62, 66), however, understands *kaf* in 2:5 as asseverative ("the Lord became an enemy"; yet see her translation of 2:4: "He bent his bow like an enemy"). Gordis ("Asseverative *Kaph*") discusses *kaf asseverativum*, but does not mention these specific verses (although he addresses 1:20; 3:22–24).

59. So explicitly Dobbs-Allsopp, *Lamentations*, 101–2. Renkema accurately distinguishes the singular form איבי in 2:22c from the plural in 1:21b. He thus rejected the Septuagint version of 2:22 as a misinterpretation, asserting that "Daughter Jerusalem's summarizing prayer is not about her enemies in the plural, it is about the one and only real enemy of her people whose very name she is afraid to mention (cf. 2:4a, 5a). She thus appeals to God against God" (*Lamentations*, 330). Jewish medieval exegesis (so Rashi, Ibn Ezra), like modern interpreters, prefers to understand איבי as alluding to human enemies; see Hillers, *Lamentations*, 108; and Berlin, *Lamentations*, 66. Ehrlich (*Randglossen zur hebräischen Bible*, 7.39) suggests that the phrase should be pointed

b. Thematic emphasis on the idea of God as an enemy and warrior without compassion

Intensifying the theme of God as an enemy, the lament emphasizes that God has not been compassionate (לא חמל) in his actions against his city and people: בלע אדני לא חמל ("the Lord has laid waste, He did not have compassion," 2:2a), הרס ולא חמל ("He has torn down, He did not have compassion," 2:17b), and טבחת לא חמלת ("You slaughtered, You did not have compassion," 2:21c);[60] neither did God regret his plan or refrain from carrying it out (2:8b; see §12.2).

c. Detailed descriptions of the people's suffering as result of God's lack of compassion[61]

Johan Renkema correctly points out a gradual intensification in the descriptions of God's lack of compassion and its results (2:9b–12, 20–22), which in its final appearance affects not cities, walls, and houses, but the people, and even more so, innocent children.[62]

d. Lack of any explicit confession of sin on the part of the people

Throughout the lament, and specifically in his descriptions of the divine deeds of destruction (2:1–9a, 17, 20–22), this author avoids any reference to sins committed by the people.[63] The only misdeeds actually mentioned in the lament can hardly bear the burden of responsibility for the severe punishment of Jerusalem: "Your seers prophesied to you delusion and folly. They did not expose your iniquity so as to restore your fortunes, but prophesied to you oracles of delusion and deception" (2:14; compare 1:8, 9, 14, 18, 22 and so sporadically in the other laments).[64] This almost

---

differently, so that both the personal pronoun and the verb refer to human enemies: איבי כלם ("my enemies had annihilated them").

60. Compare NJPS translation of לא חמל in these three verses: "without pity."

61. For the various ways in which Lamentations adduces the theme that the people's suffering surpasses the sum of their possible sins, see Dobbs-Allsopp, *Lamentations*, 31–32; and "Tragedy, Tradition, and Theology," 34–39.

62. Renkema, *Lamentations*, 326–27.

63. On the special role of the confession of sins in communal laments, see Rom-Shiloni, "Socio-Ideological Setting"; and see §11.2.3.

64. Pace Renkema ("Theodicy in Lamentations?," 425–28), who accentuates be-

complete omission of any acknowledgment of the people's sins, plus the *only* mention of such sins occurring in a nonconfessional context (2:13–17), undermines any sense of God's role as a just judge and reinforces the image of God as noncompassionate warrior. These strategies reveal the poet's implicit doubts concerning divine justice.[65]

Compassion and a lack of compassion are theologically connected with the role of God as judge. The assertion that God employed judgment without compassion, together with the omission of a communal confession of sin, reflects a major theological problem with which the author of Lam 2 struggles. But, does the author imply that God acted unjustly? The lament does not answer this question in any explicit way; however, the fierce protest against God's role, especially in the final verses, more than hints at such an implication.

Another implicit hint at the question of divine (in)justice is suggested by the portrayal of divine anger. Throughout the Hebrew Bible, and specifically in the historiography, divine wrath is understood and accepted theologically as part of the conception of just retribution. The people arouse God's anger through their unacceptable behavior or disloyalty, and this inflames him to justifiably punish them (as happens repeatedly in Judges; e.g., Judg 3:7–11). Hence, the question arises in the context of Lam 2: if God's anger is portrayed so prominently *without* any mention of its cause, does the poet imply that the divine anger has no defensible justification?

e.   Call to communal prayer

Nevertheless, and not least important, the poet exhorts Jerusalem to address God through prayer (Lam 2:18–19); and finally the city, or the poet himself, addresses YHWH in a last, highly emotional appeal (or accusation) decrying the results of the destruction God brought about (2:20–22).[66] This final segment of the lament, although it lacks the straight-

yond what is reasonable the responsibility of Jerusalem's false prophets for the destruction. Compare Dobbs-Allsopp ("Tragedy, Tradition, and Theology," 34–39), who elaborates on the unbalanced relationship between sin and suffering in Lamentations.

65. Compare for instance confessional sayings within communal laments, as in Ps 79:8 or Jer 14:7, 20. So Boase, *Fulfilment of Doom?*, 181–84.

66. Compare Hillers (*Lamentations*, 103), who suggests that Lam 2:20–22 sets forth "Zion's anguished appeal"; and he considers the entire lament as an appeal to God's compassion (108); so also Dobbs-Allsopp, *Lamentations*, 78–79. Berlin (*Lamentations*, 67, 75–76) calls it "Jerusalem's speech to God"/"Jerusalem's prayer of supplication to

forward formal petition familiar from other communal laments (e.g., Ps 44:24–27), falls within Morrow's trajectory of the rhetoric of complaint, moving into the realm of accusation.[67]

In addition to these five literary (formal and thematic) devices that constitute protest in Lam 2, a sixth feature reinforces this element of protest and locates this composition within the theological context that is typical of the (communal) laments in general.

f.   Lamentations 2's struggle with the trilemma of theodicy

Green's model of the trilemma of theodicy may usefully be employed here to understand the theological framework of this poem. Through both explicit and implicit protest, the poet seeks to mediate between the enormity of human suffering and the inadequacy of traditional conceptions of God's goodness to his people, on the one hand, and his role as lord of history, omnipotent and omniscient, on the other (see fig. 1.3).

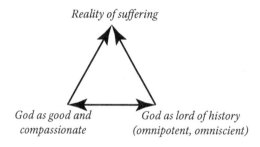

Fig. 1.3. Lamentations 2 and the trilemma of theodicy

The powerful protest of Lam 2 emerges precisely out of the poet's inability to reconcile the three points of the trilemma of theodicy. The people's distress arises out of a national military defeat; yet the role of human enemies is diminished in the poem to the point where they are primarily portrayed as using their mouths and not their weapons (2:16; also 2:7).

God" and finds these verses to be "calculated to arouse God's sympathy," yet she correctly emphasizes that the accusatory tone is retained throughout (77).

67. For the place of petition within the three segments of the lament in general, see Westermann (*Lamentations*, 95–98), who points out two "structural components": a plea that God take notice of the poet or community and a plea for effective divine intervention (97). See Morrow, *Protest against God*, 45–61; and see §3.4.3.

God's own war against Jerusalem is by far the main cause of its suffering; God shows himself to be the lord of history precisely by acting *against* the people, as their omnipotent and omniscient enemy. Through its accent on the divine wrath (2:1–2, 6, 21–22) and the lack of divine compassion (2:2, 17, 21), this lament explicitly and implicitly excludes the notion that God is good and merciful.[68] In this portrayal, God never considers sparing anyone, man, woman, or child. Nevertheless, the poet urges Jerusalem to address God in cries and prayers (2:18–22); in other words, the assumption is that, even though God has not yet acted with compassion, the people must still strive and hope to activate that quality. The author of Lam 2 clearly struggles with the three points of the trilemma of theodicy, unwilling to deny either of these central divine qualities and desperately looking for a theological reconciliation to explain the present distress.

But is Lam 2, then, to be regarded as a theodical composition? How should we describe the difference between Lam 2, with its fierce protest against God's enmity, and Jer 21:1–7, with its clear justification of God as Jerusalem's fierce enemy? Or, how are we to resolve the seeming contradictions between these two so very different contemporary reactions to the same reality?

1.3. BETWEEN JUSTIFICATION AND PROTEST: TOWARD A FRAMEWORK OF THEODICY AS DISCOURSE

The questions posed by the foregoing analysis highlight the limitations in scholarly discussion arising from the gap between the evidence of the biblical texts and prevailing modern scholarly frameworks for understanding the workings of biblical theology.[69] Three studies on Lamentations exemplify this gap. Each of these scholars finds his or her own way to address the question of theodicy in that collection of laments, and yet each is deeply disturbed by the limitations of the traditional definition of theodicy.

Johan Renkema rejects the idea that the theological reflections that characterize Lamentations are theodical in nature.[70] Renkema develops

---

68. This same dynamic characterizes Ps 74, as well as other communal laments (Pss 44, 79).

69. The insights of Boase's "Constructing Meaning" inform much of the following discussion.

70. Renkema, *Lamentations*, 58–71; and "Theodicy in Lamentations?"

three other arguments against categorizing Lamentations as a theodical composition: (1) the poets do not set out a clear presentation of the people's transgressions; thus, (2) they cannot "offer any insightful explanation of the disaster";[71] rather, (3) they offer an alternative conception of human responsibility for the catastrophe.[72] Renkema draws his main argument on his restriction of theodicy to "a (self-)justification of YHWH's actions or aloofness in the context of (significant) human suffering" and on his recognition that while all five laments focus on human suffering, "no specific allusion" to the "self-justification of YHWH" is to be found in Lamentations.[73]

Renkema understands theodicy to supply explanations limited to the arena of justice (with God as judge), that is, explanations that justify God by bringing together the notion of sinful human behavior as responsible for human distress with the idea of divine responsibility for orchestrating judgment.[74] Renkema concludes his discussion by stating:

> While the poets of Lamentations may have been aware of sin and guilt, they did not consider YHWH to be responsible for the disaster facing the people. The reason for their present situation of misery was to be sought in their own hearts. Did this insight provide them with an adequate theodicy? Given their questions and laments only in part.... The poets are thus aware of the tremendous tension that their misery must have engendered in YHWH himself.... Aware of this tension and pain they appeal to God against God. This paradox proves that the poets were

71. Renkema, "Theodicy in Lamentations?," 416.

72. Renkema, "Theodicy in Lamentations?," 416–27.

73. Renkema, "Theodicy in Lamentations?," 410. Note his discussion of 3:37–39: "The justification of YHWH's deeds is not to be located in the images of God but in the evil perpetrated by human beings. The misery with which Judah is confronted does not have its source in YHWH but rather in the unauthorized and misleading oracles of the prophets of Jerusalem. Their hollow yet attractive prophecies are the real reason for the current state of affairs.... As such, YHWH was forced to allow his word of judgment to take its course" (426). The guilt of the prophets of Jerusalem is indeed emphasized in 2:14; 4:13; and 5:7, but cannot be taken as the ultimate explanation for the destruction and the exiles. Renkema's entire explanation sounds pietistic and far from the painful laments themselves, which clearly hold God himself to be *the* agent of suffering.

74. This combination seems to draw upon a distinction between "theodicy" and "anthropodicy." In many contexts, however, this distinction appears to be an artificial one, or at least serves as only a partial explanation for the theological dynamic. Compare Crenshaw, "Introduction."

far removed from any form of theodicy. Given the immense material and especially physical and spiritual desperation, words of explanation were hardly to be expected. Any attempt to provide an answer in the songs is far exceeded by the many laments and questions . . . those who had remained faithful to YHWH were completely unable to detect the slightest divine rationale in the disaster they were being forced to undergo. . . . Their attitude is far removed from one of resignation that might have its basis in the conviction that YHWH was ultimately not responsible for everything that overcame them.[75]

I appreciate Renkema's own appreciation of the elements of theological reflection contained in Lamentations (though to my mind there is no need for that to be secondary or late), but I disagree with Renkema on a number of points, particularly on the issue of the theodical motivations of its authors. First, Renkema's point of departure, that Lamentations reflects an organized practice of temple poetry, that is, communal laments that are created to justify God, does not cohere with the lines of protest that one finds in the laments.[76] Second, Renkema argues that the poets generally find meaning in suffering and thus are able to produce a theological explanation that justified God.[77] I profoundly disagree and

75. Renkema, "Theodicy in Lamentations?," 427–28.

76. Renkema (*Lamentations*, 59–62) fiercely rejects Westermann's conception of Lamentations as comprising spontaneous reactions to the distress, as "an outgrowth of oral tradition"; see Westermann, *Lamentations*, 61–63. Renkema (62) sees Westermann's great fault in his "obsession with the original form of Lamentations as complaints of the people during the great distress of 587." Renkema argues (62) that Lamentations represents "not distress followed by lament-prayer . . . but distress followed by disillusionment! From the very outset this disillusionment was theological in nature in the sense that it was the experience of human persons who felt a terrible sense of disappointment in their God. . . . The event and the human incapacity to interpret and explain were inseparably interwoven. What they had undergone was such a contradiction of their faith in and knowledge of God, everything they had been told of him from of old." I find myself in complete agreement with Renkema's description of the horrendous theological catastrophe, but in just as complete disagreement with his conclusion that "in this equally theological catastrophe, prayer and lament seemed meaningless and even absurd. What was the point in continuing to pray to a God who had abandoned his people in such a dreadful way?!" (62). Hebrew Bible sources show that grieving laments *are indeed* the language of prayer at that time of distress.

77. Renkema, *Lamentations*, 63: "What was the reason for all this? Nevertheless, in the midst of ongoing distress they succeeded in finding a sense of theological direction, albeit an incomplete and controversial one."

perceive the poets to be struggling with these questions without finding suitable explanations.[78] Third, Renkema takes what I treat as fierce protest against God to be "self-pity"—"murmurings" that are not even addressed to God.[79] Lamentations 2 illustrates that protests against God are set side by side with justificatory reflections in the book of Lamentations (compare Lam 1 and Lam 2). Fourth, Renkema specifies the major theologoumenon of Lamentations to be "the universal kingship of YHWH."[80] I object to this conclusion; God's universal kingship does not seem to be of major interest in these five laments (see chap. 5). Fifth, Renkema is convinced that the poets confess their guilt.[81] In this area, he seems to treat the material only partially, avoiding the diverse and mutually antagonistic reflections on the questions of sin, guilt, judgment expressed in the collection. Finally, while Renkema sees some of the theological tensions within and between the five communal laments, he never concedes that these tensions might derive from protests aimed at God; this is mainly due to his point of departure concerning the task of the poets and his definition of theodicy.[82]

Studying Jer 21:1–7 and Lam 2 with the help of Green's model shows that Renkema's definition of theodicy is much too narrow. Renkema seems to have minimized the significance of the plainly stated accusation, repeated throughout Lamentations and highly intensified in Lam 2, that God *is* actively responsible for the people's distress (see also Lam 1:5, 12–15, 17, 18, 21c, 22b; 3:1–16, 42; 4:11, 16; 5:22).

A second approach is that of Frederick Dobbs-Allsopp. Dobbs-Allsopp recognizes the occurrence of the two antagonistic lines of thought (justification and protest) that oftentimes occur within one and the same context.[83] Influenced by Walter Brueggemann's conception of testimonial and countertestimonial voices, Dobbs-Allsopp applies to his study of Lamentations Zachary Breiterman's dichotomy of theodicy and "antitheodicy" proclamations distinguishable within twentieth-century post-Shoah reflections.[84] Accordingly, the proximity of these antagonistic positions marks for Dobbs-Allsopp an intentional compositional tendency:

78. See discussions of Lam 2 in §1.2.2, of Ps 44 in §8.2, and of Ps 74 in §7.1.

79. Renkema, *Lamentations*, 61–64.

80. Renkema, *Lamentations*, 67–68.

81. Renkema, *Lamentations*, 65; although it seems that Renkema purposefully avoids discussion of "sins" per se, as they are hardly specified in Lamentations at all.

82. Renkema, *Lamentations*, 69–71.

83. Dobbs-Allsopp, *Lamentations*, 27–33.

84. See Brueggemann, *Theology of the Old Testament*, 317–32. On the antithetic

The poet of Lamentations, with the future existence of the post-destruction community in Palestine at issue, searches out a middle way through to survival that continuously insists on the need to negotiate between theodic and antitheodic impulses.

Lamentations charts a middle course, which, however, theoretically incongruent, gives pragmatic warrant to love God and to protest the aversiveness of evil.

In this way, the poetry is able to give credence to both realities, the reality of sin and the reality of suffering, while at the same time insisting that these realities must be considered and weighed together. The resulting tension, though never resolved explicitly in the poetry itself, effectively frustrates any attempt to explain Jerusalem's suffering too superficially solely in terms of sin. . . . And thus, as with its depiction of God, so also Lamentations' treatment of sin is creatively heterogeneous, giving both theodic and antitheodic notions their due, without attempting, prematurely, to resolve the paradoxes that emerge.[85]

I offer three comments on Dobbs-Allsopp's analysis. First, Breiterman is very well aware of the interconnections between theodicy and antitheodicy and their unstable interpretive outlooks. Thus, I challenge Dobbs-Allsopp's tendency to project an unbridgeable antagonism between them.[86]

---

terms "theodicy" and "antitheodicy," see Breiterman, *(God) after Auschwitz*, 4, 35–59. Breiterman defines antitheodicy as "any religious response to the problem of evil whose proponents refuse to justify, explain, or accept as somehow meaningful the relationship between God and suffering" (31). He further writes that "antitheodicy mirrors theodicy in reverse . . . antitheodic statements do not do what theodic statements do. They neither justify, explain, ascribe positive meaning, account for, resolve, understand, accept, or theologically rectify the presence of evil in human affairs. . . . Rather they express anger, hurt, confusion. They do not try to silence suffering people" (37). Breiterman adds that the "classical Jewish response to the problem of evil is overwhelmingly theodic. Nevertheless, antitheodic texts are sufficiently common to justify grouping them under a heading of their own" (31).

85. Dobbs-Allsopp, *Lamentations*, 30–32.

86. Breiterman, *(God) after Auschwitz*, 5, 37, 57–59. I call attention to Breiterman's own hesitations concerning such a dichotomy: "In this spirit, I conclude this chapter with hesitation. Any given utterance by which a religious thinker responds to suffering can constitute a theodicy in one semantic context and an antitheodicy in another. Only the location of the utterance within a field of other statements determines its theodic or antitheodic significance" (57). See also 58–59, where Breiterman presents the similarities, as well as the differences, between the traditional antitheodicy of Hebrew Bible and rabbinic texts and post-Shoah antitheodicy.

Second, the search in Lamentations for a middle way is but one of many such biblical "searches" struggling with the same theological difficulties during the sixth century; hence, binary categorization, which positions justification (theodicy) and protest (antitheodicy) as mutually exclusive, does not seem adequate. Finally, Dobbs-Allsopp suggests that the middle course wends between a "pragmatic warrant to love God and to protest the aversiveness of evil." He thus fails to find a place for the obvious tendency within Lamentations to protest against God himself, not simply against a vague (or at times explicit) human-generated "evil."[87]

Elizabeth Boase is alert to the problems posed by the scholarly definitions of theodicy, and aptly criticizes both Renkema and Dobbs-Allsopp.[88] Concerning Lamentations as a whole she writes: "The poems of Lamentations are profoundly theological; God is spoken of and spoken to. Over and above this, it can also be argued that these poems are profoundly theodic. Lamentations incorporates speech which explores the relationship of God to the suffering, and while it cannot be argued that the book itself is a theodicy in its own right, it does grapple with theodic issues. In doing so, it not only reflects the present crisis, but proposes, and in turn subverts, possible theodic solutions to this crisis."[89]

Hence, recognizing the nature of the book as comprising reflections on the theodic crisis (the term borrowed from Brueggemann), Boase develops a much wider definition of theodicy "as an existential need to explain suffering and evil."[90] Using the distinctions articulated by Antti Laato and Johannes de Moor, Boase recognizes two types of theodicies operating within Lamentations: retributive theodicy (1:5, 8, 9, 14, 18, 20, 22; 3:39, 42; 4:6, 13, 22; 5:7, 16) and educative theodicy (3:25–30, 34–39).[91] Yet, Boase argues that Lamentations cannot be considered theodicy "as such."[92] She characterizes Lamentations as reflecting "a time of theodic crisis"; she

---

87. Compare Boase (*Fulfilment of Doom?*, 199–200), who points out that throughout Lamentations, God's active role as Jerusalem's destroyer is emphasized, while human agency is minimized.

88. Boase, "Constructing Meaning," 450–52.

89. Boase, "Constructing Meaning," 450.

90. Boase, "Constructing Meaning," 454.

91. Laato and de Moor, *Theodicy in the World of the Bible*, vii–liv.

92. See, for example, Boase's discussion of Lam 3:42 ("Constructing Meaning," 461): "The confession functions as an introduction to a communal lament which protests about God's inaccessibility and the action of the enemy (vv. 43–47). The movement from confession to complaint makes it difficult to see v. 42 as theodic."

locates "theodic responses" in Lamentations, but she finds them not to be fully developed:

> In light of the above analysis, is it possible to talk about theodicy in relation to Lamentations? This question can be answered in both the negative and the affirmative. Lamentations is not a theodicy in its own right, but does contain many theodic elements within its poems. . . .
>
> Lamentations does portray a period of great, arguably existential, crisis for the community. A time of theodic crisis. It does explore and express possible responses to this breakdown of meaning, and in this way can be seen as theodic. To push this too far, and to argue that the book is itself a theodicy, is to misread the purpose and meaning of the text, but to deny the existence of any theodic element is to ultimately do injustice to the struggles to construct meaning within the Jerusalem community. . . .
>
> Elements of retributive theodicy are clearly present within Lamentations, as seen by the recurring reference to the sin of the people, and the causal linking of this sin with Yahweh's action. That is not to say that this is a fully developed or wholly accepted theodic position. Too many factors in the text subvert or contradict the theodic statements for this to be so. Amongst this are those places which name Yahweh as the causal agent behind the destruction but make no reference to sin as the motivation behind Yahweh's actions (see especially ii 1–8 and iii 1–18). However, it can be asserted that one of the responses to the existential crisis is that the suffering is the result of an act of retributive justice on Yahweh's part.[93]

I want to take Boase's analysis several steps farther (and take issue with Renkema and Dobbs-Allsopp along the way). These constant transitions between rational theodical explanations (retributive or educative) and protest against God, equally representative, as they are, of the "struggles to construct meaning" in the contemporary Jerusalemite community, may best be understood not through a definition of theodicy, however expanded, but through a framework of theodical discourse.[94] In the case

93. Boase, "Constructing Meaning," 467, 468, 463.
94. On lament and even blasphemy as legitimate modes of expression within theological discourse in biblical and postbiblical Jewish tradition, see Lane, "Arguing with God."

of Lamentations specifically, I argue that from the deepest levels of their "physical and spiritual desperation" (to quote Renkema),[95] these poets are looking for explanations (or resolutions) of their intolerable spiritual situation. In different ways, they are clearly making "the effort to resist the conclusion that such a logical trilemma exists."[96]

If we place Jer 21:1–7 (as one example of a prophetic voice) side by side with Lam 2 (as one representative of the five communal laments in Lamentations and of other laments in Psalms), a more complex picture of theodical reflection emerges. One may see some lines of agreement between the prophet Jeremiah and the protesting voices in the communal laments. (1) Both highlight God's role as the one who afflicts Jerusalem (Israel/Judah), with all his might and wrath; (2) both agree concerning the lack of compassion shown by God toward his own people; and (3) both avoid, to a great extent, dealing with God's role as a just judge.[97]

Yet, the prophetic and the lamenting voices commonly differ on the question of the causal role of the people's sins in this picture. The prophets in general, and Jeremiah among them, tend to hold the people responsible for the divine judgment and thus to justify the extreme measures taken by God against Jerusalem and Judah (e.g., Jer 16:10–13). The poets treat the people's sins in various ways. While there are some direct and clear confessions (e.g., Ps 79:8; see also Jer 14:7, 20),[98] most communal laments avoid an explicit confession of sins or even proclaim the people's innocence (e.g., Pss 44:18–23; 80:19); thus they implicitly or explicitly protest against the divine judgment. Yet, and I find this crucial, like the poet of Lam 2:18–22, all the poets turn to God in prayer; that is, all these protests are marshaled in a context of prayer or, at least, a plea for salvation. Protest is part of the fabric of *communication* with God; and thus these compositions show that protest is an integral part of the religious struggle for comprehension of God's ways in times of national (and personal) distress.[99]

Between the prophecies that justify God's actions and the poetic laments that protest against him lies a rich negotiation of the theological

---

95. Renkema, "Theodicy in Lamentations?," 427–28.

96. Green, "Theodicy," 431; see §1.1.1.

97. Jer 21:8–10 does enter into the realm of God's justice, through its allusion to Deut 30:15–19, but this independent passage is attached to Jer 21:1–7 only at the redactional stage. See §6.4.

98. Jer 14:7–9 and 14:19–22 are treated in this study as two fragments of communal laments quoted by the prophet; see §7.2.

99. See Rom-Shiloni, "Socio-Ideological Setting."

challenge of justifying God (or better, of making sense of his role) in the face of disaster. I suggest framing this multifaceted deliberation as theodical discourse. While prophets and poets differ significantly in their theological perceptions and strategies, they deal with the same issues, which can be seen when the concerns of these different literatures are formulated in the terms of the trilemma of theodicy. Therefore, Lamentations in general, and specifically Lam 2, is engaged in deep theodical debate, even though most of its theological reflections do not find an answer to God's destructive actions against city and people.

If we take our cues from Hebrew Bible texts of the sixth century, it seems that we discover a disconnect between the (largely Christian) scholarly definition of theodicy (inspired by Leibniz) and the concerns of the Hebrew Bible texts themselves. In fact, the *interplay* between justification and protest, not the *antagonism* between them, is most helpful conceptually for understanding the lament literature—for seeing the theological struggles as a theodical discourse.

On the strength of this biblical record, I modestly suggest a broader definition of theodicy, based on Green's elucidation of the trilemma of theodicy and built on the understanding of justification of God as but one component of a multifaceted theodical discourse:

> Theodicy is the constant struggle to defend God, that is, to justify God's involvement in the human sphere (in both individual and national contexts), according to his roles as king, warrior, and judge. Times of crisis spurred different biblical authors to navigate in different ways the three poles of the trilemma of theodicy, guided by the anxious wish to strike a balance between the anguish of reality and recognized perceptions of God as omnipotent, omniscient, and (simultaneously) good and compassionate. Hence, the justification of God should be perceived as but one component of a theodical discourse, the product of a multifaceted deliberation within a society, which embraces a wide spectrum of opinions on the talk to and about God, from justification of God to doubt and protest against him.

This definition of theodicy is, of course, based on earlier discussions. One point of departure is the suggestion by Laato and de Moor that the sixth century is characterized by a broad spectrum of theological deliberation; they include among expressions of theodicy the "voices of those suffering in past and present," as well as those who "accuse God of injustice or cry out to Him in utter incomprehension."[100] My own framework of theodical discourse expands the concept of theodicy in two ways, both in content and in tone.

First, the broader spectrum of voices encompassed by a framework of theodical discourse allows for an understanding of theodicy as focusing on the justification of God, not only as the articulation of the ways of divine justice. This in turn suggests a wider scope for considering the different roles that God plays in events of national defeat and destruction—as lord of history, king of his people, warrior, and judge. Hence, theodical discourse encompasses the entire spectrum of divine roles and applies to all theological topics raised in consequence of national crisis.

Second, the very concept of theodical *discourse* is explicitly attentive to the tone of or, rather, the broad spectrum of voices participating in the theological discussion; this broader definition works in accordance with Green's recognition of the "effort" (or Crenshaw's "attempt") to explain or to justify God. All those who are engaged in discourse about God in the face of catastrophe struggle with Green's trilemma. Each and every one of them, whether prophet, historiographer, poet, royal official, or member of the general community, attempts to negotiate these three points in a sincere wish to find reconciliation with God. Expressions of skepticism, doubt, and protest stand side by side with the justification of God. All are necessary components of theodical discourse, that is, of the theologically explicit (or implicit) search for ways to resolve the tensions between the distress of present reality and traditional perceptions of the divine.[101]

Therefore, in answer to Renkema, Dobbs-Allsopp, and Boase, theodic crisis *is* the driving force behind both the justification of God and the challenges against God in Lamentations; both avenues attempt to come to grips with God's treatment of his nation in times of distress.

The framework of theodical discourse is easy to discern if we consider the laments from the angle of the problem of theodicy. Protest emerges from the effort to simultaneously negotiate all three points of the trilemma, whereas justification of God rests on the understanding that only two of these points serve to make intelligible God's involvement in human crises.

---

100. See Laato and de Moor, *Theodicy in the World of the Bible*, xii.

101. My inclusion of protest and doubt in theodical discourse brings me close to Obeyesekere's definition of theodicy, which, due to his interest in Hinduism, is not restricted to a monotheistic formulation: "When a religion fails logically to explain human suffering or fortune in terms of its system of beliefs, we can say that a theodicy exists" ("Theodicy, Sin, and Salvation," 11).

The crucial observation is that protest is part of the legitimate talk to (and about) God.[102]

Justification and protest thus form an indivisible pair within the Hebrew Bible's universe of theological discourse; together, they constitute theodicy as discourse. In the sources discussed here, they illuminate a confrontation with the national catastrophe of the destruction and exiles in the early sixth century and following. All voices seem to be engaging the three sides of the same trilemma. Rather than positing a binary antagonism between prophets and poets, theodic and antitheodic speakers, and their perceptions,[103] I prefer the imagery of all participants engaged in an unceasing walk on the same tracks around the three poles of the triangle established by the trilemma of theodicy, trying (mostly in vain) to reach reconciliation, to justify God in times of crisis.[104]

The recognition of the tight interconnections between opposing theological reactions, in the context of an overall search for theological justification and/or reconciliation, clarifies the complex literary and thematic evidence of our sources.[105] Even more, however, these interconnections

102. This is recognized by Westermann ("Role of the Lament," 30), who emphasizes that protest is directed at God in the national laments, in Job (p. 32), and in the laments of Jeremiah (pp. 35–36). Davidson (*Courage to Doubt*, 6–17, esp. 8) argues that the communal laments "are characterized by protest and they have nowhere to take their protest except to God."

103. I find Brueggemann's "Some Aspects of Theodicy" more in line with my suggestion, than is his courtroom imagery; protest finds a natural place under his rubrics of "theodic appeal" and "theodic protest"; see "Some Aspects of Theodicy," 264.

104. The difference between a binary system and a circular one is not only formal. These observations, then, position me closer to perspectives on the dialogical and polyphonic nature of Lamentations; see Heim, "Personification of Jerusalem"; and Boase, *Fulfilment of Doom?*, 203–44.

105. Balentine ("Prayers for Justice") discusses several prose prayers, looking at the integral connection of prayer, theodicy, and Old Testament theology. Balentine recognizes that "one of the principal functions of OT prayer is to address, clarify, and sometimes resolve theodicean issues" (598). Although he focuses on Num 14:10–21, he also discusses Gen 18:22–33; Exod 32:7–14; Josh 7:7–9; and 1 Kgs 17:17–24. Balentine argues that "these texts all revolve around the themes of crisis, prayer, resolution of crisis" (603) and that they all raise questions of divine justice within a framework of prayer; thus, "taken together they represent a significant witness to the biblical recommendation of prayer as an appropriate response for those who would stand in 'loyal opposition' to God and to God's ways of executing justice" (603; Balentine takes the term "loyal opposition" from Coats, "King's Loyal Opposition"). According to Balentine, those prose prayers have an important role in expressing the dialogical

show the benefits of adopting a framework of theodical discourse in order to sort out the theological context of the oppositional perspectives of justification and protest within Hebrew Bible texts of the sixth century.

These observations lead into two separate discussions in the next chapters. The first and broader discussion articulates the methodology of Hebrew Bible theology formulated in this study (chap. 2); the second (chap. 3) focuses on the multiplicity of theological voices in Hebrew Bible texts and their interrelationships and thus introduces the literary sources of this monograph.

---

communication between God and humanity and serve as "theodicean vehicles" (613) to allow questions to be addressed to the divine justice.

2

Studying Religious Thought

The lively scholarly search for methodological principles for studying the theologies of the Hebrew Bible spans several centuries, involving both Christian and Jewish communities of scholars. There is controversy between Christian and Jewish scholars (and theologians), as well as among Jewish scholars of Hebrew Bible theology in themselves, as to what constitutes the proper aim, principles, and content, of Hebrew Bible theology. The discussion proposes a framework for a descriptive theology of the Hebrew Bible (non-Christian and non-Jewish in its affiliation) as the most appropriate methodology to use with the variegated biblical corpus in order to decipher and reconstruct the targeted topic of theodicy as discourse.

2.1. From Biblical Theology to Hebrew Bible (Tanakh) Theology

Biblical theology as a historical discipline owes its definition to German Protestant theologian Johan Gabler, who in his 1787 inaugural address at the University of Altdorf proposed a distinction, uncommon at the time, between biblical (historical) theology and dogmatic (systematic) theology: "There is truly a biblical theology, of historical origin, conveying what the holy writers felt about divine matters; on the other hand there is a dogmatic theology of didactic origin, teaching what each theologian philosophizes rationally about divine things, according to the measure of his ability or of the times, age, place, sect, school, and other similar factors."[1]

---

1. Gabler, "Oration on the Proper Distinction," 501; the essay is translated in Sandys-Wunsch and Eldredge, "Gabler and the Distinction," 137.

Gabler presents methodological stages necessary to produce a biblical theology as a historical philological study of the "truly divine; the *dicta classica*" written by different "sacred authors" over time. By means of the careful study of their words in their ancient meanings, through which ideas could be exposed and compared within each of the many compositions (recognizing differences between the Old Testament and the New Testament), Gabler is confident that such a biblical theology could be described and only then be useful for dogmatic theology:

> For only from these methods can those certain and undoubted universal ideas be singled out, those ideas which alone are useful in dogmatic theology. And if these universal notions are derived by a just interpretation from those *dicta classica*, and those notions that are derived are carefully compared, and those notions that are compared are suitably arranged, each in its own place, so that the proper connexion and provable order of doctrines that are truly divine may stand revealed; truly then the result is biblical theology in the stricter sense of the word.[2]

This important distinction, established by the late eighteenth century, seems to have occupied Christian theologians and biblical scholars throughout the nineteenth and the twentieth centuries.[3] The historical dimension of biblical theology, framed alongside Christian dogmatics (even, to an extent, independent of the New Testament),[4] was a guideline for Gerhard von Rad in the first half of the twentieth century.[5] Nevertheless, in his influential *Old Testament Theology*, von Rad criticizes the strict

---

2. Gabler, "Oration on the Proper Distinction," 506.

3. On Gabler's contribution to formation of the discipline, see Goshen-Gottstein, "Tanakh Theology," 618, 635; and Knierim, *Task of Old Testament Theology*, 495–556.

4. The scholarly negotiation over the proper relationship between the Old Testament and the New Testament in forming biblical theology has not arrived to any agreed conceptions over more than two centuries; see Eichrodt, *Theology of the Old Testament*, 1.25–35 (entitled "Old Testament Theology: The Problem and the Method") and 1.512–20 ("Excursus: The Problem of Old Testament Theology"). Eichrodt sharply criticizes von Rad (and many others) on what he considers exaggerated historical study of biblical theology; Eichrodt's counterways draw him nearer to systematic theology, searching for typological connections and continuations (within inherent differences) between the two Testaments. See §2.2.2.

5. For an evaluation of von Rad's contribution to twentieth-century scholarship on biblical theology, see Brueggemann's introduction to von Rad's *Old Testament Theology*, 1.ix–xxxi.

historical emphasis that biblical theology took on throughout the more than 170 years from Gabler to the early to mid-twentieth century, and thus sets his goal as that of refocusing biblical theology on "Jahweh's action in revelation."[6] Von Rad articulates the core of biblical theology, its subject matter, as follows: "The subject matter which concerns the theologian is, of course, not the spiritual and religious world of Israel and the conditions of her soul in general, nor is it her world of faith ... instead it is simply Israel's own explicit assertions about Jahweh. The theologian must above all deal directly with the evidence, that is, with what Israel herself testifies concerning Jahweh."[7]

The significance of tracing the core, the subject matter, of biblical theology to the ancient Israelite talk to and about God (Gabler's words) cannot be underestimated.[8] This basic definition of biblical theology (which, nevertheless, continues to be debated) had two major consequences. It allows the field of biblical theology to be admitted as part of the critical academic study of the Bible, defined by corpus, goals, methodologies, and theological observations.[9] Subsequently, as part of the evolving academic discussions on biblical theology, the denominational borders are somewhat breached. The closed borders of this Christian, mostly Protestant, scholarly field opened first to allow Catholic and then Jewish Hebrew Bible scholars to enter the arena.

6. Von Rad, *Old Testament Theology*, 1.105–28, esp. 112–15.

7. Von Rad, *Old Testament Theology*, 1.105.

8. See further Knierim (*Task of Old Testament Theology*, 16), who likewise points out the centrality of conversation about God. He extends the focus of discussion beyond that of his teacher, von Rad (*Old Testament Theology*, 1.106), to the ongoing activity of God in history. Knierim includes all discourse about God in his relation to the cosmos, to history and society, and to human existence. From a Catholic standpoint, see Fischer, *Theologien des Alten Testaments*, 9–20. These views that specify theology as the talk of or about God may be contrasted with much broader definitions of biblical theology; for instance, Zevit ("Jewish Biblical Theology," 297–99, 305), reflecting "American parlance" as "anything related to religion"—including attitudes and actions, faith, religious lessons, etc. Under Zevit's very general definition of theology, God, as the object of study, is mentioned as but one among several other components (297), which brings his discussion much closer to a systematic theology than to a descriptive one.

9. On the history of the discipline, see Hayes and Prussner, *Old Testament Theology*, 254–76. See also Barr's opening discussion in his *Concept of Biblical Theology*, 2–17, in which he tries to precisely define biblical theology. This search for a direction, and the even more complex quest to bridge the gap between biblical scholarship and constructive theology, is the motivation behind Perdue, Morgan, and Sommer's *Biblical Theology*; see Perdue's closing chapter on hermeneutics (209–64).

This openness is only gradually achieved (and still seems to be in progress). While not at all a young field of research, biblical theology still seems to be finding its way(s) among other branches of critical study of the Bible.[10] Recent decades saw attempts from many different directions to rethink the definition of the discipline, its place in academic biblical studies, and proper methodological directions for both Christian and Jewish approaches to this field.[11]

Among the dynamics that give rise to this impulse toward redefinition is the recognition that biblical theology is an essential aspect of critical study of the Hebrew Bible. John Collins answers affirmatively the question "is a critical biblical theology possible?" and he describes the task of biblical theology as follows:

> If biblical theology is to be based on critical methodology, then its task is the critical evaluation of biblical speech about God. It is an area of historical theology. . . . It necessarily overlaps with the history of religion. It is the specialization of that discipline that deals with the portrayal of God in one specific corpus of texts. Biblical theology . . . should clarify the meaning and truth-claims of what was thought and believed from a modern critical perspective.[12]

One would think that all theologians/scholars of Hebrew Bible theology would (or could) agree on such a definition of biblical (Hebrew Bible)

10. This process is evident in the titles of several publications from the late 1970s through the present, including Gottwald, *Tribes of Yahweh*, 667–709 (entitled "Biblical Theology or Biblical Sociology?"); Barr, "Theological Case against Biblical Theology"; Collins, "Critical Biblical Theology?"; Mauser, "Historical Criticism"; and Reumann, "Whither Biblical Theology?" These questions seem not to have been solved in any satisfactory way, since conversation currently continues in Theology of Hebrew Scriptures Section (Society of Biblical Literature) and Biblical Theology Section (International Society of Biblical Literature). The most recent explorations are those of Schmid, *Is There Theology in the Hebrew Bible?*, and *Historical Theology of the Hebrew Bible*, 1–127.

11. Exemplary is the way Hasel opens his book (*Old Testament Theology*, esp. 7–9) with a discussion entitled "The Future of Old Testament Theology: Prospects and Trends": "This reader in Old Testament theology indicates that there is a multi-various and nonuniform picture regarding the sources, methodologies, nature, purpose, function, and design. Most issues are and remain debated" (reprinted in Ollenburger et al., *Flowering of Old Testament Theology*, 373); cf. Hasel's "Nature of Biblical Theology" and "Recent Models of Biblical Theology." See also Reventlow, *Problems of Old Testament Theology*.

12. Collins, "Critical Biblical Theology?," 9.

45

theology. Not surprisingly, however, and more than in any other sphere of Hebrew Bible studies, it is here, in the field of biblical theology, that a clear denominational divide exists between Christian and Jewish scholars,[13] and internally within each of those religious or nonaffiliated communities of scholars and their respective scholarship.[14] Differences are evident in five major areas, which are very much interrelated: the name of the discipline, the corpus covered, the goal, the methodologies, and the organizing systems to be invoked.[15] I add one additional area: the difference of vested interests of Christian and Jewish scholars in this scholarly field.

2.2. Six Distinguishing Criteria in Biblical/Hebrew Bible Theology

2.2.1. Name

Biblical theology is traditionally understood as the inclusive designation for a theology of the Old Testament plus the New Testament, perceived

---

13. On the profound differences of perspective between Christian and Jewish approaches to biblical theology, see Tsevat, "Theology of the Old Testament." For a programmatic statement that was influential on subsequent efforts by Jewish scholars, see Levenson, "Why Jews Are Not Interested," 38–39.

14. From a Christian point of view, see Rendtorff, "Christian Approach," who states: "The majority of Christian Bible scholars have given up the traditional Christian supersessionism when they are operating as biblical scholars. Unfortunately, when speaking about theology many of them fall back into a kind of exclusivism. They probably would not explicitly deny the theological relevance of the Hebrew Scriptures for Judaism, but they are not interested in this question because they do not see its relevance for themselves" (144). See also Pannenberg, "Problems in a Theology."

15. Lack of agreement on goals, methodology, etc., dogs internal Christian discussions as well and are repeatedly mentioned; see, e.g., Smith, *Old Testament Theology*, 72–77; Waltke and Yu, *Old Testament Theology*, 29–48, esp. 29; and Schmid, *Is There Theology in the Hebrew Bible?*, 11–47. Two studies challenge the concept of biblical theology or Jewish biblical theology as valid academic disciplines in the first place; see Moberly, *Old Testament of the Old Testament*, 152–55, 158; and Zevit, "Jewish Biblical Theology," 327–37. Yet Zevit concludes by describing what an academic Jewish biblical theology should look like (337–40) and advocates for a type of theology that "allows [for] historical and religious development and distinguishes clearly between what is meant and what it can mean" (311, 337). This is the line taken by the current study as well; see §2.3.

by Christian theologians as a single corpus.[16] Focusing on the first component, both Walter Eichrodt and Gerhard von Rad use the terminology "theology of the Old Testament."[17] But this designation does not mean a change in the conception of the canonical corpus (see §2.2.2) and does not open the floor for Jewish scholars; as Rolf Rendtorff notes: "Jewish scholars were *de facto* excluded from the academic study of their own Bible because these studies were exclusively executed as Old Testament studies in the framework of confessional Christian theological faculties."[18]

Moshe Goshen-Gottstein introduces the counterterm "Tanakh theology" to emphasize the Jewish point of departure.[19] A similar term, "Hebrew Bible theology," has come into vogue for both Jewish and Christian scholars—at least among those whom Jon Levenson characterizes as "professional academics and well-informed clergy." For Levenson, this terminology, surfacing originally in Anglo-American and now increasingly in European academic circles, demonstrates "a vibrant ecumenicity."[20] Hence, Hebrew Bible (Tanakh) theology is the term employed in the current work.

---

16. The discussion in §2.2.1 focuses on only the first component, "biblical." For a more comprehensive discussion of each of the terminological components—"Jewish," "biblical," and "theology"—see Zevit, "Jewish Biblical Theology," 292–301. A survey of conceptions of "theology" (in contrast to "religion") is set forth by Schmid, *Is There Theology in the Hebrew Bible?*, 5–47.

17. Eichrodt, *Theology of the Old Testament*, 1.24–35; von Rad, *Old Testament Theology*, 1.115–28; and Goshen-Gottstein, "Tanakh Theology," 618. Smith (*Old Testament Theology*, 72–73) articulates the difference between "the theology of the Old Testament," which is a descriptive and historical enterprise, over against "Old Testament theology," which is systematic and normative in its approach. Neither von Rad nor Eichrodt is able to set aside their understandings of the (systematic) theological messages of the Old Testament in their influential studies.

18. Rendtorff, "Christian Approach," 138. Furthermore, Rendtorff emphasizes that because Old Testament theology issued from the disciplinary context of Christian dogmatic theology, it remains in essence a Christian discipline; see Rendtorff, *Canon and Theology*, 13–14; also Levenson, "Why Jews Are Not Interested," 39.

19. Goshen-Gottstein, "Tanakh Theology."

20. Levenson, "Why Jews Are Not Interested," 34. Along these lines, the Society of Biblical Literature Theology of Hebrew Scriptures Section announced among its goals "to facilitate Jewish-Christian dialogue, creating a venue where Jewish and Christian interpreters can reflect together on a theological interpretation of the Hebrew Scriptures."

2.2.2. *Corpus*

The discipline of *biblical* theology was originally established with reference to the Christian canon and corpus.[21] Accordingly, in writing their theologies of the Old Testament, both Eichrodt and von Rad have the complete Christian canon in mind: the theology of the Old Testament is inevitably seen, at some level, as a function of its contextualization by the New.[22] A canonical approach to biblical theology (which since developed into the separate discipline of canonical criticism) is usually associated with Brevard Childs. He argues for a conceptual "switch," that gives precedence to the New Testament in determining the theological agenda.[23] This characterization of the corpus as the Christian canon frames the task of the theological discussion in two ways.

First, from a Christian point of view, this canonical definition of the corpus obligates scholars to face the question Rendtorff so clearly phrases: "Does the interpreter consider the pre-Christian (i.e., Jewish) meaning of the text to be theologically relevant or not?"[24] Rendtorff himself considers both possibilities. A negative answer leads the scholar to various conceptions of the relation of the Old Testament to the New: "He can see the Old Testament as a preliminary stage, as a pointer or path leading to the New . . . ; or he can view it as superseded; or as a necessary counterpart or antitype to the New Testament; or as the testimony of an alien religion; and so on." A positive answer requires the Christian interpreter to face

---

21. For discussion of the different approaches to the corpus in biblical theology and Hebrew Bible theology, see Rom-Shiloni, "Hebrew Bible Theology," 166–73.

22. Eichrodt, *Theology of the Old Testament*, 1.26–27; and from different perspectives, von Rad, *Old Testament Theology*, 2.309–429, esp. 428–29; Oeming, *Gesamt biblische Theologien*, 20–33, 77–80; and Barr, *Concept of Biblical Theology*, 497–505. This approach continues to typify the work of scholars following von Rad, such as Hasel (*Old Testament Theology*, 89–91), and it underlies many of the essays in the collection edited by Reumann, *Promise and Practice*; see his introductory remarks there ("Whither Biblical Theology?," 1–2).

23. Childs, *Biblical Theology in Crisis*, 91–122; and see the criticism by both Hasel (*Old Testament Theology*, 25–28) and Collins ("Critical Biblical Theology," 3–5). Tsevat ("Theology of the Old Testament," 40) argues that, from such a standpoint, "the Old Testament is henceforth a subject of theology of the New Testament alongside God, cult, salvation, and other subjects; the name biblical theology cannot conceal this." The canonical approach also typifies the work of Brueggemann; see, inter alia, "Crisis and Promise" and *Theology of the Old Testament*, 76.

24. Rendtorff, *Canon and Theology*, 14.

the Old Testament canon in its own context and articulate its theological interpretation independent of the New. Yet, Rendtorff recognizes that this leads the interpreter to "new hermeneutical tasks, ... a new theological approach, which takes the Jewish religion seriously as an independent entity and according to its own self-understanding."[25] For his own theological study, Rendtorff indeed chooses an approach quite exceptional among Christian scholars of the late twentieth century. More often than not, such a Christian canonical definition of the corpus leads Christian biblical theologians/scholars to adopt clearly supersessionist approaches to the Hebrew Bible and to Judaism in general.[26]

Second, and in more practical terms, such Christian definitions of the corpus cause the work of Jewish scholars on the Hebrew Bible always to appear partial at best. In response, Jewish scholars, and subsequently Christian theologians and scholars, advance the concept of the Tanakh/ Hebrew Bible as an independent corpus for theological research.[27]

On the conceptual level, and from a Jewish perspective, the two distinct corpora represent much more than differences in the lists and in the internal arrangement of the canonical books within Judaism (i.e., Tanakh) and Christianity (i.e., Old Testament). As Marvin Sweeney observes: "Although both traditions are based in the same scriptural books, their respective understandings of these books point to very different views of the Bible, the course and meaning of world history, and the significance of God's relationship with humanity and the world of creation."[28]

Sweeney points to two distinct general conceptions of a canon, or *the* canon, and its components. The Christian conception of Old Testament/ New Testament involves "a linear principle" in that it builds toward "the revelation of Christ as the culmination of human history." The Tanakh, on the contrary, is characterized by "a cyclical pattern," which to Sweeney is

25. Rendtorff, *Canon and Theology*, 14–15.

26. See Rendtorff's further challenges to Christian scholars in *Canon and Theology*, 15–16; similarly Barr, *Concept of Biblical Theology*, 4–5, 74; and Pannenberg, "Problems in a Theology," 276.

27. The Hebrew Bible is taken as an independent corpus for study by Collins, Hasel, Knierim, Rendtorff, Barr, and Kessler (among others); compare Fischer, who also treats the book of Baruch, the Epistle of Jeremiah, and Ben Sira in his *Theologien des Alten Testaments*. Rendtorff ("Christian Approach," 139–40) describes the significant differences between the two canons and points out that Christian scholars have long accepted the tripartite division of the Hebrew Bible.

28. Sweeney, "Tanakh versus Old Testament," 371; "Why Jews Should Be Interested"; and *Tanak*, 3–41.

structured according to a vision of "the ideal Jewish life, the disruption of Jewish life, and the restoration of that ideal."[29] I will not mount here a discussion of the contour of this cyclical pattern; the essential point is that Sweeney, like many other scholars (Jewish and Christian), feels that the Hebrew Bible can be seen as self-contained and closed in itself, whereas the Christian canon requires that linear progression from the Old Testament to the New Testament.

This conceptual difference concerning the corpus comes even more to the fore in the distinctive ways in which scholars from the two religious traditions evaluate the relationship between the Hebrew Bible and subsequent authoritative literatures.[30] Most Christian scholars and theologians are indeed committed to the authority of the New Testament as continuation of and interpretive framework for the Old Testament, with all of the risks and/or potential identified by Rendtorff.

From the Christian perspective, a useful reframing of the notion of biblical theology in relation to subsequent tradition is suggested by James Barr: "The term 'biblical theology' has clarity only when it is understood to mean theology as it existed or was thought or believed within the time, languages and cultures of the Bible itself. Only so can its difference from doctrinal theology, from later interpretation, and from later views about the Bible be maintained. . . . What we are looking for is a 'theology' that existed back there and then."[31] Barr includes within the framework of "biblical times and cultures" the time of the events, the time of the original writing of the texts, and the time of their finalization. While, as a Christian scholar, he often treats the Bible synthetically as encompassing both the Old Testament and the New Testament, he thus argues that the Old Testament and the New Testament represent two *different* sets of times and cultures.

---

29. Sweeney, *Tanak*, 24.

30. Levenson ("Why Jews Are Not Interested," esp. 45–51) maintains that the primary difference in the respective conceptions of the corpus stems from the different understanding of Scripture in each tradition. He compares the Christian, and especially Protestant, focus upon *sola scriptura*, while the traditional Jewish conception of the Bible comprises *torah shebikhtav* ("the written Torah") along with *torah shebe'al peh* ("the oral Torah"). While according to a rabbinate (mainstream Judaism) perspective these two streams indeed coalesced historically (as of the codification of rabbinic literature in the Mishnah), the relationship between the written and the oral *torah* became the core of dispute with Karaites. I argue that in academic discussions the two corpora should be kept apart.

31. Barr, *Concept of Biblical Theology*, 4.

Jewish scholars seem to choose one of three paths in articulating the relevance of Second Temple literature, rabbinic literature, and later Jewish traditions for the study of Hebrew Bible theology. On this issue, there are profound disagreements among Jewish scholars of Hebrew Bible theology—disagreements that raise questions that only begin with delineating the corpus, but eventually lead to queries about the very goal of Hebrew Bible theology. The common denominator of all three approaches is the scholar's personal negotiation of the place of the Hebrew Bible in relation to long-standing (rabbinic) Jewish tradition. The interpretive stance taken is clearly connected to the scholar's denominational/confessional commitment (at times this is even explicitly proclaimed). All contemporary Jewish biblical scholars are aware of diachronic issues and literary layers within the Hebrew Bible; and yet, some of them are ready to cross the barriers of time and trace lines of continuity (perhaps even of dialogical relationship) between the Hebrew Bible and later Jewish traditions.

The first approach is continual and dialogical, in that it conceives of an organic continuity between the Hebrew Bible and later traditions. This approach is represented by Jon Levenson, Michael Fishbane, and Benjamin Sommer, who propose in different ways that a dialogical relationship obtains between the Hebrew Bible and later Jewish traditions.

Levenson aptly asserts the independence of the Hebrew Bible from the New Testament and from Christian exegetical traditions; the latter, he suggests, stands in a revolutionary position toward the Hebrew Bible. Along these lines, Levenson opposes the Christian appellation "Old Testament." On the contrary, however, Levenson emphasizes the evolutionary nature of the relationship between Jewish traditions and the Hebrew Bible. Thus, while Levenson is very much aware of the dynamics of the historical-diachronic study of the Hebrew Bible within its ancient Near Eastern arena, he nevertheless prefers a synchronic framework for "doing" biblical theology. He considers later Jewish traditions as aimed at clarifying the plain sense of the biblical texts themselves and thus as integral to the *theological* discussion. Levenson maintains that the use of Jewish traditions in the study of Hebrew Bible theology promises a path of "novelty, even contradiction. It [i.e., the tradition] will not be fossilized, but vital, growing, and to a certain extent, changing."[32]

---

32. See Levenson, *Sinai and Zion*, 3–5, 7, 11–12; and "Why Jews Are Not Interested," 38. Levenson's synchronic/continual conception draws valid criticisms from Barr, *Concept of Biblical Theology*, 286–311, esp. 294–302.

Fishbane describes Hebrew Bible theology as a "living theology," characterized as ever evolving and accumulating through its evolutions in rabbinic tradition; thus he terms it a "Jewish hermeneutical theology."[33] Sommer takes this continual approach to an extreme, provocatively stating: "Strictly speaking, there can be no such thing as Jewish biblical theology. While many definitions of the term 'biblical theology' exist, they all accord some privileged place to the Bible. *All forms of Jewish theology, however, must base themselves on Judaism's rich postbiblical tradition at least as much as on scripture, and hence a Jewish theology cannot be chiefly biblical.*"[34]

As a Hebrew Bible scholar who is also an educator of rabbinical students at the Jewish Theological Seminary, Sommer defines his role as that of "a dialogical biblical theologian," whose primary task is to bring the Hebrew Bible "to participate in contemporary Jewish or Christian religious thought" by looking into the two traditions' long histories of exegesis. As the fine Hebrew Bible scholar that he is, Sommer structures his theological framework as a "three-way discussion" that addresses (1) ancient Near Eastern texts and the Hebrew Bible, (2) rabbinic literature, and (3) modern Jewish communities of readers.[35] The scope of his theological enterprise thus extends much beyond the literary, chronological, and spatial limits of the Hebrew Bible corpus (in its ancient Near Eastern arena).[36]

The second path in Hebrew Bible theology perceives the Hebrew Bible and Jewish traditions as distinct, but still sees the latter as in dialogue with the former, in a dependent and developmental relationship to the Hebrew Bible. This approach, represented by Marvin Sweeney, Marc Brettler, and David Frankel, is often concerned with the constructive relevance of the Hebrew Bible message to the contemporary Jewish/Israeli world.[37] Each scholar begins with a focus on Hebrew Bible texts, before going on to describe the literary dependence of later Jewish traditions on the Hebrew Bible, thus defining the relationship between the earlier and the later texts

---

33. Fishbane, *Sacred Attunement*, 39–107, esp. 43–45; and "Ethics and Sacred Attunement." For a well-taken criticism of this theological approach, see Levinson, "Review: Michael Fishbane, *Sacred Attunement*."

34. Sommer, "Dialogical Biblical Theology," 1 (emphasis added).

35. Sommer, "Dialogical Biblical Theology," 51.

36. Sommer, "Dialogical Biblical Theology," 53. I explore Sommers's dialogical approach in §2.2.3.

37. See Sweeney, *Tanak*, 3–41; Brettler, "Biblical History and Jewish Biblical Theology"; Brettler, "Psalms and Jewish Biblical Theology"; and Frankel, *Land of Canaan*, viii, 382–400.

as exegetical by nature.[38] Hence, dialogue in this framework is more of a one-way engagement of later Jewish interpreters with the foundational corpus of the Hebrew Bible.

Sweeney, for example, accepts the dialogical nature of Jewish biblical theology, but nevertheless emphasizes the differences between the Hebrew Bible and later traditions, arguing that the Bible should first be understood "in and of itself." Yet, Sweeney does not give up on the notion of dialogue. He argues that the relationship of the Tanakh to the Jewish tradition is one of an "organic and integrated process of development":

> With regard to the Tanak and the rest of Jewish tradition, it is not clear that the Tanak was composed to be in intentional dialogue with the later works, but it is clear that most of the later writings were intentionally composed to be in dialogue with the Torah and the rest of the Tanak to some degree. In order to understand that dialogue fully, it is essential to understand the literature of the Torah and the rest of the Tanak in and of itself, recognizing that the Tanak cannot function as a complete and self-contained revelation analogous to the manner in which the Old and New Testaments are read in much of Protestant Christianity. . . .
>
> When reading the Bible in relation to the larger context of Judaism, Jewish biblical theology must consider the relationship between the Bible and post-biblical Jewish tradition and literature. *Like Christianity, Judaism tends to read later literature and tradition back into the Bible. Although such a reading strategy is legitimate* insofar as it promotes full integration of the Bible into the tradition as a whole and recognizes the role of readers in the construction of literature, *it blurs the distinction and compromises a full understanding of the historical development of Judaism.*[39]

Hence, in clearer terms, this second approach emphasizes an awareness of diachronicity in its historical-critical perspective. The contemporary in-

38. Frankel maintains strict boundaries between the Hebrew Bible discussion proper and his last chapter in the book, which ranges far beyond the biblical text, tapping into rabbinic sources and contemporary theological reflections. See Frankel's explicit explanation of his approach: "Only after the biblical conceptions are accurately identified, analyzed, and categorized can one begin the process of discussing the possible relevance of these conceptions for the contemporary situation" (*Land of Canaan*, viii).

39. Sweeney, *Tanak*, 3–4, 25–26 (emphasis added). I find his last sentences on this matter somewhat confusing (4).

terest in (or confessional statement concerning) the Hebrew Bible religious world of thought stands on its own, independent of the place held by the Hebrew Bible in the long history of Judaism as a foundational component.[40]

The third path accentuates even more the diachronic differences between the Hebrew Bible and later Jewish traditions, arguing for the independence of the Hebrew Bible from its inheritors and confining the discussion of biblical theology to the canonical boundaries of the Tanakh. This approach guides the programmatic papers of Matitiahu Tsevat, Moshe Goshen-Gottstein, Isaac Kalimi, and (possibly) Zioni Zevit.[41]

Tsevat describes his own approach to the theology of the Old Testament (he uses this term exclusively) and structures it by means of two separate definitions.[42] He first defines the "theology of the Old Testament" as follows:

> I shall in the following employ the word theology in the minimal and special sense; scientific study of a literature (of a literary work, of a chapter, etc.) whose content is related to God. Note that the adjective Jewish does not appear here.
>
> . . . [The theology of the Old Testament] is part of that branch of the study of literature which has the Old Testament for its subject; it is philology of the Old Testament. It is objective (the word has already been used) in the sense and to the extent that the humanities, especially those whose primary task is understanding, are assured of the objectivity of their statements. Within the total philology of the Old Testament, theology is concerned with the understanding of its ideas, particularly, if not exclusively, the religious and, more precisely, the God-related ideas. . . . Theology so conceived is indispensable to the Old Testament research.[43]

40. Brettler ("Biblical History and Jewish Biblical Theology") emphasizes the idea of the negotiation of the corpora in the context of confessional communities. See also his "Psalms and Jewish Biblical Theology," where he continues to discuss polidoxy in the Hebrew Bible and the question of the typological relationships between Hebrew Bible and later Jewish traditions. His closing chapter in *How to Read the Bible* (279–83) brings him closer to Sommer, in terms of the dialogue he allows in both directions.

41. See Tsevat, "Theology of the Old Testament"; Goshen-Gottstein, "Tanakh Theology"; Kalimi, "History of Israelite Religion"; Kalimi, *Early Jewish Exegesis*. In his words of praise for Kalimi's approach, Zevit ("Jewish Biblical Theology," 314–17) appears to support this path of distinct Hebrew Bible theology, which he then characterized "as autonomous discipline" (311, 337, 339); and see §2.2.6.

42. Tsevat, "Theology of the Old Testament," 43–44.

43. Tsevat, "Theology of the Old Testament," 43, 48–49. This same line of argumentation is (re)introduced by Schmid, *Is There Theology in the Hebrew Bible?*, 2–3, 114–20.

But on a separate level (and recognizing the possible conflicts between the former and the latter statements), Tsevat proceeds to outline the fundamental importance of the Talmud and Midrash, along with the Old Testament, both to Judaism and for his own conceptions/beliefs. He writes: "The biblical and the talmudic literatures are for me of equal significance; despite my unequal efforts about them, they are equally near to me."[44] This is, of course, a confessional statement, by which Tsevat recognizes the place he feels obligated to give to rabbinic tradition as the "Jewish" component of his personal beliefs. Like the Old Testament, these later Jewish writings, founded on the Old Testament, function as a corpus of traditions through which Jews claim relationship to God. Tsevat recognizes the interpretive stance or function of the Talmud and the midrash in relation to the Old Testament, and thus concludes that "no theology of the Old Testament can be derived from the Talmud."[45] Tsevat's most interesting suggestion is to construct two distinct approaches to the theology of the Old Testament, the one "objective-philological" and the other "judaizing"; the second approach would thus take account of Jewish literatures and traditions based on the Old Testament.[46]

In accord with his strict linguistic approach to diachronicity, Goshen-Gottstein advocates looking forward to later Jewish traditions, but he maintains clear distinctions between these historical layers, styling Tanakh theology as a distinct enterprise: "The Tanakh theologian, like the Christian theologian, has a legitimate interest in the way a given phenomenon is mirrored, reinterpreted in a post-Tanakh structure—rabbinic, New Testament, or otherwise. The Tanakh—or Old Testament—theologian is not called upon to do the job of the student of historical layers of theology, but it is not necessary to close one's eyes to later structures even as the earlier ones are analyzed *so long as one does not confuse the facts*."[47]

From a nonconfessional point of departure, Kalimi advocates "a secular, academic-intellectual" enterprise of Hebrew Bible theology, which would first and primarily address the ancient theological meanings of the Hebrew

---

44. Tsevat, "Theology of the Old Testament," 45.

45. Tsevat, "Theology of the Old Testament," 46–48 at 48.

46. Tsevat, "Theology of the Old Testament," 48–49. Tsevat's approach is criticized by Anderson, "Response to Mattityahu Tsevat," 52–54.

47. Goshen-Gottstein, "Tanakh Theology," 633 (emphasis added). This line of thought is also adopted by Kalimi in "History of Israelite Religion" and *Early Jewish Exegesis*, 107–34, 135–63.

Bible in its contexts and only afterward be put at the service of Judaism and Christianity.[48]

I take this third path in my own study of Hebrew Bible theology. The present study emphasizes the need to preserve diachronic distinctions between the Hebrew Bible and later corpora. To borrow Barr's phrase, I am interested in describing the "theology that existed back there and then" as distinct from that of its later reframers.[49] From the point of view of determination of the target corpus, I argue that both rabbinic *and* Christian literary corpora and interpretive traditions share the same basic feature: they both stand *beyond* the times and the cultures of the Hebrew Bible with regard not only to their cultural and literary formation, but also to their respective interpretive and theological frameworks. In order to construct a Hebrew Bible (Tanakh) theology, I consider it imperative to demarcate the Hebrew Bible as a self-contained corpus, as separate from both its dependent corpora, Christian *and* Jewish.

2.2.3. Goal

Christian and Jewish scholars also debate what has been and what ought to be the goal of biblical theology, and their diverse views in turn determine the different methodologies employed.[50] Two foci of these debates concerning possible goals are germane. The first is the distinction between systematic and descriptive biblical theologies; the second is the debate concerning the intermediate place captured by a notion of dialogical biblical theology (akin to the first path outlined in the previous section) within this context. The entire discussion cuts across Christian and Jewish scholarship.

As mentioned, Gabler's initial formulation specifies the goal of biblical theology as a descriptive historical enterprise, confined to the ancient authorized (sacred) Scriptures; upon the results of this enterprise, Christian dogmatic theology was shaped and ever adapted and reformulated

---

48. See Kalimi, *Early Jewish Exegesis*, 114–18 at 114; and Zevit, "Jewish Biblical Theology," 314–16.

49. Barr, *Concept of Biblical Theology*, 4.

50. Tsevat ("Theology of the Old Testament"), for example, opens his discussion with the preliminary question of why biblical theology is traditionally a Christian domain. Tsevat goes back as far as Paul and the formative period of Christianity: "Viewed historically, the theology of the Old Testament in the Christian perspective . . . is a formulation of the relation of the Testaments to one another" (36).

according to the needs of subsequent generations.[51] Invoking this basic distinction, Krister Stendahl further develops the difference between "systematic-dogmatic theology" and "descriptive theology," which he represents as a distinction between two questions. Systematic-dogmatic theology asks "what *does* it mean?" and looks for a contemporary answer relevant to the life and beliefs of members of a faith community without regard for chronological distinctions. Descriptive theology asks "what *did* it mean?" and is thus occupied with recording and studying the ancient thought-worlds themselves, in their historical and cultural contexts. Systematic theology is founded upon philosophical methodology, whereas descriptive theology derives its methodological principles from historical-philological research.[52] Stendahl's formulation refers to Christian theologies, but these characterizations are applicable to Jewish scholars (and rabbis) just as well—yet with a significant difference. To a large extent, Christian biblical theology reflects a systematic theological outlook more than scholars generally admit,[53] whereas in Jewish circles the systematic outlook is a distinctive marker of nonacademic/noncritical study of the Hebrew Bible (i.e., as handled by rabbis in nonacademic settings).[54] Furthermore, postmodern approaches revisit the fundamental question of the

51. See §2.1. Gabler ("Oration on the Proper Distinction," 505–6) articulates, even back then, the basic notions of "reception criticism," arguing that dogmatic theology could be established only as a second step, founded on the basis of biblical theology; dogmatics needs to be understood as a separate phenomenon, changing over time in relation to the needs of various epochs.

52. Stendahl, "Biblical Theology."

53. See, for instance, Eichrodt's understanding that biblical theology should supply a unified, coherent intellectual scheme that accounts for normative claims of Christian faith (*Theology of the Old Testament*, 1.512–20); Collins, "Critical Biblical Theology?," 3–7; and Brueggemann's discussion of the "intellectual supersessionism committed in the name of Enlightenment rationality" (*Theology of the Old Testament*, 14–15), his discussion of twentieth-century scholars and scholarship (15–60), as also his designation of von Rad as representing a "'soft form' of supersessionism" (introduction to von Rad's *Old Testament Theology*, 1.xxiii–xxiv, xxvi).

54. These distinctions between dogmatic-systematic-constructive theology and descriptive theology become blurred at times, as Goshen-Gottstein observes in relation to the boundaries between the role of the theologian and that of the academic scholar of religion ("Jewish Biblical Theology," 45–64). Zevit ("Jewish Biblical Theology," 328–37) observes the growing tendency among both Jewish and Christian biblical scholars in the United States, including those who embrace critical methodology in their biblical scholarship, to presume a contemporary application for the study of biblical theology. See, inter alia, Sommer, "Revelation at Sinai."

real possibility of distinguishing "what *does* it mean?" from "what *did* it mean?" thereby sending scholars back to the starting point.[55]

Sommer's "dialogical Jewish theology" is geared to enjoying both worlds. Sommer defines the mode of dialogical Jewish theology as that of "intellectual history," which by its scope starts with "a structural phenomenology" of the Hebrew Bible (as earlier suggested by Goshen-Gottstein). Yet, the dialogical theologian does not stop with the description of such a history. At times s/he does not even begin with a biblical issue or passage, but rather with concepts expressed through the long chain of Jewish tradition from postbiblical sources up to modern ones, in a manner that is "*synthetic* in the Kantian sense."[56] Sommer enthusiastically accepts Manfred Oeming's suggestion (coming from a Christian perspective) that biblical theology should be understood as "value-related exegesis"; that is, from the Christian point of departure, exegesis that initiates a dialogical relationship between the Old Testament and the New Testament, enriching the understanding of both and discovering relevance to contemporary religious thought.[57] Another important and appreciated principle suggested by Oeming, which Sommer is happy to embrace, is the openness of Hebrew Bible theology to the exegesis of different denominations, both Christian and Jewish, and to all branches and eras of their religious traditions.[58] Sommer thus suggests that a "Jewish biblical theology" might be constructed using Oeming's approach to "individual texts and issues." He finds Oeming's approach to be very close to that of Jewish biblical scholars, with whom Sommer suggests Oeming shares "an openness to—indeed, a love of—the Bible's (protorabbinic) multi-vocality; and an awareness of . . . the synthetic rather than analytic nature of Christian measures of value applied to biblical texts."[59]

Applying these principles to the doing of "Jewish dialogical biblical

55. Brueggemann, "Biblical Theology Appropriately Postmodern."

56. Sommer, "Dialogical Biblical Theology," 22–23. The synthesis that Sommer suggests stands against what he (following Oeming) defines as the *analytic* approach, that is, an approach that retains historical and diachronic distinctions between layers of traditions. Sommer traces a biblically based conflict through transformations in rabbinic texts, medieval midrashic texts, and even the Hassidic/Mitnagdic conflict of the eighteenth century (29–43).

57. Oeming, *Gesamt biblische Theologien*, 11–19. Oeming advocates a "biblischen Theologie als wertbeziehen der Exegese" (226–41).

58. Oeming, *Gesamt biblische Theologien*, 237–41.

59. Sommer, "Dialogical Biblical Theology," 24. Sommer ends his evaluation of Oeming's approach with the remarkable note that "none of the reasons Levenson gives

theology," Sommer illustrates his approach through two examples. Suffice
it to use his conclusions to the first example: "A Jewish biblical theology
need not—in fact, should not—see for itself the goal of definitively stating
what the Bible says; rather, it should look for what the Bible invites us to
attend to, and it should examine how rabbinic and later Jewish literatures
pick up that invitation. It is by attending to the same issues, and by turning
them over and turning them over again, that Jewish biblical theology can
become part of the all-encompassing discussion that is Torah."[60] Sommer
thus designates himself as a "dialogical biblical theologian," whose major
goal in his theological studies is to set in motion a discussion that is "an
unambiguously confessional enterprise" within "confessional traditions,"
with the aim to "renew the Hebrew Bible's status as a Jewish book and
as a Christian book," highlighting the shared and distinctive traditions
of each.[61]

Sommer's thoughtful paradigm clearly constitutes an important contribution to the current discussion around constructing *contemporary* Jewish
theology. But considered in relation to the more limited boundaries of a
critical academic study of *Hebrew Bible* theology, I find two basic limits
to his methodology. The first concerns the issue of the corpus. The linear
connection of continuity and the dialogical relationship between the Old
Testament and the New Testament, suggested by Oeming for the Christian
theological context, is irrelevant to the Tanakh as the object of critical
study on its own. Later Jewish traditions do rely on the Hebrew Bible

---

for Jews' lack of interest in biblical theology would apply to a Christian biblical theology that follows Oeming's proposal" (24).

60. Sommer, "Dialogical Biblical Theology," 43. In his first example, Sommer focuses on "the primary religious value according to the Psalter and later Judaism" (29–
43). The virtuosic (or, one may say, "cherry picking") choices of sources is telling. He
starts with references in the Babylonian Talmud and Jerusalem Talmud, jumps to Has-
sidic and Mitnagdic polemics from eighteenth-century Eastern Europe that allegedly
represent a deep-rooted distinction between two Jewish "temperaments" or sets of
pious practices (liturgical religiosity versus Torah learning), and only then returns to
Ps 1 to ask: "Is the Psalter fundamentally a Hasidic or a Mitnagdic book?" (32). His answer is that the roots of these late two modes of religious experience are already within
the psalter. The final editorial process of Psalms is a Mitnagdic one, which places Ps 1
and Ps 150 as an *inclusio* to highlight the importance of piety through Torah learning
(in clear distinction from the Davidic, liturgical character of Ps 2 and many others). In
Sommer's second example on kingship and messianism, he finds innerbiblical polemics
over Davidic kingship to be early reflections of polemics that crossed generations of
Jewish traditions up to modern conflicts over ideas concerning the Messiah (43–50).

61. Sommer, "Dialogical Biblical Theology," 53.

as their foundational corpus, but the exegetical connection between the earlier and later corpora is unidirectional. The synthetic approach that Sommer advances is highly of interest and certainly has an educational-theological role in confessional contexts, but as such does not assist the critical discussion of the Hebrew Bible.[62] The second limitation concerns the dialogical jumps between late and early sources, from modern Jewish thought to the Psalms and back, enabled by Sommer's model. Sommer's examples are very clear illustrations of the possibilities that arise from reading postbiblical issues and perspectives back into the Hebrew Bible; but they thus raise the problematic possibility of mistaking externally imposed meanings for the contextually determined meaning of the biblical text. This risk of retrojection seems to me one of the most problematic aspects of Christian biblical theology. Sommer's theological model, I fear, now recasts this risk in a Jewish costume.

On the contrary, in constructing a theology of the Hebrew Bible, I consider it imperative to separate the discussion of the Hebrew Bible's theological points of view from those of the two religious traditions that gave rise to Jewish and Christian theologies. As presented time and again, synthetic approaches do not help to cut sharp distinctions between successive stages of religious thinking; they rather tend to blur the picture.[63]

Therefore, in defining my own goal for a Tanakh theology, I prefer to remain with Stendahl's descriptive question: "What *did* it mean?" and even to specify further "What *did they* [those whose voices speak in our target sources] *say* about God?" As a biblical scholar, my interest in Hebrew Bible theology is the thought-world of the Tanakh in itself, studied from a critical-descriptive point of view that uses philological tools to read the Hebrew Bible and comparative methodologies to tap its ancient Near Eastern sources. In this, I join the Jewish scholars Tsevat, Goshen-Gottstein, and Kalimi, who calls for a model of "biblical theological research" based on "secular, academic-intellectual viewpoints," the results of which would be at the service of both religious traditions.[64] Accordingly, I define the task of Tanakh theology as that of uncovering the theological statements,

---

62. This is not to devalue the need for or the achievements of such confessionally based reflections. Like Sommer, Oeming (*Gesamt biblische Theologien*, 215–25) indeed argues for the necessity of developing panbiblical theological methods, to capture a middle place combining the insights of the historical and doctrinal disciplines.

63. Here I find myself in further agreement with Sweeney (*Tanak*, 3–4).

64. See Kalimi, "History of Israelite Religion," 106.

the talk to and about God, encompassed by the Hebrew Bible, in all of its various shades and contexts.[65]

2.2.4. Methodology

A long-standing debate in the study of Hebrew Bible theology considers the relationship between the disciplines of biblical theology and history of religions, or even sociology of religions.[66] As is widely recognized, historically speaking, while Christian scholars delved into biblical theology, Jewish scholars, most notably Yehezkel Kaufmann, traditionally chose to focus upon the history of Israelite religion and privileged this field over the former.[67] Accordingly, Jewish scholars published studies devoted to Hebrew Bible conceptions of God, that is, within the field of "discourse about God" (theology), under the rubric of אמונות ודעות (*'emunot vede'ot*; literally: "beliefs and perceptions").[68]

---

65. This descriptive approach, committed to a historical and philological study, is advocated by Barr in *Concept of Biblical Theology*, 6, 15–17, 74–76. My study approximates Zevit's third type of theological studies ("Jewish Biblical Theology," 311, 337).

66. On the tension between biblical theology and the history of religion, see Goshen-Gottstein, "Jewish Biblical Theology"; note the directions in sociological analysis discussed by Gottwald (*Tribes of Yahweh*, 389–709) and especially his theoretical discussion there (667–709). See also Albertz's definition of the role of the history of the Israelite religion in *History of Israelite Religion*, 1.3–21, esp. 11–12.

67. See Goshen-Gottstein's instructive critique of Kaufmann's indifference to the methodological issues that concerned his contemporaries and predecessors ("Jewish Biblical Theology," 43–44). But compare Sommer ("Dialogical Biblical Theology," 3–6), who evaluates Kaufmann's phenomenological discussions within his study of the history of religion; and see further Sommer's important discussion of the relationship between the disciplines of biblical theology and the history of Israelite religion (15–20).

68. These studies include important contributions of major Israeli biblical scholars: Moshe Greenberg, Menachem Haran, Yair Hoffman, Jacob Milgrom, Alexander Rofé, Baruch Schwartz, Moshe Weinfeld, and Meir Weiss. Sara Japhet addresses conceptions of God more comprehensively in *Ideology of the Book of Chronicles*. She convincingly argues that the religious outlook of the book provides the foundation for the discussion of its historical narrative, as well as its national, ethnic, and geographic perspectives (10 and passim). Nonetheless, Japhet never defines her work as theological. Similarly, in *Biblical Beliefs*, Israel Knohl naturally devotes a prominent place to the figure of God and to descriptions of him, but he disregards methodological concerns pertaining to Hebrew Bible theology. What seems to be crucial is the scholar's own consciousness (or lack thereof) of her/his task of conducting a theological study. Compare Sommer ("Dialogical Biblical Theology," 3–8), who puts emphasis on the results rather than the process. In this context, Muffs's *Personhood of God* is indeed exceptional.

I accept the acknowledgment of Collins (and others) of the inevitable overlap of biblical theology with the history of religions, but I concur with Goshen-Gottstein about the necessity of emphasizing the specific contribution of the theological discussion to the historical point of view.[69] As Goshen-Gottstein himself suggests, the distinctive characteristic of Tanakh theology is its major interest in the phenomenological description of the religious world of thought, which brings the discussion into the arena of philosophy of religion. Because of its focus on descriptive observation, phenomenological methodology is ideally suited to the highly diverse theological picture presented in the Hebrew Bible. Furthermore, in contrast to the history-of-religions approach, a descriptive Hebrew Bible theology may be implemented either in a thematically driven diachronic crosscut or in a study limited by synchronic crosscuts.[70]

Stendahl's insight is that, while systematic theology is founded upon philosophical methodology, the methodological principles of descriptive theology derive from historical-philological research.[71] Beyond this basic characterization, a definitive method has not yet been established for He-

---

69. See Collins ("Critical Biblical Theology?," 9): "It is an area of historical theology. . . . It necessarily overlaps with the history of religion" (see §2.1). Goshen-Gottstein ("Jewish Biblical Theology") attempts to demarcate dividing lines between the work of the theologian and that of the scholar of religion. From his work, it is evident that despite these distinctions being appropriate and necessary, they are not at all simple or clear-cut. Compare Kalimi's characterizations of biblical theology and history of religion as separate disciplines (*Early Jewish Exegesis*, 107–10) and his arguments for their independence. In "History of Israelite Religion," Kalimi writes categorically: "There is nothing unclear in the difference between 'Old Testament Theology' and the 'History of Israelite Religion'" (106). This is either a naïve or a simplistic statement; the inevitable overlap is evident even in Kalimi's own work. See, for instance, how Sommer ("Dialogical Biblical Theology," 29–50) inclines more to the history of religion than to a phenomenological biblical theology.

70. Goshen-Gottstein, "Tanakh Theology," 628, 631. A systematic phenomenological discussion is found also in Knierim, *Task of Old Testament Theology*, 16–20, 40–41. Contra Levenson ("Why Jews Are Not Interested," 35–38), who rejects the use of "crosscuts," as an unworthy way to write biblical theology. He argues that the historian of religion is better suited than the theologian to conduct diachronic studies of biblical thought.

71. Stendahl, "Biblical Theology"; Collins, "Critical Biblical Theology?"; Goshen-Gottstein, "Tanakh Theology," 630–31; Hasel, *Old Testament Theology*, 11–28, 81–89; and Mauser, "Historical Criticism," 99–113. Tsevat ("Theology of the Old Testament," 38, 49) designates theology as a branch of philology.

brew Bible (Tanakh) theology, though there have been, and continue to be, attempts to arrive at such a method.[72]

As is evident, I find very congenial the writings of Goshen-Gottstein on this subject. His initial discussion of methodological guidelines for Tanakh theology, attentive to both philology and the history of ideas, also provides a helpful spur to my own thinking on methodological guidelines for Hebrew Bible (Tanakh) theology.[73] For Goshen-Gottstein, this discipline should involve a strictly descriptive study, which answers the essential questions "what is it all about?" or "what did Tanakh mean?" Tanakh theology should focus on "the minute study of text units," that is, it entails a philologically based, close reading of the text (632).[74] It aims as much as possible for the literal sense and evaluates *legoumena* on the basis of quantitative and qualitative criteria—that is, "the number and density of occurrences as well as the issues connected with" major themes (630)—according to their distribution in the corpus and in subcorpora, in mainstream and in peripheral contexts. Themes should be understood, "not as a static picture but in constant dynamics of ambivalence and dilemma" (628). Theological discussion should give room to the diachronic differentiation of layers of independent sources (628–29). Goshen-Gottstein suggests these guidelines in order to develop a system of qualification, which leads to an overall structure of primary and secondary issues in the religion of the Hebrew Bible (633). According to his plan, once the outlines of Tanakh theology are clarified, a diachronic theology emerges within the Tanakh (631), and clear distinctions can then be established between the Tanakh and the later literary strata of postbiblical, rabbinic, and New Testament writings (633).

---

72. Sweeney (*Tanak*, 3–4) suggests that a Jewish biblical theology should be based on "modern critical foundations" and that such could even be built on the "Christian discipline of biblical or Old Testament theology"; and yet Sweeney allows himself to articulate independent Jewish aims and presuppositions for his study, which in his own words involves "a systematic critical and theological study of the Jewish Bible" (4).

73. Goshen-Gottstein, "Tanakh Theology," 628–34. In the discussion that follows, page references to "Tanakh Theology" are given in parentheses in the main text.

74. An important contribution to the theological discussion is also put forth by Weiss in his advocacy of a method of "total (holistic) interpretation" (*Bible from Within*, 1–46). In this context, mention must be made of the comparative study of ancient Near Eastern literature and the comparison of biblical theology with the theological perspectives characteristic of ancient Near Eastern cultures; see, e.g., Knierim, *Task of Old Testament Theology*, 145–48.

Unfortunately, Goshen-Gottstein never put these guidelines to the test. Such implementation would certainly have led to refinements of his methodological suggestions.[75] Nevertheless, I find that his initial distinctions stand the test of time and are very effective as points of departure for establishing Tanakh theology as an independent domain within the academic critical study of the Hebrew Bible. Goshen-Gottstein suggests that Tanakh theology should investigate specific themes, such as the land, the Sabbath, the people Israel, national salvation, the temple (630); I prefer to focus on the central mode of theological discourse—the talk to and about God, through the prism of theodicy as discourse.

To further set the stage for study of Hebrew Bible (Tanakh) theology, I adduce here Rolf Knierim's practical suggestions. In his definition of theological pluralism, Knierim addresses the methodological challenges of Old Testament theology:

> The Old Testament contains a plurality of theologies. . . . The theological problem of the Old Testament does not arise from the separate existence of its particular theologies. It arises from their coexistence. The coexistence of these theologies in the Old Testament demands the interpretation of their relationship or correspondence, a task that is more than and different from the interpretation of each of them in its own right, which is done in historical exegesis—if exegesis does its work. . . .
>
> The Old Testament's pluralism may mean either that the various theologies are mutually inclusive, compatible, and homogeneous, or that they are mutually exclusive, incompatible, and heterogeneous. They may be subservient or dominant to one another, compete against each other, or coexist in mutual isolation from one another. The theological pluralism of the Old Testament is in principle an ambiguous phenom-

---

75. I disagree with Goshen-Gottstein on two central points. One is his determination that the scholar of theology holds "personal responsibility" to the community of believers with which he is affiliated, notwithstanding his explicit warnings to avoid the demands of faith ("Jewish Biblical Theology," 54–55; "Tanakh Theology," 629–30). Levenson criticizes Goshen-Gottstein's stance on this point ("Why Jews Are Not Interested," 38), and Brettler ("Biblical History and Jewish Biblical Theology," 566) criticizes both Goshen-Gottstein and Levenson. The second point of dispute is Goshen-Gottstein's sharp distinction between the theologian and the scholar of religion with respect to their academic approaches and their aims for the study of the Hebrew Bible and its world. It may be supposed that if Goshen-Gottstein tested the principles that he advanced in his article, he would have recognized the overlaps between these disciplines; see Goshen-Gottstein, "Jewish Biblical Theology," 50–55.

enon which may be either meaningful and justifiable or meaningless and unjustifiable.[76]

Knierim suggests basing discussion of the biblical thought-world upon "theologically legitimate priorities," that is, upon an internal biblical hierarchy of topics and perspectives. The scholar must determine which theological aspects control others, and whether a given perspective is dependent upon other perspectives or controlled by them. Ultimately, according to Knierim, the scholar must seek one dominant aspect that serves as the point of origin and criterion for all the theological perspectives. This process allows for uncovering the relationships among the various conceptions (or diverse theologies, according to Knierim) and the determination of their positions relative to other conceptions. The function of biblical theology is to evaluate the relationships between the various perspectives and to establish the theological horizon of the text in question.[77]

I constructed the present project as a descriptive theology based on the study of Hebrew Bible theology from within, that is, based on the examination of the diverse conceptions of God inherent in the Hebrew Bible itself.[78] I employ Goshen-Gottstein's initial distinctions, together with the programmatic statements of Tsevat and Collins concerning the task of Hebrew Bible(/Old Testament) theology; and I also draw on Knierim's practical suggestions concerning the plurality and internal organization of biblical theological perspectives. Thus, I learned from both Jewish and Christian scholars, and I begin from the very clear point of departure articulated by Tsevat: the study of the theology of the Hebrew Bible should

---

76. Knierim, *Task of Old Testament Theology*, 1–2, 5.

77. According to Knierim, this function is "the ultimate vantage point from which to coordinate its theologies toward *the universal dominion of Yahweh in justice and righteousness*"; *Task of Old Testament Theology*, 15 (emphasis original). Thus, for Knierim, all of the biblical theological issues and perspectives, as well as the internal relationships among them, are subtopics in a universalizing framework. See Murphy's valid critique of Knierim's proposal, insofar as it ultimately seeks a unifying thread for these diverse biblical theologies ("Response," 30–32); see also Pannenberg ("Problems in a Theology"), who raises the objection that Knierim's view seems to echo Christian theological conceptions.

78. See Rendtorff (*Canon and Theology*, 40): "Theological interpretation of the Hebrew Bible is not dependent on the theological system of the religious tradition to which the particular interpreter belongs: the Hebrew Bible is a theological book in its own right, which can be, and must be, *interpreted theologically from the inside*" (emphasis added).

be seen as part and parcel of the literary-philological study of the Hebrew Bible. In addition, I consider the internal diversity of Hebrew Bible theology both synchronically and diachronically, thereby hoping to avoid the superimposition of extrabiblical or postbiblical ideas on the thought-world of the Tanakh. The plurality of voices within the Tanakh is examined phenomenologically, which brings another topic to the table: to what extent, if any, may we establish some sort of hierarchical organization (following Knierim) for the theological proclamations in the Hebrew Bible?

2.2.5. *Organizing System*

There are three main approaches to the isolation of a possible organizing system for Hebrew Bible theology, all developed by Christian theologians or biblical scholars.

The notion of "center" (*Mitte*) holds that one central formative idea provides the core of biblical discourse about God. For example, Walter Eichrodt suggests the notion of covenant as the center of biblical theology in that it designates the relationship between God and his world, between God and his people, and between God and humanity (or the individual).[79] However, Gerhard Hasel enumerates *sixteen* topics suggested as holding this position of "*the* center," and Henning Graf Reventlow adds even more propositions to this long list.[80]

In contrast stands the notion that there is no one single core for a coherent biblical theology, and thus no central idea, but rather many independent theologies within the Bible. From his historical-critical perspective, von Rad structures his *Theology of the Old Testament* around the Tanakh's various literary compositions, showing particular sensitivity to the distinction between historical traditions and prophetic ones.[81] However, as is widely recognized, von Rad so emphasizes the notion of *Heilsgeschichte* as to effectively turn this prominent Protestant Christian theological principle of divine salvation into a central biblical idea that appears as a unifying thread in his work.

---

79. Eichrodt, *Theology of the Old Testament*, 1.14–15, 32–35. See the observations concerning Eichrodt in Brueggemann's *Theology of the Old Testament*, 27–31.

80. Hasel, "Problem of the Center," 65–69; Reventlow, *Problems of Old Testament Theology*, 126–27. See also the critique of Knierim, *Task of Old Testament Theology*, 1–20, esp. 7–8.

81. For von Rad's objections to the notion of "center," see *Old Testament Theology*, 1.106–18; and see Hasel, "Problem of the Center," 73–76.

As a student of von Rad, Knierim also attempts to identify not only a thematic hierarchy of diverse theological conceptions, but a more comprehensive systematization within these conceptions. Knierim isolates a unifying commonality within the theological pluralism and suggests that this is the universal control of God over justness and justice.[82] This, however, quite contradicts Knierim's own recognition of the "plurality of theologies."[83]

Working with the notion of a plurality of Hebrew Bible theologies, Erhard Gerstenberger and Georg Fischer each write about *theologies* of the Old Testament, though from different orientations. Gerstenberger chooses a sociological emphasis, whereas Fischer focuses on different aspects of the portrayal of God in each of the biblical books.[84]

A third course, in opposition to the other two, rejects the very concept of *any* organizing system whatsoever. Both Rolf Rendtorff and Walter Brueggemann acknowledge "multilayered pluralism," polydoxy, and contradictory theological perspectives to be inherent characteristics of biblical literature.[85] While recognizing this diversity, Brueggemann still sees the necessity for some coherence and thus suggests his courtroom metaphor, ruled by a dialectic theology of "testimonial" and "countertestimonial" positions.[86]

These different approaches, developed by Christian theologians/scholars, do more than illustrate scholarly deliberations over what is obviously a very complicated theological and literary picture. Levenson identifies this concern with systematization as another clear distinction between Christian and Jewish approaches to the Hebrew Bible: "The effort to construct a systematic, harmonious theological statement out of the unsystematic and polydox materials in the Hebrew Bible fits Christianity better than Judaism. . . . Like the different conceptions of scripture held by the two traditions, the different organization of the Tanakh and the Old Tes-

---

82. Knierim, *Task of Old Testament Theology*, 15; also 16–20, 40–41.

83. Knierim, *Task of Old Testament Theology*, 1–20; see §2.2.4.

84. Gerstenberger, *Theologies in the Old Testament*, 1–18, 297–98; Fischer, *Theologien des Alten Testaments*, 13–20.

85. Rendtorff, "Christian Approach"; Brueggemann, *Theology of the Old Testament*, xv–xvi.

86. Brueggemann, *Theology of the Old Testament*, xvi, 707–20; see discussion in §3.3. In his essay "Biblical Theology Appropriately Postmodern," Brueggemann emphasizes the impossibility of adducing a singular comprehensive idea within Hebrew Bible theology (esp. 100).

tament ensures that a biblical theology common to Jews and Christians is impossible."[87]

The present study illustrates the wide polydoxy within the Hebrew Bible itself (even apart from the polydoxy of ancient and modern Judaism). This Hebrew Bible polydoxy is largely motivated by theological deliberations concerning God and his roles in relation to the individual, the people, the nations, and the entire world he created. There seems not to be a detectable organizing system; but there is a clearly recognizable organizing hierarchy of themes, deriving from the metaphoric portrayal of God as king, in his different roles.

2.2.6. The Question of Interest, or—Are Jewish Scholars Interested in Hebrew Bible Theology?

The sixth difference between the approaches of Christian theologians/ scholars and Jewish scholars to biblical/Hebrew Bible theology may be represented as a question, as it is currently in a state of change. As many recognize, up until the 1980s and 1990s, Jewish scholars show minimal interest in "doing" theology of the Hebrew Bible. They study diverse issues of religious thought, but to a large extent refrain from engaging in the scholarly theological inquiry; this apparently stems from both internal (Jewish) reasons and external ones, given the great interest and the long-established Christian study of biblical theology.

Levenson articulates the "external" side. In his influential 1987 study and in subsequent papers, Levenson characterizes biblical theology as a profoundly Christian field, mostly Protestant in its denominational outlook, supersessionist and anti-Jewish in both explicit and implicit ways.[88]

87. Levenson, "Why Jews Are Not Interested," 51, 55. Levenson further claims: "I suspect that Judaism is somewhat better situated to deal with the polydoxy of biblical theology than is Christianity" (56). The idea of "*Mitte*-less theology" as characteristic of Jewish biblical theology is further accentuated by Brettler ("Psalms and Jewish Biblical Theology," 197), who raises the question of whether the lack of a central concept can still be considered a Jewish marker (given Christian approaches such as those of Gerstenberger, Brueggemann, and others).

88. Levenson, "Why Jews Are Not Interested"; and "Theological Consensus." Levenson offers a similar argument in his introduction to *Sinai and Zion*, 1–12. See, however, Barr's critique of what he considers to be Levenson's exaggerated and imprecise emphasis on the Protestant (and even anti-Catholic) character of biblical theology (*Concept of Biblical Theology*, 291–302); Barr notes the contributions of Catholic theologians to the study of biblical theology (297).

He stresses the understandable Jewish avoidance of participating in any aspect of such a theological discussion.[89]

Tikvah Frymer-Kensky examines "internal" Jewish facets of this disinterest, which receive less attention.[90] She explains the lack of Jewish interest in Hebrew Bible theology as a function of the role played by the Hebrew Bible in traditional Judaism and enumerates three features of this role: (1) conceptually, Jewish religious thinking does not talk "theology"; rather, talk about God is presented as part of the study of "Israel's thinking" (מחשבת ישראל), that is, "Jewish philosophy"; (2) traditional Judaism marginalizes the Bible, placing the *halakhah*, the authority of the rabbis, at the center and relegating the Hebrew Bible to the rather limited role of serving as a legitimizing foundation document; consequently, (3) traditional Judaism neglects the proper study of the Hebrew Bible on its own merits.[91]

To frame the discussion of this disinterest in terms of the academic perspective, Goshen-Gottstein presents this sketch of the development of modern Jewish biblical scholarship:

> No Jewish Bible scholar came to the academic scene as a trained "theologian," unlike many of his Christian confreres. Jewish scholars were by training Semitic philologists, historians, or archaeologists; they could have come from a rabbinical background—sometimes misnamed "theological"—or a national-secularistic one. The whole issue of "biblical theology" in its ups and downs was beyond their ken and interest. The study of Tanakh religion—historical, comparative, phenomenological—was an area of great importance for those scholars, continuing or correcting the work done by Christian scholars up to the very time

---

89. Sommer ("Dialogical Biblical Theology," 3–8) objects to Levenson's claim that Jews are essentially not interested in theology. Kalimi ("History of Israelite Religion," 110–13) emphasizes that the lack of interest among Jewish scholars applies to *Christian* biblical theology; he discusses in detail a number of examples of the profound interest of Jewish interpreters and scholars in Hebrew Bible theological views and values from the early medieval period on. Kalimi claims that the differences between Christian and Jewish scholars in this field are only the result of "the youthfulness of Jewish scholarly biblical research" (114; see a similar statement on 118). Unfortunately, this assessment is yet another oversimplification of the situation at hand.

90. Frymer-Kensky, "Emergence of Jewish Biblical Theologies."

91. Zevit ("Jewish Biblical Theology," 290) points out the great interest in theological insights of the Hebrew Bible among nonacademic Jewish thinkers (rabbis and lay) for the purpose of homiletical, rather than hermeneutical readings.

when Old Testament theology began to reassert itself. Yet the very possibility, let alone necessity, of a Tanakh theology was never as much as raised in the entire literature produced by two generations of Jewish Tanakh scholars.[92]

We are now in the fourth generation of biblical scholars in Israel, and while there was some change over the last few decades, this description is still quite accurate.[93] Nonetheless, some related developments toward new conceptions of Hebrew Bible theology may be recognized in the work of both Christian and Jewish scholars.[94]

First, there is increasing recognition of the legitimacy and independent status of a Jewish Hebrew Bible theology, as Sweeney observes:

> Although Jews and Christians share a great deal in their mutual adoption of the Hebrew Bible as scripture, the different organization and theological articulation inherent in the Tanakh and the Old Testament demonstrate that each tradition reads the Hebrew Bible very differently. The recognitions of such differences in the conceptualization of the same basic tradition points to the identities of both Judaism and Christianity as self-standing theological entities with distinctive worldviews. Theological interpretation of the Bible must take these differences and identities into account.... [This recognition] ... provides the basis for true dialogue between the two religions.[95]

92. Goshen-Gottstein, "Tanakh Theology," 621. This article is the written version of several talks Goshen-Gottstein gave at Harvard Divinity School in 1985, concerning a topic that he addressed in writing in both Hebrew and English during the 1980s. For further testimony concerning this Jewish "disinterest" in biblical theology, see Levenson's opening anecdotes in "Why Jews Are Not Interested," 33–34. Levenson notes also the philological and historical bent of Jewish scholars, and specifically the interest of secular Israeli scholars in the history of Israelite religion, rather than in biblical theology (45–51, esp. 48–49).

93. I count the generations schematically from the arrival of Yehezkel Kaufmann in 1949 at the Bible Department of the Hebrew University (established in 1925). Kaufmann had a major role in establishing the interest in Israelite/biblical history of religion in the Hebrew University and in Israeli scholarship in general. I had the privilege of studying from his students (thus counting myself as the third generation of this school). See Japhet, "Establishment and the Early History."

94. See Zevit ("Jewish Biblical Theology," 331–37), who enumerates several reasons for the rise of interest in Hebrew Bible theology among Jewish scholars in the United States. This change does not seem to have reached other Jewish scholarly communities of scholars (as yet).

95. Sweeney, "Why Jews Should Be Interested," 73–74.

Moreover, among Jewish scholars, there is a growing understanding of the necessity for the development of a Jewish biblical theology.[96] Goshen-Gottstein advocates Tanakh theology as "a Jewish option—or even necessity" in the face of what has by and large taken shape as a Christian arena.[97] He argues that "Tanakh theology can thus be conceptualized as an area common to biblical studies and the study of Jewish thought."[98]

The disruption of Christian (Protestant) hegemony over biblical theology by both Christian and Jewish (and also nonaffiliated) scholars clearly increases the legitimacy of and the interest in Hebrew Bible/biblical theology among Jewish scholars. Consequently, avenues to religious dialogue opened to processes that illustrate the importance and relevance of Hebrew Bible/biblical theology much beyond its academic study.

This renewed interest is another aspect of Sommers's programmatic framework of dialogical biblical theology; he incorporates both an intra-Jewish and a Christian-Jewish dialogical dimension as necessary elements of the theological approach:

> Dialogical biblical theology would attempt to construct a discussion between biblical texts and a particular postbiblical theological tradition. Such a theology would bring biblical texts to bear on postbiblical theological concerns—specifically, on modern Jewish or Protestant or Catholic or Orthodox or post-Christian theological concerns. A work in this field would belong to the fields of both biblical scholarship and either Jewish thought or constructive Christian theology; indeed, it ought to draw on and contribute to all these fields. . . . If biblical theology genuinely intends to participate in contemporary Jewish or Christian

---

96. This growing understanding of the necessity in the development of Hebrew Bible theology across the board of the academic community is not at all restricted to Jewish scholars; see the studies of Rolf Rendtorff, Walter Brueggemann, and Konrad Schmid. Sweeney ("Why Jews Should Be Interested," 69) considers Christian biblical theology, especially the study of Old Testament theology, to itself be presently in "a state of transition."

97. Goshen-Gottstein, "Tanakh Theology," 624–25.

98. Goshen-Gottstein, "Tanakh Theology," 629. Zevit ("Jewish Biblical Theology," 331–40) argues that Jewish biblical theology must emerge as a Jewish version of Catholic-Protestant theology. Jewish biblical theology should follow Catholic and Protestant models in its adaptation of technical language and conceptual systems, remolding these existing frameworks for "an autonomous discipline in the service of living Judaism" (338–39 at 339).

religious thought, then scholars must seek answers to these questions within each tradition's own history of exegesis.[99]

Such an approach certainly has manifold benefits, as well as social, educational, and even moral contributions, which are not at all less important (probably even much more important) than the strict academic interest. Yet, this dialogic approach is completely detached from the critical and descriptive point of departure that I wish to cultivate here for the scholarly study of Hebrew Bible theology.

Thus, the question remains: to what extent have this awakening interest and the efforts of recent years laid a foundation for a philologically based (as also, philosophically based) discipline of Hebrew Bible theology, rooted in the principles and explored using the tools of critical biblical scholarship? On the positive side, Brettler argues that the last decades saw a substantial increase in the extent of the involvement of Jewish scholars in the fields of religious thought.[100] A retrospective glance at the more than thirty years from the breakthrough papers of Goshen-Gottstein and Levenson in the mid-1980s certainly indicates a substantial change in attitude toward this area. However, in comparison to other areas of biblical scholarship, Jewish Hebrew Bible scholars still show fairly minimal interest in theological topics and even less so in the broader field of biblical theology. More importantly, there continues to be a lack of consensus on both the methodology and the goals of (Jewish) Hebrew Bible theology, framed as a distinct enterprise within biblical theology and biblical studies.

2.3. CREATING A DISTINCTIVE DESCRIPTIVE (NON-CHRISTIAN AND NON-JEWISH) HEBREW BIBLE THEOLOGY

On this basis there are two related questions. First, how can a framework of descriptive biblical theology serve the project of constructing a distinctly nonaffiliated (thus, non-Christian and non-Jewish) Hebrew Bible

---

99. Sommer, "Dialogical Biblical Theology," 21, 51. Frymer-Kensky ("Emergence of Jewish Biblical Theologies," 121) proposes another internal dialogical benefit: "Biblical theology presents an alternative source of authority to rabbinic thinking and creates a very fertile opportunity for dialogue between biblical and rabbinic ideas."

100. Brettler, "Biblical History and Jewish Biblical Theology."

theology? And second, what are the advantages as well as the challenges of such a framework?[101]

The notion of descriptive biblical theology is developed by both Christian biblical scholars working from a Christian theological framework (e.g., Stendahl, pointing to the focal question "what *did* it mean?") and by Jewish Hebrew Bible scholars working from a philological point of departure (e.g., Goshen-Gottstein and Tsevat). I basically accept the very clear point of departure articulated by Tsevat, that the theology of the Hebrew Bible (Old Testament, for Tsevat) should be considered part and parcel of the general literary-philological study of the Old Testament (see §2.2.2); however, in my designation "descriptive Hebrew Bible theology," the word "descriptive" also connotes that this enterprise is neither Christian nor Jewish in its presuppositions.

I take this counterdefinition from James Barr, who defines biblical theology as a "contrastive notion."[102] By this, Barr meant that the designation "biblical theology" "came to be used in contrast with various other modes of studying the Bible that already existed. Thus it does not have clear independent contours of its own: it depends for its existence upon that with which it is contrasted." Barr counts six such contrastive notions: (1) doctrinal (systematic, dogmatic, or constructive) theology; (2) nontheological study of the Bible; (3) history-of-religions and corresponding approaches; (4) philosophical theology and natural theology; (5) the interpretation of *parts* of the Bible as distinct from the larger complexes taken as *wholes*; and (6) the uncertain negotiation between two concepts of biblical theology: as a descriptive discipline and as "a discipline involving normative authority, personal commitment, and interpretation for the present day and the modern religious community."

My own enterprise adds a seventh contrastive notion to Barr's list; that is, a "descriptive (non-Christian/non-Jewish) Hebrew Bible theology" as a contrastive discipline to Christian biblical theology and also to postbiblical and later Jewish theologies.[103] This notion of nonaffiliation (non-Christian/

101. The following discussion differs from the way I constructed my ideas in "Hebrew Bible Theology." I am indebted to several scholarly audiences, convened in Oxford, Manchester, and Zürich over the course of 2016 (too many individuals to mention by name), whose questions and critical comments allowed me to sharpen and reconfigure these ideas.

102. See Barr, *Concept of Biblical Theology*, 5–6 and the full discussion through p. 17.

103. This nonaffiliated counterdefinition is close to Barr's sixth point (*Concept of Biblical Theology*, 15–17), but the distinction is much more than a small nuance.

non-Jewish) is not meant to exclude any scholar of any denomination from taking part in this strictly descriptive enterprise, but rather to emphasize the primary focus on the theological ideas contained in the Hebrew Bible, studied in its literary and historical context(s), on its own terms, released from later Christian *and* Jewish retrojections.

The nonaffiliated aspect of this descriptive Hebrew Bible theology functions primarily to call attention to the need for all scholars (be they Jewish or Christian) to be aware of the extent to which biblical theology was framed and is still handled as a primarily Christian enterprise, built on Christian theological categories and terminologies. The presence of Christian supersessionism in modern biblical scholarship, particularly in nineteenth- and twentieth-century theological studies of the Bible, was widely recognized in the last few decades by both Christian and Jewish scholars. From a post-Shoah perspective, supersessionism is recognized as an unacceptable stance for the academic study of the Hebrew Bible.[104] Yet, superimposition of Christian religious thought on biblical theology still takes a much more subtle form through the influence of Christian theological categories on the scholarly terminology that commonly, consciously or unconsciously, continues to be used in biblical theology.[105]

The "non-Jewish" affiliation also requires clarification. As a nonreligious Jewish scholar interested in the ancient theology(ies) of the Hebrew Bible from a delimited and critical approach, such a nonaffiliated descriptive study is essential. My personal identity and scholarly interests would probably have earned me the label "Neo-Karaite" from more than one of my respected Jewish scholarly colleagues in the discipline.[106] Yet, as a secular

---

104. See Sweeney, *Reading the Hebrew Bible*, 17–22.

105. See Rom-Shiloni, "Hebrew Bible Theology," 173–81, where I look briefly at conceptions of anthropomorphism, spirituality, immanence, and transcendence as they make their appearance in the critical study of the Hebrew Bible.

106. Levenson, for example ("Why Jews Are Not Interested," 45–51), objects to what he labels Neo-Karaite, Reform Jewish, or secular Zionist approaches, on the grounds that they all adopt "protestant" stances of advocating *sola scriptura*. My approach stands in further contrast to that of my late teacher of ancient Semitic languages, Moshe Goshen-Gottstein ("Tanakh Theology"), who argues that a Tanakh theology requires the personal commitment of "a practicing member of the community of faith" (629); in "Jewish Biblical Theology," 47–48n22, he considers Reform perspectives to raise the danger of Neo-Karaitism by applying Hebrew Bible theology to practical issues in contemporary Judaism. I profoundly disagree with Goshen-Gottstein on this point. This "Neo-Karaite" label is an improper, even misleading analogy and conveys an unfortunate derogatory connotation. It hearkens back to the longstanding conflict

Zionist I am engaged in the study of the Hebrew Bible as my foundational cultural corpus.

This contrastive task of writing a descriptive Hebrew Bible theology is not at all easy to frame. My study, though limited in its scope to conceptions of God in one particular theological arena, illustrates some of the "struggles for identity" that seem required to contextualize such a descriptive theology.[107] An important aspect of the enterprise is confrontation with Christian Hebrew Bible terminology. A descriptive (non-Christian/non-Jewish) Hebrew Bible theology has to address the very basic terms and conceptions we use and to reformulate them by means of a sensitive reading of Hebrew Bible texts, not bound to their long histories of theological interpretation in relation to later documents, be they Christian or of later Jewish traditions.[108] As presented in chapter 1, such long-accepted Christian terms and their connotations may not accord with the Hebrew Bible theological conceptions. The present book is thus an opportunity to advocate for the academic necessity of a scholarly descriptive (and non-confessional) method for the study of Hebrew Bible theology within the larger arena of modern critical study of the Hebrew Bible.

My major goal is to uncover the theological conceptions embedded within the Hebrew Bible's diverse literary compositions. These conceptions emerge in and from their literary-historical contexts; they are clearly not constructed according to some overarching theological system, and thus require an attempt to actually map out the Judean theological

---

between rabbinate and Karaite authorities over the latter's disconnection of the oral from the written *Torah*. For the Islamic-Arabic context of literacy behind the Karaite conceptions of the primacy of the written ("revealed") Scriptures over oral traditions (the Mishnah and Talmud), see Polliack, "Karaite Inversion," 243–56 (with discussion of "validation" and "invalidation" on 268). Nevertheless, in many respects (in terms of language, interpretation, literary conceptions, theology, etc.), Karaite exegesis is well informed of, and in explicit and implicit negotiation with, rabbinate language and interpretive traditions. It establishes its own traits and points of interest, as for instance in the formation of the text (Polliack, 258–61) and in using the rhetorical technique of inversion confronting both the external-Islamic front and the internal-rabbinate front (275–79, 280–86). See also Frank, "Limits of Karaite Scripturalism."

107. In *Historical Theology*, Schmid took on the ambitious task of constructing a descriptive theology of the entire Hebrew Bible; see his apt methodological considerations, xvi–xvii, 94–127.

108. Another contrastive notion of Jewish descriptive Hebrew Bible theology, which goes with Barr's first point, confronts models like Sommer's conception of Jewish dialogical biblical theology. Descriptive Hebrew Bible theology should also maintain a distinction from *constructive* Jewish (or Christian) dialogical biblical theology.

thought-world at a certain era in history under specific circumstances of crisis. Coping with the Babylonian victory and the concomitant destruction of Jerusalem and Judah causes the Judahites to draw on their rich storehouse of traditional understandings of God's actions and their relationship with him. But these understandings prove inadequate in the face of the disastrous events—the dislocation and exiles—which raises questions of doubt and despair concerning any future reestablishment of relationship with God.

Methodologically, then, this book presents a phenomenological descriptive analysis, based on a quantitative survey of the relevant sources and a qualitative identification and evaluation of the topics that fall in the realm of theological discussion. My original point of departure was the basic question: "What did they say about God?" In recognition of the multiplicity of voices participating in this theological discourse, the question itself expanded to: "How does one statement about God differ from another?" Thus, the study is attentive to theological pluralism in the biblical landscape; and thus the next step is to look at the multiplicity of voices appearing in the biblical sources.

3

MULTIPLICITY OF VOICES AND
DIVERSITY OF THOUGHT

This monograph brings together literary compositions of several genres: historiography, prophecy, and psalmodic literature. In its literary spectrum, the discussion is therefore as wide as the Hebrew Bible literature allows us to set it. The chosen sources represent independent compositions with individual histories of literary evolution. The interesting phenomenon, which should not be underestimated, is that those different and independent literary sources, created by diverse anonymous authors from different authorial circles/schools, active within about a century of time and in different places of residence, portray a relatively coherent picture constructed upon the same theological foundations. Independently, these varied sources initiate deliberations that discuss similar conceptions and reformulate them in view of the contemporary crisis. Collating these responses illustrates a lively and controversial world of thought, in which one can reconstruct implicit polemics between these literary sources, even as they work from shared conceptions of God. The challenging question is, how may we describe both the shared coherence and the diversity in the theological deliberations those sources record?

3.1. BINARY CATEGORIES OF DISTINCTION IN ANCIENT ISRAELITE RELIGION: SOME CHALLENGES

In trying to analyze the different voices within ancient Israelite religion, scholars oftentimes posit binary distinctions between them. The tendency to posit a hierarchical gap between the prophets and their contemporaries goes back (at least) as early as Abraham Kuenen (1875), who argues that a dichotomy obtained between the "ethical monotheism" of the prophets and the "popular Yahwism" of the masses. Preferring the former, he maintains that the literature of the prophets (the "spiritual aristocracy," in his words) reflects a progressive accretion of layers of religious refinement with increasingly developed ethical standards.[1] Julius Wellhausen adopts this dichotomy in proposing that the prophetic elite take an elevated stance toward the priesthood and the people. He further claims that the "Yahweh of the prophets" is different in nature from the YHWH of "institutional Yahwism."[2] Acceptance of this dichotomy constitutes a rare case in which Yehezkel Kaufmann agrees with Protestant scholarship. In Kaufmann's view, popular attitudes reflect the "folk religion" of the masses, whereas the "prophetic faith" represents the "elevated religious thought" of the enlightened and developed faith of the authors of Scripture—primarily the prophets.[3] This dismissive approach toward nonprophetic voices is exemplified in James Crenshaw's comments on the quotations of popular sayings in the prophetic literature: "On the basis of prophetic quotations, I would venture to describe Israel's popular religion in terms of arrogant

1. This basic premise appears in Kuenen, *National Religions*, 91–110, and is stated numerous times in his *Prophets and Prophecy*, 347–63. Kuenen's observations were influenced by Georg H. A. Ewald's seminal work *Prophets of the Old Testament* (*Die Propheten des Alten Bundes*) and continued to influence many Bible scholars who accept this evolutionary theory of Israelite religion but reject Kuenen's other claims, especially his denial of the divine inspiration of the prophets. For a thorough discussion of Kuenen's contribution to the scholarly discussion of prophecy, see McKane, *Late Harvest*, 65–87.

2. Wellhausen, *Prolegomena to the History of Israel*, 91; cf. his comments on Isaiah (485) and his arguments concerning the contrast between the priestly establishment and the prophets (392–425). Both Wellhausen and Kuenen were pupils of Ewald and were highly influenced by his *Prophets of the Old Testament*. See Smend, *From Astruc to Zimmerli*, 76–90, 91–102; and McKane, "Prophet and Institution." This distinction paved the way for further developments in scholarship; see McKane, *Late Harvest*, 65–113.

3. Kaufmann, *Toldot Ha-'Emunah*, 1.610, 623. Kaufmann describes "popular" belief at great length (1.589–623). Although he distinguishes between the attitudes of the prophets and those of the people (e.g., 1.600–605), he emphasizes their shared foundations and even maintains that the "higher" religion is based upon the popular one (1.610–12). In his discussion of Lamentations, Kaufmann identifies the individual author of the scroll as one of Zedekiah's officials, who expresses the ideology of the popular religion (3.594–99). Accepting this principle of hierarchical difference, Eichrodt (*Theology of the Old Testament*, 1.217) divides Israelite religion according to three groups: prophets, Priestly school, and popular thought.

confidence, spiritual insensitivity, taunting defiance, remorseless despair, painful query and historical pragmatism."[4]

From a sociological perspective, this dichotomy is seen to be just one aspect of a more complex rivalry. Rainer Albertz portrays the debate prior to the destruction as an ideological-political and theological controversy in which the "national religious circles," which adhere to the "old-style temple and king theology," oppose the Deuteronomistic proponents of "reform theology," who adhere to the "official Yahwistic religion." The former category (i.e., the "national religious circles") consists of the priesthood, the royal court, the temple priests, and the Jehoiachin exiles. The prophets Jeremiah and Ezekiel, as well as the Shaphanide family of scribes, comprise a group that opposes reformist theology prior to the destruction.[5] According to Albertz, the period of exile following the destruction is characterized by the disintegration of core systems and by internal strife among the official religious functionaries, who gradually come to recognize the significance of the prophetic message. Albertz describes the theological shift that takes place in response to the historical crisis:

> The period of the exile led to a far-reaching realignment within official Yahweh religion and a reevaluation of personal piety. The downfall of the institutions of the temple cult and the monarchy led to a far-reaching break-up of the link between the currents of religious tradition and the institutions. This opened up an opportunity for priests, prophets, officials and other intellectuals who had lost their functions to converge in various religious pioneer groups modeled on the groups formed around the pre-exilic prophets of judgment, who did theology without heed to existing institutions and power relationships, and only in relation to oral and written traditions.[6]

---

4. Crenshaw, "Popular Questioning," 392–94 at 392. Crenshaw sees the dichotomy as between "the religion of 'the man in the streets'" and "the officially sanctioned religion of Israel"—in which he includes wisdom, prophetic, and psalmodic literatures. In this regard, he uses the terms "prophetic theology" and "priestly religion" to designate theological reflections that consistently justify God in diverse ways. According to Crenshaw, "the voice of the people" should be at the center of scholarly discussion, since this brings to the fore the opinions of the "hearers," the audience that stands in dialogue with official/prophetic religion. Crenshaw further discusses the *vox populi* in *Prophetic Conflict*, 23–38.

5. Albertz, *History of Israelite Religion*, 1.231–41; 2.369–70.

6. Albertz, *History of Israelite Religion*, 2.370.

Albertz suggests a careful study from the vantage point of the sociology of religion, as a subdiscipline of the history of religion. The present study, however, addresses the various antagonistic positions from a theological phenomenological perspective and puts Albertz's model to the test. From that conceptual perspective, Albertz's binary model of the preexilic era seems too general. For example, there are some significant disagreements between Jeremiah and Ezekiel;[7] similarly, among the poets of the cult personnel and the officials from royal circles, there exist varied conceptions *prior* to the destruction and during the waves of deportation. Thus, we need to ask if the breakup of religious and traditional beliefs, which Albertz perceives as belonging to the exilic period, is already in process prior to the destruction and exiles.

Due to a literary phenomenon that particularly characterizes the prophetic books of Jeremiah and Ezekiel, it is indeed tempting to cast the literary sources of the early sixth century in a dichotomous light. As part of their rhetoric, these two prophetic books include quotations of "other voices," that is, either statements attributed to individuals (who are identified by name, title, or social circle) or popular sayings attributed simply to "the people."[8] In both books the quotations oftentimes express stances antagonistic to those of the prophets; thus they attest positions that differed from those of the prophets.[9] For these books, then, we may think of the dichotomy as between "prophetic voices" and "nonprophetic voices." The prophetic voices include the pronouncements referred to

7. See Rom-Shiloni, "Ezekiel and Jeremiah."

8. With 48 quotations in Ezek 1–39 and 136 in Jeremiah, the books of Jeremiah and Ezekiel show greater use of quotations than other prophetic books; compare Isa 1–39 (32 quotations), Hosea (11), Joel (3), Amos (7), Obadiah (2), Micah (7), and Zephaniah (3). Quotations are relatively more frequent in sixth-century prophecy: note Isa 40–55 (24), Isa 56–66 (14), Zech 1–8 (4), Zech 9–14 (3), Haggai (2), Malachi (10). See the comprehensive study of Wolff (*Das Zitat im Prophetenspruch*, 36–129), who counts 250 quotations in the prophetic corpus. In my own research, I enumerate 306 quotations; see Rom-Shiloni, *God in Times of Destruction*, 58–131.

9. The authenticity of those quotations is widely challenged. See Wolff, *Das Zitat im Prophetenspruch*, 54–90; compare Crenshaw's *Prophetic Conflict*, 34, who argues that the quotations have "a sound of authenticity" and thus should be recognized as authentic counterreactions to prophecy. Some of the quotations in Jeremiah are discussed by Crenshaw, "Popular Questioning," as well as by Overholt, "Jeremiah 2." Quotations in the book of Ezekiel receive more extensive attention in Greenberg, "Quotations in the Book of Ezekiel"; Brin, *Studies in the Book of Ezekiel*, 18–52; and Clark, "Citations in the Book of Ezekiel." See my *God in Times of Destruction*, 68–85, on the quotations as a rhetorical phenomenon in the prophecy and poetry of the sources discussed here.

Jeremiah and Ezekiel themselves, as well as passages added by followers/ tradents and redactors of their books (see §3.4.4). The nonprophetic voices quoted in the prophetic writings reflect diverse social and literary circles. But there is another nonprophetic group of authors—the poets, represented by the psalmodic literature, specifically the laments in Lamentations and in seventeen psalms (see §3.4.3). The similarities between the poetic sources and the quotations suggest that each represents a deliberate and articulated opposition to the positions expressed by the prophetic voices.[10]

Yet, closer examination of statements to and about God in sources from the sixth century leads to the recognition that binary schemes serve rather poorly to help us understand the diverse positions within these theological conflicts.[11] First, these diverse perspectives do not represent hierarchical levels of religious development, nor can the antagonistic positions be classified according to the dichotomy of piety versus heresy. Second, the nonprophetic voices, ascribed by Albertz to "nationalist religious circles," are clearly not homogeneous. Above all, most of these "nationalist religious" positions are rooted primarily in traditional religious conceptions, not distinct from those of the prophets and the Deuteronomistic historiographers. Finally, the Deuteronomistic historiographers of the book of Kings are themselves (as part of the Deuteronomistic school) also participants in this theological mix. As is recognized by scholars of the Deuteronomistic writings, while we tend to believe we know a lot about this school, scholars still struggle with determining its roots (royal, Levitical, or prophetic?) and differ on the basic conclusions as to whether it is part of the institutionalized Judean social structure or rather a movement of extreme reformers.[12] Hence, the question of where these authors belong on the theological map needs to be further discussed.

10. An example of the theological similarities between quotations and communal laments may be seen by a comparison of Jer 3:5 and Ps 103:9.

11. I came to recognize this over the last few years in the wake of my "Psalm 44" and *God in Times of Destruction.* In these earlier studies, I adopted this notion of opposition between prophetic and nonprophetic sources as my primary conceptual framework for presenting antagonistic ideologies. The present study emphasizes a more complex conceptual tapestry of perspectives.

12. To note but some of the major speakers on the multiple questions concerning the identification of the Deuteronomist(s), see Albertz, "In Search of the Deuteronomist" and the references there; Person, *Deuteronomic School,* 1–16; Hoffman, "Deuteronomist and the Exile"; Knoppers, *Two Nations under God,* 2.229–54, esp. 247–54; and Römer, "Invention of History," 261. See §3.4.2.

This picture raises a series of questions: How might we define the relationship between these different voices? How should the different voices be classified? Is it legitimate and/or even appropriate to distinguish between official and unofficial voices, orthodox and nonorthodox, or core and peripheral attitudes?[13] Furthermore, where should the prophets and the Deuteronomistic historiographers be located? Are either or both to be defined, following Albertz, as antiestablishment groups, whether in opposition to nationalist religious circles or to official Yahwistic religion? What may be said of the theological similarities between prophets and historiographers? Who should we consider to have been maintaining traditional attitudes? And who should be seen as the theological innovators in the early sixth century? Finally, what is the relationship between these divergent voices and the conventional division of Judean society into social and literary circles (priestly, royal, prophetic, historiographical, Deuteronomistic, etc.)?[14]

3.2. ALTERNATIVELY: RELIGIOUS DISCOURSE AMONG EQUALS

The present study aims to draw a map of the religious discourse of the (early) sixth century. While the time frame requires some elucidation, I first outline five general characteristics of this discourse, which I identify in the diverse literary sources that shape the structure of the specific discussions in the chapters that follow:

First, sixth-century sources share the same fundamental conceptions of God. Beyond all differences and polemics, it is remarkable to note that in prophetic, historiographic, and poetic sources alike (as well as the quotations found within prophecies), God's actions are portrayed in similar

---

13. Brueggemann (*Theology of the Old Testament*, 117–26, 400–401) suggests distinctions between official and nonofficial and core versus peripheral voices. In his reading of the book of Ezekiel, Block (*Ezekiel 1–24*, 8) discerns evidence of antagonism toward the "official orthodoxy" of Judah. For orthodox and its counterpart, nonorthodox, in the realm of religious thought, note McDonough's definition of orthodoxy: "correct or sound belief according to an authoritative norm" ("Orthodoxy and Heterodoxy"). These schematic and binary distinctions are not meant to gloss over the diversity of opinions within each circle and between them. They do, however, serve to highlight the ideological contrasts between a central stream and antagonistic expressions of thought.

14. The sociological dimension is of secondary importance to the evaluation of the theological attitudes presented by the different participating voices.

ways, through profound anthropomorphisms. *All sources(/voices) depict God as a king* who plays three primary roles: warrior, judge, and sovereign of his people and the cosmos. These three components of the shared metaphor of God as king provide the framework for the analysis of the conceptions of God in chapters 5–13. The aim of the investigation is to highlight substantial differences between the diverse sources in the deployment and meaning of this shared basic conception (see chap. 4).

Second, innovations in and reformulations of theological positions are not restricted to the prophets or to the historiographers, but, again, may be found throughout the corpus. Conversely, traditional, orthodox perspectives oftentimes characterize the pronouncements of the prophets and the historiographers as much as those of their presumed opponents. Hence, the discussions in the ensuing chapters are constructed, not on the basis of sociological divisions, but according to the deployment of the primary permutations in the metaphors for God's kingly roles. Each chapter first presents the conceptions shared across the corpus (and oftentimes beyond it, within the canonical limits of the Hebrew Bible), and then their diverse and ever new reformulations.

Third, the struggles among these diverse groups, notwithstanding their shared traditional notion of God as king, reveal important distinctions between their theological conceptions. The main theological issue under debate concerns the roles of God (as warrior, divine judge, and lord of the covenant relationship) with respect to the actions of the people and of their human enemies.

Fourth, and more generally, the deliberations found in the different Hebrew Bible sources of this era should be taken as discourse among equals. All participants may be seen to be equally as knowledgeable of traditional conceptions, as pious, and as desperate to make sense of the atrocities of the Babylonian conquest and deportations. They all search for theological explanations, and yet they supply different ones with great perseverance.[15]

---

15. These observations concerning a Yahwistically oriented discourse among equals do not negate the possibility that idolatrous and other non-Yahwistic beliefs/practices might have existed in Judah of the sixth century. The Deuteronomistic historiographers' speeches (e.g., 2 Kgs 21:10–15) and the prophetic exhortations down to Second Isaiah led earlier scholars to cast the sixth-century disputes as primarily between monotheistic prophets/historiographers and the people as adherents to syncretistic cults (e.g., Ezek 8); Second Isaiah, by the second half of the sixth century, is supposed to have introduced monotheism. I challenge this somewhat simplistic dichotomy: the Hebrew

Finally, in trying to draw some general conclusions from these differences, I put my finger on another shared motivation, which serves at times explicitly in the foreground or at other times in the background, of all these theological deliberations: all parties are struggling with the question of theodicy, the question of how to understand God's roles in the disaster. Human responses to perceptions of those roles invoke the full range of responses identified in chapter 1—justification, doubt, and protest. In at least some cases these different theological perspectives—which range from total justification of God and all of his actions, through doubt of the divine justness, to defiant protest against him—reflect the more or less stable stances of some different sociological or authorial groups among the aforementioned voices. Thus, through this avenue sociological aspects may be brought back into the discussion. In general, arguments of justification may be found primarily in the historiography of the book of Kings and within the prophetic literature, whereas protest characterizes the laments of Psalms and Lamentations and the quotations of other voices in the prophets.[16] Along the spectrum from justification to protest, all participants in these deliberations make use of both traditional materials and innovative transformations of them; taken together these deliberations comprise a theodical discourse.

3.3. THEOLOGICAL CRISIS IN THE SIXTH CENTURY: MODERN AND POSTMODERN SCHOLARLY PERSPECTIVES

Nineteenth-, twentieth-, and now twenty-first-century biblical scholars consider the framings of time and space of the Neo-Babylonian period (609–538) to mark *only* the beginnings of a great wealth of literary creativity. The traditional scholarly consensus sees the literary evolution of all the compositions discussed in this study—the book of Kings, Jeremiah, Ezekiel, Psalms, and Lamentations—as a long process that involved intensive scribal work of compilation, authorship, and editing of widely diverse

---

Bible *literary* sources from the earlier period attest to voices (and authors) who seem to be theologically on the same page in fundamental ways.

16. Raitt (*Theology of Exile*, 83–105) distinguishes between prophetic theodicy and the people's expression of doubts. But this schematization has several significant exceptions: on the one hand, the individual laments of Jeremiah (in Jer 11–20) sound a clear note of protest; on the other hand, there are currents of justification in specific communal laments (e.g., Ps 106).

compositions, in the aftermath of Judah's fall, primarily during the exilic and postexilic periods.[17] More recently, scholars tend to refer more and more of the Hebrew Bible literature to the vaguely defined late sixth/fifth centuries of the early Persian period; and in the last decades, the tendency developed to push the literary production even further, to the late Persian era, thus to the fifth and fourth centuries.

Since the goal of my study is to describe the theological deliberations that reflect on the catastrophic events that took place within a certain critical era in Judah's history, the circumstances of time and location behind the literary sources are of significance. But, as often happens in biblical studies, this is exactly the arena in which certainty is most elusive and conclusions are most debatable. In fact, literary-historical approaches may lead to scholarly dead ends, since the sources as we have them cannot be dated in any conclusively satisfactory way to the early sixth century, or even to any other specific point in that century. Redaction-history critics thus feel more comfortable dating the literary compositions to the late Persian period (or even to the Hellenistic era) than to any former points of time, although the arguments will still be scant and less than persuasive.[18]

In an effort to avoid such a dead end, I go beyond the more usual disciplinary conventions of literary-historical criticism or redaction criticism and examine two alternative approaches. These two approaches may be fruitfully integrated for the current project, that is, for the study of theodicy as discourse in the Judean thought-world of the sixth century.

3.3.1. Literary Approaches: Speaking Personae, Literary Scenarios, and Authorial Settings

Biblical scholars have long profitably integrated insights from modern literary criticism into the study of various biblical genres.[19] A helpful set of

17. See Winton Thomas, "Sixth Century BC"; and Meyers, "Babylonian Exile Revisited."

18. See, for instance, Gerstenberger (*Israel in the Persian Period*, 274–26), who argues for a late Persian period process of writing original compositions and revising others, driven by the reuse of early stages of various texts that only at that time are shaped into written books (306–9 and passim).

19. For the analysis of biblical literature, see Berlin (*Poetics and Interpretation*, 43–58), who uses diverse literary strategies, e.g., diverse points of view in biblical narrative, scenic presentation, characterization, the structuring of time (narrated time versus the time of the narrative), and so on. See Lanser, *Narrative Act*, 154, 174–84, for a further

distinctions used in poetics—for example, the concept of "scenario" rather than "setting" (*Sitz im Leben*); the distinction between speaking persona ("the implied author") and the author ("the historical author"), between the implied author and the circles of the implied audience, between narrated time and time of the narrative—promises to be very helpful for articulating the diverse theological responses and their potential relation to one another, found in this literature.

It is important to distinguish between "speaking persona(e)" and "author(s)" or between "scenarios" and "authorship" within a literary composition.[20] Biblical scholars to a large extent are alert to the evident gaps between, on the one hand, the scenarios (space, historical circumstances, sociological and theological spectrum, etc.) delineated within the biblical material and, on the other hand, the presumed point(s) in time in which these literary compositions are written and compiled, including the presumed processes of additional adaptations, revisions, and so on.

This distinction between scenarios and authorship is of paramount importance for the present task of reconstructing the theological deliberations within a certain critical era in Judah's history. It calls for the concurrent use of two distinct modes of analysis: a synchronic study of the speaking personae and a diachronic study of the process of literary development and authorship. The first method allows for examination of the interacting theological conceptions presented as held by leading figures, anonymous characters or groups, and the diverse audiences that are active in specific (literary) scenario(s). The second method is required by the apparent gap between these literary scenarios and the authorial setting(s), which have histories of their own and presumably are reflected in the ideological appropriations and transformations those conceptions underwent.

Scholars challenge the possibility of revealing aspects of the historical *realia* (including ideology and theology) behind any literary scenario, which is often treated as "invented/fictional"; they frequently choose to focus on the author's (authors') intention and on the possible audience of the final level of redaction (presuming that this part of the literary history can

---

distinction between the closed circle of the narrator (the implied author)/narratee (the implied audience) and the receptive stance of the real audience, which might actually change along with the composition's different stages of literary evolution (see also Berlin, *Poetics and Interpretation*, 52–55).

20. In invoking these distinctions and in the use of the concept of "scenario" rather than "setting" (*Sitz im Leben*), I follow Berlin's "Speakers and Scenarios."

more safely be reconstructed).[21] I suggest a middle way: using synchronic as well as diachronic methods so as to draw on the insights of both.[22]

The corpus for this study was consciously selected according to the literary speaking personae and the scenario(s) they reflect. I intentionally chose those works that themselves focus on Jerusalem's and Judah's subjugation, destruction, and dislocation and that grapple with the theological questions raised by those traumatic events. This criterion of explicit engagement of the speaking persona with this early-sixth-century complex of events thus leads to the exclusion of other prophetic compositions from consideration here (e.g., Zephaniah, Obadiah, Second Isaiah), even though, in terms of their authorial history, they probably took literary form during the sixth century as well.

3.3.2. Skepticism and Trauma Studies: Synchronic and Diachronic Approaches

For the task of tracing and evaluating the intersections, potential and actual, between speaking personae, literary scenarios, and diverse authorial settings, I find helpful the theoretical insights of skepticism and trauma studies. The study of skepticism in Israelite faith and the postmodern study of trauma as a conceptual framework for biblical interpretation produce fruitful avenues for the investigation of conceptions of God and their reformulations during these times of crises.

While skepticism (as a catchall term for both doubt in God and protest against him) is easily seen as an element of wisdom literature (especially

---

21. See Steck, *Prophetic Books*, 17–64, esp. 22–25; and in a more extreme way, Kratz, *Prophets of Israel*, vii–viii, 1–10. Interest in the late literary traditions on Jeremiah, for instance, is articulated by Carroll (*Jeremiah*, 55–64); and see Sharp, *Prophecy and Ideology*, 159–61. Alertness to the latest possible layer of the book guides the commentary of Fischer (*Jeremia 1–25*, 75–94), who dates the book of Jeremiah in the fourth century on authorial grounds and is hesitant to consider any earlier sixth-century setting for the prophetic persona.

22. Attention to both synchronic and diachronic dimensions of the text (whether poetry, prophetic, narrative, historiography, etc.) is by no means a new approach; see Berlin, *Poetics and Interpretation*, 111–34. See more extensively the collection edited by de Moor, *Synchronic or Diachronic?* Among the studies in this volume, note particularly Barr, "Synchronic, Diachronic"; and Joyce, "Synchronic and Diachronic Perspectives," 126–27, where Joyce emphasizes the independence and the equal status of each dimension (the synchronic and the diachronic) within biblical studies. Yet, the two poles are still too rarely brought together when historical-critical methods lead the discussion.

Job and Ecclesiastes), scholars also point to the presence of this strand in psalmodic and prophetic literatures, as well as within Hebrew Bible narratives, such as the accounts of the forefathers and the stories of the wilderness wanderings. From a literary-historical point of view, scholars tend to date these compositions to the exilic period, that is, to the aftermath of the destruction; thus they are seen as indirect sources of valid information concerning the theological crisis of the sixth century.[23] Although I leave aside such indirect witnesses to focus on direct and explicit reflections of the destruction and its aftermath, I find this conceptual framework helpful for thinking about my own target group of texts (see §3.4).

Of particular interest is Robert Davidson's study on skepticism. Davidson defines a crisis of faith as a theocentric crisis in which the questions not only pertain to human deeds and divine justice, but also to God himself and to the ways in which he acts.[24] In contrast to the attitudes found in literary compositions from Mesopotamia and Egypt, Israelite monotheism is unique both in its expressions of doubt and in its other responses to crisis. According to Davidson, the Israelite perspective did not call for simple, unquestioning human submission to the deity, but rather entailed a search for theological conceptions that would provide a satisfactory explanation for the events of the time.[25]

In prolific research and highly creative studies, Walter Brueggemann explores biblical perceptions of the nature of God in his relationship(s) to Israel. Focusing on the crisis of faith that followed the destruction and exiles, he examines expressions of doubt and protest.[26] Brueggemann characterizes the disagreements about God's role in these crises as a kind of court proceeding, in which expressions of doubt articulate the case for the prosecution. This ongoing dispute is both central to Israelite religion and inseparable from its coalescence.[27] Brueggemann also maintains that

---

23. See Winton Thomas, "Sixth Century BC," and a great number of studies ever since. This scholarship ties, for example, the Genesis stories of the forefathers, particularly the Jahwist strand, to the Babylonian exiles. See, e.g., Van Seters, "In the Babylonian Exile."

24. Davidson, *Courage to Doubt*, 203–13; and Davidson, "Some Aspects." See also Salters, "Scepticism in the Old Testament"; and Brueggemann, "Crisis and Promise."

25. Davidson, *Courage to Doubt*, 208; and his analysis of the destruction of Jerusalem (140–68).

26. See, inter alia, Brueggemann's "Weariness, Exile, and Chaos," 32–35; "Crisis and Promise"; and "Crisis-Evoked, Crisis-Resolving Speech"; and see §1.2.1.

27. Brueggemann, *Theology of the Old Testament*, 317–19.

the exilic and postexilic periods are times of consolidation for the biblical writings, in which ancient traditions are subjected to renewed attention.[28] He thus designates the Babylonian exile as the paradigmatic event that prompts questioning about God.[29]

Indeed, in works from the sixth century, doubt is given explicit expression in questions directed toward God, which challenge his actions or inaction; protest is addressed directly to God, and both elements are participants in the theodical discourse, along with statements that justify God's role.

Trauma studies entered Hebrew Bible scholarship fairly late in the twentieth and early in the twenty-first century, as part of a growing interest in social and psychological methods of biblical criticism (among other postmodern and postcolonial approaches).[30] The experiences of loss and of exile on the one hand and restoration on the other, over a period of approximately seventy years between the destruction of the First Temple and the dedication of the Second Temple (586–516), are gradually recognized to have nurtured the production of "trauma literature." Hence, almost naturally, the conceptual framework of trauma studies is brought to bear in biblical studies on the exilic era and the Persian period.[31] The books of Ezekiel, Jeremiah, and Lamentations, as well as the Deuteronomistic History, are all identified as trauma literature, all of them reflecting the crises of destruction, death, dislocation (thus, forced migration), refugee status, and so on in both individual and communal modalities.[32] But (as with

---

28. Brueggemann, *Theology of the Old Testament*, 74–77.

29. Brueggemann, *Theology of the Old Testament*, 321–22. Brueggemann dedicates another study (basically a revision of *Theology of the Old Testament*, chaps. 14–18) to the dialogical quality he found in the faith of the Old Testament and specifically to the portrayal of God as "dialogical character"; see his *Unsettling God*, 1–18.

30. For interesting perspectives on twentieth-century transformations in the field of trauma studies and their implications for biblical studies, see Smith-Christopher, "Reading War and Trauma," 253–59.

31. See Garber's "Trauma Studies" and "Trauma Theory."

32. Ezekiel's peculiar visions and personality originally led scholars to this conceptual framework; see Smith-Christopher, *Religion of the Landless*; *Biblical Theology of Exile*, 1–26, 75–104; and "Reading War and Trauma." Smith-Christopher integrates all traumas in the aftermath of war and dislocation under trauma studies, refugee studies, and forced migration. See also three works by Garber: "Traumatizing Ezekiel"; "Trauma, History, and Survival"; and "Vocabulary of Trauma" (dealing with Jeremiah and Lamentations). On Jeremiah, see O'Connor, *Jeremiah*. On the Deuteronomistic History, see Janzen, *Violent Gift*, 26–63. On Lamentations, see Joyce, "Lamentations and the Grief Process"; and Linafelt, *Surviving Lamentations*, 1–18, 35–61. On "literature

skepticism), the literary spectrum is further broadened to include other implicit and indirect reflections of trauma within biblical literature.[33]

As noted earlier, the present study limits itself to compositions that speak directly and explicitly of the destruction and aftermath and discuss its theological implications. These sources may thus be recognized as trauma literature, and all participants (speaking personae and authors alike) in these theological deliberations should be seen as traumatized, whether they are left in Jerusalem or dislocated to Babylon and whether they belong to the first, second, or third generations following the catastrophes.

Several aspects of trauma studies are valuable for a theological study of the sources at hand. Of the first importance is David Garber's recognition that trauma theory contributes a *perspective*, not "a method of interpretation."[34]

Second, Garber illustrates the relationship between trauma as an experience and trauma literature with an accurate metaphor: "If trauma is the initial wounding experience, trauma literature could be considered the scar—the visible trace offered by the survivor that points in the direction of the initial experience."[35] This construction of the relationship between trauma and its literary expression gained attention in psychological studies and likewise in post-Shoah literary studies; it is similarly adapted to Hebrew Bible scholarship on the ancient texts.[36]

Third, it is important to recognize that literary reactions to traumatic experience represent immediate responses, articulated during the events and shortly thereafter.[37] Studies on trauma and memory highlight that

---

of survival," see Linafelt, *Surviving Lamentations*, 19–34; and O'Connor, *Lamentations and the Tears of the World*.

33. See, e.g., Balentine, "Traumatizing Job"; Carr, "Reading into the Gap"; and sketching a much wider scope, Carr, *Holy Resilience*.

34. See Garber, "Trauma Studies," 422.

35. Garber, "Trauma Studies," 423; "Trauma Theory," 28.

36. See Smith-Christopher, "Reading War and Trauma," 253–56; Garber, "Vocabulary of Trauma"; Joyce, "Dislocation and Adaptation"; and Sweeney, *Reading the Hebrew Bible*, 228–41.

37. Against the common assumption that trauma leads first to a long shocking silence, Klawans ("Josephus, the Rabbis," 283–90) presents fairly rich data on reactions of victims/survivors to the atrocities during and shortly after 1945. Klawans (284) aptly differentiates between immediate reactions to the Holocaust (Shoah) in the late 1940s and early 1950s (famous ones by Elie Wiesel and Primo Levi, among others) and more philosophical and literary reactions that gradually appeared in the 1960s and on (e.g., Fackenheim's *Jewish Bible after the Holocaust*, Eliezer Berkowitz, Hans Jonas, and many

retellings of traumatic events may surface again and again after periods of silence, taking both literary and other forms.[38]

Fourth, the connections between traumatic experience and history, like those between traumatic experience and memory, are thoroughly investigated.[39]

For the current study, these four points characterizing trauma studies allow us to see that reflections, including theological ones, may be reworked over time and yet remain authentic throughout their repetitions.[40]

I want to linger further on these last two points, which seem to lead biblical scholars to opposite conclusions. Repeatedly, scholars base their assumptions concerning the biblical sources on a model of posttraumatic stress built on Elisabeth Kübler-Ross's influential five-point paradigm of the psychological stages following the event of loss: (1) denial and isolation, (2) anger, (3) bargaining, (4) depression, and (5) acceptance.[41] Kübler-Ross's model, which was developed to cope with death, as the title of her book indicates, is extended to apply more generally to coping with grief. According to the model, there is a progressive movement from the first shock of disaster to the final calm acceptance of the outcome, which may even bring peace and hope. This model is taken as formative for both individual and communal reactions to trauma.

Translating these psychological terms into theological frameworks, Paul Joyce and David Reimer independently discuss the application of

---

others) and notes: "It did not take any time at all for those that were so inclined to interpret the destruction of European Jewry within the traditional, covenantal theodicies. . . . The assertion, therefore, that there was a delay in responding to the Holocaust is predicated on denying the power of traditional theodicies (whether covenantal or not) and prioritizing the value of intellectual philosophizing over various important and meaningful practical responses" (285). See also Klawans's conclusion: "Jews were not shocked into silence in 1945" (287). Although the literary evidence is scant, Klawans draws the analogy back to the 70 CE destruction and presents Josephus as a response of an immediate witness (287–307). I thank Ruth Clements for introducing me to this important study. On the early literary responses to the Shoah, see Roskies, *Against the Apocalypse* and *Literature of Destruction*.

38. Caruth, *Trauma*, 1–12, esp. 2–3; Caruth, *Unclaimed Experience*, 1–10, 91–112; Erikson, "Notes on Trauma."

39. See Caruth, *Unclaimed Experience*, 10–24; and Caruth, *Trauma*, 3–9.

40. Repetition and the question of accuracy are explored in trauma studies and recognized among the clear symptoms of PTSD; see Garber, "Trauma Studies," 422.

41. Kübler-Ross, *On Death and Dying*, 10–33. I thank Christian Frevel for our conversation over this model, which brought each of us to quite different thoughts on the possible relevancy of the model to our studies.

these five stages to the book of Lamentations. While Joyce finds Kübler-Ross's model helpful for perceiving the painful, complex, and disordered nature of each of the five individual laments within Lamentations, Reimer applies the model to the collection as a whole:

- Lam 1—(denial and) isolation
- Lam 2—anger
- Lam 3—bargaining
- Lam 4—depression
- Lam 5—acceptance (although this is limited to the acceptance of the reality of suffering)

This more global application gives him insights into the redaction process of the entire scroll.[42]

The use of this linear model has additional consequences for our construal of the historical side of the literary evidence. To give one example, the progressive movement (from assumed long shocked silence to literary reactions or from denial to acceptance) leads some biblical scholars to argue that the communal laments of Lamentations constitute late poetic expressions of justification (this applies mainly to Lam 1 and Lam 3, and in general to the presumed editorial themes behind the entire scroll).[43] Thus, the composition as a whole is seen to illustrate the theological reflections of some two to three generations later, dating to the restoration period

42. Joyce, "Lamentations and the Grief Process"; and Reimer, "Good Grief?"

43. Responding to Albertz (*Israel in Exile*, 203–4) for his datings of prophetic writings to the exilic period over the sixth century on theological grounds among others (435–45), Gerstenberger argues as follows (*Israel in the Persian Period*, 307–8): "The process of coming to terms with the past takes some time, once the initial shock has been overcome, we realize this clearly from the German example after 1945, especially as it has been burdened with problems of guilt. For this reason, Albertz has to shift substantial literary efforts associated with the clarification of the historical problems to the beginning of the Persian rule." Beyond the problematic analogy, Gerstenberger seems to be carried away (along many others) by a dramatic methodological mistake. The initial German silence, deriving from shame on the part of the perpetrators of the Shoah, is both qualitatively and descriptively different from the responses of the victims, whose theological reactions and questions take shape both during and after the crisis and do not wait for it to pass. The proper parallel between the modern and ancient catastrophes—if indeed appropriate to draw—must be between the situations of the victims in each case. I can only hope that this terrible and unsound analogy, which gained axiomatic status in biblical European scholarship, will find its way out of our scholarly discussions.

and the early Persian era, that is, toward the end of the sixth century and following.[44] However, trauma studies call this linear process of resolution into question.

Mapping the elements of theodical discourse onto this linear and progressive model seems to problematize the analogy between Kübler-Ross's model of coping with grief and biblical compositions on the destruction even further. According to this model, an individual or a community would start with painful feelings of denial, isolation, and anger (stages 1 and 2), expressed by doubt and protest; would gradually move to prayer, thus to bargaining and depression (stage 3 and 4); and would finally arrive at justification, acceptance (stage 5). Theological reactions to traumatic disaster may just as well move in the opposite direction, from initial justification of God, to doubt in and protest against God. In fact, the examples discussed in chapter 1, from Jeremiah and from Lamentations itself, suggest that the linear model may be inadequate to the description of the theodical negotiations going on in these texts and that the (nonlinear) three-pole notion of trilemma may be more suited to the complexity of the scenarios represented by these texts.

The movement from justification to protest as an initial religious reaction to trauma is well documented in Jewish reflections from the period during and after the Shoah. While this observation sends us to twentieth-century thought (as this postmodern approach of trauma studies regularly does), the *Sermons from the Years of Rage* by Rabbi Kalonymus Kalman Shapira, the Piaseczno Rebbe, which he composed and wrote down in the Warsaw Ghetto during the years 1939–42, are relevant to the question of reactions to trauma in the ancient sources.[45] The Rebbe began giving over these teachings from a stance of complete justification of God and confidence in divine help; as time passed and the atrocities increased, he

---

44. Taking Lamentations as written in the exilic/postexilic era or completed only after the Second Temple is established in Jerusalem is a commonplace in European scholarship; see, for instance, Gerstenberger, *Psalms, Part 2*, 473–75. Frevel (*Die Klagelieder*, 38–45, 50–72, 79–81) is attentive to the emotional turmoil over the catastrophe (72), but considers Lamentations to reflect postexilic hopes in divine salvation and restoration (39–40, 80–81).

45. The sermons are published in a critical edition and in a facsimile edition and transcription by Reiser, *Rabbi Kalonymus Kalman Shapira*. For an English review see Diamond, "Buried, Raging Sermons"; and for a study of his theological perspectives, focusing on the Rebbe's references to divine providence, see Diamond, "Warsaw Ghetto Rebbe."

addressed God with direct petitions and an increasing element of painful protest that reflects his feelings of desertion. To the last preserved sermon, the Rebbe still asked for, or even demanded, immediate divine salvation, though he gradually realized that it would not arrive on time.

While modern and obviously culturally different from the biblical corpus, this example is worth considering for two major reasons. First, here are theological reflections expressed in the midst of crisis, under immediate and constant suffering, not at a future juncture as retrospective reflections on past events. Second, the theological expressions are very emotional and include diverse and at times contradictory feelings, which move from deep faith in God's power and in divine justice, to the wish to see immediate divine salvation, to the fear (or recognition) that there will be no divine response; and although the Rebbe has no satisfactory explanation for the tremendous suffering of the people of God, he never stops approaching God for help, in growing anger and desperation.[46] The modern example thus validates the insight suggested by the original discussion of trauma studies, that the three elements of theodical discourse—justification, doubt, and protest—need not, and probably *should* not, be seen in a linear framework of evolution.

Trauma studies perspectives, then, lend credibility to the idea that the theological deliberations found in the biblical materials reflect an actual thought-world that draws upon and shapes earlier reflections, including theological ones, stemming from the time of the crisis itself. As always happens in traumatic events, a whole spectrum of contemporary reactions reflects the theological shock and crisis as weathered by different individuals and groups. Diversity, then, is a fifth genuine feature of both individual and communal reflections on trauma (with no expectations for historical truths).

The theoretical framework of trauma studies understands reaction to trauma as a process with longevity; thus the analytical aspect of this project is not dependent on precise datings of the target corpora. This framework, then, provides a needed heuristic angle for interpreting the significance of the range of theological views expressed by this corpus, in relation to the events of destruction and dislocation.

The literary approach substantiates the distinction between speaking

---

46. To quote Diamond ("Warsaw Ghetto Rebbe," 320), who refers to the Rebbe's last sermon, of July 18, 1942: "A last attempt to divert God's gaze away from some elusive redemptive future to the desperate immediacy of the present."

personae and scenarios over against authors of literary compositions. This distinction thus opens the floor to both synchronic-contemporaneous dimensions gained from the conversation among those speaking personae and diachronic perspectives added to the distinctions between the latter and the authors, who are responsible for the literary compositions evolved over time. Trauma studies ease the urge to arrive at clear or relative datings of diverse reflections on the crisis events. Rather, trauma studies suggest the option of diverse, oppositional theological reactions as of the first generation and through their descendants.[47] Hence, these two very different approaches allow both synchronic and diachronic analysis of this selected biblical corpus.

3.4. "Checks and Balances" for the Study of Theological Diversity

I target for this study Hebrew Bible compositions that explicitly deal with the events of the destruction and dislocations: the book of Kings, Jeremiah, Ezekiel, Lamentations, and seventeen Psalms. These literary sources demonstrate a multifaceted diversity, illustrated also in their theological reflections. However, these sources show significant similarities across the corpus in terms of the issues discussed, the close connections between quotations in the prophecies and psalmodic expressions, in addition to and in contrast to the connections between the ideas of historiographers and prophets. These similarities lend validity to various conceptions as authentic reactions to the crises. Therefore, the calculated decision to limit the corpus to these direct and explicit compositions is taken even at the price of potentially confronting invented or fictional speaking personae and scenarios.

To give more credence to the evaluation of the sources at hand, I develop three lines of checks and balances by which I (1) identify the multiple speaking personae (oftentimes anonymous) in diverse literary scenarios and distinguish between their theological perspectives over the extent of

---

47. From a diachronic perspective, one might argue that a basic conventional approach to those crises would have developed over time, to which skilled authors, even long after the actual events, could have adjusted their own writings. See Berlin, *Poetics and Interpretation*, 3–5. This possibility indeed cannot be denied; though, due to the multiple authors and literary compositions involved, the idea is quite difficult to plausibly support.

the corpus; (2) differentiate retrospective perspectives from reflections that speak in and about the crisis as present reality and study them all; and (3) define guidelines for the study of the theologies of prophetic books.

3.4.1. Retrospective Perspectives Versus Contemporary Reflections

The historiography of the book of Kings, on the one hand, and the prophetic books of Jeremiah and Ezekiel along with the poetic laments (mostly communal laments) on the other, show significant differences in their points of view: retrospective versus current outlooks, relative uniformity versus a multiplicity of perspectives. These two distinguishing features cut across both synchronic and diachronic levels of discussion.

Prophecy and psalmodic laments genuinely differ among themselves and from the historiography in their literary character.[48] The two most important characteristics that they share are their sense of current or immediate theological reflection and their diversity of proclamations and thought.

The quality of immediacy expressed in these writings needs clarification. While the historiography of Kings is distinguished by its retrospective perspective, prophetic literature retains (explicitly, in most cases) the sense of speaking in and about the present.[49] The book of Jeremiah reflects (or is literarily [re]constructed to reflect) reactions of the prophet to actual events—in confrontation with kings (Jer 22; 36; 37–38); with royal officials (21:1–10; 37:3–10; and other, similar encounters throughout Jer 36–44);

---

48. Within prophetic literature, the Book of Jeremiah includes historiographical segments as well (Jer 39; 52); it also includes biographies or historical narratives (Jer 26; 36; 37–44). Not surprisingly these chapters show similarities to Deuteronomistic historiographical writings. Among many other shared features are their retrospective perspectives on the crisis events.

49. This is to differ from the well-known talmudic saying, b. Megillah 14a: "As said by the Tannaim: Many prophets served Israel, double those that left Egypt, but a prophecy that was applicable for generations was written, and the one not applied was not written." This idea is embraced also by the redaction-historical approach to explain the phenomenon of *Fortschreibung*, the ongoing adaptations of prophetic pronouncements by scribal prophets active after the prophet's own lifetime and activity; see Steck, *Prophetic Books*, 22–23. While prophecies no doubt are preserved, adapted, and revised by subsequent generations, and thus reveal the reception history of prophecy, I would not give up on the possibility of learning about the immediate role of prophecy within its time of proclamation, hence about the early stages of oral/literary transmission; see van der Toorn, *Scribal Culture*, 178–82.

with priests, prophets, and the "people" in the courts of the temple (Jer 26; 27–28); and so on.

According to the book of Ezekiel, the prophet confronts his contemporaries, the Jehoiachin exiles in Babylon, to whom he prophesies the total doom that awaits their homeland community in Jerusalem (Ezek 1–24; 33). The prophet discusses with them issues of divine justice (14:12–23; and Ezek 18; 20), the role of God in the destruction, God's presence and his involvement in the hazardous events (Ezek 8–11, crafted to respond to 8:12 and 9:9); and he addresses them with hopeful messages of restoration (compare 11:1–13 and Ezek 14–21), responding to their feelings of desertion and despair (e.g., 37:10). These speaking personae/voices and scenarios may be actual or merely literary; in any case, the authors of this prophetic literature understand the prophetic role as reacting on the spot to the immediate issues at stake and the acute emotions engendered by them.[50]

Laments comprise a separate literary category involving primarily communal laments and at times individual laments in the books of Psalms and Lamentations. In these compositions the emotional distress resulting from the catastrophe is portrayed as immediate and ongoing, agonized over by the poets themselves, as individuals or as representatives of their communities. References to the past occur only as illustrations, usually as examples of divine behavior that contrasts with present circumstances (e.g., Pss 44:2–9; 80:9–17).

Nevertheless, the laments in particular show an intentional tendency to obscure or even blur their historical scenarios (i.e., the circumstances of the original authorship) for the sake of applying the same poem to additional and even broader circumstances in the more distant future.[51] This last technique creates an unclear picture of the literarily crafted historical scenario, and it complicates efforts to determine the actual period of au-

---

50. See also Jer 42:7 for the prophet's reaction after a brief intervening period; 28:2 does not specify the intervening time. References to the past as illustrations for current circumstances may also be found in prophetic literature; e.g., Jer 7:21–28; Ezek 20:1–38; also Ezek 16 and 23.

51. This technique of blurring historical information and other recognizable details is well attested in the Mesopotamian liturgical texts, the *balag* and *ershemma* laments, which are first composed in the Old Babylonian period and continued to be copied and used down to the Neo-Assyrian, Neo-Babylonian, and Seleucid periods; see Cohen, *Sumerian Hymnology*, 40–50; Cohen, *Canonical Lamentations*, 1–46, esp. 38–39. Gabbay ("Performance of Emesal Prayers") shows that, while there is no visible connection between the content of specific *balags* and their time of performance within the ritual context, there is a common thread between the content and their performance.

thorship. Recognizing this literary technique is of great importance for setting reasonable scholarly expectations or, to state it more clearly, for minimizing expectations of deriving from the laments a complete and accurate historical report of events. Nevertheless, these psalmodic compositions are invaluable for the reconstruction of the theological world of thought.

3.4.2. The Book of Kings

While the authors' own eras generate the point of departure for their writing, the basic viewpoint of Hebrew Bible historiographers is retrospective. Their contemporary concerns are expressed only implicitly; whereas their explicit focus is on the past, from which they are interested in learning didactic lessons for the present (and, also implicitly, deriving promises for the future).[52] One of the scholarly challenges is to discover the possible time of the Deuteronomistic historiographers' vantage points.[53]

Frank Cross aptly distinguishes the book of Kings from the rest of the Deuteronomistic History and differentiates between the preexilic Josianic edition (labeled Dtr1) and the exilic layers of Kings (labeled Dtr2, mostly within 2 Kgs 21–25).[54] Across its different compositional and redactional layers (preexilic and exilic), the book of Kings draws on the repertoire of expressions, themes, and theological conceptions common to the Deuteronomistic school; but one must beware of oversimplifying a more complex

52. On the retrospective dimension of Hebrew Bible historiography, see Noth, "Jerusalem Catastrophe"; von Rad, "Deuteronomic Theology," 211–14; Halpern, *First Historians*, 219–35; Hoffman, "Reflections on the Relationship"; and Römer, "Invention of History," 264–66.

53. See, for instance, Lemaire, "Toward a Redactional History"; and Römer, "Invention of History," 264–66.

54. Cross, *Canaanite Myth and Hebrew Epic*, 287–89; followed by Nelson, *Double Redaction*, 53–90. Another influential line of scholarship distinguishes three editorial strands (labeled DtrG, DtrP, and DtrN) in the Deuteronomistic history; see Smend, "Das Gesetz und die Völker"; and O'Brien, *Deuteronomistic History Hypothesis*, 272–87. For a helpful summary of these lines of research, and a no less valuable critique of them, see Sharp, *Prophecy and Ideology*, 27–39. Where 2 Kgs 21–25 is concerned, O'Brien and many other scholars still take 23:28–25:21 as having been produced by a single historiographer. This view holds that 21:2–7, 10–14, 21–22; the reworking of 22:19, 20ab; and 23:26–27 are composed by a second, prophetic hand; and that 24:2–3; 21:8–9, 15; 22:13b, 16–17, 18a; 23:24–25; 24:20a are composed by a third, nomistic hand. Compare Seitz, *Theology in Conflict*, who points out differences between 2 Kgs 24 and 2 Kgs 25.

picture.[55] I concur with Christopher Seitz in taking the late (exilic) Deuteronomistic source known as Dtr2 (Deut 23–25) as a compilation involving several authors from among the Babylonian deportees.[56]

The destruction of Jerusalem never receives a full Deuteronomistic oration in Kings (compare the theological oration on the destruction of the Northern Kingdom in 2 Kgs 17:7–23).[57] Bits and pieces of theological reflections are evidenced in 2 Kings, though, and they help us discover that while there is quite a uniform line of argumentation within the book, there are still a number of differently nuanced ways to justify God; there is even room for great embarrassment in having to pursue this task of justification in view of the recognition that God himself is responsible for and actively participates in the catastrophe of his city and his people.

My discussion (chaps. 6, 7, 9, 10) of the historiographers' voices in the book of Kings focuses on 2 Kgs 23–25, where (following Seitz and others) I identify several authors who express a variety of theological perspectives on the role of God in the catastrophe. Yet, they are all writing within a framework of after-the-fact justification of God, in accordance with the overall outlook of the Deuteronomistic school.

---

55. An abundance of studies are dedicated to the Deuteronomistic writings in general and to the book of Kings in particular. With many other scholars, I do not accept Noth's seminal conception of the Deuteronomistic History as a unified exilic literary composition (Noth, *Deuteronomistic History*). To note a few of the different approaches, see McKenzie's discussion of the multiple voices within the late (exilic) Deuteronomistic source known as Dtr2 in *Trouble with Kings*, 135–50; Lohfink, "Was There a Deuteronomistic Movement?," 54–66; Person, *Deuteronomic School*, 1–16, 147–52; and Römer, "Invention of History," 258–71.

56. Seitz, *Theology in Conflict*, 189–200 (criticism of Cross and Nelson) and 174–78, esp. 177n170 (theological discussion of 2 Kgs 24). See also Sharp, *Prophecy and Ideology*, 38–39, 143–47 (discussion of the "Lord's servants, the prophets," in 17:7–23). Levin ("Empty Land in Kings") points out the literary growth of 2 Kgs 24–25 from a series of redactional expansions of a Jehoiachin revision, or several *golah* revisions (esp. 69–70, 81–82, 86–89). While I do not find the specific distinctions to be persuasive (neither the passages Levin considers to be an original kernel nor the differences assumed between the Jehoiachin and the *golah* revisions; see 88–89), it is clear that the two chapters comprise several hands, all of Babylonian origin. For my theological interest, this is clearly enough specificity.

57. For a discussion of the obviously biased, pro-Judean and anti-Israelite perspective of this oration, see Noth, *Deuteronomistic History*, 63–74; and Cross, *Canaanite Myth and Hebrew Epic*, 274–89. Brettler ("Ideology, History, and Theology") emphasizes the literary evolution of this passage through several stages, in Judah.

3.4.3. *Lamentations and Selected Psalms*

I treat the individual laments in Psalms and Lamentations as independent compositions, self-contained in form and content, each with its own unique religious/theological perspective; thus, they are probably written by diverse authors.

Lamentations is among the literary sources closest in time to the destruction. Lamentations 1, 2, 4, and 5 reflect the destruction of the city of Jerusalem (1:4, 7, 11, 15; 2:10–12, 19–21; 4:4–5, 8–10; 5:2–18; defeat and distress are also lamented in 3:42–47) and the deportation of its residents (1:3, 6; 2:9); but all these laments lack reference to restoration. These data suggest that the time frame for the composition of this collection is the period between Jerusalem's destruction (586) and the Edict of Cyrus (538).[58] The place of writing is probably Judah. The laments all focus on the fate of the city and its residents, looking upon the dislocation from this geographical point of departure (Lam 1:3, 6). Of further importance, there are no positive references in Lamentations to actual residence in the diaspora.[59]

Scholars indicate that the vividness of the descriptions of destruction and distress is a sign that the poems are written by eyewitnesses and that

---

58. Rudolph (*Klagelieder*, 5) suggests a variable dating of the chapters: Lam 1 is written after 598, Lam 2 and 4 after 586, and Lam 3 and 5 are later yet, though still shaped by the disaster of the destruction. Fohrer argues that all five laments are written by an eyewitness prior to the Edict of Cyrus (in Sellin, *Introduction to the Old Testament*, 298). Westermann (*Lamentations*, 104–5) suggests 550 as the latest possible date for the collection, based on reversal references to Lamentations found in Second Isaiah. Gottwald (*Book of Lamentations*, 43–45), for this same reason, argues that the scroll in its present form of five chapters is known before 538. Compare these approaches to Berlin's thoughtful discussion (*Lamentations*, 33–36); she first argues that a good poet can convey immediacy even if he is not present (33). Thus, she prefers to date the poems through arguments based on intertextual connections made in Lamentations (with Jeremiah and Ezekiel, with pentateuchal literature, and with Second Isaiah) and on linguistic data that illustrate the transitional period typical of sixth-century biblical literature. Hence, she arrives at a time frame of 571 to 538 (possibly to 520); and she is more puzzled by the purpose for its writing than by its actual dating. The linguistic data are set out by Dobbs-Allsopp in "Linguistic Evidence" and *Lamentations*, 4–5.

59. So Rudolph, *Klagelieder*, 7–8; Westermann, *Lamentations*, 55–56, 105; Hillers, *Lamentations*, 15; Re'emi, *God's People in Crisis*, 73–134; and Dobbs-Allsopp, *Lamentations*, 4–5. Compare Fohrer (in Sellin, *Introduction to the Old Testament*, 298), who argues that Lam 1, 2, 4 are written in exile, and Lam 3 and 5 in Judah. Fohrer's main argument is the many references to Ezekiel in Lam 2 and 4, which suggest the authorship of an eyewitness from among the Babylonian exiles.

they are composed to be recited on the anniversary of the destruction, in commemorative ceremonies even down to the restoration period (Zech 7:3–6; 8:19).[60] Yet, the acrostic structure and the formulaic style of the laments, which show clear resemblances (in genre, theme, and even phraseology) to Sumerian city laments and Mesopotamian *balag/ershemma* liturgical texts, raise doubts as to the historical accuracy one may ascribe to these portrayals of destruction.[61] Thus this phenomenon presents another example of the tension between literary personae and authors.[62] For the present discussion, which focuses on the theological thought-worlds evolving during and after the destruction, neither historical accuracy nor a demonstrable liturgical function is essential.

Scholars of Lamentations debate the question of whether the book shows a literary unity and a possible overall structure with Lam 3 at its core, or rather constitutes an anthology of five independent laments.[63] Likewise, questions are raised as to whether the five are the work of a single author or, rather, of up to five authors (or even more). The two questions are of importance for a theological study of the book, as they touch directly upon the question of whether Lamentations reflects one unified line of thought or whether it gives voice to multiple theological reactions. Wilhelm Rudolph argues that a single author—who could have belonged to any of the following circles: prophets, priests, political officials, or military officials—is responsible for all five laments.[64] More often, scholars

---

60. Westermann, *Lamentations*, 61–63. Fohrer (in Sellin, *Introduction to the Old Testament*, 297–98) rejects the possibility that the laments are composed for cultic use, although he does argue that this is the reason they are collected by the early Second Temple period; see Berlin, *Lamentations*, 35–36.

61. Hillers, *Lamentations*, 10, 32–39. Gwaltney ("Biblical Book of Lamentations") sets out the thematic and stylistic elements shared by Lamentations and Mesopotamian laments, but he also points out the lack of resemblance between the two corpora in structure and organization of components (207–10). In addition, Gwaltney comments on the lack of any internal evidence about the cultic function of these compositions; see Dobbs-Allsopp, *Weep, O Daughter of Zion*, 10–15.

62. See Berlin, *Lamentations*, 33–34.

63. Linafelt (*Surviving Lamentations*, 5–18) elaborates on the special place Lam 3 gains in scholarship and on the biased Christian theological perspectives it nurtures; see, e.g., Provan, *Lamentations*, 22–23. Linafelt's focus on the "figure of Zion" in Lam 1–2 and his recognition that the five laments are initially separate is closer to my own work, although I emphasize the independence of the two and the theological differences between them (§1.2.2, §9.3.1, §11.2.3).

64. Rudolph, *Klagelieder*, 7. Kaufmann (*Toldot Ha-ʾEmunah*, 3.594–99), thinks the author is one of Zedekiah's officials who held popular beliefs. For other suggestions,

presume a number of authors, and there are two major suggestions as to their social backgrounds: the authors are part of the official political or religious leadership[65] or are laypeople who did not belong to any official or professional circles, which would place the scroll within the category of popular religion of the time.[66]

On the basis of the literary data (structure, genre, and acrostic orderings), I treat Lamentations as a collection of five independent laments—five self-contained and separate poetic compositions—which thus attest to at least five different authors whose social backgrounds remain a riddle.[67] I compare each of the distinctive theological perspectives in these laments with those of the other literary sources discussed; throughout this study, I take into consideration the question of whether the laments reflect official voices and/or might be tied to specific social and literary circles.

Of the seventeen laments within the book of Psalms studied here, sixteen are categorized as laments: Pss 9–10, 42–43, 44, 74, 77, 79, 80, 89, 90, 94, 102, 106, 123, 137; and Ps 103 is categorized as a psalm of praise.[68] Formally, these psalms may use either the first-person singular (thus, individual laments) or more often the plural (thus, communal laments); and yet they all address situations of national catastrophe(s).[69] These psalms

---

see Westermann, *Lamentations*, 24–61. In this context, I note also the Second Temple and rabbinic traditions (e.g., b. Baba Batra 15b) that ascribe Lamentations to Jeremiah; the same tradition is reflected in early translations, such as the Septuagint (repeated in Vulgate).

65. To mention some of the suggestions: cult prophets (Gottwald, *Book of Lamentations*, 113–17), the Jerusalemite priesthood (Kraus, *Klagelieder*, 12–13, wavers between the official priesthood and cult prophets), or a high-ranked official in Zedekiah's court (Re'emi, *God's People in Crisis*, 81).

66. So Gunkel, "Klagelieder Jeremia" and *Psalms*, 15–17. Westermann (*Lamentations*, 56–58) suggests multiple authorship, but does not suggest a specific literary authorial circle. He feels that the laments do not accord in style with either of the known, contemporary literary circles; so also Hillers, *Lamentations*, 14.

67. Moreover, the acrostic ordering may serve to explain the proximity of independent and even contradictory statements in a single closed context; see Löhr, "Threni III" and "Alphabetische und alphabetisierende Lieder."

68. Scholars differ on the formal and thematic categorization and thus on the accurate numbers of communal and individual laments in Psalms. Ps 103 is discussed in §12.1. Kraus's inclusion of both communal and individual laments as "songs of prayer" and his formal subcategorizations of each seem appropriate to me; see Kraus, *Psalms 1–59*, 47–56. From a ritual-cultic point of view, see Gerstenberger, *Psalms, Part 1*, 9–14; and from a rhetorical perspective, see Charney, *Persuading God*, 1–15.

69. Compare Kraus (*Psalms 1–59*, 50–51), who leaves the situations of the national

may be taken as a subcategory within psalms of lament, based on their common denominator; that is, they reflect situations of distress, caused by either God or human enemies, and oftentimes explicitly refer to the destruction of Jerusalem and Judah and/or to the dislocation of its people in the aftermath of this destruction.[70]

Dating psalms by tying them to specific historical events is one of the most debated issues in the study of the book.[71] I recognize that authors of the poems that make up the anthology we call the book of Psalms intentionally obscure historical clues, avoiding the mention of specific historical figures, nations, or events that might associate these poems with any particular historical episodes. Rather, psalmodic poetry in Israel is crafted to be relevant to as many events as possible across many time periods.[72] This very characteristic is, of course, a great stumbling block for modern Hebrew Bible scholars, intrigued by the principles of literary criticism and interested in revealing the world of thought at the time(s) of the psalms'

---

distresses completely open to diverse crises but allows himself to be more specific on the individual laments (52–55). While it is clearly safer to indeed generalize the distress (and assume later reapplications of these texts to additional catastrophes), most of the selected psalms mentioned are quite clear in their references to the national catastrophe under discussion here.

70. See Broyles (*Conflict of Faith and Experience*, 11–34, 213–25) for his definition of the lament, which he sees to be constructed of three building blocks: description of the distress (with specific attention to the agent of disaster, frequently God, and at times the human enemy); interpretation of the distress; and appeal to God, an element shared by both individual and communal laments. Broyles (chaps. 2–3; summary on 221–25) distinguishes two subgroups within the laments: "psalms of plea" and "psalms of complaint"; the latter group expresses the painful theological turmoil that is the focus of the present study.

71. Psalms scholarship from the nineteenth through the mid-twentieth centuries, and specifically the Scandinavian school, assumed that most of the psalms are Second Temple period Jewish liturgical compositions. Therefore, historical references are understood as fictional retrospectives or as historicizations of mythological elements (so Kraus, *Psalms 60–150*, 203–4). This position was modified in the course of the twentieth century, and contemporary scholarship considers the collection of Psalms to reflect the literary creativity of several hundred years, not excluding the possibility of preexilic authorship; see Weiser, *Psalms*, 91–95. Broyles aptly argues that the "situational context" of each psalm contains both the historical circumstances of authorship and those of the text's possible reuse in (or adaptation for) different later occasions (*Conflict of Faith and Experience*, 17–20).

72. As more generally in the ancient Near East, see 97n51, above, and Broyles (*Conflict of Faith and Experience*, 17–22) for what he defines as "interpretations" of situations of distress.

composition (and during their early transmission). Hence, the recognition of this feature of the psalms demonstrates once again the importance of acknowledging the gap between speaking voices and authors.

Indeed, scholars of Psalms do not agree on the list of poems that might reflect the Babylonian destruction and the exiles thereafter. Yehezkel Kaufmann argues that the destruction in Nebuchadnezzar's time is not mentioned at all in the Psalms, apart from the hint in 137:7.[73] Georg Fohrer names Pss 60, 74, 77:1–16, 102, and 123.[74] Enno Jansen designates five laments as sixth-century compositions: Pss 44, 74, 89, 102; and Lam 5.[75] Arthur Weiser selects only three psalms (Pss 74, 79, 137) and argues that not every poem about a national crisis reflects Judah's destruction, and thus he does not count Ps 44 and Ps 89 in this group.[76] Hans Kraus suggests that Ps 60 reflects the events of 587. He understands Ps 44, Ps 74, and Ps 79 against the background of exile; Ps 137 as stemming from the experience of captivity in Babylon; Ps 87 as reflecting exilic or postexilic reality; and Ps 85 and Ps 126 as representing the return. In addition, Kraus flags Pss 9–10, 42–43, 77, 90, 94, 102, 103, 106, and 123 as having emerged from the exilic or postexilic eras.[77] Ralph Klein considers Pss 44, 74, 79, and 102 to be testimonies of Judean exiles.[78] Craig Broyles distinguishes communal laments by their differing descriptions of the distress and considers them all exilic and postexilic compositions. Only Pss 74 and 79 does he consider to reflect the destruction; Pss 106 and 137 reflect exile; and others designate various events: military defeat (44, 60, 80, 89, 108), social violence (10, 55, 94, 109), national distress (85, 126), and lack of salvation (107).[79]

I selected a group of seventeen psalms as foci for my theological investigation. This is not the place to discuss each psalm separately (see chaps. 6–12); suffice it to mention three common denominators that serve as criteria for choosing them.

First, fourteen of the psalms include historical and geographical information that accords with descriptions of the destruction era in the histo-

---

73. Kaufmann, *Toldot Ha-'Emunah*, 2.661 and n37.

74. Fohrer, *History of Israelite Religion*, 309. Yet Ps 60 seems to reflect political and military realities earlier than the sixth century.

75. Janssen, *Juda in der Exilzeit*, 19–20.

76. Weiser, *Psalms*, 91–92.

77. Kraus, *Psalms 1–59*, 65.

78. Klein, *Israel in Exile*, 18–22.

79. Broyles, *Conflict of Faith and Experience*, 95–99.

riography, in the books of Jeremiah and Ezekiel, and in Lamentations. To note some of the major points:

- The end of political sovereignty is described in Ps 89 as the end of Davidic rulership, although the psalm does not refer to a deportation of the defeated king.[80]
- The destruction of Jerusalem is described in Ps 79, which refers to the bloodshed in the city and its surroundings.
- The defilement of the temple and its destruction is described in Pss 74 and 79; and 74:9 bemoans the cessation of prophetic activity and the lack of communication with God, which could refer to his involvement in these historical circumstances (see §7.1 on Ps 74).
- Military defeat and deportation from the city, portrayed as divine acts, are mentioned in Pss 44, 80, and 106 (see 106:47).
- Life in exile among foreign nations is the context of Pss 42–43, which mention geographic regions in the north of Israel as distant points from which the poet is unable to reach the place of the temple (42:3; 43:3, 4).
- Both geographically and chronologically, Ps 77 hints at an exilic background.
- Psalm 102, which opens as an individual lament, exposes the psalmist's interest in the fate of Jerusalem and its people (102:13–23, 29); these verses clearly talk of Jerusalem as destroyed (102:14–17) and might also be hinting at living outside the land (102:11).
- Psalm 137 relates but few details of the distress that brought the Judeans to the rivers of Babylon, but it certainly reflects some aspects of life among the nations, including the question of whether the Yahwistic cult could be practiced in exile.

On the other hand, some psalms seem to have emerged from Judah itself during this same period, such as Pss 9–10 (see 9:12; 10:16), which reflect the concept of the divine presence as king in the city. Could these two psalms signal an internal conflict in Jerusalem during the period between

---

80. Sarna ("Psalm 89") suggests that Ps 89 reacts to the threat by the Syro-Ephraimite coalition against Ahaz (735–734). Kraus (*Psalms 60–150*, 202–4, 210–11) rejects the possibility of a postexilic dating, arguing that the voice of the king may be heard in 89:47–52. Thus he suggests that the psalm is composed prior to the destruction or at the latest during the exile.

the two crisis events, the Jehoiachin exile and the destruction?[81] From another angle, Ps 74 and Ps 89 describe the destruction and the dethronement of the Jerusalem king, but do not mention deportation.[82]

A second criterion is an identifiable complex of ideological conceptions shared by these fourteen psalms, which may then be used to identify yet other psalms that express similar theological confrontations with the realities of destruction and exile. In lieu of any identifiable historical or geographical references, these theological topics may serve to identify Pss 90, 94, 103, and 123 as germane to the discussion. Psalms 94 and 103 contain thematic connections with the books of Jeremiah and Ezekiel, which link these psalms with those calamitous events. Three elements in Ps 94 reveal the poet's concern with the fate of the entire nation: he expresses his confidence in God, who will not desert his people and land (94:14); he quotes the words of the evildoers in phrasing similar to that of Ezek 8:12 and 9:9; and he refutes them with rhetorical questions (Ps 94:8–10) and with the divine epithet יהוה אלהינו (94:23). Psalm 103 opens and closes with verses of praise that form an *inclusio* (103:1–2, 20–22). In between, in 103:8–16, we find implicit echoes of communal calamity, in which the poet is very close to Jeremian phraseology (e.g., 103:9; see Jer 3:5, 12), although he nevertheless recognizes the workings of divine mercy and salvation in times of distress (see §12.1 on Ps 103). Psalm 90 refers to a situation of national calamity as the result of divine judgment implemented by God in his wrath (90:7–10, 15), and it presents the well-known question עד־מתי in 90:13 (similarly 74:10 and 79:5). Psalm 123 opens with the poet's words to God, but then moves to the communal arena, describing the community's full subjection to God (123:2); the poet sets forth petitions for salvation (123:3; see also 9:14; 102:14), in view of the scorn and contempt the people suffer (123:3b–4; similarly Pss 42–44).

The third and final criterion that unites these psalms is a set of shared literary and formal characteristics that form-critically place them in the category of individual or communal laments. Nine of the seventeen psalms under discussion are classified as communal laments (Pss 44, 74, 79, 80, 89, 90, 106, 123, 137), and four are individual laments (Pss 9–10, 42–43). Three share some characteristics of both subgroups: they open as individual calls

---

81. Contra Kraus (*Psalms 1–59*, 193–94), who suggests a postexilic dating.

82. See Middlemas's discussions of Pss 74, 79, 89, 102; Isa 63:7–64:11; and Lamentations as literary products composed within Judah (*Templeless Age*, 35–51; and *Troubles of Templeless Judah*, 122–70, 171–228).

to God, but transform within to the plural, representing the entire people (Pss 77, 94, 102).[83] This transformation from the singular to the plural, from the individual to the communal, also characterizes Ps 103, the single psalm of praise in this group, which however implicitly gives voice to the distress experienced by the people and to a strong defense of God's role therein (103:8–9, 10–14, 17–18).

Studies of the lament genre (communal and individual) identify three main elements shared across the genre: an address to God, complaint(s) over the present distress, and petitions for salvation.[84] Segments of praise that regularly appear in these psalms usually belong with the first component, as part of the address to God. His past sovereign deeds as lord of the world (89:6–19), as lord of his people who saved them from Egypt (77:12–21), or as the lord who led his people to possess the land (44:2–9)— all build a strong basis for the contemporary complaint and the petitions for salvation that follow. The proximity of praise and complaint in these psalms, like that of praise and petitions for salvation, indicates the complexity of the theological perspectives revealed by these psalms.[85] Differ-

83. Compare Kraus (*Psalms 1–59*, 50), who categorizes Pss 44, 74, 77, 79, 80, 90, 94, 123, 137 as communal laments; 102 as an individual lament over sickness (*Psalms 60–150*, 284); 103 and 106 as songs of praise (289–90, 316–17); 137 as a Zion song (501). Or see Weiser who, faithful to Gunkel's literary categories, describes these psalms as "blends" of different generic components. Thus, he sees Pss 9–10, 94, 102 as individual laments combined with psalms of thanksgiving (*Psalms*, 84, 66–67); 77 as an individual lament combined with praise (530–31); 89 as a royal song (591); 103 as a praise and thanksgiving song (657–58); 106 as praise (679–80); and so on. Such narrow generic categorizations do not take into consideration the special nature of these (individual and) communal laments.

84. There is a diversity of opinions on fine tuning the specific characteristics of the genre. Gunkel (*Psalms*, 14–15, 32) identifies the elements of complaint, petitions for salvation, and proclamations of confidence in divine assistance. Mowinckel (*Psalms in Israel's Worship*, 1.195–204) suggests a slightly different plan: address to God, complaint, and petitions for salvation. This schema is generally accepted by Westermann, *Lamentations*, 95–98; and with minor modifications by Kraus, *Psalms 1–59*, 46–47; and Weiser, *Psalms*, 67. More importantly, Gunkel considers the elements of praise found in some communal laments to represent the interference of an entirely different genre into those laments. For a more complex discussion of the genre, see Broyles, *Conflict of Faith and Experience*, 220–21; and Morrow, *Protest against God*, 76–105.

85. See Gerstenberger, *Psalms, Part 1*, 13. Charney (*Persuading God*, 5–8) aptly emphasizes the lines of argument as building the connections between the different components; I tend to enhance this rhetorical approach and locate the theological arguments behind different steps taken and nuances presented in addressing (and thus in challenging) God.

ences in the ordering of the components or in their proportions within these psalms are taken in this study to reflect diverse rhetorical strategies and theological positions (and not as illustrations of, e.g., the literary amalgamation of different fragments of psalms). Table 3.1 demonstrates the extent to which the use of these components reflects the conventions of this literary pattern; and most importantly, it reveals the poets' freedom to use these components toward the goals of either justifying God or establishing a protest against him.

In both forms, expressed either as words of the individual or as representative of the collective (communal or individual lament), these psalms lament the present situation of distress and ask for salvation within the national arena; thus they, too, testify to the broad range of theological reflections on the destruction, coming from both Judah and Babylon.

Each psalm will be discussed individually, with attention to its own particular voice, rhetorical strategies, and points of interest. As a group, these psalms reflect a high and sophisticated poetical form and style, presumably written by professionals; thus, the poems are hardly expressions of laypersons' beliefs. More plausible is the assumption that they are composed by poets of the temple who are masters of its liturgy and who carry on their traditions in the aftermath of its destruction, in both Judah and Babylon. One of the challenges is to place those individual poets on the overall spectrum of religious reflections upon the destruction and the exiles, particularly in relation to the prophets and to prophetic literature.

3.4.4. The Study of the Theologies of Prophetic Books

The books of Jeremiah and Ezekiel pose even more nuanced challenges to the study of their theological perspectives. In contrast to the psalmodic literature (both Psalms and Lamentations), these books create the expectation that they constitute the collected proclamations of specific prophetic figures, active over several decades among specific and known audiences. Yet, critical readings of these books reveal that they reflect much more than the actual words of the individual prophets. In different ways they call attention to the need for a sophisticated analysis that takes into consideration multiple dimensions and methodological approaches within critical Hebrew Bible study.

Table 3.1. Characteristics of the Lament Genre

Psalm	Calling God's Name	Defining the Relationship	Praise	Questions	Description of Distress	Calling God to Wake Up	Petition for Help	Confession of Sins	Proclamation of Confidence and Obedience
9–10	9:2–3		9:4–19	10:1, 13	10:2–11	9:20–21; 10:12	10:14–16		10:17–18
42–43	42:2	42:2–3		42:3	42:4–6		43:3–5		43:2–5
44	44:2	44:5	44:2–9	44:25	44:10–23, 26	44:24	44:27	44:18–19, 21–22	44:18–23
74	74:12	74:2	74:12–17	74:2, 11	74:3–11	74:20			
77	77:2–3	77:4–7	77:12–21	77:8–10	77:11				
79	79:2			79:5	79:1–4, 7		79:6, 9, 11–12	79:8	79:10, 13
80	80:2–4	80:2–4	80:9–12	80:5	80:6–7, 13–14, 17	80:15	80:8, 18, 20	80:19	80:4, 20
89	89:9	89:19	89:2–19, 20–38	89:47–50	89:39–46	89:48, 51			89:2–3
90	90:1		90:2–6	90:13	90:1–7		90:14–17	90:8	90:16
94	94:1–2			94:3, 16	94:4–11			94:23	94:16–22
102	102:2		102:26–28		102:4–12, 24–25	102:3	102:2–3		102:13–29
106	106:1	106:6	106:2–5, 7–12, 13–46			106:47	106:47	106:6	106:47
123	123:1	123:2			123:3b–4		123:3a		123:2
137					137:1–4		137:7–9		137:5–6

3.4.4.1. The Book of Jeremiah

One of the major critical challenges provoked by the book of Jeremiah is the need to constantly steer between diachronic and synchronic spheres of discussion.[86] The diachronic sphere has to do with the distinction between the prophet and his followers, his tradents, and the editors of the book; the synchronic treats of the relationship between the prophet and his contemporaries.

a.   The prophet and his followers (tradents/editors)

Not surprisingly, the book of Jeremiah proves to be one of the best laboratories for form and redaction criticism. From the time of Bernard Duhm and Sigmund Mowinckel, scholars differentiated poetry from prose and distinguished "later" Deuteronomic/Deuteronomistic phrases from "authentic" Jeremian passages. Employing these distinctions, scholars tend to conclude that only a small part of the prophecies in Jeremiah (if any) may cautiously be assigned to an early-sixth-century prophet and that most of the materials in the book (specifically the prose) should be credited to Deuteronomistic tradents and editors down to the fourth century.[87] In this framework, there may be no real way to identify genuinely Jeremian

---

86. Compare Lundbom (*Jeremiah 1–20*, 141–52 at 141), who articulates a distinction between two theological perspectives in the book of Jeremiah: (1) "The theology in the book . . . refracted through the man Jeremiah, to which are added numerous witnesses to the life of faith that grow out of Jeremiah's own prophetic experience"; and (2) "the theology of the book of Jeremiah," which "contains reflections by others who look at Jeremiah's life and preaching from a distance." According to Lundbom, this perspective "supplements and expands the theology of Jeremiah" (149). This somewhat theoretical distinction still leaves us with the challenge of characterizing and distinguishing between the two levels.

87. Duhm (*Jeremia*, xi–xiv, xvi) considers only one-fifth of the book to be the "original" poems of the prophet, composed mostly in Anathoth and Jerusalem; later additions to the book portray a Torah teacher rather than a prophet (xviii). Mowinckel (*Zur Komposition des Buches Jeremia*, 17–51) contributes the concept of four sources for Jeremiah; and Thiel develops a detailed schema of the differentiation of these layers (*Jeremia 1–25*, 32–45; *Jeremia 26–52*, 91–115). Present-day redaction critics in Germany follow in these footsteps, or more often modify Thiel's ideas in significant ways, and yet the basic categorizations in terms of authorship are retained; see Stipp's "Offene Fragen"; "Probleme des redaktionsgeschichtlichen Modells"; "Sprachliche Kennzeichen jeremianischer Autorschaft"; "But into the Water"; and Schmid, *Buchgestalten des Jeremiahbuches*, 327–54; and "Jeremiah."

materials in the book, and therefore scholars rather speak of a Jeremiah tradition.[88] However, in the middle of the twentieth century, Yehezkel Kaufmann considered the same data concerning Deuteronomic/Deuteronomistic phraseology and themes to prove that "Jeremiah was the prophet of the Book of Deuteronomy."[89]

These different literary-historical perspectives on Jeremiah present a great challenge to scholars interested in a descriptive theology of the biblical book.[90] When we add theological concerns to a number of contextual questions that are usually asked, this diachronic perspective becomes even more troubling: What is the prophet's own initial theological-ideological orientation? Who are the prophet's "followers," both in Judah and in Babylon? Do they all belong to one specific, authorial-ideological circle? Is the prophet himself a part of or, rather, associated with the Deuteronomistic literary school? Or are only his followers and tradents members of that powerful authorial group, as is so often assumed in Jeremiah scholarship?

The foregoing questions highlight my own perception that the conceptual framework that relegates Deuteronomic/Deuteronomistic phrases and ideas to a Deuteronomist-Jeremiah (DtrJ) editorial level is much too simplistic. As repeatedly shown, Deuteronomic/Deuteronomistic expressions and theological conceptions are not in themselves either criteria for or literary markers of non-Jeremian units.[91]

b.   The prophet in dialogue with his contemporaries

An entirely different presentation of the theology of Jeremiah may develop when synchronic factors are introduced. From such a vantage point, the

---

88. See Carroll, *Jeremiah*, 55–64. Using quite different arguments, based mostly on intertextuality, Fischer argues: "Jer portrays the figure of an outstanding prophet, in many respects. Jeremiah appears to be a kind of summary of several important precursors in Israelite history, incorporating various features of them in his profile" ("Is There Shalom, or Not?," 360; and similarly his *Jeremia 1–25*, 65–74).

89. Kaufmann, *Toldot Ha-'Emunah*, 3.433–34.

90. It is remarkable to compare Duhm's approach to Jeremiah when discussing theological issues in his *Die Theologie der Propheten*, 69–95, with the literary-historical approach he takes in his commentary (*Jeremia*, ix–xxii).

91. For discussions of Jeremian and/or Deuteronomic/Deuteronomistic phraseology, see, e.g., Bright, "Prose Sermons of Jeremiah"; Weippert, *Die Prosareden des Jeremiabuches*, 228–34; Holladay, *Jeremiah*, 2.35–40, 53–63; Schmid, *Buchgestalten des Jeremiahbuches*, 327–54; and Rom-Shiloni, "Forest and the Trees."

book of Jeremiah supplies a wealth of diverse and oftentimes antagonistic theological perspectives on the cardinal issues at stake during the sixth century. In this framework, methodologies such as rhetorical criticism and sociological studies may help sort out the various contemporary voices.[92]

Jeremiah is famous for his struggles with his contemporaries, struggles that leave their marks on poetic passages, biographical stories, covenant speeches, and other "sermons."[93] If we align these various prophetic genres with the literary categories of Duhm and Mowinckel, we see that this dynamic operates throughout the book. No other prophet is recorded as having suffered such conflicts with his fellows (e.g., 11:18–23, poetry, thus of Mowinckel's source A) or as having debated so strenuously with officials, priests, and prophets in Jerusalem (Jer 26, 36–39, 40–44) or with the anonymous crowds (7:1–15; all prose, thus Mowinckel's sources B and C; compare Amos 7:10–17). A special feature that illustrates this dialogical quality of Jeremiah is the wealth of quotations throughout the book (see §3.1).

The important point raised here for the identification of theological aspects within the book of Jeremiah is, therefore, the recognition that theological polyphony in this book is both a synchronic matter of the prophet and his immediate audiences and a long-term diachronic interplay, representing a time span of one to three generations following the prophet, during which his adherents continued to engage his words, adapting them time and again to their ever-changing circumstances.[94]

In support of this last point, internal theological and ideological dissonances appear both in prophetic passages and in biographical and historical stories concerning the prophet and his contemporaries, in both poetry and prose.[95] Prophecies in Jeremiah show, at times, contradictory

92. Rhetorical criticism is the main methodology used by Lundbom, *Jeremiah 1–20*, 68–92. For sociological perspectives, see Wilson, *Prophecy and Society*, 1–19, 297–308, and his discussion of Jeremiah as an Ephraimite prophet on 231–51; and Overholt, *Channels of Prophecy*, 17–25.

93. For a discussion of the A source materials as reflecting the voices of different lamenters, see Biddle, *Polyphony and Symphony*, 1–14, 115–28.

94. The notion of adaptation and elaboration of the prophet's words by later tradents accords with Schmid's concept that later expansions of prophetic passages are theological in nature; see *Is There Theology in the Hebrew Bible?*, 63. I concur with Schmid's idea, but the distinctive criteria by which those elaborations are to be traced in his framework seem unclear; see Rom-Shiloni, "From Prophetic Words," 577–83.

95. See Kessler ("From Drought to Exile") for the suggestion that exilic authors also interpolate material into poetic passages. Kessler argues that Jer 7–20 is compiled by the exiles as prayers with a clear theodical role.

perspectives, which may be understood diachronically as differences between the prophet and his later followers and tradents. But considered
in terms of sociogeographical distinctions, such contradictory perspectives may also be understood as more contemporaneous (synchronic)
differences between the prophet (through his immediate followers) and
his various audiences. Here are several examples of such contradictory
conceptions:

1. The idea of the destruction as the total annihilation of the Judean
    community, with no exile to follow (e.g., Jer 27:8) versus the idea of
    a distinction between the fates of the two Judean communities, with
    exclusive priority given to the Jehoiachin exiles (Jer 24).
2. The notion that the destruction will leave/has left the land empty and
    desolated (e.g., 9:9–10), over against prophecies that predict resto-
    ration of "the remnant of Judah" in the land (42:10–12).
3. The different attitudes toward the last kings of Judah, Jehoiachin and
    Zedekiah. Compare the prophecy against Jehoiachin (22:24–30) with
    the expectation in Jerusalem for his return (Jer 27–29, esp. 28:2–4)
    and, yet again, the odd prophecy concerning Zedekiah (34:1–5).[96]
4. The different approaches toward Babylon and its king: King Nebu-
    chadnezzar is presented as God's obedient vassal for three generations
    (27:5–8; or seventy years, 25:11), which raises the demand to accept
    Babylonian subjugation and remain in the land (27:9–13; as also
    21:8–10). Yet, the symbolic action contextualized to the same event
    (on the fourth year of Zedekiah, 28:1; 51:59) predicts Babylon's fall
    (51:59–64).
5. The attention given to the people who remain in Judah (42:10–12)
    over against the Jehoiachin exiles (24:4–7; 29:16–20; 32:36–41) in
    terms of the implications of the destruction for the God-people
    relationship.
6. The fate of the Jehoiachin exiles in Babylon: Are they doomed to

96. See Seitz, *Theology in Conflict*, 205–14. Jer 34:4–5 represents a different view in
comparison to Deuteronomistic perceptions and does not accord with other prophecies addressed to Zedekiah or with the prophet's general conception of exile as a place
of no return (as in 22:24–30); but it does fit the close contacts of Jeremiah with the
last king of Judah. One may also add the topic of Jeremiah's status as part of עֲבָדַי(וֹ)
הַנְּבִיאִים ("His servants the prophets"), as examined by Sharp (*Prophecy and Ideology*,
41–80); she discerns specific features that help to distinguish Judah-based tradents over
against pro-*golah* tradents throughout the book.

death in that foreign land, as prophesied to Jehoiachin (22:24–27)? Are they to survive, even thrive, in Babylon, though still with no prospect of return (29:1–7)? Or are they the chosen continuation of the people of God (24; and fragmented in 29:16–20)?

7. The different conceptions of human responsibility for the disasters: the entire generation of the destruction (32:17–23), the exiles (16:10–13), or those who remained in Jerusalem (24:8–10; 29:16–20).

8. The notion of God's mercy, in the aftermath of the destruction, as directed to those who remained in the land (42:12) or to those in exile (12:15; 30:18).

9. Different conceptions of the reinstatement of the covenant: as a new covenant (31:31–34) and as an "eternal covenant" (ברית עולם) in prophecies addressed to the Babylonian exiles (32:36–41; 50:5).[97]

The common denominator among all these conceptual differences is the internal struggle over group-identity issues between the two Judean communities of the early sixth century and on. This struggle brings the people who remained in Judah, and the prophet Jeremiah as a leading figure among them, into confrontation with the Jehoiachin exiles, confrontations that possibly continued between Jeremiah's tradents in Judah and tradents in Babylon, be they descendants of the Jehoiachin exiles or of other subsequent deportations. While it is reasonable to assume that the words of the prophet are compiled and edited in both Judah and Babylon, the final compilation of the book is carried out in Babylon (or by Babylonian repatriates back in Yehud) and is probably completed by the end of the sixth century.[98] During the process, the authors among the exiles edited the words of this Judahite prophet and added to them their own, taking the liberty to express perspectives that are in diametric opposition to those of the prophet and his immediate followers in

97. Rom-Shiloni, "Prophecy for 'Everlasting Covenant.'"

98. See pp. 115–17, below. For the suggestion that the *golah*-edition of Jeremiah is Deuteronomistic in nature and evolved later on in the course of the Persian period, see Pohlmann, *Studien zum Jeremiabuches*, 183–97; and Schmid, *Buchgestalten des Jeremiahbuches*, 201–327. Note also the suggestion by Stipp that separate processes of Deuteronomistic redactions are carried out in centers, in Judah and in Babylon, within a relatively early time frame; see his "Das judäische und das babylonische Jeremiabuch." Hoffman (*The Good Figs*, 103–220) argues for Deuteronomistic elaborations and redaction activity in Babylon (the city) already within the prophet's activity (116–20).

Judah.[99] Thus the book of Jeremiah is an invaluable source for studying the religious worlds of thought in both Judah and Babylon during the sixth century, most notably its first half.

While many scholars of Jeremiah tend to favor redaction criticism, and thus to focus on diachronic dimensions in the evolution of the book, I suggest that—and hope that the following discussion demonstrates—unless there are good reasons to categorize a passage as either exilic in origin or as a product of the Persian period (fifth or even fourth century), it should be considered part of a relatively synchronic deliberation among the book's speaking personae, reflecting literary developments that primarily occur still within the sixth century.[100]

In this conception of the growth of the book, I thus join a growing number of scholars who, contrary to prevailing tendencies to date the final edition of the book to the late Persian period, argue that the book of Jeremiah is compiled and edited—and thus gains its final shape—by the early Persian period, still within the sixth century.[101] Among the scholars who argue for the earlier framework is Ernst Nicholson, who contends that not only do the prose sermons reveal literary and theological connections to Deuteronomy, but they are also fully embedded in ideological

---

99. In "Prophecy for 'Everlasting Covenant,'" I suggest that the book of Jeremiah contains additions and editorial work by others in addition to Deuteronomistic authors/compilers/editors. Such non-DtrJ literary activity may be suggested by Jer 34:4–5. I address this complex material in my *Exclusive Inclusivity*, 198–252.

100. This methodological point of departure goes hand in hand with Hoffman's approach to the question of authenticity; see "Isn't the Bride Too Beautiful?," 114–15; and this caution in his commentary: "One should not demand a positive definite proof that this or that verse is Jeremian, because this is impossible. A verse is referred to Jeremiah simply because of its presence in the book, unless its language, its content, or the historical background which it reflects suggests otherwise" (*Jeremiah 1–25*, 65; my translation). Even given this recognition, Hoffman nevertheless categorizes most of the prose passages in Jeremiah as DtrJ. Yet, methodologically, this approach stands in diametric opposition to that of Kratz, *Prophets of Israel*, 1–10.

101. Compare Mowinckel (*Zur Komposition des Buches Jeremia*, 55–57), who assumes that the literary evolution of the book continues until its final redaction in the end of the fifth century. In his schema, sources A and B are compiled between 580 and 480 in Egypt, whereas the Deuteronomistic C prose sermons are added in Babylon or in Yehud around 400. Duhm (*Jeremia*, xx) argues that it is impossible to determine the book's date of completion; thus one should reluctantly accept the most recent possible date, which he takes as ca. 200 BCE (in keeping with the evidence of Ben Sira's prologue). This line of argument is more or less maintained by current scholars.

issues that are central to the life of the Babylonian exiles; this causes him to date the DtrJ editorial level between 561 and 520.[102] Alexander Rofé argues that an old book of Jeremiah, which includes both prophecies and stories about the prophet, is available before the DtrJ revision and that the literary process of compilation and revision is completed by the end of the sixth century or the early fifth century.[103] Christopher Seitz even suggests the first half of the sixth century as the time of compilation, carried out simultaneously in both Judah and Babylon. Based on parallels with Ezekiel and 2 Kings, Seitz considers the DtrJ editors to have come from among the Jehoiachin exiles.[104] Mark Leuchter considers Jer 1–25 to be contextualized well in a roughly single historical context, whereas Jer 26–45 appears to be appendices and additions by character; these chapters are authored and compiled in Babylon around 570.[105] Jack Lundbom describes the creation of two versions of the "book of books," as he terms the compiled manuscript of Jeremiah—one in Egypt (a composition by Baruch of Jer 1–51, which equals the Septuagint sequence and underlying text version) and one in Babylon (a composition of Jer 1–51 by Seraiah, which is similar to the Masoretic Text). Both versions, according to Lundbom, are compiled during the early exilic period, thus roughly parallel to the Deuteronomistic compilation of Kings. Hence, the historical appendix of Jer 52 is indeed the last text to be added to the compiled book, by the mid-sixth century.[106]

These observations do not in any way reduce the plausibility of a notion of the gradual literary growth of the prophetic collection. I prefer to extend William McKane's model of a "rolling corpus" to describe a process of gradual yet constant transformation of the earliest prophetic proclamations by multiple hands, not restricted to a single DtrJ reviser (contra Rofé) or to a large-scale systematic DtrJ editorial reworking (contra Thiel).[107] I find persuasive Yair Hoffman's idea of a gradual and unsystematic growth of

---

102. Nicholson, *Preaching to the Exiles*, 117.

103. Rofé, "Studies on the Composition."

104. Seitz, *Theology in Conflict*, 222–35, 293–96.

105. Leuchter, *Polemics of Exile*, 1–24; and *Josiah's Reform and Jeremiah's Scroll.*

106. Lundbom, *Jeremiah 1–20*, 92–102, esp. 100–101. For a linguistic study of Jeremiah that further supports a sixth-century context, see Hornkohl, *Ancient Hebrew Periodization.*

107. The concept of a "rolling corpus" is coined by McKane (*Jeremiah 1–25*, l–lxxxiii) to explain the textual distinctions between the Masoretic Text and Septuagint versions of the book; he recognizes the value of this model for explaining the literary growth of the prophetic materials themselves (li–liii).

the book, mainly at the hands of Deuteronomistic authors/editors; yet in distinction from Hoffman, I broaden the model still further. I would not exclude the prophet himself or his contemporaries from involvement in the shaping and reshaping of the prophet's words.[108] Furthermore, with Seitz, I consider compilers and tradents in both Judah and Babylon to be involved in the creation of the book; and I add to this mix authors from non-Yahwist groups that seem close to the Babylonian exilic ideologies of Ezekiel (and later of Second Isaiah).[109] This more complex picture of the literary and theological growth of the book of Jeremiah accounts for the polyphonic nature of its prophetic proclamations, which adds to the lack of consistency even within the pronouncements argued to be those of the prophet himself.[110]

Both literary analytical approaches—synchronic and diachronic—provide the tools and the framework(s) for revealing the diverse theological conceptions contained in this prophetic book. The same two approaches may fruitfully be brought to the study of the book of Ezekiel.[111]

3.4.4.2. The Book of Ezekiel

This prophetic book collects the prophecies of Ezekiel son of Buzi, a member of a Jerusalemite priestly family (perhaps of Zadokite lineage) who is deported from Jerusalem with the Jehoiachin exile (597) and starts his prophetic activity five years after his arrival in Babylon in 592 (Ezek 1:2);

---

108. Hoffman, *Jeremiah 1–25*, 80–81; and note his remarks there on the linguistic formations in Jeremiah, which show late characteristics, such as Aramaisms (10:11), in only a few places. This is further analyzed in Hornkohl's *Ancient Hebrew Periodization* (esp. 370–74), who places Jeremiah (in both the Masoretic Text and the shorter Septuagint *Vorlage*) within transitional Biblical Hebrew of the sixth century. Compare to Hoffman's last book (*The Good Figs*, 202–20) where he narrows down the DtrJ work and dates its early activity to the immediate years after their arrival in Babylon (the city). I do not find this suggestion plausible or necessary.

109. Seitz, *Theology in Conflict*, 222–35, 282–96; and see Rom-Shiloni, "Prophecy for 'Everlasting Covenant.'" Compare Sharp (*Prophecy and Ideology*, 159–60), who discusses the pseudepigraphical inclusion of materials in the prophet's name by his tradents. She outlines a complicated process of literary evolution for the book, but finds it hard to identify the voice of the prophet behind or in addition to the different contradictory perspectives.

110. Biddle, *Polyphony and Symphony*, 1–14, 115–28.

111. See Joyce, "Synchronic and Diachronic Perspectives."

his last dated prophecy comes from 570 (29:17).[112] Just as with Jeremiah, we can also view Ezekiel in the synchronic and diachronic spheres.

a.   The prophet in dialogue with his contemporaries

The book of Ezekiel distinguishes clearly between two audiences: the prophet's addressees in the prophetic proclamations and the targets of the prophet's words of judgment. The first group of addressees are the prophet's "brothers" in Babylon (11:14), the immediate and explicit audience of the Jehoiachin exiles. The prophecies addressed to this community of exiles both pronounce the doom of Jerusalem (e.g., 33:23–29) and offer to the exiles the possibility of restoration (11:16–20; also 36:16–32). In contradistinction, the primary target of Ezekiel's judgment prophecies is Jerusalem, the city and its present inhabitants, who are doomed to total annihilation (as seen throughout Ezek 1–24, especially Ezek 4–5 and 33:23–29).[113] In contrast to Jeremiah's situation, Ezekiel is actually sought out by the elders of Israel and Judah among the exiles (8:1; 14:1; 20:1), as well as the exilic community in general, among whom the prophet is praised for his rhetorical skills (33:30–33). The prophet identifies with his fellow exiles in his ideological-theological outlook. Ezekiel establishes theological-ideological distinctions between the two Judean communities, those who remain in the land and those exiled to Babylon in 597. The latter group, comprised of some of the most prestigious Jerusalemite families, are seen in Ezekiel's prophecies as the true continuation of Judean existence as the people of God (e.g., 11:16–21; 20:32–38; 36:6–15).[114]

Within this synchronic sphere, the lack of any direct or explicit connections between Ezekiel and Jeremiah is a point of interest to scholars. This silence obscures a theological and ideological disagreement between these two prophets, active during relatively the same time period. Since each represents the community he lived among, one in exile and one in Jerusalem, they hold two diametrically opposed positions on the meaning of the exile and on group-identity issues.[115] In many other theological respects, the two prophets appear to be in closer agreement, which testifies

112. For the prophet's time and place of activity, see Joyce, *Ezekiel*, 3–6.

113. The prophecies of consolation themselves are almost all addressed to the exiles; the only exception within this group of prophecies is 16:59–64, which I therefore take to be a non-Ezekielian addition to this chapter.

114. Rom-Shiloni, *Exclusive Inclusivity*, 139–97, esp. 139–44.

115. Rom-Shiloni, "Ezekiel and Jeremiah."

to the shared heritage that they are reshaping in such different social and cultural circumstances.

b.   The prophet and his followers

It is widely assumed that, like other prophetic collections, the book of Ezekiel collates proclamations of diverse prophetic origins. Yet, as Paul Joyce points out, the book of Ezekiel is also considered more unified and integral, in terms of its prophetic authorship, than other prophetic books, certainly by comparison with the book of Jeremiah.[116] Nevertheless, scholarship on Ezekiel has long debated the extent of the prophet's involvement in recording his own words and the proportion of non-Ezekielian materials in the book.

The studies of Walther Zimmerli and Moshe Greenberg still illustrate the two opposite approaches to deciphering the process of the book's literary evolution. Zimmerli argues that the prophet does make his own contributions to the writing and editing of his prophecies, but that the book goes through diverse hands, over a long process of evolution;[117] whereas Greenberg holds that the broad unity of thought in the book, illustrated through its special literary style, leaves the impression of a single author active over a relatively short span of time and probably within the lifetime of the prophet.[118] Rainer Albertz argues for a broad involvement of Ezekiel's followers in compiling and editing the book, within the first two generations after the prophet's lifetime; thus, the collection as a whole reflects a relatively contemporary view of the destruction and the early exilic period.[119]

The evidence of Ezekiel's own involvement in recording his prophecies is but minimal (24:2; 37:15; 43:11). The prophet gains his authority as spokesperson for God through the symbolic act of swallowing an already written scroll (written on both sides) to illustrate that the words of God captured the prophet's interiority (3:2). Although the prophet goes through a period when silence is imposed upon him (3:26; 33:22), many prophecies stem from that same period.[120] This indication that some of

---

116. Joyce, *Ezekiel*, 7.

117. Zimmerli, *Ezekiel*, 1.68–74, esp. 68 (on the prophet's contribution to this process). For criteria to distinguish layers in the book, see Block, *Ezekiel 1–24*, 17–23; and Joyce, *Ezekiel*, 7–16.

118. Greenberg, *Ezekiel 1–20*, 3–27; and see Kasher, *Ezekiel 1–24*, 20–28.

119. Albertz, *Israel in Exile*, 360–69.

120. A lot has been written on Ezekiel's dumbness (consult commentaries); suffice it to cite one important contribution by Kasher, "Dumbness in the Book of Ezekiel."

the prophet's activity is restricted to a private sphere, together with the unified literary-rhetorical structure of the prophecies, contributes to the assumption that the prophet is himself involved in composing (and thus writing) his own prophecies before they are proclaimed in public.[121] On the other hand, as is widely recognized, there is no way to deny the involvement of later followers, tradents, authors, and editors in the book, during and probably after the prophet's lifetime.[122] Yet, in contrast to the book of Jeremiah, Ezekiel shows little evidence of grave ideological and theological contradictions between the prophet and his followers, with no indication of sociological or geographical change and with no evidence of a long process of literary evolution. The book of Ezekiel thus illustrates a quite homogeneous prophetic thought-world, well-contextualized in Babylon of the sixth century, primarily in its first half and certainly prior to 538.[123]

The books of Ezekiel and Jeremiah, along with the laments of Psalms and Lamentations, and the historiography of 2 Kings, present a complicated tapestry of sources within which we may trace the threads of the theological conceptions formed in the wake of the destruction and in the face of the realities of exile. The great challenge is both to separate the strands and to interpret the picture as a whole.

121. This is recognized by Ewald, *Prophets of the Old Testament*, 4.7–17 at 9; and thoroughly investigated by Davis, *Swallowing the Scroll*, 29–46, 47–71. Block (*Ezekiel 1–24*, 20–23) emphasizes the role of Ezekiel in writing his own prophecies and possibly in collating and arranging them within the book.

122. Even Greenberg (*Ezekiel 1–20*, 488) recognizes this in relation to 3:16b–21; and he characterizes 12:13–14 as a later revision of 17:20–21; he is followed in this by Kasher, *Ezekiel 1–24*, 27. See also Block, *Ezekiel 1–24*, 223; and Joyce, *Ezekiel*, 15–16.

123. Joyce (*Ezekiel*, 7–16) reaches this same conclusion through his discussion of seven criteria developed to distinguish layers of authorship in the book. On the Babylonian context of Ezekiel, see the collection edited by Rom-Shiloni and Carvalho, "Ezekiel in Its Babylonian Context," with contributions by Shawn Aster, Daniel Bodi, Dale Launderville, Jonathan Stökl, and Christoph Uehlinger and responses by Martti Nissinen and Madhavi Nevader. See further, Vanderhooft, "Ezekiel in and on Babylon"; Winitzer, "Assyriology and Jewish Studies"; Darshan, "Meaning of ברא"; and Rom-Shiloni, "Ezekiel among the Exiles."

SUMMARY AND A PROPOSAL

The first part of this book sets out three major issues of method. Chapter 1 lays the foundation for the overarching framework of theological deliberations in my targeted sources, which is formed around the issue of theodicy. But theodicy—the desire to justify God in the midst of catastrophe—in the sixth-century sources inspired a complex discourse that included not only justification, but also doubt in and protest against God. I designate this interplay of theological reactions as theodical discourse; the goal is to map this discourse and thereby gain a clearer picture of the thought-world of the sixth-century Judean communities coping with destruction and exile.

Chapter 2 discusses the methodology of biblical theology, or rather Tanakh/Hebrew Bible theology, showing the many differences between Christian and Jewish approaches in the field. The lack of scholarly consensus (in general, and among Jewish biblical scholars in particular) on the issue of "how to do it" requires me to explain my own choices and to formulate my theological discussion as descriptive (non-Christian and non-Jewish) in its critical orientation.

Chapter 3 focuses on several scholarly approaches to biblical texts that serve the goals of this study more adequately than traditional literary-historical criticism. Borrowing observations from poetics (to distinguish literary personae and scenarios from historical authors and settings) and trauma studies (to recognize and contextualize immediate theological reactions as well as later reflections), I emphasize the importance of invoking both synchronic and diachronic analytical perspectives. I invoke these two methodological perspectives throughout this monograph, as I analyze the book of Kings, Jeremiah, Ezekiel, Lamentations, and seventeen selected psalms.

The major goal of the second part of this study is to uncover the theological conceptions embedded within diverse literary Hebrew Bible compositions that reflect directly on the destruction and the exiles. These are seen here as the catalytic agents that shaped the Hebrew Bible literary records of the Judean religious thought-world of the (early) sixth century and on. Coping with the Babylonian victory and the concomitant destruction of Jerusalem and Judah causes the Judahites to draw on their rich storehouse of traditional understandings of God's actions and their relationship with him. But these understandings prove inadequate in the face of the continuing sequence of disastrous events—the dislocation and exiles—which raises questions of doubt and despair concerning any future reestablishment of the relationship with God.

As a descriptive Hebrew Bible theology, this book comprises a phenomenological analysis, based on a quantitative survey of the elements that make up theodicy as the broad theological issue under deliberation in the relevant sources. The following discussion maps the three theological approaches of this theological discourse—justification, doubt, and protest—aiming for a faithful reconstruction of the tapestry of religious world views in this crucial and dramatic period.

The theodical discourse uncovered in this study is best seen as a discussion among equals. My original point of departure was the basic question: "What did they say about God?" In recognition of the multiplicity of voices participating in this theological discourse, the question itself expanded to: "How does one statement about God differ from another?" Thus, the study is attentive to theological pluralism, and therefore it looks at the multiplicity of voices in the biblical sources addressed.

The sources selected for this research reflect a limited, relatively synchronic crosscut within biblical literature. This cut is demarcated by factors of time and place; I focus on biblical sources that directly address the political crises of the Neo-Babylonian period within the sixth century, composed in Judah and in Babylon. In order to describe the theological perspectives represented in this corpus, the labels "preexilic" and "postexilic" seem both arbitrary and inadequate to the complexity of the task.[1] Instead, my point of departure is the recognition that the theological transformations reflected in these works evolve in the first place through interactions between authors and schools contemporary with the cata-

---

1. For the limitations on the usefulness of the divisions "preexilic" and "postexilic," see Middlemas, *Templeless Age*, 1–9.

strophic events, and in the second place as these works and the ideas in them are constructed and reconstructed over time by later writers from among the traumatized Judean communities, even down to the second and third generations. For theological study, all these literary participants are relevant and authentic.

Part II of this book illustrates a process of continuing expansions in Israelite/Judaic religious thought, wherein older, cherished conceptions and traditions are nuanced and reshaped in the face of the current crises. This recognition requires me to first articulate the conventional beliefs about God and the God-people relationship that served the people of Judah prior to these crises, in order to then describe how these conventions are reexamined, or simply challenged, as events deteriorate over time.

The theological investigation is founded on a careful linguistic and philological analysis. I began by assembling a large database comprised of all the divine names and epithets occurring in the target corpora; I then checked the semantic fields for all the terms used to describe God's deeds and actions in the selected sources.[2] Gathering the verbal forms with God as agent, I divided them thematically according to the various divine roles they designate, and I distinguished them according to three generic contexts: prophecy, quotation, and poetry. Then I analyzed the different terms according to the various speakers (prophets and historiographers, poets, and laypeople) and according to their grammatical forms (first-, second-, or third-person).[3] The terms used to describe God were also considered in relation to their use in the human sphere, in order to illuminate the appropriation of anthropomorphic language to the realm of the talk to and about God. This foundational methodology enabled an inclusive portrayal of the multiple theological issues and diverse stances expressed in the selected corpora, and it further facilitated in the present study the exploration of the relationships among them.

My point of departure is phenomenological in that it does not focus on a certain literary composition,[4] nor on the historical period per se,[5] but rather on conceptions of God embedded in the target texts. In this respect,

---

2. Westermann proposes that descriptions of God's actions, expressed by verb structures, are the primary way to learn about biblical conceptions of God; see *What Does the Old Testament Say?*, 11–14, esp. 13; and also Mettinger, *In Search of God*, 1–2, 202.

3. This database is reproduced in my *God in Times of Destruction*, 426–502.

4. In contrast to the approach taken by Raitt, *Theology of Exile*; and Seitz, *Theology in Conflict*; as also Fischer, *Theologien des Alten Testaments*.

5. Compare, Ackroyd, *Exile and Restoration*; and Klein, *Israel in Exile*.

the methodology of the present study differs from previous scholarship on the sixth century. There is no attempt to set the theology of the book of Kings, or the book of Jeremiah as a whole, against that of Ezekiel, nor to set these together against the theology of Lamentations and Psalms, for example. Rather, the theology of each individual historiographic observation, prophetic proclamation, poetic expression, or quotation of other voices is examined phenomenologically; all expressions are considered equal witnesses to the theological deliberations.[6] At times, ideological resemblances may be discerned between the different sources; in other instances, antagonisms may be discovered between historiographers, between prophets, between each prophet and their respective audiences (including prophets and their followers/tradents), and between prophets and poets. Close examination reveals a variety of voices within a single literary composition and opens the stage to possibilities of polydoxy expressed by diverse voices within each of those prophetic, historiographic, or psalmodic compositions, as well as in successive literary stages in the evolution of this Hebrew Bible literature.

The organizing themes of my study are twofold. The major theological framework is introduced here as theodical discourse. The other broad organizing theme is the conception of God as king, which is shared by all sources and voices delineated in my study. These pervasive conceptual elements function together in the target sources. Chapters 5–13 are devoted to describing the ways in which these two conceptions intersect. The three modes of theodical discourse (justification, doubt, and protest) serve as wide enough categories, in both form and theme, to encompass the entire theological portrayal of God as king in his major roles.

Rolf Knierim notes that the dominant aspect in each statement about God in the Hebrew Bible is the relationship between God and reality and between reality and God. This dominant aspect, according to Knierim, occurs in relation to three arenas: the cosmos and nature; the situation of humanity in general, including Israel; and the personal human condition.[7] Sources from the period discussed in this study show concern with the second of these arenas, that is, the relationships between God and the national historical situation of Judah and its people, and the relationship

6. Caution is necessary in evaluating the quantitative evidence, since the stances of the prophets in the books bearing their names will naturally receive greater representation. For this reason, I refrain from guessing whether this or that conception gained prevalence within the Judean world of thought.

7. Knierim, *Task of Old Testament Theology*, 10–12.

between the people in these historical and social circumstances and God. Universal and personal perspectives are less represented, or rather belong to the fairly large group of indirect reflections on this era (see introduction). In the national and social contexts of the early sixth century and on, God is portrayed as king—acting as warrior, as judge, and as sovereign. This portrayal is the focus of the second part of my investigation.

PART 2

*Theodicy as Discourse in the
Face of Destruction*

5

GOD AS KING

Since there was only One God now, He necessarily had to take over all—and I emphasize the word *all*—of the powers, functions, and obligations of the old multideitied pantheon. . . .

He was a whole pantheon in Himself. He was not only God the father, God the husband, the king and ultimate master but also God the spice maker, architect, interior decorator of the *mishkan* (Tabernacle), artist. God the teacher, God the scribe; God the gynecologist, God the midwife, God the veterinarian. God the creditor, God the debtor, God the playwright, God the sublime chess player who delights in playing moral games with His son, man, created in His image. God occasionally laughed and more often cried; He was consoled by prophets, and His anger was cooled by prophets and zealots. He walked, rested, and slept, but He was always awake.

—Yochanan Muffs, *The Personhood of God*

The talk to and about God in the Hebrew Bible in general, and in sixth-century sources in particular, is thoroughly anthropomorphic. The foundational conception of God as king may be seen in its metaphorical anthropomorphic portrayals. The wide range of functions of this anthropomorphic metaphor in sixth-century sources suggests that the metaphor of God as king serves as the preeminent conception of God in these texts, shared by all speakers, whether poets or prophets, historiographers or laypeople. God's several perceived roles as king, warrior, judge—thus sovereign over his people—are likewise challenged by all biblical speakers in face of the events of the early sixth century (see chaps. 6–12).

5.1. The Conception of God and Anthropomorphism as Metaphor

Comparative religious studies draw a distinction between "the conception of god" (*Gottesvorstellung*) and "the image of god" (*Gottesbild*).[1] *Gottesvorstellung* refers to the thought of a person or a nation about its god, whereas *Gottesbild* comprises the system of symbols employed to represent the deity in terms that are familiar to human beings from their world.[2] The image of a god is constructed in two ways: by direct descriptions of the deity, either verbal or pictorial, or by implicit descriptions that may be deduced from the cult[3] or from the temple architecture.[4] These direct and indirect descriptions together comprise the image of a god, from which it is possible to gain a sense of how people conceived their deity, his (her) appearance and actions.[5]

---

1. See Mettinger's "Study of the *Gottesbild*" and references there; *In Search of God*, 201–7; and "Gudsbildens gestaltning" (following Olsson's "Gudsbild"). Note some challenges raised by Loeland, *Silent or Salient Gender?*, 27–29. The *Gottesbild* and its implications for the *Gottesvorstellung* in Mesopotamia, Ugarit, and Israel are discussed by Dietrich and Loretz, *Jahwe und seine Aschera*, 1–6, 183–88.

2. Mettinger ("Study of the *Gottesbild*," 135–36) defines the *Gottesbild* as "the expressed form in which the concept is communicated in texts (language), rites (gesture and body language), and iconography (art)." The distinction between the image and the concept of god is borrowed from the field of semiotics, which deals with "symbol" and "object" and their relationships to the conception behind them. See Langer, *Philosophy in a New Key*, 53–78, who writes: "Symbols are not proxy for their objects, but are *vehicles for the conception of objects*. . . . In talking *about* things we have conceptions of them, not the things themselves; and *it is the conceptions, not the things, that symbols directly 'mean'*" (60–61; emphasis original); and note her observations on the relationship between concept and symbol: "A concept is all that a symbol really conveys. But just as quickly as the concept is symbolized to us, our own imagination dresses it up in a private, personal *conception*, which we can distinguish from the communicable public conception by a process of abstraction" (71–72). So also Lyons, *Semantics*, 1.95–119, esp. 95–105, 110.

3. The cult as a key to conceptions of God is emphasized by Haran in "Ark and the *Kerubim*" and "Divine Presence." For Deuteronomic and Priestly conceptions of God, see Weinfeld, *Deuteronomy and the Deuteronomic School*, 191–243; and note Milgrom's criticisms in "Alleged 'Demythologization and Secularization.'"

4. Hurowitz, *I Have Built You*, 328–37.

5. Although decoding the image of a god exposes much of the information scholars may gain, it does not reveal all the aspects within the conception of the god. In Egypt and Mesopotamia, there is a distinction between the deity's idol and his/her nature and character. Frankfort (*Ancient Egyptian Religion*, 12) calls the pictorial expressions of the

In ancient Near Eastern religions, images of gods are formed in four ways. Each of these four could take on a pictorial-tangible shape in art or be expressed in words in literary compositions:

a. Theriomorphism, describing the deity as an animal, is common in Egypt and also found in Mesopotamia.[6]

b. Therianthropism, describing the deity as part animal and part human, is known in Egypt and Mesopotamia: as deities with the body of a man and either the head of an animal or with mixed facial features, comprising characteristics of animals and humans; or the reverse — the Egyptian sphinx had the body of an animal and the head of a man.

c. Anthropomorphism is the most common type of description of the deity in ancient Near Eastern religions, a type of personification in which the god is depicted as human in appearance, character, and function.[7]

d. Aniconic representations of a deity indicate the presence of the god by a symbol or a religious artifact without an image (such as a stele, for example) or conversely emphasize the avoidance of an image,

---

gods "ideograms," whereas Hornung (*Conceptions of God*) argues that "pictures of gods should not be understood as illustrations or descriptions of appearances, but rather as allusions to essential parts of the nature and function of deities" (114; complete discussion on 125–42; and the terminology that designates the deity on 54–56). In addition, Hornung emphasizes (124, 128–35) that, despite the vast iconographic expressions at hand, much is still unknown in terms of the characters and conceptions of the gods. In reference to Mesopotamian religions, Jacobsen develops the understanding of Mesopotamian religion in general as metaphor (*Treasure of Darkness*, 3–21); also "Pictures and Pictorial Language," where Jacobsen points out the relationships between the pictorial images of the gods and the metaphoric imagery that appears in their names and epithets. He concludes that the pictorial language expresses only partially the characters of the gods and their fields of responsibility.

6. See Hornung, *Conceptions of God*, 100–109; and Jacobsen, *Toward the Image of Tamuz*, 16–38, esp. 17. Barr ("Theophany and Anthropomorphism," 31) convincingly argues that there are no theriomorphisms in Hos 5:14; Amos 1:2; or elsewhere in the Hebrew Bible.

7. The term "anthropomorphism" is borrowed from the Greek and has been used in modern scholarship since the eighteenth century, though it earlier functioned as a technical term in Greek philosophy and in early Christian exegesis. See Werblowski, "Anthropomorphism." Jacobsen (*Toward the Image of Tamuz*, 17–19) points out that anthropomorphism captured the major place within the religions of Mesopotamia because of the wish to portray the deity as a ruler and sovereign (see §5.2.3).

leaving a blank space instead of erecting a statue (e.g., the space between or above the cherubim in the Solomon's Temple or above the
calves in Beth-El and Dan).[8]

The general trajectory of development seems to be from zoomorphic
to anthropomorphic imagery, but both types are found alongside one another in Egypt and Mesopotamia and even combine with one another
in the same time period.[9] Moreover, aniconism is not the last type in a
chronological sequence, but one of four synchronic methods in the ancient
Near East of the second and first millennia. As Tryggve Mettinger shows,
aniconism is established in the Bronze Age in the ancient Near East and
specifically in Canaan; thus we may presume that Israel adopted this as a
representational convention upon its encounter with Canaanite societies.[10]

8. Mettinger (*No Graven Image?*, 16–27) distinguishes between two types of aniconism: "material aniconism" and "empty-space aniconism" (23–27).

9. Hornung (*Conceptions of God*, 110–13) presents a sequential development in the
use of hieroglyphic symbols and in Egyptian iconography in general along the following spectrum: fetishistic symbols, zoomorphic images, anthropomorphic images.
Nevertheless, he argues that this is not a chronological development, since there are
synchronic iconographic expressions for these ways of imaging the gods. For instance,
Hathor appears synchronically through four different images: woman, cow, a theri-
anthropomorphic image of a woman's body with a bull's head, and the same image
with the mixed facial features of a woman and a cow. These images occur along other
zoomorphic representations of Hathor as lioness, snake, hippopotamus, or tree. The
diverse images signify distinctions between the image and the concept of the goddess
(see *Conceptions of God*, 33–42, 100–125); and these distinctions are further demonstrated in the terminology used to describe her functions (45–56). Jacobsen (*Toward
the Image of Tamuz*, 17) argues that the symbols that designate natural phenomena
in Mesopotamia continue to serve as their symbols alongside anthropomorphic descriptions; he notes, by way of example, the many depictions of Inanna ("Pictures and
Pictorial Language," 1–8).

10. Mettinger (*No Graven Image?*, 17) argues that "Israelite aniconism seems to
be as old as the Solomonic temple, and may antedate it by centuries" (also 135–40,
191–97). In Egypt aniconism occurs in the imagery pertaining to only two gods, Atun
and Ammon, over a limited period of time and restricted to the theology of El-Amarna
(49–54, 46). In the Mesopotamian context, aniconism appears only sporadically within
a clearly anthropomorphic cultic world, evident in artifacts from Assyria and from the
Cashite dynasty in Babylon. Mettinger raises the possibility that the priests of the god
Ashur argue for aniconic representations of the god as a counterclaim against the anthropomorphic cult of Marduk (55). Ornan ("Idols and Symbols") develops functional
distinctions between the synchronic use of anthropomorphic images and aniconic representations in Neo-Assyrian and Neo-Babylonian art.

In Hebrew Bible compositions, the God of Israel is depicted in but two of the four modes noted here, anthropomorphically and aniconically.[11]

5.2. Anthropomorphism in the Hebrew Bible: The Great Paradox and the Scholarly Challenges

The use of anthropomorphism in Hebrew Bible literature accrues great scholarly interest. The most troublesome issue arises from the conflict between the prohibition against making any pictorial image of God and the widespread and common use of verbal anthropomorphisms throughout the literary compositions.

The prohibition in the second commandment, ‏לא תעשה־לך פסל וכל־‏ ‏תמונה‏ ("you shall not make for yourself a sculptured image, or any likeness," Exod 20:4; Deut 5:8), is given additional emphasis in each of the law collections of the Pentateuch (Exod 20:22–23; 34:17; Lev 19:4; 26:1; Deut 4:1–18; 27:15). It is enacted by the absence of a statue in Solomon's Temple and by the placement of aniconistic symbols of God (the cherubim and calves) and even supported by archeological finds in the temple at Tel Arad.[12] This prohibition, however, seems to counter the abundance of anthropomorphic phraseology in the Hebrew Bible corpus. Thus, the question is: How can one explain the paradox of a marked decline in iconism and image worship and an abundance of casual talk to and about God in anthropomorphic language?

A variety of answers to this paradox, and explanations for the existence of verbal anthropomorphisms in the Hebrew Bible, are suggested, ranging over a broad spectrum. Yehezkel Kaufmann minimizes this contradiction, arguing that popular thought clearly assumes the existence of a divine im-

---

11. According to Mettinger (*Dethronement of Sabaoth*, 25), anthropomorphism and aniconism join together in the descriptions of God as king in Zion.

12. The question of whether pictorial anthropomorphism operated in Israelite religion still occupies scholars, as presented in the collection edited by van der Toorn, *Image and the Book*, published following Mettinger's *No Graven Image?* In this collection, Hendel's article "Aniconism and Anthropomorphism" compares what he considers the unique anthropomorphic conception in Israelite religion with the notion of patron gods in ancient Near Eastern religions (esp. 206–12, 220–23). His observations fit, however, only a limited number of Hebrew Bible sources (i.e., those focusing on the danger of *seeing* God) and do not account for the many anthropomorphisms that are part of the routine language of narrative, prophecy, and poetry.

age (דימוי הדמות);[13] this conception is generally embraced by authors and even by prophets, who unreservedly use "the colors of the popular imagination."[14] Mettinger, on the contrary, highlights the paradox, which becomes the point of departure for his discussion of aniconism within the framework of tangible representation of the image of God.[15]

Gerhard von Rad and subsequently Robert Carroll suggest a sociological distinction in the use of (or the prohibition against) images. They maintain that the prohibition is limited only to the cultic sphere and does not apply to the biblical thought-world, which generally attributes a human image to God. Both scholars assert that the "theology of idols" is eventually superseded by the "theology of the word" (to employ Carroll's terminology).[16] Even if this distinction exists, however, it cannot account for the presence of anthropomorphic language in the poetry of Psalms and Lamentations, which are by their very nature anchored in cult liturgy.

From a historical point of view (both literary and archeological), anthropomorphism is of high interest and importance for understanding the development of ancient Israelite religion and the crystallization of monotheism, as reconstructed from the Hebrew Bible and from extrabiblical evidence.[17] In introducing a broad definition of monotheism as "a belief that there exists one supreme being in the universe, whose will is sovereign over all other be-

13. Kaufmann, *Toldot Ha-'Emunah*, 1.221, 229–31.

14. Eichrodt (*Theology of the Old Testament*, 2.16–23) contrasts naïve, popular (uneducated) thought with "prophetic influence," which gradually modified natural mythology and human representations of God "by more spiritual ways of thinking" (2.20). Eichrodt categorizes different (self-)representations of the transcendent God as devices that enable God to express, or to declare, his presence within the human realm; this technique of representation "serves to uphold the historical realism of the revelation" (2.32–33, over against the more abstract notion of *kabod*). See also 2.35–39 with regard to the language of *panim*; and finally see 2.40–42 on the divine name, which Eichrodt finds to totally exclude the notion of visual appearance, representing the conception of the divine presence as an independent function.

15. Mettinger, *No Graven Image?*, 13–17, esp. 15.

16. See von Rad, *Old Testament Theology*, 1.217–19; Carroll, "Aniconic God."

17. It is beyond my scope to specify the abundance of studies that focus on the significance of this prohibition in the history of Israelite religion. Suffice it to mention only von Rad (*Old Testament Theology*, 1.217–19), who sees the prohibition against idols as the beginning of a transcendental conception of an invisible God. Von Rad considers this a unique Israelite conception, which became fully developed in Second Temple literature. But transcendence is not an Israelite innovation, as von Rad himself argues (1.213–14) and as is shown by Hornung in the case of Egypt and by Jacobsen in that of Mesopotamia (see note 9, above).

ings,"[18] Benjamin Sommer aptly suggests the important distinction between conceptions of God in ancient Israelite religion and the portrait of God in Hebrew Bible literary records, which he terms "biblical religion."[19] For Sommer, the Hebrew Bible itself is clearly monotheistic (rather than monolatric) in outlook, whether this is expressed descriptively or at times prescriptively.[20] Sommer points out two ideals that the Hebrew Bible sets as key pillars of its religion: "the ideal of monolatry" and "the ideal of aniconism." The two are intertwined from the very first revelation in Sinai (Exod 20:3–4).[21]

Sommer rejects the possibility that anthropomorphism is treated metaphorically in the Hebrew Bible. Rather, Sommer writes about an unabashed and corporeal anthropomorphism, and his point of departure is that when the ancients speak about the body of God, they really mean that God had a body, or actually bodies, although Sommer admits that this assumption is an argument from silence.[22] Sommer points out the distinct conceptualizations of gods in the ancient Near East (including Israel) over against the Greek culture with respect to the notions of divine body(ies) and the fluidity implied by its/their ability to appear in several places simultaneously (in Sommer's words: "For ancient Near Eastern religions, gods could have multiple bodies and fluid selves").[23] Nevertheless, Sommer presents what he considers to be a varied attitude toward divine embodiment within diverse biblical sources, such that the Hebrew Bible as a corpus presents both "material" and "nonmaterial" anthropomorphic conceptions of the body of God. Sommer emphasizes that both the Deuteronomic school and the Priestly school rejected earlier (Yahwist and Elohist) conceptions of divine body and fluidity in different ways. The Priestly school and Ezekiel, for instance, perceive the *kabod* as God's actual one body (not susceptible to fragmentation and fluidity).[24] For the

---

18. Sommer, *Bodies of God*, 145–74, esp. 146.

19. Sommer, *Bodies of God*, 148–49, and the entire chapter. I find Sommer's discussion of monotheism and this broader definition of it very important and helpful.

20. Sommer, *Bodies of God*, 172, where he concludes that it is "monotheism and not merely monolatry," although he admits it is an argument from silence.

21. Sommer, *Bodies of God*, 150, esp. 159–74.

22. Sommer (*Bodies of God*, 4–10) criticizes at some length contemporary scholarly approaches to the corporeality of God in the Hebrew Bible; see especially his counter-suggestion on 8–9, where he applies Lorberbaum's questions, addressed to rabbinic literature, to the Hebrew Bible; see Lorberbaum, *Image of God*, 12–26, 101–4, 469–75.

23. Sommer, *Bodies of God*, 12 and the discussion on 12–37.

24. Sommer, *Bodies of God*, 68–78; see also Sommer's discussion of "the fluidity model" on 38–79.

Deuteronomic school, by contrast, anthropomorphic conceptions of God are transformed into the *shem* theology, which serves as "a sign of divine presence, not a manifestation of God Himself."[25] Hence, Hebrew Bible sources treat the issue of anthropomorphism as divine body and self in diverse ways, while still retaining an older "fluidity tradition," which is oftentimes hidden behind this or that veil.[26] Sommer asserts that those who claim that anthropomorphism is (merely) metaphorical or allegorical language themselves bear the burden of proof.[27]

One such proof may be learnt from a comparative perspective. The paradoxical relationship between pictorial and verbal portrayals of the divine in the Hebrew Bible leads both Tallay Ornan and Barbara Porter to discuss anthropomorphism and aniconism in Mesopotamian artistic and literary compositions of the second and first millennia.[28] Interestingly, Ornan argues for a decline in the use of anthropomorphism in pictorial representations of deities, which creates an imbalance between pictorial and verbal-literary anthropomorphisms, which resembles what characterizes the Hebrew Bible literature.[29] Porter accentuates the divergence inherent in Mesopotamian religion concerning deities who may be represented by anthropomorphic and nonanthropomorphic forms at one and the same time, in the same way that material objects (such as musical instruments, buildings, etc.), natural phenomena, and even illnesses are treated as nonanthropomorphic deities, a status conferred by the DINGIR determinative. Through a "transfer of qualities from owner to object," these items gain the status of deities (even their "supernatural 'chargedness'"), although they do not hold "the full range of divine powers and responsibilities of that owner god."[30] This diversity of representations establishes the

25. Sommer, *Bodies of God*, 62 and see 62–78 (on the presumed dichotomy between these two schools).

26. Sommer, *Bodies of God*, 124–26.

27. Sommer, *Bodies of God*, 9.

28. Ornan, *Triumph of the Symbol*, 168–82; Ornan, "In the Likeness of Man"; Porter's introduction to *What Is a God?* (1–13) and "Blessings from a Crown."

29. Ornan, *Triumph of the Symbol*, 171–73. See also Keel and Uehlinger, *Gods, Goddesses*, 135–40, 173–75; Machinist, "Anthropomorphism in Mesopotamian Religion"; and Smith, "Ugaritic Anthropomorphism."

30. Porter, "Blessings from a Crown," 191, and also her introduction to *What Is a God?* Sommer (*Bodies of God*, 10) refers to and quotes Smith (*Origins of Biblical Monotheism*, 87–88); it is important to note, however, that Smith gives a long list of anthropomorphisms as *images* of diverse gods in Ugarit, Mesopotamia, and subsequently Israel. These anthropomorphisms express superhuman strength and size; the deities are portrayed as

understanding of anthropomorphism as one type of metaphoric portrayal of the gods in both the ancient Near East and the Hebrew Bible.

The current study focuses on the Hebrew Bible literary evidence, understanding anthropomorphism as a theological-phenomenological element in verbal representations of God.[31] In an even more specific way, I am interested in defining the place and the role of anthropomorphism in shaping conceptions of God. Thus, in answer to this paradox, Israelite/Hebrew Bible religion seems to distinguish between these two broad types of anthropomorphic descriptions of God. It prohibits pictorial iconography in sculpture and drawing, but at the same time, it permits literary verbal descriptions of God using human imagery.[32] As noted by Ornan and Porter in relation to ancient Near Eastern religions more generally, such gaps between pictorial and verbal representations of the gods are well attested over the first millennium BCE. Hence, the question is addressed to the literary compositions, where the verbal description of God in human terms is the very language of the talk about God.

Even within verbal descriptions there are diverse conventions for describing God anthropomorphically, and the apprehension of approaching too close to a pictorial iconography causes individual authors to set specific idiosyncratic limits for their verbal portrayals. Phenomenologically, there is a constant negotiation in Hebrew Bible materials between anthropomorphism and aniconism (or even anti-iconism). Accordingly, anthropomorphism is set alongside other representations of God, such as *kebod yhwh*, the pillar of cloud and of fire, and so on.[33] While anthropomorphism pictures a concrete physical image of God, the other representations try to

---

engaged in human activities and as assuming human forms (*Origins of Biblical Monotheism*, 84–88). Indeed, Smith says that the Mesopotamian descriptions "heighten the anthropomorphism to make the deity transcend the basic analogy between humans and deities. . . . In this way anthropomorphism is both affirmed and relativized" (88). Smith uses the explicit phrase "anthropomorphic imagery" (89; see 91). I argue (and, I believe, Smith does as well) that in both the ancient Near East and Israel these images are but symbols.

31. In this respect, I follow scholars who address anthropomorphism on the basis of its theological-phenomenological characteristics, in particular Barr, "Theophany and Anthropomorphism"; Mettinger, *In Search of God*, 201–7; Hendel, "Aniconism and Anthropomorphism in Ancient Israel"; Kasher, "Anthropomorphism, Holiness, and Cult"; and Hamori, *When Gods Were Men*, 26–64, 150–56.

32. From the perspective of the history of religions, Werblowski ("Anthropomorphism," 317) points out the discordance between verbal anthropomorphism and iconography in Buddhism and in the Shintu.

33. See Weinfeld, "כָּבוֹד *kāḇôḏ*"; Aster, *Unbeatable Light*, 258–315; and Sommer,

cover up such physical and mental characteristics, to designate presence but blur its human contours, as if God were "behind curtains," hiding any of the deity's detailed descriptions. But does this mean that these authors do not use anthropomorphic language (or imagery) behind that curtain?[34]

Three primary, and very different, scholarly approaches explain the use of personifying language in the Hebrew Bible.

5.2.1. Anthropomorphism as a Stage of Historical Development in Religious Thought

The paradigm of development from the concrete to the abstract was introduced in nineteenth- and twentieth-century scholarship. The model proposes a linear development from a popular mindset that imagines the deity in concrete terms to a more abstract conception that refrains from ascribing a physical human image and prefers to refer mental states and emotions to God, to assertions of God's presence in which anthropomorphic terms are completely absent.[35] This line of development is based on the evidence found within the Hebrew Bible itself: the prohibition against making idols reflects the superiority of Israelite belief over against the nations' worship of wood and stone (e.g., Deut 4:12–20; Isa 44:9–20).[36] The literary evidence of the Hebrew Bible is aligned with a presumed development of abstraction in the biblical conception of God, along with the innovativeness of the monotheistic outlook. Scholars of religion point out that many other "primitive" religions undergo this same course of refinement, moving from the concrete to the abstract. Scholars argue that this refinement occurs by way of a natural tendency to limit the use of physical anthropomorphism; on this trajectory, language that personifies emotions

---

Bodies of God, 1–11, 38–57, 58–79. While Sommer focuses on the pentateuchal literature, the present study engages other corpora, mainly prophecy and poetry.

34. See Mettinger, "Veto on Images."

35. See Jevons, "Anthropomorphism"; and Werblowski, "Anthropomorphism."

36. Hurowitz ("Make Yourself an Idol") explains the polemic articulated between Israel and the nations in Jer 10, Second Isaiah, and Deut 4 as the joining of Hebrew Bible authors into an internal debate within Assyrian religion over the essence of idols, since an ambivalent attitude to statues of gods characterizes Mesopotamian religions (see Jacobsen, "Graven Image"). Mettinger (*No Graven Image?*, 21–23) conducts a comparative examination of aniconic trends among iconic cults across the ancient Near East, including Egypt and Mesopotamia, and mostly connected to the West Semitic aniconism, taking the anti-iconic (iconoclasm) attitude as a genuine Israelite development, "Israel's *differentia specifica*" (196, 14, 135–40, 191–97).

and other mental processes (anthropopathism) signifies a distinct and more advanced stage in the linear development toward abstraction.[37]

Scholars argue that this progression appears in different layers within the Hebrew Bible corpus; it is seen as an indicator of diachronic development and as a marker of synchronic hierarchical difference between authors who are supposed to represent defined social circles. To put it into more concrete terms with regard to our sources, the relatively abstract conception of God is attributed to prophets, historiographers, and authors of later biblical writings, over against presumably earlier and more popular personifying conceptions, which are said to be preserved primarily in poetry; this presumption, however, fails to account for the abundance of anthropomorphisms found in the prophetic books themselves. This abundance is customarily explained as an intentional adaptation by which the prophets shape their words or their rhetoric style, in order to reach out to various circles holding to more traditional conceptions.[38]

Likewise, anthropomorphism is used to distinguish different literary schools. Weinfeld finds that the anthropomorphic view of God characterizes Priestly sources, but that a more abstract conception of God operates in Deuteronomic/Deuteronomistic sources.[39] Compare his position to that of von Rad, whom Weinfeld relies upon and who argues that Priestly traditions, like Deuteronomistic ones, reflect a long literary process and thus attest to a spectrum of conceptions. Thus, the Priestly "*kabod-moed* conception/theology" is more elaborated and abstract than earlier, anthropomorphic layers of Priestly traditions and serves as a corrective to those earlier conceptions.[40] Or compare Eichrodt, who as part of the German school, holds that the Priestly layer in the Pentateuch, along with the au-

---

37. Along this developmental trajectory, Jevons ("Anthropomorphism," 573–74) discerns five stages of religious thinking, from the personifying description to the rejection of such descriptions as improbable and unfit for the description of the deity.

38. See Eichrodt, *Theology of the Old Testament*, 1.216–17; Kaufmann, *Toldot Ha-'Emunah*, 1.221.

39. Weinfeld, *Deuteronomy and the Deuteronomic School*, 191–209; with Milgrom's criticism in "Alleged 'Demythologization and Secularization.'" I add two examples that clearly stand against Weinfeld's argument of abstraction in Deuteronomy: the conception of God as "a jealous God" (אל קנא), which elaborates on the second commandment (5:9; also 4:24; 6:15; 29:19; 32:16, 21); and the conception of war, with God walking in front of the human troops (20:4).

40. Von Rad, *Studies in Deuteronomy*, 39–41, esp. 40–41. Von Rad defines the Priestly conception of the tabernacle as "neither the dwelling place of Jahweh himself nor of his name, but the place on earth where, for the time being, the appearance

thors of Chronicles, Ezra-Nehemiah, and the cultic liturgy, all put forth an abstract portrait of God, with a tendency to silence naïve anthropomorphic conceptions.[41] Israel Knohl complicates this picture; he examines the use of personifying language in the redactional layers of Priestly writings and observes that, while the Priestly source attempts to minimize such language, the Holiness school, which he dates as relatively later, uses personification abundantly.[42]

If such is the case, then these alleged differences in the use of anthropomorphism cannot represent the consequences either of diachronic development or of hierarchical distinctions in religious thinking. The prophetic literature—including both poetry and prose prophecies and also including prophetic quotations of other voices—uses physical and mental anthropomorphisms to describe God, with no traces of refinement for what at times may be considered "enlightened circles."[43]

Furthermore, these distinctions between literary schools leave their marks in different attitudes toward the personification of God in the books of Jeremiah and Ezekiel, in light of the connection of the former to the Deuteronomistic school and of the latter to Priestly circles.[44] I have no intention of blurring substantial differences between the prophetic books of Jeremiah and Ezekiel, particularly not in their distinct conceptions of God, their different presentations of theophany, and so on. But both prophets use anthropomorphic language, physical and mental, as their basic rhetorical mode for describing God and his actions (with certain distinctions); and yet, there is no evidence for a substantial difference between them, in terms of a transition from physical to mental personification.[45]

---

of Jahweh's glory meets with his people" (39); he delineates the diversity within the Priestly sources (40).

41. Eichrodt, *Theology of the Old Testament*, 1.217–18; see also 2.33–35. Eichrodt (1.218–19) sees this tendency in the early versions, particularly the Aramaic Targumim, in the form of "corrections" that tone down the language of divine personification.

42. See Knohl, *Sanctuary of Silence*, 121–31, 160–63. Sommer (*Bodies of God*, 38–79) further complicates this question and suggests a more synchronic approach to the distinctions between Priestly and the Deuteronomist, which should together be seen over against earlier Yahwist and Elohist "traditions of fluidity."

43. Eichrodt (*Theology of the Old Testament*, 1.211–12, 216–17) argues that, in contrast to other literary sources, the prophets use many anthropomorphic descriptions; he finds them to be most apparent in the late prophecies within Isa 40–66.

44. Weinfeld, *Deuteronomy and the Deuteronomic School*, 198 and n3.

45. For a specific discussion of anthropomorphism in Jeremiah, see Rom-Shiloni, "Challenging the Notion."

I give two brief and intertwined examples. The first concerns Ezekiel and his use of the Priestly term and conception כבוד יהוה ("the presence of God"). In the Priestly materials, כבוד יהוה connotes an aniconic representation of God, in which the divine presence is represented by light.[46] Ezekiel, however, uses the term in a clearly anthropomorphic sense. In his commission prophecy, above the "expanse" (רקיע, 1:25), he sees the image of the man(-king) seated on his throne דמות כמראה אדם (1:26-28), which is identified as הוא מראה דמות כבוד־יהוה ("that was the appearance of the semblance of the presence of YHWH," 1:28). The same vision (מראות אלהים, 1:1; 8:1-3; 43:3) and the same language describes God entering and leaving his house, the temple (כבוד אלהי ישראל/יהוה, 9:3; 10:4, 18-19; 11:22; 43:1-9).[47] What should have been a nonanthropomorphic description of כבוד יהוה becomes, in Ezekiel's description of the divine, unequivocally anthropomorphic—indeed, the imagery is somewhat hidden and in many formal ways remote and unclear (note the use of approximations: כדמות, כמראה, etc.); but behind all these restrictions, there is a physical shape of a man.[48] Ezekiel thus moves between aniconic language, which he draws from Priestly sources, and an anthropomorphic physical image of his own creation; in quite a surprising way, the prophet succeeds in integrating them both.[49]

46. The semantic field in which כבוד occurs implies an aniconic meaning; note זהר, נגה, הוד, הדר, תהלה, and also the Akkadian term *melammu*. Thus, in both Priestly and non-Priestly sources, כבוד is an aniconic symbol for the presence of God, similar to the ark (1 Sam 4:21), or even without its first meaning in the epithet מלך הכבוד (Ps 24:8, 10). According to Priestly sources, מראה כבוד יהוה appears as fire (Exod 24:16-18), enwrapped in or covered by a cloud (Exod 16:10; 40:34-36; 1 Kgs 8:11), and only once without any hiding device (Lev 9:23); in none of these passages is there a reference to a human image.

47. Compare Ezek 43:5-9, which uses anthropomorphic terms to describe God, to Exod 40:34-36, describing the cloud. Exceptions are the occurrences of כבוד יהוה in Exod 33:18, 22 (Yahwist/Elohist), where it refers to an anthropomorphic image of God (see Isa 17:4; 10:16). So Greenberg, *Ezekiel 1-20*, 51; and Zimmerli, *Ezekiel*, 1.124. For the independent status of כבוד יהוה in Ezekiel as hypostasis of YHWH as a divine king, see Strong, "God's *Kabod*"; Aster, *Unbeatable Light*, 301-13; and Sommer, *Bodies of God*, 58-62, 68-78.

48. See van Wolde, "God Ezekiel Envisions."

49. Kasher ("Anthropomorphism, Holiness, and Cult") considers Ezekiel's anthropomorphic conception (in his terminology) "innovative," in that, although he relies on Priestly traditions, he does not privilege either the Priestly or Holiness Legislation materials, but chooses independently from both and combines them in unique ways (see esp. 203-8). Since Weinfeld (*Deuteronomy and the Deuteronomic School*, 201) does

The use of anthropomorphisms in the Hebrew Bible in general, and in the prophetic literature in particular, is by no means unified or one-dimensional; the opposite would be closer to the truth. My second example is further connected with the theophany in Ezek 1. There are clear differences between the theophanies experienced by the three major prophets upon their commission (Isa 6; Jer 1:4–10; Ezek 1). Isaiah son of Amoz sees God sitting on his throne in the temple (is it a heavenly temple or the earthly one?); the skirts of his robe fill the temple, and he is surrounded by seraphs who cover him (or themselves? Isa 6:2), who are proclaiming God's universal majesty (6:3).[50] It is intriguing that even in this most anthropomorphic presentation, there is no real description of God that could be translated into a pictorial presentation. I consider this syntactical vagueness concerning the details intentional.[51] Ezekiel 1:26–28 puts forth a different presentation of God's theophany. It portrays God in both human terms דמות כמראה אדם ("there was the semblance of a human form," 1:26) and as remote, above the expanse of the heavens. Of even more significance is that although two human body parts are mentioned (ממראה מתניו ולמעלה וממראה מתניו ולמטה, "from what appeared as his loins up . . . and from what appeared as his loins down," 1:27), no further specific physical details are given; on the contrary, those two parts are characterized as כמראה־אש ("what looked like a fire," 1:27a–b) and

---

not distinguish between Ezekiel and the Priestly source, he considers the latter to employ כבוד as a physical image of God and not as a term designating presence; thus, for Weinfeld, the term is not an "abstract" and therefore *not* parallel to the Deuteronomic conception. Furthermore, it seems that Weinfeld does not consider the distinction between anthropomorphism and aniconism and the significant gap between them.

50. Luzzatto (*Isaiah*, 62–64) aligns with traditional interpretation and by analogy with Ezek 1:11, argues that the seraphs covered themselves in awe of God (see also Rashi, Qimhi, Ibn Ezra, and others on Isa 6:2); yet Luzzatto recognizes that "if it had not been for Ezekiel, it might have been interpreted that the seraphs cover God's face and feet with their wings, so that the divine would not be seen." Childs (*Isaiah*, 55) suggests that this anthropomorphic scene transforms the Jerusalem temple into a heavenly one and argues that the seraphs cover themselves to keep themselves from seeing God, so that they can serve God properly in "worship and praise." Watts (*Isaiah 1–33*, 73–74) and Seitz (*Isaiah 1–39*, 54) argue along similar lines. Hamori (*When Gods Were Men*, 26–32) refers to this scene as transcendent anthropomorphism.

51. Vagueness in the description of the scene characterizes the Aramaic Targum to Isa 6:2–3. This is carried further by medieval and modern Jewish commentators; see, e.g., Luzzatto, *Isaiah*, 62–63. Kaiser (*Isaiah 1–12*, 74–75) notes that "the prophet does not actually describe Yahweh himself" (74).

as surrounded by radiance (ונגה לו סביב, 1:27).[52] Jeremiah's call is of an audial, not visual character (Jer 1:4–10; esp. 1:4). But is this truly a more abstract encounter, when at the crucial moment, the hand of God touches the prophet's lips (1:9)?[53]

Each of these three prophetic books seems to be negotiating the "proper" way to describe God in anthropomorphic terms; that is, they each search for and find their own ways of doing it, but when carefully read, they all cover more than they reveal. Jeremiah is no less concrete, no more abstract, in his use of anthropomorphic language than Isaiah son of Amoz, Ezekiel, or any other of their contemporaries.[54]

Rather, the differences between the three prophets in reference to their portrayals of God may be defined along the spectrum of iconic/anti-iconic language. Isaiah son of Amoz and Ezekiel portray only in very general terms a picture that is close (but clearly not identical) to iconographic anthropomorphism. It may plausibly be surmised that due to its similarity to

---

52. See Greenberg, *Ezekiel 1–20*, 50–51. Greenberg further argues (52–53) that "like the appearance of" denotes exactness (the *opposite* of vagueness), which "does not signify a reservation with respect to looks but with respect to substance." He bases his argument on Judg 13:6 and claims that such precise anthropomorphic language is allowed in a vision. The combination of diverse modes in describing the divine appearance symbolizes, according to Greenberg, "powerfully, and in concentrated form, God's support of and intimate presence with the prophet" (54; see 80–81). Compare Eichrodt (*Ezekiel*, 58–59), who briefly mentions that "of the figure to be perceived upon the throne we get only a vague outline. Isaiah, too, shows a similar restraint in his description." In reference to Ezek 8–11, Eichrodt (*Ezekiel*, 116–17) argues that "the imagery of the vision in Ezekiel 1 made it possible to regard the object standing in the holy of holies as a mere outward shadow of a transcendental reality, the doxa of which was not touched by earthly catastrophes, but could, when the temple was destroyed, be taken up into the heavenly sphere." Blenkinsopp (*Ezekiel*, 22–23) outlines a pious Christian perspective on God "in humanity's image."

53. The question of anthropomorphism is rarely raised in reference to Jer 1:9, although scholars do address the more general question of whether it is an audial or a visual theophany. See McKane, *Jeremiah 1–25*, 9–10; and Lundbom, *Jeremiah 1–20*, 234, 236–37; compare Isa 6:7 and Ezek 2:8–9. For a broader discussion see Zimmerli, "Visionary Experience in Jeremiah." Phenomenologically, the hand sent to the prophet is a partial representation of the divine, as so often seen in Jewish art of the Roman-Byzantine periods; note, for example, the hand of God in the Dura Europos synagogue (third century CE) and the Beit Alpha synagogue (sixth century CE) mosaics, among many examples.

54. I apply this observation to the entire collection of conceptions of God in Jeremiah, as I do not see signs of abstraction in any of them, contra Weinfeld, "Jeremiah and the Spiritual Metamorphosis," 26; see Rom-Shiloni, "Challenging the Notion."

a pictorial representation, this verbal description is toned down by each of the prophets, so to express only a very general outline or partial or remote description; but they each portray God in anthropomorphic terms, even if behind a thick veil.[55] Jeremiah clearly refrains from describing God as appearing before him in a full human image, and in this he differs from the prophets who preceded him—Amos (7:7; 9:1), Isaiah son of Amoz (Isa 6), Ezekiel (1, 8–11, 43)—and especially from portrayals of Moses (i.e., Exod 33:12–23), who in many respects serves as a model for Jeremiah.[56] It is more accurate to define an anti-iconic tendency in the book of Jeremiah that permeates even literary descriptions. But Jeremiah's reservations concerning a fully anthropomorphic representation of God (even in words) bear no relation to a rejection of anthropomorphism altogether, to an abstract concept of God, or to a tendency toward transcendence and away from immanence; rather, all these are but expressions of a rejection of iconism. Jeremiah does use both physical and mental anthropomorphisms, references to different spheres of human activity, and so on (such as the hand of God in Jer 1:9). Thus, it is possible to hone the distinctions between the prophets over the descriptions of God as residing on the differences between anthropomorphism, iconism/aniconism, or even anti-iconism.

Anthropomorphic language in sixth-century literature does not accord with the paradigms of linear development from concrete to abstract, nor with distinctions of religious development among Judean authorial circles. It does, however, signal an awareness of the literary options for and limitations to be observed in describing God verbally, in ways that almost touch upon pictorial-iconic anthropomorphism. David Aaron writes: "There is no progression from concrete to abstract, literal to metaphorical, plurality of meaning to singularity of meaning. All of these are natural byproducts of the human struggle to make sense."[57] His words are very apt for the sixth-century theological deliberations and representations presented in this study.

55. On this notion of anthropomorphism behind a veil, see Barr, "Theophany and Anthropomorphism," 35.

56. See Holladay, "Jeremiah and Moses." The avoidance of an actual vision of God (contrast Num 12:6–8) might be due to the clear hierarchical distinction Jeremiah sets between Moses and himself. For Jeremiah, visions and visionaries belong to the denigrated camp of the "peace prophets" (Jer 23:16); and the prophet similarly rejects dreamers (23:25). This, of course, runs counter to Num 12:6 and other pentateuchal passages that see dreams and visions as legitimate prophetic activity.

57. Aaron, *Biblical Ambiguities*, 199.

5.2.2. Anthropomorphism as Lack of Awareness of Tension between Anthropomorphic Expressions and Monotheistic Belief

A second explanation for the systematic use of personifying language in the Hebrew Bible is suggested by Yehezkel Kaufmann, who argues that the abundant use of personifying language in the Hebrew Bible, including prophetic literature, proves that the practitioners of Israelite religion are unaware of such tension.[58] Kaufmann claims that portrayed images of God and monotheistic belief coexist in Israelite religion throughout its history and that the search for a move toward abstraction in the conceptions of God is anachronistic:

> The conception of monotheism is, according to our terms, among the most abstract ideas of human thought. According to our conceptions, this idea is bound with abstractions of all the many phenomena in which the world is revealed to us, and with perceiving all according to a mysterious unity beyond comprehension. . . . The biblical literature in its entirety, with no distinction of source or layer, portrays an image of God, and finds no fault in this whatsoever. There is no abstract notion of God in the Hebrew Bible, and there is no ambition for abstraction. . . . The question of image and abstraction is beyond the boundaries of the biblical problematic.[59]

Kaufmann makes some important observations here, both in his justified opposition to the notion of an abstract conception of God in the Hebrew Bible and in his claim that anthropomorphism is not a deficiency in

---

58. Kaufmann, *Toldot Ha-'Emunah*, 1.227–31. Moreover, Kaufmann denies the existence of an internal conflict between pictorial and verbal descriptions. He argues that the prohibition against idols is connected only to the worship of other gods and that the question of symbolizing God in any tangible way is not at all discussed in the Hebrew Bible. Kaufmann thus disregards the testimony of Deut 4:12 and Isa 40:18 (*Toldot Ha-'Emunah*, 1.230–31 n11) and does not refer to Deut 27:15 (see von Rad, *Old Testament Theology*, 1.215). But his observations on this point cannot be accepted; see Hurowitz, "Make Yourself an Idol."

59. Kaufmann, *Toldot Ha-'Emunah*, 1.221, 226, 229 (my translation). Kaufmann surveys the occurrence of the idea of abstraction in postbiblical sources and refers its appearance in Jewish thought under the influence of Greek philosophy on Jews as of the Hellenistic period and up to the peak of this influence in Medieval Jewish philosophy (*Toldot Ha-'Emunah*, 1.231–44, 249–54). See also Eichrodt, *Theology of the Old Testament*, 1.210–14; and Goshen-Gottstein, "Body as Image."

the eyes of Hebrew Bible authors as a whole. Nevertheless, two of his other points require criticism. Kaufmann proposes that anthropomorphism is nothing more than a careless habitual use of language and a product of popular imagination. However, the description of God's role in the destruction of Jerusalem in Jeremiah and Ezekiel demonstrates the opposite. The prophets (even more than the other sources) make conscious and prominent use of anthropomorphic language, and there is no reason to attribute lack of intention to them; the discussion in §5.2.1 serves as but one example of the great sensitivity shown by the prophets (as well as other authors) to the degree of personification in their pronouncements, and yet they clearly speak in anthropomorphic terms. "Careless" and "unintentional" are clearly not fitting descriptors for their work.[60]

5.2.3. Anthropomorphism as Metaphor

The foregoing observations lead to the third explanation for the widespread use of anthropomorphism, physical and mental, in the Hebrew Bible. This explanation is based upon examining the place of anthropomorphic description in semantic-semiotic study. As a verbal representation of the human image of God, anthropomorphism is constructed in the manner of metaphor.[61]

Studies that challenge the definition of talk about God as metaphor inform a sense of dissatisfaction that this definition appears to limit the scope of theological discussion in various ways. Thus, plenty of other terms are at hand, such as "God-related idioms" (David Aaron) or "God-language" (from Tryggve Mettinger to Hanne Loeland).[62] With many other scholars,

---

60. See Uffenheimer, "Biblical Theology."

61. Jevons ("Anthropomorphism," 576–77) defines anthropomorphism as a metaphor. From a comparative perspective, Jacobsen (*Treasure of Darkness*) presents anthropomorphism as a major theme within "the religious metaphor" of "the Numinous," whose purpose is "to point beyond itself and the world from which it is taken" (3–5 at 5). Divine images, portrayed in human form as of the third millennium, are among the different devices that are intended to insure the divine presence in the physical world (14; along with cult dramas, religious literature, and temples). Since the third millennium BCE, the gods of the Mesopotamian pantheon are perceived as rulers (and then as parents), and their shifting portrayal reflects social changes in Mesopotamia (165–220). Within religious studies, anthropomorphism as metaphor is discussed, along with cognitive and ideological aspects of religion, by Guthrie, *Faces in the Clouds*, 62–90, 177–204; and Benavides, "Cognitive and Ideological Aspects."

62. For "God-related idioms," see Aaron, *Biblical Ambiguities*, 1–22. The term "God-

I retain the use of metaphor, both for the linguistic values it holds and for the adequate relationships it supplies between image and conception.

A metaphor is a figurative verbal expression for a concept that cannot be captured adequately by precise vocabulary. As such, the metaphor fills a vacuum in the selection of words available to a speaker by bridging two diverse conceptual entities.[63] Ivor Richards and Max Black define the relationship between a metaphorical expression and its content.[64] Black suggests that this relationship may be framed in three ways, all of which may be used in deciphering the meaning of a metaphoric phrase: (1) substitution—the metaphor substitutes for a literal sense of the target concept; (2) comparison—the metaphor requires comparison of the two items; oftentimes a significant contribution to the meaning of the metaphor arises exactly from the discordance between them;[65] and (3) simultaneous interaction—the metaphor creates an interaction between the "vehicle" (the figurative device that usually conveys the content) and its "tenor" (the content of the metaphorical statement), which the author and then the listener/reader simultaneously play within their mind, as this interaction produces "associated commonplaces" that the two share.[66] In relation to this last alternative, Richards emphasizes the interaction be-

---

language" is suggested by Mettinger, *In Search of God*, 204–7; and Strawn, *What Is Stronger than a Lion?* 1–15. See Loeland's explanation of her choice of "god-language" in *Silent or Salient Gender?* 25–26.

63. The place of metaphor within semantic and semiotic study is discussed by Lyons, *Semantics*, 1.102–6. Black (*Models and Metaphors*, 25–47) discusses the function of metaphor in adding content to the literal meaning of the word or phrase, including its role in catachresis (30–34). For additional definitions of metaphor, see Brettler, *God Is King*, 17–28; Brettler, "Metaphorical Mapping of God"; Loeland, *Silent or Salient Gender?* 23–55; and Aaron, *Biblical Ambiguities*, 9–15.

64. Richards, *Philosophy of Rhetoric*, 89–138.

65. Black, *Models and Metaphors*, 30–45. See also Richards, *Philosophy of Rhetoric*, 124–27; and Brettler, *God Is King*, 18–21. For a criticism of the comparative component within metaphor, see Fogelin (*Figuratively Speaking*, 33–66), who challenges the concept of an expected overlap between the vehicle and the tenor (or the source and the target) and prefers to recognize "salient features" that correspond between the two and are necessary to allow the metaphor (61–66, 67–92); see the careful discussion of this aspect by Loeland (*Silent or Salient Gender?*, 31–47), who also notes the necessity of inconsistency between the components of the metaphor as an aspect of its function (40–47).

66. Black, *Models and Metaphors*, 30–47; this interaction is emphasized by Richards, *Philosophy of Rhetoric*, 100. Dille (*Mixing Metaphors*, 2–4, 14–20) holds the dynamic of interaction to be central to the associated relationships between clusters of

tween the tenor and the vehicle. Even though the vehicle may be unusual (or even alien) to the literal meaning in the context where it occurs, the interaction between it and the tenor gives additional meaning to the metaphorical expression.[67] A broader definition of metaphor is proposed by George Lakoff and Mark Johnson (and by Lakoff and Mark Turner), who emphasize the conceptual aspects of metaphors within language, of what they call "everyday metaphorical thought."[68] They observe metaphor as a "spatial conceptualization of linguistic form" that develops similarities along "cross-domain correlations" between the "source domain" and the "target domain." Accordingly, "source-to-target mapping" allows one to trace interactions of the new understandings that the metaphor, as source, contributes to its conception, the target.[69]

As is widely recognized, these definitions of metaphor are very helpful for the study of theology, and specifically for talk to and about God.[70] In addition, biblical metaphorical language may provide insights into the life situations of those who produced it. Leo Perdue, looking at the book of Job, describes the "metaphorical process" as built on the following stages: absurdity, disorientation and destabilization, mimesis, transfor-

---

multiple and diverse metaphors found in a single context (and throughout Isa 40–55), where each contributes to a highly diverse and rich portrayal of God.

67. Richards, *Philosophy of Rhetoric*, 95–112. The exceptional status of the metaphor (the vehicle) in reference to the literal meaning of the phrase in its context is discussed by Black, *Models and Metaphors*, 27–28.

68. See Lakoff and Johnson, *Metaphors We Live By*, 126–38, 147–55 at 243, 245.

69. Lakoff and Johnson, *Metaphors We Live By*, 243–74 esp. 246–47. Lakoff, *Women, Fire, and Dangerous Things*, 57–64 at 59: "A metaphor with the name A is B is a mapping of part of the structure of our knowledge of source domain B onto target domain A"; and see Lakoff and Turner, *More Than Cool Reason*.

70. See Soskice (*Metaphor and Religious Language*, 142–61), who argues that metaphors give us "two ideas for one"; and thus metaphoric language enlarges our knowledge about conceptions of God. Dille (*Mixing Metaphors*, 18) argues that all language about God is ultimately metaphoric or analogic; thus, all God-language involves complex interactions between multiple metaphors in portraying God. Loeland (*Silent or Salient Gender?*, 31n6) accepts the idea that all God-language is figurative or metaphorical and uses this as one of her presuppositions. But note that both Dille (*Mixing Metaphors*, 18–19) and Loeland (*Silent or Salient Gender?*, 51–54) challenge the idea that this understanding of metaphor brings us closer to actual knowledge of God; if all God-language is metaphorical, the tenor, God's self, remains unknown. All metaphors are built in turn upon other metaphors that have become commonplace; hence the interaction is a mix between metaphors of different status.

mation, and restabilization.[71] Considered in this light, my proposed focus on metaphoric language for God in the sixth-century sources may prove a particularly apt window onto the spiritual-theological crises brought on by the disorienting events of the sixth century.

All three definitions of metaphor prove essential for the task of distinguishing between anthropomorphic language and conceptions of God and, most importantly, for revealing the interaction between the two. Anthropomorphic metaphors fill the gap between human understanding and lexicon, by which humans can describe God, who is not bound by any human limitations and thus not graspable by either concept or language. The tenor (or the target domain) is the conception of God, and anthropomorphism is the vehicle (or the source domain). Lines of similarity and lines of distinction between God and human beings may be drawn by means of substitution of, comparison of, and interaction between that which characterizes humans and that which is understood as characterizing God.[72] The role of anthropomorphism in the Hebrew Bible, on the level of both literary description and conception, is thus similar to the role of anthropomorphism in pictorial descriptions in other religions—it serves as the image of God, but is not in itself a conception of the divine.[73] Defining anthropo-

---

71. Perdue, *Wisdom in Revolt*, 22–27.

72. This distinction accords with the medieval Jewish definition of such language: דברה תורה כלשון בני אדם ("Scriptures have spoken as/in human language")—a definition that takes personification language as necessary for human comprehension. Rabbi Judah Ibn Kuriash (Algeria, tenth century CE), in his letter to the Jews of Fez, explains Isa 48:9's phrase למען שמי אאריך אפי ("for the sake of My name I control My wrath"), saying: "And as this phrase, which is used concerning humans, the created, and the mortal [לגשמיים לברואים ולבני תמותה], so it is said of God the Great and Mighty. But this is all only a human style [סגנון בני אדם], to suit what they understand according to their spirit and soul, as the Rabbis said: 'Scriptures have spoken as human language' (*b. Berachot* 31). . . . All these are, as we said, to draw [those phrases] closer to human understanding, according to their comprehension of their issues and their qualities, and all is under: 'Scriptures have spoken as/in human language'" (Katz, *Book of Rabbi Judah Ibn Kuriash*, 52 [my translation]). Ibn Kuriash's words are quoted in Rashi's interpretations of Isa 48:9 and Exod 15:8; see also Qimhi on Jer 14:7; and Maimonides, הלכות יסודי התורה, chap. 1: הלכות no. 9, 12.

73. See Jacobsen, "Pictures and Pictorial Language," 6–8. This semantic-semiotic understanding of metaphor differs from psychological-cognitive approaches in religious studies such as that of Guthrie (*Faces in the Clouds*, 65), who argues that religious conceptions in themselves are as anthropomorphic and function as a means to explain the entire nonhuman world. A series of experiments at Cornell University, with over fifty graduate and undergraduate students of different denominations as subjects, con-

morphism as a vehicle in a metaphor illustrates this important difference between anthropomorphism per se and conceptions of God, which is like the difference between a sign and the object it represents; biblical anthropomorphism thus may also be seen in terms of the distinction between an image of God (*Gottesbild*) and a conception of God (*Gottesvorstellung*), discussed at the outset of this chapter.[74]

This distinction between image and conception is crucial, for instance, to explain how a transcendent conception of God can coexist with anthropomorphic representations of the divine (as in Ezek 1) and how immanence and transcendence can be found simultaneously in Ezekiel's thought and also be represented in anthropomorphic language (as in Ezek 8–11).[75]

---

cerns their use of anthropomorphic concepts of God. The investigators distinguish between "theological concepts" (i.e., theoretical beliefs) and "concepts used in everyday life"; see Barrett and Keil, "Conceptualizing a Nonnatural Entity." Their summary of the results is: "These three studies reveal that subjects do use anthropomorphic concepts of God in understanding stories, even though they may profess a theological position that rejects anthropomorphic constraints on God and God's activities. It appears that people have at least two parallel God concepts that are used in different contexts, and these concepts may be fundamentally incompatible" (240; see also 243–44). These results raise the possibility that this incompatibility might have been otherwise construed if the investigators considered anthropomorphism not as a concept of God, but as a vehicle for God's representation in speech/language.

74. Much is written on symbol and object, on their interrelationships, and on their relevance to metaphor; see §5.1 and Preminger and Brogan, *New Princeton Encyclopedia*, 1250–54. Compare Sommer (*Bodies of God*, 8–9) and §5.2.1; see also Hamori (*When Gods Were Men*, 3–4) in her discussion of the two "אִישׁ theophanies" (Gen 18:1–15; 32:23–33); she argues for an "anthropomorphic realism," which she defines as "tangible, physical human form, not in a metaphor, or in a vision, or in a dream, but in a body" (3). I consider both passages as different points on the spectrum of anthropomorphic metaphor.

75. See Hamori (*When Gods Were Men*, 26–32), who establishes separate categories for "immanent anthropomorphism" and "transcendent anthropomorphism." Typologically, there is no difference between these two types of anthropomorphic description; that is, God is presented in both conceptions in terms of metaphorical anthropomorphisms. It seems that this distinction is needed, however, to counter *scholarly* suppositions (especially Christian ones); see, for instance, Eichrodt's discussion of anthropomorphism (*Theology of the Old Testament*, 1.206–27, esp. 206–10 and 212–14). Eichrodt calls his discussions "God as Personal" and "God as Spiritual"; though in his discussion of the Hebrew Bible sources, he actually deals with everything *but* the spiritual nature of the divine (and indeed says that it is only through Jesus Christ that the Christian faith succeeded in recognizing divine spirituality; 212). He considers anthropomorphic phrases to be part of the "personhood" of God, which for him is entwined with the conception of immanence. Eichrodt defines the theological

Similarly, the distinction between image and conception can explain the juxtaposition of different metaphors for God; at times personal and impersonal metaphors may be brought together in one and the same context (e.g., Deut 32:4, 15, 18, 30, 31, 37). Kirsten Nielsen suggests an approach to biblical theology (both Old Testament and New Testament, as the Christian canon) based upon the many metaphors for God.[76] Nielsen is mostly interested in impersonal metaphors for God and discusses one of them, God as a rock, focusing on two texts (Deut 32 and 2 Sam 22). While Nielsen concedes that the root metaphors are those she categorizes as "personal metaphors"—the metaphors for God as king, father, shepherd, and so on—the very variety of these metaphors in itself makes a theological statement, which Nielsen phrases as follows: "God is more and God is different"—underscored by such a variety of metaphors being needed to portray the different aspects of divine activity. While the personal metaphors carry the burden of representing the relationship between God and human beings, the impersonal metaphors, according to Nielsen, have a different, special function "to remind us that there is more to be said about God than just saying that God is like a human. God transcends the

---

problem developed through this "personhood" of God as follows: "The immanence of God threatened to overshadow his transcendence" (211). The "threat" grows with the many anthropomorphic and anthropopathic phrases Eichrodt recognizes throughout the Hebrew Bible. God accordingly is presented as having a "super-human personality" (213), mostly because he is not confined by human limitations (214–15). I believe the point is clear: it is not only that Eichrodt's whole discussion is saturated with Christian theology, but that it lacks the distinction between image (anthropomorphism) and conceptions (immanence, transcendence, etc.). Eichrodt concedes the possibility that the expression *panim* (God's face) might have a "metaphorical sense," mostly in the context of the cult, but also as an expression of God's "personal involvement" or "direct intervention"; for Eichrodt, however, all these uses denote "speaking of God's personal activity in veiled language" (2.35–39, esp. 37, 39).

76. See Nielsen, "Metaphors and Biblical Theology." In her general discussion of biblical theology, Nielsen presents two approaches that from her perspective pertain to the Christian canon (Old Testament and New Testament). One approach stresses diversity, the second looks for unity among the various documents by locating one theme or point of view that runs throughout. Nielsen argues that this approach allows one to see both continuity and change, since Old and New Testament share two root metaphors for God. In the Old Testament, the primary metaphor is God as king; in the New Testament the metaphor of God as father comes to the fore. But the two appear in each Testament, and side by side with them there are plenty of other metaphors in service, including impersonal ones.

boundaries of human life."[77] For Nielsen, the challenge of biblical theology, then, is to find ways that combine or balance between personal and "beyond personal" metaphors, to insure that the result does not designate any exclusive identification of God with "anything else," following Exod 20:4. Although I greatly appreciate Nielsen's observations, my study nevertheless focuses on personal metaphors for God.

5.3. Anthropomorphic Metaphors for God

Anthropomorphic metaphors for God in the Hebrew Bible in general, and particularly within sixth-century literature, touch upon all the spheres of human existence and activity. Physical anthropomorphism makes reference to the limbs and organs of the body, to actions involving the senses and actions performed by humans. Mental anthropomorphism pertains to the realm of thought, emotion, will, and human characteristics. In addition, anthropomorphic expressions drawing on occupations, professions, and customs of life are borrowed from human behavior.

The examples given are restricted in number and in scope in that they are drawn from the sources dealt with in this study; hence, from the historiography of Kings, from the prophetic literature in Jeremiah and Ezekiel, from quotations in the two prophetic books, and from selected laments in Psalms and Lamentations.[78] Thus, although the information does not exhaust the phenomenon throughout the Hebrew Bible, I do not expect this data to differ substantially from the general occurrence of anthropomorphism in other Hebrew Bible compositions.

5.3.1. Physical Anthropomorphisms: Limbs and Organs of the Body

God's Hand or Arm. Both Jeremiah and Ezekiel make frequent reference to the hand or the arm, in expressions that describe both the martial activity of God against his people and against the nations, and his destructive involvement in national and international affairs, for example, in the

---

77. Nielsen, "Metaphors and Biblical Theology," 264, 265, 268. This mixture of personal and impersonal metaphors in one and the same context adds another facet to the dynamic of interaction between metaphors, as presented for instance by Dille, *Mixing Metaphors*, 173–78.

78. On Jeremiah see Rom-Shiloni, "Challenging the Notion."

phrase נטה ידו על ("I will stretch out My arm against," Jer 6:12; 15:6; PAN Jer 51:25; Ezek 6:14; 14:9, 13; 16:27; PAN Ezek 25:7, 13, 16; 35:3).[79] God's oath to his people is regularly indicated by the phrase נשא ידו להם ("I gave My oath to [literally: I lifted My hand up for]," Ezek 20:5). Against the claim that these are merely empty expressions (or dead metaphors), both prophets, in their respective commissioning prophecies, state that the "hand of the LORD" is extended to them (Jer 1:9; Ezek 2:9). Once in Jeremiah (15:17) and three times in Ezekiel (1:3; 3:14; 33:22), the "hand of the LORD" is the tangible expression used to indicate the resting of the divine spirit upon the prophet (see the role of this phrase in the symbolic vision in Jer 25:15, 17); the representation of the nation as clay in the hand of the potter, that is, God (18:6); and the image of Jehoiachin as a stamp on the right hand of the God the king (22:24). In poetic sources, YHWH's hand or arm signifies the military might of God (Ps 89:11, 14), God's assistance to a king in warfare (89:22), and his battles against the nations for his people (44:3–4; 77:16). His seeming inactivity during the destruction is expressed either in the phrase למה תשיב ידך וימינך מקרב חיקך כלה ("Why do You hold back Your hand, Your right hand? Draw it out of Your bosom!," Ps 74:11; Lam 2:3) or, negatively, as לא־השיב ידו מבלע ("He did not hold back His hand from destroying"; NJPS: "[He] refrained not from bringing destruction," Lam 2:8; 3:3).

God's Face. God's role in the destruction is depicted using phrases that refer to the face: ונתתי את־פני בהם ("I will set My face against them," Ezek 15:7; 14:8) and שים פניו ב־/לרעה (Jer 21:10; 44:11). On the other hand, reassurance within a consolation prophecy is phrased in the promise לוא־אפיל פני בכם ("I will not look on you in anger [literally: I will not put My face down upon you]," 3:12).[80] The political and military defeat is a result of God's turning his face away from the people (Ezek 7:22); exile is described as casting off or expelling the people from before the face of God (2 Kgs 24:20; Jer 7:15; 15:1; 23:39; 32:31; 52:3); and the destruction

---

79. נטה ידו על also occurs in Isa 5:25; Zeph 1:4; PAN Zeph 2:13; and note the phrase הניף ידו על־הגוים in Isa 11:15 and Zech 2:13. While this is a clear anthropomorphic image, the divine deed to which it points may be a cosmic action that brings total annihilation (e.g., Exod 7:5; 15:12).

80. The phrase פני יהוה occurs nineteen times in judgment prophecies against Israel in Jeremiah and in four prophecies of consolation (e.g., 30:20; 31:36; 33:18; 35:19). Similarly, it occurs nine times in Ezekiel, as in ונתתי את־פני בהם ("I will set My face against them," 15:7; 14:8); the political and military defeat is a result of God's turning his face away from the people (7:22).

and the deportations are a result of the "hiding of the face" (Jer 33:5; Ezek 39:23, 24, 29; Pss 44:25; 102:3; and הסתיר פניו, Ps 10:11, in a citation of the words of the evildoer). The prophet as a devoted servant stands before his lord (Jer 18:20); the kings serve before him in diverse ways (26:19; 34:15, 18; 49:19; 50:44; as a future hope in 36:7; and consolation prophecies in 30:20); and the people are promised that they will continue being a nation before God (31:36; also 33:18; 35:19; compare 33:24). In all of these passages, the face of God is the image (the vehicle, the source), whereas the conception behind the image is that of God's presence (4:1; 5:22; 7:10), as may be deduced from the parallelism between "Me" and "My face" (2:22; 5:22).

Organs Located in the Face. Among the organs located in the face, the one that is most frequently mentioned in both prophecy and poetry is the "nose of the LORD" (אף יהוה). The nose functions as a signifier for divine wrath—in 2 Kings (23:26; 24:20), Jeremiah (חרון אף, 4:26), and Ezekiel (כילה אף, 5:13; שילח אפו, 7:3). Among other phrases, there is a repeated parallel between אף and חמה (e.g., Jer 7:20; 32:31; 33:5; 42:18; 44:6; Ezek 22:20; 38:18; PAN 25:14). אף יהוה occurs once in a Jeremian paraphrase of an individual lament: אל־באפך פן־תמעטני ("not in Your wrath [literally: nose], lest You reduce me to naught," Jer 10:24; compare Pss 6:2; 38:2); and in various phrases in many communal laments (Pss 74:1; 77:10; 90:7, 11; Lam 2:1, 6; 3:43). Once released, the divine wrath brings total devastation, often portrayed as a consuming fire (Jer 4:4; 21:12), which God never regrets, (לא שב (חרון) אף (יהוה ממנו) (4:8; 23:20).

The "eyes of the LORD" in Jeremiah see the good and bad actions of humankind (32:19); by means of his eyes, God sees the people's transgressions: כי עיני על־כל־דרכיהם לא נסתרו מלפני ("for My eyes are on all their ways, they are not hidden from My presence," 16:17). In Ezekiel, God's eyes represent God's lack of pity in the proclamation of punishment (5:11; 7:4, 9; 8:18; 9:10); and the opposite, God's pity (20:17). This metaphor seems to be completely detached from any action connected with the actual act of sight (seeing). It rather includes the entire movement from seeing, to interpreting the sight, to the action taken as its result. The phrase ושמתי עיני עליהם לטובה ("I will look [literally: I will lay my eye] upon them favorably," Jer 24:6) specifies benevolence toward the exiles with Jehoiachin.

The "ears of God" are mentioned only in poetic supplications for salvation (Pss 10:17; 102:3; Lam 3:56).

Finally, the "mouth of God" appears only in 2 Kgs 24:3 and in the prophecies of Jeremiah (9:11, 19; 15:19) and Ezekiel (3:17; 33:7), as the organ of divine speech.[81]

Of the five senses, two are used in anthropomorphic metaphors for God. The sense of sight appears in the verbs ראה, הביט, השקיף in Jeremiah and Ezekiel (Jer 13:27; 18:17; 23:24; PAN Jer 46:5; Ezek 16:6, 8); in a saying put by Ezekiel into the mouths of the elders in Jerusalem (8:12; 9:9); and in calls for divine assistance in communal laments (Pss 94:9; 102:20; Lam 2:20; 4:16). Similarly, the sense of hearing, expressed by שמע and הקשיב, is attributed to God in Jeremiah (8:6; 14:12) and in the communal laments (Ps 106:44; Lam 3:56, 61); the two senses, sight and hearing, are found together in Ps 106:44 and Lam 3:60–61.

God's "Soul, Substance"—the נפש *of God.*[82] Three times in Jeremiah, נפשי designates the active (or reactive) dimension of God in his judgment against Israel: אם בגוי אשר־כזה לא תתנקם נפשי ("shall I not bring retribution on a nation such as this?" 5:9, 29; 9:8; and once in an oath in PAN Jer 51:14). Note also the collocation תקע נפשי ("lest I come to loathe you," 6:8; see also Ezek 23:18 [2x]). God's rejection of his people is expressed in a rhetorical question within a fragmented communal lament: געלה נפשך (Jer 14:19, invoking Lev 26:11, 15, 30).

5.3.2. *Everyday Actions of Human Life*

Physical anthropomorphisms also encompass everyday human activities particularly in the communal laments, for example: sleeping and awakening, עורה למה תישן אדני הקיצה אל־תזנח לנצח ("Rouse Yourself; why do You sleep, O Lord? Awaken, do not reject us forever!," Ps 44:24); or taking action: הרימה פעמיך ("bestir Yourself [literally: pick up your feet]," 74:3) and קומה עזרתה לנו ("arise and help us," 44:27; 74:22).

---

81. פי יהוה occurs several times in the Pentateuch as a synonym for "the word of God" (e.g., Num 14:41). 2 Kgs 24:3 MT uses פי יהוה where the Septuagint has ἐπὶ τὸν θυμὸν κυρίου (and the Peshitta has והוה רוגזא רבא על יהודה) to denote anger; these renderings of 2 Kgs 24:3 may reflect the reading of or an analogy to על אף יהוה (so also in the long addition to 2 Chr 36:5, LXX 5c).

82. נפש occurs in the Hebrew Bible with the physical meaning "throat" (e.g., Ps 107:9; Prov 25:25) or in a metaphorical sense to express breathing (2 Sam 16:14); from this sense is derived the meaning "soul" and "life," designating physical existence (Jer 17:21; Lam 2:19). נפש also designates mental operations, such as the wish or passion for food and drink (Hos 9:4). See Seebass, "נֶפֶשׁ *nepeš*."

5.3.3. Mental Anthropomorphisms

Mental anthropomorphism covers a wide range of actions, emotions, desires, and so on. In the area of thought, Jeremiah uses the epithet גדל העצה ("wondrous in purpose," 32:19). Divine omniscience is expressed in Jeremiah through ידע and חשב, as in כי אנכי ידעתי את־המחשבת אשר אנכי חשב עליכם נאם־יהוה מחשבות שלום ולא לרעה ("for I am mindful of the plans I have made concerning you—declares YHWH—plans for your welfare, not for disaster," 29:11, 23; similarly 1:5; 18:8, 11; PAN Jer 48:30). ידע occurs also in Ezek 11:5 as divine knowledge of the people's thoughts.[83] God plans his destructive deeds, זמם, and is determined to activate his מזמות accordingly, so as to reach a complete and hazardous calamity (Jer 4:28; 23:20; 30:24; PAN Jer 51:12).[84] God remembers (זכר) the distant and obedient past (2:2) as well as the present, long-lasting disobedience (31:34), and this divine ability guarantees future salvation in a consolation prophecy (31:20).[85] In Lam 2, God plans and executes the destruction (2:2, 17). With respect to the quality of understanding, evildoers in Ps 94 are quoted as casting aspersions on God's understanding: לא יראה־יה ולא־יבין אלהי יעקב ("the LORD does not see it, the God of Jacob does not pay heed [literally: does not understand]," 94:7). Common in communal laments are references to God as (not) remembering and forgetting (לא זכר/שכח in Pss 10:11; 42:10; 44:25; Lam 5:1, 20).

The realm of emotions comprises manifestations of divine anger (e.g., Lam 5:22) as well as references to mercy and benevolence (3:22, 32). למען הכעיסני (Jer 7:18, 19; 8:19) is one phrase in the rich inventory of rage phraseology, as for instance the parallel nouns קצף and זעם (10:10) or the triad אף, חמה, and קצף (21:5; 32:37; only קצף in PAN Jer 50:13).[86] The

---

83. Compare the repeated demand to know God (e.g., Jer 9:23; 24:7).

84. This planned evil action is thus the source of protest in Lam 2:17. זמם occurs thirteen times in the Hebrew Bible; in six of them God is the agent initiating destructive deeds or restoration (also Zech 1:6; 8:14, 15). Of the nineteen occurrences of מזמה in the Hebrew Bible, only the three occurrences in Jeremiah and in Job 42:2 refer to God as agent.

85. The verb זכר (לא) occurs often in Jeremiah and in Ezekiel, where the people are accused of not remembering God (Jer 17:2; Ezek 6:9; 16:22, 43, 61, 63; 20:43; 21:28, 29; 23:19; 36:31; Lam 1:7, 9). Once, in an individual lament (Jer 20:9), the prophet raises the hypothetical option that he would not remember God, would not be his messenger.

86. To give some statistics: forty-seven of the fifty-four occurrences of the verb כעס in the Hebrew Bible refer the anger to God, and only seven use כעס to convey a human reaction (as in 1 Sam 1:6). However, only four of the twenty-one occurrences

period of the destruction and exile blatantly demonstrates the absence of divine grace and mercy: לא חמל לא חס ולא רחם (e.g., Jer 13:14; see Ps 77:10). God gathers his favor, grace, and compassion away from the people: אספתי את־שלומי מאת העם־הזה נאם־יהוה את־החסד ואת־הרחמים ("for I have withdrawn My favor from that people—declares YHWH—My kindness and compassion," Jer 16:5); and while his quality as עשה חסד is repeated (9:23; 32:18), this is clearly inactive during the critical time of destruction. God's mercy (see chap. 12) for his people is saved for prophecies of consolation to Israel (12:15; 30:18; 33:26), and it is depicted by means of the metaphor of a father's relationship to his son (31:20). God's anguish and sorrow are given expression by means of rhetorical questions in Jeremiah (e.g., 2:31–32) and in the prophetic passages that mix complaint and accusation (e.g., 3:19–21; 8:4–7; 18:13–15).[87] Such expressions of divine sorrow do not appear in Ezekiel; God's sorrow is not referred to in the quotations within Jeremiah and Ezekiel nor in the laments within Psalms and Lamentations.

With respect to will, Jeremiah's definition of the divine role in the time of the destruction is that ויהוה לא רצם ("so YHWH has no pleasure in them," 14:10, 12). More common are descriptions of divine remorse, reversal of an initial plan and intention, expressed in the phrase ניחם יהוה על (42:10) and in pleas within communal laments (Pss 90:13; 106:45).[88]

5.3.4. Roles, Occupations, and Customs of Life

Two further components should be added to this varied array of human metaphors, physical and mental. One touches upon the roles in which human beings serve or occupations in which they engage, and the second

---

of the noun כעס refer to divine anger (1 Kgs 15:30; 21:22; 2 Kgs 23:26; Ps 85:5). The *hiphil* infinitive form להכעיס את־יהוה (as in 1 Kgs 14:9; 16:13) is common in Deuteronomistic compositions; see Weinfeld, *Deuteronomy and the Deuteronomic School*, 340. The other occurrences of this construction in Jeremiah are 11:17; 25:6, 7; 32:29, 30, 32; 44:3, 8. The verb קצף occurs sixteen times as a divine action, and the noun קצף appears twenty-seven times as a divine emotion of fierce anger. The verb קצף does not appear in Jeremiah, but the noun repeats four times in the book; and see Lam 5:22.

87. See Fretheim, *Suffering of God*, 115–26.

88. ניחם in the meaning "regretted" or "turned away from his initial intent" occurs in Judg 2:18; 1 Sam 15:35; and more. Regret as a human quality occurs in Jer 8:6; 31:19; Ezek 14:22; PAN Ezek 32:31. In its second meaning, "be appeased from anger," this verb only rarely occurs in reference to God. An exception is Ezek 5:13; the two meanings function together in a closed context in Ezek 14:22–23 and in Jer 31:13.

pertains to daily or customary habits of life. Accordingly, God is portrayed as a father (Jer 31:9, 20) or as a husband (2:2; 3:1–5; Ezek 16 and 23); both may also occur together (Jer 3:19–21 and in the quotation at 3:4).[89] God is further described as performing different human occupations: builder and farmer (24:6),[90] fisher (PAN Ezek 29:4–5), cook (Ezek 24:9–12), butcher (PAN Jer 51:40), or smith (Jer 9:6; Ezek 22:17–22). But by far the most dominant image of God reflects his supreme status: he is compared to a king, the human figure of the highest social status, taking the roles of sovereign, warrior, and judge.

Anthropomorphism is a general phenomenon that cuts across all the sources of this study: the historiography of Kings and, in greater measure, the prophetic literature and the poetry of the selected Psalms and Lamentations. Furthermore, there does not seem to be a distinction of use between physical or mental anthropomorphisms; both arenas are widely used by all. Anthropomorphism is the sixth-century way to talk about God.

5.4. God as King: A Pervasive Metaphor

In accordance with the qualities of a human king (its vehicle or source domain), we may identify three components of the anthropomorphic metaphor of God as king: (a) the epithet "king" for God and the verb מלך ("reign"); (b) symbols of governance (throne, crown, scepter, etc.); and (c) descriptions of actions and deeds that tell of the roles and functions that designate God's kingship.

While the metaphor of God as king is recognized as of major importance, scholars question its place within the theology of the Hebrew Bible

89. Within the metaphoric marital description of the God-people relationships, plenty of verbal phrases are taken from punishments of a husband against his wife according to the divorce laws, such as קצף ("I cast her off," Jer 3:8; see 3:1) and נתן ספר כריתותה אליה ("handed her a bill of divorce," 3:8). Ezekiel 16 and 23 use this metaphor against Jerusalem, presumably invoking phraseology used in laws against adultery, גרע חוקה ("withhold . . . maintenance," 16:27), or the descriptions of the judgment against the adulteress in 16:35–43 (see Day, "The Bitch Had It Coming").

90. Several verbal phrases with God as agent take actions from agriculture as metaphors for God's action: אסף (literally: "gather," with a double meaning, the second of which is presented by NJPS: "I will make an end of them," Jer 8:13; 16:5), הפיץ כקש ("so I will scatter you like straw," 13:24), מילא וניפץ נבל יין ("fill and smash jar of wine," 13:12–14), הוריד מן הקן ("pull down from a nest," PAN Jer 49:16).

and particularly within sixth-century literature.[91] This opposition rests mainly on the evidence for category (a), that is, on the relatively infrequent use of the root *mlk* with God as agent in the Hebrew Bible (as epithet or verb) and on its clear restrictions by genre. However, other scholars, with whom I concur, argue that reliance on category (a) alone gives a misleading impression as to the place captured by this metaphor and the religious conception of God as king in Israelite thought.[92]

I present the problem of the metaphoric representation of God as king through the use of the root *mlk* in the Hebrew Bible and challenge several scholarly suggestions that are raised to explain this seemingly limited representation. Only then do I return to consider this conception through a much larger database, tapping into categories (b) and (c) for an expansion of the literary indications of the use of this metaphor.

5.4.1. The Problem: Distribution and Date

There are only thirteen occurrences of the verb מלך with God as agent in the Hebrew Bible: one in the historiography, eight in the psalmodic poetry, and four in prophecy.[93] The epithet "king" (*melek*) for God appears forty-two times: once in the historiography, twenty-three times in the poetry, and eighteen times in the prophecy.[94] There are also nine occurrences of the abstract nouns מלוכה or מלכות in reference to God, in either prophecy

---

91. On the importance of the metaphor, see Mettinger, *In Search of God*, 92–93; and concerning the role of this metaphor in Mesopotamian religion, see Jakobsen, *Treasure of Darkness*, 77–92.

92. Mettinger ("Fighting the Powers of Chaos") argues that the relatively rare occurrences of *mlk* with God as agent in the Hebrew Bible is probably the reason for the limited attention given to the conception of divine kingship in broader theological studies. Indeed, von Rad does not allot a separate discussion to this topic in the two volumes of his *Old Testament Theology*; Eichrodt (*Theology of the Old Testament*, 1.194–202) deals with *mlk* only as one among God's epithets; and Zimmerli (*Old Testament Theology in Outline*, 41–43) deals with this conception at the end of his discussion of God as creator, where he asserts that it is borrowed from the Canaanites.

93. Historiography: 1 Sam 8:7; poetry: Exod 15:18; Pss 47:9; 93:1; 96:10 || 1 Chr 16:31; Ps 97:1; 99:1; 146:10; prophecy: Isa 24:23; 52:7; Ezek 20:33; Mic 4:7.

94. Historiography: 1 Sam 12:12; poetry: Num 23:21; Deut 33:5; Pss 5:3; 10:16; 24:7–10 (5x); 29:10; 44:5; 47:3, 7, 8; 48:3; 68:25; 74:12; 84:4; 89:19; 95:3; 98:6; 99:4; 145:1; prophecy: Isa 6:5; 30:33; 33:22; Second Isa 41:21; 43:15; 44:6; Jer 8:19; 10:7, 10; 46:18; 48:15; 51:57; Mic 2:13; Zech 14:9, 16, 17; Mal 1:14; Dan 4:34; and note also Zeph 3:15 LXX (βασιλεὺς Ισραηλ κύριος ἐν μέσῳ σου).

or poetry.[95] Therefore, excluding two occurrences in 1 Samuel, the use of the root *mlk* with God as subject is confined to poetic and prophetic passages.[96] This relatively minor number of occurrences and their distribution within Hebrew Bible literature do not support the claim of centrality within Hebrew Bible theology.

Furthermore, although poetic sources are notoriously difficult to date, the distribution of the prophetic books that feature the root *mlk* may be somewhat more assured. The main use of this root comes from the second half of the eighth century to the end of the sixth century, with Isaiah son of Amoz and Micah in the earlier group and with Obadiah and Zephaniah, Second Isaiah, Second Zechariah, and Malachi in the later (and note the reoccurrence of the root in the much later Daniel). The data leave us with a clear impression of an increase in the use of the epithet "king" in prophecies from the second half of the sixth century onward. Even as early as the first part of that century, the root *mlk* appears six times in Jeremiah (five in the words of the prophet: 10:7, 10; 46:18; 48:15; 51:57—all suspected of being redactional or Masoretic elaborations—and once in a quotation attributed to the people, 8:19–20) and once in Ezekiel (20:33).

5.4.2. Scholarly Solutions

The data on the root *mlk* with God as agent in the Hebrew Bible, particularly the relative abundance of the root in the poetry and prophetic writings, give rise to significant and influential studies on several tracks of comparative research. Beginning with Sigmund Mowinckel, scholars focus upon the *Sitz im Leben* of the יהוה מלך psalms, on their cultic and liturgical background in a presumed festival of YHWH's enthronement, which is said to have been celebrated at the start of the agricultural year.[97]

95. Prophecy: Obad 21; Dan 3:33 (2x); 4:31; poetry: Pss 22:29; 103:19; 145:11, 12, 13. In addition, ממשלה refers to God's sovereignty in Pss 103:22; 145:13.

96. The two occurrences in the historiography are in the two speeches concerning kingship in 1 Sam 8:7 and 12:12, but the words ויהוה אלהיכם מלככם are not represented in the Septuagint, and thus are suspected of being a Deuteronomistic expansion; see Hertzberg, *I and II Samuel*, 99.

97. Mowinckel argues for traces of YHWH's enthronement festival in the psalms; see *Psalmenstudien*, 2.44–145; and *Psalms in Israel's Worship*, 1.1–41. Among those who follow Mowinckel is Morgenstern, "Cultic Setting." This suggestion certainly enriches the scholarly discussion with both fans and opponents; see Weiser, *Psalms*, 23–35; Kraus, *Psalms 1–59*, 60–62; and Seybold, "מֶלֶךְ *melek*," 371–72.

Martin Buber is a dissident opinion, arguing that divine kingship is an Israelite conception even prior to their settlement in Canaan.[98] The governing scholarly perspective, however, holds that the conception of divine kingship is borrowed from the Canaanite (or possibly the Mesopotamian) arena by the early monarchic period. Thus, studies focus on the origin of the supposed enthronement festival and the conception behind it, on its Canaanite and perhaps Mesopotamian background, and on the ways in which it is assimilated into Israelite thought.[99]

Side by side with this comparative interest, the distribution of occurrences of this root in poetry and prophecy leads scholars to propose sociological distinctions between prophets and circles of priests and poets (as representatives of the masses). Otto Eissfeldt relates the late occurrences to a postexilic prophetic polemic against beliefs in demonic forces, although he argues that the conception of God as king is in use throughout the biblical period and, based on Num 23:21, that it is an ancient popular conception.[100] Walter Eichrodt thinks that the conception of God as king is widespread in priestly circles in Jerusalem, whereas prophetic circles avoid it until Josiah's reforms. The reforms, according to Eichrodt, engender a change of attitude toward the conception of divine kingship among the prophets, expressed in an increased use of this conception in late prophecy.[101]

In studies dedicated to the idea of the kingship of God, John Gray suggests a different sociological distinction.[102] He maintains Eissfeldt's suggestion that the conception of God as a king is borrowed from Canaanite culture by popular Israelite religion; this popular use explains its occurrences in poetry, whereas the prophets avoid it because of its Canaanite origins. Gray adds that the preexilic prophets, as early as the eighth century, modify the popular conception of God's kingship by emphasizing the element of cosmic warfare (as in the concept of the day of YHWH). Thus, they replace the Canaanite foundations with clearly Israelite ideas taken from the salva-

---

98. Buber, *Kingship of God*, 99–107.

99. See Alt, "Gedanken über das Königtum Jahwes"; Eissfeldt, "Jahwe als König"; and Seybold, "מֶלֶךְ *melek*," 368. This scholarly perspective is also accepted by Mettinger, "Study of the *Gottesbild*," 139–40; see the discussion of the work of John Gray later in this section.

100. Eissfeldt, "Jahwe als König."

101. Eichrodt, *Theology of the Old Testament*, 1.194–202.

102. See Gray's "Hebrew Conception"; "Kingship of God"; and *Biblical Doctrine of the Reign of God*.

tion history. The traditions of the covenant with and election of Israel, the centrality of Jerusalem, and the preeminence of the house of David hold a central place in the prophetic message and push aside the idea of divine kingship.[103] Gray emphasizes the difference between the perspectives of the prophets Jeremiah and Ezekiel and those of contemporary popular circles in Jerusalem. In his opinion, Jeremiah's opposition to the Molech worship in the Ben-hinnom Valley (7:30–34; 32:35) demonstrates that the prophet lobbied vigorously against conceptions of God as king and that his origins in Anathoth lead Jeremiah to emphasize salvation traditions.[104] Gray contrasts Jeremiah's outlook with that found in the book of Ezekiel, where he identifies a more developed expression of the conception of God as king (Ezek 1–3; 8–11; 43), as well as Canaanite foundations for the conception of God's kingship in the prophecy of the war of God against Gog (Ezek 38–39); but he nevertheless argues that the conception of the covenant fills the primary role in that prophet's message as well.[105]

Hebrew Bible academic research on the *metaphor* of God as king blossomed in the 1980s.[106] Tryggve Mettinger defines this metaphor as a "root metaphor"; that is, one that sustains a network of metaphors that supply ideas associated with one another and that influence the general shaping of the image of God in biblical thought. As a root metaphor, God's kingship reflects a key concept in the thought-world of the Hebrew Bible, and thus it is possible to learn from it about conceptions of God in themselves.[107] Examining the Canaanite background of this metaphor in the Hebrew Bible,

103. Gray, *Biblical Doctrine of the Reign of God*, 117–57.

104. According to Gray ("Kingship of God," 20), the exceptional prophecy in Jer 10 is the sole evidence for the assumption that Jeremiah even knew the Canaanite tradition.

105. Gray, *Biblical Doctrine of the Reign of God*, 158–60. Gray further explains the relatively frequent use of this conception in Second Isaiah as a borrowing of the hymnic pattern found in the Psalms (160–81).

106. There are only a few discussions or comments on the metaphoric character of phrases concerning divine kingship earlier than the 1980s; see Johnson, *Sacral Kingship in Ancient Israel*, 233. See Brettler's explanation of this scholarly restraint (*God Is King*, 26–28). The metaphoric treatment of divine rulership in Mesopotamian religion is suggested by Jacobsen, *Treasure of Darkness*, 75–91 (see p. 131 n. 7 above).

107. Mettinger, *In Search of God*, 92–122; and "Fighting the Powers of Chaos." However, in his later studies on iconography in the Hebrew Bible and in extrabiblical sources, Mettinger is careful not to propose a fully analogical connection between the symbol and the object. Mettinger borrows the term "root metaphor" from the American philosopher Stephen Pepper (*World Hypotheses*, 84–114), who applies it to the metaphor of God as king in the Hebrew Bible; see Mettinger, *In Search of God*, 92–93; and Mettinger, "Study of the *Gottesbild*," 138–40.

Mettinger identifies two facets borrowed from descriptions of the deities El and Baal and applied to the image of YHWH, which point to two of God's main roles: God as sovereign is borrowed from the image of El, and God as warrior is taken from the image of Baal.[108]

Marc Brettler investigates the metaphor of God as king on the basis of similarities and differences between a human king and God. He addresses the similarity in both the epithets and secondary metaphors used for each, which suggest parallels in characteristics, in symbols of rulership, and in the roles of the human king and of God within the domestic-political sphere.[109] In all instances, he finds that the metaphor of God as king presents God as superior to any king, since none of the human weaknesses are ever attributed to him. In this way, the metaphor is maximally extended, such that the statement that *God* is a king implies that God is much more than a king.[110] Brettler differentiates metaphorical depiction from literal language, distinguishing them by two types of statements: "God is not *really* a . . ." (shepherd, in Brettler's example) and "God is *like* a . . ." (shepherd).[111] This difference between the *real* and the *like* allows the biblical writer to retain God's incomparability, presenting God as the ultimate paradigm, significantly different from the human pattern invoked in the metaphor.[112] Another highly important observation by Brettler concerns the vitality of the metaphor. In reference to the "associated commonplaces" of a basic metaphor, Brettler points out that "metaphor in the broad sense functions as a storehouse of entailments, only some of which will be adduced in particular contexts as appropriate."[113] That is, the biblical authors could pick from a multiplicity of descriptors associated with a basic metaphor in order to address a given rhetorical situation. Indeed, this "storehouse of entailments" is certainly not exhausted in Brettler's own discussion of

---

108. Mettinger, "Study of the *Gottesbild*," 139–40.

109. Brettler, *God Is King*, 26. The "domestic affairs" that Brettler discusses are the approach to the king and to the royal court, royal personnel, the king as judge, the king as builder, and the king as head of the royal treasury (89–124).

110. Brettler, *God Is King*, 162–64.

111. Brettler, "Metaphorical Mapping of God," 222.

112. Brettler, "Metaphorical Mapping of God," 222–25.

113. Brettler, "Metaphorical Mapping of God," 228, but see also 222, 224. To quote Brettler again: "If a metaphor is alive, the author gives it *particular* meaning by using it in a *particular* way in a *particular* context" (223). Suggesting a more general methodological path, Brettler calls for what he admits to be "a large-scale project" of "metaphorical mapping of God" (225) and sets out some of the complexities this initiative would set before the adventurous scholar (225–29).

the metaphor of God as king. He is very brief in his discussion of the role of God as judge and refrains altogether from addressing the roles of God as ruler and warrior.[114]

For at least two reasons, there is a need to further advance the reevaluation of the conception of divine kingship through the investigation of the metaphor of God as king. First, as a follow-up on the studies of Mettinger and Brettler, it is appropriate to further investigate the gap between the avoidance of the use of the root *mlk* and a whole range of metaphorical representations of God as king in the Hebrew Bible in general and in sixth-century sources in particular; this broader range is based on the two other components of this metaphor: symbols of governance and descriptions of God's actions and deeds—categories (b) and (c) in §5.4. It may indeed be possible to explain the infrequent use of the root *mlk* for God as a deliberate avoidance of the epithet "king" because of proximity to Canaanite religions. However, the small number of occurrences of this root cannot measure the extent to which this metaphor and accordingly the conception are used in Hebrew Bible compositions and certainly should not limit our recognition of this metaphor in other forms. Second, in contrast to the sociological distinctions made by earlier scholars (Eissfeldt, Eichrodt, and Gray, among others) it appears that all speakers in the sixth-century sources discussed in the current study, be they poets, priests, prophets, historiographers, or laypeople, frequently portray God as king.

The metaphor of God as king is the major metaphor for God, shared by all voices within Judean communities during the period of destruction and its aftermath. The metaphor is given wide expression specifically in relation to the symbols of sovereignty and particularly in descriptions of God's major roles as warrior, judge, and sovereign over his people within a covenant framework. Moreover, the interest in God's status as a national deity and in the maintenance of the covenant is not exclusive to the prophets. This is a central topic in the thought of the period, common to prophets and poets alike.

To further establish that the metaphor and the concept of God as king are cardinal and shared by all speakers, it is thus appropriate to examine the characteristic expressions of this anthropomorphic metaphor and its contribution to the formation of the conception of God as king, first within the communal laments and then within Jeremiah and Ezekiel.

---

114. As explicitly mentioned, Brettler, *God Is King*, 89. In "Images of YHWH," Brettler addresses the metaphor of God as warrior through a limited investigation of Pss 3, 46, 83, 144.

5.4.3. The Metaphor of God as King in Psalms and Lamentations

Seven psalms of praise are defined as "יהוה מלך psalms" (Pss 47, 93, 95–99).[115] These psalms are the point of departure for Gray in claiming the existence of an Israelite conception of God as king in other sources within the Psalms and in prophetic literature.[116] According to Gray, three elements from the Canaanite conception of Baal's kingship enter Israelite religion and are found in these psalms: (1) the fight against the forces of chaos and victory over them, (2) the establishment of world order and announcement of the divine kingship, and (3) the promise of moral order in the world by means of universal justice. The Israelite elements in these psalms include the itemization of the wonders and acts of God in the history of Israel from the exodus through the settlement of the land[117] and the emphasis on the supremacy of God over all other gods.[118] The integration of clearly Israelite components in almost every one of those psalms illustrates the unique development of the Israelite faith as it adapts the Canaanite view. Such mixture of components is also found beyond the framework of the יהוה מלך psalms—in other psalms of praise,[119] in psalms of Zion,[120] and in individual and communal laments.[121]

Thus, five of the communal laments that allude to the destruction (Pss

115. Mowinckel (*Psalmenstudien*, 2.6) explains the repeated formula יהוה מלך as a reannouncement of God's becoming king, of his enthronement; thus, he translates the expression "Jahwe ist (jetzt) König geworden"; and so also Weiser, *Psalms*, 617. Compare Eissfeldt ("Jahwe als König," 189), who translates it exactly with the phrase rejected by Mowinckel: "Jahwe ist König"; followed by Kraus, *Psalms 1–59*, 45–46.

116. Gray, "Kingship of God."

117. Gray ("Kingship of God," 7, 13) shows that elements of the history of salvation are taken into these psalms and received special emphasis in their new contexts. This becomes for Gray a major distinction between the kingship of God in Psalms and the appearance of this idea in the prophets.

118. For elements of praise in the יהוה מלך psalms, see Pss 47:3–4; 93:4; 96:4–5; 97:7 and note the epithet עליון (47:3; 97:9).

119. Pss 24, 29, 104. See Weiser (*Psalms*, 52–66) for the list of common roles associated with the kingship of God, including creator, universal sovereign, warrior-savior, judge, etc.

120. In the seven Zion psalms (46, 48, 76, 84, 87, 122, 132) the following motifs recur: God is king in Zion (48:3; 84:4); the city (Jerusalem) is his city and dwelling place (46:5; 48:2; 76:3; 84:8; 87:2; 122; 132:13–14); God fights the nations as savior of his city and people (46:2, 8, 12; 48:5–8; 76:4–8; 87:4 in creation; 132:17–18); God is judge (76:10). See Kraus, *Psalms 1–59*, 58.

121. The motifs associated with the conception of divine kingship within individual

9–10, 44, 74, 89), together with the hymn in Ps 103, share features connected with the metaphor of God as king:

a. the epithet מלך (10:16; 44:5; 74:12; 89:19; 103:19)
b. symbols of governance: God sits on a throne (9:8; 89:15), he resides in Zion (9:12; 74:2) where his temple stands (74:7), and he has servants in his heavenly abode (89:6–8; 103:20–22)
c. actions and deeds that designate God's kingship: God is the supreme God above all others (89:6–9), creator and sovereign of nature (74:12–17; 89:10–13), ruler of all nations (9:4–13, 16–21; 44:3–4; 89:14–15; 103:19–22), and supreme universal judge (9:9, 20; 10:16–18; 74:19–23; 89:14–15)

In addition, even without the epithet "king," a few components of the primary metaphor of God as king appear sporadically in six additional communal laments: Pss 42–43, 77, 79, 80, 137. In Pss 42–43, God's "place" in Jerusalem functions as a symbol of governance (42:5; 43:3); God plays the role of the national ruler (43:1; also Pss 9–10; 74), a role that can also be inferred from the words of the enemy ("where is your God?" 42:4, 11) and from the pressure exerted by the enemy (42:10; 43:2). In Ps 77 God acts as both a sovereign over gods and the forces of nature (77:14–15, 17–20) and as a national ruler (77:16, 21). In Ps 79 the symbol of governance mentioned is the place of God in his domain, in his sanctuary in Jerusalem (79:1). His role is that of a national sovereign, and his subjects are emphatically termed "his servants" and "his adherents" (חסידיו, 79:2, 10), "his nation" and "his flock" (עמו וצאן מרעיתו, 79:13). Again, this same role is implied in the question asked by the nations: "Where is their God?" (79:10). God also plays a role as a warrior, "the God of our salvation" (79:9), and he is called upon to save his people (79:6, 9–13), to act "as befits Your great strength" (כגדל זרועך, 79:11–12). Psalm 80 features a plethora of leadership roles. In 80:5 God acts as a national ruler, responsible for his nation's establishment and well-being in the land (80:9–12); he is called "the shepherd of Israel" who "leads Joseph like sheep" (80:2); he is a world leader "enthroned on the cherubim" (ישב הכרובים, 80:2); he expels the nations from the land in order to plant his nation in their stead (80:9). God as a warrior is called upon to save his people by his might (80:3). The complaint against God

---

laments are presented by Gray (*Biblical Doctrine of the Reign of God*, 85); for the elements of praise within individual laments, see Weiser, *Psalms*, 66, 68–83.

recalls that he helps the enemy, acting as an enemy of his people (80:13, 17). In Ps 137 God is called upon to wage battle on behalf of his people, against the Babylonians (137:7–9), as a national ruler and warrior. His actions bring appropriate retribution against his people's enemies, which in turn derives from his role as judge (137:8).

On the basis of these three components (divine epithet, symbols of governance, and God's actions and deeds), the complete linguistic inventory of the metaphor of God as king appears to be broader than the parallels to Canaanite conceptions adduced by Gray.[122] Furthermore, in three characteristics these communal laments (and Ps 103) differ from the יהוה מלך psalms:

1. Four of the psalms focus explicitly on the status of God as sovereign of the covenant (44, 74, 89, and 103; 95:7 only an implicit reference to this feature).[123]
2. Both the יהוה מלך psalms and communal laments use the image of God as warrior who saves his people from their enemies (e.g., 44:2–9); but it is only within the communal laments that God is further described as an enemy who fights against his *own* people (89:39–46) or delivers them into the hands of their enemies (44:10–17; 80:13, 17).
3. In distinction from the יהוה מלך psalms, where God's status as a universal judge is highlighted, in the communal laments of Pss 9–10, 74, 89, 103 judgment is a factor within the struggle between Israel and the nations (its enemies), and the people's judgment is delivered as in a courtroom action (103:6–13, esp. 103:10).

The common denominator in these laments, which are presumably from the time of the destruction, is the focus upon the role of YHWH as a national God. For each of the three functions—sovereign, warrior, and judge—his role is integrated into two circles, one nested in the other. The

122. Pss 9–10, for instance, do not accord with Gray's observations, as they do not allude to the struggle with chaotic forces at all, the feature that Gray emphasizes as characterizing the Canaanite myth ("Kingship of God," 4). Nevertheless, the metaphor of God as king is still the major metaphor within these psalms.

123. In five of the יהוה מלך psalms God is portrayed as a national sovereign (Pss 47, 95, 97, 98, 99). God is the shepherd of his flock/people (95:7–11), the one God of his people (97:7–8), the king establishing מישרים as also משפט וצדקה ביעקב (99:4, 6–7; see Weinfeld, *Justice and Righteousness*, 12–25), and the warrior who fights his people's wars (47:3–5; 98:1–3).

inner circle relates to his role as the national God, and the outer, broader circle pertains to his role as universal God. As a sovereign, God is the universal ruler, creator of the universe, but there is a special place set aside for his role as national God of Israel. As a warrior, he acts in both the national and universal spheres as the savior of his people from foreign enemies, but he is also portrayed in battle against his own people, the head of the enemy armies arrayed against Jerusalem. Finally, as a judge in the global context, he is the protector of the poor and downtrodden, and in this capacity he adjudicates on behalf of his people against the nations that oppress it. At the national level, his people's distress is explained as resulting from the verdict of God the judge against his people on the basis of the quality of justice. Therefore, all of the actions of God in both aspects, on behalf of his nation and against it, are described by means of the metaphor of God as king.

The components of the metaphor of God as king in the five communal laments (Pss 9–10, 44, 74, 89), in the thanksgiving hymn (103), and in isolated parts of six additional psalms (42–43, 77, 79, 80, 137) serve as an inventory for the components of the metaphor of God as king in the poetic compositions that can be dated to the sixth century. This metaphor serves the needs of the psalmists, who react to the roles played by God in the events of the destruction and the exiles. Moreover, these metaphoric components in psalmodic poetry are similar to those in the books of Jeremiah and Ezekiel.

5.4.4. The Metaphor of God as King in Jeremiah and Ezekiel

In both prophetic books, the description of God through the primary functions of the king in his actions and deeds as sovereign, warrior, and judge (c) is significantly more prevalent than the two other components of this metaphor: (a) the occurrences of the root *mlk* and (b) the symbols of governance. Chapters 6–12 of this study give full presentations of each of these elements. At this point, I make a few preliminary observations on the occurrences of the epithet מלך and expressions using symbols of governance in each of the two books.

a.   The epithet מלך

The rarity of the root *mlk* with YHWH in Jeremiah and Ezekiel is quite similar to that which is found in the other prophetic books, and in both books it is possible to establish the authenticity of the use of this root as part of the prophet's own repertoire.

The only appearance of *mlk* in the book of Ezekiel is in the disputation speech in 20:1–38. Here, the prophet refutes a quotation statement by the exiles (נהיה כגוים כמשפחות הארצות לשרת עץ ואבן, "we will be like the nations, like the families of the lands, worshiping wood and stone"), who desperately ask whether exile designates an end to their national-religious existence, such that would bring assimilation within the nations (20:32).[124] The refutation is formed as an oath: "As I live—declares YHWH God—I will reign over you [אמלוך עליכם] with a strong hand, and with an outstretched arm, and with overflowing fury" (20:33). The use of the verb מלך is integral to Ezekiel's counterargument (20:32–44), which comprises a declaration of YHWH's relationship to the Babylonian exiles. The description of God's kingship corresponds to the three functions. As sovereign, God will obligate the people anew in מסרת הברית ("and I will bring you into the bond of the covenant," 20:37). As warrior, God overpowers his people with his strong hand and outstretched arm, by which he will bring them forth from their places in exile to the desert and ultimately to the land of Israel (20:34–38). The redemption from the foreign lands is described by means of clear allusions to the exodus tradition, especially to the period of wandering in the desert, and illustrates the universal power of God. Finally, God will act as a judge of his people in the "wilderness of the peoples" and will sort out from their midst those who are unfaithful to him (20:38).[125]

Of the six occurrences of the root *mlk* for God in the book of Jeremiah, the epithet occurs once in a citation attributed to the people: "Hark! The outcry of my poor people from the land far and wide: 'Is not YHWH in Zion? Is not her King within her? Why then (did they anger Me with their images, with alien futilities?) Harvest is past, summer is gone, but we have not been saved'" (8:19–20; see §7.2). God's presence in Zion raises the expectation of divine salvation, and thus the deteriorating situation broadens the scope of the people's protest from questioning God's fulfillment of his role as warrior-savior to the question of his presence in Zion at all.

The other five occurrences of מלך as an epithet for God are within the prophet's proclamations: the phrases מלך הגוים and מלך עולם (10:7,

---

124. For a full discussion of Ezek 20:1–38, see Rom-Shiloni, *Exclusive Inclusivity*, 156–62.

125. See Hoffman, *Doctrine of the Exodus*, 57–60.

10) and the epithet within the repeated formula נאם־המלך יהוה צבאות
שמו (PAN Jer 46:18; 48:15; 51:57), which occurs in three of the prophecies
against the nations.[126] All these occurrences are considered inauthentic.
The initial argument against their authenticity is textual. Jeremiah 10:6–8,
10 is not represented in the Septuagint (or in 4QJer[b]); and in the Septuagint versions of two prophecies against the nations, the epithet מלך does
not occur (46:18 LXX and 48:15 LXX), which leaves 51:57 as the only occurrence of this epithet in Septuagint Jeremiah.[127] The second argument is
literary: because of similarities to Second Isaiah, the formula יהוה צבאות
שמו is supposed to have been borrowed from Second Isaiah by followers/
editors of Jeremiah.[128] In this way, scholars discount even further the occurrences of this divine epithet and consider it a non-Jeremian theological
conception. It seems, however, that both the data and the conclusions
gathered from it need reevaluation.

The formula יהוה צבאות שמו occurs twelve times in the Hebrew Bible,
four in Second Isaiah and eight in Jeremiah;[129] within Jeremiah the formula occurs in four different contexts, whereas the occurrences in Isaiah
function in only two.[130] These diverse contexts show that this formula is

126. Janzen, *Studies in the Text of Jeremiah*, 121, 132; and Tov, "Jeremiah Scrolls from
Qumran."

127. The Septuagint equivalent of Jer 46:18 MT is 26:18, and its phrase ζῶ ἐγώ,
λέγει κύριος ὁ θεός misses the equivalents to מלך, שמו, and צבאות. Janzen considers
Masoretic phrases to be secondary elaborations (*Studies in the Text of Jeremiah*, 78, 216
and n22). He is followed by Holladay, *Jeremiah*, 1.324; and McKane, *Jeremiah 26–52*,
1130. The Peshitta has a different word order but the same components: אמר מריא
מלכא צבאות שמה instead of נאם־המלך יהוה צבאות שמו. Holladay (*Jeremiah*, 1.400)
considers 51:57 MT to be a secondary prose elaboration.

128. In Jer 46:18 this formula has a literary-rhetorical function—it opposes God to
pharaoh king of Egypt (46:17); the other two occurrences in the prophecies against the
nations (48:15; 51:57) are presumed to be secondary elaborations in the Masoretic Text
under the influence of this prophecy against Egypt; so Rudolph, *Jeremia*, 273. Cassuto,
in a minority position, suggests that the borrowing went in the opposite direction (from
Jeremiah to Second Isaiah); *Biblical Literature and Canaanite Literature*, 35–51; see also
Holladay, *Jeremiah*, 2.86–88.

129. Second Isa 47:4; 48:2; 51:15; 54:5; Jer 10:16; 31:35; 32:18; 46:18; 48:15; 50:34;
51:19, 57. To these might be added the formulas יהוה אלהי־צבאות שמו, Amos 4:13;
5:27; יהוה שמו, Amos 5:8; 9:6; Exod 15:3; Jer 33:2; and perhaps יהוה זכרו, Hos 12:6.

130. Three of the five contexts in which the formula יהוה צבאות שמו occurs are
words spoken by God: (1) declaring his commitments toward his people in a consolation prophecy (Jer 31:35); and (2) designating his commitment to save his people from
his enemies in consolation prophecies embedded within prophecies against the nations

well anchored in Jeremiah; and there are no good enough arguments to consider it alien to the prophet's (or to his immediate tradents') theological conceptions of God as sovereign of his people, warrior, and creator of the world.[131] Stylistically, this formula modifies the standard prophetic formula נאם־יהוה (46:28; 48:12).[132] Thematically, as is common in the prophecies against the nations, God is portrayed as warrior who fights for his people against the nations (PAN 46:20–21; 48:15–16; 51:53–57). Therefore, the formula נאם־המלך יהוה צבאות שמו refers to the role of God as warrior-savior of his people, using the common epithet צבאות and the unique epithet מלך.[133]

(Jer 50:34; Isa 51:15). (3) In the three prophecies against the nations in Jeremiah, the elaborated prophetic formula (נאם־יהוה) designates either an oath (PAN 46:18) or a divine commitment to the prophecy's validity (48:15; 51:57). The other two contexts in which this formula occurs express human praise: (4) Three times at the closing of a passage of praise, Jeremiah uses this formula to proclaim the uniqueness of God, the Lord of Israel (10:16; 32:18; PAN 51:19). The formula appears in a similar context at the end of the doxologies in Amos (4:13; 5:8, 27; 9:6) and in the corrupted text in Jer 32:2. (5) Second Isaiah uses the phrase יהוה צבאות שמו in proclamations by the people or the prophet to express assurance of divine salvation (Isa 47:4; 54:5) and to reinforce an oath by the people (48:2).

131. The epithet יהוה צבאות on its own appears quite frequently in the Masoretic Text of Jeremiah—eighty times in the prophet's own words and twice in quotations (26:18; 28:2); the Septuagint expression θεοῦ παντοκράτορος, on the other hand, translates only twelve of those occurrences and twice uses this epithet where there is no Masoretic equivalent (3:19; 49:18). I concur with Rofé ("Name YHWH Ṣĕbā'ôt"), who considers the Masoretic Text reading preferable to that of the Septuagint in this specific example, as also in general. In the literary sphere, the formula יהוה צבאות שמו occurs in Second Isaiah in only two of the five contexts (see previous note), and one of them is actually expanding on the Jeremian formula (Isa 47:4; 54:5). This suggests that the direction of influence runs from Jeremiah to Second Isaiah to Jeremiah, contra Crenshaw, "*YHWH Sᵉba'ot Šemo*," 173–74. Crüsemann (*Studien zur Formgeschichte*, 96) recognizes the uniqueness of this formula in the three prophecies against the nations in Jeremiah, although he judges them to be a late linguistic addition of the editor of the prophecies against the nations in Jeremiah.

132. נאם־יהוה (like כה אמר יהוה) is frequent in the prophetic use of the exilic and postexilic period, and according to Meier (*Speaking of Speaking*, 314) its distribution reflects the prophets' obsessive motivation to present God's words directly and accurately.

133. The authenticity of Jer 10 (including 10:7, 10) is challenged time and again, but the two מלך epithets hardly garner attention (see Holladay, *Jeremiah*, 1.324–30; Carroll, *Jeremiah*, 354–59); compare Margaliot ("Jeremiah x 1–16"), who argues for the prophecy's authenticity and yet discusses God's portrayal as king only very briefly (303–4). These epithets and the entire passage present God as a warrior who, as the cosmic

The epithet מלך appears in three of the eight occurrences of יהוה
צבאות שמו in Jeremiah—thus expressing God's ultimate control as unique
among the gods of the nations, the God who conducts the world orders of
creation and settles human orders, as sovereign of his people who defends
them from their enemies. In all these contexts, God is portrayed acting as
a king, and thus there is no good reason to exclude the epithet מלך from
Jeremiah's linguistic world.

b.   Symbols of governance

The book of Ezekiel describes the divine revelations as "visions of God"
(1:1–3:15; 8:1–11:24; 43:1–7), and the book mentions the following symbols
of governance, as seen in these visions: the divine throne (1:26; 10:1; 43:7)
and the temple, designated as "my temple" (8:6; 9:6), "My holy mountain"
(20:40), "the House" that the כבוד יהוה enters and leaves (9:3; 10:4, 18–19;
43:4; 44:4), the place of "My throne" and "the soles of My feet" (43:7).
God further appoints the prophet as his messenger (2:3–4); and the cult
personnel approach him לפני יהוה (44:3–31). While Ezek 1 does not use the
root *mlk*, God's chariot symbolizes the divine cosmic control by the God-
king, enthroned in a heavenly throne above the firmament (1:26–28).[134]

In the book of Jeremiah, the temple is termed "My house," and it may
be presumed that God is conceived as present there, prior to his announcement of his departure (12:7); in similar fashion God leaves his place in
Shiloh and destroys it (7:12).[135] The "throne of YHWH" appears once in
Jeremiah, in a consolation prophecy (3:14–18).

In addition, Jeremiah refers to the heavenly council (23:18),[136] in which
the legitimate prophet gains a special place and from which the peace

----

sovereign and creator, subdues both nature (10:10a) and humans (10:10b) and whose
position as cosmic sovereign comes from his being its creator (10:11, in Aramaic). מלך
עולם is a *hapax*; a close parallel in style and theme is Ps 10:16.

134. Kaufmann (*Toldot Ha-'Emunah*, 3.543–47 and 488–90) points out the "cos-
mological symbolism" of the divine chariot. This is recognized as "kingly" imagery by
Zimmerli, *Ezekiel*, 1.53. On Ezekiel's use of Mesopotamian iconography in this description, and yet its accordance to Israelite religion, see Greenberg, *Ezekiel 1–20*, 54–59;
and van Wolde, "God Ezekiel Envisions."

135. בית־יהוה is mentioned also in Jer 19:14; 26:9. This is observed as a significant
difference from the Deuteronomistic phrase and conception of the temple as "this
House which bears My name" (7:10, 30; 32:34; 34:15).

136. סוד means "council," as in סוד עמי (Ezek 13:9), סוד מרעים (Ps 64:3), סוד יש׳
רים ועדה (111:1), and so also in reference to the heavenly council: סוד־קדשים (89:8),

prophets are excluded (23:22).[137] Within his fierce polemic against the peace prophets in this passage (23:9–40), Jeremiah seems to get closer to Isaiah son of Amoz's description of the divine council (Isa 6:8–9) and makes use of an explicitly anthropomorphic imagery of God as king.

5.5. SUMMARY

The evidence of the Psalms, the quotations found in Jeremiah and Ezekiel, and the writings of the two prophets and their followers/tradents contravene the sociological distinction drawn by Eichrodt and Gray (among others) between prophetic circles and their priestly or lay audiences, with respect to the use of the metaphor and conception of God as a king. This metaphor constitutes a shared set of images and a pervasive conception that runs through the sixth-century sources. The popular image of God, like that of the poets, is not substantially different from that of the prophets Jeremiah and Ezekiel and their followers/tradents. It appears that all parties share the conceptions of God portrayed mainly (not exclusively) through the metaphor of God as king. The ideological-theological struggles between these groups result from their efforts to bring these shared conceptions and metaphorical conventions to bear in different ways on the catastrophic events of the sixth century.

This metaphor and the conceptual world of God as king serve as the organizing theme of the theological discussion that follows. They are my point of departure from which to locate and distinguish the various voices on the talk to and about God in the selected sources that face or reflect on the sixth-century events. In the biblical literature of this period, God is seen as the king of his people, as a warrior, and also as a judge. However,

---

קהל קדשים (89:6), and עדת־אל (82:1). סוד also means "the word of God and his plan" in Amos 3:7 and Ps 25:14.

137. So Bright, *Jeremiah*, 152; Holladay, *Jeremiah*, 1.634; Carroll, *Jeremiah*, 462–63; and McKane, *Jeremiah 1–25*, 581–82. A vision is mentioned only in Jer 23:18 and 4:23–26. Otherwise Jeremiah receives his prophecies only through audial channels (1:4–10). Thus the Masoretic Text of 23:18 (וירא וישמע את־דברו, "and seen, and heard His word") seems to be harmonistic (compare the Septuagint, which lacks וישמע and is better balanced poetically, with sight in the first stich and hearing in the second). McKane (*Jeremiah 1–25*, 580–81) suggests that וישמע is a corrective gloss for the exceptional phrase (יהוה)ראה דבר־, which otherwise occurs in 2:31 and means "understand," with no connection to a prophetic vision; see also בסוד אלוה שמע (Job 15:8).

God's perceived activity or inactivity in the events surrounding the destruction of Jerusalem leads biblical authors to push the limits of the conventional assumptions about the God-people relationship that undergird this metaphorical thought-world. Expressions of doubt about or protest against God's deeds and misdeeds, as well as justifications of his actions, provide an entry point into the entire spectrum of theological topics, into the use and the transformations within this metaphorical field, and, not least, into the disagreements raised in reaction to this national crisis.

6

God as Warrior

The overwhelming political and military defeat of the kingdom of Judah, the destruction of Jerusalem and, above all, the demolition of God's temple, give rise to a cluster of questions concerning the role of God and the role of human beings in these events. This chapter lays out the fundamental conceptions of God's role in war as shared by all voices/sources; chapters 7–9 discuss the different theological perceptions of the events of the war within this framework.

6.1. Divine and Human Roles in War:
The Victory and the Defeat

The use of human metaphors to describe God's roles as sovereign and warrior (e.g., as the head of the army in Isa 13:4) makes clear that God's role as warrior is subordinate to that of his kingship, a means of realizing God's sovereignty over his people and the world.

In his persona as ruler, God the warrior acts in one of two ways: as a savior who brings victory or as an enemy who generates calamity.[1] God's

---

1. The idea of God as savior is commonly examined within the framework of either a historical or a mythological conception of war in the Hebrew Bible. In both frameworks, scholars deal with the place of war in the cult. For studies that focus on the historical conception of war, see Schwally (*Der heilige Krieg*, 1–3) and von Rad (*Holy War*, 52–73), who argues that the tribal federation (the amphictyony) is the setting in which the theological conception of war takes root. In contradistinction, Smend (*Yahweh War and Tribal Confederation*, 109–19) attributes this development to the tribes of Rachel. See also Stolz (*Jahwes und Israels Kriege*), who investigates God's involvement in the wars of Israel from the desert wanderings until the salvation from Sennacherib

involvement in war as savior of his people is celebrated in the Hebrew Bible, recurring in the historiography, the prophecy, and the psalmodic literatures (e.g., Judg 4–5; Ps 96:2; Deut 33:29). Accordingly, scholars thoroughly discuss God's powers of deliverance and concentrate on his salvific deeds. The biblical emphasis on praise of God as savior causes scholars as early as Friedrich Schwally to focus on only that side of the biblical representation of war. Subsequently, Gerhard von Rad builds his entire Old Testament theology on the idea of God's relationship with his people as constructed within a framework of "salvation history."[2] Biblical perceptions of the role of God in the people's defeat, the negative side of military confrontation, are almost unnoticed in the many studies dedicated to God's role in war.[3] Study of the theological reflections on Judah's

in 2 Kgs 18 (in a similar vein, see Talmon, "YHWH's Wars"). For comparative studies, see Weippert ("Heiliger Krieg") and Kang (*Divine War*), who explores the historical context of the concept of "holy war" in Mesopotamia, Anatolia, Syro-Palestine, and Egypt, before examining the biblical sources from the exodus down to David's wars. The mythological conception of war in the Hebrew Bible is illuminated by Cross (*Canaanite Myth and Hebrew Epic*, 91–111) and Miller (*Divine Warrior*, 166–75), who focus their attention on similarities between the Hebrew Bible and Canaanite mythology. According to Mettinger ("Fighting the Powers of Chaos," 22–29), the mythical conception fulfills a central function in the shaping of the war motif in the theology of Zion and the cultic tradition of Jerusalem.

2. See von Rad, *Old Testament Theology*, 1.105–15; von Rad, *Holy War*, 74–93; and Craigie, *Problem of War*, 38–40. Compare Eichrodt (*Theology of the Old Testament*, 1.228–32), who argues that salvation is only one aspect of God's activity as warrior; as king of his people he can act in favor, but also against, his own people. This idea is clearly closer to the Hebrew Bible evidence.

3. References to God's role as an enemy of his own people are rarely presented and at best receive minimal attention. Fredriksson (*Jahwe als Krieger*, 92–94) mentions the portrayals of God as conqueror in Lam 2 and Amos; von Rad (*Holy War*, 108–14) notes this only in his discussion of Amos 2:14–16. Von Rad's survey of the concept of holy war in the prophets is restricted to passages in Micah, Ezek 38, Haggai, and Zechariah detailing God's acts of salvation. He does not pay attention to conceptions of war in Jeremiah or Ezekiel, specifically the passages dealing with defeat. Lind, on the other hand (*Yahweh Is a Warrior*, 109–13), discusses briefly the "theology of defeat"; and Craigie (*Problem of War*, 75–79) devotes five pages to the "meaning of defeat in battle" and remarks that God's involvement in war is part of the description of the worldwide sovereignty of God as king (43). To further illustrate this scholarly Christian bias, see Miller ("God the Warrior"), who struggles with Christian theology that occasionally runs into apologetics over questions such as: "How can the divine Warrior of the Old Testament be reconciled with the God of love so forcefully presented in the New Testament? What kind of God would order the wholesale slaughter of groups of people?" (41). In such a context, studying texts where God is portrayed as the enemy of his own people appears to be far beyond consideration.

destruction requires me to focus on the talk to and about God in times of defeat, when salvation is clearly not in view.

Within both ancient Near Eastern cultures and Israel itself, military-political conflicts are accompanied by theological proclamations—to support the king and his armies, to guarantee victory. Defeats in war are critical events that challenge the conceptions of the national god as warrior in two major areas—the scope of divine activity and the actual power of the god.

6.1.1. *The Sphere of Divine Activity*

From a theological point of view, the arrival of the enemy's army in the land is an international event taking place throughout a wide geographical area that breaches the boundaries of the opposing kingdoms. Such an event requires an explanation. Explanations address the gods'/God's role in spurring the onset of the human enemy or in permitting the enemies' entry into his land; such explanations need to account for either the deity's uncharacteristic actions in or perhaps absence from the human arena.[4] The questions generated by such a defeat relate to the deity's role as the national god, but also to his/her function as the god of human history—the god who propels kings and their armies, who stands behind their political activities, and who may even give victory to his people's enemies.[5]

6.1.2. *Divine Power*

In the religious thought of both Israel and the ancient Near East, the nation's defeat is also the defeat of its god(s), an evidence of the deity's weakness or absence, just as, to the contrary, a military victory expresses the victory of the people's deity over the enemy and their god(s).[6] A blatant example

4. Ideological explanations and theological justifications characterize royal Assyrian inscriptions; Oded, *War, Peace, and Empire*. Note specifically Oded's references to the involvement of Ashur and other Assyrian gods in instructing the king and granting him powers, weapons, etc. (9–28, 83–100).

5. Reports on defeats (or even on a lack of military successes) are for known reasons almost absent from royal Assyrian inscriptions; see Tadmor, "Sennacherib's Campaign to Judah" and *With My Many Chariots*, 653–76; Laato, "Assyrian Propaganda." Nevertheless, we do have limited evidence of theological reflections on defeat, reflecting the Babylonian side, from the Assyrian-Babylonian conflicts of the seventh century; see Gadd, "Inscribed Barrel Cylinder."

6. Albrektson (*History and the Gods*, 53–67) and Saggs (*Encounter with the Divine*, 64–92) show that no substantive difference exists between the biblical conception of God and that of the major deities in Mesopotamian religion with regards to the

of this idea in the Hebrew Bible is the framing of the saving acts of God in Egypt. YHWH's victory is an expression of his greatness and power over other deities (Exod 18:9–11); the struggle is at times presented as God's war against the Egyptian gods, in order to liberate the children of Israel from the hands of their enslavers (12:12).[7] Conversely, in the accounts of the war waged by Assyria against Israel (2 Kgs 18–19; Isa 36–37), the challenging words of the Rabshakeh illustrate the confidence of the Assyrians in their ability to best the gods of the populations they targeted for conquest (2 Kgs 18:33–35; Isa 36:19–20).[8] From the enemy's perspective, the king of Assyria is the representative of the god Ashur, the executer of his battles. So, the Rabshakeh claims (2 Kgs 19:10–13; similarly Isa 37:10–13):

[10] Tell this to King Hezekiah of Judah: Do not let your God, on whom you are relying, mislead you into thinking that Jerusalem will not be delivered into the hands of the king of Assyria. [11] You yourself have heard what the kings of Assyria have done to all the lands, how they have annihilated them; and can you escape? [12] Were the nations that my predecessors destroyed . . . saved by their gods?	[10] כה תאמרון אל־חזקיהו מלך־יהודה לאמר אל־ישאך אלהיך אשר אתה בטח בו לאמר לא תנתן ירושלים ביד מלך אשור. [11] הנה אתה שמעת את אשר עשו מלכי אשור לכל־הארצות להחרימם ואתה תנצל. [12] ההצילו אתם אלהי הגוים אשר שחתו אבותי.

The continuation of the prophetic story in 2 Kings (and in Isaiah) proves God's superiority to these other gods: by way of a miracle, God removes the Assyrian forces from his city. Thus, this is the story of how God, counter to the expectations of the Assyrians (based on their defeat of the

---

involvement of the divine in world history, just as there is no need to categorize such universal perspectives of the divine to late periods.

7. Interestingly, conflicts between Israel and its imperial enemies are more often presented as conflicts between God and the human emperor, not his gods; note the multiple references to conflict between YHWH and the pharaoh (Exod 7:17; 8:6, 18; 9:29–30), with but a few references to battle against the gods of Egypt. The same obtains in passages dealing with Assyria and Babylonia. On the former, note prophetic passages that use royal Assyrian ideology, boasting of the king's victory over other nations and their gods (Isa 10:5–19, esp. 10:9–10; 36:18–20); on the latter, see Jer 27).

8. On this conception of war in Assyrian royal ideology, see Oded, *War, Peace, and Empire*, 13–20. At the same time, it is worth noting that the Rabshakeh makes a claim at odds with this ideology; that is, that the king of Assyria has come against the city as the messenger of the God of Israel (2 Kgs 18:25; Isa 36:10).

other nations and their gods), saves his people from the king of Assyria and even brings about Sennacherib's death (2 Kgs 19:32–36; Isa 37:33–38).[9]

This conception of God's power over enemy kings, and even over the enemy's gods, is further attested in the prophecies against the nations in the book of Jeremiah. The essential expression of the subjugation of Moab and Babylon is God's vanquishing of their gods—Chemosh, Bel, and "the idols of Babylon" (Jer 48:7, 13; 51:44, 47). But when it comes to the God of Israel and to Jerusalem's defeat, historiographers and prophets avoid the language of divine defeat or absence. It is only through a remarkable assertion repeated in quotations in Ezekiel ("for they say, 'The LORD does not see us; the LORD has abandoned the country,'" 8:12; 9:9) and in questions that are put into the mouths of Israel's enemies ("where is your/ their God?," Pss 42:4, 11; 79:10; 115:2) that we know that the God of Israel did not escape troubling challenges to divine power and presence. These quotations convey the idea that the catastrophic circumstances of subjugation, defeat, and exile testify to God's weakness, to his absence, or to his dissociation from his people, in the land or in exile, before and after the destruction.

The theological deliberations I discuss in chapters 6–9 use the imagery of God as warrior (and traditional assumptions associated with that image) to try to understand the events and aftermath of the Babylonian invasion, siege, and capture of Jerusalem and Judah. The use and transformations of this imagery by a variety of speakers illustrate the wide range of perspectives on God's role in these events from justification of God's perceived actions to doubt as to God's power to save or even to his continuing presence with his people, and to protest against God's disinvolvement and lack of salvation.

At the heart of the theological discourse stands the constant tension between the divine involvement in war and human actions (of both the people and the enemy). While all parties agree—historiographers, prophets, poets, and people—that the Babylonians and their subservient allies fought against Judah, all parties likewise perceive that the defeat, the destruction, and the exiles are primarily acts of YHWH (or at least as acts in which

9. This version of the prophetic story of Sennacherib's campaign combines two different historical events—the military campaign of 701 and the death of the Assyrian king, which took place twenty years later in 681—in order to illustrate the confirmation of Isaiah's prophecy. For the genre of "prophetic story" and its structure in its two versions (or as a single story that is supplemented secondarily), see Rofé, *Prophetical Stories*, 78–83; and Cogan and Tadmor, *II Kings*, 240–44.

YHWH is involved or from which deliverance is expected). Nonetheless, no unity of thought exists concerning the part that God plays in comparison to that played by the human enemies in bringing about these crises.

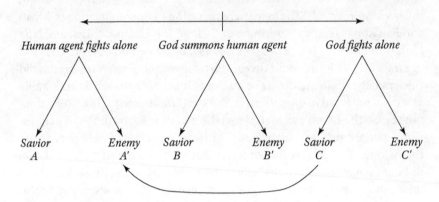

Fig. 6.1. **God and human roles in war: seven options for victory and defeat**

Figure 6.1 represents the entire theological spectrum of perspectives that links the actions of God and of human beings in war. At the center of the continuum is the perspective that harmonizes the historical event of human armies on the battlefield and the theological interpretation that it receives. God as warrior summons the armies of the people and their enemies and is responsible for their activity. However, at the two ends of the continuum, emphasis is given to only one plane of activity—the human or the divine. At each of these three points, God or human agents may function as either saviors or enemies, thus advancing deliverance (A, B, C) or destruction (A′, B′, C′), and occasionally complaining of a human enemy's threat from which God is called to save his people (A′ → C). While developed for the study of sixth-century sources, this diagram is valid for all reflections on war in the Hebrew Bible and helps to illustrate perceptions in both victory and defeat.

6.2. EXPLANATIONS FOR VICTORY IN WAR

(A)   A human hero/king acts alone.

The concept of victory due to human heroism, strategic brilliance, and courage appears in a relatively limited number of biblical descriptions of victory. Heroic deeds are related in short anecdotes, such as those that tell us about David's heroes (2 Sam 21:15-22; 23:8-23), as well as in some epic poetry, such as the Song of Lamech (Gen 4:23-24), the fragmented victory song over Benjamin (Judg 20:43, MT), and David's lamentation over Saul and Jonathan (2 Sam 1).[10] God's participation is not mentioned at all, and certainly is not a primary component, in these "stories of the heroes," the purpose of which is to glorify the human warrior.[11]

> *(B)   YHWH appoints a savior for Israel (and assists him).*

The human savior acts in battle by means of divine empowerment, and even though the stories articulate the hero's courage, war strategies, and decision-making powers, victory would not have been attained without divine intervention.[12] According to this perspective, which is widespread throughout Hebrew Bible literature (and likewise in ancient Near Eastern sources), the human deeds are intertwined with divine support or even with God's own critical actions, alongside the fighting forces and as their

---

10. On the other hand, in the Song of Deborah, the role of YHWH is fused together with the role of the human heroes (Judg 5:23). The independent status of this explanation of victory may be learned, for instance, from the alternate stories concerning the victory over Sihon: in Num 21:21-26, the people are responsible for the victory, while in Deut 2:26-37 success is said to have come from God.

11. Seeligmann ("Human Heroism," 74-75) claims that this solely human focus is original; only as a result of a secondary literary development is God's involvement added. In his opinion, the traditions about David's heroes are closest to the heroic traditions of other nations, while 1 Sam 19:4-5; 14:45; 2 Sam 23:2 are remnants of human savior traditions to which God's salvation is secondarily added. Human saving acts appear in the list of Saul's wars (1 Sam 14:46-48) and, in an expanded fashion, in the stories of the judges, such as those that venerate Ehud's cleverness (Judg 3:15-16; see 20:16) or Samson's tactics and might. Specific stories relate human saving acts to Othniel (3:10-11), Ehud (3:29-30), Gideon (8:28), and Tola son of Puah (10:1). However, in these last stories, statements that accentuate divine intervention are interwoven into the hero stories, creating a perception of "double causality." Such elements include the spirit of YHWH (which falls upon the hero; 11:29), YHWH's role in raising up the human savior (e.g., Ehud in 3:15 and Othniel in 3:9). These descriptions are closer to the center of the continuum.

12. "YHWH raised a champion" in Judg 3:9, 15; 1 Sam 9:16; 2 Sam 8:14; 10:9-12; 2 Kgs 13:5; Neh 9:27. See also Deut 7:21 and 9:3.

leader.[13] Sometimes, historical events are explained on the basis of "double causality," that is, as a result of both human and divine activity.[14]

(C) YHWH fights alone against the enemy.

YHWH's singlehanded activity is expressed by the absence of any description of human action in the war between Israel and its enemies. Relatively few examples are found of this third mode, which depicts the saving act of God while the people passively stand and observe (e.g., Exod 14:14, 30–31). Only after the victory do soldiers join in, to pursue those who are trying to escape (Judg 7:23–25) or to take booty (2 Chr 20:25).[15]

This threefold model of divine/human participation in war develops, expands, and significantly modifies models proposed by distinguished scholars on Hebrew Bible ideologies of war, beginning with Friedrich Schwally.[16] In his focus on God's involvement in victory, Schwally suggests a diachronic evolution in biblical conceptions of war. In his schema, due

13. This conception corresponds to the ancient Near East ideologies of war; see Kang, *Divine War*, 108–10; and Oded, *War, Peace, and Empire*, 13–18. See also ויהך הדד קדמי ("and Hadad went before me"); Tel Dan inscription, line 5; see Lipschitz, "'Beit David' Polemic," 40.

14. Idioms that denote the synergy between YHWH and Israel in war include YHWH marching with the armies and fighting for them (Deut 20:4), going before the armies to fight for them (1:30), marching before the warring armies (Judg 4:14; 2 Sam 5:24), causing the enemy to lie slain before Israel (Josh 11:6), routing the enemy before Israel (Judg 20:35). In like fashion, note the protective function of the ark in passing over the Jordan River (Josh 3:11) and in war (Josh 6; 2 Sam 11:11). Similarly, in prophecy, "the Lord of Hosts is mustering a host for war" (Isa 13:4). See von Rad, *Holy War*, 41–49; and Seeligmann, "Human Heroism," 74–81; and the discussion of Seeligmann on p. 183. Other examples of double causality might be added; e.g., Josh 10:42 (also 10:14; 23:10); 2 Sam 7:14; 1 Kgs 12:15; 2 Kgs 14:27–28.

15. See also Num 10:35–36; 23:21–22; Josh 10:8–13; 2 Chr 20. Descriptions in which God's actions take on a cosmic aspect appear in Deut 33:2–3; Judg 5:4–5; Hab 3:3–6; Ps 68:18. Second Isaiah describes the impression of YHWH's acting alone in war, upon "all flesh" (40:3–6; 52:7–12).

16. Schwally, *Der Heilige Krieg*, 1–3. The term "holy war" does not occur in the Hebrew Bible. Schwally borrows it from the *jihad* of Islam. The closest biblical term would be מלחמות יהוה (1 Sam 18:17; 25:28; Num 21:14). Von Rad uses "holy war" and is criticized by Smend, *Yahweh War and Tribal Confederation*, 26–42; Stolz, *Jahwes und Israels Kriege*, 9–16; Weippert, "Heiliger Krieg," 483–93; and Kang, *Divine War*, 1–7; see further Ollenburger's introduction to von Rad, *Holy War*, 22–33. Miller ("God the Warrior") accepts von Rad's perspectives on holy war and discusses this term in relation to Christian faith.

to developments in piety and the increasing wish to praise God as warrior, late historiography elaborates on divine deeds and minimizes the role of human forces, so as to lay stress on the divine role in war.[17] These evolving lines of religious thought are further elaborated by Gerhard von Rad, who notes the distinction between sources in which God summons the enemy and those in which God acts alone.[18] Von Rad also argues for a diachronic development from the synergistic descriptions to those of YHWH acting alone, noting that the latter develops in prophetic circles. However, von Rad does not expand on this divergence, nor does he entertain the third possibility: the human being as the sole hero—conception (A).[19]

Isaac Seeligmann is the first to articulate this three-part paradigm for the relationship between human heroism and divine salvation in historiographic compositions and prophetic literature.[20] In considering the interrelationships between the three modes of action, Seeligmann adapts the evolutionary model, and he does not consider the issue of divine and human roles in defeat.[21] He explains the three ways of depicting victory in the Hebrew Bible as the results of a process of diachronic development in historiosophic thinking. Even though they appear more than once side by side, these three ways reflect different layers in the stories' crystallization. Seeligmann holds that "the stories of the heroes" are remnants of national folktales or of ancient historiosophy, while the two other ways represent more developed theological-historiosophic thinking.

The need to significantly modify these earlier models arises from two observations. First, limiting the discussion of God's roles in war to occasions of victory allows but a partial presentation of the Hebrew Bible evidence;

---

17. Schwally, *Der Heilige Krieg*, 108–11.

18. Von Rad, *Holy War*, 41–52; and similarly Seeligmann, "Human Heroism." Compare the unique and at that time different position of Fredriksson (*Jahwe als Krieger*, 107–9), who focuses on the portrayal of God as warrior, differentiating between two modes: "Jahwe als Heerführer" and "Jahwe als Einzelkämpfer." In the first mode, God as king operates as the head of the people's armies. In this context, Fredriksson notes (78–79, 110–11) that God could also activate the kings of foreign peoples against Israel (as in Isa 10:5–6), just as he could use forces of nature and cosmic powers. In the second mode of action, God acts alone. Fredriksson considers this mode to occur relatively rarely, confined to descriptions of God fighting the forces of chaos (*Chaoskampfe*).

19. Von Rad, *Holy War*, 94–114.

20. Seeligmann, "Human Heroism," 81.

21. This diachronic evolutionary model characterizes most discussions on the ideologies of war in the Hebrew Bible. See, among others, Niditch, *War in the Hebrew Bible*, 134–49.

the model is clearly ill fitted to reflections on events of defeat. Second, the paradigm of diachronic evolution from conceptions of human heroism to divine salvation does not fit the biblical evidence of responses to the destruction. In explanations for the Babylonian destruction of Jerusalem, the three theological modes appear synchronically, used by different contemporary speakers; they diverge thematically one from the other, but there are interconnections between them that clarify that such a diachronic distinction is unfounded. The three modes of conceptualizing the divine-human equation in defeat are mirror images of the three mode for reflecting on victory.

6.3. Explanations for Defeat in War

(A')   A human enemy/king initiates war against Israel.

In a parallel to the situation of the human hero who defeats the enemy by his powers alone—conception (A)—a few military crises are portrayed in which the enemy invades Israel or Judah, seemingly without God's involvement, thus designated (A'). For example, two prophecies of Isaiah son of Amoz relate to the military initiative of the enemy: the Syro-Ephraimite war against King Ahaz of Judah (735–733)[22] and Sennacherib's campaign against Hezekiah (701).[23] The prophet does not attribute the wars to God and mentions only the initiatives of the enemy kings (Isa 7:1–2; 36:1; 2 Kgs 18:13). In the former instance, Isaiah gives the cause of the conflict as the political interests of the Syro-Ephraimite coalition (7:5–6). In the latter, according to the account of 2 Kings, Hezekiah's rebellion is the impetus to the Assyrian king's punishment campaign against him (2 Kgs 18:7, 14).

The reactions of both King Hezekiah and the prophet to the Assyrian threat are indicative of the relationship between explanations (A') in events of defeat and (C) in events of victory. As a response to the words of the Rabshakeh, Hezekiah tears his clothes, covers himself with sackcloth, and goes to the house of God, where he subsequently prays for salvation (2 Kgs 19:1–2, 14–19; Isa 37:1–2, 14–20). Additionally, he sends a delegation of high officials and priests to the prophet (2 Kgs 19:2–7; Isa 37:2–7).[24] Not-

22. 2 Kgs 16:5–18; 2 Chr 28:5–25; Isa 7:1; 8:22; cf. 8:23–9:6. For a historical study of the political interests at play here, see Oded, "Historical Background"; see also Thompson's detailed study of the different sources for this war (*Situation and Theology*).

23. 2 Kgs 18–19; Isa 36–39; 2 Chr 32:1–23. See Cogan and Tadmor, *II Kings*, 240–51.

24. The rebellion is positively evaluated in 2 Kgs 18:7, but there is no parallel in Isa

withstanding the significant differences between the responses of kings Ahaz and Hezekiah to these distinct crises (Isa 7:11–12 in comparison with 2 Kgs 19:1–4 and Isa 37:1–4), the prophet Isaiah takes the same position regarding both events in terms of YHWH's role vis-à-vis the external threat:[25] YHWH responds favorably to the king's prayer and will act categorically as savior of the people, the king, and the city from the hands of their enemy, event (C) (Isa 7:3–9; 37:6–7, 21; 2 Kgs 19:6–7).[26]

These examples point to a thematic and functional divergence between victory and defeat. In victory, the stories of the heroes depict human war in order to lionize the heroes. In defeat, the stories of the enemies emphasize their brutality and base behavior. The military distress described in these accounts serves as motivation either to seek divine deliverance through prayer or to predict such deliverance through a prophecy of salvation. Thus, while God is not responsible for the (impending) defeat, he is asked to intervene by saving his people from the military crisis in which they are trapped. Consequently, the one who prays or the prophet who prophesies expects that the threat of destruction by this enemy acting without divine support (A') will be transformed into an event of divine salvation and victory (C).

In sources of the sixth century, this line of thought is found in pronouncements of the king and his royal officials, in communal laments, and in prophecies of the peace prophets. Do Jeremiah and Ezekiel consider this option to hold in the contemporary situation (chap. 7)? And if so, where if at all do they give it room in their prophecies (chap. 8)? Hence, the discussion of this theological explanation reveals an issue under debate between the prophets and several groups of their contemporaries.

> (B') *YHWH summons an enemy against Israel (and*
> *assists him/them).*

36–39 to the chronistic information in 2 Kgs 18:13–16 (see Cogan and Tadmor, *II Kings*, 240–41, 246–51).

25. The book of Kings treats the two kings completely differently from how Isaiah son of Amoz presents them. In Kings, Ahaz is depicted as a total sinner (2 Kgs 16:2–4), while Hezekiah is portrayed as obedient to YHWH (18:3–8). See Tadmor, "Ahaz and Tiglath-Pileser"; and Na'aman, "Criticism over Willful Subjugation."

26. Similarly, Isa 37:30–38; 2 Kgs 19:29–37; cf. Deut 33:29. Divine intervention on behalf of the people in the Syro-Ephraimite War appears only as a suggestion (Isa 7:7–9), which Ahaz rejects (7:10–12), while in 2 Kings, Ahaz prefers to rely on the help of the Assyrian king (16:7–9).

In an inversion of mode (B), where YHWH is seen as appointing (and supporting) a savior for his people, he is portrayed in events of defeat as handing his people over to the enemy (B'). The armies of the enemy king are successful only because of God's support for their actions; this support is usually perceived as punishment for the people's disloyalty to God (Deut 32:27–30; Judg 4:2; 6:1). So announces the prophet Isaiah in relation to the Assyrian army (10:5–6); and the same is implied by the Assyrian officer, the Rabshakeh (36:10).

In sources of the sixth century, this line of argumentation is widely used. It serves the historiographers in 2 Kings, the prophets Jeremiah and Ezekiel, and the poets of communal laments (in Psalms, Lamentations, and passages embedded in the prophetic literature); it even appears in anonymous quotations of "the people" cited by the prophets. Hence, almost all speakers use this (B') concept. (Chapter 8 looks at the special distinctions between these speakers.)

(C')   YHWH fights alone against his people.

In contradistinction to the image of God as the sole savior of his people at times of crisis—conception (C)—God is portrayed in events of defeat as the only (or primary) enemy of his people, who acts against them without the involvement of human armies (C'). This radical description appears in a number of examples in classical prophecy of the eighth–seventh centuries.[27]

In sixth-century sources this conception may be found only rarely in poetry (e.g., Lam 2); but it is surely the dominant model in the books of Jeremiah and Ezekiel for the depiction of YHWH's role in the Babylonian destruction and exiles. (Chapter 9 explores the choice made by prophets and poets of this extreme position.)

All three conceptions of divine and human roles in war, and specifically in times of defeat, are used simultaneously, synchronically, in Jerusalem of the early sixth century. They are used by different speakers, who may individually combine two or even all three conceptions. Hence, the traditional scholarly hierarchical or diachronic parameters used to estab-

---

27. Examples of God as his people's enemy appear in Isa 1:24–28; 2:6–22; 9:18–20; figuratively in 5:1–7; 10:33–34 (and Second Isa 42:25); Hos 1:4–5; 4:1–3; 5:14; 8:14; 11:8; 13:7; metaphorically in Hos 2:1–15; Amos 2:5; 3:13–15; 4:6–13; 5:27; 7:9; 8:9–11; as doxology in Hos 4:13; 5:8–9; 9:5–6; Mic 1:2–7, 12; 6:13–16; Zeph 1:1–10, 12–14, 17; Zech 1:2–6; 7:14; 8:14–15; 13:7–9.

lish distinctions between the various sixth-century constituencies do not seem to supply efficient answers for the theological interrelationships between them.

The distinctive characteristics between these three configurations of divine and human roles in events of defeat serve as points of departure for chapters 7–9. Chapter 7 focuses on portrayals of the defeat as the human enemies' initiative (A') from which God is called to save (C), that is, the (A' → C) conception; chapter 8 begins at the midpoint of the continuum (B'), accordingly, as God summons the Babylonian emperor and his troops against his own people and enables their military success; and chapter 9 considers the adaptation of the most radical position, that God himself has acted as Israel's enemy (C').

The challenge for the following discussions is to point out both similarities and distinctions between these three conceptions in order to evaluate the functions they serve for the diverse sixth-century authorial groups. Three arenas—theology, sociology, and function—provide the parameters within which to examine the unique features of each of the three conceptions of defeat in war. Theologically, each of these three conceptions illuminates God's activity and power in the events by means of specific literary and thematic features. Sociologically, each of these conceptions is mobilized by almost all speakers, yet in different measures of use and with distinct emphases. Hence, functionally, these three conceptions each may serve multiple rhetorical purposes, as determined by the different speakers. The multiple functions of these conceptions brings our discussion to the spheres of justification, doubt, and protest. The interplay between these conceptions give us a window into sixth-century theodical discourse, the talk to and about God seeking to fathom God's role in the disaster.

The presentation that follows cannot be exhaustive. I choose only exemplary texts, by which I intend, nevertheless, to give as complete a picture as possible of the rich and highly polemical theological deliberations concerning this major issue: the roles of God and of human beings in the national catastrophe.

6.4. Appendix: Theological Perspectives on Jeremiah 21:1–10

Jeremiah 21:1–10 in conjunction with 37:3–10 further illustrates the contemporaneity of these different theological perceptions of divine and human roles in war (see §1.1.2). These two passages are pivotal for the study of the literary growth of the book of Jeremiah. Attention to the conceptions of God's role(s) in 21:1–10 substantiates the argument that the passage combines two independent prophetic passages (21:1–7 and 21:8–10). The traditional distinction sees 21:1–7 as "redactional-theological" and 37:3–10 as "biographical-historical." The plethora of theological perspectives used simultaneously within Jeremiah requires different solutions to explain these distinct prophetic passages in the book.

Jeremiah 21:1–10 narrates a confrontation between Jeremiah and Zedekiah's officials. The confrontation turns explicitly on the distinct assumptions of the protagonists concerning the roles of YHWH and the Babylonian enemy during a period of actual political and military distress, presumably during the last siege of Jerusalem. Zedekiah, via his officials, requests divine deliverance from the Babylonian enemy (21:2). Their request for divine performance of wonders (עשה נפלאות) reveals their faithfulness in God and communicates their trust in God's ability to rescue them from the current crisis (see §1.1.2). Furthermore, their request illustrates their knowledge of and reliance upon the traditions of Israel's national history, particularly that of the exodus from Egypt. The officials thus use conception (A')—that is, they expect that the actions of the enemy are *not* sanctioned by God, and they present a plea for salvation based on conception (C).

Jeremiah presents the opposite picture: he claims that YHWH is the real enemy of Jerusalem, and he alone will fight against it (21:3–7). The prophet uses the exodus tradition to contradict the officials' assumptions, on the basis of conception (C'). The prophet's polemic against the officials' position is constructed through a combination of literary features in his proclamation of YHWH's answer to them:

1. The prophet responds to the circumstances presented by the officials in their request, that is, "for King Nebuchadrezzar of Babylon is attacking us," by countering that God is their true enemy: "And I Myself will battle against you" (21:5).

2. The prophet inverts the exodus tradition's outstanding expression of divine deliverance, ביד חזקה ובזרוע נטויה (Deut 5:15), into an expression of the power with which God will act *against* his people: ביד נטויה ובזרוע חזקה ("with an outstretched hand and with mighty arm, with anger and rage and great wrath," Jer 21:5).[28]

---

28. The phrase ביד נטויה ובזרוע חזקה in Jer 21:5 is unique; see §1.1.2.

3. The prophet uses verbs (in the first-person) taken from the semantic field of war (21:3–7). Thus, Jeremiah declares that YHWH is the key enemy of Jerusalem and it is he alone who will fight against the city (21:5–6). Nebuchadrezzar, the powerful emperor, and other human enemies are mentioned only subsequently; they will benefit as scavengers and will kill any refugees from "the pestilence, the sword, and the famine" (21:7).

These rhetorical features illustrate the polemic between the prophet and the court officials over the essential question: Will God deliver his people from the Babylonian king? Or, exactly what role is God playing in this situation of military distress? The prophet chooses to respond to the officials' plea for salvation with the most extreme theological response: God is Jerusalem's foe.

Jeremiah 21:8–10, on the other hand, takes yet a different track. While YHWH is seen as ultimately responsible for the destruction, the actual devastation of the city is carried out by the Babylonian king and his army, under divine orders—that is, conception (B'): "For I have set My face against this city for evil and not for good—declares YHWH. It shall be delivered into the hands of the king of Babylon, who will destroy it by fire" (כי שמתי פני בעיר הזאת לרעה ולא לטובה נאם־יהוה ביד־מלך בבל תנתן ושרפה באש, 21:10).

According to the scholarly consensus, 21:1–10 contains two separate prophecies.[29] The arguments for distinguishing 21:8–10 from 21:1–7 are both literary and thematic: (1) in 21:8–10, the words of the prophet are addressed to the people, while in 21:1–7 they are an answer to the king through his offi-

---

29. The common scholarly perception differentiates between the two passages, presuming only one to be authentic. Duhm (*Jeremia*, 168–71) considers 21:8–10 to be the original prophetic proclamation, since these verses contain direct advice to the people on how to behave at this time of crisis (in parallel with 38:2); on the other hand, 21:1–7 provides a theological explanation for God's course in war, and thus, Duhm identifies it with the Deuteronomistic redaction. However, Rudolph (*Jeremia*, 134–36) maintains that 21:8–10 is also inauthentic, i.e., the words of an editor. Berridge (*Prophet, People*, 204–5) recognizes in 21:8–10 three phrases that are distinctive to the book of Jeremiah: "the way of life" and "the way of death"; "sword, famine, pestilence"; and והיתה־לו נפשו לשלל ("and his life shall be for him plunder"). I add a fourth phrase—שים פניו ב־ ("set His face against")—found, besides Jeremiah (here and 44:11), only in the Holiness Legislation (Lev 20:5) and in Ezekiel (14:8; 15:7). All of these, in his view, support the authenticity of Jer 21:8–10 and strengthen the connection between this passage and what is said in the previous verses.

cials; and (2) 21:8–10 encourages the people to choose life, which requires subjugation to the Babylonians under the realization of the expected conquest of the city, while 21:3–7 prophesies complete annihilation to the inhabitants of the city—both human and animal—as a result of pestilence (21:6) or of the three paradigmatic evils: pestilence, sword, and famine (21:7).[30] I propose a third difference between these literary units: (3) 21:8–10 uses conception (B')—YHWH summons the Babylonians to the city, and they, as his agents, are the ones who set it on fire (21:10). On the other hand, according to 21:3–7, God is the city's enemy and the people's destroyer, and the participation of the Babylonians is minimized—conception (C').[31]

The relationship between these two units within 21:1–10 is also addressed through consideration of their resemblance to two prophetic units in Jer 37–38 (37:3–10; 38:2–3).[32] Jeremiah 37:3–10, like 21:1–7, portrays the visit to the prophet of a deputation of officials. Four elements tie the two descriptions together: (1) the time: the siege of Jerusalem; (2) the composition of the delegation: two officials, with Zephaniah son of Maaseiah the priest taking part in both; (3) the objective: to seek YHWH's help on behalf of the people (21:2) or to pray to YHWH on their behalf (37:3); and (4) the prophet's response in both prophecies: calamity is to overtake the city. It is precisely at this last point, however, that the prophetic units differ one from the other, in their descriptions of the role God will play in the catastrophe. In 21:1–7 God fights alone, conception (C'); whereas in 37:3–10 God endows the Babylonians with astounding strength to continue to fight against Jerusalem, thus the (B') conception, in which God summons and supports the enemy.

The correlation between the units is explained in different ways. They could represent two faithful descriptions of two different (historical) occasions in which court officials approach the prophet in the name of the king during the months-long siege, as suggested, for example, by John Bright.[33]

---

30. Rofé ("Studies on the Composition," 7) adds to this list of differences also their divergent depictions of the fall of Jerusalem. However, he does not identify the different points of view concerning God's role in the war.

31. The aforementioned differences negate Hoffman's idea (*Jeremiah 1–25*, 438–44) that 21:1–10 is a single unit.

32. Jer 38:2–3 clearly resembles 21:8–10, but see Lundbom (*Jeremiah 37–52*, 66), who suggests the possibility that the prophet might repeat his own words (thus no need to emend the passage or delete it as secondarily intruded; pace Duhm, *Jeremia*, 302, and others).

33. Bright (*Jeremiah*, 216–17) suggests that Jer 21:2 comes from the first months of

Alternatively, they could be two depictions, from two different hands, of the same historical event. This is the view of Duhm, Mowinckel, and many others. In this view, 37:3–10 is a faithful historical depiction, written by a historian (Jeremiah's biographer, whoever he is), of the confrontation between the officials delegation and the prophet.[34] In complement to this evaluation, the prophecy in 21:1–7 is identified by Alexander Rofé, for example, as "an anachronistic portrayal" of the same event, as a prophecy *ex eventu* (i.e., after Zedekiah had fallen into the hands of the Babylonians), or even as a Deuteronomistic theological adaptation by a student who "was more faithful to the mission of Jeremiah than Jeremiah himself."[35] A third way to understand the relationship between the units is as two tellings of an anecdote of no historical value or, in McKane's language, "a pious invention."[36]

Generally speaking, the evidence of Jeremiah regarding conceptions of YHWH's role in the destruction (see chaps. 7–9) leans most often to the first or last explanation. From this theological perspective, the prophetic materials in Jeremiah certainly do not support the hierarchical or diachronic distinctions between a presumed historical explanation in 37:3–10 and its proposed theological redaction in 21:1–7. It appears that the two

---

the siege, while 37:5 speaks about the lifting of the siege during the summer months (see McKane, *Jeremiah 26–52*, 940–41). The temporary relief from the Babylonian siege upon Judah due to Egyptian aid is alluded to again in Jer 34:21–22 and Ezek 30:20–26. Lundbom (*Jeremiah 21–36*, 95; *Jeremiah 37–52*, 51, 55) accepts Bright's observation that the passages are not literary doublets, but separate descriptions of distinct events; see further Avioz, "Historical Setting of Jeremiah 21:1–10."

34. So Duhm, *Jeremia*, 296–97; and Wanke, *Untersuchungen*, 100–102.

35. Rofé, "Studies on the Composition," 8–11. Those who hold that the subject of both passages is the same event attribute the prophecy in Jer 21 to the editorial layer and explain its placement as governed by the juxtaposition of related units, placed after the mention of Pashhur in 20:1–6 (Rudolph, *Jeremia*, 135) or as an introduction to the prophecies to the Judean kings (Thiel, *Jeremia 1–25*, 230–31). However, Holladay (*Jeremiah*, 1.570) maintains the independence of the prophetic unit in Jer 21 and explains the presence of three parallel units as the work of different collectors who, each in his own way, expand the "reminiscences" of Jeremiah. The following discussion supports Holladay's position.

36. McKane, *Jeremiah 26–52*, 943 (discussion on 940–45). Goldstein (*Life of Jeremiah*, 186–93) elaborates on this third possibility and suggests that both passages may have undergone DtrJ revisions, in the process of historicizing the stories concerning the prophet in the broader description of Jerusalem's fate. Goldstein still accepts Jer 21:1–10 as relying on 37:3–10 (following Rofé, and others), but he finds the two revisions to be closer than previously thought.

theological conceptions, (B') and (C'), served the prophet, his followers, and the book's editors; that is, neither of these approaches is exclusive to any particular group among the tradents of the book.

If we look at the distinctive portrayals of the roles of God and the human enemies in this war, 21:1–7 and 37:3–10 stand as separate proclamations. While the officials and the king present the same viewpoint in both units (21:2; 37:3), conception (A' → C), Jeremiah's responses concerning YHWH's involvement in the destruction differ between the two passages: in 21:8–10 and 37:6–10, YHWH summons the enemy to the city, conception (B'); in 21:3–7, God acts alone as the adversary against city and people, conception (C').

The proximity of conceptions (B') and (C') in the prophetic collections, in both Jeremiah and Ezekiel, is one of the genuine features of each of these two books. Thus, there is no reason to exclude either proclamation from the materials pertaining to the prophet (or his followers/tradents). I suggest two reasons for the editorial attachment of 21:8–10 after 21:1–7. The first is literary—the desire to expand the prophet's message from the king to the people. The second reason is theological—an attempt to modify the prophet's extreme projection of Jerusalem's annihilation by balancing the depiction of God as sole enemy against his people, with the historical circumstances of the clearly human, Babylonian siege of Jerusalem.

In other words, traces of editorial work *may* be found in 21:1–10; the major one is the attachment of the prophetic passage in 21:8–10 to 21:1–7. Yet, there is no reason to doubt the independent authenticity of both passages; just as there is no problem with considering the different perspectives of 21:1–7 and 37:3–10 as two distinct proclamations of the prophet himself (or his contemporaneous followers). If there is room or a need for historical explanations for the repeated proclamations, it is certainly possible that the officials might have been sent to the prophet twice (probably even more times; see 37:17; 38:14) during those distressful months of the Babylonian siege, and that they might have received different responses from the prophet, in accordance with the ad hoc circumstances that prompted the visit and with the language of the request.[37]

The confrontations in 21:1–7 (21:8–10) and 37:3–10 thus demonstrate

---

37. This same line of argument may serve scholars who wish to find in Jeremiah only later editorial traditions. See Goldstein, *Life of Jeremiah*, 205–41; and §3.4.4.1. By focusing on theological conceptions, I am not persuaded by arguments of style that attempt to distinguish "Jeremian" from DtrJ literary levels. My discussion challenges any simple model of literary evolution.

that the dispute concerning the human and divine roles in political-military events derives from the lively and painful rethinking of taken-for-granted religious worldviews. The three conceptions outlined in this chapter (and varied nuances within them) come into play simultaneously in Jerusalem and among the exiles in Babylon (possibly in Egypt as well) at least from the first decades of the sixth century and on. It is possible to identify theological, sociological, and functional distinctions in the ways various groups make use of these conceptions, but the discussion of these differences needs to be released from hierarchical and chronological paradigms that too often govern the scholarship of Hebrew Bible theology and ideology.

7

God Is Called Upon to Fight
for His People

In this theological framework, the defeat (and destruction) of Judah is seen as the outcome of a human enemy's initiative, against which God is called to react in keeping with his role as savior of his people in times of distress, the (A' → C) configuration (see fig. 7.1).

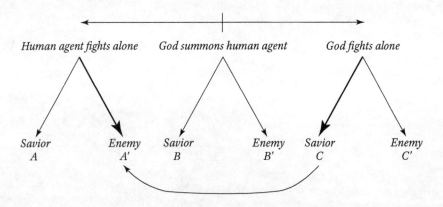

Fig. 7.1. Human enemy wages war; God is called to fight for his people

The expectation of divine assistance in the face of the Babylonian campaign against Judah is seen in Zedekiah's request, via his officials, for the word of God during the last Babylonian siege against Jerusalem (Jer 21:2), where the Babylonian king acts alone in launching a war against Judah, and

God is asked to deliver.[1] This (A' → C) configuration is primarily found in communal laments (Pss 74, 79, 94, 137; Lam 1, 3, 4, 5; Jer 14:7–9, 19–22) as well as in a few popular sayings invoked in the book of Jeremiah (8:19–23). All these passages feature, in some form, the two basic components of the lament genre: (1) a description of the distress coupled with a complaint about the lack of salvation and (2) a plea for divine deliverance. From the point of view of theological function, all these passages illustrate either doubt or protest addressed to God in the face of the deteriorating circumstances in Jerusalem and Judah prior to the destruction, during the events, or in their aftermath, as the speakers confront the reality of dislocation and exile.

Of special interest is the question whether this model of the human and divine roles in the defeat serves also to justify God's role (or his seeming inactivity) in the events. On this point, the prophetic literature mounts a scathing polemic. Only in quotations of the "peace prophets" do we hear justifying voices, primarily within Jeremiah and at a few points in Ezekiel. The theological positions of this group are decisively delegitimized by both Jeremiah and Ezekiel, who use this model in a very limited fashion, in prophecies against the nations and in consolation prophecies.

This (A' → C) configuration is seen in three types of material: expressions of protest, expressions of doubt within quotations in Jeremiah, and prophetic justifications of God as warrior, as savior of his people in times of distress.

7.1. Protest: "O God, My King from of Old" (Psalm 74)

Psalm 74 addresses God with the questions "why?" (74:1, 11) and "until when?" (74:10). The poet describes the present distress as the destruction of God's sanctuary (74:3–8) and as the cessation of cultic and religious institutions (74:8–9); not of least importance is the theological distress of the people, who feel deserted in this crucial crisis by an inactive God—whom the poet nevertheless continues to address in pleas for salvation (74:3a, 18–23).[2] This communal lament, thus, features all three components of the

---

1. See §1.1.2 and §6.4. Compare Jer 37:2 and also 37:17; 38:14, where the dialogue between the king and the prophet seems to reside on the (B') conception.

2. Dating of Ps 74 varies, although all suggestions rest on the clear description of

lament genre: complaint about the present distress, praise for past acts of salvation, and pleas for future deliverance.

As meticulously presented by Meir Weiss, the first verses of this psalm (74:1–3) capture this timeline of present, past, and future as the core of the poem, which is then developed in its other three segments:[3]

[1] Why, O God, do You forever reject us,	¹ למה אלהים זנחת לנצח
do You fume in anger at the flock that You tend?	יעשן אפך בצאן מרעיתך.
[2] Remember the community You made Yours long ago,	² זכר עדתך קנית קדם
Your very own tribe that You redeemed,	גאלת שבט נחלתך
Mount Zion, where You dwelt.[4]	הר־ציון זה שכנת בו.
[3] Bestir Yourself because of the perpetual tumult,	³ הרימה פעמיך למשאות נצח
all the outrages of the enemy in the sanctuary.	כל־הרע אויב בקדש.

Weiss argues that there is a chronological symmetry between 74:1–3 and 74:4–23 in their time references to the *present* distress (74:1, 4–11), to the divine deeds of salvation in the *past* (74:2, 12–17), and to salvation re-

---

the destruction of cultic center(s). Suggestions for late datings tie the psalm to the Hasmonean period, based on (1) the presumed connections to 1 Macc 2:7–9; 4:38; 2 Macc 5:16, 21; 8:35; (2) the mention of the failure of prophecy, in accordance with 1 Macc 4:46; 9:27; 14:41; and (3) the lack of any hint of the circumstances of exile. Gunkel and Begrich (*Introduction to the Psalms*, 98) criticize this late dating and argue that Ps 74, like Pss 44, 79, and others, refers to desecration and burning of the First Temple; and yet they consider this particular psalm postexilic, within the timeframe between Ezra and Alexander the Great. Kraus (*Psalms 60–150*, 97) also contests the Hasmonean dating, arguing that the burning of the temple is tied to the Babylonian destruction, thus 587/586, and the period thereafter. Furthermore, Kraus explains the lack of actual reference to the exile by suggesting that the psalm is written substantially after the destruction (74:1, 3, 9); he therefore suggests composition between 587 and 520, probably closer to that later date. The psalm might have been used in the liturgy of laments over the destruction (Jer 41:5; Zech 7:1–3; 8:18–19; see Kraus, *Psalms 60–150*, 97). For another sixth-century dating, see Hossfeld and Zenger, *Psalms*, 2.243.

3. Weiss, *Bible from Within*, 281–93.

4. Compare NJPS: "where You dwell," while the other two *qatal* forms of 74:2 are aptly translated in the past (perfect mode): קנית and גאלת ("you made yours . . . you redeemed"). See Hossfeld and Zenger, *Psalms*, 2.239: "Mount Zion here, on which you have set your dwelling."

quested for the *future* (74:3, 18–23).[5] To pursue this structural observation even further, I suggest that the poet builds the contents of his lament on two concentric structures (1–3, 4–23) that tie the theological turmoil into the chronological-symmetric structure to describe the God-people-enemy relationship:

Time reference and theological turmoil	Opening verse	Entire psalm
The people's distress over God's *present* neglect	74:1	74:4–11
Divine deeds of salvation, drawing on a mythic *past*	74:2	74:12–17
The enemies' current destruction of the temple spurs a call for divine intervention in the *future*	74:3	74:18–23

Through this threefold structure of the opening verses and the entire psalm, the major complaint is repeatedly emphasized, highlighting the feeling of eternal divine neglect that echoes dramatically throughout (74:1, 10–11, 18–23). The special structure of this opening segment, which unfolds in both a symmetric and a concentric order, constructs the feeling that the three components—the complaint, the praise, and the pleas for salvation—are intertwined in what sounds like a chaotically emotional lament. Indeed, this turmoil represents protest motivated by the intention to justify God's role—an intention that is nevertheless left unfulfilled.

The people's present distress (74:1, 4–11) stems from two causes: the expression of a sense of permanent divine desertion (74:1, 10–11) forms a first *inclusio* around the description of the enemy's deeds of destruction (74:4–9):

[1] Why, O God, do You forever reject us, do You fume in anger at the flock that You tend? . . .	¹למה אלהים זנחת לנצח יעשן אפך בצאן מרעיתך.
[4] Your foes roar inside Your meeting-place; they take their signs for true signs. [5] It is like men wielding axes against a gnarled tree; [6] with hatchet and pike they hacked away at its carved work.	⁴שאגו צרריך בקרב מועדך שמו אותתם אתות. ⁵יודע כמביא למעלה בסבך עץ־קרדמות. ⁶ועת (ק: ועתה) פתוחיה יחד בכשיל וכילפת יהלמון.

5. Weiss, *Bible from Within*, 290–93.

197

[7] They made Your sanctuary go up in flames;	שלחו באש מקדשך [7]
they brought low in dishonor the dwelling-place of Your presence.	לארץ חללו משכן־שמך.
[8] They resolved, "Let us destroy them altogether!"	אמרו בלבם נינם יחד [8]
They burned all God's tabernacles in the land.	שרפו כל־מועדי־אל בארץ.
[9] No signs appear for us;	אותתינו לא ראינו [9]
there is no longer any prophet;	אין־עוד נביא
no one among us knows for how long.	ולא־אתנו ידע עד־מה.
[10] Till when, O God, will the foe blaspheme,	עד־מתי אלהים יחרף צר [10]
will the enemy forever revile Your name?	ינאץ אויב שמך לנצח.
[11] Why do You hold back Your hand?	למה תשיב ידך [11]
Draw Your right hand out of Your bosom![6]	וימינך מקרב חיקך כלה.

There is a clear order (in both sequence and hierarchy) between those two sources of distress. Psalm 74:4–9 focuses entirely on the human enemy that brutally destroys the most holy place(s) of God.[7] With loud shouts and horrific physical acts, they first destroy the temple's special wood carvings, before they set fire to the entire structure.[8] As regularly occurs in Psalms, the identity of the enemy is not specified; the poet gives only a few details by which to picture this enemy. One clear fact is that, according to the poet, the initiative to destroy the temple came from the enemy alone; God had no causative role, conception (A') (see §6.1.2).

Moreover, in these verses, the poet disregards the effects of the enemy's actions on individuals, the city, or the nation as a whole. Human suffering is totally absent from the poet's description (compare 79:1–4, which stresses the horrific fate of the people, after mentioning the destruction of the

---

6. According to the Masoretic Text accentuation, 74:11 divides after וימינך, as reflected in NJPS: "Why do You hold back Your hand, Your right hand? / Draw it out of Your bosom!" (למה תשיב ידך וימינך / מקרב חיקך כלה). In contrast, I concur with the division that places וימינך with the second part of the verse and thus read it as a complaint and a plea (compare Ps 44:4); see Hossfeld and Zenger, *Psalms*, 2.240.

7. The holy site (sometimes in plural) is mentioned using various terms over the course of these verses (74:3, 4–8): קדש מועדך, מקדשך, משכן, שמך, along with מועדי־אל in the plural. See Gelston, "Note on Psalm lxxiv,8."

8. Ps 74:5–6 is interpreted in a variety of ways. The target of the destruction is seen as either the carvings on the gates of the temple (פתוחים, read and understood as פתחים by the Septuagint and Peshitta) or wooden carvings elsewhere; כשיל וכילפת are understood to be axes and pickaxes, based on the similarity to Akkadian *kalappu* (plural *kalappāti*) and Hittite *kullupi* ("axe"). See Hossfeld and Zenger, *Psalms*, 2.245–47.

temple in 74:1).[9] Rather, Ps 74 stresses that the enemies act against *God's* temple; in so doing, they blaspheme *God*, and they are thus termed *God's* enemies, who act against *his* institutions (74:4, 7, 10–11 and 74:18–23). No other aspect of the destruction has a place in this lament.

An exception in this context is 74:9, which argues that the destruction terminates not only cultic activity (74:8), but also that all signals of communication with God through signs or prophets consequently cease. This is where the complaint reaches back to God. Psalm 74:10–11 echoes 74:1, and yet the verses express two counterpoints: (1) in response to the question "Why . . . do You fume in anger at the flock that You tend?" (74:1b),[10] 74:10 mentions explicitly the enemy's sins of blasphemy. Divine anger is indeed justified, but it should be aimed at the enemy. (2) While the poet feels, or worries, that God deserts his people eternally/constantly (לנצח, 74:1a), it is the enemy who constantly defames God's name (לנצח, 74:10b). This latter situation indeed deserves divine intervention, yet God at this stage is continuously inactive. He seems to step away from any action on behalf of his people (השיב ידו מ־, 74:11; implied in 74:9), and thus he avoids taking steps against those who indeed act directly against him (74:10).[11]

Rhetorically, the *inclusio*, containing this presentation of the enemy's destruction of the temple, constructs an implicit call to God to rise to action, to serve as savior of his people. According to conception (C), YHWH may be expected to fight alone against the enemy (see §6.2 and §9.1). Protest here emerges from the sense that God is avoiding action on behalf of his people/his name. The next segment of this communal lament introduces yet another rhetorical strategy to awaken God's response.

---

9. Compare Weiss (*Bible from Within*, 291–93), who explains the focus on the temple as setting a gradual growing judgment presented within the introduction (74:1–3) from God, to his community, to Mount Zion, to the sanctuary. I do not find this explanation convincing.

10. In Ps 74:1b יעשן אפך בצאן מרעיתך is aptly translated as an additional question: "Do You fume in anger at the flock that You tend?" For the use of fire imagery to convey divine wrath, see two other questions of protest addressed to God: תבער כמו־אש קנאתך ("will Your indignation blaze like fire?," 79:5) and תבער כמו־אש חמתך ("will Your fury blaze like fire?," 89:47).

11. Hossfeld and Zenger (*Psalms*, 2.247–48) consider this accusation of divine inaction to be the climax of accusation in this psalm. The destruction and exile are repeatedly described as sources of disgrace for God in Ezekiel (e.g., 36:20–23) and communal laments (e.g., Jer 14:7–9, 19–22). Disgrace (using the verbs בוש, חרף, and כלם and the nouns בושה, חרפה, and כלמה) also repeats in individual laments (e.g., Pss 55:13; 69:8, 20–21).

Psalm 74:2 and 74:12–17 move to the past—a glorious past, for which God is clearly praised as the one who delivers and saves, again conception (C). Psalm 74:2's call to remember the people established in the ancient past (קדם) is further developed in 74:12–17. The passage begins with a pious declaration, by which the poet expresses his long and steady commitment to God, using the phrase מקדם ("from of old," 74:12):[12]

[2] Remember the community You made Yours long ago,	[2]זכר עדתך קנית קדם
Your very own tribe that You redeemed,	גאלת שבט נחלתך
Mount Zion, where You dwell. . . .	הר־ציון זה שכנת בו.
[12] O God, my King from of old,	[12]ואלהים מלכי מקדם
who brings deliverance throughout the land;	פעל ישועות בקרב הארץ.
[13] it was You who crumbled the sea with Your might,[13]	[13]אתה פוררת בעזך ים
who smashed the heads of the monsters in the waters;	שברת ראשי תנינים על־המים.
[14] it was You who crushed the heads of Leviathan,	[14]אתה רצצת ראשי לויתן
who left him as food for the denizens of the desert;	תתננו מאכל לעם לציים.
[15] it was You who released springs and torrents,	[15]אתה בקעת מעין ונחל

12. For מקדם ("from of old") in reference to the poets' expression of personal relationship with God, see Pss 77:6; 119:152; 143:5. The declaration in 74:12 is at a first glance quite similar to that of 44:5: אתה־הוא מלכי אלהים צוה ישועות יעקב ("You are my king, O God; decree victories for Jacob!"). Weiss (*Bible from Within*, 278–81), however, aptly outlines significant differences between the two statements: (1) In 44:5 God is directly addressed in the second-person, whereas in 74:12 he is spoken about in the third; (2) in Ps 44 this declaration comes after the praise of God for his past deeds and thus reflects an unshaken confidence; in 74:12 declaration proceeds from the protesting question: "Why do You hold back Your hand?" (74:11). Therefore, according to Weiss, 44:5 is indeed a declaration of faith, whereas 74:12 is a groan, an argument, and a challenging protest. I see both proclamations as declarations of faith and agree with Weiss that 74:12 represents a more painful mood of expression.

13. Compare NJPS: "It was You who drove back the sea with Your might." But פרר *piel* means "crumble" (Isa 24:19) and as a divine action occurs otherwise only in Job 15:4; 16:12 (not including the *hiphil* form in the phrase הפר ברית, Gen 17:14; Deut 31:16; Jer 11:10; 14:21).

it was You who made mighty rivers run dry;	אַתָּה הוֹבַשְׁתָּ נַהֲרוֹת אֵיתָן.
[16] the day is Yours, the night also;	לְךָ יוֹם אַף־לְךָ לָיְלָה 16
it was You who set in place the orb of the sun;	אַתָּה הֲכִינוֹת מָאוֹר וָשָׁמֶשׁ.
[17] it was You who fixed all the boundaries of the earth;	אַתָּה הִצַּבְתָּ כָּל־גְּבוּלוֹת 17 אָרֶץ
summer and winter—it was You who made them.	קַיִץ וָחֹרֶף אַתָּה יְצַרְתָּם.

It is of great interest, however, that 74:13–17 does not cite any of God's salvific deeds in the history of his people "from of old," but rather hearkens back to creation-combat traditions. In 74:13–17 the poet uses the independent personal pronoun אתה seven times in phrases that declare the praise of God: "it was You who. . . ." Four components of these creation traditions receive attention in these verses: (1) the combat with chaos, represented by the forces of the sea (74:13–15); (2) establishing the order of day and night with the appropriate sources of light (74:16); (3) establishing the borders of the world (74:17a); and finally, (4) creating the major (meteorological/)agricultural seasons, winter and summer (74:17b). Thus, God's deeds of "deliverance" in the land (פעל ישועות בקרב הארץ, 74:12) are acts that establish order in all of these areas.[14] Nevertheless, the first and highly accentuated element in the sequence is the cosmic combat with the forces of chaos.[15]

The combination of these two divine acts—establishment of the people (74:2, with vague echoes of Exod 15:13, 17) and creation of the world and its divisions through combat (Ps 74:13–17)—is a standard combination in psalms of praise (e.g., Ps 136), as well as in two other communal laments (Pss 77, 89).[16] Psalms 74, 77, and 89 are the only three of our target group

14. See also Ps 89:6–14, which uses the (B') conception; and 89:39–46, which offers a protest against God.

15. Resemblances to the Canaanite myth of creation in these psalms (among others) are suggested by Mowinckel, *Psalms in Israel's Worship*, 1.114–15. See Mettinger, "Fighting the Powers of Chaos"; and Day, *God's Conflict with the Dragon*, 88–140.

16. The relationships between mythic theophany traditions (or chaos-combat traditions) and the exodus traditions have long been under scholarly debate, and Ps 74 and Ps 77 play major roles in those discussions. In any event, 77:16–21 refers to Exod 15; note the echoes in גאלת בזרוע עמך (Ps 77:16) and נחית כצאן עמך (77:21) as compared to נחית בחסדך עם־זו גאלת נהלת בעזך אל־נוה קדשך, Exod 15:13; see also the pairing of חיל and רגז in Ps 77:17 and Exod 15:14. See Loewenstamm's "Shiver of Nature" and *Tradition of the Exodus*, 107–9, followed by Weiss, *Ideas and Beliefs*, 109–25; for a different position, see Fenton, "Differing Approaches," 359.

of seventeen psalms (see §3.4.3) that use the chaos-combat myth for the portrayal of God as warrior; otherwise, this portrayal is governed by the anthropomorphic metaphor of God as a warrior-king.[17]

The creation traditions, including the chaos-combat myth, shed light on the image of God as warrior, the characterization of the enemy, and the nature of salvation, and they have three functions in these psalms. First, this mythic picture is introduced following a declaration of God's greatness and incomparability (77:14; 89:9) or following the recognition of his kingship from the days of old (74:12; 77:15). The chaos-combat serves as an excellent example of God's past acts of deliverance, which are called by various terms: ישועות ("deliverance," 74:12); עלילותיך, and פעלך, פלאך, מעללי-יה ("the deeds of the LORD," "Your wonders," "Your works," 77:12, 13, 15); and חסדי יהוה, and פלאך, and אמונתך ("the LORD's steadfast faithfulness," "Your wonders," "Your faithfulness," 89:2, 6). Likewise in Ps 74, God is portrayed through the use of second-person verbs as active and sole warrior: "It was You who crumbled, smashed, crushed, left him as food for the denizens of the desert, caused to burst/split, dried out" (תתננו, רצצת, שברת, פוררת, בקעת, מאכל לעם לציים, and הובשת, 74:13–15). Second, these recollections of the chaos-combat myth add another argument against the human enemies—they are now implicitly characterized as analogous to the chaotic forces that in days of old threatened God and the orderly world.[18] Finally, as a combination of these two aspects of the argument, and since this is a combat in which God proved victorious, God is implicitly requested to reactivate his abilities of old in the current distressing situation.

Hence, using these traditions is a forceful expression of faith; these three psalmists (of Pss 74, 77, 89) expect an immediate deliverance, analogous to that original deliverance at the beginning of times. In these three psalms, God's war against the powers of nature provides an example *a minori ad maius* of his potential ability to act against the human enemies of his people. In this manner, the creation-chaos-combat myth serves the

17. Such use clearly shows the positive regard in which these originally Canaanite and Mesopotamian mythic traditions of creation in combat are held among Israelite authors down to the sixth century; this observation holds true for both poetry and prophecy (e.g., Jer 4:23–28; 5:22); see Fenton, "Differing Approaches," 340–51.

18. For the invocation of the forces of chaos to delegitimize the enemy and configure them as God's enemies, see Isa 5:30; 8:7–8; 17:12–14; 59:19; Jer 6:23 ‖ 50:42; 47:2–3; 51:42, 55; Ezek 29:3; 32:2; Hab 3:8–9, 14–15; Pss 46:3–8; 65:8; 124:4–5; see Fenton, "Differing Approaches," 351–55, 379–80. Fenton (346–49) therefore considers this mythic perspective to be of ongoing relevance by the early Neo-Babylonian period.

human need to seek a change in the historical reality. Therefore, 74:12–17 intentionally connects the universal sovereignty of God with his sovereignty over the national history (74:2) by proclaiming that the God of Israel is responsible for the cosmic world order. Sovereignty and power are the main topics on the scope of the divine activity in the postdestruction era and are needed qualities for the future confrontation with the enemies (74:18–23).[19] Of even greater significance in the context of these three communal laments, however, these verses of praise for past salvation provide an argument against current feelings of divine negligence (74:1; 77:8–10). In Ps 89, which uses the (B') conception, God's praise forms the background to the protest that expresses surprise at God's seeming withdrawal from his covenant with/oath to David (89:4, 20–38), as a result of which God seems to have empowered the enemies against the king (89:39–43). This perception of God's refusal of divine deliverance, or at least the complaint about its delay, is shared by the three psalms (74:1, 10–11, 18–23; 77:8–11; 89:47–50). In all three, the poets call out to YHWH in order to awaken him and to spur him to action in the national sphere (74:2, 20–22; 77:2–3; 89:51–52). All three communal laments particularly emphasize remembrance (זכר/שכח), investing great efforts in reminding God of his obligations to the people (74:2, 18, 23; 77:4–7, 12–14 versus 77:10) or his covenant with the king (89:2–5 and 89:48, 51). Hence, the expression of magnificent praise becomes the basis of a powerful implicit protest.

With 74:3 and 74:18–23, Ps 74 reaches its final section, the plea for future salvation. The latter section expands 74:3's call for God's intervention, describing the enemy's actions as directed against God himself, hence the (A' → C) configuration:

[3] Bestir Yourself because of the perpetual tumult,	הרימה פעמיך למשאות נצח [3]
all the outrages of the enemy in the sanctuary. . . .	כל־הרע אויב בקדש.
[18] Remember this,	זכר־זאת [18]

---

19. Ps 77:14–21 combines the chaos-combat myth with the Egypt-exodus traditions. Compare this use to the invocation of creation-chaos-combat myths to establish Marduk's divine status as head of the pantheon in Mesopotamian religion; see Michalowski, "Presence at the Creation"; Lambert, "Mesopotamian Creation Stories"; and Katz, "Reconstructing Babylon."

it is the enemy that blasphemes the LORD,[20]

how base people revile Your name.

[19] Do not deliver Your dove to the wild beast;

do not ignore forever the band of Your lowly ones.

[20] Look to the covenant!

For the dark places of the land are full of the haunts of lawlessness.

[21] Let not the downtrodden turn away disappointed;

let the poor and needy praise Your name.

[22] Rise, O God, champion Your cause;

Remember that You are blasphemed by base men all day long.

[23] Do not ignore the shouts of Your foes,

the din of Your adversaries that ascends all the time.

אויב חרף יהוה

ועם נבל נאצו שמך.

[19] אל־תתן לחית נפש תורך

חית ענייך אל־תשכח לנצח.

[20] הבט לברית

כי מלאו מחשכי־ארץ נאות חמס.

[21] אל־ישב דך נכלם

עני ואביון יהללו שמך.

[22] קומה אלהים ריבה ריבך

זכר חרפתך מני־נבל כל־היום.

[23] אל־תשכח קול צרריך

שאון קמיך עלה תמיד.

Furthermore, 74:18–23 creates a second *inclusio* structure that draws on 74:1–3 as a whole. It expresses a protest against God's desertion and wrath (74:18–21, echoing 74:1–2); it calls God to remember that it is the enemy who has blasphemed him (74:18, echoing 74:2–3); and in 74:22–23, the poet draws on the introductory call of 74:3: הרימה פעמיך ("bestir Yourself"), asking God to act against his enemies.

In these closing verses, protest turns into pleas for divine action, for affective intervention on behalf of the people. Yet, the pleas address the negligence of God in even clearer way. Psalm 74:20 calls to God explicitly: הבט לברית ("look to the covenant!")—God has obligations toward his people, and the protestor accuses him directly of not living up to them. In his implicit accusation of God as backing away from his covenant commitments, the poet thus takes a different stance than that usually taken by historiographers and prophets, who tend to lay responsibility for the distress on the people's disloyalty to God and to his covenant. According to this communal lament, God needs to be reminded of his longstanding

20. My translation maintains the structural parallel with 74:2, as in the Hebrew; compare NJPS: "Be mindful of how the enemy blasphemes the Lord." Hossfeld and Zenger (*Psalms*, 2.240) translate: "Oh, remember: YHWH, the enemy has scoffed"; and see Hacham (*Psalms*, 19) for these interpretations of the verse, along with two others.

commitment to his people (74:2, 20), just as God seemingly also needs to be reminded of the identity of the *true* enemies (74:4–9, 18, 23). זכר־זאת אויב חרף יהוה ("remember this, it is the enemy that blasphemes YHWH") sets a parallel and a contrast to 74:2: זכר עדתך קנית קדם ("remember Your community You made Yours long ago") and empowers dramatically (though implicitly) the accusation that God has forgotten. As part of this reminder, the poet stresses again that the enemy's actions and blasphemy are directed against God himself (74:18, 22b; see 74:10); God should be motivated to fight for his own sake (ריבה ריבך, 74:22a). As in the earlier description of the enemies' deeds of destruction (74:4–11), mention of the people's own suffering is completely avoided, such as we find described in Lamentations and in other communal laments within Psalms (Pss 79, 89, 137; also 44).[21] The only clues to any distress are expressed in Ps 74 through the most general psalmodic conventions of literary opposition between the poor or the pious (עניים, 74:19; דך נכלם עני ואביון, 74:21) and the base people (עם נבל, 74:18, 22), who turn the land into נאות חמס מחשכי־ארץ ("the dark places of the land are full of the haunts of lawlessness," 74:20).

The different strategies and arguments for awakening God to action presented in Ps 74 are proofs both of the poet's piety and of his full acquaintance with the diverse traditions that shaped the conception of God as warrior in Hebrew Bible literature. The poet has not given up the idea that God is preeminently the savior of his people in times of need—God is still his king. In bitterness of spirit, out of a desire to hope, and in conviction of YHWH's power to save his people, the poet of Ps 74 (like the poets of Ps 77 and Ps 89) returns to the myth of creation in combat—the greatest of God's past deeds (74:13–17; 77:12).[22] Both in the scope of his activity and in his powers, God is portrayed in this communal lament as an omnipotent savior. The only unsolved issues, then, are why God continues to be inactive in the current crisis, and how much longer this question needs to be asked.

---

21. As often in communal laments, both the afflicted and the enemy are portrayed using socioeconomic categories. See further Pss 9–10; and Kraus, *Psalms 1–59*, 92–99.

22. Mettinger ("Fighting the Powers of Chaos," 33–34) reconstructs the historical evolution of the use of the chaos-combat myth and argues that in face of the 586 crisis, authors clung even more powerfully to this conception as a foundation for the promise of the future. As examples of such use, he mentions Lam 5:19; Ps 74:12–17; and Isa 51:9–10. Mettinger makes two additional notes of interest: first, the absence of this warlike motif from the Deuteronomistic History is ascribed to the demythologizing tendency of the entire composition; and, second, the scholarly disinterest in the chaos-combat as an acceptance of this Deuteronomistic tendency is somehow normative.

But these unsolved issues become even more complicated, and the implicit protest echoes louder. Psalm 74 says nothing at all concerning any sins committed by the people; as often within communal laments, the psalm has no confession of sins (see §11.2.3.), which thus accentuates even more the inexplicability of the divine negligence. Although this is implicit in comparison to 44:18–23, Ps 74 presents quite the same thought as that passage—here is a loyal people who reminds God that *he* is bound by a covenant that *he* seems to have not kept; according to that covenant, his major task is to be the savior of his people in times of need (10:1).

Thus, Ps 74 constitutes yet another text (like Pss 44, 77, 89) that establishes my conviction that the Hebrew Bible presents us with a "discourse among equals," both in terms of commonly held religious conceptions and intellectual acquaintance with shared national (and possibly ancient Near Eastern) traditions. These poets are not inferior in any bit from their contemporaries, prophets or historiographers, nor do they differ from them in their sincere wish to find a theological explanation for the present situation. Rather, Ps 74 gives another rich example of the painful negotiation of the trilemma of theodicy. Its author refuses to relinquish either his traditional understandings of God or his conviction of the people's faithfulness under suffering; thus, he is unable to find a theological explanation for the distressing reality.

7.2. The People's Doubts: Quotations in Jeremiah and Fragmentary Communal Laments (Jeremiah 8:19–20, 21–23; 14:7–9)

Doubt has long been acknowledged as an important component in the crystallization of religious thought and is the result of the clash between two opposing conceptions or of the state of indecision between two antithetical perceptions (see §1.2.1). Expressions of doubt are not easy to locate in Hebrew Bible writings or to distinguish from expressions of protest. The discussion below characterizes doubt in the Hebrew Bible as expressed in quotations and communal laments, that is, in speeches of the people, addressed to God,[23] and locates forms, rhetorical features, and themes that shape these expressions as well as the ways in which doubt is refuted.

In terms of form and rhetoric, doubt is expressed by means of interrog-

23. For the significance of quotations in Jeremiah and for criteria for the evaluation

ative sentences, either in the simple mood (Jer 5:19; 9:11; 13:22; 16:10; and attributed to the nations in 22:8)[24] or in rhetorical questions (8:19–20, 21–22; 14:7–9, 19–22).[25] There is an interesting congruity between form and content in the use of these two kinds of questions in Jeremiah. Straightforward questions challenge the workings of divine justice and the role of God as judge, using the interrogative expressions מדוע ("why?," 13:22), על־מה ("for what?," 9:11; 16:10; 22:8), and תחת מה ("because of what?," 5:19). To give but one example (5:19):

And when they ask, "<u>Because of what did the LORD our God do</u> all these things?" You shall answer them, "<u>Because you forsook Me and served alien gods on your own land, you will have to serve foreigners in a land not your own</u>."	והיה כי תאמרו <u>תחת מה</u> עשה יהוה אלהינו לנו את־ כל־אלה ואמרת אליהם כאשר עזבתם אותי ותעבדו אלהי נכר בארצכם כן תעבדו זרים בארץ לא לכם.

The prophet's response indicates the reason for God's forceful acts of destruction and dislocation: they constitute an appropriate retaliation for the people's sins (according to the *lex talionis*, "measure for measure").[26]

Rhetorical questions, on the other hand, challenge God to act as savior of his people in times of need. Hence, they refer to God's roles as warrior and as lord of his people, using the three-part rhetorical model ה . . . אם מדוע . . . (8:19–20, 21–22; 14:7–9, 19–22).

Thematically, then, doubt is expressed in Jeremiah by means of complaints over the absence of divine deliverance in the face of the national

of their use (in Jeremiah as well as in other sixth-century compositions), see Rom-Shiloni, *God in Times of Destruction*, 58–131, and bibliographical references there.

24. A question-and-answer sequence similar to Jer 22:8–9, attributed to "the nations" or an anonymous "them," occurs also in Deut 29:23; 1 Kgs 9:8–9; 2 Chr 7:21.

25. This line of questions occur in three passages within the individual laments in Jer 11–20; see 12:1; 15:18; 18:20.

26. See §10.2. Long ("Two Question and Answer Schemata," 130–34) argues that the question-and-answer structure reflects a literary convention that originates in the Deuteronomistic historiography. Several formal characteristics point to the rhetorical shaping of this saying: (1) the sequences imply a measure-for-measure structure; and (2) the three components that designate Jerusalem's sins—abandonment of the covenant, bowing down to other gods, and worship of other gods—all invoke the second commandment (Exod 20:3–5; Deut 5:7–9; see Jer 16:11–12). Compare other quotations attributed to foreign passersby or enemies, concerning God's actions against Jerusalem (Lam 2:15–16; see 4:12).

distress, side by side with pleas for salvation. But these characteristics are to a large extent also shared by expressions of protest. Three anonymous quotations in the book of Jeremiah clarify the definition of doubt, with its unique characteristics and the controversies it reveals.[27] Jeremiah 8:19-20 introduces doubt through a rhetorical question posed by the people but yet interrupted by the prophetic voice, which thus allows us to see the polemic between them. Jeremiah 8:21-23 raises another such question; it is, however, cast in the first-person, which raises the question of whether this idea might have been Jeremiah's own. Finally, 14:7-9 may represent a fragment of a communal lament that the prophet set within his prophecy (and perhaps even contributed to in a mild way). These three passages not only clarify the distinctions between doubt and protest, but provide additional examples of the interplay of theodical discourse between prophets and their contemporaries.

Jeremiah 8:19-20 is a short prophetic unit within 8:4–9:25, a cluster of judgment prophecies against Jerusalem that articulates the prophet's rebuke of the people's sins, which lead to their punishment (8:4-17), using the (B') conception; coupled with quotations that voice the people's desperation in facing the enemies' invasion (8:14), the (C') conception; or laments expressed by God or the prophet over the total destruction (9:9-10), the (C') conception. Jeremiah 8:19-20 introduces yet another kind of cry into this context, said to be spread throughout the land or all around (הנה־קול שועת בת־עמי מארץ מרחקים); it is phrased as a three-part rhetorical question:[28]

---

27. Another context in Jeremiah where doubt is expressed is within the individual laments in Jer 11–20 (called, inappropriately, "confessions"), for instance, 12:1-3. See Davidson, *Courage to Doubt*, 121-39, who argues that this passage expresses "an inner turmoil of doubt" (Davidson's term is "vocational crisis") side by side with "outward courage and assurance" (122). Jeremiah confronts God over his sense of the failure of his ministry, even experiencing the sense of being unsure of God (129-39), to the point where he feels "caught somewhere between heaven and hell in that struggle for faith" (138).

28. מארץ מרחקים is difficult. It is inconceivable to take this question as said by the exiles, just as it is unreasonable to assume that the prophet is away from the city. Therefore, I accept the suggestion of Holladay: "The people on every hand cry out" (*Jeremiah*, 1.293); and similarly Carroll, *Jeremiah*, 234-35: "the people from the length and the breadth of the land" (both of them following Duhm, *Jeremia*, 92: "Land weiter Ausdehnungen," as in Isa 33:17). NJPS likewise offers a similar alternative: "Hark! The outcry of my poor people from the land far and wide." Compare McKane (*Jeremiah 1-25*, 193): "coming from a distant land"; and Lundbom (*Jeremiah 1-20*, 528, 531): "a cry

¹⁹ Hark! The voice of my people on every
hand cries out:
"<u>Is</u> not the LORD in Zion?
<u>Is</u> not her King within her?
<u>Why then</u> did they anger Me with their images,
with alien futilities?
²⁰ "Harvest is past, summer is gone,
but we have not been saved."

¹⁹ הנה קול שועת בת־עמי
מארץ מרחקים
הַיהוה אין בציון
אִם־מלכה אין בה
מַדוע הכעסוני בפסליהם
בהבלי נכר.
²⁰ עבר קציר כלה קיץ
ואנחנו לוא נושענו.

Rhetorical questions are among the unique stylistic techniques of the book of Jeremiah. They are used in fourteen questions spoken by God through his prophet, and in five quotations coming from the anonymous "people."[29] By their nature, rhetorical questions set up a contrary-to-fact premise; thus they express rebuke when used by God/the prophet and can indicate doubt and/or subtle protest against present circumstances when attributed to the people. But most important for our purposes, they express polemical views in relation to the topic at hand, through their ironic and even sarcastic tone. Thus, these quotations indicate conflicts between speakers and audience and express anger and/or antagonism on the part of the questioner.

Like most of the rhetorical questions in Jeremiah (six of the fourteen attributed to God/the prophet and four of the five quoting the people),

---

of my dear people from a land far off." Both consider this passage to be an exilic expansion; Lundbom (529–30) accepts an earlier suggestion by Volz (*Der Prophet Jeremia*, 110: "aus fernem Land") and thinks the prophet is crying for his people in both 8:19–20 and 8:21–22.

29. Six three-part rhetorical questions in which God is the speaker all occur in the poetry: Jer 2:14, 31–32; 8:4–5; 15:5; 22:28 plus the construction ה . . . אם . . . הלוא in the question attributed to God in 23:23–24. In addition, within the God-talk (or the prophet-talk) the two-part question ה . . . אם is found in 5:22; 18:14–15; 31:20; אם מדוע . . . in 30:6; and אם . . . אם in 48:27; with a one-part question מה in Jer 5:22 and interlocutive ה in 22:15. Four rhetorical questions said by "the people" addressed at God in quotations are structured as three-part questions: 8:19–20, 21–22; 14:19, 22 (ה . . . אם . . . הלוא), with another quoted two-part question in 3:5 (ה . . . אם). Based on this distribution, Holladay ("Deuteronomic Gloss") argues that the rhetorical questions constitute an indication of authenticity; but Long ("Two Question and Answer Schemata," 137–39) relates this very style to "a deuteronomistic redactor" of Jeremiah and finds it to be "a useful tool in deuteronomistic rhetoric" (138). On the value of quotations for the theological reconstruction and, not least, the challenges of authenticity, see §3.1.

8:19–20 is constructed in three parts. Structurally, the first two components suggest a reduction *ad absurdum* of the issue at stake, while the third (8:20) component expresses the motivation of the entire question and its main message; thus, this third part functions as the climax of the question (similarly, for instance, to 2:31–32).[30]

From the perspective of doubt and protest, the first two components of the cry in 8:19–20 suit the people's feelings of desperation on the eve of destruction. They raise *doubt* at the seemingly absurd possibility that God the king must have abandoned his city. But the continuation of the construction in 8:19b–20 suggests at face value two different possible completions of the three-part rhetorical question: 8:19b sets a *justification* of the divine judgment, whereas 8:20 expresses *protest* against God, as the people's expectations of salvation are not met.

As scholars of Jeremiah have long recognized, thematically and grammatically, the third component of this rhetorical question is meant to be 8:20: עבר קציר כלה קיץ ואנחנו לוא נושענו ("harvest is past, summer is gone, but we have not been saved"). This statement, in first-person plural, presents the logical continuation to the first two questions concerning God's absence; this last component connects God's absence with the people's long wait for salvation. Together, the two parts of the question reveal the basic conception of the speakers concerning the role of God as king and warrior—had he been in his city, their salvation would have been guaranteed. Thus they clearly adhere to the conception that God is (expected to be) the savior of his people in times of need (A' → C).

Yet, as (also) widely recognized, this threefold structure is interrupted by a divine rebuke: "[Why] then did they anger Me with their images, with alien futilities?" This component clearly does not fit the grammar of the rhetorical question, but rather responds to it (or at least to the two opening statements). While scholars often consider 8:19b to be a DtrJ gloss, William Holladay argues for Jeremianic authorship and considers this additional question to be an intentional interruption into the quoted words.[31]

30. These functional distinctions between the parts of the rhetorical questions is developed by Held ("Rhetorical Questions"), who argues that the third component of the question states the core of the argument. Van Selms ("Motivated Interrogative Sentences") considers the third part to express the motive of the entire question. Avishur ("Patterns of Double and Triple," 447) also considers the third component to be the excuse for the entire construction, such that the first two components are quite superfluous to it.

31. For 8:19b as a DtrJ gloss, see Thiel, *Jeremia 1–25*, 135. Holladay ("Deuteronomic

I concur with Holladay; here as elsewhere, the interplay of contemporary (synchronic) theological perspectives may be obscured by the historical-critical tendency to ascribe the differences between such perspectives to editorial layers within the book. This intrusion may very well be that of the prophet himself (or one of his immediate followers), who, in quoting the people's doubting outcry (8:19a and 8:20), could not wait to its end without objecting against its implications. Theologically, this interruption is of interest, since it suggests a *justification* of God's withdrawal; in answer to the expression of doubt that challenges God's apparent absence and failure to save his people, the prophet bursts in with the well-known accusation of the people as responsible for their own fate.

Three observations are in order. The first concerns the use of the rhetorical questions in Jeremiah as a source for discovering theological polemics. The literary study of 8:19–20 reveals the distinct theological perspectives at play. The prophetic intrusion into the three-part rhetorical unit allows us to identify the question itself as a genuine, nonprophetic position, which the prophet (or one of his immediate followers) could not disregard. The doubt concerning God's presence in Zion and failure to save is clearly not the attitude of the prophet, but rather a perception articulated by his audience in Jerusalem, which the prophet molds into the form of the threefold rhetorical question.

Second, this passage demonstrates that doubt arises in the clash of two opposing theological conceptions, particularly when theological certainties conflict with undeniable (and seemingly impossible) circumstances. The rhetorical question of 8:19a and 8:20 is motivated by the close connection between the roles of God as king and warrior and the expectation of his presence in Zion. These two background assumptions, that God is present and that God will save, which govern the "theology of Zion," seem no longer to operate at this crucial time.[32]

Third, this passage can tell us much about the shape of the theodical

---

Gloss") argues for the Jeremianic authorship of 8:19b and considers it an intentional interruption within the threefold rhetorical question, as part of the "poetic effect of the oracle" (495). This line is also taken by Lundbom, *Jeremiah 1–20*, 528–29, 532. I agree with Holladay ("Deuteronomic Gloss," 496–97) that the form (the threefold rhetorical question) and the vocabulary do not support DtrJ authorship, but rather constitute a Jeremianic echo of Deut 12:3 (498).

32. On the theology of Zion in Jeremiah, see Rom-Shiloni, "Challenging the Notion"; compare Wessels, "Zion, Beautiful City"; and Mettinger, *Dethronement of Sabaoth*, 62–66.

discourse among the prophet and his contemporaries. The secondary intrusion creates an asymmetric interplay between justification, doubt, and protest. The intrusion does not at all negate the issues raised concerning God's seeming absence from Zion and the lack of divine help. On the contrary, it either accepts both as given or completely avoids them, and it rather transforms the discussion into the arena of divine justice, adding another component that lays responsibility for the distress upon the people themselves. This line of argumentation, followed in the intrusion, accords with the well-known biblical phenomenon of justifying God's punitive measures as judge (e.g., Ezek 8–11; and see chap. 10 and §11.2); thus, the intrusion indicates that we are indeed witnessing here a lively (and literary) example of theodical discourse.[33]

Jeremiah 8:21–23 features another three-part rhetorical question. This one is couched in the first-person singular, framed as the prophet's lament over his people. Should, however, this rhetorical question actually be attributed to the prophet?[34]

[21] Because my fair people is shattered I am shattered,	²¹על־שבר בת־עמי השברתי
I am dejected, seized by desolation.	קדרתי שמה החזקתני.
[22] Is there no balm in Gilead?	²²הַצרי אין בגלעד
Can no physician be found?	אם־רפא אין שם
Why has healing not yet come to my fair people?	כי מדוע לא עלתה ארכת בת־עמי.
[23] Oh, that my head were water,	²³מי־יתן ראשי מים
My eyes a fount of tears!	ועיני מקור דמעה
Then would I weep day and night	ואבכה יומם ולילה
for the slain of my fair people.	את חללי בת־עמי.

Jeremiah 8:21 and 8:23, with their repetition of בת־עמי, serve as an *inclusio* that expresses the prophet's agony over the destruction of his people at a time when the city is *already* filled with "the slain of my poor people" (8:23).[35] Jeremiah 8:22 interjects another cry of desperation, formed as a

33. This theological observation supplements the fine rhetorical studies of this passage as a dialogue between the prophet, the people, and God; see Lundbom, *Jeremiah 1–20*, 528–30; and Fischer, *Jeremia 1–25*, 344–45.

34. Contra Holladay, *Jeremiah*, 1.290; Carroll, *Jeremiah*, 235–36; Lundbom, *Jeremiah 1–20*, 533–34; and Fischer, *Jeremia 1–25*, 344–45.

35. This analysis, then, sets out an alternative suggestion for the division of the text,

three-part rhetorical question, which in its turn expresses doubt concerning God's presence and his ability to save the people from the tough circumstances in Jerusalem. The same basic issues raised in 8:19-20 are now expressed through an alternative metaphor, using medical imagery: balm from the Gilead as herbal medicine and God as a physician, a specialist in healing the people of their injuries.[36] As in 8:19a and 8:20, the questions that form the first two components stem from the expectation that when God is present, he acts for his people (in this case as a compassionate healer); they thus raise doubt about God's presence. The third component once again complains about or protests against the lack of salvation. But in difference from 8:19b, there is no hint in 8:22 that the people are in any way to blame for their suffering. Finally, as in the preceding passage, this quotation does not see God as responsible for the distress. Thus, in its theological approach 8:22 also adopts the (A' → C) conception and expresses a desperate call for salvation.

These rhetorical questions (8:19a, 20 and 8:22) take the same position; they exemplify the horrors of the destruction, which Jeremiah vividly adduces by quoting the lamenting cries. This second cry of lament, however, differs from the first in that the prophetic voice does not intrude into the quotation. On both theological and literary grounds, this rhetorical question in 8:22 is also a quoted lament; it does not represent Jeremiah's own position. This recognition requires a wider survey of anonymous quotations in Jeremiah that feature fragmentary laments.

In contrast to the communal laments, these short lament texts are fragmentary in nature, in that they generally include only one of the two literary components of the lament: cries of despair in the face of distress (usually part of the complaint) and (rarely) pleas for salvation. Given their truncated form, they rarely exemplify a full theological framework. However, these fragmentary quoted laments share the (A' → C) conception with the communal laments, as they question God's presence and (in)action in face of a distress caused by human enemies. Apart from 9:16-20, which mentions the wailing women of Jerusalem, the quotations are all anonymous. They occur as first-person plural cries of despair (4:8b, 13b, 19-20;

---

which may account for the distinct voices within these verses. Compare Lundbom (*Jeremiah 1–20*, 528–39), who divides the prophetic units between 8:21 and 8:22 (i.e., 8:18–21 and 8:22–9:2).

36. Medical imagery appears as a metaphor for military defeat in Jer 14:18; 51:8–9; God is described as a physician in Exod 15:26; Hos 5:13; 6:1; 7:1; 11:3; 14:5. For balm (צרי) as a curative herb, see Jer 46:11.

9:16–21); first-person or second-person singular, feminine constructions (4:29–31), personifying the lament of the city; and first-person singular (4:19–21; 8:21–23; 10:19–25; 14:17–18). The laments of this last group express the views of the prophet himself, in his role of praying for the people (14:11; 15:1; 16:5).[37]

If those laments express the prophet's own sentiments, however, one must show that the basic perceptions behind these fragments are expressed elsewhere by the prophet. Yet, neither of the theological problems identified here—either the possibility of God's absence from his city or his seeming inability to save his people—is standard for Jeremiah's prophecies against Judah or in the prophecies against the nations, which generally use conceptions (B') and (C') (discussed in chaps. 8–9). Although the notion of divine abandonment is well situated in ancient Near Eastern sources concerning destruction of cities and temples, Jeremiah refers explicitly to such a notion in only one passage (12:7).[38] Furthermore, if we consider these fragments in light of the two governing explanations of God's roles in war found in Jeremiah, we may note that the prophet commonly expresses the opposite perspective—he clearly emphasizes God's presence in the city and the land, along with his people and their enemies, and accentuates God's own role in the destruction. In light of this difference and Jeremiah's general antipathy to the (A' → C) framework, none of these fragmentary laments can represent the prophet's own ideas.

Therefore, the lament in 8:22, as well as these other fragmentary laments and cries of doubt and despair, may be presumed to represent genuine sentiments or laments, expressed by the prophet's contemporaries, which are secondarily put into judgment prophecies or into larger edited units of oracles (such as 8:4–9:25) in order to sharpen the impression of the catastrophe. It is quite remarkable that although there is a significant gap between the prophet's conceptions and those expressed in the rhetorical question of 8:22, Jeremiah (or his immediate followers/tradents) had no difficulty placing it within the prophet's cry over his people.

Jeremiah 14:7–9 provides a more extended example of the prophet's

---

37. See Reventlow, *Liturgie und prophetisches Ich*, 199–201; and Hoffman, *Jeremiah 1–25*, 177–79. Carroll (*Jeremiah*, 167, 261, 263) judges only 8:21–23 to be the prophet's own words, while the others (4:19–21; 10:19–21, 23–25) are, for him, communal laments or laments of the city. Finally, Holladay (*Jeremiah*, 1.147, 149, 290, 293, 310–12, 436–37) considers all to be fragments of actual laments.

38. For divine presence, absence, and abandonment, see Rom-Shiloni, "Challenging the Notion."

reuse of such a cry. These verses constitute the second passage within the unit 14:1–15:4, which is headed by the superscription עַל־דִּבְרֵי הַבַּצָּרוֹת ("concerning the drought," 14:1).[39] This unit is built in two symmetrical sections (14:1–16 and 14:17–15:4), with four components in each: description of distress (14:2–6, 17–18), communal lament (14:7–9, 19–22), prohibition against praying on behalf of the people (14:11–12; 15:1), and God's judgmental response (14:10, 13–16; 15:2–4).[40] However, from 14:7 on the remaining subunits do not refer to drought. Rather, the prophet, the people, and God in his responses discuss the horrors of a military-political threat and raise or challenge the expectation that God will intervene to save the people. Within this larger context, 14:7–9 presents a partial communal lament:

[7] Though our iniquities testify against us,	אִם־עֲוֺנֵינוּ עָנוּ בָנוּ [7]
act, O Lᴏʀᴅ, for the sake of Your name;	יְהוָה עֲשֵׂה לְמַעַן שְׁמֶךָ
though our rebellions are many	כִּי־רַבּוּ מְשׁוּבֹתֵינוּ
and we have sinned against You.	לְךָ חָטָאנוּ.
[8] O Hope of Israel,	מִקְוֵה יִשְׂרָאֵל [8]
Its deliverer in time of trouble,	מוֹשִׁיעוֹ בְּעֵת צָרָה
why are You like a stranger in the land,	לָמָּה תִהְיֶה כְּגֵר בָּאָרֶץ
like a traveler who stops only for the night?	וּכְאֹרֵחַ נָטָה לָלוּן.
[9] Why are You like a man who is stunned,	לָמָּה תִהְיֶה כְּאִישׁ נִדְהָם [9]
like a warrior who cannot give victory?	כְּגִבּוֹר לֹא־יוּכַל לְהוֹשִׁיעַ
Yet You are in our midst, O Lᴏʀᴅ,	וְאַתָּה בְקִרְבֵּנוּ יְהוָה
and Your name is attached to us—	וְשִׁמְךָ עָלֵינוּ נִקְרָא
Do not forsake us!	אַל־תַּנִּחֵנוּ.

39. For similar superscriptions to other prophetic units in Jeremiah, see 46:1; 47:1; 49:34. The title here specifies drought as the thematic focus of the passage, even though 14:2–6 is the only segment that refers to this crisis (although 14:22 brings a call for rain). On the aspect of drought in this passage and generally in Jeremiah, see Hareuveni, *New Light*, 27–53.

40. From the literary and thematic points of view, Uffenheimer ("On Drought") presents the symmetrical structure of this unit and argues that it constituted the prophet's lament and innerdialogue with his God. The structural and literary similarities between the two parts of this unit are set out by Volz (*Der Prophet Jeremia*, 162–63) and Holladay (*Jeremiah*, 1.422). From the perspective of literary-history criticism, Duhm (*Jeremia*, 127–33) considers this unit to be comprised of independent and detached oracles; similarly Skinner, *Prophecy and Religion*, 128. From the liturgical aspect, Boda ("From Complaint to Contrition," 188, 193) argues for the unity of this entire passage.

The unit begins with a confession of sins (Jer 14:7; compare Ps 79:8–9),[41] followed by complaints against God's neglect and seeming dysfunction (Jer 14:8–9a; compare Ps 79:5, 10), and concludes with declarations of piety and a plea for salvation (Jer 14:9b; compare Ps 79:11–13). Formally, in their larger context, these components could have applied to Jer 14:2–6 as a possible description of the distress; however, 14:7–9 seems to be detached from the horrors of drought. It is thus more plausible that these verses are a fragment of a communal lament focused on a disaster caused by a military threat, where God's assistance as a warrior is expected.[42]

Two epithets in 14:8 are used in apposition to describe God: מקוה ישראל and מושיעו בעת צרה. The relationship between them resembles the structural relationship between the other subunits of this collection. מקוה in its double meaning as "water source" (Jer 17:13) and as "hope" (Ezra 10:2) alludes to the two distinct sources of distress. In the first sense, it stands as a metaphoric epithet that portrays God as a source of living water and corresponds with the setting of drought, while the root קוה in the sense of hope for divine help also activates the sphere of a military threat (although תקוה is the more common noun form in prayer contexts). This double meaning also serves Jeremiah in 17:13, and it seems that it is intentionally invoked.[43]

The second epithet, מושיעו בעת צרה ("savior in times of need"), clearly belongs with the military distress. In the present discussion, it provides yet another example of the prevailing theological expectation that God

41. Confession of sins is a component that occurs in only a few communal laments (as in Ps 79:8). In Jeremiah, such a declaration is heard only in 14:19–20 and in another liturgical text quoted in 3:22–26. See §11.2.3.

42. Boda ("From Complaint to Contrition," 194) suggests its possible *Sitz im Leben*, and even actual dating, and argues that 14:7–9 and 14:19–22 are part of a liturgy composed in the days of Zedekiah, during the siege, which is combined with the larger unit concerning drought (though 14:2–6 must be prior to the destruction of Jerusalem).

43. קוה occurs in the Hebrew Bible in two homonymic roots. 1קוה with ל־/אל־ of the person means "wait, hope for" and with God as the object: "wait for God, wish for his assistance" (as in Isa 8:17; Hos 12:7). The noun מקוה otherwise occurs in Jer 17:13; Ezra 10:2; and 1 Chr 29:15 and is taken as derivative of 1קוה (Koehler, Baumgartner, and Stamm, *Hebrew and Aramaic Lexicon*, 626). The most common noun form is תקוה, with God as its source (e.g., Ps 9:19; Jer 29:11; 31:17; and in a quotation of despair, Ezek 37:11). Compare 2קוה, which means "gather" (Gen 1:9) and is used specifically to denote gathering water. That the two homonymous roots have identical nominal forms allows the play of the double meaning here and in Jer 17:12–13.

will act as to save his people from their human enemies in keeping with the (A′ → C) framework.[44]

In its immediate context, the second epithet sets the stage for two structurally parallel rhetorical questions that use two quite shocking images of God:

[8] Why are You like a stranger in the land,	⁸למה תהיה כגר בארץ
like a traveler who stops only for the night?	וכארח נטה ללון.
[9] Why are You like a man who is stunned,	⁹למה תהיה כאיש נדהם
like a warrior who cannot give victory?	כגבור לא־יוכל להושיע.

The question "why would you pretend to be like . . ." or "present yourself as . . ." captures the essence of doubt in this communal lament.[45] The poet chooses images as different as possible from the divine qualities suggested by the epithet מושיעו בעת צרה. The first question challenges God's presence by using the images of a stranger and a passing guest.[46] These two represent marginal members of a human society, either resident outsider (גר) or an occasional visitor who stays for only a short period of time before heading on to his next stop (ארח). The common denominator of the two is their foreign identity—they do not belong—which is mainly illustrated by the lack of any commitment or sense of responsibility to the place they are in and detachment from the social activity taking place in the core society. Comparing two such figures to the God of Israel—who gave his own land to his people to settle in and who is considered to be involved in all aspects of his people's life in this land—creates a sense of absurdity: could God conceivably behave as such an outsider at this time of need?

---

44. The epithet מושיע for God also occurs in 2 Sam 22:42 ‖ Ps 18:42; Isa 43:3, 11; 45:21; 49:26; 60:16; Hos 13:4; and Ps 106:21. Compare the passages in which God summons a human savior for his people (Judg 3:9, 15; 2 Kgs 13:5; Neh 9:27). In all these contexts the distresses are political-military ones. This is also the appropriate context for the use of the epithet גבור for God: גבור יושיע (Zeph 3:17). Fredriksson (*Jahwe als Krieger*, 61–64) takes Jer 14:8–9 as evidence for the frozen use of the epithet גבור, which he thinks is detached from the context of war. I reject this argument.

45. למה תהיה כ to introduce an image also occurs in Song 1:7: שלמה אהיה כעטיה על עדרי חבריך ("For why would I be like one who pastures with your friends' flocks covered (in modesty)"; see Zakovitz, *Song of Songs*, 53. See also למה יהיה ל־, 1 Chr 21:3.

46. The Septuagint's αὐτόχθων ("citizen") seems harmonistic, employing here the known pair גר/אזרח, as in Lev 17:15.

The second question addresses God's power in images taken from human war. It adduces two categories of ineffective warriors, one who is stunned with fear (איש נדהם) and another who is powerless, "a warrior who cannot give victory."[47] As in the previous question, the two images are as far as possible from the qualities suggested by the epithets of God as warrior.

To enhance the power of these expressions of doubt even more, the two questions are answered by the proclamation: "You are in our midst, O Lord, and Your name is attached to us" (14:9b). Although these troubling feelings embrace him, the poet still expresses confidence in God; he declares that God is present among his people and is thus expected to be involved on their behalf (as in Num 14:14; Deut 7:21; 23:15).[48] This communal lament concludes with the people's plea: "Do not forsake us."[49]

Although fragmentary, Jer 14:7–9 exemplifies in the most powerful way the expression of doubt that emerges through the clash between two profound theological ideas—the certainty of God's presence and the absolute trust in his powers as warrior-savior—in the face of the present distress. Formally, doubt is expressed in rhetorical questions, which here present extreme, absurd images of God in his roles as king (and as warrior), taken from the human arena and specifically from either marginal social characters or antiheroic figures. The comparison of God to these figures illustrates the great gap between what is theologically expected and the incomprehensible circumstances in which the poet and people find themselves. The declaration of confidence, which accentuates the people's

47. איש נדהם is a *hapax*. The root appears only in an epigraphic evidence from Yavneh-Yam: [ולא תדהמנ[י, interpreted "do not leave me powerless"; see Ahituv, *Ha-Ketav VeHa-Miktav*, 143–49. The Septuagint's ἄνθρωπος ὑπνῶν ("a sleeping man") is a harmonistic suggestion, built upon descriptions of God using the language of ישן and עור (Pss 44:24; 78:65; 121:4; רדם is not used in reference to God).

48. יהוה בקרבנו is an expression for divine protection granted by God's presence in war (1 Sam 4:3, where the ark serves as symbol of God's presence) and promised in Joel 2:27 and Zeph 3:15. Compare Mic 3:11, where it denotes a false hope for salvation; and in Zeph 3:5, God's presence guarantees justice. On the negative side, see Num 14:42 and Deut 1:42, where God's absence from the battlefield amounts to the threat of defeat; compare Deut 6:15 and Amos 5:17, where God's presence "among you" represents a risk or danger.

49. אל-תנחנו suggests a unique use of נוח ("leave") in the semantic field of desertion (otherwise expressed by עזב, זנח, etc.); this meaning seems to be much more stark than simply to "leave someone behind," as this root denotes in the human sphere (e.g., 1 Kgs 19:3). Compare the benevolent divine care expressed by נוח, as in the phrase יהוה הניח ל-/מכל-איביו מסביב (Josh 23:1), which stands for "cause to rest" in the aftermath of military success.

perception that God is nevertheless in their midst, adds additional weight to this painful lament.

These theological expressions that move from the questions—the imageries, the declaration of faith and the plea—describe the literary-rhetorical ways in which Jeremiah represents doubt. They reveal feelings of insecurity that jeopardize the people's certainty in regard to the long-held theological traditions concerning God's presence and his ability to deliver in times of distress (clearly close to 8:19–20 and 8:22).

As an antithesis to such expressions, the consolation prophecy in Zeph 3:14–17 provides a telling example:[50]

[14] Sing, Fair Zion, shout aloud, Israel.	¹⁴ רני בת־ציון הריעו ישראל
Be glad and exult with all your heart, Fair Jerusalem.	שמחי ועלזי בכל־לב בת ירושלים.
[15] YHWH has commuted your sentence,	¹⁵ הסיר יהוה משפטיך
He has cleared away your foe.[51]	פנה איבך
<u>The King of Israel, the Lord, is in your midst,[52]</u>	<u>מלך ישראל יהוה בקרבך</u>
You will no longer fear evil.	לא־תיראי רע עוד.
[16] On that day it will be said to Jerusalem: Do not be afraid;	¹⁶ ביום ההוא יאמר לירושלים אל־תיראי
To Zion: Do not be disheartened.	ציון אל־ירפו ידיך.
[17] <u>The Lord your God is in your midst.</u>	¹⁷ <u>יהוה אלהיך בקרבך</u>
<u>A warrior who brings victory.</u>	<u>גבור יושיע</u>

50. The translation of Zeph 3:14–17 is by Berlin, *Zephaniah*, 141. The entire passage includes 3:18–20 as well; see Sweeney, *Zephaniah*, 193–208. A question under debate is the relationship between Zephaniah and Jeremiah; this passage provides one example of the great differences between the two prophets. Sweeney adduces the arguments often presented for a postexilic dating of Zeph 3:14–20 and then argues that they are not "a firm basis" for such a dating (196). Sweeney prefers to date this passage to the time of Josiah's reform and to see it as part of the expectations for a close-at-hand return. I cite this passage here for phenomenological comparison; thus I do not attend to major questions concerning the passage.

51. פנה איבך is a *hapax*. The Septuagint suggests a contextual interpretation, using λυτρόω, which is otherwise an equivalent of פדה (Jer 15:21; 31:11 [= 38:11 LXX]; see Exod 13:13; 15:13; 34:20; Deut 15:15) or of גאל (Zeph 3:1; Jer 50:34; see Exod 6:6; Lev 25:25, 30). In addition, Septuagint, Peshitta, and Aramaic Targumim use the plural איביך.

52. See also Mic 4:7. While Berlin (*Zephaniah*, 143) treats God as the (present) king, scholars often suggest that the text should be corrected to a verbal *yiqtol* form: ימלך

He rejoices over you with gladness,   יָשִׂישׂ עָלַיִךְ בְּשִׂמְחָה
He keeps silent in His love;   יַחֲרִישׁ בְּאַהֲבָתוֹ
He delights over you with song.   יָגִיל עָלַיִךְ בְּרִנָּה.

In Zephaniah's words, God is indeed "a warrior who brings victory" (3:17; compare Jer 14:9ab)—an idea closely related to the emphasis on his presence amidst his people (Zeph 3:15, 17)—this presence guarantees salvation, security, and joy.[53] Jeremiah 14:7–9 is a remarkable example of the opposite side—the theological crisis that develops once this orderly tradition crashes on the hard rocks of reality. At that crucial and painful moment, doubt first arises—examining these traditional perceptions and questioning them one by one.

The lament in 14:7–9 seems to be part of a communal lament that is borrowed by the prophet for the needs of his prophecy, thus of a status similar to that of other anonymous quotations in the book. Jeremiah cannot be considered its author, although he may have contributed two of his own phrases to this liturgical text (מִקְוֵה יִשְׂרָאֵל and מְשׁוּבוֹת).[54] This distinction of voices (of authorship) is essential to the task of drawing further distinctions between the diverse theological conceptions brought together and at times intertwined in Jeremiah.

The independence and non-Jeremianic character of this communal lament is apparent in several themes and phrases, being otherwise unknown in the book (*hapaxes*): יהוה עֲשֵׂה לְמַעַן שְׁמֶךָ ("act, O Lord, for the sake of Your name") otherwise occurs in Ezek 20:9, 14, 22; 36:22; Isa 48:9;

(likewise Mic 4:7; see BHS and commentaries), which turns divine kingship into eschatological expectation. Sweeney (*Zephaniah*, 199) treats מֶלֶךְ as referring to the human king, suggesting that it designates Josiah and only metaphorically refers to "YHWH's protection of Jerusalem from danger." I do not see that this phrasing denotes a human king mediating divine kingship over the city. For declarations of faith that praise God's kingship, see Pss 44:5 and 74:12.

53. Sweeney (*Zephaniah*, 197) points out the close connection and familiarity of Zephaniah with temple liturgy and with "formal temple worship." This might explain his emphasis on Jerusalem and on Zion theology. Smith (*Micah, Zephaniah, and Nahum*, 143–44) is even more specific and argues that the prophecy has the structure and the vocabulary of the enthronement Psalms (47, 95, 97), which explains many of its features, including the promise of salvation. Surprisingly, the connections to Jeremiah seem not to attract the attention of these scholars.

54. מְשׁוּבָה (and its plural מְשׁוּבוֹת) occurs twice in Hosea (11:7; 14:5), once in Proverbs (1:32), and ten times in Jeremiah. Jer 14:7 is the only reference of מְשׁוּבוֹת in a quoted passage. On מִקְוֵה יִשְׂרָאֵל, see discussion earlier in this section.

66:5; and more frequently within psalmodic literature (Pss 79:9; 106:8) and in individual laments (23:3). The expectation that God will surely save, and the doubting of his presence and/or his power, do not accord with Jeremiah's perspective. Jeremiah vigorously refutes such ideas; particularly he distinguishes God's presence from a notion of certain salvation and argues that God may be present amidst his people, but yet act as a foe (e.g., 21:1–7).

This fragment of an otherwise unknown communal lament may contribute a substantial dimension to the role of Jeremiah as one who prays for his people (11:14; 14:11; 15:1). Jeremiah is clearly acquainted with prayer literature and as part of it presumably also knew communal laments (10:19–25), if we can assume that some of those are composed during his time of activity. Expressions of doubt and protest are part of this language of prayer.

The prophet seems to have used such phrases, from individual verses up to larger segments of several verses, in his prophecies. It appears that he accepts these expressions as they are and places those laments in new contexts, interfering in their content and structure in very minor ways. In their prophetic contexts, these quoted voices reinforce the prophetic message concerning the severity of the imminent or present catastrophe by demonstrating the people's feelings of doubt and distress (8:19–20, 21–22; 14:7–9, 19–22).[55] Thus, (1) the use of such quotations should be seen as an identifiable literary technique native to the prophet's own arsenal; and (2) these quotations demonstrably never showcase the prophet's own sentiments, and therefore they should not be taken as reflecting the prophet's own theological conceptions. Therefore, these fragmentary laments are of great importance for the reconstruction of the theodical discourse of this period, precisely because they reflect different perspectives from those of the prophet.

In summary, expressions of doubt in Jeremiah occur in only a few anonymous quotations within the book, introduced as challenges in the form of interrogative sentences—rhetorical questions or simple ones. Simple questions are raised in order to be immediately refuted by the prophet (5:19; 9:11–15; 13:22b–27; 16:10–13; 22:9); and the rhetorical questions stem from fragmentary communal laments that the prophet quotes as "other" contemporary reactions circulating in Jerusalem of the early sixth century.

Two major issues are in the frontline of the contemporary theologi-

---

55. Within Jer 11–20 only three such questions raised in individual laments are secondarily connected to the prophet himself.

cal discourse concerning the role of God as warrior—God's presence and God's powers in war (see §10.2 and §11.3 on expressions of doubt). They stem from the basic conception (A' → C) that God is the savior of his people from their enemies in times of military distress (and logically speaking, not the source or instigator of that distress). Doubt evolves from the prior *acceptance* of these theological givens, in the face of the realization that expected salvation is not forthcoming. If the theological framework is irrefutable, questions must arise about God's presence and/or powers. As vehicles of doubt, the rhetorical questions, in particular, allow the speakers to present the extreme improbability of the seeming divine inactivity in the current context, in an effort to encourage God to recommit himself to his role as king and savior of his people.

Within these expressions themselves, we have a clash between the conceptual framework of (A' → C) and the experienced reality, introducing questions concerning God's roles as lord (king) and warrior. If God is the king of Jerusalem and is present in his city, how could he not save his people in this time of need?[56] This seemingly unresolvable problem, however, is not to be construed simply as a result of conflict between cherished conceptions of God and distressing reality.[57] While situations of distress are certainly the fertile and necessary soil for doubt, the recurring phenomenon in Jeremiah of expressions of doubt reflects a conflict between two conceptions of God (i.e., presence and power). In such expressions, questions are raised concerning one or even both conceptions, suggesting the option that one conception reinforces over the other (i.e., God is absent, therefore, he does not use his powers to save), or that one of the conceptions (or even both) seems inactive and thus is(/are) challenged (i.e., God is present, but has lost his powers, thus he cannot save). The prophet argues in response for a significant transformation in one or in both conceptions.[58]

Doubt is clearly an integral element of the wider contemporary theodical discourse, and so it is used by the prophet. It starts from a deep piety and belief in God's benevolence, in his role as savior in times of need, and

56. Similarly, doubt is apparent in the clash between God's roles as warrior and as judge: if God is solely responsible for wreaking destruction upon his people (as implicitly understood in Jer 5:19; 16:10–13), how does that action square with God's attributes of justice and compassion? See §10.2.

57. Compare Davidson (*Courage to Doubt*, 8), who argues that the conflict emerges between cherished conceptions of God and historical reality.

58. The prophetic refutation of such doubts may be seen also along this clash of conceptions: God is present and has not lost his powers, but uses them all against his people; see §9.1 and §9.4.

it seeks a theological reconciliation between conceptions of God's control over history and over his people and the present situation of human suffering and distress brought on by the war.

7.3. JUSTIFICATION THROUGH POLEMIC: THE "PEACE PROPHETS" VERSUS JEREMIAH AND EZEKIEL

The perceptions that the destruction is an event that the enemies had initiated and fought with no divine assistance (A'), and that God indeed might be expected to save his people from them (C), are expressed by the "peace prophets," quoted in the books of Jeremiah and Ezekiel and fiercely refuted by them.[59] The following discussion has three goals: (1) to show that the peace prophecies should be categorized as justifications of God; (2) to argue that the proper way to express justification of God is the cardinal source of polemic between Jeremiah and Ezekiel and the other prophets; the question adduced, then, is what exactly distinguishes them theologically? and (3) to discuss Jeremiah's and Ezekiel's alternatives, that is, how did the two prophets treat (if at all) the (A' → C) conception of God and man in war?

Ten short and fragmentary peace prophecies are quoted in Jeremiah and Ezekiel, from one word to several verses long. The prophecies promise salvation in connection with three major facets of the political-military crises that marked the deteriorating state of Judah over the years 604–586.[60]

a. The peace prophets assure the people that the Babylonian threat against Jerusalem and Judah will not be realized.

The peace prophecies disregard the Babylonian threat, arguing that it will never materialize (Jer 14:13, 15; 37:19). They counter it with the promise summarized in one word שלום: "peace, well-being"—that is, a lasting se-

---

59. I use the term "peace prophets" in this discussion. The Septuagint constantly presents those prophets as ψευδοπροφητῶν ("false prophets"), adopting the perspective of their opponents.

60. The peace prophecies discussed here are Jer 6:14; 8:11; 14:13, 15; 23:17; 27:9, 14, 16–22; 28:2–4; 37:19; Ezek 13:10. A few additional quotations fall outside this group: Jer 23:25 refers to dreams as a basis for prophecy; 23:33–40 features a quasi-dialogue about משא יהוה. The quotation in 7:4 is not attributed to a prophetic speaker, though it is considered to comprise "illusions" (so NJPS) or "false words" that the people count upon (7:4, 8).

curity guaranteed for the king and the people in their place (Jer 6:14 ‖ 8:11 with minor textual differences; 23:17; Ezek 13:10).[61]

1. Jeremiah 6:13–14

[13] For from the smallest to the greatest,	כִּי מִקְּטַנָּם וְעַד־גָּדוֹל ¹³
They are all greedy for gain;	כֻּלּוֹ בּוֹצֵעַ בָּצַע
Priest and prophet alike,	וּמִנָּבִיא וְעַד־כֹּהֵן
They all act falsely.	כֻּלּוֹ עֹשֶׂה שָּׁקֶר.
[14] They offer healing offhand	וַיְרַפְּאוּ ¹⁴
For the wounds of My people,	אֶת־שֶׁבֶר עַמִּי עַל־נְקַלָּה
Saying, "<u>All is well, all is well</u>,"	לֵאמֹר <u>שָׁלוֹם שָׁלוֹם</u>
When nothing is well.	וְאֵין שָׁלוֹם.

2. Jeremiah 14:13

[13] I said, "Ah, Lord YHWH! The prophets are saying to them, 'You shall not see the sword, famine shall not come upon you, but <u>I will give you unfailing security in this place</u>.'"	וָאֹמַר אֲהָהּ אֲדֹנָי יְהוִה ¹³ הִנֵּה הַנְּבִאִים אֹמְרִים לָהֶם לֹא־תִרְאוּ חֶרֶב וְרָעָב לֹא־ יִהְיֶה לָכֶם כִּי־<u>שְׁלוֹם אֱמֶת</u> <u>אֶתֵּן לָכֶם בַּמָּקוֹם הַזֶּה</u>.

3. Jeremiah 14:15

[15] Assuredly, thus said YHWH concerning the prophets who prophesy in My name though I have not sent them, and who say, "<u>Sword and famine shall not befall this land</u>"; those very prophets shall perish by sword and famine.	לָכֵן כֹּה־אָמַר יְהוָה עַל־הַנְּבִאִים הַנִּבְּאִים בִּשְׁמִי וַאֲנִי לֹא־שְׁלַחְתִּים וְהֵמָּה אֹמְרִים <u>חֶרֶב וְרָעָב</u> <u>לֹא יִהְיֶה בָּאָרֶץ הַזֹּאת</u> בַּחֶרֶב וּבָרָעָב יִתַּמּוּ הַנְּבִאִים הָהֵמָּה.

4. Jeremiah 23:16–17

[16] Thus said YHWH of Hosts:	כֹּה־אָמַר יְהוָה צְבָאוֹת ¹⁶

61. The promise of "peace, well-being" is attested in Neo-Assyrian prophecies; see *šulmu* in *Chicago Assyrian Dictionary* Š 3.247–56; Parpola, *Assyrian Prophecies*, 1.9 lines 26, 29; 3.1 lines 9–12.

Do not listen to the words of	אל־תשמעו על־דברי
the prophets	הנבאים
Who prophesy to you.	הנבאים לכם
They are deluding you,	מהבלים המה אתכם
The prophecies they speak are from their own minds,	חזון לבם ידברו
Not from the mouth of YHWH.	לא מפי יהוה.
[17] They declare to men who despise Me:	[17] אמרים אמור למנאצי
YHWH has said:	דבר יהוה
"All shall be well with you";	שלום יהיה לכם
And to all who follow their willful hearts they say:	וכל הלך בשררות לבו אמרו
"No evil shall befall you."	לא־תבוא עליכם רעה.

5. Jeremiah 37:19

[19] And where are those prophets of yours who prophesied to you that the king of Babylon would never move against you and against this land?	[19] ואיו (ק: ואיה) נביאיכם אשר־נבאו לכם לאמר לא־יבא מלך־בבל עליכם ועל הארץ הזאת.

6. Ezekiel 13:10

[10] Inasmuch as they have misled My people, saying, "It is well," when nothing is well, daubing with plaster the flimsy wall which the people were building.	[10] יען וביען הטעו את־עמי לאמר שלום ואין שלום והוא בנה חיץ והנם טחים אתו תפל.

b. The prophets promise divine deliverance from the ongoing subjugation to Babylon.

7. Jeremiah 27:9

[9] As for you, give no heed to your prophets, augurs, dreamers, diviners, and sorcerers, who say to you, "Do not serve the king of Babylon."	[9] ואתם אל־תשמעו אל־נביאיכם ואל־קסמיכם ואל־חלמתיכם ואל־ענניכם ואל־כשפיכם אשר־הם אמרים אליכם לאמר לא תעבדו את־מלך בבל.

8. Jeremiah 27:14

[14] Give no heed to the words of the prophets who say to you, "Do not serve the king of Babylon," for they prophesy falsely to you.

14וְאַל־תִּשְׁמְעוּ אֶל־דִּבְרֵי הַנְּבִאִים הָאֹמְרִים אֲלֵיכֶם לֵאמֹר לֹא תַעַבְדוּ אֶת־מֶלֶךְ בָּבֶל כִּי שֶׁקֶר הֵם נִבְּאִים לָכֶם.

9. Jeremiah 28:1–4, 10–11

[1] The prophet Hananiah son of Azzur, who is from Gibeon, spoke to me in the House of YHWH, in the presence of the priests and all the people. He said: [2] "Thus said YHWH of Hosts, the God of Israel: I hereby break the yoke of the king of Babylon. [3] In two years, I will restore to this place all the vessels of the House of YHWH which King Nebuchadnezzar of Babylon took from this place and brought to Babylon. [4] And I will restore to this place King Jeconiah son of Jehoiakim of Judah, and all the Judean exiles who went to Babylon—declares YHWH. Yes, I will break the yoke of the king of Babylon."
. . .
[10] But the prophet Hananiah removed the bar from the neck of the prophet Jeremiah, and broke it; [11] and Hananiah said in the presence of all the people, "Thus said YHWH: So will I break the yoke of King Nebuchadnezzar of Babylon from off the necks of all the nations, in two years." And the prophet Jeremiah went on his way.

1אָמַר אֵלַי חֲנַנְיָה בֶן־עַזּוּר הַנָּבִיא אֲשֶׁר מִגִּבְעוֹן בְּבֵית יְהוָה לְעֵינֵי הַכֹּהֲנִים וְכָל־הָעָם לֵאמֹר. 2כֹּה־אָמַר יְהוָה צְבָאוֹת אֱלֹהֵי יִשְׂרָאֵל לֵאמֹר שָׁבַרְתִּי אֶת־עֹל מֶלֶךְ בָּבֶל. 3בְּעוֹד שְׁנָתַיִם יָמִים אֲנִי מֵשִׁיב אֶל־הַמָּקוֹם הַזֶּה אֶת־כָּל־כְּלֵי בֵּית יְהוָה אֲשֶׁר לָקַח נְבוּכַדְנֶאצַּר מֶלֶךְ־בָּבֶל מִן־הַמָּקוֹם הַזֶּה וַיְבִיאֵם בָּבֶל. 4וְאֶת־יְכָנְיָה בֶן־יְהוֹיָקִים מֶלֶךְ־יְהוּדָה וְאֶת־כָּל־גָּלוּת יְהוּדָה הַבָּאִים בָּבֶלָה אֲנִי מֵשִׁיב אֶל־הַמָּקוֹם הַזֶּה נְאֻם־יְהוָה כִּי אֶשְׁבֹּר אֶת־עֹל מֶלֶךְ בָּבֶל. . . .

10וַיִּקַּח חֲנַנְיָה הַנָּבִיא אֶת־הַמּוֹטָה מֵעַל צַוַּאר יִרְמְיָה הַנָּבִיא וַיִּשְׁבְּרֵהוּ. 11וַיֹּאמֶר חֲנַנְיָה לְעֵינֵי כָל־הָעָם לֵאמֹר כֹּה אָמַר יְהוָה כָּכָה אֶשְׁבֹּר אֶת־עֹל נְבֻכַדְנֶאצַּר מֶלֶךְ־בָּבֶל בְּעוֹד שְׁנָתַיִם יָמִים מֵעַל־צַוַּאר כָּל־הַגּוֹיִם וַיֵּלֶךְ יִרְמְיָה הַנָּבִיא לְדַרְכּוֹ.

c. The prophets promise that King Jehoiachin, the temple vessels, and the people exiled in 597 will all soon return to Jerusalem (Jer 28:2–4; 27:16–22 MT).

10. Jeremiah 27:16–18[62]

[16] And to the priests and to all that
people I said: "Thus said the LORD:
Give no heed to the words of the
prophets who prophesy to you, 'The
vessels of the House of YHWH shall
shortly be brought back from Babylon,' for they prophesy falsely to you.
[17] Give them no heed. Serve the king
of Babylon, and live! Otherwise this
city shall become a ruin. [18] If they
are really prophets and the word of
YHWH is with them, let them inter-
cede with YHWH of Hosts not to let
the vessels remaining in the House of
YHWH, in the royal palace of Judah,
and in Jerusalem, go to Babylon!

[16] ואל־הכהנים אל־כל־העם
הזה דברתי לאמר כה אמר
יהוה אל־תשמעו אל־דברי
נביאיכם הנבאים לכם לאמר
הנה כלי בית־יהוה מושבים
מבבלה עתה מהרה כי שקר
המה נבאים לכם. [17] אל־
תשמעו אליהם עבדו את־
מלך־בבל וחיו למה תהיה
העיר הזאת חרבה. [18] ואם־
נבאים הם ואם־יש דבר־יהוה
אתם יפגעו־נא ביהוה צבאות
לבלתי־באו הכלים הנותרים
בבית־יהוה ובית מלך יהודה
ובירושלים בבלה.

62. The Septuagint equivalent of Jer 27:16–22 MT is 34:16–22; it is much shorter
than the Masoretic Text and diverges significantly from it. But in terms of the current
discussion, the quotations of the peace prophets do not differ between the two in
either 27:9 or 27:16, though the quotation in 27:14 is lacking in the Septuagint. The
differences are even more apparent in 27:19–22, which seems to be a secondary elaboration in both the Septuagint and Masoretic Text and does not contain an additional
quotation of a peace prophecy. For the reconstructed Hebrew *Vorlage* of the Septuagint, see Janzen, *Studies in the Text of Jeremiah*, 45–48. Janzen considers 27:16–22 to
be completely distinct from 27:1–15, which focuses only on the temple vessels and
(originally) the question of their return (not the time of their return); thus עתה מהרה
in 27:16 is an elaboration in the Masoretic Text that completely changes the question
of the previous passage, whether the vessels will be returned to when this will occur
(45). In Janzen's understanding, 27:17 MT is a plus based on 27:12–14 and 27:18bb MT
is taken from 27:21–22; but here Janzen concedes that the most reasonable explanation
for the difference would be that the Septuagint suffered haplography. Nevertheless,
Janzen concludes that 27:19–22 MT "is so awkward and overloaded with repetition
that it cannot be original" (46). Rather, he suggests that the Masoretic Text is in itself
a conflation of several variants and overloaded with expansions (47). Cf. Lundbom
(*Jeremiah 21–36*, 305, 321–25), who discusses in detail the scholarly divide over the
relationships between the Masoretic Text and Septuagint in this chapter and makes the
altogether opposite suggestion, arguing for the deficiency of the Septuagint suffering
of omissions due to haplography and *homoeoarcton/homoeoteleuton*. I find Lundbom's
position more convincing.

The fragmentary character of these quoted prophecies and their being scattered in diverse contexts within Jeremiah (and several times in Ezekiel) raise difficulties for relating these prophecies to specific events within the two decades of subjugation to Babylon. Three historical anchors might actually be in view here. First, the general promises of peace and the references to those who negate the Babylonian threat (Jer 6:14 || 8:11; possibly 14:12–13) may be connected with subjugation to Babylon in general, at any point of time from 604 on, when Judah became a Babylonian vassal kingdom (2 Kgs 24:1; *Babylonian Chronicles*, no. 5).[63]

A second potential anchor is the fourth year of Zedekiah (593/592; particularly the prophecies included in Jer 27–29; esp. 28:1 and 27:1).[64] At that time, Judah has been a Babylonian vassal for more than ten years; King Jehoiachin, his royal court, and a significant community of Jerusalem elites are already in exile (2 Kgs 24:8–17), and King Zedekiah heads a regional coalition against King Nebuchadnezzar of Babylon (Jer 27:1–4). Furthermore, Jeremiah gives additional information about the activity of peace prophets in Babylon among the Jehoiachin exiles, mentioning at least three by name (Ahab son of Kolaiah and Zedekiah son of Maaseiah in 29:21; and Shemaiah the Nehelemite in 29:24). But we have only indirect information about their message, which might also have focused on the duration of the Jehoiachin exile (29:24–29; see Jeremiah's prophecy in 29:1–9).

The third point of reference is the final Babylonian siege against Jerusalem, when the actual threat of war, destruction, and deportation became vivid, and the promises of divine salvation held an even more urgent role. This last context suits the description of the secret meetings between Zedekiah and Jeremiah during the long Babylonian siege, in the course of which a peace prophecy is quoted (37:19); This crisis might provide another possible anchor for the general promises of peace and likewise for the rejection of a real threat of war (14:13–15; 23:17; Ezek 13:19). The one chapter given to illegitimate prophets in Ezekiel (Ezek 13, plus a criticism of this group in 22:23–31) does not clarify the picture. Therefore, the dis-

---

63. See Grayson, *Assyrian and Babylonian Chronicles*, 99–102 no. 5. For discussions of the exact year Judah is subjugated to Babylon and the accompanying historical circumstances, see Oded, "When Was the Kingdom of Judah Subjugated?"; and Galil, "Babylonian Calendar."

64. Sarna, "Abortive Insurrection."

tinctions of content leave the actual historical data as vague as the books of Jeremiah and Ezekiel present it, and clearly less relevant.

If one focuses on the theological conceptions employed in these prophecies, Hananiah son of Azzur's prophecy (Jer 28:2–4, 11), the longest of the extant quotations, presents all the stylistic and thematic markers of a full-fledged prophecy. The prescript כה־אמר יהוה צבאות אלהי ישראל (28:2) uses one of the common introductory formulas in Jeremiah (7:3, 21; 9:14; 16:9; 18:13; 25:27; 29:4, 10, 21, 25; 31:23). The main body of the prophecy consists of an *inclusio* enclosing a repeated promise of deliverance: שברתי את־על מלך בבל (28:2b) and כי אשבר את־על מלך בבל (28:4b); and yet another *inclusio* on the repeated promise to return the vessels, the king, and the people אני משיב אל־המקום הזה (28:3–4).[65]

Furthermore, in breaking the yoke of the king of Babylon, Hananiah not only reacts to Jeremiah's symbolic action of wearing the yoke on his neck (27:2), but more so, he is invoking (or even restoring) a well-known metaphor, used by Isaiah son of Amoz (Isa 9:3; 10:27), by Jeremiah himself (Jer 30:8–9), and by Nahum (Nah 1:13) to describe release from subjugation as an act of divine deliverance. The same metaphor appears in Lev 26:13 and is alluded to in Ezek 34:27–28. With the exception of Isa 10:27—the only passage where such release is achieved through a human warrior summoned by God (10:26)—these texts portray God as the sole warrior, saving his people and releasing them from the yoke of their human subjugators.

Thematically, Hananiah combines all three topics. He describes God as warrior, who within two years will subdue the Babylonian king; by doing so, God will release the people of Judah from subjugation and will bring those exiled—the king, the temple vessels, and the people—back to Jerusalem. Hence, although we generally have only fragmentary information concerning the prophecies of the peace prophets (and assuming that they are a cohesive group), it seems safe to characterize them as belonging to the (A' → C) approach.

What is then the cardinal issue under debate, the crux of the polemic, between the prophets in the early years of the sixth century, which seems to have been a highly intensive and lively period of prophetic activity? The promises of salvation from the Babylonian threat, and especially the reliance on the prophecies of Isaiah son of Amoz, lead scholars to propose

---

65. Much is written on Hananiah's prophecy; for a careful literary study, see Brin, *Prophet in His Struggle*, 83–104.

that debates over Zion theology form the core of controversy between the prophets.[66] I find this suggestion problematic, since Jerusalem is clearly not the primary focus of these prophecies; it is mentioned in only two of them (Jer 14:16; Ezek 13:16). Other prophecies either refer to the entire area of Judah (Jer 14:15; 37:19) or lack any spatial reference whatsoever (14:13; 23:17), yet all of these prophecies cannot but expect divine assistance at this time of need. What seems rather to be at stake in this conflict is the different expectations concerning God's role in the war waged by human forces against Jerusalem and Judah, and thus in the projected fate of the city.[67]

Evidence for this suggestion may be seen in the theological conceptions with which Jeremiah and Ezekiel refute these prophecies. In five of the passages that quote the peace prophecies, Jeremiah and Ezekiel counter with judgment prophecies in which God fights as the sole enemy—conception (C')—causing grave disaster to the people, along with those deceiving prophets, as for instance: "Assuredly, they shall fall among the falling [יפלו בנפלים]; they shall stumble at the time when *I* punish them [בעת־פקדתים יכשלו]—said YHWH" (Jer 6:15). Counter to the promises of the peace prophets, God himself is to bring not salvation but sword and famine upon the land, through which both the people and the prophets will be totally annihilated: "Those very prophets shall perish [יתמו] by sword and famine" (14:15–16);[68] alternatively, the storm will be the divine weapon of war: "Lo, the storm of YHWH goes forth in fury, a whirling storm, it shall whirl down upon the heads of the wicked" (23:16–22 at 23:19). According to Ezekiel, it is God (and God alone) who will bring to ruin both the city and the deceiving prophets within it (Ezek 13:14–15). In three other passages, God summons Babylon as his agent to subjugate Judah and the entire region (Jer 27:5–13, 14–22; 28:12–14), conception (B').

The polemic between the prophets originates from their different understandings of God's role in the war against Jerusalem. The peace prophets hold to their belief that God continues to be committed to serve as savior of his people in times of need; thus, they expect his immediate inter-

---

66. So Buber, *Prophetic Faith*, 168–70; and Sisson, "Jeremiah and the Jerusalem Conception." See also Eichrodt, *Ezekiel*, 167–68.

67. I concur on this point with Quell, *Wahre und falsche Propheten*, 58–61; Osswald, *Falsche Prophetie*, 18–23; and Overholt, "Jeremiah 27–29."

68. Compare בעת פקדתם, Jer 8:12. McKane (*Jeremiah 1–25*, 187–88) discusses the textual differences between 6:15 and 8:12 and considers the formal difference between פקדתים and פקדתם to reside in the active role assigned to God in the former.

vention on behalf of the people in face of the Babylonian threat. Jeremiah and Ezekiel, on the other hand, consider the Babylonian subjugation and then the war to be divine initiatives: God himself acts as the sole (or at least primary) foe of Judah and Jerusalem.

This distinction between prophetic conceptions of God's role in the war gives rise to a yet more fundamental question concerning this conflict among sixth-century prophets. In refuting those peace prophecies, it seems clear that Jeremiah and Ezekiel are aware of the (A' → C) conception of divine and human agency in war, so the question is: did they make use of this conception in their prophecies? The answer to this question is positive, and may be demonstrated by two groups of prophecies in the two books—prophecies against the nations, on the one hand, and consolation prophecies to Israel, on the other.

1.   Prophecies against the nations in Jeremiah and Ezekiel

Fourteen prophecies against the nations in Jeremiah and ten in Ezekiel explicitly picture war as God's action on behalf of his people;[69] note, for example, the epithet גאלם חזק יהוה צבאות שמו ("their Redeemer is mighty, His name is YHWH of Hosts," Jer 50:34; also 51:36).[70] In their message to Israel (and to the nations), these prophecies portray God, either explicitly or implicitly, as a warrior who saves his people from their enemies.[71] Three

---

69. The prophecies against the nations in Jeremiah considered in this discussion are 49:1–2; 50:6–7, 9–10, 14–16, 17–20, 21–27, 28, 29–30, 33–34; 51:6–10, 11–14, 24, 36–37, 59–64. Those in Ezekiel are 25:1–5, 6–7, 8–11, 12–14, 15–17; 26:1–6; 29:1–16, 17–21; 35:5–9, 10–15. Other prophecies against the nations in Jeremiah and Ezekiel use the other two conceptual models to portray the defeat; see §8.1.2 and §9.1.

70. גאל occurs only twice in Jeremiah: as an epithet for God in this verse, and as a verb in 31:11. A connection with the context of war is suggested by its use in other contexts—in the epithet גאלם מיד־צר ("He redeemed them from adversity," Ps 107:2) and by the proximity of גאל and ישע in 106:10; but note the similarities with Prov 23:11.

71. The complicated issues concerning the messages conveyed by the prophecies against the nations to both Israel and the nations is studied by Raabe, "Why Prophetic Oracles?" The explicit and, just as important, implicit messages of the prophecies against the nations are discussed by Kaufmann (*Toldot Ha-'Emunah*, 3.40–46, 415–24). Hoffman (*Prophecies against the Nations*, 35–37) argues that the prophecies against the nations genre does not convey an explicit message of salvation to Israel and that such a message is certainly not required by the genre. According to Hoffman (290, 294–98), explicit or implicit references to the opposite fates of the nations and Israel mark a postdestruction (exilic) development of this (preexilic) genre. Among his examples are Jer 50–51; Ezek 25; 28:20–24; 35. However, the proximity of prophecies against

points characterize these prophecies in both books, with a fourth element found only in Ezekiel.

(a) According to the sequence of events found in the prophecies against the nations, the nations' destruction of Jerusalem and Judah resulted solely from human initiative, conception (A') (e.g., Ezek 25:12; 26:2). In Jeremiah the Babylonians are called שׁסי נחלתי ("you who plundered My possession," 50:11) or שׁביהם ("their captors," 50:33); and the people that suffer from their actions are designated עשׁוקים ("oppressed," 50:33). The military action against Judah is described as an attack of lions against scattered sheep (50:6–7, 17–18). The nations' war against Israel is not portrayed as a result of divine initiative or as judgment against Israel. There is no hint of God's involvement in bringing over the nations against Jerusalem and no mention of Judah's sins against God. The one exception, which proves the rule overall, is 50:7. Whether 50:7b is part of the quotation (and thus the enemies are those who accuse Judah of sins against God and use this as an excuse for their attack on it)[72] or whether 50:7b is a prophetic reaction to the nations' confidence (invoking 2:3), in any event, in the context of 50:4–7, the prophet annuls the nations' proclamation as inadmissible, as just an excuse for the Babylonian actions against Judah, and he enforces the line of divine deliverance and benevolence (50:4–5; also 50:8–10).[73]

(b) God's war against the nations is described in one of two ways. Most of the examples portray God as fighting the nations alone, conception (C), with nine instances in Jeremiah and six in Ezekiel.[74] Only a few prophecies

---

the nations and consolation to Israel may also result from doublets, where a passage occurs once in prophecies of consolation (e.g., Jer 30:10–11) and once in the prophecies against the nations against Egypt (46:27–28). The Septuagint has this passage only in the prophecies against the nations. But since, according to the Septuagint order of the book, the prophecies against the nations precede the consolation prophecies, the single occurrence of this passage says nothing of its original placement; see McKane, *Jeremiah 26–52*, 762–63. Holladay (*Jeremiah*, 2.160) considers 30:10–11 to be one of three Judean elaborations of the first edition of the consolation collection (along with 30:16–17 and 31:7–9a) and argues that all three passages are authentic and antedate the destruction. Therefore, their occurrence in two collections is indeed evidence of the book's complicated process of evolution. Finally, in Ezekiel, 28:25–26 and 29:21 are the only examples of the proximity of consolation passages to prophecies against the nations.

72. Jer 50:7 raises questions as to the borders of the quotation, whether it is limited to two words (לא נאשׁם) (see Lundbom, *Jeremiah 37–52*, 377, 379) or possibly stretches to 50:7b (argued by Bright, *Jeremiah*, 340, 354).

73. For the place of Jer 50:4–7 in the context of Jer 50 and for the structural connection between these verses and 50:17–20, see Holladay, *Jeremiah*, 2.402–3.

74. God's fighting alone against the nations—the (C) conceptio,,"appears in Jer

state that, following God's solo campaign, or along with it, human forces will be summoned to war, conception (B'), with four instances in Jeremiah and four in Ezekiel.[75]

(c) In justification of the divine war against the nations, the prophecies often state that the war is a judgment against these nations for either their sins against God (Jer 49:12) or their deeds against Israel.[76] Among the nations' particular sins are the political interests that motivated their invasion of Judah in order to seize its (desolated) territory (Jer 49:1–2; Ezek 26:2; 35:10; 36:2, 5) or "simply" the expression of eagerness to destroy Judah (Ezek 25:12, 15; 35:5, 10). A more general sense of the nations' sins against God and Israel is stated in terms of retribution (גמול הוא משלם לה, "He will deal retribution to her," Jer 51:6): God repays Babylon for all her deeds ("pay her back for her actions, do to her just what she has done," 50:29–30), for the evil that she did to Israel ("for all the wicked things [כל־רעתם] they did to Zion before your eyes," 51:24). God's actions against Babylon are his revenge: נקמת יהוה ("this is YHWH's vengeance. Take vengeance on her, do to her as she has done!," 50:15; also 50:28 [2x]; 51:6, 11 [2x]; Ezek 25:14, 17); it is "the hour of their doom!" (Jer 50:27, 31; 51:18).[77]

(d) Finally, and only in Ezekiel, God's war against the nations captures a central role in the universal recognition of God's power and involvement on the international stage. Ezekiel concludes his prophecies against the nations with the repeated recognition formula וידעו כי־אני (אדני) יהוה (25:5, 7, 11, 17); he accentuates the idea that God is to be sanctified in the eyes of the nations through his actions against them: ונקדשתי בם לעיני הגוים ("and I have shown Myself holy through them in the sight of the nations," 28:22, 25).[78]

49:1–2; 50:18, 28, 33–34; 51:6–10, 11–14, 24, 36–37, 59–64 and Ezek 25:6–7, 13, 15–17; 29:1–16; 35:1–9, 10–15.

75. God's summoning a human enemy against the nations—the (B') conception—appears in Jer 50:9–10, 14–16, 21–27, 29–30 and Ezek 25:1–5, 8–11, 14; 26:1–6; 29:17–21.

76. The prophecies against the nations are constructed in measure-for-measure units; see, for instance, Jer 50:15, 29; Ezek 35:5–6. But the destruction of the nations is also portrayed without mention of their sins (Jer 49:23–27, 28–33, 35–39; Ezek 30:20–26; 32:17–21; also Isa 14:1–2, 24–27, 28–32; Zech 9:1–8). See Hoffman, *Prophecies against the Nations*, 34–55.

77. Other sins ascribed to the nations are their mockery of Judah in its distress (e.g., Jer 50:31–32; Ezek 25:3, 6, 8) and hubris (Jer 48:7, 14, 26, 29, 42; Ezek 27:2).

78. God's sanctification among the nations is further mentioned in Ezek 38:16, 23. This phrase is also recalled in prophecies of consolation to Israel that forecast the ingathering of the exiles from among the nations (20:41; 36:23; 39:27).

The combination of these three or four elements illustrates the rich use of the (A' → C) approach by both Jeremiah and Ezekiel in the context of the prophecies against the nations.

Jeremiah 51:59–64 demonstrates the close conceptual similarity between the pronouncements of Jeremiah and the peace prophets on the issue of God's role as savior of his people from the Babylonian foe:

⁵⁹ The instructions that the prophet Jeremiah gave to Seraiah son of Neriah son of Mahseiah, when the latter went with King Zedekiah of Judah to Babylonia, in the fourth year of [Zedekiah's] reign. Seraiah was quartermaster. ⁶⁰ Jeremiah wrote down in one scroll all the disaster that would come upon Babylon, all these things that are written concerning Babylon. ⁶¹ And Jeremiah said to Seraiah, "When you get to Babylon, see that you read out all these words. ⁶² And say, 'O YHWH, You Yourself have declared concerning this place that it shall be cut off, without inhabitant, man or beast; that it shall be a desolation for all time.' ⁶³ And when you finish reading this scroll, tie a stone to it and hurl it into the Euphrates. ⁶⁴ And say, 'Thus shall Babylon sink and never rise again, because of the disaster that I will bring upon it. So they tire themselves.'"⁷⁹

Thus far the words of Jeremiah.

⁵⁹הדבר אשר־צוה ירמיהו
הנביא את־שריה בן־נריה בן־
מחסיה בלכתו את־צדקיהו
מלך־יהודה בבל בשנת הרבעית
למלכו ושריה שר מנוחה. ⁶⁰ויכתב ירמיהו את כל־הרעה
אשר־תבוא אל־בבל אל־ספר
אחד את כל־הדברים האלה
הכתבים אל־בבל. ⁶¹ויאמר
ירמיהו אל־שריה כבאך בבל
וראית וקראת את כל־הדברים
האלה. ⁶²ואמרת יהוה אתה
דברת אל־המקום הזה להכריתו
לבלתי היות־בו יושב למאדם
ועד־בהמה כי־שממות עולם
תהיה. ⁶³והיה ככלתך לקרא
את־הספר הזה תקשר עליו אבן
והשלכתו אל־תוך פרת.
⁶⁴ואמרת ככה תשקע בבל
ולא־תקום מפני הרעה אשר
אנכי מביא עליה ויעפו.

עד־הנה דברי ירמיהו.

79. The translation of ויעפו (omitted in the Septuagint) follows Lundbom (*Jeremiah 37–52*, 42; compare NJPS: "and [nations] shall have wearied themselves [for fire]"). Lundbom (*Jeremiah 37–52*, 502–3, 509) points to ויעפו in 51:58 and 51:64 as a scribal "catch line" closing a passage he considers to be "Seriah's colophon." Seraiah son of Neriah son of Mahseiah, "the official of the resting place" (51:59), might have been a member of this scribal family and Baruch's brother (32:12); see McKane, *Jeremiah 26–52*, 1354.

This passage serves a unique function within Jeremiah. It comprises the closing passage of the words of Jeremiah (51:64b), as well as the final passage in the collection of prophecies against Babylon (Jer 50–51);[80] it is said to have been proclaimed in the fourth year of the reign of Zedekiah (593; 51:59), the same year as Hananiah's prophecy of salvation (28:1).[81] Jeremiah 51:59–64 says nothing of the circumstances that lead Zedekiah to send officials to Babylon in his fourth year, a time that is connected with his attempts to rebel against Babylon (Jer 27–28; 29:1–7). Likewise, we know nothing of any other members of this delegation, its goals, or its achievements.[82]

When compared to Hananiah's prophecy, each of these two prophecies accompanies a symbolic act that reinforces God's words (28:11; 51:63). Breaking the yoke from Jeremiah's neck, Hananiah proclaims salvation (28:10–11); in a parallel act, after reading the scroll, tying it to a rock, and throwing it into the Euphrates, Seriah is to say: ככה תשקע בבל ולא־תקום מפני הרעה אשר אנכי מביא עליה ("thus shall Babylon sink and never rise again," 51:64).[83] Jeremiah (through Seriah) promises the fulfillment of God's prophecies against Babylon, prophecies of total annihilation (51:62); salvation for Judah is only implicit here. In this respect, Jeremiah's pronouncement clearly differs from Hananiah's elaborate prophecy of the

80. For a similar closing formula at the end of the prophecies against Moab, see Jer 48:47. This postscript is unique in the prophetic literature, one of several other similar editorial comments in the book of Jeremiah. See 36:1–8 and Jer 45 for two other suggested colophons (Lundbom, *Jeremiah 37–52*, 503), and note the prescripts in 22:6; 23:9; 30:1–4; compare Ps 72:20.

81. The question of authenticity is often raised in discussions of Jer 51:59–64. Holladay (*Jeremiah*, 2.433–34) considers this passage to be the kernel of the prophecies against Babylon. But more often it is categorized as a non-Jeremian passage that is secondarily placed in this location. According to Mowinckel (*Zur Komposition des Buches Jeremia*, 65) it is connected to the biographical materials, the B source passages; so also Carroll, *Jeremiah*, 855–56; and McKane, *Jeremiah 26–52*, 1350–59.

82. See Malamat, "Twilight of Judah"; Kahn, "Some Remarks," 139–57, esp. 143–44. Hoffman (*Jeremiah 26–52*, 831) accepts as authentic the historical context and gathers from it that objection to Hananiah's prophecy does not necessarily connote a positive attitude toward Babylon. Yet, on the other hand, he prefers dating Jeremiah's prophecy at 51:59–64 to the time following the destruction, during the exile. I do not see the grounds for that.

83. The explanation of the symbolic action is introduced in both by the comparison word ככה, also used in Jer 13:9; 19:11; 28:11; see Lundbom *Jeremiah 37–52*, 509. See McKane (*Jeremiah 26–52*, 1357–58) for the apt criticism of the scholarly debate as to whether this proclamation constitutes a symbolic act or a magical curse; he argues that "it is far from clear that this difference of terminology creates a significant distinction" (1357).

return of the king, the temple vessels, and the people (28:2–4). They also differ in that Jeremiah's symbolic action functions as a magical curse.[84] The other contrast between them is in their timeframes: Hananiah specifies a two-year limit, whereas Jeremiah does not limit the arrival of distress over Babylon.

Jeremiah 51:59–64 is exceptional in the book of Jeremiah. While it does not promise salvation to Judah (or the return of the 597 deportees), it does predict the imminent fall of Babylon. This idea contrasts with the idea put forth in Jer 27–29 that Babylon is to stay in control for three generations (27:11; also 25:11–12; 29:10) and also with Jeremiah's consistent demand to accept Babylonian subjugation (21:9; 27:6–8, 11–13; 38:2–4, 17–18; after the fall 42:10–12).[85] This prophecy remains a riddle to me. Formally and thematically, 51:59–64 closes the prophecies against the nations collection in Jeremiah, recalling 25:15–38, where Babylon is positioned the head of the nations (25:26). But, while recognizing the editorial aspects of the function of the passage in its present form, rejecting it as non-Jeremian does not seem to ease the difficulties.[86] Hence, while not solving this riddle, and if this prophecy may be considered Jeremian (or of any other of his followers and tradents), this unique prophecy contributes to the notion that by the early sixth century all these various Judean prophets are working comfortably with the same theological conception, the (A' → C) framework. This shared conception may also be found in prophecies of consolation to Israel within Jeremiah and Ezekiel.

2. Consolation prophecies to Israel: Jeremiah

Eight consolation prophecies in the book of consolations (Jer 30–31) and in the prophecies against Babylon (Jer 50–51) promise that God will save

---

84. Although pronounced through Seriah (and not directly by the prophet), Lundbom considers these words to be a curse (*Jeremiah 37–52*, 509). The borders of this curse are under debate. Scholars argue for the secondary nature of מפני הרעה אשר אנכי מביא עליה (McKane, *Jeremiah 26–52*, 1358); but Lundbom (*Jeremiah 37–52*, 509) considers this to be a Jeremianic expression alluding to 6:19.

85. I reject Friebel's explanation of this disjunction (*Jeremiah's and Ezekiel's Sign-Acts*, 154–69); he argues (164–69) that these are words of consolation to the exiles. As Friebel himself admits, this has no textual grounds, and I do not think it may be even inferred.

86. Compare McKane, *Jeremiah 26–52*, 1358–59, with references there to other scholars who consider this passage non-Jeremian.

his people from its captivity in exile.[87] In these prophecies, divine deliverance is configured as a divine war against the nations. Six of these prophecies explicitly recall deliverance from an enemy in the past (30:5–7, 8–9, 10–11 [with its doublet in 46:27–28]; 31:7–9a, 10–14); two indicate that God's action on behalf of his people constitutes a judgment against the nations (30:18–22; 50:17–20).

Three points support the argument that God's deliverance of the people is framed as a divine war against the nations. (a) Salvation is described in phrases taken from the semantic field of war (e.g., "I will make an end [אעשה כלה] of all the nations," Jer 30:11; 31:10–14). (b) Salvation is accompanied by judgments taken against the nations; note the phrase פקד על/אל (30:20; 50:18) and the announcement that in contrast to his care for Israel, God will annihilate the nations (30:11; 46:28b). Salvation thus calls forth a display of joy and power before the nations (31:7). (c) The aim of God's saving acts is that "Jacob should again have calm and quiet with none to trouble him" (30:10b; 46:27b). Imagery in the consolation passages is taken from the semantic field of peace and security, the opposite of war (Lev 26:6; Ezek 34:27–28); these prophecies focus on receiving YHWH's gifts—cultivating the land once again and enjoying its fruits (Jer 31:11–12).

3.   Consolation prophecies to Israel: Ezekiel

Consolation prophecies in Ezekiel capture a smaller place in comparison with Jeremiah,[88] and God's war against the nations appears in only two prophecies of consolation in the book.[89] In 34:25–30, as part of the re-

---

87. For a comprehensive discussion and bibliography on authorship and dating for the prophecies of consolation in Jeremiah, see Rom-Shiloni, "Group-Identities in Jeremiah."

88. The main verb of deliverance in Ezekiel is הציל, which occurs 14x in the book, but only 5x referring to God as the savior of this people (13:21, 23; 34:10, 12, 27); ישע occurs 3x in consolation prophecies (34:22; 36:29; 37:23); גאל appears only in the phrase אנשי גאלתך (11:15; the Septuagint reads καὶ οἱ ἄνδρες τῆς αἰχμαλωσίας σου); and פדה is not used in Ezekiel. Salvation and deliverance are thus prospected in only six chapters in Ezekiel (11, 13, 20, 34, 36, 37); in two, the enemies (or the major obstacles) are "internal"—corrupt leaders: the shepherds (34:10, 22–23) or prophetesses (13:20–23)—and twice God delivers Israel from all of their cultic (religious) defilements with no reference to a context of war (36:29; 37:23); in five prophecies (11:14–21; 20:32–38, 41–42; 34:11–16, 17–31; 36:22–36; 37:1–14, 15–28) a cluster of verbs portrays bringing the exiles back to their homeland: לקח, הוציא, אסף, קיבץ, הביא in addition to הושיע, הציל.

89. There is no reference to the metaphor of God as warrior in the following proph-

institution of the "covenant of peace," God is to be acknowledged for the deliverance of his people from the enemies who subjugate them: "They shall know that I am YHWH, when I break the bars of their yoke and rescue them from those who enslave them" (34:27).[90] The prophecies against the nations collection in Ezek 25–28 address the six nations of the surrounding regions in Syria-Israel-Cisjordan. Ezekiel 28:25–26 closes the collection with words of consolation to Israel.[91] The proximity of the prophecy against Sidon (28:20–24) and the consolation words to Israel (28:25–26), together with the phrases repeated between them, illustrate the rhetorical opposition between the secured settlement of Israel upon its land and the punishment that God will level upon all those nations that had despised it (28:26).

These features call to mind Jer 30:8–9, a prophecy of consolation that shows similarities to Hananiah's announcement: "I hereby break the yoke of the king of Babylon" (28:2, 4, 11):

[8] In that day—declares YHWH of Hosts—<u>I will break the yoke from off of your neck and I will rip off your bonds</u>. Strangers shall no longer make slaves of them; [9] instead, they shall serve YHWH their God and David, the king whom I will raise up for them.	[8] והיה ביום ההוא נאם יהוה צבאות <u>אשבר עלו מעל צוארך ומוסרותיך אנתק</u> ולא־יעבדו־בו עוד זרים. [9] ועבדו את יהוה אלהיהם ואת דוד מלכם אשר אקים להם.

Deliverance is presented through the metaphor of breaking the yoke and ripping off the bonds of subjugation.[92] Jeremiah 30:8–9 reverses 27:2, and while indeed it is close to Hananiah's prophecy (28:2–4, 11), this passage, as well as Ezek 34:27b, allows us to see the larger thematic context of this metaphor.

Prophetic traditions from the time of Isaiah son of Amoz used this imag-

---

ecies of consolation in Ezekiel: 11:16–21; 16:59–63; 20:39–44; 34:11–16, 20–24; 36:1–15, 22–32; 37:11–14, 19–23, 24–28; 39:25–29. See Raitt, *Theology of Exile*, 132.

90. I discuss Ezek 34:25–30 in *God in Times of Destruction*, 212–14, 372–74.

91. Zimmerli (*Ezekiel*, 2.99) finds the connector מכל סביבתם השאטים אותם in 28:24, with modest distinctions in 28:26 (בעשותי שפטים בכל השאטים אתם מסביבותם, "when I have meted out punishment to all those about them who despise them"), to mark 28:25–26 as the concluding passage to Ezek 25–28. שאט/שוט ("disdain, despise") and the phrase שאט את־מסביב are unique to Ezekiel (verb in 16:57; noun, noted בשאט נפש, in 25:6, 15; 36:5). See Bodi, *Ezekiel and Erra*, 69–81.

92. The image of breaking the yoke is also used by Jeremiah in judgment prophecies (e.g., 2:20). See Rom-Shiloni, "How Can You Say."

ery to symbolize divine deliverance from subjugation to the Assyrians (Isa 9:3; 10:27; Nah 1:13). In the new historical context, both Jeremiah (30:8–9) and Ezekiel (34:27b), independently of one another, take this metaphor a step further than Hananiah's prophecy. To the idea of release from bondage, these two prophecies add the notion of transforming subjugation to human rulers into the worship of God, the ultimate king. זרים ("strangers") in Jer 30:8 holds a double meaning, based on a Janus parallelism: looking backward it refers to the human ruler, whose yoke will be broken; looking forward it designates other gods.[93] This theme of freedom from human rulers in order to serve God echoes the repeated call in the exodus tradition: שלח את־עמי ויעבדני במדבר ("let my people go that they may worship Me in the wilderness," Exod 7:16; also 7:26; 8:16; 9:1, 13; 10:3); it is also celebrated in the Holiness Legislation: "For it is to Me that the Israelites are servants: they are My servants, whom I freed from the land of Egypt, I YHWH your God" (Lev 25:55).[94] The portrayal of God as deliverer of his people from human subjugation thus invokes the paradigmatic salvation from Egypt and is also invoked in the Decalogue (Exod 20:2–5; Deut 6:12–13). Leviticus 26:13 (Holiness Legislation) uses the following unique formulation: "I YHWH am your God who brought you out from the land of the Egyptians to be their slaves no more, who broke the bars of your yoke [ואשבר מטת עלכם] and made you walk erect" (this formulation seems to be invoked by Ezek 34:27b). These thematic references within the two prophetic books collate the release from (Egyptian) bondage with the commitment to worship God, accepting him as the ultimate king.[95]

The exodus tradition, the paradigmatic divine salvation, thus serves for both Jeremiah and Ezekiel as the foreground of the (A' → C) conception; in view of the lack of any evidence to the contrary, we may surmise that

93. For זרים as "other gods," see Deut 32:16; Jer 2:25; 3:13. The phrase עבד ב־ designates subjugation to a human ruler in Jer 25:14 (lacking in the Septuagint; with the alteration of את־ and ב־ in 27:7). Therefore, the Septuagint translation of 30:8 (= 37:8 LXX) as καὶ οὐκ ἐργῶνται αὐτοί is harmonistic, reflecting the translation of the more common phrase עבד את, as in 30:9. See Becking, *Between Fear and Freedom*, 135–64.

94. See Hoffman, *Doctrine of Exodus*, 115–47, esp. 129–33.

95. The restoration of Davidic rulership (Jer 30:9b) may be a genuine part of this prophecy, as part of an early layer of the consolation book: Judean in its geographic arena and addressed to the remnant of the Northern kingdom; see Rom-Shiloni, "Group-Identities in Jeremiah," 25 and n31. Other scholars consider 30:9b to be a later addition to the prophecy, as it expands the thematic horizon and adds the restoration of political independence under Davidic kingship. This future hope is similarly expressed in 23:5–6; 33:14–16, 17, 21–22, 26.

Hananiah son of Azzur shared this traditional conception as well. Yet there is a significant difference between Jeremiah and Hananiah in their conceptions of exile. Hananiah considers the Jehoiachin exile to be a temporary situation, from which God will deliver the people more or less immediately (within two years), whereas Jeremiah's consolation prophecy (30:8–9) has no concrete historical horizon.[96]

Jeremiah, Ezekiel, and the peace prophets agree upon two points. They all argue that they express the words and will of God, and they all predict the future, though they arrive at opposing visions as to what that future holds.[97] A third point of agreement between them is the conception of God as warrior and savior of his people from their enemies. These points of agreement may explain the fierce struggle between them, and the great efforts they make to undermine their opponents' legitimacy.

The book of Jeremiah echoes an accusation that occurs a few times against Jeremiah's legitimacy: his opponents argue that he was never sent by God to prophesy (26:9). This accusation is implicit in the prophet's response: "It was YHWH who sent me to prophesy.... For in truth, YHWH has sent me to you" (26:12–15; also 29:25–28; 43:2–3). A much fiercer and more elaborate picture may be traced of the arguments raised independently by Jeremiah and Ezekiel against contemporaneous colleagues. Nine accusations are leveled by these two prophets (separately and independently) against the peace prophets, in the attempt to delegitimize their status and message:

96. The ahistorical perspective of this consolation prophecy raises difficulties for scholars, who try to establish a historical context for this expectation of national restoration. See Nicholson (*Preaching to the Exiles*, 87–91), who suggests that this prophecy belongs with other prose passages, as an expression of hopes that arose among the Deuteronomistic exiles following the release of Jehoiachin from his prison (2 Kgs 25:27–30).

97. From the aspect of content, prediction of the future is the only role expressed in the fragmentary quotations of the peace prophets, and yet it is but one of the roles practiced by those considered to be true prophets. There seems to be no distinction in principle between short-term and longer-term predictions, and they are all legitimate prospects delivered by the prophets, who may feature both: "shortly" (עתה מהרה) in Jer 27:16 (lacking in the Septuagint); "in two years" (בעוד שנתים ימים) in Hananiah's prophecy in 28:3, 11; "forty years" (ארבעים שנה—a generation or a human lifespan) in Ezek 29:11, 12, 13; "seventy years" (שבעים שנה) in Isa 23:15, 17; Jer 25:11, 12; 29:10; or three generations (ועבדו אתו כל־הגוים ואת־בנו ואת־בן־בנו) in Jer 27:7. See Greenberg, *Ezekiel 21–37*, 606; and *Ezekiel 1–20*, 104–5.

1. They prophesy in the name of God, though they are never sent by God: לא שלחתים ולא צויתים ולא דברתי אליהם ("I have not sent them or commanded them. I have not spoken to them," Jer 14:14–15; Ezek 13:6).

2. Their words are false, coming out of their own hearts, that is, imaginations: חזון שקר . . . ותרמות (Jer 27:14b, 16b); כי שקר הם נבאים לכם (ק: ותרמית) ("a lying vision, . . . the deceit of their own contriving," Jer 14:14; 23:16 [חזון לבם ידברו]; Ezek 13:2); חזים שוא וקסמים להם כזב ("they prophesy falsely and divine deceitfully for them," 22:28); and עשה שקר (they "act falsely," Jer 6:13).

3. They delude the people (מהבלים המה אתכם, Jer 23:16; הטעו את־עמי, Ezek 13:10; בכזבכם לעמי, 13:19; טחו להם תפל, 22:28).

4. They steal words from one another, hence lack originality in their proclamations: מגנבי דברי איש מאת רעהו ("the prophets . . . who steal My words from one another," Jer 23:30).

5. They perform other forbidden divinatory practices, such as dreams (Jer 23:25–28, 32) and magical divination (וקסם ואלול, "worthless divination," Jer 14:14b;[98] Ezek 13:6–9; 22:28). Therefore the list that follows is broader and includes side by side with prophets other illegitimate practitioners: אל־נביאיכם ואל־קסמיכם ואל חלמתיכם ואל־ ענניכם ואל־כשפיכם ("to your prophets, augurs, dreamers, diviners, and sorcerers," Jer 27:9).

6. They prophesy and encourage audiences of sinners and blasphemers (Jer 23:14, 17).

7. They are ethically sinners—"they are all greedy for gain" (Jer 6:13)— and adulterers (together with the priests who support and encourage them; 23:10–11).

8. They encourage the people ineffectually: "They offer healing offhand for the wounds of My people" (Jer 6:14). Ezekiel uses a different imagery: "They daub the wall for them with plaster" (Ezek 13:12; 22:28). He accuses the prophets of not fulfilling their roles in the day of crisis: לא עליתם בפרצות ותגדרו גדר על־בית ישראל לעמד במלחמה ביום יהוה ("You did not enter the breaches and repair the walls for

---

98. The second of three phrases in Jer 14:14b, וקסם ואלול (ק: ואליל), is a hendiadys (the other two phrases are nominal constructions) and is translated "worthless divinations" by McKane (*Jeremiah 1–25*, 324) and "an empty divination" by NJPS; for אליל as "worthlessness," see Ps 96:5 (Holladay, *Jeremiah*, 1.420).

the House of Israel, that they might stand up in battle in the day of YHWH," 13:5).

9. Finally, and worst of all, prophets in both Jerusalem and Samaria prophesy in the name of the Baal (Jer 2:8): ־הנבאו בבעל ויתעו את עמי את־ישראל ("They prophesied by Baal and led My people Israel astray," 23:13, alluding to Deut 13:2–6); they cause the people to go astray and worship other gods: החשבים להשכיח את־עמי שמי בחלומתם ... כאשר שכחו אבותם את־שמי בבעל ("those who plan to make My people forget My name, with their dreams . . . as their fathers forgot My name through the Baal," Jer 23:27).[99]

These fierce accusations attempt to confront and overturn the recognition that these prophets receive from their audiences, and thus confirm that the prophets consider themselves to be and are acknowledged by their contemporaries as messengers of God. Here again, the example of Hananiah son of Azzur is telling. In Jer 28, he is repeatedly designated simply as "the prophet"; Jeremiah leaves the debate embarrassed, unable to refute the possible validity of Hananiah's words (28:11b).[100] The fundamental similarities between the prophets show that they are all relying on one and the same tradition, on one and the same conception of God as savior of his people in times of need (A' → C). Their roads divide as the situation in Jerusalem deteriorates: the peace prophets continue to hold to the traditional conception, hoping for divine salvation; they are confident that it would eventually occur.[101]

In contrast to the peace prophets, Jeremiah and Ezekiel each independently conceive of God's involvement as savior of his people on a chronological continuum. They recognize that this quality has a paradigmatic past (represented by the exodus traditions) and a promising future— expressed in prophecies against the nations and in prophecies of consolation for the people. However, both prophets (independent of each other) also perceive that God is not taking the role of savior in their own historical

99. Following the translation of Lundbom, *Jeremiah 21–36*, 202.

100. Compare the postbiblical exegetical tradition, exemplified in the Septuagint translation, which consistently adds the title ὁ ψευδοπροφήτης ("false prophet") to Hananiah's name (Jer 6:13; 26:7, 8, 11, 16 [= 32:7, 8, 11, 16 LXX]; 27:9 [= 34:9 LXX]; 28:1 [= 35:1 LXX]; 29:1, 8 [= 36:1, 8 LXX]; Zech 13:2).

101. According to the limited information we have, these peace prophets do not mention questions of justice, and thus do not pay attention to that aspect of divine justice in the theological discussion.

present—that is, within the period of the destruction, God is *not* acting as his people's savior. While very difficult to accept theologically, this is a remarkable justificatory argument—neither prophet gives up this important divine role, but they recognize that the role is God's alone to activate. It is God's choice to be present and involved, but he may also choose not to save; that is, he may even choose to be his own people's foe.

The conception that human enemies are solely responsible for the destruction of Jerusalem and Judah and that God would surely save his people from their threatening hands (A' → C) remains a conception held by the people, the king, and his officials throughout the last years of Jerusalem. In their voices this is the ground for presentations of doubt and of protest by anonymous speakers quoted in the prophetic books and by poets. But this same conception is at the core of the debate among the prophets. The peace prophets follow previous traditions and continue to identify God as the savior of his people. However, neither Jeremiah nor Ezekiel (in their separate locations) can resort to this conception to explain God's role in the present political distress. Rather, these two prophets (and the followers, tradents, editors who compiled their books) choose one of the two other options, either conception (B'), where God summons enemies against his people, or conception (C'), the very extreme portrayal of God himself as the destroyer of Jerusalem.

8

God Summons the Enemy

The idea that God summons the Babylonian emperor and his troops, the enemies of his own people, and has control over the outcome of their actions, suggests theologically the synergistic point of a human action guided by the divine. The (B') concept, the midpoint of the continuum described in chapter 6—supplies the most convenient explanation for the arrival of the enemy armies and certainly for their military (political) success (see fig. 8.1).

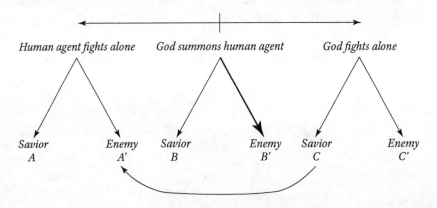

Fig. 8.1. God summons the enemy

This perception of God's control of the situation is the basis of the efforts by the historiographers (2 Kings) and the two prophets, Jeremiah and Ezekiel, to justify God—that is, to account for the enemy's presence, the people's distress, and God's seeming refusal to fight for his people. The same conception is at the base of certain poetic compositions (Pss 44; 80;

89; 106; Lam 1–2) that plead for divine salvation and protest against God's delivering his people into the hands of their enemies.

8.1. JUSTIFICATION OF GOD (2 KINGS 21–25; JEREMIAH AND EZEKIEL)

8.1.1. *The Deuteronomistic Historiographers (2 Kings 21–25)*

The Deuteronomistic historiographers use only this conception, (B'), in their retrospective handling of defeat, the Judean destruction included.[1] The destruction of Judah never received the kind of full Deuteronomistic elaboration accorded the destruction of the Northern Kingdom (2 Kgs 17:7–23; see §3.4.2). Nevertheless, even the meager evidence on this point shows that this same shared conception leads to a variety of ways to justify God's role in the present distress, as seen in the different theological responses to God's role in the catastrophe from 2 Kgs 21–25, all within justificatory proclamations.

(a) Explicit presentations of the connection between cause and effect, between sin and punishment, characterize limited number of passages that relate to the fall of Judah. In 2 Kgs 21:10–15; 23:26–27; 2 Kgs 24, the fate of Judah is described as a well-planned divine punishment for either the sins of Manasseh (21:10–11; 24:2–4) or the sins of the entire people (21:12–15; 24:20).[2] God's anger against Judah and Jerusalem motivates God to expel them from his presence (להסיר מעל פניו, "to banish them from His presence," 24:3; עד־השליכו אתם מעל פניו, "so that He cast them out of His presence," 24:20).[3]

(b) Second Kings 24 suggests an *implicit* juxtaposition of sin and pun-

---

1. I restrict my comments to 2 Kings, though this conception of God's role in times of defeat and subjugation governs all the compositions within the Deuteronomistic writings.

2. The presence of these two different perpetrators of sins (i.e., the kings or the people) is one of the major factors in distinguishing late (exilic) Deuteronomistic writing from early (Josian) Deuteronomistic writing (labeled Dtr2 and Dtr1). See Cross, *Canaanite Myth and Hebrew Epic*, 287–89; and Nelson, *Double Redaction*, 123. 2 Kgs 24:3–4 does not clarify the ambiguity concerning the agent of אשר שפך וגם דם־הנקי (24:4), which, following 24:3 might be related to Manasseh and not to Jehoiakim. Yet, the accusation of shedding innocent blood goes well with Jer 22:17, addressed to Jehoiakim; and this identification is made explicit in the elaborated text of 2 Chr 36:5 LXX.

3. Based on its occurrences, Nelson (*Double Redaction*, 59) counts הסיר מעל פניו

ishment in references to the last kings of Judah: Jehoiakim (23:36–24:3), Jehoiachin's short term under siege (24:8–10), and Zedekiah's era (24:18–20).[4] Following the general pattern of the book of Kings, mention of the kings' religious disobedience (23:37; 24:9, 19) closes the introductory descriptions of their reigns, after which the historiographers asyndetically mention the military distress that the king and his people faced (24:1, 10–17; 25:1–2). Both Jehoiakim and Zedekiah rebel against the Babylonian king, and thus the military campaigns have political motivations.[5] But through the proximity of these two components (religious disobedience and human political-military threat) the historiographers present the Babylonian campaigns as the working out of divine punishment in retaliation for the kings' *religious* disloyalty. Second Kings 24:2 MT explicitly refers to God as the chief commander who sends the different troops against Judah.[6]

These explicit and implicit literary techniques by which the historiographers establish the sin-punishment connection on a national level draws into the discussion the metaphor of God as judge (chap. 10). Here, however, I call attention to the sin-punishment connection in terms of its function in these descriptions of God's role as warrior.

The short oration in 21:10–15 explicitly sets out the connection between Manasseh's sins and the decree of punishment against the people; it is attributed to anonymous prophets and couched in Deuteronomistic language:

[10]Therefore YHWH spoke through His servants the prophets: [11]"Because King Manasseh of Judah has done these abhorrent things—he has outdone in wickedness all that the Amorites did before his time—

---

as a Dtr2 expression (i.e., the exilic Deuteronomistic source); see 2 Kgs 17:18, 23; 23:27; 24:3.

4. This asyndetic proximity of religious disobedience and the military distress is frequently reiterated in the book of Kings; see 2 Kgs 15:18 and 15:19; 15:28 and 15:29; 16:3–4 and 16:5; 17:2 and 17:3. The proximity of events may be specified by temporal phrases like אז in 16:5 or בעת ההיא in 24:10, but oftentimes has no temporal anchor at all. This technique of juxtaposition serves in Kings also to relate religious faithfulness to political success (as in 2 Kgs 18:1–8).

5. For the historical circumstances of the rebellions of both Jehoiakim and Zedekiah, see Cogan and Tadmor, *II Kings*, 307–9, 322–24.

6. 2 Kgs 24:2 LXX lacks יהוה, thus leaving punishment to the human arena, to a punitive Babylonian campaign in response to Jehoiakim's rebellion. See Cogan and Tadmor, *II Kings*, 306.

and because he led Judah to sin with his fetishes, [12]assuredly, thus said YHWH, the God of Israel: *I am going to bring such a disaster* [הנני מביא רעה] on Jerusalem and Judah that both ears of everyone who hears about it will tingle. [13]*I will apply to* [ונטיתי על] Jerusalem the measuring line of Samaria and the weights of the House of Ahab; *I will wipe* [ומחיתי את] Jerusalem clean as one wipes a dish and turns it upside down. [14]*And I will cast off* [ונטשתי את] the remnant of My own people *and deliver them into the hands of their enemies* [ונתתים ביד איביהם]. *They shall be plunder and prey to all their enemies* [והיו לבז ולמשסה לכל־איביהם] [15]because they have done what is displeasing to Me and have been vexing Me from the day that their fathers came out of Egypt to this day." (emphasis added)[7]

Three characteristics of God's role may be highlighted in this passage. (1) A hierarchy is set between God and the human enemy. God initiates war and summons the human enemy against his people (21:12–13); the enemy is a subordinate and agent (21:14). A sequence of first-person verbal phrases tells of divine involvement in the event, beginning with the threat to bring distress upon Jerusalem (הנני מביא רעה על־ירושלים ויהודה, 21:12). God is depicted as a ruler who stands at the head of the fighting armies. Yet, (2) God is active and his activity is not limited to "administrative responsibility" only. Second Kings 21:13 mentions the massive punishment God himself will bring upon the city and people (ונטיתי על־ירושלים את קו שמרון ... ומחיתי את־ירושלים), which will leave Jerusalem as an empty plate placed upside down.[8] After all this (3) God will go even further and

---

7. 2 Kgs 21 is recognized as a product of at least two redactional layers, with 21:1–2a and 21:16–18 stemming from the earlier stage. The prophetic oration in 21:10–15 is generally recognized as of the later exilic layer of Kings (Dtr2, or exilic Deuteronomistic layer); it compares Jerusalem and Judah to Israel of the Ahab dynasty (21:13) and adds bloodshed to the long list of Manasseh's sins (21:16). Nevertheless, scholars debate the detailed analysis of 21:3–15, tracing two major editions and possible later supplements. Nelson (*Double Redaction*, 66–69) identifies Dtr2 phrases within 21:1–9. Compare Hobbs (*2 Kings*, 300–303), who criticizes Cross and Nelson (among others) and argues against the presence of multiple or even double editorial layers within Kings (see xxii–xxv). Hobbs considers 2 Kgs 21 to be typical of Deuteronomistic writing and a united piece (see xxvi–xxx; on repetitions for accentuation, see 303), which aims at presenting Manasseh and Judah as following in the footsteps and thus the fate of Ahab and Israel (301 and xxv).

8. On the two images in 2 Kgs 21:13, see Cogan and Tadmor, *II Kings*, 269. Hobbs (*2 Kings*, 307) argues that the images in this verse originate in two different social mi-

desert the remnant of his people (ונטשתי את שארית נחלתי, 21:14), which may well refer to Judah, those who remained after God's rejection of the Northern Kingdom (17:18).[9] This remnant of those who manage to survive God's earlier actions will then be delivered into the hands of human enemies (21:14). Hence, the human enemies are brought into the picture at the very last moment, to complete the defeat and to take the booty.[10]

From the perspective of divine and human participation in war, the division of forces in this passage is such that God holds the major role in destroying Judah, a more significant one than that taken by the actual human enemies he will summon against it. This presentation of the divine actions in the destruction is adjoined from beginning to end with different statements concerning the sins that caused this great divine anger. Second Kings 21:10–11 points to Manasseh's abominations, to which he succeeded in attracting the entire people of Judah; but 21:15 makes a more general accusation of long-term disobedience that raised divine anger, from the time of the exodus till this very day.[11]

Second Kings 24 juxtaposes explicit and implicit justifications of God's actions. This literary technique serves to legitimize God's ongoing responsibility for the military distress; God actively determines Judah's fate, in particular the 597 Jehoiachin exile, which is seen here as the culminating catastrophe. The hierarchal distinction between God and the human enemy is retained within the opening and the closing verses of 2 Kgs 24—it is the God of Israel who takes action against his disloyal king and kingdom (24:2–3, 20). God is the one who expels them away from his presence,

---

lieus, the first coming from prophetic circles (see Amos 7:7–8) and the second being a popular proverb. See §9.1.3.

9. Cogan and Tadmor, *II Kings*, 269. Hobbs (*2 Kings*, 308) argues that this passage denotes a reversal of the divine protection promised to the remnant during the 701 crisis (but note the difference in terminology in 2 Kgs 19:30–31, which uses שארית ופליטה); he also points out similarities with Jeremiah, considering Jeremiah to be the borrower of this idiom from Kings (Jer 12:7; 2:14–19).

10. והיו לבז ולמשסה designates the horrendous consequences of defeat and subjugation (Num 31:32; Isa 42:24; Jer 2:14; Ezek 26:5; Zeph 1:13). Compare Num 13:31 and Deut 1:39, where this threat (against the people) serves as a source of divine protection, and so in consolation prophecies, Jer 30:16; Ezek 34:22 (see 34:8); 36:4.

11. The differences between 2 Kgs 21:11 and 21:15 mitigate against the possibility of a single author (pace Hobbs, *2 Kings*, 308) and support Nelson's arguments in *Double Redaction*, 66. On the merismatic borders of time from the exodus to present, see 1 Sam 8:8; Jer 7:25; and §10.1.

not the Babylonian king who actually brought Jehoiachin and his court to Babylon, along with the professional artisans of Jerusalem (24:12–16).[12]

(c) A third justifying voice can be traced in 2 Kgs 25, the chapter that relates the very end of Jerusalem, as well as of Judean existence in the land (25:22–26).[13] Second Kings 24:20a is the last point where God is mentioned explicitly, as standing behind Jerusalem's destruction.[14] Throughout 2 Kgs 25 God is absent. He is not there when Nebuchadrezzar, his officials headed by Nebuzaradan, and his troops finally burst into the city (25:3–4), take action against the king (25:5–7), or destroy and burn the city houses, including the house of the Lord and the city walls (25:8–10). He is not mentioned when Nebuzaradan leads into exile those who survive, leaving a poor remnant in the land (25:11–12), or in the context of the copper vessels taken away from the temple (25:13–17). He is absent from the description of the capture of the priests and other officials taken to Riblah and executed there (25:18–21); this final step in the catastrophe of destruction and deportation is followed by the closing formula: ויגל יהודה מעל אדמתו ("thus Judah was exiled from its land," 25:21b). Finally, God is not mentioned in two appendixes that relate the fate of the remnant in Mizpah under Gedaliah (25:22–26) and tell of Jehoiachin's release, thirty-seven years into his exile (25:27–30).[15] Second Kings 25 gives a very detailed description of the atrocities in Jerusalem from the siege and onward; but in contrast to the

12. The phrases הסיר מעל פניו (2 Kgs 17:18, 23; 23:27; 24:3; but see Jer 52:3) or השליך מ(על) פניו (2 Kgs 17:20; 24:20) are to be taken as the theological rationalization for deportation; see also Deut 4:27; 28:36, 64. 2 Kgs 24:12–16 presents no less than four (mostly repetitive) lists of deportees.

13. Seitz (*Theology in Conflict*, 189–98, 199–200, 218–19) considers 2 Kgs 24 and 2 Kgs 25 to be two different descriptions, the products of two distinct authors, both settled in Babylon; the first represents the Jehoiachin exiles in Babylon, and the second adds the 587 events, still from a marked pro-Jehoiachin perspective (as may be seen from his selection of episodes and the concluding passage; 25:27–30).

14. Seitz (*Theology in Conflict*, 193) argues that 24:18–20 represents the conclusion of the book, before 2 Kgs 25 is secondarily appended. As the connecting bridge between the two chapters, 24:18–20 functions not only as a conclusion, but as an introduction to the reign of Zedekiah, as in Jer 52:1–3.

15. The question of whether this note on the release of Jehoiachin represents a good or a bad ending to the book of Kings is of major interest to scholars of Kings; see von Rad, *Studies in Deuteronomy*, 74–91; Noth, "Jerusalem Catastrophe"; Becking, "Jehoiachin's Amnesty"; and Schmid, "The Conquests of Jerusalem." The absence of God in these passages may suggest that the author considers these incidents to represent continuing distress, not salvation.

previous descriptions (2 Kgs 21–24), the entire description remains on the level of actions by the human enemy.[16]

Thus, the author of 2 Kgs 25 seems to choose quite a different theological way from the authors (and redactors) of 2 Kgs 21–24. Although this is an argument from silence, it is based on the contrast between 2 Kgs 25 and those passages that explicitly emphasize God's role in events (21:10; 23:26–27; 24:2–3, 20). With all due caution, I define the perspective of 2 Kgs 25 as "theological silence." Instead of producing explicit or implicit statements about God's involvement in the destruction, this historiographer invests his writing skills in depicting in copious detail the events caused by human agents. He thus leaves God out of the domain of human cruelty.

Arguments from silence are always difficult. Nevertheless, a similar theological silence may be traced elsewhere in the historiography of 2 Kings, in the passage concerning Josiah's death (23:28–30).[17] Again, the technique used is a kind of chronistic style of presenting the facts, narrating all the details from the king's fortunes in the war, through his death and burial and through the coronation of the royal prince.[18] It is thus remarkable that nothing is said theologically concerning the death in battle of the most righteous Davidic king.

In view of what we know about the Deuteronomistic school of authors—whose primary aim is to write a theological history of Israel and Judah, from the early days of the Davidic royal house and the construction

16. Seitz (*Theology in Conflict*, 192) notes the silence of 2 Kgs 25 regarding Zedekiah's first nine years of reign and the lack of any mention of Jeremiah (although he considers Jeremiah traditions to be in the background of 2 Kgs 24–25). But Seitz does not address the theological silence described here.

17. The theological silence concerning Josiah's death is maintained in the commentaries, which for the most part follow the biblical lead and focus on the historical background that leads to this tragic end, skipping over the grave theological difficulty it raises; see Gray, *I and II Kings*, 747–48; and Hobbs, *2 Kings*, 339–40. Cogan and Tadmor (*II Kings*, 291–302) close their detailed historical study with a short reference: "The historian could not reconcile Josiah's death with his world view of just retribution" (302); they then adduce 2 Chronicles, 1 Esdr 1:28–29; and Josephus, *Jewish Antiquities* 10.78, as references for explicit justifications for the king's death.

18. This theological silence is, of course, not retained in 2 Chr 35:20–27, which elaborates on the terse account of 2 Kings's Deuteronomistic History to create a fully independent story. See Japhet, *I and II Chronicles*, 1041–44. From a theological perspective, the Chronicler indeed has "'good reasons' to change the description" of Josiah's death (1042)—it seems that he could not comprehend the inexplicable fate of Josiah; he therefore finds a way to accuse him of hubris, for which purpose he even borrows and refers to the death of none other than Ahab (1042–43).

of the temple (1 Kgs 1–11) to the destruction of the temple and the kingdom (with brief reference to the fortunes of the last remnant of the royal house)—these silences are deafening—particularly the avoidance of mentioning God and his role in the events that led to Jerusalem's destruction, from the Babylonian siege onward.

The silence of 2 Kgs 25 may cover over a deep theological embarrassment at the inexplicability of the atrocities. Such a reaction to God's perceived role in the destruction of Jerusalem does not stand against the conception of the destruction as a justified judgment to a sinful people (24:20). But it does, like the silence in relation to Josiah's death, convey the inexplicability of the extent of this judgment, no matter how justified, upon God's chosen city and people. This theological silence is even more powerful in comparison to voices heard in parallel sources, which explicitly protest against God's active participation in Jerusalem's fall (compare this passage to Lam 2:20–22).[19]

Thus, the last chapters of 2 Kings feature three distinct justifications of God's actions as warrior against his people: from the loud and clear oration (21:10–15 and comment in 23:26–27), to the implicit view of God as acting behind the scenes (24:1–3, 9–10, 19–20), to the theological silence that seeks to relegate catastrophic events to the sphere of human cruelty (2 Kgs 25).

8.1.2. *The Prophetic Sources, Jeremiah and Ezekiel*

The idea that God himself summons and directs the enemy's actions is also found in two genres within the books of Jeremiah and Ezekiel: judgment prophecies against Judah and prophecies against the nations.[20] Sim-

---

19. The lack of a full oration concerning Judah's destruction in 2 Kings may be another argument from silence to this theological embarrassment. Could this also reflect a conscious literary choice to keep silent in face of this crisis?

20. This (B') concept of war is found in forty judgment oracles (against Judah) in Jeremiah: 1:13–16; 4:5–8, 15–18; 5:10–11, 15–17; 6:1–5, 6–8, 22–26; 8:10–12, 16–17; 12:7–13; 13:15–17; 15:1–2, 3–4, 11–14; 16:16–18; 17:1–4; 18:13–17, 19–23; 19:1–13; 20:1–6; 21:8–10; 22:6–7, 24–27; 25:8–14; 27:1–8, 9–15, 16–22; 28:12–17; 32:1–5, 16–25, 26–35, 36–41 (though consolation is promised to the exiles, 32:36 refers to the deliverance of Jerusalem into the hands of the Babylonian king); 34:1–7, 8–22; 37:3–10, 17–21; 38:1–13, 14–28; 40:1–6; and six in Ezekiel: 7:20–27; 11:1–13; 16:36–43; 21:23–29; 23:22–31, 46–49. Similarly, there are twenty-seven instances of this (B') concept in Jeremian prophecies against the nations: 25:15–29, 30–38; 43:8–13; 44:30; 46:14–24, 25–26; 47:2–7; 48:1–10, 11–17, 18–28; 49:1–6, 7–11, 12–22, 28–33; 50:2–3, 8–10, 14–16, 21–27, 29–30, 41–43, 44–46; 51:1–5, 11–14, 27–33, 47–48, 52–53, 54–57; and sixteen prophecies against the

ilar to the historiographic passages, these features comprise both shared elements and characteristics unique to each of these prophetic collections. This approach to the defeat is characterized by five formal and thematic features:

a. The human enemy is clearly subordinate to God. YHWH as sovereign is responsible for the initiation and progress of the military campaign. Part of this divine responsibility is expressed in God's inaction, insofar as he does not fight for his people. In this respect, God practically, although indirectly, assists the enemy forces.

b. God and the human enemy alternate in action. God's actions as sovereign and warrior, leading the human forces into battle, are related in passages that use the literary technique of interchanging God and the human enemy as alternative subjects of the verbs within the same prophetic unit.

c. As the head of the fighting armies, God summons the human enemies and instructs them strategically. Those strategic instructions occur mostly in Jeremiah (and in Ezek 9).[21] Yet, once the summons is given and answered, the enemy has some leeway in conducting his own campaign.[22]

God's hostile involvement in the battle is further intensified in these prophecies by the presence of two features that are much more prominent in the (C′) concept of war, where God is portrayed as the sole enemy:

d. The human enemy at times appears as but one of the destroying forces that God may activate.

e. The consequences of war are total destruction of people and city and an empty land.

---

nations in Ezekiel: 21:33–37; 25:1–4, 8–11, 12–14; 26:1–6, 7–14; 28:1–10, 11–19; 29:17–21; 30:1–9, 10–12, 20–26; 31:1–14; 32:1–10, 11–12, 17–32. The number of prophetic units is counted here on the basis of small oracular units, following the divisions suggested in Carroll's commentary on Jeremiah, to which I added a further distinguishing criterion according to the distinction between divine and human deeds.

21. See Bodi, *Ezekiel and Erra*, 95–110.

22. This strategic independence of the human enemy is recognized also by Isaiah in relation to the Assyrians (10:5–11), and it will also be the reason for the later punishment of this human agent (10:12–19; Jer 25:12–13).

Thematically, the two prophetic books share a common denominator in their presentation of God as the one who summons the Babylonians against Jerusalem. The prophetic voices (the prophets, their followers, and their editors), in both poetic and prose passages, justify God through their portrayal of God as warrior, in their emphasis that the defeat clearly came through God's will and activity. From this perspective, the events of the Babylonian campaign show God to be active and present, a powerful warrior and sovereign. It is unquestionably God who leads the enemy against his people and directs their actions. This theological accentuation of the divine activity and power in war is likewise apparent when it comes to the prophecies against the nations. The prophecies against Judah and against the nations are replete with phrases taken from the military milieu.

The poetic passage Jer 4:5–8 serves to illustrate four of the five features of this configuration:

[5] Proclaim in Judah,	⁵הגידו ביהודה
announce in Jerusalem, and say:	ובירושלים השמיעו ואמרו
"Blow the horn in the land!"	ותקעו (ק: תקעו) שופר בארץ
Shout aloud and say: Assemble,	קראו מלאו ואמרו האספו
and let us go into the fortified cities!	ונבואה אל־ערי המבצר.
[6] Set up a signpost: To Zion.	⁶שאו־נס ציונה
Take refuge, do not delay!	העיזו אל־תעמדו
For I bring evil from the north, and great disaster.	כי רעה אנכי מביא מצפון ושבר גדול.
[7] The lion has come up from his thicket:	⁷עלה אריה מסבכו
the destroyer of nations has set out,	ומשחית גוים נסע
has departed from his place,	יצא ממקמו
to make your land a desolation;	לשום ארצך לשמה
your cities shall be ruined, without inhabitants.	עריך תצינה מאין יושב.
[8] For this, put on sackcloth,	⁸על־זאת חגרו שקים
mourn and wail;	ספדו והילילו
for the blazing anger of YHWH has not turned away from us.[23]	כי לא שב חרון אף־יהוה ממנו.

---

23. Carroll (*Jeremiah*, 159–62) aptly considers the original prophetic unit to be limited to 4:5–8, with two responses appended in 4:9–10 and 4:11–12; so also Lundbom (*Jeremiah 1–20*, 332–35), who considers the following prose verses (4:9–10) "an added

The prophecy describes a concrete military-political threat, still not specified by name (as also 1:14), but only portrayed as evil from the north (compare 4:6; 6:1) or as a nation coming from the land of the north (6:22).[24] Although Jeremiah (and possibly his tradents) had experienced Babylonian rule, the descriptions of enemy troops invading the land are highly conventional, and the enemy remains anonymous.[25] This anonymity seems to accentuate an enormously severe human threat, yet . . .

1. The subordination of the human enemies to God is clearly established; it is YHWH who brings the human emperor from afar and who is responsible for the initiation of the military campaign (כי רעה אנכי מביא מצפון ושבר גדול, 4:6b).[26] The enemy force is described as highly trained: משחית גוים ("the destroyer of nations," 4:7a; see also 5:15–17).

2. God and the human enemy alternate as the subjects of the verbs in this unit. While the human enemy will actually destroy the land (4:7),[27] it is God's wrath that motivates that total destruction (4:8).

3. As the head of the fighting armies, God summons the human enemy and instructs them strategically. In 4:5–8, the role God plays in the military threat against Judah is twofold: he is both the source of the catastrophe (4:6b) and the one who warns the people in Judah and in Jerusalem to hide within the fortified cities for safety (4:5–6a; also 6:1). This quite contradictory twofold maneuver illustrates the theological complexity in presenting God as the originator of distress for his own people.[28]

---

dialogue between Yahweh and Jeremiah" (334), to be distinguished from the poetry of 4:5–8. This initial reaction expands on the wrath that affects all leading social circles: the king, officials, priests, and prophets (4:9); it constitutes one of the very few places where Jeremiah raises a direct protest against God (4:10), accusing him of no less than deceiving the people, having promised peace when total defeat is approaching.

24. Different identifications are suggested for this human enemy: (1) Scythians, following Greek historian Herodotus, *History* 1.104–6; (2) Babylonians, who are the imperial ruling force from 605 and on; (3) both Babylonians and Scythians; (4) diverse enemies (Jer 25:26). To most scholars none of these identifications seem satisfactory; see Holladay, *Jeremiah*, 1.42–43.

25. For other conventional descriptions of enemy actions in Jeremiah, see 4:13–18; 5:15–17; 6:1–8, 22–26; 10:22.

26. The northern enemy in Jeremiah is also the source of military threats against Egypt (46:6, 10, 24), Philistia (47:2), and even Babylon itself (50:3, 9, 41).

27. משחית גוים is also used by Jeremiah to refer to Babylon in those prophecies *against* Babylon that recall its task as the divine agent of destruction (51:20).

28. Compare Schmid ("How to Date the Book of Jeremiah"), who considers 4:5–8 from a redactional-critical perspective.

Anxiety is felt, expressed in 4:5–6, through the cluster of verbs that illustrate the terror and raise the emotional tone yet higher, calling the people to gather into fortified cities. This anxiety is further accentuated through the metaphor of the enemy as a hunting lion (4:7a).

The result of the war (e, above), the consequences of the enemy's actions, is complete destruction, a land emptied of its inhabitants (4:7b).[29] This description of profound ecological disaster brought upon the land represents turning this step beyond the atrocities of human-directed war. Its use in these prophecies that feature the human enemy as God's agent illustrates further the interchangeability of God and human in this (B') concept; thus it underscores the idea that the destructive human actions take place on God's orders. In consequence, mourning is called for, as the people realize that the political events designate divine wrath (4:8).[30]

Other prophetic passages within Jeremiah and Ezekiel broaden the picture of each of those features.

a.   The subordination of the human enemy to God is emphasized by the use of the first-person to indicate God's actions; only rarely are they described using second- or third-person.

These actions begin with a summons to the enemy, as for instance in כי הנני קרא לכל־משפחות ממלכות צפונה ("for I am summoning all the peoples of the kingdoms of the north," Jer 1:15); they develop through God's statement of what he plans to do: הנני מביא עליכם גוי ("lo, I am bringing against you a nation," 5:15); מאתי יבאו שדדים לה ("the ravagers would come against her from Me," PAN Jer 51:53); and in the second-person: כי־תביא עליהם גדוד פתאם ("when You bring sudden marauders against them," 18:22). God is responsible for the victory of the enemy's armies against his people. The common phrase יהוה נתן את־ביד ("YHWH gave the city/king/people into the hand of . . .") appears seventeen times in Jeremiah, but only four times in Ezekiel.[31] Other phrases demonstrate the primacy of God over the enemy, for example, "I will scatter them before the enemy" (Jer 18:17).

---

29. עריך תצינה מאין יושב; see Jer 2:15; and for the use of נצה, see McKane, *Jeremiah 1–25*, 92. See §9.1.3.

30. The first-person plural ממנו suggests that this is a quotation of the people, crying out in their despair. Jeremiah interjects such short cries of lament into his judgment prophecies in other places (4:13, 31; 6:24, 26b).

31. The occurrences of the construction יהוה נתן את־ביד "(YHWH) gave X into the hand of Y" in Jeremiah are distinguished according to the object: the city (20:5; 21:10; 32:3, 28, 36, 43; 34:2; 38:3, 18), the king (22:25; 32:4; 34:3, 21; 37:17), the people

In retaliation for the people's cultic disloyalty (Jer 19:3–5), God leads the human enemies to act as executors of his judgment; God brings distress upon this place (הנני מביא רעה על־המקום הזה, 19:3).[32] This dynamic of the enemy as God's agents is further elaborated in 19:7 (והפלתים בחרב לפני איביהם וביד מבקשי נפשם, "I will cause them to fall by the sword before their enemies, by the hand of those who seek their lives") through the collation of two phrases: הפיל (בחרב) לפני אויב (Jer 20:4; Isa 31:8; 37:7) and the elliptical phrase (lacking the initial verb): נתן את־ביד מבקשי נפשו. The construction becomes a characteristic marker of Jeremian adaptation.[33]

Similarly, the prophecies against the nations feature both direct and indirect declarations of God's actions, for example: "I will break Elam before their enemies" (PAN Jer 49:37). The combined phrase השבית את־ביד ("put an end to X by the hand of Y") assigns the action of destruction to YHWH, but its execution to the enemy; for example, "I will put an end to the wealth of Egypt by the hand of King Nebuchadrezzar of Babylon" (PAN Ezek 30:10). In like fashion, God brings desolation upon the land through strangers: "I will deliver the land into the hands of evil men. I will lay waste the land and everything in it by the hands of strangers" (PAN Ezek 30:12; compare 29:12). As commonly seen in this synergy between God and the human agent that YHWH summons to wage war, the human force is fully capable of conducting the fiercest combat.[34]

b. God and the human enemy alternate in action.

God's continuing responsibility for the human enemies' deeds is accentuated through verbal descriptions of warfare given in the first-person, which frequently alternate with portrayals of the human campaign conducted by the enemy force (Jer 15:11, 14; 22:7; 34:22; PAN Jer 51:2). YHWH ei-

---

(20:4; 34:18–20), or the king and the people (21:7). Three occurrences in Ezekiel refer to the people (23:9, 28; 39:23) and one, allegorically, to Jerusalem: "I will deliver you into their hands" (16:39). An analogous phrase is נתן את־/ל/למורשה ("deliver X to Y as a possession," PAN Ezek 25:4, 10).

32. ובקתי את־עצת יהודה וירושלים ("and I will frustrate the plans of Judah and Jerusalem," Jer 19:7) presents bqq as a pun on baqbuq ("jug"), though it is only here and in Isa 19:3 that this verb appears in an abstract context; compare Isa 24:1, 3; Jer 51:2.

33. נתן את־ביד אויב וביד מבקשי נפשם is a uniquely Jeremianic construction (21:7; 22:25; 34:20, 21; 38:16; PAN 44:30; 46:26). נתן את־ביד also occurs in both Priestly (Num 21:2, 34) and Deuteronomic texts (Deut 1:27; 2:24; 7:24) in the Pentateuch; and it is a very common phrase in the historiographic books (e.g., Josh 6:2).

34. So also Jer 6:1 and 6:4–5, quoting the enemy.

ther gives the enemy the authority to subject his people after the defeat (27:5–8) or himself initiates the subjugation of his people in their countries of exile: "I will make you a slave to your enemies in a land you have never known" (17:4). A remarkable feature of the terrible description within Jer 19 is the sustained emphasis on God's own deeds, through a long list of verbs of war in first-person in 19:7–9 and then again in 19:11–13. The only exception is 19:9b, which refers to the human enemies as the immediate cause of their distress.[35] Likewise, the alternation between God and the human enemy as the subject of verbs of aggression is often tempered by the enemy's act of war being credited to YHWH (as in 25:8–14), through verbs of which he is the subject: "I will exterminate them and make them a desolation, an object of hissing—ruins for all time. And I will banish from them the sound of mirth and gladness" (25:9b–10).[36]

c.   As the head of the fighting armies, God summons the human enemy and instructs them strategically.

YHWH himself commands the armies that are then to conduct their own campaigns against the nations (PAN Jer 47:7; 50:21) or against his own people (Ezek 9:11). YHWH gives strategic instructions to the fighting armies, which are transmitted in the imperative, like the words of a king to the heads of his army:[37] "Go up against her vines and destroy; lop off

35. במצור ובמצוק אשר יציקו להם איביהם ומבקשי נפשם ("because of the desperate straits to which they will be reduced by their enemies, who seek their life," Jer 19:9) is a collation of two phrases. The opening of the statement is borrowed from Deut 28:53, 55, 57; but איביהם ומבקשי נפשם represents the Jeremian adaptation of the allusion (see discussion of Jer 19:7; also 21:7; 22:25; 34:20–21; 44:30; 49:37). Additional units are characterized by transpositions of YHWH and the human enemy: Jer 7:1–8; Ezek 7:10–27; 11:1–13; 16:35–45; PAN Jer 43:8–13; 49:28–33; and especially PAN Ezek 25:1–7, 8–11, 12–14; 26:1–6, 7–14; 30:10–12; 32:1–10, 16–17.

36. Jer 25:9–11 is usually ascribed to the DtrJ editor; see Thiel, *Jeremia 1–25*, 272–73. However, Holladay (*Jeremiah*, 1.665–66) sees these verses as authentic to the prophet. The words "declares YHWH" and "for My servant, King Nebuchadrezzar of Babylon" (25:9) are absent from the Septuagint; thus in this version YHWH summons only "the families of the north" and not Babylon. "The king of Babylon" is also missing from 25:11–12 LXX; similarly, the phrase "the land of the Chaldeans"—along with other phrases—is lacking in 25:12. Nonetheless, the Septuagint, like the Masoretic Text, describes the action as YHWH summoning the human enemy's armies.

37. Compare the military instructions of a king to the heads of his armies prior to going out to war (e.g., 2 Sam 18:1–5). Bach (*Die Aufforderungen zur Flucht*, 44–50, 92–95) notes that this is the common derivation in prophetic passages of divine directives in

her trailing branches, . . . but do not make an end" (Jer 5:10); "hew down her trees and raise a siegemound against Jerusalem" (6:6). God is thus profoundly involved in all the stages of the war waged against his people (Ezek 9:11). Similar instructions are found in the prophecies against the nations, for example, against Edom: "Assemble, and move against her, and rise up for war" (PAN Jer 49:14); and similarly the prophecies against Kedar and the kingdoms of Hazor (PAN Jer 49:28, 31) and against Babylon (PAN Jer 50:14–16): "Range yourself round about Babylon, all you who draw the bow; shoot at her, don't spare arrows" (50:14); "raise a shout" (50:15); "make an end in Babylon of sowers" (50:16); "ruin and destroy after them to the last . . . do just as I have commanded you" (50:21). The human enemy is the instrument of YHWH's anger and is required to do the following: "Come against her from every quarter; break open her granaries, pile her up like heaps of grain, and destroy her . . . destroy all her bulls, let them go down to slaughter" (50:26–27). In PAN Jer 47:6–7, instructions are given to the sword as if, metaphorically, it acts on its own.[38]

God's military directive against Israel is portrayed in Ezek 23:46–47 through the use of four different verbal forms—imperative, infinitive absolute, *conversive waw* with the perfect, and imperfect (future):

[46] For thus said the Lord GOD: Summon an assembly against them, and make them an object of horror and plunder. [47] Let the assembly pelt them with stones and cut them down with their swords; let them kill their sons and daughters, and burn down their homes.	[46] כי כה אמר אדני יהוה העלה עליהם קהל ונתן אתהן לזעוה ולבז. [47] ורגמו עליהן אבן קהל וברא אותהן בחרבותם בניהם ובנותיהם יהרגו ובתיהן באש ישרפו.

These instructions to the human armies are parallel to the orders given by YHWH earlier in Ezek 9 to the "person clothed in linen" (from the celestial retinue), who is called to act against Jerusalem and who returns to YHWH and proclaims that he completed his mission (9:3–7, 11).[39]

---

war before going out to battle (1 Kgs 22:6, 12, 15–23) or during battle (20:13, 22, 28). He also argues that calls to flee from battle, which are mostly found in the prophecies against the nations (PAN Jer 48:6–8, 28), belong to a single literary category originating in the holy war.

38. For other examples of military orders that God gives to the fighting forces against his people, see Jer 12:9; PAN Jer 50:29. See also another instance of orders given to the sword in Ezek 21:13–16.

39. So Zimmerli (*Ezekiel*, 1.479). Compare Qimhi, who explains the infinitive forms

d.   The human enemy at times appears as but one of the destroying forces that God may activate.

Images of natural forces—storms (Jer 4:13) and predators (lion in 4:7; lion of the forest, wolf of the desert, and leopard by the city gates in 5:6; eagle in 4:13; and similarly in PAN 48:40; 49:22)—reinforce the terror.[40]

e.   The consequences of war are total destruction of people and city, and an empty land.

Because it is under divine sovereignty, the city, its houses, and its population will suffer a conclusive punishment, which is symbolized in Jer 19, for instance, by both the broken jug and the renaming of the *Topheth*, the cultic site in the Valley of Ben-hinnom, which will be called the Valley of Slaughter (19:6).[41] Among the inflictions that God intends to bring upon the city is its complete desolation, as indicated by 19:8: "And I will make this city an object of horror and hissing [ושמתי את־העיר הזאת לשמה ולשרקה]; everyone who passes by it will be appalled and will hiss over all its wounds."[42]

These examples show that, in the prophetic framework, everything done by the enemies is simply the manifestation of the divine plan and instructions. The human enemies are tools of war in God's arsenal, as depicted in the prophecy against Babylon: "YHWH has opened His armory and brought out the weapons of His wrath; for that is the task of my Lord, YHWH of Hosts, in the land of the Chaldeans" (PAN Jer 50:25). The parallels between the descriptions of God's functions and activity in judgment prophecies against Israel and in prophecies against the nations illustrate that

---

in Ezek 23:46 as connoting first-person speech, as if God is saying, "I shall go up and I shall give." This is also how Greenberg translates the verse (*Ezekiel 21–37*, 473, 487). The diverse use of the verbal forms stands out against the contrasting background of 16:40, where the actions are executed by the human enemies.

40. The image of the destroying lion is also found in in Jer 2:30 and Joel 1:6.

41. The designation of the *Topheth* as the Valley of Slaughter is also mentioned in Jer 7:31–33, and the relationship between the two prophecies is debated. See Carroll, *Jeremiah*, 224–26, 388–89; and Lundbom, *Jeremiah 1–20*, 492–503.

42. The desolation is configured here as a divine action against the city. שים לשמה ולשרקה is a clear Jeremian phrase (2:15; 18:16; 19:8; PAN 25:9–10). כל עבר עליה ישם וישרק על־כל־מכותה occurs twice in PAN Jer 49:17 and 50:13; otherwise only in 1 Kgs 9:8. Compare Jer 7:34, which uses other phrasing to express desolation (alluding to Lev 26:44).

the concept of God as sovereign, meting out punishment, extends throughout the entire universe and is not limited to actions against Israel.

8.2. PROTEST: "ALL THIS HAS COME UPON US, YET WE HAVE NOT FORGOTTEN YOU" (PSALM 44)

The idea that God is responsible for the distress, and acts by summoning the human enemies, leads poets in Psalms and Lamentations to express complaints and direct accusations against God.[43] Three characteristics of this (B') concept of war are regularly present, both in protests and in laments:

a. The subordination of the human enemy to God is recognized by the poets through the placement of YHWH as initiator of and responsible for the distress.

b. God and the human enemy alternate in action, and thus the agents of verbs of aggression interchange between God and the human enemy.

c. As the head of the fighting armies, God summons the human enemy and instructs them strategically.

The metaphor of YHWH as the military chief portrays God as the one who leads the human armies to their success—that is, to accomplish his own people's defeat and annihilation. What served the prophets in justifications of God's activity and power, becomes in the poets' words the ground of a painful protest.

Psalm 44 is an important example of protest in the Hebrew Bible—of its traits as a mode in the talk to God, of its polemical nature, and of its roots in theodical discourse—and it focuses on human and divine roles in war. The psalm opens with praise for past salvation and continues with complaints in regard to the current distressing circumstances of exile. Both praise and complaint invoke conception (B') of our divine-human model.[44]

---

43. This (B') concept of God's role in the destruction is not found in popular sayings quoted in the books of Jeremiah and Ezekiel.

44. Ps 44 is discussed here in order to illustrate the (B') conception, but see also the discussion of divine justice in §11.3.2. For a more extensive treatment, see Rom-Shiloni, "Psalm 44."

Protest is expressed throughout this psalm in both formal and thematic features. Most important, the voice of the psalmist speaks directly to God, using second-person verbal phrases suffixed by pronominal/object pronouns of the first-person plural.[45] This formal-stylistic device is used with verbs of both salvation (44:2–9; e.g., הושעתנו ["You give us victory"], 44:8) and desertion/defeat (44:10–17; אף־זנחת ותכלימנו ["yet You have rejected and disgraced us"], ולא־תצא בצבאותינו ["You do not go with our armies"], תשיבנו אחור ["You make us retreat"], תתננו כצאן מאכל ["You let them devour us"], זריתנו ["You disperse us"], תשימנו ["You make us," 2x, 14, 15]; and 44:20: כי דכיתנו ["You cast us crashed"], ותכס עלינו בצלמות ["You covered us over with deepest darkness"]). But this stylistic feature, which at the outset does indeed highlight the close relationship between God and his people, comes to accentuate the perception of conflict between God and his people, first in 44:10–17 and even more so in 44:18–23, where these verbal phrases present the people as victims of affliction brought about by God's actions.

Thematically, the antagonistic relationship between God and the people is masterfully constructed through the structuring of the psalm into its three main segments of praise, complaint, and petition.[46] The psalm opens with praise (44:2–9), which in turn is divided into two parts.[47] Psalm 44:2–4 recalls God's past salvific deeds, particularly the settlement in the land. Throughout the generations, parents tell the story to their children (44:2), so that the people's attitude of appreciation is maintained over time.[48] In the second section, 44:5–9, praise for past events develops into the psalmist's declaration of present piety ("You are my king, O God," 44:5) and closes

45. In addition, God is thrice addressed by means of two of his designations: אלהים (44:2, 9) and אדני (44:24).

46. Haar ("God-Israel Relationship," 31, 105–32) highlights the articulation of the God-people relationship in seven communal laments, among them Ps 44 (pp. 32–36). Yet, Haar overlooks the element of protest discussed here. In this psalm, the statements describing God's actions against his people are a much more prominent feature than the questions directed to God (apparent in 44:24–25). Such questions are usually seen as the main characteristic of doubt and protest; see Miller, *They Cried to the Lord*, 70–75.

47. The positioning of praise before the request is a unique feature of the poetic compositions of Psalms and Lamentations and contrasts with the form of the short prose prayers. See Greenberg, *Biblical Prose Prayers*, 10; and b. Berakhot 32a. For parallels in the Sumerian and classical literature, see Crow, "Rhetoric of Psalm 44," 395–96.

48. Retelling the story to one's children is of major importance in Exod 10:2; 12:26; 13:8; Deut 6:20–25. The events of the exodus through the settlement are the focus of praise in other communal laments, such as Ps 80, while Pss 74, 77, 89 draw on the struggle with primeval chaotic forces.

with the praises of the entire community ("in God we glory constantly, and praise Your name unceasingly," 44:9).[49] In these two subsections, verbal phrases convey praise for deeds of deliverance. God guarantees his people's settlement in the land (44:3–4) as well as their victories since that time (44:5–9), so that God's leadership and power in the past guaranteed the people's victory (see 44:6–7: "through You we gore our foes; by Your name we trample our adversaries"). The psalmist minimizes the role of the human Israelite warriors in the past, in order to celebrate assistance of the divine king—whom he currently feels is still his king (44:5).

The complaint in 44:10–23, the core of this psalm, is similarly divided into two parts, each of which refers differently back to the verses of praise. The first subunit, 44:10–17, describes the present distress as political-military defeat, destruction, and exile. Using a series of verbs in the second-person, the author reproves God for his active involvement in the people's suffering. In contrast to God's past salvific deeds, "deeds *You* performed in their days, in days of old" (44:2), God's present (mis-) deeds express his desertion of the people: "Yet *You* have rejected and disgraced *us, You* do not go with *our* armies" (44:10). Moreover, God's actions contribute to the enemies' success ("*You* make *us* retreat before our foe," 44:11); this amounts to delivering the people into the enemy's hands ("*You* sell *Your people* for no fortune," 44:13) and to consigning the people to disgrace, shame, and mockery ("*You* make *us* the butt of our neighbors, ... *You* make *us* a byword among the nations," 44:14–15).[50]

This literary structure closes with a chiasmically structured opposition between 44:16–17 and 44:9. The expression of constant praise in 44:9, באלהים הללנו כל־היום ("in God we glory constantly [NJPS: at all times]," gives way to one of permanent self-contempt: כל־היום כלמתי נגדי ("I am constantly aware of my disgrace," 44:16), and the only voice heard is "the sound of taunting revilers" (44:17).[51]

---

49. Ps 44:5–9 is also distinguished by rapid alternation between first-person singular and plural (so also 44:16). For discussion of the features of this passage, see Morrow, *Protest against God*, 96–101.

50. God's active responsibility for the people's disgrace is further illuminated when Ps 44:14 (also 80:7) is compared to 31:12; 79:4; 89:42; Deut 28:37; Lam 5:1. God afflicts his people with disgrace (חרפה) in Hos 12:15; Jer 24:9; 29:18; Ezek 22:4 in the same way that he acts against the nations (PAN Jer 49:13; Ps 78:66).

51. Kessler ("Psalm 44," 198) points out the contradiction between the elements of perpetual praise in 44:9 and perpetual disgrace in 44:16–17. This contrast also calls for a deeper appreciation of כלמה and חרפה in 44:10–17, which at face value appears to apply to the shame of the people of God (also Isa 51:7; Zeph 2:8), but in the present

The second part of the complaint, 44:18–23, is not less painful, as the psalmist here insists on the people's innocence. Loren Crow shows that 44:18–23 forms a parallel construction (A-A-B ‖ A-A-B in 44:18–20 ‖ 44:21–23), in which proclamations of the people's piety (A in 44:18–19 ‖ 44:21–22) are set in opposition either to God's deeds against his people or to the consequences of these deeds for the people's present situation (B in 44:20 ‖ 44:23).[52] The opposition between God and the people is given further formal expression in the verbal phrases of this passage. But in contrast to 44:10–17, God and people here switch grammatical places. With the exception of 44:20 (דכיתנו... ותכס עלינו), in 44:18–23 the people are the agents of the verbal phrases and thus appear in the first-person plural; God becomes the object of action, presented through second-person objective pronouns: ולא שכחנוך ולא־שקרנו בבריתך ("yet *we* have not forgotten *You*, nor [have *we*] been false to *Your* covenant," 44:18) and כי־עליך הרגנו ("it is for *Your* sake that *we* are slain," 44:23; compare 44:10, 17 with 44:20). This grammatical feature reinforces the thematic opposition suggested in these verses—the people are loyal to God and to his covenant, yet God takes fatal actions against them. This proclamation thus brings forcefully to the fore the question of divine justice (see §10.2).

These verses gain even further force in comparison with the psalm's previous segments. Psalm 44:23, which concludes this subunit, features the third occurrence of כל־היום ("constantly"). This third iteration of the phrase marks the general movement through the psalm as it expresses the decline in the people's condition, which starts with praise (44:9), changes to disgrace (44:16), and concludes in defeat and death (44:23).[53]

Psalm 44 ends with petition in 44:24–27, which calls on God to intervene once again on behalf of his people. Using language that further emphasizes God's inactivity in the present circumstances, they constitute additional implicit protest. First, the petitions call upon God to awaken, a figure of speech that implies that God has long neglected his people: "Rouse Yourself; why do You sleep, O Lord? Awaken, do not reject [us] forever!" (44:24).[54] Second, God continues to hide his face (44:25); that is,

---

context may also denote their blasphemy against God himself (2 Kgs 19:22; Isa 37:23; also Zeph 2:10).

52. Crow, "Rhetoric of Psalm 44," 397–99; see Kessler, "Psalm 44," 198–99.

53. For this and other "keyword plays," see Kessler, "Psalm 44," 202–4.

54. Batto ("Sleeping God," 159–64) points out the use of divine "sleep as a symbol of divine authority" in mythic creation episodes. Yet, with the exception of Ps 74, which ties together creation and exodus traditions, most of the individual (Pss 7, 35) and communal laments (Pss 44, 59) do not develop this image of God as creator, but

he is present, but appears to choose not to act according to his capabilities. Finally, in contrast to the loyal people, who continuously praise God for his past salvation (44:2–4) and who even in these times of distress have never forgotten him (44:18), it is God who forgets the people's affliction ("*You* forget *our* affliction and *our* distress," 44:25). By using the nouns עֲנִי and לַחַץ the psalmist alludes to the exodus traditions, which became the paradigmatic examples for God's benevolent response to his people's agony (Exod 3:6–9; Deut 26:7); the allusion further underscores the break with past precedents in the present situation.

The psalmist completes his plea with a final call for help.[55] From the midst of the people's distress, which has brought them as low as the dust of the ground (Ps 44:26), the psalmist calls upon God to (once again) help and redeem his people: "Arise and help us, redeem us as befits Your faithfulness" (44:27). God is still considered to be, and can still prove to be, the savior of his people.

The two basic segments—praise (44:2–9) and complaint (44:10–23)— form a symmetry, after which the psalm closes with petitions for help that tie together the two preceding units (44:24–27). The organizing element of the entire psalm is the relationship between God and people, portrayed in chronological perspective—from past salvation, through present abandonment and consequent distress, to a plea for (imminent) future deliverance.[56]

This structure highlights the mental turmoil in which the protestor-psalmist is trapped.[57] Throughout the psalm, the poet declares his faith in God, his devotion to him, and his continuing bond with the community of believers (44:5, 23). Yet, in his proclamation of innocence and obedience (44:18–23), the psalmist poses for himself the trilemma of theodicy. He struggles with how to reconcile God's role as lord of history, God's character of goodness and benevolence, and the (incomprehensible) present distress and suffering of the people (see §1.1.1, §1.3, and §11.3.2). In describing the current distress, the poet agonizes over the warlike actions

---

rather present God as lord of history, in the character of warrior, sovereign, and king (note also 78:65; compare Batto, 169–72). This difference, however, is not noticed in Mrozek and Votto's criticism of Batto in "Motif of the Sleeping Divinity."

55. Requests for help appear regularly at the end of communal laments; see Pss 74:22; 80:4, 8, 20; 89:47.

56. Compare Crow's concentric trajectory ("Rhetoric of Psalm 44," 394); and Kessler ("Psalm 44," 194–95), who suggests a chiastic structure.

57. A similar example of protest occurs in Ps 77; see Weiss, *Ideas and Beliefs*, 114–17.

God takes against his people—God abdicates his role as warrior-savior and instead delivers his people into the hands of their enemies. The poet recognizes God's role as warrior, doubting neither his omnipotence nor his omniscience as lord of history; yet he protests against the enmity that God is presently exhibiting against his own people.[58] An even greater tension arises from the poet's assertion that the people remain loyal to God and to his covenant. The poet measures the present political distress through the concept of retribution; therefore, he struggles with the presumption that God is a good and benevolent judge.[59]

Nevertheless, and of great importance, the psalmist's anxiety does not obscure his address to God in prayer, his pious understanding that God is his king (44:5), and his pleas for salvation (44:24–27). The goal of his final plea (like the goal of the lament in general) is to bring about a change, to cause God to act once again in favor of his devoted, suffering, and innocent believers, as in the remembered past. From that pious position arises his protest, his orderly criticism, which is addressed to God and is therefore apparent throughout this psalm (and as typical also in other laments, both communal and individual).[60]

Psalm 44 is among the few communal laments that lay the responsibility

58. See Westermann, "Role of the Lament," 24–28; and Miller, *They Cried to the Lord*, 86–114, esp. 97–114. Yet Ps 44 differs both from the general structure for communal laments identified by Westermann (lament-petition-praise; see "Role of the Lament," 26–27) and from Brueggemann's cognitive pattern (orientation-disorientation-reorientation). Brueggemann's model (in *Psalms*, 3–32) is adapted from Paul Ricoeur's dialectic of disorientation and reorientation, applied to the study of the function of the Psalms. Yet in Brueggemann's analysis Ps 44 fails to reach the final stage of this model; the praise section functions merely as an introduction, adducing national memories of past salvation. Therefore, Ps 44 falls into Brueggemann's category of un-answered complaints, exemplified by Ps 88 (*Psalms*, 56–57). Brueggemann emphasizes "the direct accusation against God" in these psalms, as well as the intensification of the elements of desperation.

59. Two additional comments concerning the nature of protest in Ps 44 should be mentioned: (1) its polemic against prophetic accusations of the people's disloyalty against and forgetfulness of God and (2) its polemic against wisdom conceptions of retribution. Furthermore, this psalm draws also the limits of protest, that is, limitations that the poet seems to take upon himself in crafting his direct accusations against God. See Rom-Shiloni, "Psalm 44," 690–97.

60. Most of the complaints in the communal laments differentiate between the source of distress, commonly identified as the human enemies, and God, who, being uninvolved in the distress, is the addressee of petitions for help (Pss 74, 79, 137). See §7.1.

for the actual destruction and exile upon God, as the one who summons the human enemies against Judah and delivers his people into their hands; the human enemies play only minor roles in the affliction. Other psalms that take this line of argumentation are Pss 80, 89, and 106. This (B') conception is also found in sporadic passages in Lam 1–2. In all of these contexts, the three basic characteristics of the (B') conception are apparent:

a.   The subordination of the human enemy to God is emphasized by the primacy of God as the sovereign who summons the human enemies against his land, people, or king (Pss 80:13–14, 17; 89:41–46; 106:41–42; Lam 1:5–6, 14, 17; 2:3, 7, 17).

b.   God and the human enemy alternate in action, as illustrated through the interchangeability between God and the human enemy as the perpetrators of acts of war (Ps 89:41–46; Lam 1:5, 13–15).

c.   As the head of the fighting armies, God summons the human enemy and instructs them strategically (Ps 89:41–46).

Functionally, this presentation of the role of God in the defeat comprises the component of the complaint against the present distress. Like Ps 44, these passages, whether one-verse proclamations or entire psalms, articulate the great current distress and express a direct protest addressed to God, concerning his perceived role in the destruction and its aftermath. Thus, they accept the idea that God is both sovereign and warrior—and this is exactly the source of their agony. Nevertheless, all protestors still call upon God and expect his future deliverance (Ps 106:47).

In contrast to this (B') concept of war, which integrates human military activity with the theological view that sees divine intervention as the cause of human events, conception (C') views the destruction as the sole product of divine activity.

9

GOD AS THE ENEMY

The third conception of God's role in Jerusalem's destruction sees God himself as the sole initiator and executor of the catastrophe (see fig. 9.1). This (C') conception discounts any human role in the events (or profoundly limits its scope) and thus presents an explanation that is to a great extent detached from historical realities. Furthermore, this conception stands in diametric opposition to the (A' → C) framework, which conceptualizes the human enemies as those who initiate the war, and God as his people's sole savior.[1]

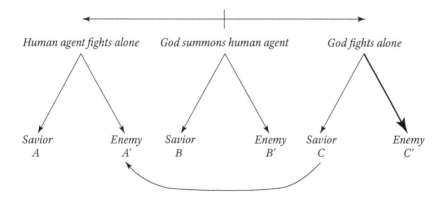

Fig. 9.1. God is the enemy

This explanation for the disaster occurs mainly in the prophecies of Jeremiah and Ezekiel. In (C') passages, God's control over the disaster is seen

1. See discussion of Jer 21:1–7 in §1.1.2 and the opposition between the (A' → C) framework and the (C') conception in §6.4.

to be absolute; the destruction of city and land is portrayed as his warlike activity and as a sign of his power, that is, his fury unleashed on his own people. While the two prophets use this conception in many similar ways, a careful look at the two prophetic books reveals significant differences between them in style and in theme, primarily in their interpretations of the meaning of the total annihilation when seen from this perspective. These prophetic justifications of God's actions as sole enemy of his people are built on the thematic and formal characteristics of this approach, and the radical stances of both Jeremiah and Ezekiel mount a fierce polemic against their contemporaries, who continue to try to "rescue" God's image as savior of his people along the (A' → C) conception of war. This conception is found both in poetry (Pss 90, 102; Lam 2; 1:21–22; 3:1–16) and in some speeches attributed to "the people," whose words are quoted in the book of Jeremiah to express doubt and protest.[2]

The (C') conception is used in contexts of justification of God's role and in expressions of doubt and protest; therefore it has implications for the reconstruction of the overall theodical discourse. The (C') conception constitutes the most extreme approach to the destruction, as that executed by God himself, acting in great wrath and absolute power. The consequence of such destruction is total annihilation, not only of the people, but also of the land itself, which is portrayed as desolate and empty. Thus, while the theological origin of the notion of the empty land is a highly debated issue in scholarship, the (C') conception of God's role in war puts this debate in context.

One of the most fascinating questions that surfaces is the question "why?"—Why do the prophets choose to justify God as the sole foe of his own people? This theodical choice calls for an explanation of the prophetic voices on the basis of a theological description.

9.1. Justification: The Argumentation and Its Price in Jeremiah and Ezekiel

The conception of God as the sole enemy of Jerusalem forms the primary theological basis for the judgment prophecies of both Jeremiah and Ezekiel.

---

2. Six anonymous quotations of "the people" in Jeremiah express this conception: 5:19; 8:14; 9:11; 13:22; 14:19–22; 16:10. A similar sentiment is put into the mouth of the "nations" (22:8). See §9.2.

Statistically, this conception appears almost two times more in Jeremiah's judgment prophecies against Israel/Judah than the (B') conception occurs in that context discussed in chapter 8,[3] and five times more than the (B') conception occurs in Ezekiel's judgment prophecies against Jerusalem.[4] In the prophecies against the nations, by contrast, the (C') conception is of minor importance, occurring much less frequently;[5] and thus, the (B') conception seems to govern in prophecies against the nations in both prophetic books. The statistical data illustrates the clear prophetic preference for the (C') conception in explaining the theological meaning of the destruction of Jerusalem and Judah for the Judean communities themselves, a preference exhibited by both prophetic books (separately and independently).

The theodical approach based on this conception is characterized by three features:

a.   God is the sole executor of the destruction, and in most cases there is no mention of the actions of human enemy armies.

This feature is essential; on occasion, following the description of the main events of the divine war, human enemies are mentioned as completing the victory (Jer 21:7; Ezek 5:12; PAN Ezek 25:12–14), taking the booty, or sim-

---

3. I count sixty-two occurrences of (C') conception of war in judgment prophecies against Israel in Jeremiah: 1:11–12; 4:3–4, 23–28; 5:1–6, 7–9, 12–14, 18–19, 26–29; 6:9–11, 12–15, 16–21; 7:12–15, 16–20, 29, 30–34; 8:1–3, 13; 9:6–8, 9–10, 11–15, 24–25; 10:17–21; 11:9–14, 15–17, 21–23; 12:14–17; 13:1–11, 12–14, 20–27; 14:10, 11–12, 13–16; 15:5–9; 16:1–9, 10–13, 14–15; 17:19–27; 18:1–12; 19:14–15; 20:16; 21:3–7, 11–12, 13–14; 23:7–8, 9–12, 13–15, 16–22, 33–40; 24:1–10; 26:1–10; 29:1–7, 16–19; 32:42–45; 35:1–17; 36:3, 30–31; 39:15–18; 42:9–17, 18–22; 44:1–6, 11–14, 26–28. This passage division relies on Carroll's divisions in his commentary on Jeremiah, which I further refine by invoking the three categories of distinction between the deeds of God and human beings in war.

4. There are thirty-two instances of the (C') approach in Ezekiel's judgment prophecies against Israel: 4:1–17; 5:1–4, 5–17; 6:1–10, 11–14; 7:1–4, 5–9, 10–19; 9:1–11; 11:14–21; 12:1–16 (an exceptional example in which, over against the human deeds presented, it is God who judges Zedekiah); 12:17–20, 21–25, 26–28; 13:1–16, 17–23; 14:1–11, 12–20; 15:1–8; 17:16–21 (see note on 12:1–16); 18:21–32; 20:1–29 (throughout this historical retrospective of Ezek 20 there is no mention of human enemies); 21:1–5, 6–10, 13–22; 22:1–16, 17–22, 23–31; 24:1–14, 15–27; 33:23–29, 30–33.

5. The (C') approach appears in sixteen passages in Jeremiah's prophecies against the nations: 9:24–25; 12:14–17; 46:27–28; 48:29–39, 40–47; 49:23–27, 35–39; 50:11–13, 31–32; 51:6–10, 24, 25–26, 36–37, 38–40, 41–43, 59–64. The (C') approach is represented in ten passages in Ezekiel's prophecies against the nations: 25:6–7, 15–17; 26:15–21; 27; 28:20–24; 29:1–16; 30:13–19; 31:15–18; 35:1–9, 10–15.

ply enjoying the outcome (Lam 2:16–17). The placement of the actions of human enemies *following* God's own warlike deeds seems to constitute an editorial principle in Jeremiah; for example, in Jer 5 (C') passages alternate with (B') passages:

C'	5:7–9
B'	5:10–11
C'	5:12–14
B'	5:15–17
C'	5:18–19

b. God as warrior uses natural forces (at times combined with human troops) in fighting his war.

These natural forces may be called in from the outside or may be local natural forces that God manipulates. Stormy winds (סערת יהוה ["a great storm is unleashed from the remotest parts of earth"], Jer 23:19) are enlisted to cause a war involving many nations (25:32).[6] Likewise, God may bring from outside the forces of pestilence and death to send among his people (21:6). Within the land, God may "light fire" in towns and in peripheral areas (Jer 17:27; Ezek 21:3);[7] he may summon local predators to attack (5:17; 14:15)—among them lions of the forest, wolves of the desert, and leopards from the lands around the towns of Judah (Jer 5:6). In addition, God may blight the ecology and agricultural conditions of the land and by this cause hunger (Jer 14:15, 16, 18; 42:14, 16; Ezek 5:16; 14:13; and reversed in consolation prophecies in 34:29; 36:29–30).

Descriptions of God summoning these nature forces to war parallel, at face value, his summonses to human agents—the (B') conception. Compare,

---

6. The רוח משחית ("destructive wind," PAN Jer 51:1, 11) is evoked to arouse nations against Babylon (51:2); thus it is used also with the (B') conception. In the Mesopotamian city laments, in which Enlil is the major deity that causes the destruction, the storm is his primary agent. On the relatively few appearances of the destructive storm in biblical sources, see Dobbs-Allsopp, *Weep, O Daughter of Zion*, 55–66.

7. Other phrases that refer to God as the one who kindles fire are ביער (אש) ("I the Lord have kindled it," Ezek 21:4) and באש עברתי כליתים ("I will consume them with the fire of My fury," 22:31). The metaphor נתן לאש (as in 15:6: "I have designated [them] as fuel for fire") portrays the consuming fire as a semi-independent force, with God as the first cause. Fire serves often as metaphor for divine anger in Jeremiah, as in יצאה כאש חמתי ("lest My wrath break forth like fire," 4:4).

for instance, the phrase והעברתי את־איביך בארץ לא ידעת ("and I will bring your enemies by way of a land you have not known," Jer 15:14), which refers to bringing a human army against Judah, to לו־חיה רעה אעביר בארץ ("if I were to send wild beasts to roam the land," Ezek 14:15), which uses the same verb (עבר את־/ב *hiphil*) to describe bringing animal predators against it. In a somewhat different vein, PAN Jer 51:1 uses (יהוה) העיר רוח משחית to describe arousing natural forces ("see, I am rousing a destructive wind against Babylon"), which is immediately elaborated to mean sending foreign armies against it (51:2). This same phrase is used elsewhere in the prophecies against the nations to describe God summoning human armies against Babylon: העיר יהוה את־רוח מלכי מדי ("the LORD has roused the spirit of the kings of Media, for His plan against Babylon is to destroy her," 51:11); it is also used with no mention of a wind at all: כי הנה אנכי מעיר ומעלה על־בבל קהל־גוים גדלים ("for see, I am rousing and leading an assemblage of great nations against Babylon," PAN Jer 50:9; also Ezek 23:22).

Such formal and semantic similarities cause Hennig Fredriksson to classify the use of both natural and human forces as illustrations of the notion of God as the head of armies (*als Heerführer*).[8] But thematically, this very use of natural forces in war is *the* significant feature that characterizes the war waged by God himself in the (C') conception, thus distinguishing God's own war from situations in which God summons human forces and they conduct the war using human strategies in the (B') approach. The uniqueness of this (C') conception is that it portrays God as acting directly from his position as creator of the world and its absolute ruler; thus he mobilizes all created forces in order to guarantee the war's total and complete results.

c.   The result of the war in which God is the sole enemy is total destruction, that is, desolation of agriculture life and emptying of the land of both human and animal.

The unleashing of God's forces afflicts the people, the city, and the land; the consequences are horrendous in that they profoundly transform the entire ecological system. Such consequences could not have been caused by human forces and therefore clearly result from God's warlike actions.[9]

8. See Fredriksson, *Jahwe als Krieger*, 47–50; and Dobbs-Allsopp, *Weep, O Daughter of Zion*, 57.

9. Natural forces are sometimes invoked in support of the (B') conception as well, where they are summoned in support of the human enemies he summons from other lands. See §8.1.2.

Element (a) defines the (C') conception, while the other two features often accompany it to enforce God's role as the sole warrior. Three texts (among many others) illustrate these three features and various nuances of this conception in the prophets: in Ezek 5 we see elements (a) and (b)—God as the sole executor of the destruction and God as warrior who uses natural forces (at times combined with human troops) in his war. Jeremiah 9:9–10 and 4:23–28 portray element (c)—the consequences of God's war as a sole enemy: total destruction and an empty land.

9.1.1. *God as the Sole Executor of the Destruction (Ezekiel 5)*

Ezekiel 4–5 presents a series of symbolic acts that show forth the siege against Jerusalem and its consequences. Ezekiel 4:1–3 pictures the setting of the siege and 4:4–8 its prolongation; 4:12–15 switches gears by depicting the defiling conditions of exile, and 4:16–17 returns to the intensifying hunger in Jerusalem. Finally, in 5:1–4, the prophet is told to portray Jerusalem's destruction:[10]

[1] And you, O mortal, take a sharp knife; use it as a barber's razor and pass it over your head and beard. Then take scales and divide the hair. [2] When the days of siege are completed, destroy a third part in fire in the city, take a third and strike it with the sword all around the city, and scatter a third to the wind and unsheathe a sword after them. [3] Take also a few [hairs] from there and tie them up in your skirts. [4] And take some more of them and cast them into the fire, and burn them in the fire. From this a fire shall go out upon the whole House of Israel.	¹וְאַתָּה בֶן־אָדָם קַח־לְךָ חֶרֶב חַדָּה תַּעַר הַגַּלָּבִים תִּקָּחֶנָּה לָּךְ וְהַעֲבַרְתָּ עַל־רֹאשְׁךָ וְעַל־זְקָנֶךָ וְלָקַחְתָּ לְךָ מֹאזְנֵי מִשְׁקָל וְחִלַּקְתָּם. ²שְׁלִשִׁית בָּאוּר תַּבְעִיר בְּתוֹךְ הָעִיר כִּמְלֹאת יְמֵי הַמָּצוֹר וְלָקַחְתָּ אֶת־הַשְּׁלִשִׁית תַּכֶּה בַחֶרֶב סְבִיבוֹתֶיהָ וְהַשְּׁלִשִׁית תִּזְרֶה לָרוּחַ וְחֶרֶב אָרִיק אַחֲרֵיהֶם. ³וְלָקַחְתָּ מִשָּׁם מְעַט בְּמִסְפָּר וְצַרְתָּ אוֹתָם בִּכְנָפֶיךָ. ⁴וּמֵהֶם עוֹד תִּקָּח וְהִשְׁלַכְתָּ אוֹתָם אֶל־תּוֹךְ הָאֵשׁ וְשָׂרַפְתָּ אֹתָם בָּאֵשׁ מִמֶּנּוּ תֵצֵא־אֵשׁ אֶל־כָּל־בֵּית יִשְׂרָאֵל.

10. The symbolic actions in Ezek 4 open with וְאַתָּה and an imperative verbal form (4:3, 4, 12). Ezek 5:1–4 continues the repeated structure and opens with the similar formula: וְאַתָּה בֶן־אָדָם קַח־לְךָ ("and you, O mortal, take," 5:1). I discuss these symbolic actions, including 5:1–4, in the broader context of Ezekiel's prophecies against Jerusalem in Rom-Shiloni, *Exclusive Inclusivity*, 173–78. Here I focus only on the portrayal of God as the sole enemy of Jerusalem.

The prophet is instructed to take a sharp knife to be used as a razor to cut his hair. Then, in a clearly schematic way, he is to divide the hair into three parts, each to be destroyed by a different means in a different place. One third is to be burnt by fire within the city; the next third is to be stricken by the sword in the area immediately around it; the last third is to be scattered to the wind (5:2, 12), and God's sword will pursue it (5:2). Hence, fire, sword, and dispersion to the wind are to be inflicted upon the entire population of Jerusalem, with no survivors. The meager remnant that the prophet bundles in his skirt is eventually itself to be thrown into the fire; this fire will engulf the entire house of Israel (5:4).[11]

The symbolic action is interpreted in the subsequent verses. Ezekiel 5:5–17 makes three statements of accusation (5:5–6, 7, 11a) that justify God's action in bringing this harsh judgment against his city. Each repeats the same key accusation—Jerusalem sins even more than the foreign peoples surrounding it, who are never even committed to God (5:6a, 7).

Following each accusation is a statement of judgment (5:8–9, 10, 11b–15).[12] These statements need particular attention, because they encapsulate Ezekiel's portrayal of God as the sole enemy of Jerusalem:

[8] Assuredly, thus said the Lord GOD: <u>I, in turn, am going to deal with you, and I will execute judgments in your midst</u> in the sight of the nations. [9] On account of all your abominations, <u>I will do among you what I have never done, and the like of which I will never do again.</u>	⁸לכן כה אמר אדני יהוה <u>הנני עליך גם־אני ועשיתי בתוכך משפטים לעיני הגוים.</u> ⁹<u>ועשיתי בך את אשר לא־עשיתי ואת אשר־לא־אעשה כמהו עוד</u> יען כל תועבותיך.

11. For this pessimistic perspective on Jerusalem's fate and its total destruction, see Rom-Shiloni, *Exclusive Inclusivity*, 176.

12. The general structure of Ezek 5 is therefore as follows: two statements of accusations (5:5–6, 7) precede two statements of judgment (5:8–9, 10; using the structure of כלל ופרט). These two sections are followed by 5:11–15, which first states another accusation and then explains in concrete meaning the symbolic act at the opening of the chapter (5:11–12), along with the consequences of this total annihilation (5:13–15). I take 5:16–17 to be a secondary elaboration. Compare Greenberg (*Ezekiel 1–20*, 119), who suggests that 5:11–17 consists of an interpretation of the symbolic act (5:11–12) along with three coda statements (5:13, 14–15, 16–17); and Zimmerli (*Ezekiel*, 1.154, 174–76), who understands both 5:11–13 and 5:16–17 as "a secondary interpolation of the text," thus leaving 5:14–15 (together with 5:4b–6, 8–9) to be part of "the original text" (154). Block (*Ezekiel 1–24*, 196) considers 5:5–17 to be "fragments or summaries of the oral explanations" of the different sign acts within Ezek 4–5.

¹⁰ Assuredly, parents shall eat their children in your midst, and children shall eat their parents. I will execute judgments against you, and I will scatter all your survivors in every direction. ¹¹ Assuredly, as I live—said the Lord GOD—because you defiled My Sanctuary with all your detestable things and all your abominations, I in turn will shear [you] away and show no pity. I in turn will show no compassion: ¹² One-third of you shall die of pestilence or perish in your midst by famine, one-third shall fall by the sword around you, and I will scatter one-third in every direction and I will unsheathe the sword after them. ¹³ I will vent all My anger and satisfy My fury upon them; and when I vent all My fury upon them,¹³ they shall know that I the Lord have spoken in My passion. ¹⁴ I will make you a ruin and a mockery among the nations round about you, in the sight of every passerby. ¹⁵ And when I execute judgment upon you in anger and rage and furious chastisement, you shall be a mockery and a derision, a warning and a horror, to the nations round about you: I the Lord have spoken.

¹⁰ לכן אבות יאכלו בנים
בתוכך ובנים יאכלו אבותם
ועשיתי בך שפטים וזריתי
את־כל־שאריתך לכל רוח.
¹¹ לכן חי־אני נאם אדני
יהוה אם־לא יען את־
מקדשי טמאת בכל־שקוציך
ובכל־תועבתיך וגם־אני
אגרע ולא־תחוס עיני וגם־אני
לא אחמול. ¹² שלשתיך
בדבר ימותו וברעב יכלו
בתוכך והשלשית בחרב
יפלו סביבותיך והשלישית
לכל־רוח אזרה וחרב אריק
אחריהם. ¹³ וכלה אפי
והנחתי חמתי בם והנחמתי
וידעו כי־אני יהוה דברתי
בקנאתי בכלותי חמתי בם.
¹⁴ ואתנך לחרבה ולחרפה
בגוים אשר סביבותיך לעיני
כל־עובר. ¹⁵ והיתה חרפה
וגדופה מוסר ומשמה
לגוים אשר סביבותיך
בעשותי בך שפטים באף
ובחמה ובתכחות חמה אני
יהוה דברתי.

---

13. והנחמתי suggests the *hitpael* of נחם, meaning "plot revenge" (Koehler, Baumgartner, and Stamm, *Hebrew and Aramaic Lexicon*, 689); see also Gen 27:42; Isa 1:24; 57:6. Compare Greenberg (*Ezekiel 1–20*, 115), who suggests that this phrase should be read as a question ("should I quiet myself in spite of these things?"); he adduces Ezek 16:42 as another example of a similar four-component string. Note, however, that 5:13 and 16:42 bear opposite meanings, a fact that may indeed support the suggestion to understand 5:13a as a rhetorical question. Ezek 5:13 introduces a long list of divine deeds following והנחמתי, whereas in 16:42 הניח חמה ב־ serves as a summary statement for the judgment upon Jerusalem detailed in the preceding verses (16:39–41) and speaks of the abatement of God's wrath (וסרה קנאתי ממך), followed by ושקטתי and ולא אכעס עוד). Compare Zimmerli (*Ezekiel*, 1.152), who prefers to explain this difficult verbal form with the semantic value of "comfort" as "a simple, erroneous scribal repetition of והנחותי."

The central feature of the (C') conception, the portrayal of God as the sole executor of the destruction, is highly accentuated in Ezek 5. Lexical, morphological, and syntactical features all contribute to this character-ization. Lexically, the verb עשה ("do, execute"), though not specific to the semantic field of war, is nevertheless one of the more commonly used verbs in both Ezekiel and Jeremiah for portraying God's role in the events. It attributes to God the defeat, the destruction, and the deportation—with no mention of any human enemy. In Ezekiel עשה occurs twenty-five times, either on its own, or in the phrases עשה שפטים/משפטים ב־ and עשה ב־ נקמות גדלות. Thematically, the phrase עשה שפטים ב־ is a reversal of God's paradigmatic salvific deed of the exodus tradition, thus the (C) conception of war, in which God inflicts the Egyptian gods, the enemies of his people (Exod 12:12; Num 33:4). Ezekiel transforms this phrase and conception to designate God's judgment over his own people, thus the (C') conception.[14] Morphologically and functionally, עשה appears mainly in the first-person in judgment prophecies against Israel, nine times in prophecies against the nations and three times in prophecies of consolation.[15] Ezekiel also juxta-poses the divine words of judgment with descriptions of their execution, to reinforce the notion that the destruction is the exact fulfillment of the di-vine word; note the recurring phrase דברתי ועשיתי (e.g., 17:24), especially in the most emphatic statement: "But whenever I the Lord speak what I speak [אדבר את אשר אדבר דבר], that word shall be fulfilled [ויעשה]

---

14. עשה שפטים in the meaning "execute judgment upon" occurs further in Ezek 5:10, 15; 11:9; 16:41 (carried out by humans); PAN Ezek 25:11; 28:22, 26; 30:14, 19; oth-erwise only in 2 Chr 24:24. עשה משפטים in this meaning occurs only in Ezek 5:8; see Greenberg, *Ezekiel 1–20*, 113; and Zimmerli, *Ezekiel*, 1.151.

15. In Ezekiel עשה with God as agent occurs in the first-person thirteen times in judgment prophecies against Israel (5:9 [3x]; 6:10; 14:23 [2x]; 16:59; 22:14 [2x]; plus four times in the phrase עשה שפטים/משפטים ב־—see previous note); once in the second-person (עשה כלה, 11:13); nine times within prophecies against the nations (e.g., עשה, 35:11, 14, 15, and עשה ב־ נקמות, 25:17); and three times in the first-person in prophecies of consolation to Israel (20:44; 36:27; 37:22). In Jeremiah עשה occurs four times in the first-person (7:14 [2x]; 19:12; 42:10); twice in consolation prophecies (29:32; 46:28); and twice in the third-person (21:2 [עשה נפלאות]; PAN Jer 51:12). It occurs in the second-person in a communal lament, thus in a context of protest (14:22), and in one quotation of passersby (22:8). The verb also occurs twice in Lamentations with God as agent: 1:12 (second-person) and 2:17 (third-person).

without any delay; in your days, O rebellious breed, I will fulfill every word I speak [אדבר דבר ועשיתיו]—declares the Lord GOD" (12:25).[16]

Ezekiel 5, then, is one of those passages in which the prophet repeats the verb עשה twice or even thrice in one verse to stress his point. A total of six occurrences of first-person עשה announce that God is to execute judgment against Jerusalem. The phrase ועשיתי בתוכך משפטים in 5:8 and the three repetitions of עשה in 5:9 frame God's actions as a *talio* in proportion to Jerusalem's sins as portrayed in 5:7 (ואת־משפטי לא עשיתם). The phrase עשה שפטים (משפטים) בך reappears in 5:10 and 5:15 to frame the explanation of the symbolic act given in 5:11–14.[17]

Both Ezek 5 and other (C') passages in Ezekiel and Jeremiah make use of a long list of other verbs more directly related to the semantic field of war to depict God's warlike actions against Israel and against the nations (in prophecies against the nations), as well as verbs that refer to deportation and exile.[18]

---

16. Note also the parallelism of זמם and עשה in PAN Jer 51:12 and Lam 2:17.

17. In other (C') passages in Ezekiel, those phrases with עשה serve as conclusions at the close of the prophecy; see 6:10; 14:23 (2x); PAN 25:17.

18. The relevant verbs and their occurrences within (C') passages:

- איבד in the first-person (Jer 15:7; PAN 12:17); even more common is האביד, Jer 1:10; 18:7; 31:28; PAN Ezek 25:7, 16.
- כילה in Jer 9:15; 14:12; PAN/consolation to Israel in 30:11; 46:28; Ezek 22:31; in the second-person in 11:13; in the third-person in Lam 2:22; and negated in consolation prophecies (or corrections) as לא עשה כלה in Jer 4:27; 5:18; 30:11; 46:28 (in the past in Ezek 20:17).
- הכרית in the infinitive, though as part of God's warlike actions in Jer 44:7, 8, 11; PAN 51:62; in the first-person (or infinitive) in Ezek 14:8, 13, 17, 19, 21; 21:8, 9; PAN 25:7, 13, 16; 29:8; 30:15; 35:7. This is one of the verbs that commonly portray God's war against the nations (e.g., Deut 12:29; Josh 23:4; and so in prophecy: PAN Amos 1:5, 8; Zech 9:6); it occurs otherwise against Israel only in Isa 9:13; Zeph 1:3, 4; and negated in Isa 48:9.
- השבית in Jer 7:34; 16:9; PAN 48:35; Ezek 34:10, 25.
- שיחת in Ezek 43:3 (and in a third-person protest in Lam 2:5, 6); more common is השחית in Jer 15:6; 13:9, 14 (in infinitive; note the reversal in comparison to Deut 10:10 or to the phrase of prayer in 9:25); PAN Jer 51:20; in the second-person (Ezek 9:8); this verb occurs also in (B') passages (e.g., PAN Jer 51:11, 20).
- שיכל in Jer 15:7 (and otherwise as a divine deed against his people only in Hos 9:12).
- השמיד in Ezek 14:9 and PAN 25:7 (and in the second-person in Lam 3:66); this use of השמיד in prophecies against the nations occurs also in Mic 5:13 and Hag 2:22.
- התם occurs in the first-person in Ezek 22:15 and oftentimes as impersonal

In terms of morphology, God's direct involvement as executor of the destruction is emphasized by the piling up of first-person verbal forms—God announces his own program of action. From Ezek 5:8 on, with its elaborate construction הנני עליך גם־אני ("I, in turn, am going to deal with you"), we find twenty-seven verbal forms in the first-person—five in 5:8–9, fifteen in 5:10–15, and seven more in 5:16–17. The same concentration of first-person forms can be seen in other passages of judgment against Israel that employ the (C′) conception, as well as in prophecies against the nations and in consolation prophecies.[19]

Finally, in terms of syntax, the explicit use of the first-person pronoun אני (and אנכי in Jeremiah), usually prior to the verb, adds a double emphasis to God's role as the lone actor. Constructions like הנה אני/

---

agent (e.g., Jer 14:15; 44:12, 27, although the implicit agent is clearly God; see the people's complaint in 44:18). This verb is also used in (B′) passages, as in Jer 27:8 (following Josh 8:24; 10:20).

· החרים once in judgment prophecy against Israel (Jer 25:9), otherwise used to describe God's actions only against the nations (PAN Jer 50:21, 26; 51:3) and in other instances in prophecy (Isa 11:15; 34:2; Mic 4:13; Zech 14:11).

· גלה in Jer 29:4, 7 and reversed in consolation in 29:14 (otherwise גלה with God as agent only in Amos 5:27 and 1 Chr 5:41).

· זרה in Jer 15:7 and in consolation prophecy in 31:10 and PAN 49:32, 36, where God is the one who scatters, yet within (B′) passages (Ezek 5:10, 12; 6:5, 8; 12:14, 15). The phrase הפיץ אותם בגוים וזרה אותם בארצות occurs in 12:15; 20:23; 22:15; PAN 29:12; but 30:23, 26—within a (B′) passage—and in one consolation prophecy in 36:19.

· הטיל occurs in Jeremiah and Ezekiel only as a verb of expulsion away from the land, with God as agent (Jer 16:13; 22:26, 28 [passive]; PAN Ezek 32:4).

· הדיח is typical of Jeremiah, where the action is almost always a divine deed (e.g., Jer 8:3 and 24:9; the only two exceptions are 23:2 and 50:17, where the agents are human). הדיח with אבד designates complete annihilation (Jer 27:10, 15); but in consolation prophecies this is reversed (16:15; 23:3, 8; 30:17; 32:37; 46:28).

· הפיץ occurs as a divine deed four times (of ten) in Jeremiah and nine times (of nineteen) in Ezekiel (all in the first-person): Jer 9:15; 13:24; and in one consolation prophecy (30:11); but also in a (B′) passage (18:17); Ezek 11:16 (with הרחיק); with זרה (see זרה above); in consolation prophecies with קיבץ (Ezek 20:41; 28:25; PAN Ezek 29:13).

· השליך in Jer 7:15 and in the passive in 22:28, but see 22:26 with God as agent of exile in a (B′) passage.

19. Clusters of first-person verbs are markers of this (C′) conception of war; see previous note and next note.

הנני אל/על and often הנני/הנה אני with a participle are very common in both Jeremiah and Ezekiel.[20] In Ezek 5:8 הנני עליך opens the proclamation of judgment, and in 5:15 the emphatic construction אני יהוה דברתי ("I the LORD have spoken," and again in the secondary 5:17) closes the unit.[21] It is remarkable that, as we see from the data presented here, similar linguistic techniques are used to depict God's actions across the three genres—judgment prophecies against Israel, prophecies against the nations, and consolation prophecies. All three invoke the same metaphor of God as warrior, expressed through shared linguistic formulas independent of the genre or the circumstances of the prophetic proclamation. Rather, there seems to have been a general conception, and conventional linguistic ways, to express the metaphor of God as warrior in his two roles, as savior in prophecies of consolation and as an enemy in prophecies of judgment to Israel and to the nations. It seems that, for both Jeremiah and Ezekiel, the conventions for expressing God's direct action *on behalf of* his people—the (C) conception of war—are eminently adaptable to expressing God's direct action *against* his people—the (C′) conception. The use of these linguistic conventions in the two prophetic books sharpens the portrayal of God as the sole destroyer of the city, the kingdom, and the people.

---

20. הנני על occurs in Ezek 5:8 and PAN 28:22; הנני אל occurs in 13:8, 20; 21:8; 34:10. For other phrases with the construction הנני + participle, see 16:37; 21:3; 22:19; 24:16, 21; as also in prophecies against the nations: 25:7 (with a verb in the perfect form); 29:8; and note הנני אני מביא עליכם חרב, 6:3. These constructions appear also in prophecies of consolation; e.g., הנני אליכם in 36:9 (also 36:6) and הנה אני + participle in 37:5, 12, 19, 21. The book of Jeremiah presents an even longer list of phrases with these constructions (more than twenty); as in Ezekiel, they occur in judgment prophecies against Israel; e.g., הנני אל (Jer 21:13) and other constructions, e.g., / הנני (הנה) אנכי / אני + participle (6:19; 9:14; 16:9; 21:4; 23:39; 39:16) in prophecies against the nations (e.g., 49:5, 35; 50:31), consolation prophecies (e.g., 29:11; 32:37, 42), and proclamation אני משיב, 28:3–4.

21. Use of the first-person pronoun אני is especially typical of Ezekiel. It appears 110 times in the book, 61 of them in the formula וידעתם(ו)/כי־אני יהוה/אדני יהוה (e.g., 6:7) and 45 times in a variety of syntactical constructions where the pronoun stands before or after verbs in the *qatal* form (5:13; 14:9), the *yiqtol* form (5:11 [2x]), the participle (20:12), or the infinitive (20:42, 44).

9.1.2. God as Warrior Uses Natural Forces (at Times Combined with Human Troops) in His War

Ezekiel 5:10–15 allows us to explore the second feature of the (C') conception in both Ezekiel and Jeremiah: the enlistment of diverse natural (and human) forces to afflict the people—affliction that illustrates the totality of the destruction.

Within the *inclusio* that repeats the basic threat—ועשיתי בך שפטים (5:10, 15)—the prophet mentions first the horrific situation of cannibalism during the siege. God is said to be the agent of the actions taken in the city and responsible for the expulsion of the survivors to the wind (5:10). In addition, following the schematic three-part division of the population by affliction and place established through the symbolic act (5:2), 5:12 gives specific and somewhat different names to those afflictions, which it presents according to the triad: דבר-רעב-חרב (pestilence, famine, sword). The first two are unleashed within the city; the sword is employed in its surroundings; and a fourth force, the wind, disperses the remainder, after which another sword is unsheathed against them (5:12b).

The triad חרב (ו)רעב ודבר and the pair רעב וחרב / חרב ורעב are among the expressions that join together natural and human forces as God's entire arsenal of forces in war, and these phrases are nearly unique to the books of Jeremiah and Ezekiel (with only a few occurrences in other Hebrew Bible compositions).[22] The triad חרב (ו)רעב ודבר occurs fifteen times in Jeremiah.[23] Ezekiel uses the formula five times, and in five other passages he elaborates it with a fourth component (or more). Table 9.1 shows that while Jeremiah maintains an orderly sword-famine-pestilence pattern in the use of these components (albeit with minor changes), Ezekiel makes much freer use of the pattern's components, which may change places rather freely, according to the rhetorical needs of the specific context.

---

22. חרב (ו)רעב ודבר is reflected in 2 Sam 24:13, pronounced explicitly in 1 Chr 21:12, and in a four-component string in 2 Chr 20:9. The pair otherwise occurs in inverted order in Lam 4:9; see Isa 51:19; Job 5:20.

23. Jeremiah also uses a four-component formula: מות חרב רעב ושבי (15:2; see 15:3). The pair חרב ורעב is exclusive to Jeremiah, where it occurs thirteen times, nine of them within the prophet's words (11:22; 14:15, 16, 18; 16:4; 18:21; 42:16; 44:12 [2x]; also 51:13, 27 LXX), three times in quotations (5:12; 14:13, 15), and once implicitly (42:14).

Table 9.1. The triad "sword, famine, and pestilence"

		Sword	Famine	Pestilence	Other
Jeremiah	14:12	1	2	3	
	21:7	2	3	1	
	21:9	1	2	3	
	24:10	1	2	3	
	27:8	1	2	3	
	27:13	1	2	3	
	29:17	1	2	3	
	29:18	1	2	3	
	32:24	1	2	3	
	32:36	1	2	3	
	34:17	1	3	2	
	38:2	1	2	3	
	42:17	1	2	3	
	42:22	1	2	3	
	44:13	1	2	3	
Ezekiel	5:12	3	2	1	4 winds
	5:17	4	1	3 + blood	2 wild beasts
	6:11	1	2	3	
	6:12	2	3	1	
	7:15a	1	3	2	
	7:15b	1	2	3	
	12:16	1	2	3	
	14:13–20	3	1	4	2 wild beasts
	14:21	1	2	4	3 wild beasts
	33:27	1		3	2 beasts

In the sequence of events in a human war, the initial step of laying siege to a city brings ecological ruin to the surrounding area and aggravates hunger within the besieged city, which in turn is followed by the rapid spread of disease. By contrast, Jeremiah and, even more starkly, Ezekiel portray these three disasters as afflicting the city and the land all at once; they have equal status as destructive agents, and thus they convey the sense that the totality of the catastrophe hit city, land, and people in one blow. This triad is clearly not used to represent a historical situation of gradual deterioration.[24] A look at the way these disasters are depicted confirms

24. Compare Eph'al, *City Besieged*, 57–64.

this claim: famine and pestilence may appear as a single catastrophe and may appear independently of the sword, that is, of the human involvement in war (Ezek 5:16; Jer 21:6); either famine (Ezek 5:12; 14:13) or pestilence, coming from afar (6:12), can lead off the sequence of afflictions; or the sequence may interchange chiastically for the case of style (6:11–12).[25] Jeremiah 21:6 mentions pestilence as the single infliction God will bring, to annihilate both humans and beasts in Jerusalem; and then 21:7 lists the triad (pestilence, sword, famine) as afflictions that will already have decimated Jerusalem's inhabitants, before God himself gives them into the hands of their human enemies.

Therefore, the sword-famine-pestilence triad (with its elaborations and permutations) has theological, rather than historical, significance—it symbolizes the divine war that God is waging against the city (and/or the people), using the various forces at his disposal: "sword" is a metonym for war and stands for divine activation of human enemies; "famine" is the immediate result of the ecological transformation God causes to the land during the war; and "pestilence" represents the natural forces God brings from outside to strike in and around the city and land.

The equalization of natural and human forces through this rhetorical triad allows Jeremiah and Ezekiel to ascribe the destruction directly to God, not merely in the fashion of a ruler over human armies, as in (B′) conception of war. God's active role in the war is conveyed through the triad of the three afflictions (and their expansions), along with the more general phraseology of disaster. He activates against his people both human armies and the natural forces at his disposal. The (C′) conception brings to prominence God's own warlike deeds, so that the human enemy either completely disappears from the literary description of war or appears in a dramatically diminished role, under the anonymous rubric of "sword." Thus, the human enemy becomes simply one of the weapons used by God, the ultimate warrior.

Returning to Ezek 5:12, then, the order of these three components in this context is determined by the spatial distinction of these three afflictions within the symbolic action of 5:2: in the midst of the city, in its closer

---

25. Interestingly, Ezek 6:12 coordinates the affliction with its victims in terms of distance: those far away from the city will die through pestilence, those nearby by the sword, those remaining besieged in the city through famine. This, however, differs from 7:15, which takes pestilence and hunger to be within the city and sword on the outside. Compare Zimmerli (*Ezekiel*, 1.191), who finds Ezekiel's triad here to be "not particularly skillful." I prefer Block's apt reading of this trio (*Ezekiel 1–24*, 235–36).

surroundings, and farther away.[26] Accordingly, in 5:12, Ezekiel freely combines and rearranges: pestilence and famine strike as the initial force in the middle of the city (representing the "fire" of 5:2); the sword takes care of those who escape to the immediate surroundings; and any remnant is dispersed to the winds but even so, pursued by the sword. It is clear throughout, that God is the agent of destruction.

Ezekiel 5:16–17 closes this chapter with yet another pledge of disasters to come, a secondary expansion of the core prophecy:[27]

[16] When I loose the deadly arrows of famine against those doomed to destruction, when I loose them against you to destroy you, I will heap more famine upon you and break your staff of bread. [17] I will let loose against you famine and wild beasts and they shall bereave you; pestilence and bloodshed shall sweep through you, and I will bring the sword upon you. I the LORD have spoken.	<div dir="rtl">16 בְּשַׁלְּחִי אֶת־חִצֵּי הָרָעָב הָרָעִים בָּהֶם אֲשֶׁר הָיוּ לְמַשְׁחִית אֲשֶׁר־אֲשַׁלַּח אוֹתָם לְשַׁחֶתְכֶם וְרָעָב אֹסֵף עֲלֵיכֶם וְשָׁבַרְתִּי לָכֶם מַטֵּה־לָחֶם. 17 וְשִׁלַּחְתִּי עֲלֵיכֶם רָעָב וְחַיָּה רָעָה וְשִׁכְּלֻךְ וְדֶבֶר וָדָם יַעֲבָר־ בָּךְ וְחֶרֶב אָבִיא עָלַיִךְ אֲנִי יְהוָה דִּבַּרְתִּי.</div>

The secondary nature of this passage has long been recognized by scholars, due to (1) the *inclusio* pattern that nicely rounds out the previous prophetic passage (וְעָשִׂיתִי בָךְ שְׁפָטִים, 5:8, and בְּעָשׂוֹתִי בָךְ שְׁפָטִים, 5:15); (2) the concluding formula אֲנִי יְהוָה דִּבַּרְתִּי, which is used in 5:15 (and as a penultimate assertion in 5:13) and then repeated in 5:17; and (3) these verses opening with the infinitive construct, which introduces two additional lists of afflictions, including disasters that are not found in either 5:2 or 5:12. Ezekiel 5:16–17, then, seems to have been adjoined rather abruptly to a closed literary unit.[28] The accumulation of additional judgments beyond those already mentioned in 5:2 and 5:12 is the most substantial argument for these verses' secondary nature. More specifically, 5:16–17 emphasizes famine—it is the only disaster named in 5:16 and leads off a longer list in 5:17 (wild beasts, pestilence, blood, sword). Famine does not appear in the symbolic action (5:2), but is part of the explanatory

26. On the correspondences between 5:2 and 5:12, see Block, *Ezekiel 1–24*, 210.

27. Greenberg (*Ezekiel 1–20*, 119, 127–28) designates 5:16–17 as "coda 3" for this passage, recognizing the repetitive and elaborative nature of this prophecy, which he explains as "calamities and expressions of wrath come in heaps" (127).

28. For different presentations of the literary structure and history of Ezek 5 and the categorization of 5:16–17 as secondary within this passage, see note 12, above.

prophecy (5:12). Ezekiel 5:16–17 seems to fill out the description of this component, bringing no less than three phrases that contain רעב (famine): twice שילח רעב ב־ and הוסיף רעב על and even a fourth reference using the phrase שבר מטה־לחם ("break your staff of bread," Lev 26:26; Ezek 4:16; 14:13; otherwise only Ps 105:16).[29]

In contexts other than Ezek 5, the (C') conception may also be marked by another formulaic phrase that describes God's war as a simultaneous combination of human and natural forces: יהוה הביא/דבר רעה אל/על. This phrase is typically Jeremian, occurring seventeen times in that book, but only once in Ezekiel (14:22).[30] This nonspecific "evil," or better "distress," may target either a particular group among the people (Jer 11:23) or the people of Judah in general (6:19); it may be brought against "this place" (19:3) or against the nations (PAN Jer 49:37; 51:64). Twelve of the occurrences of this construction do not mention the nature of the disaster, and the abstract term רעה serves as a general indicator. All of these occurrences fall within passages that describe God as sole warrior, with no mention of active human enemies, thus the (C') conception.[31] In two of these passages, רעה is accompanied by either the pair חרב ורעב (11:22–23) or the triad חרב רעב ודבר (42:17); in others, as a consequence of this disaster, the land is left desolated and empty of man and beast (19:3, 6–9; 44:21–23). רעה, the disaster, is the means by which God executes his plan: חשב לעשת רעה (36:3), יצר רעה וחשב מחשבה (18:11), דבר רעה (11:17),[32] עשה רעה (42:10), החל להרע (25:29), שם פניו ב־/לרעה (21:10; 44:11), and שפך על רעה (14:16). This general use of רעה to articulate the (C') conception may be set against the four passages in Jeremiah in which disaster (הרעה) is elaborated only as the bringing of human enemies against the

---

29. Greenberg (*Ezekiel 1–20*, 116) suggests that 5:16–17 is a "variation on classical threats of doom in Deuteronomy and Leviticus." He specifically notes that the markers אספה עלימו and חצי הרעב הרעים ורעה אסף עליכם in these verses echo the phrasing ויספתי עליכם and חצי אכלה־בם רעות as well as מזי רעב in Deut 32:23–25, along with מכה in Lev 26:21. Block (*Ezekiel 1–24*, 213, no. 89) demonstrates additional intertextual connections between Ezek 5 and Deut 32.

30. Jer 4:6; 6:19; 11:11, 17, 23; 16:10; 19:3, 15; 23:12; 32:42; 35:17; 36:31; 42:17; 44:2; 45:5; PAN 49:37; 51:64. Note also the similar phrases: הביא עליהם יום רעה (17:18) and הנני מביא את־דברי אל־העיר הזאת לרעה (39:16).

31. The twelve units that display conception (C') are Jer 6:16–21; 11:9–13; 16:10–13; 19:14–15; 23:9–12; 32:42–45; 35:1–19; 36:1–32; 42:7–17; 44:2–6, 20–23; 45:1–5.

32. דבר רעה also occurs in Jer 11:17; 16:10; 19:15; 35:17; 36:31; but only three times in (B') passages: 26:13, 19; 40:2. Ezek 6:10 uses דבר לעשות להם רעה.

city—conception (B'): 4:5–8; 19:1–13; 21:8–10; PAN Jer 49:37–39 (note also הקרא את הרעה אל, 32:23–24).

In justifying God's actions, Ezek 5 focuses on Jerusalem and her sins, which brought upon her the well-deserved punishments that she is now to suffer (5:5–6, 7, 11a). But the point of this passage is not only to justify God's actions from the perspective of divine justice (see §10.1 and §11.2), but also to emphasize God's sole involvement in executing this justified judgment upon the city.

Ezekiel 5 also illustrates the third feature of (C') conception: *the consequences of the divine war in total destruction* of the people, the city, and the land itself. This prophecy of Ezekiel presents Jerusalem's judgment as complete—it includes the entire population, divided into three schematic parts, and punished in three different spatial arenas: in the city, in its agriculture surroundings, and farther away from it. The punishment is also holistic in terms of the scope of the destruction caused by the triad of natural and human forces that God calls into service; and the final two weapons—wind and sword—ensure that not even a remnant will survive.

9.1.3. The Consequences of God's War: Total Destruction and an Empty Land (Ezekiel 25:3; Jeremiah 9:9–10)

Ezekiel and Jeremiah refer to the destruction of Jerusalem and Judah in order to underscore the fate of the people, both the inhabitants of Jerusalem and the exiles deported to Babylon; but in addition, the two prophetic books refer to the fates of the city and the land in their own right.

In prophecies against the nations, Ezek 25:3 quotes the mocking words of the Ammonites:

[3] Say to the Ammonites: Hear the word of the Lord GOD! Thus says the Lord GOD: Because you cried "Aha!" over My Sanctuary when it was desecrated, and over the land of Israel when it was laid waste, and over the House of Judah when it went into exile.	³ואמרת לבני עמון שמעו דבר־אדני יהוה כה־אמר אדני יהוה יען אמרך האח אל־ מקדשי כי־נחל ואל־אדמת ישראל כי נשמה ואל־בית יהודה כי הלכו בגולה.

The end of the religious-political existence of Judah is marked, even in the eyes of the surrounding nations, not only by the destruction of the temple and the deportation of the people, but also by the devastation of the land. חרבה ("ruin") is the general term used to describe the destruction of the temple (Jer 22:5; Isa 64:10), the city (Jer 27:17; Ezek 5:14), Jerusalem and the cities of Judah (Jer 25:18; 44:2, 6), and the entire land (7:34; 25:11; mountains of Israel in Ezek 38:8).[33]

The (C') passages that describe the destruction of city and land use four elements to characterize the disaster, all of which are found in Jer 9:9–10. These two verses lament the destruction of both rural and urban areas of Judah; they move from east to west, from the rural areas in the Judean Desert (which Jeremiah intimately knew) to Jerusalem and then westward to the cities of Judah.[34] The prophet portrays the profound ecological disaster each area suffers:[35]

[9] For the mountains I take up weeping and wailing,	⁹עַל־הֶהָרִים אֶשָּׂא בְכִי וָנֶהִי
for the pastures in the wilderness, a dirge.	וְעַל־נְאוֹת מִדְבָּר קִינָה
They are laid waste; no man passes through,	כִּי נִצְּתוּ מִבְּלִי־אִישׁ עֹבֵר
and no sound of cattle is heard.	וְלֹא שָׁמְעוּ קוֹל מִקְנֶה
Birds of the sky and beasts as well have fled	מֵעוֹף הַשָּׁמַיִם וְעַד־בְּהֵמָה
and are gone.	נָדְדוּ הָלָכוּ.
[10] I will turn Jerusalem into rubble,	¹⁰וְנָתַתִּי אֶת־יְרוּשָׁלִַם לְגַלִּים
into dens for jackals;	מְעוֹן תַּנִּים
and I will make the towns of Judah	וְאֶת־עָרֵי יְהוּדָה אֶתֵּן
a desolation without inhabitants.	שְׁמָמָה מִבְּלִי יוֹשֵׁב.

33. חָרְבָּה ("ruin") is similarly used in the prophecies against the nations to designate the fate of the cities and lands of the nations (PAN Ezek 25:13; 29:9; 35:4). The pair חָרְבָּה and שְׁמָמָה ("ruin" and "desolation," as in Jer 44:6; PAN Ezek 29:9) is also used differentially to distinguish the fate of the city ("ruin") from that of the rural areas ("desolation") (PAN Ezek 35:4).

34. See Holladay (*Jeremiah*, 1.303–5) on the form of this short unit, which he considers to be "a passage where divine pathos and judgment are blended" (304). The identity of the speaker (is God or the prophet represented by the first-person verbs of 9:9 and 9:10?) is a problem for the early versions and is subsequently addressed by scholars. See McKane (*Jeremiah 1–25*, 203–4), who describes the Septuagint's plural λάβετε (9:9) as "an attractive solution" and thus a theological emendation, which he assumes is then adopted by the Peshitta.

35. Compare this aspect to the description of the fate of Jerusalem in (B') prophecies, in which God summons the Babylonian king against Jerusalem—following the city's capture, the Babylonian king destroys it by fire (Jer 21:10; 34:2, 22; 37:8; 38:3, 17, 23; Ps 74:7; Lam 4:11). Destruction by fire is also forecast for Babylon (PAN Jer 50:32). Fire in Jerusalem is recorded in 2 Kgs 25:8–9 and in the parallel accounts in Jer 52:13 and 2 Chr 36:19.

(a) The destruction of the houses in the city turns the city into גלים ("rubble," Jer 9:10), עיים ("heaps of ruins," Jer 26:18), or ישבי חרבות החרבות, Ezek 33:24 and 35:4).[36]

(b) The profound transformation of the ecology of both the land and the city turns each of them into a desolate place. Jeremiah 9:9 focuses first on the desert areas east of Jerusalem, the mountains that are regularly home to herds, shepherds, and wild beasts and birds. The destruction is portrayed as a profound ecological disaster that affects those mountains and "the pastures in the wilderness." The phrase נדדו הלכו (NJPS: "have fled and are gone") pictures the sudden and complete disappearance of living creatures due to the divine act of destruction. The imagery is that of migrating birds, which spread their wings and fly away in a very short time.[37] I thus translate נדדו הלכו as "they have migrated and gone."

Jeremiah 9:9–10, like other (C′) prophecies, proclaims that God is the sole agent of this disastrous ecological transformation, which affects not only the city and its houses, but the rural areas surrounding the city as well.[38] The first-person verbal form designates God himself as the agent who makes Judah desolate: "And I will make [אתן] the towns of Judah a desolation without inhabitants [שממה מבלי יושב]" (9:10b). Note the similar constructions: פן־אשימך שממה ארץ לוא נושבה ("lest I make you a desolation, an uninhabited land") in 6:8 and והשמתי את־פתרוס ("I will lay Pathros waste") in PAN Ezek 30:14. God is the initiator of this dramatic

---

36. גלים occurs only three times in the Hebrew Bible, two of them in Jeremiah (9:10; PAN 51:37, concerning Babylon) and once in Job 15:28. The singular (גל) in Isa 25:2 and the plural in Hos 12:12 refer to destroyed sanctuaries. עיים designate ruins of a city (Mic 3:12; Ps 79:1); it is used in the singular עי השדה (Mic 1:6). The destruction of houses, fortresses, and walls is mentioned in Lam 2:2; prophecies of the reconstruction of those ruins are found in Ezek 36:10, 33; Mal 1:4; and Second Isa 49:19; 52:9; 58:12; 61:4.

37. Compare Skinner, *Prophecy and Religion*, 50, who argues that Jeremiah chooses this imagery because of his fondness for birds; and so Holladay, *Jeremiah*, 1.166. While this possibility cannot be denied, of course, I prefer to explain this apt choice as rooted in the ecological phenomenon of bird migration, which Jeremiah presumably knows from observation. Jeremiah in his place in Anathoth is at a middle point between the two major routes of bird migration that were, as they still are, the paths for millions of birds flying over the Shefelah on the west or the Judean Desert and the Jordan Valley on the east. For bird migration routes, see Leshem and Yom-Tov, "Routes of Migrating Soaring Birds."

38. For God as the agent of the ecological transformation, see Jer 6:8; 7:34; 9:9, 11; 12:4, 10–11; 18:16; 25:11; 32:43; 45:4.

change, through which agricultural areas become a desert (also Jer 12:10), and the desert becomes a total vacuum (9:9).[39] The passage employs an anthropocentric, or rather ethnocentric, approach, which depicts God as destroying the fauna and flora of Judah as a consequence of the affliction of people (compare Jer 7:20; 21:6; 36:29).[40]

(c) The desolation in Jerusalem results when it is emptied of humans and animals. Again, Jer 9:10 is one example of the emphasis that this change will result from a divine deed, thus proclaimed in the first-person: "I will turn [ונתתי] Jerusalem into rubble.... And I will make [אתן] the towns of Judah a desolation without inhabitants." To make this description even more vivid, the city is pictured as a "den of jackals" (מעון תנים; also 10:22)—predators that enter human residential areas only if they are completely deserted.[41] Thus, their presence in the ruined city is the best sign of the profound change that is to take place in the aftermath of the destruction (see Ezek 13:4). Along with these dramatic changes we also see the transformation of the urban area into a rural field (Jer 26:18; Mic 3:12) and even to an uncultivated field that thus can grow only thorns (Isa 34:13).

(d) Finally, the complete destruction of Jerusalem and Judah causes either God or the prophet in Jer 9:9–10 to lament at the sight of the desolation.[42] In other passages, anonymous passersby, foreigners, even nations react to and reflect on this catastrophe. Cries of astonishment, of lament, of surprise, even of mockery are expressed by diverse spectators, from among the people or from the outside, who cannot fathom the fate of Jerusalem,

---

39. See McKane, *Jeremiah 1–25*, 204. For (C') descriptions of the land as desolate, see Jer 4:23–28; 7:30–34; 9:9–10, 11–15; 12:4; 32:42–45; 45:1–5; Ezek 12:19–20; 15:8; 33:27–29. This description occurs also in (B') passages (Jer 6:6–8; 12:10–11; 18:13–17; 25:8–14); the element of ecological transformation is also apparent in Ezek 7:1–9. Other terms of desolation include חרב (as in the quotation in Jer 33:10), שממה (10:22; 34:22), or שמה ("a desolation," 19:8); Jerusalem and the cities of Judah are נשמות (33:10).

40. This general affliction of humans and animals in the course of destroying Judah for its sins stands in diametric opposition to the promises of Gen 8:21–22 and 9:8–17. But this feature is indeed characteristic of judgment prophecies in general and is not a sign of the lateness of the Genesis stories in comparison to the prophetic literature; see Gertz, "Noah und die Propheten." See §9.1.4.

41. מעון תנים designates in Jeremiah also the destruction of Hazor (PAN Jer 49:33) and of Babylon (PAN Jer 51:37). See מקום תנים in Ps 44:20, which may thus allude to Jerusalem as well.

42. Jer 9:9 LXX omits נהי. Holladay (*Jeremiah*, 1.304) offers an interesting note on the redactions of this broader unit in the Masoretic Text—with ונהי בכי (9:9) at the middle, after the prophet's/God's "weeping" in 8:23 (בכה) and before the general "wailing" in 9:17–19 (נהי).

who cannot comprehend the deeds of God in her midst.[43] These expressions further accent the scope of the disaster: "And I will make this city an object of horror and hissing; everyone who passes by it will be appalled and will hiss over all its wounds" (Jer 19:8).

These four elements demonstrate in a clear way that God is the sole actor in the destruction of Jerusalem and the land of Judah. Human enemies are completely absent, and the scope of the affliction is much beyond that of human war. From the theological point of view, these descriptions establish God's absolute power over events of war. God's destructive actions are illustrations of his control over his world—the natural resources of the earth, waters and winds of the heavens. As the one who determines the agricultural fertility of the land, God alone may engineer its desolation, may empty it of flora, fauna, and human life.

The description of war initiated by the national God/god, which leaves in its wake total destruction and an empty and desolate land, is part of a literary tradition shared by Hebrew Bible authors and ancient Near Eastern scribes from other cultures. The evidence for such literary conventions is abundant on both the phraseological and thematic levels. Innerbiblical parallels consist of phrasing shared by judgment prophecies against Israel, judgment prophecies against the nations, and the communal laments in Psalms and Lamentations, which describe the destruction of the city, the people, and the land. Extrabiblical parallels show clear thematic connections between those Hebrew Bible sources and other literature of the ancient Near East, primarily Sumerian city laments. These thematic connections (which appear in widely different times and cultures) illustrate the common theological challenge faced in these very different cultural settings: the need to find theological explanations for inexplicable political defeats and their aftermath, to understand the role of God/the gods in the calamity.

Several types of shared terminology and phrasing may be recognized within our target biblical corpora:

a. The description of the sword sent to annihilate Judah, ‫ושלחתי אח־‬ ‫ריהם את־החרב עד כלותי אותם‬ ("and I will dispatch the sword after them until I have consumed them," Jer 9:15), is repeated word for word in a prophecy against Elam (PAN Jer 49:37).

43. Other cries of surprise are seen in Lam 2:13–16; 4:12; as also Jer 22:8–9; see Deut 29:23; 1 Kgs 9:8–9.

b. The total annihilation brought upon the people is described in meris-
    matic expressions (Jer 16:6; Lam 2:10–11).

c. The phrase /שמם/שת/שם/) נתן יהוה (ארצם) כל הארץ (היתה/שת/שם/)
    לשמה appears three times concerning Jerusalem and the cities of
    Judah: שם את העיר שממה/לשמה ("that the towns of Judah may be
    made a desolation," Jer 10:22; 19:8; 34:22). It occurs fifteen times in
    other biblical passages, also in reference to a land, Judah or another
    ("so their land will become a desolation," e.g., Jer 18:16; PAN Jer
    49:13; Ezek 12:20; 33:28–29; PAN Ezek 32:15).

d. Jeremiah 18:16 says that the land of Israel will be שרוקת עולם
    (ק: שריקת) ("an object of hissing for all time," 19:8). Elsewhere, Bab-
    ylon is said to have become שממות עולם ("a desolation for all time,"
    PAN Jer 51:26, 62); this same phrase is used by Ezekiel in reference to
    Mount Seir (PAN Ezek 35:9).

e. Several expressions that describe the absence of human beings or
    animals from Jerusalem and Judah are also used of other lands: מאין
    אדם ומאין יושב ומאין בהמה refers to desolate Jerusalem ("without
    any person, without any inhabitant, without any animal," Jer 33:10,
    12; also מאין אדם ובהמה, 32:43) and Babylon (PAN Jer 50:3); מאין
    יושב by itself describes desolated Noph in Egypt (PAN Jer 46:19);
    מבלי־איש עבר designates the emptiness of Judah ("no one passes
    through," 9:9, 11) and also the fate of cities in Babylon (היו עריה
    לשמה ארץ ציה וערבה ארץ לא־ישב בהן כל־איש ולא־יעבר בהן בן־
    אדם ["her towns are a desolation, a land of desert and steppe, a land
    no man lives in and no human passes through"], PAN Jer 51:43; also
    2:6).

f. It is said that Jerusalem will become "a den of jackals" (Jer 9:10;
    10:22); the same is said of Hazor and Babylon (PAN Jer 49:33; 51:37).
    Lamentations 5:18 agonizes that Mount Zion became a place where
    foxes prowl.

Extrabiblical parallels are found primarily in five laments over the destruction of the cities of Sumer, their inhabitants, and their land, from the
close of the third millennium.[44] Four general categories provide thematic

44. The laments are for Ur (Kramer, *Lamentation over the Destruction of Ur*; Samet,
Lamentation over the Destruction of Ur), Sumer and Ur (Michalowski, *Destruction of
Sumer and Ur*), Nippur (Tinney, *Nippur Lament*), Eridu (Green, "Eridu Lament";
Peled, "New Manuscript of the Lament for Eridu"), plus the *Curse of Agade* (Cooper,
Curse of Agade). Hymnology and laments over destroyed temples are collected in Co-

parallels between these laments and Hebrew Bible materials, in the books of Jeremiah and Ezekiel as well as Psalms and Lamentations:[45]

a. Destruction of the cities—the cities are described as turned into rubble; emptied of their residents, they become dens for a variety of wild animals (snakes, jackals, foxes, dogs) or places of refuge for rebels.[46] The *Curse of Agade*, for instance, closes by saying that the city is totally empty, with no inhabitants, because there is no longer any place for them to reside.[47]

b. Annihilation of the cities' inhabitants—the laments portray death on a vast scale within those cities. The *Ur Lament* expresses the scope of the deaths in merismatic pairs (mother and father, woman and child, sister and brother, woman and toddler); the corpses of the dead fill the streets, and blood floods the ditches.[48] In the *Lament over Sumer and Ur*, death is all-encompassing and does not distinguish righteous from wicked.[49] Furthermore, death is caused by sword and famine— by sword outside the city and by famine within[50]—and there is a complementary parallel between those slain by the sword and those sick with famine.[51] The magnitude of the disaster is so great because Enlil

---

hen's *Sumerian Hymnology* and *Canonical Lamentations*, vol. 1. In addition to these sources, descriptions of destruction may be found in the curses that close political treaties; see Hillers, *Treaty Curses*, 43–79; Weinfeld, *Deuteronomy and the Deuteronomic School*, 109–16; and Dobbs-Allsopp, *Weep, O Daughter of Zion*, 66–72.

45. The relationships between the city lament and Hebrew Bible literature, and particularly Lamentations, are thoroughly discussed in the commentaries of Hillers and Dobbs-Allsopp; in addition, see Gwaltney, "Biblical Book of Lamentations"; and Samet, "Sumerian City Laments." For parallels to prophetic literature, see Dobbs-Allsopp, *Weep, O Daughter of Zion*, 1–96, 157–63.

46. See Kramer, *Lamentation over the Destruction of Ur*, line 422; Michalowski, *Destruction of Sumer and Ur*, lines 143–46, 222, 346–49; Cooper, *Curse of Agade*, lines 257, 259; Green, "Eridu Lament," *kirugu* 1, lines 18–27; and Tinney, *Nippur Lament*, lines 12, 102.

47. Cooper, *Curse of Agade*, lines 279–80. The aspect of total annihilation is mentioned as of line 225; see also Tinney, *Nippur Lament*, lines 12, 32–33.

48. Samet, *Lamentation over the Destruction of Ur*, lines 400–403, 213–18, 219–36.

49. Michalowski, *Destruction of Sumer and Ur*, lines 110–11; compare Ezek 21:8. The *Curse of Agade* addresses also the demolition of the social orders (Cooper, *Curse of Agade*, lines 190–95).

50. Michalowski, *Destruction of Sumer and Ur*, lines 399–401; see Jer 14:17–18; Ezek 5:2, 12; Lam 1:20.

51. Michalowski, *Destruction of Sumer and Ur*, line 389; see Jer 14:18; Lam 4:9.

summons a multidirectional attack by human enemies.[52] Finally, the city laments repeatedly mourn the terrible silence of destruction—the cessation of worship, the transformation of the joyful sounds of the liturgy into the wailing sounds of lament.[53]

c. Destruction of outlying agricultural areas—the *Ur Lament* broadens the description of the destruction from the city to its fields, orchards, and plain, to "possessions" that include its flocks, precious metals, and gem stones.[54] The consequence of the destruction in the *Lament over Sumer and Ur* is elaborately presented as a complete end to the daily routine in all respects, with the destruction of water resources, fields, orchards, and domestic animals.[55] Within this portrayal, affliction in the ecological sphere is mentioned, expressed in terms of the cessation of agricultural growth and its products—wheat does not grow, fruits do not ripen, and there is no beer, wine, or honey. Water canals are empty, there is no ship movement, and roads on the sides of the river are no longer traversable.[56]

d. Involvement of god/the gods in the destruction—in all of the city laments it is Enlil, the storm god, who is responsible for the destruction. The *Lament over Eridu* opens with "the storm/sandstorm" and then reveals Enlil as the agent behind it (*kirugu* 1, line 26); in the *Ur Lament*, Anu, god of the heavens, joins Enlil. The *Curse of Agade* states that the vast destruction is the result of an attack against the Ekur, Enlil's temple (lines 225–26); the attack causes the storm, as also eight other gods curse Uruk and the land of Agade (lines 210, 222).[57] The destruction is made possible by the gods' abandonment of their temples and cities; this abandonment is at times explained explicitly as a consequence of divine anger.[58]

---

52. Michalowski, *Destruction of Sumer and Ur*, lines 251–61.

53. Michalowski, *Destruction of Sumer and Ur*, lines 314–16; Tinney, *Nippur Lament*, lines 14, 38–41, 54–56, 77 (and compare descriptions of restoration in lines 193–95); see Lam 2:6; and compare Ps 74:4–9, where the destruction is done by human enemies.

54. Samet, *Lamentation over the Destruction of Ur*, lines 271–81.

55. Michalowski, *Destruction of Sumer and Ur*, lines 126–32.

56. Michalowski, *Destruction of Sumer and Ur*, lines 309–13, 322–28; such a vast calamity characterizes also the closing curses in Cooper, *Curse of Agade*, lines 225–80.

57. Green, "Eridu Lament," lines 5–10; and Cooper, *Curse of Agade*; note the curses of the gods in lines 227–80.

58. Tinney, *Nippur Lament*, lines 79–81; for abandonment conceived as punishment, see line 196. In the lament over Eridu, Mullil and Gashananna are said to have destroyed Sumer and the city of Uruk respectively. The repeated line *zag h[e'-b]i-in-*

The role of the human armies in the destruction in relation to the role of the god(s) differs from one lament to the other. In the *Ur Lament*, for instance, the destructive actions of the human enemies, the Sutu and the Elamites, are mentioned in only one line (244) of the 436 lines of this lament; throughout, the role of Enlil in the destruction is emphasized far beyond, and in total detachment from, the actual human war. Likewise, in the *Lament over Nippur*, the human enemies are referred to in three lines (129, 157, 263) of 323. In the *Lament over Eridu*, the Subrians and the Elamites are mentioned once (*kirugu* 4, line 10). In contrast, in the *Lament over Sumer and Ur*, Enlil is said to summon the enemies from the four corners of the world (lines 254–65); the human enemies enter the temples and defile them.[59] Finally, in the *Curse of Agade*, Enlil summons the Gutium to destroy the city and the land, and they are responsible for the disaster (lines 152–72), although the annihilation is caused by the divine curses (lines 225–80).

All these innerbiblical and extrabiblical materials suggest that the theme of the empty land originates as a component in the theological portrayal of total destruction inflicted upon a city, its inhabitants, and its surroundings, when God (or the gods) acts as warrior(s) against his (or their) people. Descriptions of the land empty of humans and animals, desolate and uncultivated, serve as an integral part of the portrayal of God's/the gods' exclusive role in profoundly transforming the natural character and the agricultural characteristics of the land—a transformation that human armies could not have caused.[60] These descriptions evolve from (or reflect) the theological conception of the omnipotence adduced to the destroying god (whether YHWH or Enlil or another), and they are part of the conceptions of God's/ the god(s)' absolute power over his (their) creatures, from humans to animals, to the earth itself.[61]

---

tag šu li-bi'-in-dag ("he(/she) destroyed it (but) he(/she) did not abandon it"; Green, "Eridu Lament," *kirugu* 6, lines 7', 24') is of great interest.

59. Michalowski, *Destruction of Sumer and Ur*, lines 197–98; compare Pss 74:4–8; 79:1.

60. A transformation of the opposite sort is highlighted and elaborated on in the *Lament over Nippur*, in the account of the gods' restoration of the land under the reign of Ishme-Dagan. See Tinney, *Nippur Lament*, *kirugu* 7; note, in particular, the references to the city and the temple (lines 190–206, 299–304), to the city's inhabitants (lines 207–10), and to the coming of the "good day" for Sumer and Akkad and for the wider surroundings (lines 247–61).

61. Theological/religious conceptions are addressed by Sumeriologists; see Samet,

9.1.4. *The Ethnocentric Conception of the Land in (C') Judgment Prophecies (Jeremiah 4:23–28)*

Widespread ecological disaster is an important component of the destruction wrought by God in passages that cast God as the sole enemy, in conception (C'); thus, such destruction plays a major role in judgment prophecies against Israel (and to a lesser extent also in prophecies against the nations). Jeremiah 4:23–28 illustrates one theological context for the development of the idea of ecological destruction as an element of punishment of Judah:

[23] I look at the earth,	ראיתי את־הארץ [23]
it is unformed and void;	והנה־תהו ובהו
at the skies,	ואל־השמים
and their light is gone.	ואין אורם.
[24] I look at the mountains,	ראיתי ההרים [24]
they are quaking;	והנה רעשים
and all the hills are rocking.	וכל־הגבעות התקלקלו.
[25] I look: no man is left,	ראיתי והנה אין האדם [25]
and all the birds of the sky have fled.	וכל־עוף השמים נדדו.
[26] I look: the farm land is desert,	ראיתי והנה הכרמל המדבר [26]
and all its towns are in ruin—	וכל־עריו נתצו
because of YHWH,	מפני יהוה
because of His blazing anger.	מפני חרון אפו.
[27] (For thus said the Lord:	כי־כה אמר יהוה [27]
The whole land shall be desolate,	שממה תהיה כל־הארץ
but I will not make an end of it.)	וכלה לא אעשה.
[28] For this the earth mourns,	על־זאת תאבל הארץ [28]
and skies are dark above—	וקדרו השמים ממעל
because I have spoken, I have planned,	על כי־דברתי זמתי
and I will not relent or turn back from it.	ולא נחמתי ולא־אשוב ממנה.

This prophecy is unique in the book of Jeremiah in its presentation of the destruction as a retreat to a precreation cosmic state (4:23–25), as it begins with what seems to be a clear literary allusion to Gen 1. This allusion causes scholars to consider this poetic passage a late addition to the

---

"Sumerian City Laments," 97–100; Gabbay, *Pacifying the Hearts of the Gods*; and Gabbay, "Performance of Emesal Prayers."

book of Jeremiah.[62] From the picture of cosmic chaos, the camera zooms in to the destruction in Judah itself, specifically in two rural regions east of Jerusalem: the Carmel and the Desert (4:26).[63]

In a four-part vision (ראיתי והנה), the prophecy borrows the Gen 1 schematic description that moves from cosmic elements to living creatures.[64] Accordingly, the destruction is a return to chaos on earth, to the absence of light from the sky (ואין אורם, Jer 4:23). Only then does it refer to leaving creatures, twisting the order of creation, but yet emphasizing that the land is empty—no human being (אין האדם) and no birds (וכל עוף השמים נדדו, "and all the birds of the sky have migrated [NJPS: fled]," 4:24).[65] As in 9:9, this choice to represent the entire animal world by birds

62. The use of the cosmic imagery and the relationships to the Genesis text are treated in various ways (see Qimhi). Childs ("Enemy from the North") ties these verses to theomachy, but there are no signs of conflict with sea monsters in this passage. Fishbane ("Jeremiah iv 23–26") notes a chiastic parallel between this description and Gen 1:1–2:4, with the Sabbath, the seventh day, standing in parallel to Jeremiah's portrayal of the destruction as God's deed of wrath (Jer 4:26). Furthermore, Fishbane explains the cosmogenic descriptions in Jer 4:23–26 and Job 3:3–13 as related to magic and cult, following parallels in Mesopotamian and Egyptian literatures (155–67). Finally, Eppstein ("Day of Yahweh in Jer 4:23–28"), followed by Carroll (*Jeremiah*, 168) among others, categorizes this passage as a late addition of an apocalyptic passage; see counterarguments in Holladay, *Jeremiah*, 1.164; McKane, *Jeremiah 1–25*, 108; and Lundbom, *Jeremiah 1–20*, 357.

63. The boundaries of this oracle are defined differently in the commentaries. Holladay (*Jeremiah*, 1.148) separates 4:23–26 from 4:27–28 on the basis of a presumed change in speakers: that is, the prophet speaks in 4:23–26 (using the genre of vision report, as in Amos 7:7–9); while Jer 4:27–28 constitutes "Yahweh's confirmation of that vision": שמים and ארץ occur in 4:23 and 4:28; כל־הארץ in 4:27 refers to all creation as presented in 4:23–25; and שמם is a plus in 4:26 LXX (ἠφανίσθησαν, i.e., נשמו) that occurs again in 4:27, both Masoretic Text and Septuagint. Hence, Holladay sees here a structural parallel to 4:19–22. While this division is accepted by Lundbom (*Jeremiah 1–20*, 356–59), he nevertheless considers 4:27–28 a supplement, a prose addition (359), yet not necessarily by a postexilic editor (pace Duhm, *Jeremia*, 53–54; and Carroll, *Jeremiah*, 170–71). Compare McKane (*Jeremiah 1–25*, 106–11), who follows Duhm and understands 4:23–26 as separate and independent of its surroundings (106), with 4:27–29 focusing on "devastation and flight."

64. For a similar type of prophetic vision, see Jer 24:1; Amos 7:1, 4, 7; Ezek 1:4, 15; 2:9; Zech 1:8; 2:1, 5, etc.

65. On עוף השמים see also Jer 9:9 and §9.1.3. Holladay (*Jeremiah*, 1.163) argues that Jer 4:25 comprises another allusion to Gen 2:5; thus he raises the possibility that both the Priestly and Yahwist traditions are available to the prophetic author (thus implying that the passage is late). I do not see the resemblance to Gen 2:5, and the negation אין האדם should be taken as reversal of Gen 1. Combinations of "man" and "beast" occur

of the sky is very appropriate. It uses the picture of avian migration when thousands of birds (or more) disappear from sight in a matter of minutes— and then are completely gone.

But it is of even greater interest that this prophecy is not circumscribed by its references to Gen 1 and in a very significant way does not accord with the Priestly tradition about creation.[66] The second vision, Jer 4:24, refers to the trembling of the mountains and the hills. This element, not represented in Gen 1, is among those elements reminiscent of mythic traditions about theomachy, creation through combat.[67] Jeremiah's knowledge and use of this "other" creation tradition is similarly apparent in 5:22 in reference to water forces. Hence, as in many other instances, Jeremiah uses a Priestly tradition about creation and harmonizes it with other traditions, clearly unconcerned about the thematic contradictions that scholars emphasize between the two.[68] Thus, the complicated allusion to Gen 1 is in keeping with the compositional style of the prophet and his immediate followers, not an indication of a late addition, and the passage may be dated to the era of the prophet.

Another intriguing issue that Jer 4:23–26 raises is the connection between the cosmic return to a precreation state and the regional focus of 4:26—why does the prophet (or a follower) begin with a cosmic, universal description, and where exactly does the national and regional interest in Judah come into play? William Holladay suggests that this prophecy works via a long historical retrospective, starting with creation, continuing

---

in Jer 21:6; note the string of four components in 7:20: עַל־הָאָדָם וְעַל־הַבְּהֵמָה וְעַל־עֵץ הַשָּׂדֶה וְעַל־פְּרִי הָאֲדָמָה ("My wrath and My fury will be poured out upon this place, on man and on beast, on the trees of the field and the fruit of the soil"). Holladay (*Jeremiah*, 1.256) argues that the pairing of "man" and "beast" characterizes both the Yahwist and Priestly traditions; he raises the possibility that Jeremiah is influenced by Zeph 1:3.

66. This point eludes Fishbane ("Jeremiah iv 23–26") and Lundbom, *Jeremiah 1–20*, 358. Holladay (*Jeremiah*, 1.165) refers to the collapse of hills and mountains due to God's deeds (as in Ps 65:7 and 46:3), but does not see that as a problem in relation to the echoes to Gen 1 (and 2) found in this passage.

67. For the trembling of mountains and hills as an element of creation through combat traditions, and thus as part of the portrayal of God as warrior and/or sovereign, see Nah 1:4–5; Hab 3:6; Ps 104:32; Prov 8:25 (and Ps 46:4 for the inclusion of creation theomachy within the Zion theology). As a framework for Jer 4:23–26, I prefer this context over the suggestion to see in 4:24 a different tradition concerning theophany (as in Ps 114:4, 6). Compare Holladay, *Jeremiah*, 1.165.

68. Holladay (*Jeremiah*, 1.163n69) mentions the reference to the Priestly tradition of this creation tradition. On Jeremiah's use of Priestly traditions, see Rom-Shiloni, "How Can You Say"; "Compositional Harmonization"; and "Forest and the Trees."

through the settlement in the Carmel (2:7) and in its towns, and ending in destruction.[69] I suggest a different line of thematic contact between 4:23–25 and 4:26. All of these judgment proclamations employ an ethnocentric approach to the land, which uses ecological observations to serve theological conceptions.

According to the ethnocentric approach to the land, the punishment of this one small nation that defaulted on its covenant obligations toward its God is expressed in terms of a divine judgment that harms creation as a whole, to the point of de-creation. The story of the deluge provides another good example of the clash of cosmic ecological systems and theological conceptions. The deluge, as a punishment against sinful human beings, afflicted all living creatures, which are totally destroyed and then reestablished (Gen 6:7; 7:23). The rising waters threatened an even more substantial destruction of plant life; this is avoided only when God stops the waters (8:11) and the climatic change proves temporary. The story of the deluge closes with God promising to himself to avoid causing such destruction in the future (8:21–22). Yet, this promise is not reiterated in other places within the Pentateuch or in the Prophets. (One exception within a consolation prophecy is Isa 54:9–10.) Instead, judgment prophecies against Israel and against the nations use the very same conception of cosmological-ecological disaster to describe the impending fate of Judah (e.g., Jer 9:9–10, 11–15), as well as other enemy kingdoms (e.g., 31:35–36, 37).[70]

Jeremiah 4:23–26 bridges cosmic creation traditions and the historical-national realm. These verses present a thematic flow that indeed starts with a cosmic perspective. Beginning with elemental entities (earth, sky, mountains and hills), moving on to the realm of living creatures (humans and birds), the prophecy finally hones in on the area close to Jerusalem—the Carmel, which designates a cultivated region and its settled towns.

Jeremiah 4:26 uses an asyndetic construction, ראיתי והנה הכרמל המדבר, which denotes the transformation of the Carmel into a desert. Linguistically, this interpretation is confirmed because only one region

---

69. Holladay, *Jeremiah*, 1.166. Compare Lundbom (*Jeremiah 1–20*, 360), who takes הכרמל as a general term for "the garden land," thus standing for "the promised land."

70. This ethnocentric conception and its diverse references in the Hebrew Bible deserve a separate discussion. Examples are just as valid in the Sumerian city laments; see, e.g., Michalowski, *Destruction of Sumer and Ur*, lines 126–32, 309–13, 322–28; and Cooper, *Curse of Agade*, lines 257, 279–80. Stipp ("Concept of the Empty Land," 124–32) does not go beyond mentioning an "early origin of the narrative" from a Babylonian ideological proclamation.

is referred to in 4:26b: וכל־עריו נתצו; that is, all the cities of the Carmel region are demolished.[71]

The Carmel is a narrow geographical strip about five to ten kilometers in width, running from north to south, between the Benjamin and Judah hills and the Judean Desert. This is the very region where Jeremiah is born and raised, in the area of Anathoth (and likewise the birthplace of Amos of Teqoa; Amos 1:1–2). Because of its rich soil and plentiful rains (250–400 mm per year), the Carmel generally allows agriculture and permanent settlement. Yet, years of drought may easily turn the Carmel into a desert, that is, transform its geographical conditions so that it will not sustain cultivation (i.e., with less than 250 mm rain per year; see Amos 4:7–8). Such a lack of water would cause the region's permanent settlements to be deserted as well, which would plunge the region into complete desolation, indistinguishable from the Judean desert that borders it.[72]

Jeremiah is clearly familiar with these geobotanical conditions, and they operate in the background of his prophecy. That is, the prophet is sensitively aware of the fluctuating conditions of the Carmel and the constant danger of its becoming a desert; and these conditions might be the reason for his focus on that region in his prophecy. Constructing a prophecy of consolation, Isa 32:15—והיה מדבר לכרמל והכרמל ליער יחשב ("and wilderness is transformed into farm land, while farm land rates as mere brush")—refers to the same regions, describing transformation in the opposite direction, from total desolation to the highest plants in the Israel *ya'ar* ("forest/thickets").[73] Hence, Isaiah, Jeremiah, and even Amos (see 1:2) all use the geobotanical local contexts of the Carmel and the (Judean)

---

71. The Septuagint reads ὁ Κάρμηλος ἔρημος ("the Desert of the Carmel"), defining the geographical region first and foremost as "the desert"; see McKane, *Jeremiah 1–25*, 107.

72. נתצו in Jer 4:26 suggests three different roots: (1) נתץ in the Masoretic Text (and so also Peshitta and Vulgate) designates destruction of walls (Jer 39:8; 52:14), houses (33:4), and city (Judg 9:45). As a divine deed destroying cities, it occurs only in Jer 4:26 and in the infinitive (1:10; 18:7; 31:28). (2) The Aramaic Targum's וכל קרוותה צדיאה reflects the root נצה in the *niphal*, meaning "make into ruin" (Jer 4:7; also 2 Kgs 19:25; Isa 37:26). (3) The Septuagint's ἐμπεπυρισμέναι πυρί reads נצתו באש, thus יצת (Jer 17:27; 21:14; PAN 43:12; also without "fire" in 9:11; PAN 46:19). This textual evidence suggests an opposite picture in Jer 2:15: עריו נצתה (ק: נצתו) מבלי ישב, where the Septuagint reads κατεσκάφησαν, the regular equivalent of נתץ. Based on this complicated and ever-changing textual evidence, Holladay (*Jeremiah*, 1.143) suggests that Jeremiah himself plays with those different roots to create such multiple meanings.

73. See Blenkinsopp, *Isaiah 1–39*, 434.

desert. The crucial point that ties Jer 4:23–25 with 4:26 in this prophecy seems to be the basic ethnocentric conception of the land. This theological conception portrays the divine judgment over Judah as the total unmaking of all ecological systems, from elements to vegetation to animals to human, leaving an empty land.

Jeremiah 4:23–26 utilizes the conception of the empty land in two main points. First, it depicts the consequences of actions as taken by God (/the gods) when he is the sole warrior, who alone is capable of destroying his land and bringing annihilation. Second, the consequence of God's act of war is a profound change in the ecological and agricultural nature of the land, a change that is much beyond what human kings and their forces could have brought about. The notion of the empty land serves here and in other judgment prophecies as a theological topos. In both Hebrew Bible and ancient Near Eastern sources, affliction is described as affecting all the ecological systems: mountains, hills, and valleys; precipitation and water systems; vegetation; and subsequently all living creatures, human and animal. The divine actions leave the land empty and desolate of all life.

Therefore, the question that occupied scholars of biblical history and archeology over the last few decades concerning whether such wholesale destruction actually takes place (or whether this rhetoric rather represents the so-called myth of the empty land) may be set in a different light when examined from the perspective of the broader ancient Near Eastern theological context in which it appears to have taken shape.[74] The rhetoric of the empty land as it appears within judgment prophecies serves first and foremost a theological aim: it styles the forecast destruction as carried out directly by God, thus total and final. Therefore, the conception of the destruction as leaving the land desolate and empty has its origin much earlier than the Persian era or even the exilic period. It is clearly part of the theological and rhetorical arsenal of the judgment prophecies by the early sixth century in Judah; the conception and the language are available to Jeremiah as well as prophets in Babylon, such as Ezekiel (33:23–29). The political use of this older theological conception by Ezekiel, as a representative of the Jehoiachin exile (early sixth century and throughout

74. See Carroll, "Myth of the Empty Land"; and Barstad, *Myth of the Empty Land*, 77–83. On the gap between the biblical portrait and apparent demographic reality (based on a few excavations but mostly on archeological surveys), see Lipschits, *Fall and Rise of Jerusalem*, 206–71. For a counterposition see Oded, "Myth of the Empty Land?"

the fifth century), should thus be understood as secondary use; that is, this theological perception is transformed to serve as a strategy in the sociopolitical struggles between Judeans in their *two* exilic centers, Judah and Babylon.[75]

9.1.5. Divine Wrath as a Force in Combat

Jeremiah 4:26 concludes with a phrase that explains the entire vision of destruction as a result of the divine wrath.

Divine wrath is clearly one of those concepts that make Hebrew Bible theologians feel uncomfortable. Christian scholar Ralph Smith, for example, devotes ten pages to this topic, with five of these pages allotted to the presentation of texts that illustrate that "wrath is not God's last word in the Old Testament."[76] He emphasizes that "the anger of God should not be treated in isolation from other aspects of His nature or from human sin," which is "the apparent reason for the anger of God."[77] Smith presents his pious observation in a question: "Is God's anger only temporary, secondary part of His nature which leaves no lasting effects on His relationship or dealings with people?" to which he finds an answer in Walther Eichrodt's words: "Unlike holiness and righteousness, wrath never forms one of the permanent attributes of the God of Israel; it can only be understood as, so to speak, a footnote to the will to fellowship of the covenant God."[78] Smith concludes his discussion by assuring his readers that God's wrath "is the counterpart, not the antithesis, of his love," and he goes on to adduce sources to show that God's anger should not be identified with evil.[79]

---

75. The concept of the empty land is used by both the exiles in Babylon and the repatriates in Yehud to argue for their exclusive status as the people of God. See Rom-Shiloni, *Exclusive Inclusivity*, 253–76.

76. Smith (*Old Testament Theology*, 205–15, esp. 205–6) begins with the lexical equivalents of rage and wrath in Egyptian, Akkadian, and Greek religion; he concludes this extrabiblical survey with the notion of the fear of the gods in "primitive religions." He focuses on statistics, noting twenty different words for wrath (of which he presents זעם, אף, חרון, and נקם); the number of times these terms occur; and the significant difference in frequency between references to God's wrath and to human wrath in the Hebrew Bible (references to divine wrath occur three times more). Nevertheless, Smith finds ways to explain this data in a typical Christian theodical way.

77. Smith, *Old Testament Theology*, 210, 211.

78. Eichrodt, *Theology of the Old Testament*, 1.262.

79. Smith, *Old Testament Theology*, 214, 215.

Nowhere in his discussion does he adduce a specific Hebrew Bible text to phenomenologically describe divine wrath.

Within Jewish scholarship, this unease with divine wrath causes Abraham Heschel, for one, to argue that wrath in the Hebrew Bible is an action, a deed performed by God, but not in itself a divine quality.[80] Furthermore, Heschel accentuates the temporary or limited duration of divine wrath, over against God's eternal benevolence.[81] But, Moshe Greenberg aptly criticizes Heschel for presenting only a partial picture and completely disregarding Ezekiel, who paints divine wrath as a special force, to the point that the only way to calm down divine anger is by Jerusalem's total destruction (Ezek 8:13; 16:42).[82] Jeremiah 4:26 and 4:27–28 are but two examples of this phenomenon in Jeremiah. The two prophets (along with poetic sources) present divine wrath as an element of the portrayal of God as a warrior, who fights against his people and against the nations. For sixth-century historiographers, prophets, and poets, God's wrath is a live theological concept.

In both the Hebrew Bible and ancient Near Eastern religions, the metaphor of a/the wrathful God (or gods) serves in the portrayal of the role of God(/the gods) in his(/their) people's defeat and in the destruction of his(/their) temple(s). A famous nonbiblical example is the Mesha Stela, where the military success of the Israelite king, who subjugated Moab for a long period of time, is explained as due to Chemosh's anger against his kingdom:[83]

Omri King of Israel has afflicted Moab for many days, <u>because Chemosh was angry with his land.</u>	עמרי מלך ישראל ויענו את מאב ימן רבן כי יאנף כמש בארצה

Similarly in Mesopotamian sources, political and military distress are the result of divine wrath, which led the god to abandon his kingdom and

80. Epithets such as ארך אפים or רב חסד among others, support such an argument; yet two divine epithets take wrath as a divine quality: אל זעם (Ps 7:12, which the Septuagint reverses, elaborates, and negates: καὶ ἰσχυρὸς καὶ μακρόθυμος μὴ ὀργὴν ἐπάγων καθ᾽ ἑκάστην ἡμέραν) and בעל חמה (Nah 1:2).

81. Heschel (*Prophets*, 2.69–71) mentions Isa 26:20; 54:7–8; 57:16–19; Jer 31:3; 33:11; Hos 2:21; Mic 7:18); but he either ignores or relegates to the notes other references that evince the opposite, such as Jer 17:4 and Mal 1:4.

82. Greenberg, "Anthropopathism in Ezekiel." Greenberg is not aware of the distinction between Ezekiel's treatment of Jerusalem and those who remain there and the Jehoiachin exiles. Thus in Ezek 1–24, divine wrath is activated against Jerusalem to bring total calamity; whereas it is transformed into words of hope for the exiles in 20:32–33. See Rom-Shiloni, "Ezekiel as Voice of the Exiles."

83. Mesha Stela, lines 4–6; see Ahituv, *Ha-Ketav VeHa-Miktav*, 377–94, esp. 383–84.

land.[84] The cylinder of Marduk-Apla-Iddina II is one of the exceptional testimonies among Assyrian and Babylonian royal inscriptions reflecting the Assyrian-Babylonian conflicts of the seventh century, which includes the theological reflections of those defeated or subjugated:

[8] [i]-nu-šú bēlu rabu(ú) ᵈMar-duk it-ti ᵐᵃᵗAkkadiᴷᴵ ki-mil-tuš is-bu-us-ma [9] [MU-x]-ᴋᴀᴍ-ma ᵃʷᵉˡnakru lim-nu ᵃʷᵉˡSubaru(ú) ina ᵐᵃᵗAkkadiᴷᴵ ep-pu-uš be-lu-tu [10] [a-d]i(?) u₄-me im-lu-u ik-šú-da a-dan-na [11] [bēlu] rabu(ú) ᵈMarduk a-na ᵐᵃᵗAkka-diᴷᴵ šá ik-mi-lu ir-šu-ú sa-li-ma	[8] At that time the great lord Marduk <u>had turned in wrath from the land of Akkad,</u> [9] and for [X] years the evil enemy, the Subarean, had exercised lordship in the land of Akkad, [10] until(?) the days were fulfilled, the hour had come [11] (when) <u>the great (lord) Marduk had (re)gained contentment towards the land of Akkad, which he had been wroth withal.</u>[85]

The Babylonian king explains that due to the shameful state of his temples, Marduk leaves his land in anger, bringing a dark period in which Babylon is subjugated to the Shubratu. Change comes with the reign of Marduk-Apla-Iddina II, who by reinstituting Marduk's temples appeases the god; Marduk now returns to his land and in his favor brings it to political and economic recovery.

The Babylonian example helps us to recognize the not insignificant role played by divine anger in the Hebrew Bible. Divine wrath is described three times more than human wrath in Hebrew Bible compositions; the semantic field includes nouns and verbal phrases of the roots אנף, זעם, חמה־יחם, חרה, כעס, עבר, עשן, קנא, and קצף.[86] In addition, two signif-icant issues should be stressed. First, God's wrath does not necessarily cause him to leave his city and people; the presence or absence of God is one of the issues under debate between the different authorial parties in

---

84. Such a divine self-exile is recorded in Neo-Assyrian and Neo-Babylonian in-scriptions as well as in the Cyrus Cylinder of the Persian period. See Kutsko, *Between Heaven and Earth*, 103–9. For further examples of divine wrath in Assyrian royal in-scriptions, see Oded, *War, Peace, and Empire*, 18–20, 125–31.

85. Gadd, "Inscribed Barrel Cylinder," 123–24. The noun *kimiltuš* designates "divine wrath" or "divine dissatisfaction"; the verbs *kamālu* (*Chicago Assyrian Dictionary* K 372) and *sabāsu/šabāsu* (*Chicago Assyrian Dictionary* S 1.4) mean "be angry"; *rāšu sālima*, on the other hand, stands for "be appeased from anger" (see von Soden, *Akkadisches Handwörterbuch*, 2.961; and *Chicago Assyrian Dictionary* S 102–3).

86. See Johnson, "אָנַף *'ānaph*," 356. For discussion of these occurrences, see Rom-Shiloni, *God in Times of Destruction*, 454–60 (appendix 3.C).

Jerusalem.[87] Second, divine wrath serves as a component in the metaphor of God as warrior, in one of two ways. It functions either to motivate the warlike actions God then executes against his people or side by side with warlike language (and at times substituting them) to designate God's acts in and of itself. These two modes correspond to the two main conceptual approaches to the role of God in war, (B') and (C'):

> (a) *Divine wrath motivates (or explains) God's warlike*
> *actions against his people.*

Inflicting judgment upon the people (or individuals) may be expressed by holding back God's favor and benevolence. חרון אפו (God's "blazing anger") creates drought (עצירת גשמים), which brings agricultural disaster and hunger in its wake (Jer 12:13; see Deut 11:17). But even more frequently, divine wrath functions in descriptions of God's roles in war and in explanations of the people's defeat. For example, God's wrath may cause him to abstain from helping his people in war, an inaction that allows enemies to overpower Israel (Judg 2:20–23); or, due to his anger, God may summon the enemy against his people (Isa 10:5–6). In either case, we see here a pattern with three components:

> human sin → divine wrath → judgment: defeat in war

In this pattern, divine wrath stands on its own, either initiating war or explaining it. In contrast to human anger, which causes a loss of control and extreme actions stemming from a place of unreason (Amos 1:11), the metaphor of divine wrath portrays God's action as an expected step, a reasonable consequence of human iniquity (of Israel and the nations alike), in accordance with the measure of justice.

This pattern is common in the books of Jeremiah and Ezekiel, in judgment prophecies against both Israel and the nations that use the (B') conception, while it appears only sporadically in (C') prophecies.[88]

---

87. See the quotations of other voices in Ezek 8:12 and 9:9, and compare Ezekiel's prophetic refutation in Ezek 8–11, where he emphasizes that God has only now left the temple and the city, due to its iniquities (Ezek 8–9), and yet still remains on the Eastern Mountain (11:23).

88. (B') passages that mention God's wrath prior to his summoning the enemy: Jer 4:5–8; 15:10–14; 17:1–4; 18:18–23; PAN Jer 49:34–39; 50:17–21; 51:45–53; Ezek 16:26–29, 38–42; 23:22–27; PAN Ezek 25:12–14. This divine anger preceding the infliction is, however, relatively rare in (C') passages; see Jer 25:34–38; Ezek 8:17–18; 24:1–14. In

> *(b)   Expressions of wrath serve side by side with warlike*
> *language or substitute for it.*

In Lamentations, expressions for divine wrath appear extensively in Lam 2 (2:2, 3, 4, 6, 21, 22) and sporadically in all of the other laments (1:12; 3:1; 4:11; 5:22; see §1.2.2). Like similar examples in Psalms (e.g., 80:17; 90:7, 9, 11), divine anger functions as a force that brings calamity, as a divine weapon in and of itself, mostly within (C') passages, that is, when no human army conducts the war for God.[89] None of these occurrences of such expressions present the divine anger as motivating or explaining God's actions.

These data from the poetry correspond with the many occurrences within Jeremiah and Ezekiel where divine anger is not the motivation for, but rather one component of, the war itself.[90] In these sources one can detect a two-part pattern, where expressions of divine wrath are intertwined with the language of war:

human sin → war that ends in defeat

This pattern is typical of (C') passages in both prophetic books. It is not found at all in (B') passages in Jeremiah and occurs only once in such a

---

addition, the phrase הכעיסני (מען) ל designates God's wrath as an explanation for the divine judgment in several of the (C') passages in Jeremiah, although oftentimes the actual punishment is not specified beyond the threat of pouring divine wrath over Jerusalem and Judah, or general phrases concerning the prospected coming evil (Jer 7:16–20 [at 7:18–19]; 8:19; 11:15–17; 25:6, 7; 44:3, 8). Compare 7:29–34 (at 7:29), where the total destruction is detailed; or 32:26–35 of the (B') concept, where four references to the divine anger in one prophetic passage (32:29, 30, 31, 32) justify God's summoning Jerusalem into the hands of the Babylonians. In the two (C') passages in Ezekiel that mention God's wrath, anger is the result of the people's abominations, and it precedes divine infliction (8:17–18; 24:1–14 [at 24:8]). In the (B') concept in Ezekiel, להכעיסני is the motivation for giving the people into the hands of their enemies (Ezek 16:26–29 [at 16:26]; 16:38–42 [at 16:42]; 23:22–27 [at 23:25]; and PAN 25:12–14 [at 25:14]). This pattern is also behind Ps 106:40–46 and the quotation in Jer 2:35.

89. For divine anger within psalms that use the (B') conception, see, e.g., 106:40–46.

90. Eighteen such passages in Jeremiah use the (C') conception: 4:3–4, 23–26; 6:9–11; 7:16–20; 10:10, 25; 12:13; 21:1–7, 11–12; 23:19–20; 25:34–38; 30:23–24; 32:37; 33:5; 42:18–22; 44:2–6, 7–10; PAN Jer 50:11–13. Seventeen such passages may be seen in Ezekiel: 5:7–15; 6:11–14; 7:1–9; 9:1–11; 13:13–15; 14:12–23; 20:1–38; 21:19–22; 22:23–31; 24:1–14; 36:16–36; 38:18–23; PAN Ezek 25:15–17; 30:13–19; 35:10–15; 36:1–12; and note also 22:17–22, where expressions of wrath are coupled with the imagery of melting in fire, rather than expressions of war.

passage in Ezekiel (PAN Ezek 25:12–14). Such passages incorporate divine wrath in one of three ways.

First, expressions of divine wrath occur side by side with war language, thus incorporating wrath into the divine war arsenal, as seen, for instance, in Jer 21:5: "And I Myself will battle against you with an outstretched hand and with mighty arm [ונלחמתי אני אתכם ביד נטויה ובזרוע חזקה], with anger and rage and great wrath [ובאף ובחמה ובקצף גדול]." The three expressions of wrath add up to God's hand and arm, and this long string is tied together by the repetition of the *beth instrumentalis* (for a similar construction, see 32:37).[91] Such use of the *beth instrumentalis* is also the case where anger and wrath are the devices of war alongside devastating forces of nature, as in Ezek 13:13–15:

[13] Assuredly, thus said the Lord GOD: <u>In My fury</u> I will let loose hurricane winds; <u>in My anger</u> a driving rain shall descend, and great hailstones <u>in destructive fury</u>. [14] I will throw down the wall.... [15] <u>And when I have spent My fury</u> upon the wall and upon those who daubed it with plaster....	[13] לכן כה אמר אדני יהוה ובקעתי רוח־סערות בחמתי וגשם שטף באפי יהיה ואבני אלגביש בחמה לכלה. [14] והרסתי את־הקיר ... [15] וכליתי את־חמתי בקיר ובטחים אתו תפל ...

The phrase מ(פני) חרון אף יהוה ("because of His blazing anger") recurs in several different contexts in Jeremiah (4:26; 12:13; 25:34–38; 30:24; PAN Jer 49:37; 51:45). Notwithstanding the causal construction, the phrase does not explain the motive for the divine action. Rather, it describes and accentuates the *manner* in which God acts in these passages. Note the structural parallelism in 25:36–38:

[36] Hark, the outcry of the shepherds, and the howls of the lords of the flock! For the LORD is ravaging their pasture.	[36] קול צעקת הרעים ויללת אדירי הצאן כי־שדד יהוה את־מרעיתם.

---

91. For *beth instrumentalis*, see Gesenius, Kautzsch, and Cowley, *Gesenius' Hebrew Grammar*, §119o–q. Compare examples where the divine wrath appears prior to and as the motive of the outstretched hand/arm of God, as in על־כן חרה אף־יהוה בעמו ויט ידו עליו ויכהו ("that is why the Lord's anger was roused against His people, why He stretched out His arm against it and struck it," Isa 5:25a) and in the repeated phrase בכל־זאת לא־שב אפו ועוד ידו נטויה ("Yet his anger has not turned back, and His arm is outstretched still," 5:25b; 9:11, 16, 20; 10:4).

³⁷ The peaceful meadows shall be
wiped out
by the fierce wrath of the LORD.
³⁸ Like a lion, He has gone forth from
His lair;
the land has become a desolation,
because of the oppressive wrath,
because of His fierce anger.

37 וְנָדַמּוּ נְאוֹת הַשָּׁלוֹם

מִפְּנֵי חֲרוֹן אַף־יְהוָה.

38 עָזַב כַּכְּפִיר סֻכּוֹ

כִּי־הָיְתָה אַרְצָם לְשַׁמָּה

מִפְּנֵי חֲרוֹן הַיּוֹנָה

וּמִפְּנֵי חֲרוֹן אַפּוֹ.

The first stitch of each verse describes the fate of the shepherds in the face of the massacre and subsequently the terrible silence of desolation that prevails in those previously cultivated areas till their destruction. The second stitch of each verse presents God as the initiator of this catastrophe. Jeremiah 25:36 uses שדד ("devastate, despoil, destroy"), which often in Jeremiah designates the action of human forces (as in 4:13); placing 25:37 and 25:38 in parallel suggests that the two expressions of anger in 25:38 (מפני חרון היונה ומפני חרון אפו) stand in clear apposition to each other, placing the divine anger as acts of war in themselves.[92]

Second, expressions of anger intensify descriptions of warlike activity by serving as adverbs in verbal phrases of war: גדע בחרי־אף ("in blazing anger He has cut down," Lam 2:3), היכה באפו ובחמתו ("I struck down in My anger and rage," Jer 33:5), הרס בעברתו ("He has razed in His anger," Lam 2:2), and עשה שפטים באף ובחמה ובתכחות חמה ("when I execute judgment upon you in anger and rage and furious chastisement," Ezek 5:15).[93]

---

92. The closing sentence of Jer 25:38 MT (= 32:38 LXX) is difficult, for several reasons: (1) חרון היונה is a *hapax*. The Septuagint reads τῆς μαχαίρας τῆς μεγάλης, "the great sword," in translation of חרב היונה (cf. 46:16 [= 26:16 LXX] and 50:16 [= 27:16 LXX]); Peshitta's מן קדם רוגזה דמריא reads מפני חרון יהוה. Holladay (*Jeremiah*, 1.687) explains היונה as a participle of ינה with the meaning "oppress" (Jer 22:3). (2) The Masoretic Text has a double expression of wrath, but the second expression is lacking in the Septuagint. Carroll (*Jeremiah*, 506) explains this double expression as reflecting two different forces behind this anger. חרון היונה designates anger expressed by the human enemy (following Jer 46:16), whereas חרון אפו refers to the divine anger. Yet this distinction cannot be accepted in this context, which accentuates that God alone stands behind the disaster (C'). (3) The connections between 25:38 and the previous verses are somewhat tenuous. Rudolph (*Jeremia*, 168) argues that 25:38 is secondary, though he does not specify the reasons. Indeed, 25:38 differs in its theological conception concerning God's absence and anger, as it brings together language of desertion (עזב) with anger (חרון). Jer 25:34–37, on the other hand, emphasizes the divine presence and involvement in the destruction.

93. The same adverbial use may be seen in verbal phrases that are not from the se-

Third, expressions of anger may either substitute for expressions of warlike action or precede descriptions of total annihilation (to designate the warlike action that brought about such desolation). This is often the case with the imagery of wrath as an inextinguishable fire that consumes everything in its path: פן־תצא כאש חמתי ובערה ואין מכבה מפני רע מעלליכם ("lest My wrath break forth like fire, and burn, with none to quench it, because of your wicked acts," Jer 4:4; 21:12); a similar use may be seen in a prophecy against Babylon: מקצף יהוה לא תשב והיתה שממה כלה ("because of the LORD's wrath she shall not be inhabited," PAN Jer 50:11–13).[94]

Recalling 4:23–26, this cosmic destruction concludes with the words "because of the LORD, because of His blazing anger," which is the phrase that lays responsibility for the cosmic events on God, or specifically on his rage. The apposition in 4:26 between מפני יהוה and מפני חרון אפו tells that this blazing anger itself functions as an engine of war.[95]

This interchangeability between expressions of anger and expressions of war may be illustrated by comparing Jer 7:20 and 21:6:[96]

My wrath and My fury will be poured out upon this place, on man and on beast, on the trees of the field and the fruit of the soil. It shall burn, with none to quench it. (7:20)	הנה אפי וחמתי נתכת אל־המקום הזה על־האדם ועל־הבהמה ועל־עץ השדה ועל־פרי האדמה ובערה ולא תכבה.
I will strike the inhabitants of this city, man and beast: they shall die by a terrible pestilence. (21:6)	והכיתי את־יושבי העיר הזאת ואת־האדם ואת־הבהמה בדבר גדול ימותו.

---

mantic field of war; e.g., יעיב באפו ("the Lord in His wrath has shamed," Lam 2:1) or וינאץ בזעם־אפו מלך וכהן ("in His raging anger He has spurned king and priest," 2:6).

94. In twenty-seven of twenty-nine occurrences of the noun קצף in the Hebrew Bible, God is the agent, and so it appears in Jer 21:5 and 32:37 against Israel; against Babylon in PAN 50:13; and once in the doxology at 10:10 aside זעם (see also Ps 102:11). The verb קצף occurs also in Lam 5:22; and as the people raising God's anger in Ps 106:32. The verb is not attested in Jeremiah and Ezekiel; otherwise, in sixteen of its occurrences in the Hebrew Bible God is the agent.

95. Jer 4:26 LXX adds the verb ἠφανίσθησαν ("ruin, destroy") after מפני חרון אפו. Holladay (Jeremiah, 1.143) accepts the Septuagint as reflecting the original reading on the basis of formal and lexical arguments: the Septuagint has a complete chiasmic structure and refers to 4:9 and 4:27, where שמם appears. These two arguments could just as well designate a secondary harmonistic version.

96. Compare also 42:18–22 and 24:8–10; 44:6 and 7:34.

God's anger poured over this place (7:20) plays a similar role as the divine warlike affliction of the city (21:6). In both descriptions, God causes total devastation to both humans and animals.

To conclude, (B′) passages use the concept of divine anger as a component of the hierarchy of divine and human forces. Divine wrath stands on its own in these contexts; in many (not all) occurrences it is presented as God's justified reaction to human sins and thus motivating his warlike actions. As a consequence of his aroused (and justified) wrath, God summons human armies to execute his plan of punishment.

Expressions of divine wrath are much more common in (C′) passages, where it may (or may not) be justified as a response to human sins.[97] This distinction thus signals a significant difference between (B′) and (C′) passages: in the first, divine wrath typically either motivates or explains God's actions; whereas in the second, expressions of wrath function as components within the divine arsenal of actions and weapons.

This descriptive discussion of divine wrath illustrates the breadth of this theological theme in sources of the sixth century. Unfortunately (and in opposition to Christian perspectives as represented by Smith or Jewish perspectives as represented by Heschel), prophets and poets of the sixth century did consider the wrath of God to be a real, active, and destructive force that could cause total calamity, as a final step in God's execution of judgment. All speakers of the time were aware of this terrifying quality of YHWH, which is acknowledged and configured in different ways in expressions of justification, doubt, and protest (chap. 10).

9.1.6. Summary: The "Why" Question

At the outset of this chapter, I posed the "why" question—why would prophets choose to present God as the sole foe of his own people? Three characteristics of the (C′) conception of war emerged: (a) God is the sole agent of the destruction, (b) God uses all the forces of nature in his war (including human troops), and (c) the consequences of this divine war are disastrous—total calamity is brought upon the people and ecological disaster empties the land, turning it into a desolate territory with no living

---

97. The component of justification of the divine wrath is not obligatory and signals a significant difference between (C′) prophetic passages and quotations or communal laments, which protest against God's wrath. See §11.2.3 (confession of sins), §1.1.2 (on Jer 21:1–7), and §1.2.2 (on Lam 2).

things, human or otherwise, settled upon or growing in it. Divine wrath is an actual weapon of war wielded by God in his role of sole warrior.

These unusual and extreme features of the (C') passages point to a radical position adopted by both Jeremiah and Ezekiel in order to justify God's role in the destruction of his city and people. The (C') passages show that God is entirely omnipotent, entirely in control—of the cosmos, of history, and of the fate of his city and people. The distribution and extremity of these passages show that the destruction is of a polemical nature (see §8.1.2 and the lists of references in the footnotes at the start of this chapter). As presented in both prophetic books, the (C') conception is the governing explanation for the role of God in Jerusalem's destruction. This high distribution is not less than amazing, precisely because this explanation is clearly detached from the historical events that most of the speakers may be presumed to experience themselves or that, at most, take place one to three generations before the books are given their final literary shape. In any event, authors of the sixth century know that it is the Babylonians who physically destroy Jerusalem and put an end to Judah's existence, deporting substantial segments of its population to Babylon. Nevertheless, the prophets choose to describe this defeat and destruction as the consequence of deeds of a war conducted by the God of Israel alone.[98]

The prophetic polemic concerning the roles of God and the human enemies in the war waged against Jerusalem and Judah is only rarely explicitly exposed (e.g., Jer 21:1–7 on the debate between Jeremiah and two of Zedekiah's officials; similarly 37:3–10). These polemical contexts are implicitly leading and shaping the argumentation of Jeremiah and Ezekiel. The prophets feel called upon to fight two distinct, even antagonistic, lines of thought, which, we may assume, are prominent among Judean theological worldviews.

The first view is the expectation that God would certainly deliver his people from the Babylonian foe, as he had done before. This expectation, the (A' → C) conceptual approach, is held by the king and his officials (e.g., Jer 21:2); it underlies poetic pronouncements of doubt and protest at the deteriorating situation in Jerusalem (e.g., 14:7–9) and is also supported by the peace prophets (e.g., Hananiah's prophecy in 28:2–4, 11; Ezek 13:1–16).

---

98. In view of the Sumerian city laments, this type of presentation should certainly not come as a surprise, but should rather be seen as partaking in the common conceptions and conventions of descriptions of defeat in different cultures of the ancient Near East. See §9.1.3.

Neither Jeremiah nor Ezekiel could stay calm in the face of this expectation, in view of their own seeming convictions that defeat, not victory, is imminent.

A second view, and not less problematic in its threat to undermine God's power and role in historical events, is the idea that God is either absent or impotent in the current crisis, and thus unable to save (see §6.1.1 and §6.1.2). In prophetic sources, this conception is explicitly used, though only in relation to other gods. In Jeremiah, it is restricted to six prophecies against the nations: against Moab (48:7–9, 12–13), Ammon (49:1–6 MT = 30:17–22 LXX),[99] and Babylon (50:2–3; 51:41–44, 47–49). Five of these passages reflect the (B') conception; God will summon either a "ravager" (שדד, 48:8; 51:48b; see 48:12; 49:3) or an "enemy from the north" (50:3);[100] the projected devastation is described as so vast that it will leave the land in complete desolation (48:8b, 9b; 49:2; 50:3b; see §8.1.2). PAN Jer 51:41–44 uses the (C') conception:

[41] How has Sheshach been captured,	אֵיךְ נִלְכְּדָה שֵׁשַׁךְ [41]
the praise of the whole earth been taken!	וַתִּתָּפֵשׂ תְּהִלַּת כָּל־הָאָרֶץ
How has Babylon become	אֵיךְ הָיְתָה לְשַׁמָּה
a horror to the nations!	בָּבֶל בַּגּוֹיִם.
[42] The sea has risen over Babylon,	עָלָה עַל־בָּבֶל הַיָּם [42]
she is covered by its roaring waves.	בַּהֲמוֹן גַּלָּיו נִכְסָתָה.
[43] Her towns are a desolation,	הָיוּ עָרֶיהָ לְשַׁמָּה [43]
a land of desert and steppe,	אֶרֶץ צִיָּה וַעֲרָבָה
a land no man lives in	אֶרֶץ לֹא־יֵשֵׁב בָּהֵן כָּל־אִישׁ
and no human passes through.	וְלֹא־יַעֲבֹר בָּהֵן בֶּן־אָדָם.
<u>[44] And I will deal with Bel in Babylon,</u>	<u>וּפָקַדְתִּי עַל־בֵּל בְּבָבֶל [44]</u>

99. The Masoretic Text of 49:1 and 49:3b reads מלכם ("their king"), rendered in the Septuagint (= 30:17, 19) as Milkom, the Ammonite god. The Vulgate, Peshitta, and most commentators follow the Septuagint reading. See, e.g., Volz, *Der Prophet Jeremia*, 414–15; Rudolph, *Jeremia*, 286; Holladay, *Jeremiah*, 2.366, 368; McKane, *Jeremiah 26–52*, 1204; and Lundbom, *Jeremiah 37–52*, 315–16; and note Rashi on this verse, who glosses it "the Ammonite god who is called 'king.'" Compare, however, Fischer (*Jeremia 26–52*, 536–37), who prefers the Masoretic Text because of the phrasing in 49:3 ("their king, his prophets, and his priests"); 48:7b; and also Amos 1:15. McKane (*Jeremiah 26–52*, 1204) suggests that Amos 1:15 influenced both Jer 48:7b and 49:1–6. Isa 46:1–2 proclaims that the gods of Babylon will be taken into captivity.

100. Ironically, the nation of the north (גוי מצפון) is more than once the source of threat (Jer 6:22–26; PAN Jer 50:9, 41). This typological presentation cannot be matched with the historical Persian-Elamite foe, which came against Babylon from the east.

and make him disgorge what he has swallowed,	והצאתי את־בלעו מפיו
and nations shall no more gaze on him with joy.	ולא־ינהרו אליו עוד גוים
Even the wall of Babylon shall fall.	וגם־חומת בבל נפלה.

The passage opens in a lament fashion (51:41), which, similar to Lam 1:1; 2:1, agonizes over the reversal of the fame and honor of the destroyed city, but here the prophet ridicules the agony over Babylon's destruction.[101] The force that subdues Babylon is the sea and its waves (Jer 51:42). Not a human enemy, but this powerful natural force causes total desolation (51:43; see 2:6). Jeremiah 51:44 MT projects a confrontation between YHWH and Bel (Marduk's main epithet in the Neo-Babylonian period), the devouring monster (compare also 51:34, where Nebuchadrezzar is the enemy that devours Zion and Jerusalem is a monster).[102] God will rescue Bel's prey from inside his very mouth; this action will have its consequences both for Marduk's position among the nations and for the immediate state of Babylon, causing the shattering of its wall. Marduk will thus be stripped of his devouring powers and even of his ability to protect his own city.[103]

In all six of these prophecies against the nations, the national gods, and specifically their idols, are mentioned as either going to exile with their priests and officials (PAN Jer 48:7; 49:3), as having crashed down at the time of the destruction (Jer 50:2; possibly 51:44, 47), and as disappointments to their people (48:13; 51:44, 47).[104] Jeremiah rebukes these nations

101. For the motive of reversal in the glory and fame of the destroyed city, see Dobbs-Allsopp, *Weep, O Daughter of Zion*, 38–42; and Berlin, *Lamentations*, 47–51.

102. The Septuagint does not represent בל ב and thus omits this confrontation altogether. See Janzen (*Studies in the Text of Jeremiah*, 119) and Lundbom (*Jeremiah 37–52*, 479), who suggest that this omission is due to haplography. For the epithet Bel for Marduk, see Jer 50:2; Isa 46:1; and Lundbom, *Jeremiah 37–52*, 370.

103. This note is another indication of the early dating of this passage; the reference clearly predates the reign of Nabonidus, the last king of Babylon, who established Sin as the city's primary deity. Lundbom (*Jeremiah 37–52*, 481) dates this passage (51:34–44) to the period following the deportation of 597 on the basis of 51:35, which assumes that people remain in Zion to curse the Babylonian king.

104. The Moabites' disappointment in Chemosh (Jer 48:13) is set in parallel to Israel's disappointment in "Bethel, on whom they relied" (48:13b). Scholars debate two possible interpretations of this statement: is Bethel a divine name or a toponym? If Bethel stands for the place, the statement might focus on the people of Northern Israel, who relied on King Jeroboam's temple at Bethel (1 Kgs 12–13; 2 Kgs 17) and who

and their gods for hubris (Moab in 48:7, 11; Ammon in 49:4) and mocks their projected fall; in 50:2–3 Bel-Marduk is brought to ridicule Babylon's major gods (also 51:44, 47). Jeremiah also injects denigrating references to Babylon's idols and fetishes, using the terms עצבים and גלולים (50:2) and פסילים (51:47).[105] The patron gods of these other nations all lost their powers, their places, and their peoples; their land becomes totally desolate. According to Jeremiah (adapting a theme common in the ancient Near East), the fall of Moab and Ammon, and the capture of Babylon, mean first of all the physical shattering of their idols, but even more important the powerlessness, dismay, fear, and shame brought upon their primary gods. But Jeremiah cannot allow such thoughts when it comes to YHWH, the God of Israel.

Jeremiah and Ezekiel mount counteroffensives to both the conception that God will certainly save the people from the Babylonians and the idea that God is unable to save (or absents himself for this reason). In presenting God as a warrior who alone fights against his own people, with all his might, rage, and forces (Jer 21:5; and even in a message of consolation in Ezek 20:33–34), the prophets retain God's qualities of omnipotent sovereign. It is God himself who initiates this judgment against his people, and he is the sole executor of this judgment. His sovereign status as creator and lord of the entire world is expressed in his ability to mobilize the entire cosmos, all its natural and human forces, to bring total destruction upon Judah (just as he can act against the nations). In a paradoxical fashion, the total annihilation of Judah, caused by God himself, serves the two prophets as the major proof that these divine qualities are still intact. Thus, this conception in itself serves as a radical justification for God—as omnipotent sovereign and creator; that very action confirms his omnipotent status.

The polemical quality of the (C') conception of God's role as sole enemy, ultimately responsible for Jerusalem's and Judah's destruction, may be further illuminated by taking another look at expressions of doubt, protest, and even denial.

---

are constantly blamed for worshiping other gods (17:7–23). This comparison to Northern Israel is also made in Jer 48:27. The cultic center in Bethel is utterly destroyed by Josiah by 621 (2 Kgs 23:15–16) and thus may reveal that at least some sections of these prophecies against Moab are among Jeremiah's earliest proclamations. Note, however, the discordance between the Moabite god and the Israelite sanctuary. It is possible that this comparison implicitly expresses some late-seventh-century theological reflections at the destruction of Samaria (of 721).

105. עצב is an idol made of clay (Jer 22:28); the term designates worship of other gods (Hos 8:4). גלולים is a *hapax* in Jeremiah, but common in Ezekiel (6:4; 8:10; 14:3).

9.2. Doubt, Argument, and Challenge: "It Is You Who Made All These Things" (Jeremiah 14:22)

Questions quoted within the book of Jeremiah, together with a fragment of a communal lament in 14:19–22, shed light on the use of the (C') approach among nonprophetic voices. Six questions presented as quotations of "the people" (5:19; 8:14; 9:11; 13:22; 14:19–22; 16:10) and one put in the mouth of the nations (22:8) challenge the justice of the punishment meted out and implicitly challenge God's actions as judge, using the interrogative words מדוע ("why?," 13:22), על־מה ("for what?," 9:11; 16:10; 22:8), and תחת מה ("because of what?," 5:19).[106] But the very act of questioning indirectly reflects recognition of God's sole responsibility for the distress currently faced by the people.

The speakers of these questions refer to two features seen in other (C') passages. First, they all recognize God as the sole executor of the destruction; none of them refer to any human enemies. Two of the questions—Jer 5:19 and 22:8—use the verb עשה ("do, execute"; see §9.1.1):

And when they ask, "Because of what <u>did YHWH our God do</u> all these things?" you shall answer them, "Because you forsook Me and served alien gods on your own land, you will have to serve foreigners in a land not your own." (5:19)	והיה כי תאמרו תחת מה <u>עשה</u> <u>יהוה אלהינו</u> לנו את־כל־אלה ואמרת אליהם כאשר עזבתם אותי ותעבדו אלהי נכר בארצכם כן תעבדו זרים בארץ לא לכם.
And when many nations pass by this city and one man asks another, "<u>Why did YHWH do thus</u> to that great city?" (22:8)[107]	ועברו גוים רבים על העיר הזאת ואמרו איש אל־רעהו על מה <u>עשה</u> <u>יהוה ככה</u> לעיר הגדולה הזאת.

106. Barr ("Why? in Biblical Hebrew") argues that Jeremiah uses questions quite often and in diverse functions; see his discussion of למה and מדוע in Jeremiah (pp. 9–10, 12–13). See §10.2.

107. This question, put in the mouth of the nations, also occurs in Deut 29:23; 1 Kgs 9:8–9; 2 Chr 7:21. Long ("Two Question and Answer Schemata," 130–34) argues that the question-and-answer structure reflects a literary convention originated in the Deuteronomistic historiography. Two formal and thematic elements facilitate the claim that Jer 5:19 is not an authentic Jeremian formulation: (1) the measure-for-measure structure; and (2) the three components that designate Jerusalem's sins: abandonment of the covenant, bowing down to other gods, and worshiping them—all invoke the second commandment (Exod 20:3–5; Deut 5:7–9; see Jer 16:11–12). I challenge both arguments. Compare other quotations of the exclamations of foreign passersby or en-

This recognition is also repeated in the final words of the fragmentary communal lament quoted in 14:19–22, which addresses God in the second-person: כי־אתה עשית את־כל־אלה ("for it is You who did all these things").[108]

Jeremiah 16:10 uses דבר על to proclaim that the disaster is God's intention and that the destruction is simply the execution of his plan:[109]

"Why has <u>YHWH decreed upon us</u> all this fearful evil? What is the iniquity and what the sin that we have committed against YHWH our God?"	על־מה דבר יהוה עלינו את כל־ הרעה הגדולה הזאת ומה עוננו ומה חטאתנו אשר חטאנו ליהוה אלהינו.

A second feature, implicit in all of these questions, is the characterization of the "land desolate and empty" in the wake of the total destruction and dislocation. Jeremiah 9:11 presents this issue explicitly:[110]

What man is so wise	מי־האיש החכם
that he understands this?	ויבן את־זאת
To whom has YHWH's mouth spoken,	ואשר דבר פי־יהוה אליו
so that he can explain it?	ויגדה
Why <u>is the land in ruins,</u>	על־מה <u>אבדה הארץ</u>
<u>laid waste like a wilderness,</u>	<u>נצתה כמדבר</u>
<u>with none passing through?</u>	<u>מבלי עבר.</u>

This question is styled by Jeremiah as a challenge to the wise and to the pretentious prophet and thus clearly does not reflect the prophet's own dilemma, but it does reflect an issue under debate.[111] This reference to

---

emies over God's deeds against Jerusalem (Lam 2:15–16; 4:12). This could very well be a convention the prophet (or his followers) used.

108. Compare NJPS: "for only You made all these things," which accentuates God's role as well.

109. דבר with the meaning "think, plan" also occurs in Jer 4:28; 11:17; 18:7–9; 32:24; 51:12; and in quotations in 16:10; 40:2. It also occurs in Ezek 5:13–17; 6:10; 12:25; 17:19–21; it is emphasized in the formula דברתי באה ועשיתי (24:14).

110. אבדה הארץ ("the land has been destroyed") refers to the ecological crisis; compare Exod 10:7: אבדה מצרים ("Egypt is lost") following the plague of hail. The expression conveys the ruin of agricultural life in the land and its transformation into desert; see Jer 9:9; 4:26; §9.1.3 and §9.1.4.

111. The address to a wise man and a prophet is close to Hos 14:10, but there the parallel is between the wise and the prudent (חכם ונבון). For wise men as opponents

the ecological disaster is indeed unique among these questions; more often they either allude to the calamity only in general phrases, such as כל־הרעה הגדולה הזאת ("all this fearful evil," 16:10) or את־כל־אלה ("all these things," 5:19; 14:22), or focus on the fate of the city (22:8).

The thematic common denominators of these questions and the fragmentary communal lament are, first, their reflections on the gravity of the disaster; second, their sense of desperation, stemming from the lack of any explanation of the reasons for the catastrophe; and, finally, their attribution of the distress directly to God. They do not question God's exclusive role in causing the current suffering. Laying the question or the lament totally at God's doorstep, they completely omit any reference to human foes involved in the war against Jerusalem. Thus, doubt arises from that unresolvable conflict stemming from the pious recognition of God's absolute power as omnipotent and present sovereign, who thus must have caused the disaster himself. These questions do not doubt the source of the agony, but await answers supplying the reasons, the excuses, for God's fierce judgment.

Jeremiah 13:20–27 is the last of three independent passages (13:15–17, 18–19, 20–27) brought together to emphasize that Judah's judgment is brought about by its hubris.[112] It is first mentioned within the symbolic action of the linen loincloth buried and ruined in the Perath (13:1–11). "Fame, praise, and splendor" (ולשם ולתהלה ולתפארת, 13:11) could have been the share of the houses of Israel and Judah, yet the people exploited those for pride (גאון יהודה גאון ירושלים, "the overweening pride of Judah and Jerusalem," 13:9). This fault of pride governs 13:15–27. Accordingly, 13:15 exhorts the people to "be not haughty" (אל־תגבהו), but rather to give honor to God (13:16), for *God* has spoken (כי יהוה דבר, 13:15b).[113] Likewise,

---

of Jeremiah, see Jer 8:8–12. Jeremiah's close connections with wisdom literature are apparent in both his poetry and prose and may be due to the shared background of Jeremianic and Deuteronomistic circles; see Weinfeld, *Deuteronomy and the Deuteronomic School*, 244–74.

112. Hubris is a repeated accusation in Jer 13. Hubris is often labeled in the prophets, including Jeremiah and Ezekiel, as the sin of the nations; see PAN Jer 48:29; 49:16; Ezek 28:2–5; 29:3; 30:6, 18.

113. Viewing hubris as the thread that ties these three passages together may also explain the editorial order of this chapter; note the proximity of these prophecies to the symbolic action involving the linen loincloth (13:1–11) and the accusation in 13:9. Compare Lundbom (*Jeremiah 1–20*, 669), who suggests that exile is the common thread for 13:15–27 and that pride and exile probably should be kept together, like sin and

13:18–19 refers to the king and his mother, who are called upon to humble themselves (השפילו שבו) in the face of the catastrophe that reached to their "glorious crowns" (עטרת תפארתכם).

²⁰ Raise your eyes and behold	²⁰ שאו (ק: שאו) עיניכם וראי
those who come from the north:	(ק: וראו) הבאים מצפון
Where are the sheep entrusted to you,	איה העדר נתן־לך
the flock you took pride in?	צאן תפארתך.
²¹ What will you say when they appoint as your heads	²¹ מה־תאמרי כי־יפקד עליך
those among you whom you trained to be tame?	ואת למדת אתם עליך אלפים לראש
Shall not pangs seize you	הלוא חבלים יאחזוך
like a woman in childbirth?	כמו אשת לדה.
²² And when you ask yourself,	²² וכי תאמרי בלבבך
<u>"Why have these things befallen me?"</u>	<u>מדוע קראני אלה</u>
It is because of your great iniquity	ברב עונך
that your skirts are lifted up,	נגלו שוליך
your limbs exposed.	נחמסו עקביך.
²³ Can the Cushite change his skin,	²³ היהפך כושי עורו
or the leopard his spots?	ונמר חברברתיו
Just as much can you do good,	גם־אתם תוכלו להיטיב
who are practiced in doing evil!	למדי הרע.
²⁴ So I will scatter you like straw that flies	²⁴ ואפיצם כקש־עובר
before the desert wind.	לרוח מדבר.
²⁵ This shall be your lot,	²⁵ זה גורלך
your measured portion from Me	מנת־מדיך מאתי
—declares the LORD.	נאם־יהוה
Because you forgot Me	אשר שכחת אותי
and trusted in falsehood,	ותבטחי בשקר.
²⁶ I in turn will lift your skirts over your face	²⁶ וגם־אני חשפתי שוליך על־פניך

judgment, since indeed exile designates humiliation (671). So Qimhi (on 13:4); and compare further Friebel (*Jeremiah's and Ezekiel's Sign-Acts*, 110–11n81), who considers גאון to have a possible positive connotation in this context: "The excellence and majesty which the people would be unable to enjoy because of its removal" (111). This meaning is hard to accept in the context of these three passages in Jer 13; in addition, hubris is specified as Judah's sin in Ezek 7:24 and 16:56.

and your shame shall be seen.	וְנִרְאָה קְלוֹנֵךְ.
[27] I behold your adulteries,	[27] נִאֻפַיִךְ וּמִצְהֲלוֹתַיִךְ
your lustful neighing,	זִמַּת זְנוּתֵךְ
your unbridled depravity, your vile acts	עַל־גְּבָעוֹת בַּשָּׂדֶה
on the hills of the countryside.	רָאִיתִי שִׁקּוּצָיִךְ
Woe to you, O Jerusalem,	אוֹי לָךְ יְרוּשָׁלַיִם
who will not be clean!	לֹא תִטְהֲרִי
How much longer shall it be?	אַחֲרֵי מָתַי עֹד.

Jeremiah 13:20–27 hearkens back to Jerusalem (or Judah) and the entire people, who are called "the flock you took pride in" (צֹאן תִּפְאַרְתֵּךְ, alluding to 13:11).[114] The repeated distress is connected in all three passages to the deportation of the entire flock (13:17, 20), and likewise of the king and his mother (probably referring to Jehoiachin and Nehushta, 13:18–19; see 2 Kgs 24:8, 12).[115]

As an element of the hubristic behavior at issue here, Jer 13:22 quotes a seemingly quite ignorant question: "Why have these things befallen me?" Yet, Jerusalem's question may be the only question that conveys doubt as to the source of the distress. The accusation in 13:22b, מַדּוּעַ קְרָאֻנִי אֵלֶּה, with its passive form קְרָאֻנִי ("have befallen me"), is grammatically neutral, leaving open the possibility that the disaster is perceived as stemming from either divine (C') or a human (A') initiative.

---

114. The feminine imagery for Jerusalem (or Judah) alternates between depictions of the city as a shepherd responsible for the flock given her to guard (13:20); as a caring mother, even in labor (13:21); and as God's adulterous consort (13:25–27); all these images are known from Jer 2–3. In addition, these verses alternate in their grammatical references between the second-person singular feminine and the second-person or third-person plural verbal forms. See, for instance, 13:20, where the Masoretic Text *qere* and *ketiv* present a mixture (*ketiv* שְׂאִי עֵינֵיכֶם וּרְאִי); compare the Septuagint, which introduces a grammatical harmonization and reads: Ἀνάλαβε ὀφθαλμούς σου, Ἰερουσαλημ, καὶ ἰδέ. This reading identifies the object as Jerusalem and accepts the *ketiv* version of the second-person singular feminine verbs referring to יְרוּשָׁלִים. See McKane (*Jeremiah 1–25*, 306–7) for an explanation of the Septuagint that accounts for the rapid grammatical interchanges.

115. This reference to the king and his mother gives rise to several suggestions for identification. Most common is the presumption of an allusion to Jehoiachin and his mother in the deportation of 597 (2 Kgs 24:8–17; Jer 22:26); see, for instance McKane, *Jeremiah 1–25*, 303–5; and Hoffman, *Jeremiah 1–25*, 339, 342. See Carroll (*Jeremiah*, 301–2) for other suggestions (from Jehoiakim to Zedekiah), and his general perspective that due to the lack of clearer details, the prophecy may be applied to different occasions.

The prophetic rebuke elaborates on the reasons why and thus sets out the city's or the people's responsibility for their own distress (13:21, 23, 25b). The heart of the proclamation, however, is the statement of judgment in 13:24–26, particularly its explanation in 13:25a that clarifies the agent of distress: זה גורלך מנת־מדיך מאתי נאם־יהוה ("this shall be your lot, your measured portion from Me—declares the LORD"). The prophetic response (13:22b–26) leaves no doubt as to the agent of judgment. Jeremiah accentuates grammatically that the historical events of deportation are "from Me." He uses the object pronoun (מאתי), along with a sequence of first-person active verbs. ואפיצם ("I will disperse them," 13:24) refers to the people's deportation; earlier references to captivity and exile in this passage (13:17, 19, 20) use only passive forms. Returning to the adultery imagery, the prophet uses another first-person active construction: וגם־אני חשפתי שוליך על־פניך ("I in turn will lift your skirts over your face," 13:26). It is God himself who will bring public disgrace upon his people and his city, in contradistinction to the glory, the pride, and the hubris repeatedly stressed in 13:15, 18, 20.

9.3. FORMS OF PROTEST (LAMENTATIONS 1; JEREMIAH 5:12–14)

9.3.1. *God as the Enemy in Lamentations 1*

Four of the laments in Lamentations use the (C′) conception, but they differ in the weight given to this explanation of the disaster.

Lamentations 2 is by far the most elaborated communal lament, presenting God as warrior and as *the* enemy of his own people.[116] In both explicit imagery (2:4–5) and a long list of verbal phrases drawn from the semantic field of war and presented in the third- and second-person, God is portrayed as the executor of the destruction: a fierce warrior who does not respect mercy (2:2a, 17b, 21c) and who has worked his plans out (2:8, 17). Warlike actions perpetrated by human enemies are mentioned only three times in this entire chapter (2:3b, 7b, 17c); the human enemies are portrayed as forces that benefitted from God's summoning them, having empowered them, or simply having allowed them to enjoy the results of his deeds (2:16). The peak of the expressions of agony and protest in Lam 2

---

116. The phrase איבי כלם at the close of this lament may be another reference to God as the ultimate foe (see §1.2.2).

is in its closing verses, 2:20–22, where instead of pleas for salvation, the poet addresses God with further cries against God's horrific deeds. The stress in this lament is on the role of God as a warrior and foe, omnipotent indeed, but clearly not compassionate; although this is only implicit, the lament questions the workings of divine justice. Yet God is the only one to be addressed in prayer and to be constantly confronted with the great suffering he himself caused (2:19–20).

The closing verses of Lam 1 present a significantly different perspective in terms of theodical discourse.[117] The lament closes with the following recognition:

[20] See, O YHWH, the distress I am in!	²⁰ראה יהוה כי־צר־לי
My heart is in anguish,	מעי חמרמרו
I know how wrong <u>I was to disobey.</u>	נהפך לבי בקרבי <u>כי מרו מריתי</u>
Outside the sword deals death;	מחוץ שכלה־חרב
indoors, the plague.	בבית כמות.
[21] When they heard how I was sighing,	²¹שמעו כי נאנחה אני
there was none to comfort me;	אין מנחם לי
all my foes heard of my plight and exulted.	כל איבי שמעו רעתי ששו
<u>For it is Your doing:</u>	<u>כי אתה עשית</u>
<u>You have brought on the day that You threatened.</u>	<u>הבאת יום־קראת</u>
Oh, let them become like me!	ויהיו כמוני.
[22] Let all their wrongdoing come before You,	²²תבא כל־רעתם לפניך
<u>and deal with them</u>	<u>ועולל למו</u>
<u>as You have dealt with me</u>	<u>כאשר עוללת לי</u>
<u>for all my transgressions;</u>	<u>על כל־פשעי</u>
for my sighs are many,	כי־רבות אנחתי
and my heart is sick.	ולבי דוי.

Lamentations 1:20–22 makes a further statement of the distress (1:20–21) and a plea for revenge upon the human enemies (1:21cb–22),[118] using two

---

117. Other (C') passages may be seen in Lam 3:1-16; 4:16, 22.

118. The versions disagree about the parsing of 1:21c. The Masoretic Text's הבאת יום־יום־קראת suggests a further complaint about the distress, so that the call for revenge starts only in ויהיו כמוני (1:21cβ). Instead of הבאת, the Peshitta reads the Syriac imperative איתא, which signals the beginning of the pleas for revenge in 1:21c; this is accepted by Westermann (*Lamentations*, 138), who suggests that the Hebrew text

intriguing elements. First, concerning the roles given to the enemies and those to God on the matter of their involvement in the destruction—the enemies *hear* what God has *done* (1:21b). In distinction from earlier verses in this lament (1:2c, 3c, 5a, 7c, 10a–c, 16c, 17a, 19a), the closing segment uses second-person verbs to accentuate that *God* is the one who executes the destruction, in accordance with his earlier proclamations (אתה עשית הבאת יום־קראת). The human enemies are not named as the actual warriors or even as active participants in causing the distress. The plea for salvation in this lament is, therefore, the request that God do to the enemies just what he has done to Jerusalem, to his own people (ועולל למו כאשר עוללת לי).[119]

Second, throughout the lament and particularly in these final verses, Lam 1 features the confession of sins (1:5b, 8a, 9a, 14a, 18, 20 [כי מרו מריתי], 22 [על כל־פשעי]). Thus, the poet justifies God's judgments against Jerusalem by tying them to the behavior of the people.[120]

This feature provides an appropriate point of comparison between Lam 1 and Ps 79:8–9. The latter is a typical protest using the (A' → C) framework. Psalm 79:1–4 describes the distress caused by the human enemy's troops, who destroy God's temple and city and slaughter its inhabitants. God is not involved in causing this horrendous distress; it is entirely the doing of the human enemy. Rather, God is addressed with pleas for salvation and revenge in its aftermath (79:6, 10–13). The confession of sins in this psalm is offered in the hope that it will hasten the divine intervention. While both compositions contain confessions of sins, they differ in their perspectives on the role given to God. Lamentations 1 gives pride of place to the (B') conception, describing God's summons of human enemies against the sinful city (1:5, 7, 9, 10, 13–15, 17). In the final plea for salvation, however (and even while confessing the peoples' sins; 1:20b), the author of this lament employs both the (C') conception and its flip side—God the warrior-enemy could still act as savior, if his actions are aimed at the human enemy of his city and people (1:21c, 22a–b). This jumble of themes may be sorted out with reference to Green's "trilemma of theodicy" (see §1.1.1 and fig. 9.2).

---

should be corrected. But Albrektson (*Text and Theology*, 84) aptly doubts the possibility that יום־קראת could be addressed to the foreign nations. I therefore prefer to see the transition from the complaint to the final pleas for salvation only in 1:21cβ.

119. Pleas for revenge against the enemy are frequent in both individual (see Ps 6:11) and communal (79:12; 83:14–15) laments. See Westermann, *Lamentations*, 84.

120. This is one remarkable difference between Lam 1 and Lam 2, which lacks this component of confession of sins. Lam 2:14 does not play this role; see §1.2.2 and §11.2.3.

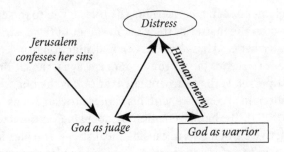

Fig. 9.2. Lamentations 1 and the trilemma of theodicy

The poet recognizes that God is sovereign and warrior—it is God who causes the present distress, and it is he whom the poet addresses in pleas for salvation, for similar measures to be this time taken against the human enemies of Jerusalem. The poet further recognizes God to be a just judge; the people/the city indeed sinned gravely and deserve punishment. These two qualities of God are piously acknowledged, even as the poet confesses the people's sins. In negotiating the three poles of the triangle, the poet of Lam 1 chooses to emphasize the people's suffering. Since God's qualities are acknowledged as given, the only pole that could be more freely manipulated is the reality of the people's suffering, in hope that the description of this suffering will cause God to wake up to the needs of his people.[121] The accentuation throughout this lament on the severe distress and suffering constitutes a protest against the delayed salvation. Although, in comparison to Lam 2, this first lament seems quite subtle, it does not seem to have solved the trilemma of theodicy.

9.3.2. Denial, "It Is Not He!" (Jeremiah 5:12–14)

Jeremiah 5:12–14 is the only passage where, within a quotation, God's role in the predicted war is categorically denied; the speakers actually refute the entire threat of war:

[12] They have been false to YHWH and said:	כחשו ביהוה ויאמרו[12]
"It is not He!	לא־הוא

---

121. For distress as a motivation for the communal laments in general, see Dobbs-Allsopp, *Lamentations*, 41–44. Dobbs-Allsopp also presents the comparative materials on the emphasis given to the destruction in its multifaceted effects; see *Weep, O Daughter of Zion*, 66–72. This is clearly accentuated in Lam 1; see Berlin, *Lamentations*, 47–48.

No trouble shall come upon us,	ולא־תבוא עלינו רעה
we shall not see sword or famine.	וחרב ורעב לוא נראה.
[13] The prophets shall prove mere wind	[13] והנביאים יהיו לרוח
for the Word is not in them;	והדבר אין בהם
thus-and-thus shall be done to them!"	כה יעשה להם.
[14] Assuredly, thus said YHWH, the God of Hosts:	[14] לכן כה־אמר יהוה אלהי צבאות
because they said that,	יען דברכם את־הדבר הזה
I am putting My words into your mouth as fire,	הנני נתן דברי בפיך לאש
and this people shall be firewood, which it will consume.	והעם הזה עצים ואכלתם.

The meaning of the two first words of this quotation, that is, the identity of הוא (is it God or an impersonal pronoun for "the Word"?), and likewise the boundaries of the quotation (does it stop at 5:12 or also include 5:13a or 5:13b?), are already under debate by the versions and, following them, between interpreters. The solutions to both literary difficulties are dependent on the contents one finds in this quotation.

לא־הוא is understood differently by the Masoretic Text and Septuagint.[122] In the Masoretic Text, following the introductory designation of the quotation as כחשו ביהוה ("they have denied YHWH"), God is the agent implied by the third-person pronoun.[123] Robert Carroll aptly presents לא־הוא as the obvious opposite of אני הוא (Deut 32:39; Isa 43:10, 13).[124] The negation לא־הוא would thus signify negation of God's involvement in the human sphere or, as some argue, the negation of his very existence.[125] The Targum seems to go along with this alternative, with its interpretive translation: לא מן קדמוהי אתיא עלנא טבתא ואף לא תיתי עלנא בשתא ("not from before Him, do good things come upon us. Moreover, evil will

---

122. This distinction is highlighted by Sutcliffe, "Note on לא הוא."

123. כחש ביהוה expresses "denial or rejection of Yahweh" (Isa 30:9; Prov 30:9); see Schunck, "כָּחַשׁ *kāḥaš*," 134; Holladay, *Jeremiah*, 1.186–87; and compare NJPS: "They have been false to the Lord."

124. Carroll, *Jeremiah*, 182.

125. A similar line of denying the very existence of God (or "just" his presence and involvement) is found in Pss 10:4; 14:1; 53:2, put in the mouth of the "wicked" or "benighted." In reference to אמר נבל בלבו אין אלהים (53:2), Dahood (*Psalms 1–50*, 81–82; and *Psalms 51–100*, 19) prefers the translation "God is not present" to "there is no God." What seems clear is that the people "are living as if he does not matter" (Holladay, *Jeremiah*, 1.186).

not come upon us"), which is also suggested to stand behind Zeph 1:12: לא־ייטיב יהוה ולא ירע ("YHWH will do nothing, good or bad").[126] The Septuagint, however, translates לא־הוא in Jer 5:12 as οὐκ ἔστιν ταῦτα ("that is not so"), which denies the words of God and clearly does not "touch" God himself. It seems that the Septuagint here represents an attempt to cope with the theological difficulty raised by the Masoretic Text.[127]

The boundaries of the quotation are conceived according to two interpretive perspectives.[128] One ends the quotation at Jer 5:12, where 5:13 is either God's or the prophet's response against them; literarily this is similar to 14:15 and to the distinctions between prophets in 23:25–29.[129] The other suggestion extends the quotation through 5:13a; this characterizes the denigrated prophets as "true" prophets of God, just like Jeremiah himself, with their judgment in 5:13b.[130]

For three thematic reasons, this quotation includes all of 5:12–13:

a. The quotation in those two verses is structured against God (כחשו ביהוה) and is actually targeted at three objects of address: the power of God, his words, and his messengers. Thus 5:13 refers to the "true" prophets, and כה יעשה להם expresses a threat of judgment against them (calling "true" prophets to judgment is recorded in Jer 26).

126. See Rashi. Qimhi (on Jer 5:12) suggests that in לא־הוא the speakers deny divine providence and oversight, as also divine judgment, as threatened by his (true) prophets (and so refers to other passages such as Jer 12:4; Ezek 8:12; Ps 94:7); but then he interprets Jer 5:13 (with the Targum and Rashi) as addressed at the false prophets proclaiming their judgment. See Berlin, *Zephaniah*, 88.

127. The third-person pronoun הוא as designating the word of God occurs in 2 Kgs 15:12. This line of interpretation for our verse is accepted by Duhm, *Jeremia*, 60; and preferred by Sutcliffe, "Note on לא הוא," 290. This is also reflected in the Septuagint and is followed by NJPS: "It is not so!"

128. Duhm (*Jeremia*, 60) takes the opening words לא־הוא out of the quotation as well, thus according to him the quotation opens with ולא־תבוא. This is improbable from the standpoint of both form and content. In form, ויאמרו regularly introduces direct speech (e.g., Jer 4:5; 5:19).

129. The Aramaic Targum complements the prophets in 23:13 with the attribute ונבי שקרא (i.e., "false prophets"), making their words false prophecies; this is followed by Rashi and Qimhi; as also Holladay, *Jeremiah*, 1.187. Carroll (*Jeremiah*, 182) prefers the solution that sees 23:13 as the prophet's reaction.

130. So Duhm (*Jeremia*, 60–61), who also suggests that the words כה יעשה להם should be transposed to 5:14, after צבאות, as proper to the introduction of the judgment pronouncement. Thus also McKane, *Jeremiah 1–25*, 121. The Septuagint's Codex Alexandrinus does not have these words at all.

b. Jeremiah's extant pronouncements against the peace prophets do not feature a parallel to והנביאים יהיו לרוח ("the prophets shall prove mere wind"). Jeremiah uses terms like שקר ("false," 23:14, 26) or הבל ("vain," 23:16) in reference to their words; he prophesies annihilation against them (14:15), but this phrasing in 12:13 is clearly unique.[131]

c. The struggle over legitimacy between the prophets is the background to this saying. Jeremiah 5:12–13 not only refutes the prophetic words (as in 14:13–15), but furthermore it touches upon the sender (God) and through him upon the messengers (the prophets), who are threatened to be harmed.

In light of all these factors, the quotation represents words of the people (who would then be the hidden subject behind כחשו).[132] This suggestion may be established on the basis of 5:14, which pronounces judgment upon the entire people and not upon the peace prophets alone.[133] Moreover, 5:14 diametrically opposes to these words of denial, in terms of all three topics addressed in the quotation (and thus this verse constitutes a fourth argument for extending the borders of the quotation to 5:12–13). In the quoted passage, the speakers take a stand in the struggle between the peace prophets and Jeremiah (or possibly other "true" prophets);[134] their provocative words are spoken against God himself, against his threatening words as conveyed by the prophets, and against his messengers themselves. Jeremiah 5:14 puts God's words directly in the prophet's mouth (thus le-

131. והדבר אין בהם is read differently by the Masoretic Text and the Septuagint. The Septuagint translates καὶ λόγος κυρίου οὐχ ὑπῆρχεν, which clarifies the reading as דבר ("word of God"). The difference resides on the similarity between the homograph nouns: דִּבֵּר ("speech") and the common noun דָּבָר ("word").

132. Compare Lundbom (*Jeremiah 1–20*, 389), among others, who considers the peace prophets to be the antecedent.

133. Compare the emphasis on punishing the prophets in particular, but within the general judgment (Jer 14:15–16), and afflicting the prophets specifically (23:30–32).

134. והנביאים יהיו לרוח, referring to the "true" prophets, is exceptional (and still preferable). It is of great interest that within this struggle over legitimacy between prophets, the true prophets never present themselves (nor are they presented by their tradents) as part of a contemporary group. This is one of those points where the silence between Jeremiah and Ezekiel could have been broken; see Rom-Shiloni, "Ezekiel and Jeremiah." Jer 28:7–9 is the only place where Jeremiah explicitly locates himself in a long (diachronic) tradition of prophets and thus isolates that single prophet who prophesies "shalom"; other such examples would be expressions of continuity with Samuel and mostly with Moses (15:1; also 1:4–10).

gitimizing him as messenger); these fiery words will consume the entire people—in response to לֹא־הוּא ("not he!"); and it is God the sole warrior who will act against his people (C'), not even through human enemies.[135]

From this interpretive standpoint, this quotation should represent proclamations of the people influenced by peace prophets, and לֹא־הוּא should deny any role to God in causing the distress.[136] Thus, this is a direct refutation of Jeremiah's repeated threats that God is about to either summon the Babylonians against Judah (B') or fight his people without human instruments (C'). But while the peace prophets consistently attributed the distress to human enemies (A') in expectation of divine salvation (C), the words quoted here clearly do not expect such favorable intervention. The quoted words seem to reflect a complete disregard of the deteriorating political situation, and in their ignorance of the atrocities ahead, they leave God out of the events entirely.[137]

9.4. Summary: Conceptions of God as Warrior and Their Implications for Theodical Discourse

The differing depictions of the roles of God and human beings in war, in times of victory and defeat, led me to develop a model to frame the multifaceted theological deliberation taking place in sixth-century Judah—among historiographers, prophets, poets, and members of "the people," whether designated by name, like kings and their officials, or anonymous.

---

135. See McKane (*Jeremiah 1–25*, 122), who considers 5:14 to be a response to "an allegation that he lacked the power to enforce his judgments"; according to Lundbom (*Jeremiah 1–20*, 389), this is a response to a denial of "Yahweh's activity." In this respect Jer 5:12 differs from Mic 3:11 and presents a more widely drawn denial of divine action.

136. This would than stand against the interpretive option that these words denote the denial of God's existence; see note 125, above.

137. There are at least two explanations for leaving God out of the events: (a) to argue for the sovereignty of other gods (as otherwise only in Jer 44:15–19) or (b) to attest to a perspective that considers war to be solely a human prerogative (implied in the hope for human assistance in 37:7). In neither case is God portrayed as leading historical events. Zeph 1:12 may substantiate the first alternative: (1) the judgment prophecy in 1:4–6 recalls worshipers of other gods; (2) Zephaniah's refutation (1:13–18) accentuates the role of God in bringing the distress in the context of "the day of YHWH." Von Rad (*Old Testament Theology*, 2.263–64) finds in 1:12 expression of the deep crisis over questions such as whether YHWH "was still in control of the events," of his power, his plan, etc., which are typical of the Judean society in both Judah and in exile during the sixth century. Von Rad argues that this mode of the era appears in the books of Jeremiah, Ezekiel, Zephaniah, and Second Isaiah.

Three major theological conceptions of God's role in the defeat—(A' → C), (B'), (C')—are used in different ways by these diverse speakers to express justification of God, doubt, and protest (and even in one case, denial). This complicated presentation requires some conclusions.

a.   Distribution among speakers

All three approaches to the role of God and human beings in defeat appear to be used by both prophets and poets, shaped according to their rhetorical needs. Some contemporaries use only a single conceptual framework. Thus the historiographers of 2 Kings use only the (B') conception; whereas quotations in the book of Jeremiah avoid this conception in their addresses to God and make use of the two conceptions (A' → C) and (C'); the peace prophets use only the (A' → C) framework and not any of the others.[138]

Beyond these general tendencies, any statistical data about the different approaches is highly problematic; this is mostly due to the limited information we have of other voices, which appear only within short quotations that serve particular rhetorical functions within the arguments of their quoting authors. Hence, there is no way (and no pretension) to take this picture of distribution at face value, as a valid quantitative evidence for the precise history of thought in the early six century. Rather, as in so many other aspects of Hebrew Bible literature, we have a selected corpus of theological reflections, and we must at least presume that our information is incomplete. Nevertheless, in qualitative terms, that is, from the standpoint of theological conceptions and themes, this discussion may allow us to draw several lessons from the theological deliberations we do have, to discern the shape of the theodical discourse developed between them.

b.   Theological deliberations

The three conceptions on the roles of God and human in war—(A' → C), (B'), (C')—seem well established in the literary sources we have. They share recognizable characteristics, that all speakers are aware of and use "properly." Hence, all speakers are equal participants in the theological discourse in terms of their acquaintance with national and religious traditions and beliefs. They all share the concept of God as king and use the highly anthropomorphic metaphors of God as a human king who fights in a humanlike war, either as savior or as foe. Furthermore, within the (A' → C)

---

138. For the specific data, see Rom-Shiloni, *God in Times of Destruction*, 262–63.

framework, poets recall creation-combat traditions, which supply another set of metaphors for the portrayal of God as warrior (Pss 74, 77), with Ps 89 using the (B') conception.

c.   Polemics

The theological deliberation is cast in highly polemical terms. The (B') conception moderates the synergism between God and human beings in events of defeat and destruction and is thus used by almost all speakers (except for quotations in prophetic passages) to express the clear involvement of God in the events. This conception functions within historiographic and prophetic *justifications* of God, as well as in painful poetic protests against his deeds (Ps 44). Such protests initiate an implicit polemic with prophetic voices. The two other conceptions each seem to serve the rhetorical and conceptual needs of distinct constituencies, and thus appear as polemicizing against one another (as in Jer 21:1–7). The (A' → C) framework used by the peace prophets, who expect immediate salvation, is no less than a red flag to Jeremiah and Ezekiel, who refute each quoted peace prophecy with fierce (B') and (C') pronouncements. The (C') conception lies at the base of the polemic between Jeremiah and Ezekiel concerning the fate of the divided people in the aftermath of the exiles and destruction: the aspect of total annihilation of land and people comes to serve both Ezekiel and the Babylonian-exilic editors of Jeremiah as a basis for denying the existence of a remnant Judean community in Jerusalem and Judah following the 597 exile.[139]

d.   Theodical discourse

Each of these three conceptions may be used to express justification, doubt, and protest. The three theological perspectives draw on the same shared theological conceptions of God as king and sovereign, and they take their point of departure from his role as omnipotent warrior. Within this framework, God is expected to save his people in times of need—although he may also turn out to be his people's fiercest enemy. The people's distress is thus theologically addressed by making use of one of these two oppositional images of savior or foe.

Doubt and protest arise from a clearly pious point of view within the

---

139. The diverse conceptions and implicit polemics between Jeremiah and Ezekiel as part of the internal struggle between those who remain in Judah and the Babylonian exiles are the focus of my *Exclusive Inclusivity*.

theological crisis. In asking questions of doubt or raising laments of protest, the speakers express recognition of God's omnipotence and omniscience in his roles as both warrior and judge. Hence, there is no difference between the speakers in their religious piety (be they historiographers, prophets, poets, or the people). Expressions of doubt and protest, just like expressions of justification, are proclaimed by pious members of the Judean communities who seek a theological explanation for the inexplicable.

e.   Theodical motivation

Having seen a large number of texts as representatives of the three theological perspectives of justification, doubt, and protest, it is clear that all speakers also share the motivation to find a theological explanation for the role of God in the destruction. They all very much want to understand and justify God in his actions against his own people; and therefore, the discourse in which they participate is by definition theodical. They all recognize both God's power and his active presence during the destruction (most of the speakers would agree that God did not leave or abandon his land and people); they differ on the ways to explain his presence, his actions, his powers; and they differ in their capability to indeed find a reconciling solution.

Using Green's trilemma of theodicy seems a helpful way to map the relationships between these different theological expressions. While all the different voices use (to different extents) the three conceptions of divine and human roles in war—(A' → C), (B'), (C')—the following examples show that each of these voices treat somewhat differently the three poles of the trilemma (even when using the same conception).

1.   The (A' → C) conception: God is asked to dispel the human enemy.

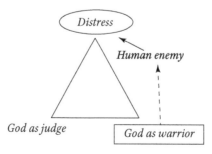

Fig. 9.3. Jeremiah 21:2—official plea for salvation

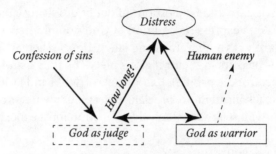

Fig. 9.4. Psalm 79—protest out of confession

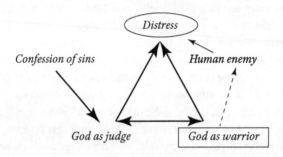

Fig. 9.5. Jeremiah 14:7–9—doubts

In three texts—Jer 21:2; Ps 79; and Jer 14:7–9—emphasis is laid on the people's current suffering (explicit in Jer 21:2 and Ps 79:1–4); this is aimed at awakening God, the omnipotent warrior, to save his people. Both the king's officials (Jer 21:2) and the psalmist (Ps 79:5) recognize God's ability and powers as a warrior and plead for his salvation (illustrated in the broken arrows in figs. 9.3, 9.4, and 9.5). The two differ, however, in Ps 79 including a confession of sins (79:8, 9b), whereas the officials do not see that as a necessary step in their approach to God through the prophet. Furthermore, 79:5–13 challenges the role of God as judge, asking how long would his anger sustain (79:5)? The poet expects that the people's confessions of sins and proclamations of piety will assuredly result in God's involvement on their behalf (79:8, 9b, 13); and if not for his people's sake, God should save them for his own name (79:9–10). In contrast to these two passages, Jer 14:7–9 minimizes the role of the human foe. The political-military distress is only implicit, gathered from the questions of doubt addressed directly to God. The questions in this fragmentary communal lament challenge the aspect of God as warrior-savior, questioning God's presence and powers. Nevertheless, this passage also introduces a confession of sins (14:7b) and expresses confident loyalty to God, as a basis for asking for his help (14:9b).

2.   The (B') conception: God summons the human enemy.

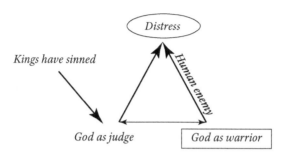

Fig. 9.6. 2 Kings 24:2–3, 20—justification

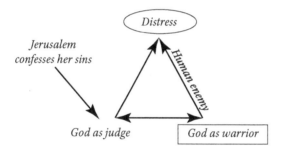

Fig. 9.7. Lamentations 1—torn between justification and protest

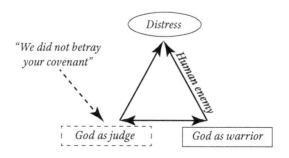

Fig. 9.8. Psalm 44—protest

Three texts—2 Kgs 24:2–3, 20; Lam 1; and Ps 44—illustrating the (B') conception recognize that the distress is caused by God, who summons the human enemies against Jerusalem and Judah, against his people.

Second Kings 24:2–3, 20 justifies God for bringing on the enemy by placing responsibility for the catastrophe on the people, because of their kings' religious disobedience (see fig. 9.6). Lamentations 1 confesses the people's sins and presents the distress as comprising justified measures taken by God (1:5, 8, 17, 18; see fig. 9.7). Yet at the same time, the poet pleads to God to attend to the city's distress (1:9c, 11c) and even protests against the grave suffering God causes (1:12–16). The poet seems to be torn between justification and protest. Psalm 44 asserts the people's loyal *obedience* to God (44:18–23) and thus (implicitly) protests against God as judge (see fig. 9.8). The psalmist recognizes God as his king even in present circumstances (44:5–9); he praises God for his past assistance as warrior, before he turns to his fierce protest against God's seeming desertion of the people and enumerates God's actions against his obedient people (44:10–17, 20, 23).

3. The (C') conception: God himself is the agent of his people's destruction.

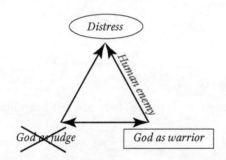

Fig. 9.9. Jeremiah 21:3–7—justification

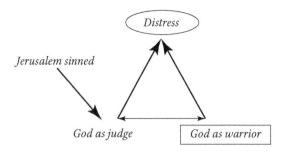

Fig. 9.10. Ezekiel 5—justification

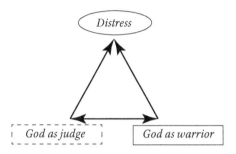

Fig. 9.11. Lamentations 2—protest

Prophetic proclamations use the (C') conception in two different ways. Both take for granted God's prerogative to act entirely from his purview as warrior and judge and disregard any notion that God must be benevolent or compassionate, thus allowing for the (unthinkable) possibility that God should be seen as the sole foe of his own people. There are difficulties in choosing this conception to justify God's role in his people's destruction and in giving prominence to this conception within Jeremiah and Ezekiel. Jeremiah 21:3–7, taking one approach (see fig. 9.9), emphasizes that the cause of the turmoil is actually God himself and not the Babylonian king, as claimed by the officials. The prophecy focuses on the qualities of God as warrior (omnipotent and lord of history) and on the prospect of total annihilation, and it completely ignores the sphere of divine justice and mercy. Ezekiel 5, on the other hand, chooses a much more common approach (see fig. 9.10), explaining the distress as the result of deserved judgment—Jerusalem sinned and must be punished; her current troubles not only demonstrate the quality and prerogatives of God as warrior, but also the appropriate divine response from the criterion of justice. For the prophets, this conception clearly represents the lesser of two evils. They abandon the notion of divine compassion altogether, to emphasize the presence and the omnipotent powers of the divine warrior addressed at his own people.

The (C') conception is also used in complaints, where it serves to accentuate the extent of the distress. Lamentations 1:21–22 confesses the people's sins, at the same time acknowledging God's prerogatives as sovereign, warrior, and judge, but mounting complaints and protest against the delay of deliverance. Much fiercer is the protest of Lam 2, which emphasizes God's lack of compassion in his role as warrior, as the enemy of his people (see fig. 9.11). But the lament neither confesses sins nor presents God as righteous; only implicitly does it express its protest over what seems to be injustice.

The ambiguous, somewhat trivial, theological explanation that lays responsibility for the catastrophe entirely on the people deserves a note. In historiographical or prophetic accusations, and likewise in self-confessional sayings in communal laments, this line of argumentation leaves both divine qualities in power and poses both confession and the human distress itself as remedies for effecting reconciliation with God. But this line of explanation functions differently in different contexts. In contexts of justification—conceptions (B') or (C')—the distress is the result of divine judgment in retaliation for the people's sins of disloyalty. The catastrophe exemplifies God's action as both warrior and judge and is not a result of the human enemy's initiative. In texts of doubt and protest, confession of sins takes the major role, in the hope to arouse God to act as warrior and judge on behalf of his people, whose distress is now caused by the human foe, conception (A').

An interesting dimension is added to the trilemma of theodicy in expressions of doubt and protest where confession of sins may be lacking and/or where clear statements of loyalty and devotion are proclaimed (e.g., Pss 44:18–23; 74:12). In these contexts, blaming the people does not seem to be an effective strategy for configuring rupture and reconciliation. Rather, the psalmists are left with the need to revisit God's own qualities and roles to resolve the trilemma; it is at these points that questions arise concerning God's functions as warrior (Jer 14:7–9) or as judge (implicitly in Ps 44:18–23; Lam 2).

In all these different cases, it is the perception of the people's position in relation to God and God's commands—devotion or disloyalty, obedience or its opposite—that provides the key to the ways the various speakers negotiate the trilemma of theodicy in the crisis of the destruction. The most important difference between the justifying voices and those that express doubt or protest is that the former find ways to supply theological explanations and avenues of reconciliation, whereas the passages that presume the people's loyalty and thus express doubt and protest are marked by an embarrassing lack of explanations for God's roles in his people's destruction, and they therefore lack avenues of reconciliation.

10

God as Judge and Divine Justice

Within sixth-century theodical discourse, the conceptions of divine justice, of God as good and compassionate, complement the conceptions of God as Lord of history, omnipotent and omniscient. Together they constitute the basic beliefs of ethical monotheism (discussed in §§ 1.1, 1.3, 9.4). The seeming clash between the expected divine justice, the role of God as warrior, and the perceived reality of human suffering within sources discussed here gives rise to diverse theological reflections and reveals explicit and implicit theological struggles among different voices.

This chapter delves more deeply into the ways in which the workings of divine justice are perceived by different speakers, looking at the shared metaphor of God as judge and laying down the fairly wide spectrum of debatable conceptions.

10.1. God as Judge: The Metaphor

Judge is one of the major roles attributed to God within the metaphorical field of divine kingship.[1] God's establishment on his royal throne is the symbol of his sovereignty,[2] and in the manner of a human king, God acts

---

1. Tsevat, "God and the Gods in Assembly," 127; and Brettler, *God Is King*, 109–16. In certain passages, the dynamic involvement of God in the metaphorical trial context is created by verbs like נצב and עמד (Ps 82:1, 8; Isa 3:13). From a comparative perspective, see Kang (*Divine War*, 108), who demonstrates that in Hittite and Mesopotamian sources war is configured as a divine judgment for violation of international treaties; thus, Kang argues that the gods are perceived as both warriors and judges.

2. This can be seen in the psalms that reflect the destruction and exiles (9:5, 8, 17;

as supreme judge.[3] Accordingly, God is called to decide questions of right and wrong in interpersonal relationships and likewise in international conflicts among nations;[4] in both spheres of human society, God is depicted as protector of the underprivileged, the weak, and the poor.[5] God thus acts as judge of the individual against his accuser(s), as demanding justice in the national sphere for his people, and as universal judge who calls all nations to judgment.[6]

In court, God may act in one of two opposing ways: he may activate his quality of harsh judgment (מידת הדין), or he may show pity and benevolence (מידת הרחמים). Both spheres activate the same vocabulary. Among the shared words and phrases used are פקד, נקם, דן דין, שילם גמול, גמל, שפט, רב ריב, and עשה משפט. Among the nouns, only משפט serves both contexts (Jer 9:23; 10:24; 12:1; 30:11; 46:28); צדקה, חסד, and רחמים ap-

---

89:15; 103:6, 19), as also in other psalms outside those discussed in this study (97:2; 98:9; 99:4).

3. The transferal into the divine realm of the portrait of the human king as judge and the connections between the human and divine judge are shared by different cultures in the ancient Near East (and beyond). See Holtz ("Praying as a Plaintiff") for linguistic parallels between Akkadian prayers and Neo-Babylonian legal procedures; such "courtroom language" is also known from prayers within the Hebrew Bible. In *Neo-Babylonian Court Procedure*, Holtz presents legal and administrative texts coming from private and temple archives of the seventh to fifth centuries, in which court procedures or litigation proceedings may be seen in their everyday contexts.

4. שפט with the meaning "decide controversy, discriminate betw[een] persons, in civil, political, domestic and religious questions" (Brown, Driver, and Briggs, *Hebrew and English Lexicon*, 1047) appears in requests for divine judgment in favor of one of the two sides in a conflict, as between Sarai and Abram (Gen 16:5) or between Jacob and Laban (31:53); as also in individual laments (Pss 7:9; 9:5, 9; 10:18; 17:2; 26:1; 35:24; 119:84; 143:2), hymns (111:7; 146:7; 149:9), and psalms of God as king (96:13; 98:9). For passing judgment on behalf of a person as a role of the human king, see 2 Sam 15:4; the same role is in the background of the cases brought to David, Solomon, and the "anonymous" kings of Israel (2 Sam 14:1–20; 1 Kgs 3:16–27; 2 Kgs 6:24–31).

5. See Deut 10:17–18; Pss 103:6; 146:7–9; and this is also the theme of Ps 82. The role of the human king as defender of the weak repeats in royal psalms (45:5; 72:1–2; 101; 122:5) and Prov 31:9. Dereliction of this duty is counted among the sins of the kings of Jerusalem (Jer 21:12; 22:3, 15–16; Ezek 34). Justice and protection for the poor is one of the things expected of the future king (Isa 9:6; 16:5; Jer 23:6).

6. In psalms of God as king: Pss 67:5; 82:1; 96:10–12; in prophecy: Isa 3:13; 26:9; 41:1; Jer 25:31; and in eschatology (Isa 2:4; Mic 4:3). The divine role of bringing about and safeguarding justice among nations served the Assyrian kings as one of their ideological arguments for waging war; see Oded, *War, Peace, and Empire*, 101–20.

pear only in the benevolent sphere.[7] In most cases, these phrases designate the divine protection given to the individual or to the people in the face of their enemy or enemies; only the people as a whole, however, seem to be the target of divine judgment. דן (דין) illustrates this dual function; it labels God's salvation of his people from enemies (Deut 32:36; Ps 135:14) or his saving of orphans and widows (68:6). When דן (דין) refers to God's actions *against* human beings, its object is almost always foreign peoples, that is, those considered enemies of God's people (Gen 15:14; Isa 3:13; Ps 9:9–10). Much less frequently does the verb דין denote God's deeds *against* his own people. This use, particularly in reference to Judah's destruction, is found only in Jeremiah (30:13).[8]

Another such root is שפט, which occurs as a verb with God as agent only twice in Jeremiah. Both instances are in the *niphal*. In one, judgment is pronounced upon Jerusalem (2:35), and in the other, upon all nations/human beings (25:31). The noun משפט (or plural משפטים) denotes judgment (1:16; 4:12; PAN 48:21, 47; 49:12); it portrays a legal procedure, where God pronounces the sentence and where the destruction is its execution.[9]

---

7. חסד ורחמים occur as a pair in Jer 16:5; and an opposition between עשה חסד and משלם עון (32:18) configures the two poles of judgment. Ezekiel uses neither חסד nor רחמים, and משפטים denotes divine judgment rendered against the people (Ezek 5:8; 39:21). See chap. 12.

8. I give two additional examples. גמל occurs ten times in the Hebrew Bible in reference to a divine deed on behalf of (Isa 63:7) or against (Pss 18:21 [directed at the individual]; 103:10) God's people. On the other hand, שילם גמול (PAN Jer 51:6, 56; Ps 137:8) denotes God's justified acts of war against Babylon (similarly Isa 59:18; 66:6; Joel 4:4; the only positive use of שילם גמול occurs in Prov 19:17, referring to the individual). נקם portrays God as executing the judicial ruling he handed down. Divine revenge against God's own people is cast in particularly harsh language (Lev 26:25; Deut 32:35; Isa 1:24; Ps 99:8); and God's deeds against Israel are likened to his actions against the nations (Deut 32:41, 43; Judg 11:36; 2 Sam 22:48; Ps 18:48; 149:7; Isa 35:4; Nah 1:2 [3x]; Mic 5:14 [עשה נקם]). In Jeremiah and Ezekiel, it designates a divine deed against God's people in one case (Ezek 24:8) and three times as a rhetorical question on the option that God will act in revenge against his own people (Jer 5:9, 29; 9:8). Otherwise, נקם appears in both Jeremiah and Ezekiel only in prophecies against the nations (Jer 46:10; Ezek 25:12, 15; as also Nah 1:2). Thus, God's actions against Babylon are "times of revenge" (PAN Jer 51:6, 36), whether God executes the judgment himself or summons human enemies toward that goal (PAN Jer 50:15; 51:11; Ezek 25:12). Note also the psalmist's request for revenge against the nations (Ps 79:10), the individual's request for revenge in various settings (Jer 11:20; 15:15; 20:12; Lam 3:60), and the epithet אל־נקמות (Ps 94:1–2). God's assistance to Israel in its wars is presented as revenge in Num 31:2 and Josh 10:13.

9. דיבר את משפטים occurs also in contexts where human beings are judges (Jer

In comparison, Ezekiel uses the verb שפט with God as agent twenty-four times (more than any other prophetic book). Twenty-one of these occurrences designate actions against Israel, referred to as the entire people (7:27), often specified as the people who remained in Jerusalem (7:3, 8; 11:10, 11; 16:38; 22:2 [2x]; 23:36) or its king (17:20). Less so שפט is addressed at the Babylonian exiles' community (20:4 [2x], 35, 36 [2x]; 36:19) or individuals of that exilic community (18:30; 33:20; and with a consoling tone in 34:17, 20, 22). Only three occurrences mark prophecies against the other nations (PAN Ezek 21:35; 35:11; 38:22).[10] In all of these instances, Ezekiel portrays God not only as the judge, proclaiming his judicial verdict, but also as the executor of this judgment.[11] Furthermore, in most of these occurrences, it is God alone who does both; only three times (in the Masoretic Text) does God summon the nations to execute his judgment (23:24, 45; 24:14).[12] In three instances of this metaphor, Ezekiel's choice of שפט to designate the prophetic exhortation locates the prophet, as God's messenger, as a participant in the judicial context. In 20:4 the prophet is commanded התשפט אתם ("arraign, arraign them, O mortal! declare to

---

39:5; 52:9; compare וידברו אתו משפט, 2 Kgs 25:6). These passages point to the judicial context from which this phrase is transferred to the realm of the God-people relationship. In Jer 12:1 the prophet is positioned as a plaintiff in court, asking the help of the just judge (similarly Mic 3:8). A different meaning of משפט in parallelism to דרך is repeated in Jer 5:4, 5; 8:7, where it designates God's request for obedience to his commandments.

10. The phrase שפט את־כדרכיו ("[God] judges one according to one's ways") is repeated six times in Ezekiel, all referring to Israel (7:3, 8; 18:30; 24:14; 33:20; 36:19); the phrase שפט את־במשפטי occurs once (7:27); and the phrase עשה משפטים/שפטים ב־ ("[God] executes judgments against you") occurs a total of ten times, four addressed to Jerusalem and its residents (5:8, 10, 15; 11:9) and another six to the nations (PAN Ezek 25:11; 28:22, 26; 30:14, 19; 39:21). Besides these occurrences in Ezekiel, עשה שפטים ב־ occurs only rarely elsewhere in the Masoretic Text—three times in Exodus (6:6; 7:4; 12:12) and once each in Num 33:4; Prov 19:29; and 2 Chr 24:24.

11. So Greenberg, *Ezekiel 1–20*, 113. See שפט and משפט in Brown, Driver, and Briggs, *Hebrew and English Lexicon*, 1047–48; also Koehler and Baumgartner, *Lexicon in Veteris Testamenti*, 1623, 1625. This same meaning occurs in Isa 35:4 in a prophecy against Edom.

12. In contradistinction to Ezek 24:14 MT, where the agents of שפטוך are human enemies (23:45), the versions suggest that God himself is the agent. See the Septuagint's κρινῶ σε, Peshitta's אדונכי, and Targum's אתפרע מניך (all in accord with the construal of this expression in 7:3, 8 MT). Greenberg (*Ezekiel 21–37*, 503) holds that the versions reflect an ancient variant. The prophetic passage leading up to 7:14, where God acts alone, does corroborate this line of thought.

them the abhorrent deeds of their fathers"); the object here is the elders of Israel, representing the Jehoiachin exiles who have come to the prophet. In 22:2 the command is directed against Jerusalem: התשפוט את־עיר הדמים ("arraign, arraign the city of bloodshed; declare to her all her abhorrent deeds"); and in 23:36 it is directed against the two sinful sisters, Jerusalem and Samaria: התשפוט את־אהלה ואת־אהליבה ("O mortal, arraign Oholah and Oholibah").[13]

It is evident from the foregoing that all groups—historiographers, prophets, poets, and the people (i.e., laypeople)—share two basic conceptions. First, they share the overarching metaphorical portrayal and conception of God as judge. Second, the majority of the sources agree that the political-military events of subjugation, destruction, and exiles constitute divine act of judgment, inflicted on the people in retribution for their sins.[14] This recognition of the workings of justice, however, does not prevent calls of protest. Exceptions to this broad agreement on God's involvement in causing the distress may be found in several communal laments (Pss 74:3–8; 79:1–3), as well as the eleven fragmentary prophecies of the peace prophets. The latter do not lay responsibility on God for bringing the enemy upon the land, but reserve for God the role of savior; in addition, they lack any reference to the issue of divine justice. This *argument ex silencio* is, of course, problematic from the outset, but such a lack might be connected to the peace prophets not seeing the enemies' approach as a divine judgment (see §7.3). Hence, all these different voices—those that see divine justice as activated in the events and those who struggle against this explanation—share the traditional conception of retribution, which sees a direct correlation between human deeds and divine reactions; and all of these speakers transform and apply this conception to the national sphere.

---

13. See Greenberg, *Ezekiel 1–20*, 363. The versions struggle with the correct way to translate שפט in these three passages. The Targum chooses the same phrasing to translate in all three places: התוכח (יתהון) ("polemicized [with them]"). The Septuagint, on the other hand, does not show a single equivalent. Ezekiel 20:4 uses ἐκδικέω meaning "punish" (see Cooke, *Ezekiel*, 223–24); but 22:2 and 23:36 use κρίνω, which means to "judge, set a sentence, decide."

14. To give but a few examples, in the historiography see 2 Kgs 24:2–3, 20; among prophetic passages see Jer 1:13–16; 5:1–6; Ezek 5 and 17; and among the communal laments see Ps 89:39–46 (note the call for divine grace in 89:50); Lam 1:5, 8, 9, 14, 18, 22; 3:40–45; 4:6, 22; 5:7, 16.

10.2. God as Judge: The Polemics Concerning Divine Justice

Growing out of this shared conception, there are, nevertheless, explicit (and implicit) traces of sharp polemics between these various groups by the early sixth century, around several questions concerning the role of God as judge, questions that challenge the workings of divine justice. These polemics may be traced in three literary contexts. First, they are indicated by the explicit questions addressed to God and quoted by Jeremiah (e.g., 13:22) or included within communal laments (e.g., Ps 74:1). Second, they appear as clear statements of doubt and of protest, quoted alongside disputation speeches in Ezekiel (18:2, 19, 25, 29; 33:10). And, finally, polemics may be assumed to implicitly stand behind any prophetic voices that are motivated by the need to refute prevalent conceptions within the Judean communities of the Neo-Babylonian era.

The diverse and sporadic questions that are quoted (or formulated as hypothetical questions) in the book of Jeremiah and within communal laments in Psalms allow us to reconstruct aspects of the theological struggle.[15]

Jer 13:22	And when you ask yourself, "<u>Why</u> [מדוע] have these things befallen me?"
Jer 9:11	What man is so wise that he understands this? To whom has the Lord's mouth spoken, so that he can explain it: "<u>Why</u> [על־מה] is the land in ruins, laid waste like a wilderness, with none passing through?"
Jer 16:10	And when you announce all these things to that people, and they ask you, "<u>Why</u> [על־מה] has the Lord decreed upon us all this fearful evil? <u>What</u> [ומה] is the iniquity and <u>what</u> [ומה] the sin that we have committed against the Lord our God?"
Jer 22:8	And when many nations pass by this city and one man asks another, "<u>Why</u> [על־מה] did the Lord do thus to that great city?"
Jer 5:19	And when they ask, "<u>Because of what</u> [תחת מה] did the Lord our God do all these things?"

15. The questions quoted here from Jeremiah are those that quote "other voices," not those of the prophet himself. For other "why" questions, see §9.2.

The prophet's answers to each of these questions shed light on three issues under debate among his contemporaries:

a. The nature of sin—all five of these prophetic passages answer the questions by specifying the people's sin as disobedience to God, in accord with the political metaphor of God as sovereign. The people are accused of abandoning God, his Torah, or his covenant (9:12; 16:11; 22:9), forgetting God (13:25), or preferring other gods (5:19; 13:25).

b. The quality of judgment—in three of Jeremiah's responses to these questions, the prophet emphasizes rhetorically that God acts according to the retributive principle of "measure for measure" (מידה כנגד מידה); note the correspondence between the structure of the question על מה and that of the answer על-אשר/על (9:11–12; 16:10–11; 22:8–9). The loss of the land, the distress that has befallen the people, and the destruction of the city are all the expected (and entirely justified) consequences of the people's sins. In the other two passages, the rhetorical balance is struck between the two parts of the prophet's answer, which set the people's deeds against the consequences of those divine acts of retaliation: "Because you forsook Me and served alien gods on your own land [כאשר עזבתם אותי ותעבדו], you will have to serve [כן תעבדו] foreigners in a land not your own" (5:19); and: "This shall be your lot, your measured portion from Me [זה גורלך מנת-מדיך מאתי]—declares the LORD. Because you forgot Me and trusted in falsehood" (13:25).[16] In both structures, the present distress is the balanced consequence of the people's sins.

c. The present generation's responsibility—Jeremiah 16:10 raises the challenge of timing—asking for the reasons that caused God to inflict his judgment on "us." Jeremiah's response emphasizes not only the constant, long-term iniquities of previous generations (16:11), but also the responsibility of the destruction generation for its own fate (16:12).

---

16. Another issue raised and presented through a rhetorical question concerns the reasons for King Jehoiachin's exile and his fate (Jer 22:24–30). This passage is a compilation of prose and poetic units; see Holladay, *Jeremiah*, 1.604–9, and other commentaries. In form and content, the prophet's answer is structured here as a dirge quoted by the prophet (22:29–30) to enhance the rhetorical power of the expressed divine judgment (see Rudolph, *Jeremia*, 143).

The communal laments in Psalms repeat the interrogative word למה ("why?") in search of the reason for the destruction (80:13);[17] mainly, however, the term appears in passages that challenge possible reasons for the ongoing distress in its aftermath:[18]

Ps 80:13 <u>Why</u> [למה] did You breach its wall so that every passerby plucks its fruit?

Ps 10:1 <u>Why</u> [למה], O Lord, do You stand aloof, heedless in times of trouble?

Ps 42:10 I say to God, my rock, "<u>Why</u> [למה] have You forgotten me, <u>why</u> [למה] must I walk in gloom, oppressed by my enemy?"

Ps 43:2 For You are my God, my stronghold; <u>why</u> [למה] have You rejected me? <u>Why</u> [למה] must I walk in gloom, oppressed by the enemy?

Ps 44:24–25 Rouse Yourself; <u>why</u> [למה] do You sleep, O Lord? Awaken, do not reject us forever! <u>Why</u> [למה] do You hide Your face, ignoring our affliction and distress?

Ps 74:1, 11 <u>Why</u> [למה], O God, do You forever reject us, do You fume in anger at the flock that You tend? . . . <u>Why</u> [למה] do You hold back Your hand, Your right hand? Draw it out of Your bosom!

The struggle concerning the reasons for the destruction and the workings of divine justice is further accentuated in several communal laments

---

17. For the communal laments discussed in this study, see §3.4.3. See Barr, "Why? in Biblical Hebrew." Barr confronts Jepsen ("Warum?") and suggests that למה and מדוע are interchangeable: "Surprise, wonder, amazement, compassion, blame, reproach, and anger all form one single continuum in the meanings of Hebrew 'Why?'" (8). Yet Barr sees aptly that "why?" questions are commonly a reflection of "something wrong" and a sign of trouble (though clearly this negative meaning is not exclusive, as Barr shows on 23–24). Barr also suggests that these questions feature distinctions of style and function (23–33); for example, questions addressed directly to God in the second-person are relatively rare, but typical of Psalms (there are seventeen למה such questions in the book) and that they characterize complaint (32–33). I focus on the theological dimensions of those questions, to which, quite surprisingly, Barr barely gives attention in his detailed paper.

18. See also questions using עד־מה ("how long?," Ps 89:47) or עד־מתי ("how long?," 74:10; 90:13) and the interrogative particles ה . . . אם (77:8–10), all of which tell of the struggle with the continued suffering, with feelings of desertion, where God is challenged as no longer involved in the fate of his people.

by the lack of any reference to the people's sins (Pss 9–10, 42–43, 74) or by elaborated confessions of sins (79:8 for instance) that might have served as possible justifications for divine judgment. Moreover, 44:18–23 and 80:19, on the contrary, emphasize the people's ongoing *obedience* to God; in these poems, the question of divine *in*justice is at stake.

These references join other communal laments (Pss 77, 102, 123, 137) where there is no mention of either the people's sins or an explicit reference to divine justice.[19] It is thus remarkable that within the seventeen psalms that refer to the sixth-century destruction and exiles, only four include a confession of sins (Pss 79, 90, 103, 106).[20] It seems safe to argue that the issue of justifying God in his role as judge is under debate or on the table, negotiated by diverse speakers of that era.

Another question asked explicitly in Jeremiah concerns the quality of divine mercy (מידת הרחמים). At the end of a passage that discusses the covenant relationship between God and his people, the prophet quotes the people as saying: "Does one hate for all time [הינטר לעולם]? Does one rage forever [אם־ישמר לנצח]?" (3:5a). The two rhetorical questions are negated in 3:12, assuring the people that לוא־אפיל פני בכם כי־חסיד אני נאם־יהוה לא אטור לעולם ("I will not look on you in anger, for I am compassionate—declares the LORD; I do not bear a grudge for all time").[21] Similarly, Ps 103 contextualizes this question of when God's mercy will once again be exercised within the broader context of God's role as judge (103:6–13), by turning doubt into a justificatory statement: לא־לנצח יריב ולא לעולם ינטור ("He will not contend forever, or nurse His anger for all time," 103:9). Such statements shine light on another aspect of the challenges raised about God's role as judge during the destruction and in the exilic period thereafter. His actions against his people are accepted as executions of judgment in its fullest force, but what is then to be said about

---

19. An implicit reference to God's role as judge who releases prisoners occurs in Ps 102:20–21. Ps 94 refers explicitly to God as judge (94:2) and further expresses obedience to God (94:17–19) and full confidence in the divine help in saving his people from the evils (94:9–15, 22–23); thus there is no room for challenging the divine justice or for confession of sins.

20. The end of Ps 89 also features an implicit confession (89:51–52). Confessions of sins occur to varying extents in Lamentations (1:5, 8, 9, 14, 18, 22; 3:40–45; 4:6, 22; 5:7, 16; and implicitly in 2:14). See §11.2.3.

21. Jer 3:12–13 responds to (even reverses) 3:1–5, the passage that serves as the kernel of several poetic and prose prophetic passages in 3:6–4:2; see McKane, *Jeremiah 1–25*, liii–lv, lxii, 69–72; Rom-Shiloni, "Covenant in Jeremiah," 163–69.

his benevolence and mercy? This question joins others concerning the nature of repentance and whether God would be able to forgive the people for their sins, questions that are part of the deliberation between Jeremiah and his audience (e.g., Jer 2:20–25, 35).

The overall picture that comes clearly out of the explicit questions within Jeremiah and the communal laments is that of a lively (and painful) discussion around the issue of God's role as judge. The prophetic voices may be polemical responses (subtle or outspoken) to the diverse other voices that explicitly challenged God and his actions as judge (e.g., Jer 5:1–9). Three major issues are raised within the sources studied:

1. The exercise of judgment and its correspondence to the people's sins.[22]

2. The culpability of the generation of the destruction and the question of divine justice.[23]

3. The attribute of divine mercy and the question of whether it is activated during the destruction and throughout the deportations.[24]

---

22. The quality of divine judgment is discussed in Jer 9:11–12; 16:10–11; 22:8–9.

23. The status of the current generation is reflected in Jer 16:10–13; Ezek 18:2, 18, 25, 29; 33:17–20; as also Pss 44:18–23; 80:13; Lam 5:7. See chap. 11.

24. Deliberation over the measure of divine mercy occurs in Jer 3:5 and Ps 103:9 and is mostly refuted in the prophets. See chap. 12.

11

God Visits the Guilt of the Parents upon the Children, the Present Generation

Two pairs of oppositional concepts are identified as governing ideas of retribution in the Hebrew Bible: the first pair is collective versus individual retribution, the second is immediate retribution against the sinner versus retribution visited upon succeeding generations (transgenerational). The major distinction between these two pairs is chronological—the first presumes a synchronic relationship between behavior and punishment, the second a diachronic one.

To give one example, the chronological distinction marks a major difference between biblical historiographers, that is, between the historiographic compositions of Kings and Chronicles. According to Kings, the destruction is a divine judgment against sins committed in the past—either by many of the kings of Judah, from Solomon (1 Kgs 11:1-13) to Zedekiah (2 Kgs 24:19), or by Manasseh, the fourth-generation ancestor of Zedekiah (2 Kgs 21:1-15; 23:26-27; 24:2-3). Although the entire kingdom is punished, only rarely are the sins of the people themselves mentioned (e.g., 12:4; 15:4; 17:7-23; 21:8-9, 11, 14-15). A contrasting current in Kings portrays retribution as immediate and *not* simply suspended to future generations. Except for King Manasseh of Judah (2 Kgs 21), each of the Davidic kings who sins faces a military-political crisis during his years in power. Either through narrative proximity or by means of tense particles and phrases, such as אז or בעת ההיא, the historiographers present the crisis as the immediate outcome of transgression (e.g., 1 Kgs 15:3-6; 2 Kgs 16:2-6; and similarly 23:37-24:2; 24:9-17; 24:19-25:7). Hence, the book of Kings throughout uses both the immediate and the transgenerational conceptions of retribution. The book also takes for granted the notion of collective retribution, that is, the idea that the kings' personal disobedience determines the fate of their subjects and the kingdom.[1] The only exception is the story of the fate of righteous Josiah, in which the historiographer implicitly struggles with the notion of individual retribution and chooses "theological silence."[2]

Different nuances come together within the book of Kings, aligning conceptions of retribution held by diverse Deuteronomists over time. Scholarship on Kings and on the Deuteronomistic History in general distinguishes between Josian and exilic editors (labeled Dtr1 and Dtr2), in articulating their conceptions of retribution (see §3.4.2). I purposefully take them together, since phenomenologically they have much more in common than what divides them. Theologically, all of these conceptions provide answers to the challenge of Jerusalem's destruction—but while they all justify God, none seem to provide an entirely satisfactory explanation.[3]

By way of comparison, Chronicles presents the destruction as immediate punishment for the sins perpetrated by Zedekiah the present king, his officials, and the people (2 Chr 36:11–16). Hence, the Chronicler, as consistently throughout his composition, argues that retribution entails immediate judgment upon those who sin. The Chronicler also emphasizes the shared responsibility of the entire generation of the destruction for their own fate—they all sinned tremendously and thus face this collective punishment within their own lifetimes.[4]

---

1. On this conception of collective retribution in the Hebrew Bible, which groups kings with their subjects, see Kaufmann, *Toldot Ha-'Emunah*, 3.595–600. On Manasseh as solely responsible for Judah's fate (according to the late exilic Deuteronomistic historiographer, labeled Dtr2), see Sweeney, "King Manasseh of Judah." The idea of the god who acts against violators of a loyalty oath in a political treaty is well recorded in Assyrian royal inscriptions; see Oded, *War, Peace, and Empire*, 83–94.

2. Compare Chronicles' presentation of Josiah's death; see Talshir, "Three Deaths of Josiah." Another possible theological silence occurs in reference to Azariah's affliction with leprosy, which remains unexplainable (2 Kgs 15:5 = Uzziah in 2 Chr 26).

3. Sweeney ("King Manasseh of Judah," 275) aptly argues for a deliberate incoherency in the Deuteronomistic History concerning what he terms "divine culpability" in these diverse explanations for Judah's destruction, by which he means inconsistency between notions of divine and human culpability or conflation of the two. He judges this phenomenon to reflect an actual struggle within exilic and postexilic Judean thought.

4. Japhet, *Ideology of the Book of Chronicles*, 165–76, 364–73.

11.1. TRANSGENERATIONAL RETRIBUTION IN THE CONTEXT OF EXILE: THE QUESTION OF EZEKIEL

From a descriptive, phenomenological point of view, I argue that these two pairs of retribution conceptions should not be kept apart. The study of retribution conceptions should take into consideration a richer portrayal of different constellations of the four elements (future and transgenerational versus immediate retribution, collective versus individual). Sources from the early sixth century demonstrate that the question of the responsibility of the destruction generation for its fate is examined primarily in light of the diachronic distinction between transgenerational and immediate retribution (often understood as collective); the collective versus individual retribution pair captures only a minor role, oftentimes adjoined to the diachronic framework.[5]

In addition, I suggest that the theological presumption shared by all voices, which all speakers lean upon as a foreground tradition, is the well-known divine epithet from the Decalogue (Exod 20:5–6; also Deut 5:9–10):

[5]Visiting the guilt of the parents upon the children, upon the third and upon the fourth generations of those who reject Me, [6]but showing kindness to the thousandth generation of those who love Me and keep My commandments.	[5]פקד עון אבת על־בנים על־שלשים ועל־רבעים לשנאי. [6]ועשה חסד לאלפים לאהבי ולשמרי מצותי.

This divine epithet, which constitutes one of the thirteen divine names and epithets in Exod 34:6–7, was long ago recognized as two of those divine qualities that spurred controversy throughout the biblical literature; see, for instance, Deut 7:9–10, which is then taken further by Jer 32:18.[6] Many other references to this epithet, mostly implicit, show the various angles from which this formulation is enlisted to understand the causes

---

5. For a comprehensive study of the formative history of scholarship on the retribution concept(s) and mainly for the plurality of thought in the Hebrew Bible, see Weiss, *Scriptures in Their Own Light*, 458–510, esp. 458–89.

6. The intertextual connections between these passages and their relative chronological order are of course under debate. I follow here Weiss, *Scriptures in Their Own Light*, 495–98, esp. 491–94. Weiss illustrates how those epithets are each modified to serve in the different contexts, and yet he argues that this epithet is genuine to the Decalogue reference and that this is the invoked text (492–94).

of the present crisis: is the disaster a response to the sins of past generations or to those of the present one? Daniel Block identifies this epithet
as "the traditional doctrine" that stands behind Ezek 18:2;[7] I widen this
claim and suggest that this epithet (and the conception it reflects) forms
the theological point of departure for the entire theological discussion of
the destruction, as we may discern this discussion in Hebrew Bible sources
of the Neo-Babylonian era.

The troubling aspect in this divine epithet is the first clause: "visiting
the guilt of the parents upon the children." What is the status of the children—are they sinners themselves? Or could they be innocent, yet suffer
vicariously for the sins of the previous generations? This unclarity seems
to stand behind the entire theological deliberation.[8] Both explicit (Ezek
18:2) and implicit references to this divine epithet grapple with the status
of the current generation; and theologically even more troubling, such
references open up the discussion of the relationship between this divine
attribute and the nature of divine justice. The Judean generation that suffered the destruction is identified by all speakers throughout the sixth
century as "the children" (or even a later generation) of sinning ancestors.
But these diverse speakers differed on the degree of responsibility allotted
to the children themselves. Our sources from historiography, prophecy,
and poetry expose four different positions on the culpability of the destruction generation, which represent the full spectrum of justification,
doubt, and protest:

1. The children sinned like their ancestors; thus it is appropriate
   that they themselves be judged. Although sins are committed
   throughout the generations, the destruction generation had its own
   share in this sinful transgenerational history, and therefore they
   deserve punishment.
2. The children did not sin; the destruction is a divine judgment brought
   unjustly upon the current generation.
3. The children sinned far beyond their fathers, which explains why the destruction occurs only in the time of the
   contemporary generation.

7. Block, *Ezekiel 1–24*, 559.
8. The responsibility of the sons for their fate occupies ancient, medieval, and modern commentators, who emphasize the contrast in Exod 20:5–6 between לשנאי and
לאהבי ולשמרי מצותי, asking whether these labels refer to the fathers or to the sons.
See, for instance, Weiss, *Scriptures in Their Own Light*, 495–98.

4.   The children do not carry the burden of their parents' sins. The
     destruction is a divine judgment in immediate retaliation for
     contemporary sins.

These four perspectives are all motivated by the wish to find a theological explanation for the divine judgment in accordance with the divine
attribute of God as a just judge. Thus, they participate in the theodical discourse, taking different positions on the operation of this divine quality in
the current crisis. The first and the second explanations stand in diametric
opposition—the former justifies God as "visiting the guilt of the parents
upon the children," the latter raises doubts and protests against divine injustice. The third statement accentuates contemporary sins and thus lays
a heavier burden on those who actually suffer the punishment. Implicitly
this third formulation reflects discomfort with this epithet, yet a real effort
to sustain a belief in it, so to still justify God. The fourth statement is also
motivated by justificatory intentions but takes a different tack, rejecting
the notion of long-term retaliation for one of immediate retribution.

Several passages in Ezekiel (14:12–23; 18:1–20, 21–31; also 3:16–21;
33:10–20) appear to polemicize explicitly against this notion of transgenerational retribution. The three-generational pattern of 18:1–20 launches
the rule: "Consider, all lives are Mine; the life of the parent and the life of
the child are both Mine. The person who sins, only he shall die" (18:4).
This passage is often accepted as innovative in its conception of individual
retribution, as a central innovation developed within the Judean religious
thought of the postdestruction and exilic eras. In evaluating this innovation, two questions are asked. The one examines its content: did Ezekiel indeed aim at a notion of individual retribution in opposition to the national-
collective one? And the other concerns the Hebrew Bible context: did
Ezekiel innovate a concept that is not adduced prior to himself?

Walther Eichrodt answers both questions positively. He claims that Ezekiel, not as a theologian but as a prophet, initiates a significant change in
Israelite religion, by countering the epithet of the second commandment.[9]
Eichrodt interprets the rule "the person who sins, only he shall die" (18:4)
as countering the idea of transgenerational retribution with a notion of
"individual responsibility." According to him, the use of legal style is a
device meant to enhance "the absolute validity" of this proclamation of a

9. See Eichrodt, *Ezekiel*, 235–37; Cooke, *Ezekiel*, 200–201; and von Rad, *Old Testament Theology*, 1.392–94.

new divine word, by imitating earlier established legal formulas that proclaim "the will of God."[10] According to Eichrodt, the concept of individual retribution developed among the Babylonian exiles (Ezekiel among them), who feel that they suffer "severer punishment than their compatriots who still remained in Jerusalem."[11] Eichrodt identifies Ezekiel's contribution in 18:6–8 as that of leading the exiles from the feeling of despair "under the wrath of God," to a new sense of hope as the emerging community in Babylon, "by God's grace."[12] Eichrodt argues that Ezekiel "sets up a norm for moral and social life, which can provide a firm basis for a man's relations with his neighbor in a foreign land":

> Here and now in this heathen land everyone who believes the word of the prophet is given room and freedom to break out the collective guilt of past generations to a new beginning which puts him into a personal relationship of service and loyalty to the God of his fathers. . . . This is nothing less than the breaking of that iron ring of collective guilt within which all hopes die, and the opening of the road to freedom, along which the individual, stirred by God's word with its summons of decision, may be brought into a new association with God and with his fellow men. . . .
>
> This is not an expression of extreme individualism. . . . We might name that form personalism, if we wanted to state the motive power which forms its central core.[13]

---

10. Eichrodt, *Ezekiel*, 237–41 at 238. Many scholars try to reconstruct the historical development of the concept of so-called individual retribution in Ezek 18. Lindars ("Ezekiel and Individual Responsibility") argues that Ezekiel's ideas regarding individual responsibility are not new; the prophet's contribution is in transforming the personal element of the criminal law into a notion of divine retribution against the entire people. Matties (*Ezekiel 18*, 115–16) reconstructs six stages in the development of the notion of individual retribution; the last stage is represented by Ezek 18. Matties emphasizes Ezekiel's similarities to Deuteronomy, the distance between his ideas and Exod 34:6–7, and the distinction between Ezekiel and the notion of transgenerational retribution in the Holiness Legislation (Lev 26:39–40).

11. Eichrodt, *Ezekiel*, 236. Eichrodt (239) further distinguishes between Ezek 18 and the list of sins addressed to the inhabitants of Jerusalem in 22:6–12. The latter, however, illustrates a synchronic polemic between the two Judean communities, not a transgenerational matter.

12. Eichrodt, *Ezekiel*, 240.

13. Eichrodt, *Ezekiel*, 239–41.

According to Eichrodt, Ezekiel's concept of "personalism" contributed significantly to Judean (Jewish) thought for generations to come.[14] In this spirit, Rimon Kasher sees the Jehoiachin exile as the framework that brings Ezekiel to his innovative and individualistic perspective; to Kasher's mind, this first wave of deportation shatters traditional and unifying collective-national conceptions.[15]

But it seems that a negative answer should rather be given to both questions—to whether individual retribution is at all dealt with, in contrast to national-collective retribution in the book of Ezekiel, and to whether Ezekiel may be held as the initiator of this presumed retribution concept. First, although Ezekiel addresses both collective and individual responsibility for sin, as well as divine retribution, Paul Joyce aptly shows that Ezek 18 does not deal with any tension between individual and collective retribution.[16] Rather, Ezekiel here makes chronological distinctions between three generations and thus interrupts the transgenerational connections for better or for worse (also exemplified in 14:12–23; see §11.4.1.2). As Walther Zimmerli argues, the singular forms that Ezekiel adopts in his prophetic speech in Ezek 18 and elsewhere are based on the legal style he chooses and even more particularly on Priestly and Holiness Legislation formulas, structured as legal precedents.[17] Not only does this legal style (of the criminal

---

14. Eichrodt does not pay attention to the quotation in Ezek 18:2 being framed as words of those in Judah (עַל־אַדְמַת יִשְׂרָאֵל, "on the land of Israel"); he also misses the transgenerational distinction between fathers and sons, focusing on the conflict between the exiles and those who remain in Judah. See Joyce's criticism on this point ("Individual Responsibility in Ezekiel 18?," 188). Along similar lines to Eichrodt, Fishbane ("Sin and Judgment") argues that Ezekiel presumes a notion of individual responsibility when addressing the Babylonian exiles, but a notion of collective judgment in his prophecies of calamity against those who remained in Judah.

15. Kasher, *Ezekiel 1–24*, 120; on the innovative perspective of Ezek 18, see 362.

16. Joyce, "Individual Responsibility in Ezekiel 18?," and *Divine Initiative*, 35–60. This line of thought is formulated by Peake, *Problem of Suffering*, 24; and also adopted by Greenberg, *Ezekiel 1–20*, 341–42; and Block, *Ezekiel 1–24*, 556–57.

17. According to Zimmerli (*Ezekiel*, 1.374–77), the legal Priestly style appears in Ezek 18 in three formal features: (1) precedents for legal rulings, given in relation to each generation, e.g., וְאִישׁ כִּי־יִהְיֶה צַדִּיק ("thus, if a man is righteous," 18:5); compare Lev 13:40 or the double phrase אִישׁ אִישׁ כִּי יִהְיֶה in 15:2; (2) representations of judgment, using phrasings such as חָיֹה יִחְיֶה ("such a man shall live," Ezek 18:9); this formulation itself does not specifically appear in the Priestly or Holiness Legislation within the Pentateuch but its antonym מוֹת יוּמָת in Ezek 18:13 is well attested (e.g., Lev 20:2, 9, 15), and the formula נָשָׂא עָוֹן in Ezek 18:19–20 is known from Lev 17:16; and (3) the list of sins. Zimmerli (1.302–6) points out similar linguistic features in Ezek

law) indicate divine authorship (divine validation, in Eichrodt's language), but to Zimmerli and Joyce, the analogy to the forensic thought-world is an important feature that justifies God as a just judge in the circumstances of national defeat.[18] From this standpoint, the question of the supposedly innovative references to individual retribution becomes irrelevant, mainly because this idea is not at all at the focus of attention in 18:1–20 (and rarely otherwise in Ezekiel; see §11.4.1.3). Joyce concludes his discussion of collective and individual responsibility, arguing that "the view that the contribution of Ezekiel marked a crucial stage in the evolution of individualism in Israel not only misrepresents the evidence concerning Ezekiel but also attempts to impose an excessively simple pattern upon language about collective and individual responsibility in the Old Testament as a whole."[19]

Indeed, Yehezkel Kaufmann argues that the distinction between reward and punishment directed to either the nation or the individual is found in diverse biblical sources in relation to both transgenerational and immediate concepts of retribution.[20]

Going beyond Ezekiel (and beyond the scholarly appreciation for this prophet's innovative thoughts on retribution) and by broadening the perspective on conceptions of retribution, we can place Ezekiel and his ideas within a broader historical context. Ezekiel's diverse perspectives may be evaluated more accurately in relation to the context of other contemporary Hebrew Bible compositions. Such a wider view shows, for instance, that Ezekiel operates with three of the perspectives; that is, he uses separately the notion of transgenerational retribution (e.g., 2:3–4; 20:1–38) and the notion of immediate retribution (3:17–21; 18:21–32; 33:10–20), whereas in

---

14:1–11. Note that in the lists of sins, Ezekiel adapts phrases from all of the pentateuchal codices; see Joyce (*Divine Initiative*, 38–41), Greenberg (*Ezekiel 1–20*, 327–32, 341–44), and Levitt-Kohn (*New Heart*, 86–104).

18. Joyce, *Divine Initiative*, 41. Although Ezekiel's discussions of retribution are portrayed schematically, and thus almost give the impression of being theoretical elaborations, Brin (*Studies in the Book of Ezekiel*, 102–5), Joyce, and Matties among others, agree that these discussions emerge for practical reasons, that is, in response to the crisis of faith within the Babylonian exilic community.

19. Joyce, *Divine Initiative*, 79–87 at 86–87.

20. Kaufmann, *Toldot Ha-'Emunah*, 3.595–600. Nevertheless, Kaufmann considers Ezekiel to have discussed individual retribution (3.553–54). Brin (*Studies in the Book of Ezekiel*, 101–5) refutes the idea that Ezekiel should be seen as an innovator and argues that the only innovation here is in tying the abstract notion of repentance to the practical perception of retribution, in order to emphasize that through the action of individuals, national salvation would come.

other contexts he annuls the existence of any transgenerational retribution altogether and remains in the collective arena (14:12–23; 18:1–20).

Does the prophet address the notion of collective versus individual retribution at all? The instances of attention to individual retribution in Ezekiel are minimal and oftentimes are the result of stylistic legal formulations rather than conceptual innovations. In addition, Joyce points out the substantial methodological difficulties in tracing out a conception of individual retribution in the Hebrew Bible in general and in Ezekiel in particular; Ezek 21:6–10 stands clearly against such a notion.[21]

Retribution among the protagonists of the destruction generation may be seen through the lenses of Jeremiah, Ezekiel, the quoted words in the prophecy and the communal laments, along the theodical discourse from justification to protest. All four components of the retribution conceptions—communal, individual, transgenerational, and immediate—are addressed to find answers to the disaster that inflicts the destruction generation.

11.2. Justification: The Destruction Is Divine Judgment upon a Generation That Sinned Just Like Its Ancestors

The idea that the current generation sins, in continuity with its ancestors, governs the historiography of 2 Kings (e.g., 24:2–3, 19–20), the prophecies in Jeremiah and Ezekiel, and the communal lament genre: it appears in several confessions of sins found in fragmentary communal laments quoted in Jeremiah (3:25; 14:20; 31:18) and likewise in the rebellious words of "the remnant of Judah" (44:17) and in two confessions of sins in communal laments in Psalms (79:8–9; 106:6). All these sources hold the generation of the destruction responsible for its own fate. Although this generation is the final link in a long chain of sinners, in comparison to previous generations' misdeeds, those who suffer the calamity carry on this long legacy of sin. Therefore, as the lord of history who brings about destruction, God acts

---

21. Joyce, *Divine Initiative*, 79–87. From a more substantial standpoint, Joyce objects to the evolutionary framework that guided scholars to reconstruct a line of gradual development from collective to individual retribution; he argues for a development in the opposite direction (85–87). In his view, there is a consistent tension in the Hebrew Bible between the individual and the collective (the nation); this is why antagonistic statements such as Ezek 9 and 21:8–9 exist side by side. Due to their importance, 18:1–20 is further dealt with in §11.4.1 and 21:6–10 in §11.4.1.3.

justifiably; and the accumulation of sin over the course of the generations explains the harsh measure of judgment.

Several streams within prophetic literature use the metaphor of God as judge to describe God's treatment of his people as a juridical event, using both linguistic devices (lexical and formal) and literary elements of structure, genre, style, and theme. In such passages, the destruction and the exiles are portrayed as the executions of a divine verdict, resulting from legal accusations that God previously announces through his prophets (e.g., Jer 7:25; 25:4).

The juridical expression of God's involvement in historical events is prevalent among the judgment prophecies and is further reflected in three genres: the *Rib*-pattern, the retribution essays in Ezekiel, and the watchman passages. All are exemplary uses of the metaphor of God as judge; that is, they present the prophetic message as a description of a juridical event.

a.   Presentations of juridical events in the *Rib*-pattern

Although limited in its occurrences, the *Rib*-pattern has long been recognized as either an independent genre within prophetic literature or as an independent theological elaboration of the accusation component found in judgment prophecies.[22] In contrast to the judgment prophecies, the *Rib*-pattern, which occurs in Jer 2:4–13 (also Mic 6:1–8 and fragmentarily in Isa 1:2–3; 3:13–15), does not end with a proclamation of punishment but leaves open the possibility of repentance.[23] Nevertheless, this prophetic genre portrays a juridical event:

1. It opens with the call שמעו ("hear," Jer 2:4; Mic 6:1) aimed at the addressees.
2. Albeit this feature is absent from Jer 2:4–13 (except possibly 2:12),

---

22. Scholarship on the *Rib*-pattern mainly discusses two issues, neither of which is at the core of the present study: the formation and evolution of this genre (see Huffmon, "Covenant Lawsuit"; Limburg, "Root ריב"; and Westermann, *Basic Forms of Prophetic Speech*, 182) and the rhetorical setting of the genre (see Limburg, "Root ריב"; and Nielsen, *Yahweh as Prosecutor and Judge*, 1–26). Here I focus on the metaphoric use of the image of God as judge (see Nielsen, *Yahweh as Prosecutor and Judge*, 39–42, 73–77).

23. Another instance of this pattern within prophetic literature is Hos 4:1–3 (although it barely shows the typical features); in poetry, note Deut 32 and Ps 50.

the *Rib*-pattern calls the mountains and cosmic entities (heaven and earth) as witnesses (Isa 1:2–3; Mic 6:2; Deut 32:1).[24]

3. As a prosecutor, God presents a complaint against the people's offense, opening with a rhetorical question (Jer 2:5; Mic 6:3).

4. God reflects on the past, recalling his paradigmatic salvific deed of bringing the people out of Egypt and leading them through the desert to the good land (Jer 2:5–7; Mic 6:4–5).

5. Rhetorical questions enhance the people's blame, highlighting the mistaken understanding or their guilt (Jer 2:6, 8; Mic 6:6–7). In Jer 2 the argument points toward a failure to address God in times of distress, giving preference to other gods over him.[25]

6. The *Rib*-pattern concludes with a divine reaction that promises that this juridical struggle will continue for generations to come (Jer 2:9). Hence, the conception of transgenerational retribution is established as a foundation for the entire discussion.

b. Juridical events in Ezekiel's retribution essays

In retribution essays (14:12–23; 18:1–20, 21–32) and in the watchman passages (3:17–21; 33:10–20), Ezekiel constructs schematic patterns that at face value detach the prophet and his audience from the contemporary context and portray God as judge (see §11.4.1.2 and §11.4.1.3):

1. The point of departure is presented as a juridical precedent, such as "if a land were to sin against Me and commit a trespass" (14:13) or "if a man is righteous and does what is just and right" (18:5, 21), or suggests a guiding rule, such as "the righteousness of the righteous shall not save him when he transgresses, nor shall the wickedness of the wicked cause him to stumble when he turns back from his wickedness" (33:12; only implied in 3:17–21).

2. The prophet establishes a transgenerational dynamic (14:12–20; 18:5–20) by alluding to a popular saying (18:2) or to known, typ-

---

24. According to Huffmon ("Covenant Lawsuit") calling heaven and earth as witnesses and the historical review are the two major components of the *Rib*-pattern. Holladay (*Jeremiah*, 1.73, 75) argues that the call to heaven in Jer 2:12 (as part of 2:10–25) is secondarily added to 2:4–9 from the second scroll.

25. The question "where is God?" in Jer 2:6 (and in a shorter form in 2:8) is similar to questions put in the mouths of foreigners (as in Pss 42:4, 11; 79:10) and in the words of Gideon (Judg 6:13). A similar question occurs as divine speech in Isa 63:11–13. Compare the challenge quoted in Mic 6:6–7 concerning the proper conduct of the cult.

ical heroes (Noah, Daniel, and Job in 14:12–20). Differently, the prophet plays on the opposition between the types of righteous and wicked to amplify on the lifetime of one generation (18:21–32 and in the watchman passages).

3. Relying on pentateuchal legal formulas, Ezekiel articulates rules for divine engagement that are phrased as permanent and not subject to change, regardless of specific historical circumstances (18:5, 20; 14:14, 16, 18, 20; see §11.4.1.2).

c. Judgment prophecies in Jeremiah and Ezekiel

Thematically, the judgment prophecies share with the *Rib*-pattern prophecies and with the retribution essays a reliance on the traditional concept of retribution, which presumes a direct connection of cause and effect between human transgression and divine reaction. The forms and rhetorical structures, however, are distinct—in Ezekiel's retribution essays (14:12–23; 18:1–20), the two poles of retribution—judgment and reward—are schematized, whereas in the judgment prophecies of both prophets this issue seems to be rhetorically presented in a much simpler way (e.g., Jer 26:3–6, 13; 36:3), and likewise in Jeremiah's admonition prophecy to the Rechabites (35:12–19).

The judgment prophecies bring the metaphor of God as judge to bear on the fate of Judah in the early sixth century. Two issues are discussed here. The first is the formal devices used to portray the strict correlation between action and result that structure the argument as one of "measure for measure." These rhetorical structures lay the groundwork for the prophetic justification of God in one exceptional passage in each book: Jer 16:16–18 and Ezek 21:6–10. The second is the different ways Jeremiah and Ezekiel deploy the transgenerational retribution conception: Jeremiah addresses the question of when transgression actually began, to which he supplies no less than three different points in the past as answers; and Ezekiel, the supposed innovator of individual retribution, struggles with the question of divine justice and appears to be using the transgenerational conception of retribution throughout his book.

11.2.1. Prophetic Justification Based on the Principle "Measure for Measure"

The traditional conception of retribution is perfectly suited to the two-part structure of the judgment prophecies, comprised of accusation and judgment. The judgment prophecies use a variety of formal devices to establish the correlation between action and consequence and thereby to justify God's punitive responses.[26] Of special importance are passages that illustrate this correlation by employing the structural principle of מידה כנגד מידה ("measure for measure"). These are formally characterized by three stylistic devices, often intertwined.

a.   Metonymic transposition of judgment and sin

In many phrases, the accusation becomes the judgment. That is, the terms that designate sinful actions (דרכים, משפטים, and תועבות) are used to refer specifically to the infliction of punishment, and the correlation is accentuated through the use of a personal pronoun: (יהוה) נתן את־דרכיו עליו ("but I will requite you for your ways," Ezek 7:9); (יהוה) נתן דרכו בראשו ("I will pay you back for your conduct," 16:43); (יהוה) שפט את־כדרכיו ("I will . . . judge you according to your ways," 7:3); (יהוה) נתן על־את כל־תועבותיו ("I will requite you for all your abominations," 7:3); (יהוה) שפט את־במשפטיו ("I will judge them according to their deserts," 7:27). The phrase איש בעונו recurs twice in Ezekiel to signify this strict correlation between judgment and sin prior to the city's destruction (7:13, 16).[27]

b.   *Kaf parallelis* correlating judgment with sin

Kaf parallelis occurs, for example, in Jer 17:10; Ezek 7:3, 8, 9; 36:19; PAN

---

26. Among these devices are (1) the use of particles and prepositions to connect sin and consequence: ב־ (Jer 15:13), בגלל (11:17; 15:4), בגלל and על (15:4), יען (Jer 5:14; Ezek 5:9), כי (Jer 4:17–18; Ezek 5:6), מפני (Jer 4:4), על (Jer 16:18; Ezek 33:29), and תחת אשר (Jer 29:18–19; Ezek 36:34 [with a different meaning]); (2) the use of לכן to mark the movement from accusation to judgment (Jer 7:17–20; PAN 51:36; also in prophecies of consolation in Ezek 11:16–17); (3) the transformation of the word order (subject/predicate) and the verbal tenses to illustrate the opposition between the people's transgressions and the divine reaction (Jer 14:10; 34:17–21); (4) the use of conditional sentences to link accusation and judgment (4:1–2; 26:4–6); (5) the use of temporal clauses to link the present distress and the judgment (Ezek 21:30, 34; 35:5; see Rashi on בעת עון קץ in 21:30, and Greenberg, *Ezekiel 1–20*, 433); and (6) the use of rhetorical questions to introduce judgment (Jer 5:7–9, 26–29; 9:6–8).

27. The phrase איש בעונו occurs only once in Jeremiah (at 31:30), but it is much more frequent in Ezekiel, where בעונו expresses the correlation between sin and judgment (3:18, 19; 33:6, 8, 9); see §11.2.2.2.

Jer 50:29; PAN Ezek 35:11. Other correlation formulas are also employed: כן . . . כ/כאשר/ככל אשר (Jer 5:19; PAN Jer 50:15, 19; PAN Ezek 35:14).

c.   Components of the sin repeated in the proclamation of judgment

This usually occurs by means of a linguistic or associative pun. The first example is Jer 14:15–16:

<table>
<tr>
<td>

[15] And they say, "<u>Sword and famine shall not befall</u> this land"; those very prophets <u>shall perish by sword and famine.</u> [16] And the people . . . <u>shall be left lying</u> in the streets of Jerusalem <u>because of the famine and the sword,</u> with none to bury them—they, their wives, their sons, and their daughters. I will pour out upon them the requital of their wickedness.

</td>
<td dir="rtl">

¹⁵והמה אמרים חרב ורעב
לא יהיה בארץ הזאת
בחרב וברעב יתמו הנביאים
ההמה. ¹⁶והעם . . . יהיו
משלכים בחצות ירושלים
מפני הרעב והחרב ואין
מקבר להמה המה נשיהם
ובניהם ובנתיהם ושפכתי
עליהם את־רעתם.

</td>
</tr>
</table>

In reaction to the quoted words of the peace prophets, judgment is presented as the reversal of their prophecies, through two proclamations (see fig. 11.1). The first, 14:15b, proclaims the judgment of the prophets themselves and sets their punishment apart from that of their adherents. The repetition of חרב ורעב emphasizes that the prophets' punishment falls appropriately upon them; that is, upon those who promised salvation from these very calamities (see §7.3). The third mention of this pair, in 14:16, refers to the fate awaiting the entire people.

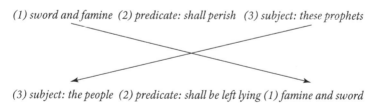

(1) sword and famine (2) predicate: shall perish   (3) subject: these prophets

(3) subject: the people (2) predicate: shall be left lying (1) famine and sword

Fig. 11.1. "Measure for measure" and the peace prophets

In its reversed order, רעב וחרב emphasizes the chiastic structure of the prophecy as a whole and adds accentuation to the measure-for-measure scheme as a total punishment.

As seen in Jer 23:2, the correlation between the shepherds' sins and their fate is built on the two opposing meanings of פקד.

Assuredly, thus said the LORD, the God of Israel, concerning the shepherds who should tend My people: It is you who let My flock scatter and go astray. You gave no thought to them [literally: you did not count them], but I am going to punish you, for your wicked acts—declares the LORD.	לכן כה־אמר יהוה אלהי יש־ ראל על־הרעים הרעים את־ עמי אתם הפצתם את־צאני ותדחום ולא פקדתם אתם הנני פקד עליכם את־רע מעלליכם נאם־יהוה.

The shepherds neglect the flock (לא פקד את). That is, they do not count them (as in Num 3:16), do not remember them (as in Gen 21:1; Exod 3:16; 4:31), and thus do not pay proper attention to their needs.[28] In retaliation, God is going to punish those leaders (פקד על; similarly Jer 13:21).[29]

The two opposing verbal phrases are both typically Jeremian (under the possible influence of Hosea (see יזכר עונם ויפקד חטאותם, Hos 8:13; 9:9; Jer 14:10). Most of the occurrences of פקד with God as agent depict God as deciding the fates of human beings, his people or other peoples. The governing meaning of פקד על is "remember for the worse" or "punish." This meaning is common in the Hebrew Bible and particularly in Jeremiah (occurring fifteen times in prophecies of judgment against Israel [e.g., 21:14] and thirteen times in prophecies against the nations [e.g., 25:12]). Only four times does this negative meaning occur with פקד את (6:15; 14:10; PAN Jer 49:8; 50:18); and only four times in Jeremiah does פקד את bear the meaning "remember for the better" or "favor" (15:15; 27:22; 29:10; 32:5). These two antagonistic meanings (together with the concrete basic meaning "count" and the more abstract meaning "remember") thus serve this prophecy in the most efficient way. The two opposing constructions craft a direct measure-for-measure balance between the sin and its consequence.

In Jer 28:15–16, the pun on שלח is another example of the effort to create a deliberate correlation between sin and judgment:

28. See the detailed description of the shepherds' responsibilities in Ezek 34:1–6 and Gen 31:38–40.

29. For the function of these oppositional meanings of פקד, see Andre, *Determining the Destiny*, 191–98; and Begg, "Yahweh's 'Visitation.'" Andre (234–35) emphasizes the legal nature of פקד in contexts of obedience or disobedience to God and even suggests a ritual-cultic setting to his nuance of the term. Compare Ezekiel, where פקד occurs only once (PAN Ezek 38:8).

¹⁵Listen, Hananiah! <u>The LORD did not send you</u>, and you have given this people lying assurances. ¹⁶Assuredly, thus said the LORD: <u>I am going to banish you from off the face of the earth</u>. This year you shall die, for you have urged disloyalty to the LORD.

¹⁵שמע־נא חנניה <u>לא־שלחך</u> <u>יהוה</u> ואתה הבטחת את־ העם הזה על־שקר. ¹⁶לכן כה אמר יהוה <u>הנני משלחך מעל</u> <u>פני האדמה</u> השנה אתה מת כי־סרה דברת אל־יהוה.

Hananiah's sin is his persistence in unsanctioned (and untruthful) prophecy (indicated by the use of *qal* שלח ["send"] with a negative; compare the positive use of this form as a verb of commissioning in 26:15); his death sentence is phrased as being "sent" off the face of the earth (using in the intensive form, *piel* שלח; this form is otherwise used in reference to deportation in 24:5 and 29:20).³⁰

Only two exceptions to this mode of measure for measure occur, once each in Jeremiah and Ezekiel. The first example is Jer 16:16–18:

¹⁶Lo, I am sending for many fishermen
—declares the LORD—
And they shall haul them out;
And after that I will send for many hunters,

And they shall hunt them
Out of every mountain and out of every hill
And out of the clefts of the rocks.
¹⁷For My eyes are on all their ways,
They are not hidden from My presence,
Their iniquity is not concealed from My sight.
¹⁸<u>I will pay them in full—</u>
<u>Nay, doubly for their iniquity and their sins—</u>
Because they have defiled My land
With the corpses of their abominations,
And have filled My own possession
With their abhorrent things.

¹⁶הנני שלח לדוגים
(ק: לדיגים) רבים נאם־יהוה
ודיגום
ואחרי־כן אשלח לרבים
צידים
וצדום
מעל כל־הר ומעל כל־גבעה
ומנקיקי הסלעים.
¹⁷כי עיני על־כל־דרכיהם
לא נסתרו מלפני
ולא־נצפן עונם מנגד עיני.
¹⁸ושלמתי ראשונה
משנה עונם וחטאתם
על חללם את־ארצי
בנבלת שקוציהם
ותועבותיהם מלאו
את־נחלתי.

---

30. Other examples of this wordplay to establish a correspondence of measure for measure between sin and punishment are found in Jer 5:19; 16:10–13; PAN Jer 50:15, 29; Ezek 7:27; 11:3–11; 36:6–8; PAN Ezek 35:15 (which develops the core of the prophecy of 35:14; see Kasher, *Ezekiel 1–24*, 116–17); and 35:5–6 (which shows a thematic correlation between sword and bloodshed that would pursue Edom as its fitting punishment).

This prophecy forecasts complete calamity in the land, and it portrays God as the one who summons the fishermen and hunters to carry out the punishment.[31] Scholars question whether 16:18 is original in this context, feeling that (1) it is redundant in light of the two necessary components of this judgment prophecy: the punishment (16:16) explained as retaliation for their sins (16:17); in addition, (2) the term שקוצים (16:18) is unusual in Jeremiah.[32] Even given these literary and lexical difficulties, traditional and critical interpreters are baffled more by the theological difficulty here concerning the divine justice, a difficulty that seems to express an exceptional perspective within Jeremiah.[33]

"I will pay them in full—nay, doubly for their iniquity and their sins" proclaims a double intensity of judgment in relation to the measure of sin, which appears to indicate an unbalanced retaliation from the side of God and jeopardizes the equity of divine justice. Yet, for four reasons this saying should not be dissociated from the prophet himself: (1) Jeremiah uses משנה in the sense "double affliction" in his request for divine vengeance against his enemies: משנה שברון שברם ("and shatter them with double destruction," 17:18). This phrasing, however, does not garner an "inter-

31. So Rudolph, *Jeremia*, 112; and Holladay (*Jeremiah*, 1.477), both of whom reject the idea that these verses refer to a judgment of exile. In identifying those enemies, Rudolph (112) suggests that the fishermen and the hunters refer to the two sieges against Jerusalem (in 597 and 586), whereas Holladay (1.478) suggests that these characters represent Egypt and Babylon respectively, and dates the prophecy to 609–605.

32. For the first argument see Rudolph, *Jeremia*, 112. Although the phrase נבלת שקוציהם is indeed a *hapax* in Jeremiah (פגרי גלוליכם in Lev 26:30 is a close parallel), שקוצים does occur in Jer 7:30; 13:27; 32:34. Moreover, it seems that the meaning of this phrase is twofold, and the double meaning is very much in line with the prophet's messages. First of all, the phrase denigrates the ineffectiveness of other gods and thus is quite similar to other Jeremian references; see שקר (5:2; 10:14; 13:25) and הבל (8:19; 10:3, 8, 15). On another level, this phrase suggests the profanation of the land as result of the widespread death resulting from the destruction (7:33; 16:4; 34:20; 36:30). Therefore, there is no need to assume an allusion to some sort of death cult here (pace Carroll, *Jeremiah*, 346). Holladay argues that 16:18 is secondary, but that it is added by the prophet himself, to refer back to 16:16. Thus, Holladay dates this addition to the time soon after the Jehoiachin exile or even after the destruction itself. I do not exclude this option.

33. An additional textual difficulty may be seen in 16:18, in the occurrence of ראשונה in the Masoretic Text and its absence from the Septuagint. Rudolph (*Jeremia*, 112–13), Holladay (*Jeremiah*, 1.477, 479), and Carroll (*Jeremiah*, 345) argue that it is a secondary gloss, explaining the chronological relationship between the judgment prophecy of 16:16–17 and the consolation prophecy of 16:14–15.

pretive defense" in the individual-lament context of 17:14–18.[34] (2) The possibility that divine retaliation may not stand in direct correlation to human deeds is also expressed in contexts of salvation (Isa 61:7; Zech 9:12; Job 42:10). Therefore, there is no need to deny this possibility in reference to judgment, especially when the prophet is portraying complete annihilation as the retaliatory response. (3) In addition, a double judgment over Jerusalem's sins also opens the prophecies of Second Isaiah: כי לקחה מיד יהוה כפלים בכל־חטאתיה ("for she has received at the hand of the LORD double for all her sins," Isa 40:2).[35] (4) A similar theological paradox—the prophet's relationship to God when God acts as the enemy of his people—is a central component of Jeremiah's prophetic message.[36]

The second exception to the mode of measure for measure is Ezek 21:6–10:

[6] Then the word of the Lord came to me: [7] O mortal, set your face toward Jerusalem and proclaim against her sanctuaries and prophesy against the land of Israel. [8] Say to the land of Israel: Thus said the Lord: I am going to deal with you! I will draw My sword from its sheath, and I will wipe out from you both the righteous and the wicked. [9] In order to wipe out from you both the righteous and the wicked, My sword shall assuredly be unsheathed against all flesh from south to north; [10] and all flesh shall know that I the Lord have drawn My sword from its sheath, not to be sheathed again.	[6] ויהי דבר־יהוה אלי לאמר. [7] בן־אדם שים פניך אל־ ירושלים והטף אל־מקדשים והנבא אל־אדמת ישראל. [8] ואמרת לאדמת ישראל כה אמר יהוה הנני אליך והוצאתי חרבי מתערה והכרתי ממך צדיק ורשע. [9] יען אשר־הכרתי ממך צדיק ורשע לכן תצא חרבי מתערה אל־כל־בשר מנגב צפון. [10] וידעו כל־בשר כי אני יהוה הוצאתי חרבי מתערה לא תשוב עוד.

34. A similarly extreme request for vengeance appears in the individual lament in Jer 12:3; see McKane, *Jeremiah 1–25*, 414.

35. Is it possible to assume that Second Isaiah here interprets Jeremiah's prophecy of 16:18? If that could be proven, it would be another clue, at least, to the way that later prophets understood Jeremiah. This example is not mentioned in the lists of allusions and innerbiblical exegesis between Second Isaiah and Jeremiah documented by Holladay, *Jeremiah*, 2.86–88; Sommer, *Prophet Reads Scripture*, 57–58; and Paul, *Isaiah 40–66*, 53.

36. Compare Ps 103:10–14, which accepts judgment to the point it is presented as even less than fit for the transgressions. See §12.1.

This passage not only contradicts the measure-for-measure conception but appears to contradict the very foundations of divine justice. The sword unsheathed symbolizes a total, collective destruction, inclusive to the utmost, to the point that it does not distinguish the righteous from the wicked; "all flesh" are its targets. Zimmerli argues that צדיק ורשע is a merism that stands for the entire population and that by this inclusive phrase the theological difficulty is somewhat resolved.[37] But, this stylistic suggestion does not dissolve the great theological challenge this prophecy poses to interpreters.[38] Rather, this theological challenge is unique and stands in clear contradiction of other prophecies in Ezekiel (e.g., 9:3–10; 14:12–23; 18:1–20). As in other areas, these characteristics evolve from the ad hoc circumstances of each prophetic proclamation.[39]

While very different, these two prophecies (Jer 16:16–18; Ezek 21:6–10) illustrate the prophets' need to emphasize both the exclusive role of God in the destruction of his people and the totality of his actions. These thematic needs seem to overpower the measure-for-measure principle of divine justice and even to work against it. Yet, the general transgenerational framework maintains the justification of the divine action—the accumulation of sins by the present generation in continuity with those of the previous generations brings about this severe divine judgment.

11.2.2. Jeremiah's and Ezekiel's Uses of the Transgenerational Retribution Conception

Jeremiah's and Ezekiel's respective uses of the retribution conception encompass separate references to its two components, sin and judgment, that may be mapped in chronological sequence. Sin constitutes the starting

37. Zimmerli, *Ezekiel*, 1.424. See Qara (to 21:8) for the suggestion that the prophet's contemporaries are in view—Jehoiachin's generation as the righteous, and Zedekiah's as the wicked—which avoids a schematic understanding of the language.

38. Greenberg (*Ezekiel 21–37*, 420, 446–47) suggests that Ezekiel here alludes to Abraham's negotiation with God (Gen 18:23). In addition, Greenberg argues that in כל-בשר the prophet refers to the entire world population and that this universalistic perspective is among the unique features of Ezek 21:1–12.

39. So Greenberg, *Ezekiel 21–37*, 446–47; also Joyce, *Ezekiel*, 156. I find this suggestion more plausible than that of Cooke (*Ezekiel*, 228), who seeks to distinguish between systematic and schematic prophecies, on the one hand, and prophecies of more narrow perspective, formed under the influence of the prophet's mental distress, on the other. In this respect Ezek 9:3–10 clearly does not accord with the other schematic prophecies. Zimmerli (*Ezekiel*, 1.422), in contrast, refers 21:1–12 to the Ezekiel school.

point, but from which juncture within the national history are the people held responsible for their current fate? Judgment frames the end point, and yet, what is the responsibility of the current generation ("the sons") for the destruction and exiles that have been inflicted upon them? Unsettled questions, then, arise on both ends, and these appear to be addressed in both prophetic books.

11.2.2.1. Jeremiah: When Did Transgression Begin?

The notion of a starting point for transgression in generations past is presented in prophetic and nonprophetic sources in two different ways. The first refers to past events in only a very general way that does not pinpoint the actual sinners, whether these are from the parents' generation or some previous generation, for example, the references in communal laments to עון אבתינו ("the iniquity of our fathers," Jer 14:20)[40] or עונת ראשנים (either "iniquities of the forefathers" or "former iniquities," Ps 79:8).[41] Of special interest is the use of the metaphoric term מנעורינו, which conjoins past and present in כי ליהוה אלהינו חטאנו אנחנו ואבותינו מנעורינו ועד־היום הזה ("for we have sinned against the LORD our God, <u>we and our fathers from our youth to this day</u>," Jer 3:25; the same term, מנעורינו, appears in 3:24 and, quoting Ephraim, in 31:19). נער in the Hebrew Bible refers to an infant's first months (Moses in Exod 2:6), a suckling toddler (Samuel in 1 Sam 1:22–26), a child who is just acquiring knowledge and language skills (Isa 7:16; 8:4), a young boy (Solomon in 1 Kgs 3:7; and Jeremiah at the time of his commissioning in Jer 1:6).[42] In all these instances, נער indicates a

---

40. All of the occurrences of the phrase עון אבות emphasize that the sons sin like their predecessors (see also Lev 26:39–40; Isa 65:7; Ps 109:13–16; Dan 9:16; Jer 11:10).

41. עונת ראשנים may be interpreted with two different syntactical constructions. The Septuagint reads ראשנים as an adjective, and likewise NJPS: "our former iniquities." In this construction, the earlier iniquities are those of the current generation. The phrase may also be understood as a construct "iniquities of the forefathers/former generations"—which conveys a more long-term perspective. In Jer 11:10 עונת אבותם הראשנים clearly stands for earlier generations; see Targum and Ibn Ezra on Ps 79:8; as also Weiser, *Psalms*, 543; Kraus, *Psalms 60–150*, 132; and Zenger in Hossfeld and Zenger, *Psalms*, 2.302–3, 306. In any case, 79:8 clearly ties the current generation with its predecessors.

42. In strings of nouns, נער takes different positions: נער–בחור–זקן (Ps 148:12; Lam 2:21), נער–איש–זקן (Josh 6:21), or נער–בחור–איש–זקן (Jer 51:22); compare עולל– בחור–איש–זקן–מלא ימים (Jer 6:11). Hence there is a parallel between נער and עולל. For the different meanings of נער, see Fuhs, "נַעַר *naʿar*."

young age, prior to maturity and self-understanding. This is also the case with regard to the noun נעורים, which indicates youth, inexperience, immaturity, and dependency (Num 30:17; Ps 71:5–6, 17–18).[43] It is thus hard to accommodate these uses of נער and נעורים with the metaphor concerning the people's life. Does נעורים designate the period after the exodus but prior to the settlement; or should it be understood as the early settlement period? This metaphor is clearly built upon a chronological anchor within the human life cycle, so that sins from the נעורים period *should* refer to the early period of the God-people covenant relationship. Yet, in Jer 2:2, חסד נעוריך, for instance, points to the wandering period, whereas 2:5–7, which describes this early covenant relationship, specifies three periods of time: the exodus, the desert wanderings, and the settlement. This metaphorical language, therefore, seems to be shared by confessions of sins in communal laments and by the prophet; and in both corpora, this time reference is intentionally blurred and inconclusive as to the starting point of sin.

Other passages in Jeremiah give no less than three specific, and yet different, starting points for the people's transgression: the day of the exodus, the period of settlement, and the time when Jerusalem is built.[44] These three points are mentioned in poetic units (Jer 2:2; 22:21), but they are mostly found in prose passages; and thus literary criticism may explain these differences diachronically.[45] All three points form part of the justification of God for his imposition of transgenerational retribution.

a. *The day of the exodus*

In four prose passages, the prophet specifies that the people's covenantal obligations began ביום הוציאי אותם/העלותי/החזיקי בידם להוציאם מארץ מצרים ("on the day I took them out of/brought them out of/took them by

---

43. Note the use of נעורים in individual proclamations of obedience to God (1 Kgs 18:12; Ps 71:5, 17). נעורים also designates the "youth" of the nation. It points to times of national sin (Isa 47:12; Ezek 16:22, 43, 60) and of national obedience (Hos 2:17; Jer 2:2; 3:4 [in a quotation]).

44. Compare the designation of transgenerational transgression against God without a specific starting point, which is indicated, for instance, by the prophetic formula שלח . . . השכם ושלח, Jer 35:15; also 7:25; 25:4; 26:5; 29:19; 44:4; and with minor variations in 11:7; 32:33; 35:14.

45. Hence, Mowinckel (*Zur Komposition des Buches Jeremia*, 20, 31) relegates Jer 2:2 and 22:21 to his source A, but considers the prose verses from the C source, the non-Jeremian prose sermons. See §3.4.4.1.

the hand to lead them out of the land of Egypt," Jer 7:21–28 at 7:22; 11:1–14 at 11:4, 7; 31:31–34 at 31:32; 34:8–22 at 34:13).[46] From that point on, says the prophet, the people are committed to general obedience (11:1–8), to specific laws (six of the ten commandments, 7:9), and to other selected obligations, cultic and social (7:3–5, 21–28), including laws concerning manumission of slaves (34:14). From that point until the present, however, they are repeatedly disobedient to God (ולא שמעו, 7:24, 26, 27; 11:7–8; 34:13–14).[47] According to the prophet, the people betrayed the first covenant immediately upon its initiation and continued in that path ever since (31:32).[48] The laws alluded to in these passages serve as paradigms for the covenantal obligations and the people's disobedience.[49] In beginning with the initial establishment of the covenant relationship, the prophet contracts the time elapsed between that first event and the current generation sitting in Jerusalem.[50]

b. The settlement in the land

According to two passages (Jer 2:4–9; 32:16–25), the history of divine benevolence begins with the exodus, continues in the desert wanderings,

46. For a thorough discussion of this formula, which I argue is a distinctive Jeremian formulation based on Priestly formulas and covenant conceptions, see Rom-Shiloni, "On the Day."

47. The statement of sending the prophets השכם ושלח refers twice to the exodus (Jer 7:25; 11:7) and once to the relatively short period from Jeremiah's commission to the fourth year of Jehoiakim (25:3). Disobedience to the Sabbath (17:21–22, 24) is presented as having been disobeyed in Jerusalem from of old (17:22–23), under the general rubric אבותיכם.

48. Jeremiah ignores Sinai/Horeb in his prophecies concerning the God-people covenant; in our passages, he uses the Priestly conception that the people are obligated to specific commandments during the day/night when the exodus took place (e.g., Exod 12); see Rom-Shiloni, "On the Day," 14–24.

49. For the use of pentateuchal legal traditions in Jeremiah, see Rom-Shiloni, "Actualization of Pentateuchal Legal Traditions"; "How Can You Say"; "Compositional Harmonization"; and "Forest and the Trees."

50. אבות occurs in several prophecies within Jeremiah as a general retrospective term, mostly combined with an allusion to the current generation. This phrasing may be used to explain and/or describe the severe judgment of exile (e.g., אתם ואבותיכם, Jer 9:15; 16:12, 13; 44:3, 21); to designate past promises with a present significance, such as the promise of the land (7:7; 11:5; 16:15; 30:3; 32:22); or to emphasize continuity throughout the generations in the place (7:14), the city (23:39), and the land (24:10; 25:5; 35:15). While not limited to the retribution concept, these phrases add to Jeremiah's conception of transgenerational national responsibility.

and is brought to completion with settlement in the land (2:6–7), when the promise of the land is fulfilled (32:16–25). These narratives of God's salvation and care highlight the people's ingratitude, which starts with settlement in the land (2:7). This same technique of chronological constriction, telescoping hundreds of years of disobedience into a continuous present, constitutes the climax of the historical review in Jeremiah's prayer in 32:20–23:[51]

[20] You displayed signs and marvels in the land of Egypt with lasting effect, and won renown in Israel and among mankind to this very day. [21] You freed Your people Israel from the land of Egypt.... [22] You gave them this land that You had sworn to their fathers to give them, a land flowing with milk and honey, [23] and they came and took possession of it. But they did not listen to You or follow Your Teaching; they did nothing of what You commanded them to do. Therefore you have caused all this misfortune to befall them.	[20] אֲשֶׁר־שַׂמְתָּ אֹתוֹת וּמֹפְתִים בְּאֶרֶץ־מִצְרַיִם עַד־הַיּוֹם הַזֶּה וּבְיִשְׂרָאֵל וּבָאָדָם וַתַּעֲשֶׂה־לְּךָ שֵׁם כַּיּוֹם הַזֶּה. [21] וַתֹּצֵא אֶת־עַמְּךָ אֶת־יִשְׂרָאֵל מֵאֶרֶץ מִצְרָיִם ... [22] וַתִּתֵּן לָהֶם אֶת־הָאָרֶץ הַזֹּאת אֲשֶׁר־נִשְׁבַּעְתָּ לַאֲבוֹתָם לָתֵת לָהֶם אֶרֶץ זָבַת חָלָב וּדְבָשׁ. [23] וַיָּבֹאוּ וַיִּרְשׁוּ אֹתָהּ וְלֹא־שָׁמְעוּ בְקוֹלֶךָ וּבְתֹרוֹתֶךָ (ק: וּבְתוֹרָתְךָ) לֹא־ הָלָכוּ אֵת כָּל־אֲשֶׁר צִוִּיתָה לָהֶם לַעֲשׂוֹת לֹא עָשׂוּ וַתַּקְרֵא אֹתָם אֵת כָּל־הָרָעָה הַזֹּאת.

Jeremiah 32:23 opens with mention of the settlement in the land and closes with "this misfortune," which is further explained in 32:24 as the arrival of the Babylonian army and its siege against Jerusalem. The two events are far away from each other by hundreds of years, and yet they are brought together in a seamless move from past to present.

---

51. The prayer in Jer 32:16–25 is for the most part considered by scholars to be non-Jeremian, seen instead as DtrJ in its character; see Thiel, *Jeremia 26–52*, 31–33. Carroll (*Jeremiah*, 625) finds this prayer to be a faithful representative of penitential prayers of the Persian period or even later (similar to Neh 9:6–37; Dan 9:3–19); see also McKane, *Jeremiah 26–52*, 842–45, esp. 845. Other scholars agree upon the secondary nature of some of its verses (32:17ab–23); e.g., Bright (*Jeremiah*, 298) thinks these highly conventional prayer expressions are secondary intrusions; while Holladay (*Jeremiah*, 2.208–9) and Lundbom (*Jeremiah 21–36*, 499–502) attribute the compilation of the prophetical passages in Jer 32 to Baruch and consider the prayer to correspond to the events of 587. In the present context, I argue that this prayer reworks several Deuteronomic/Deuteronomistic conceptions, crafted by the prophet or by a slightly later follower not necessarily of the DtrJ layer.

Jeremiah 32:18 introduces this telescoped history by reshaping the divine epithets of the second commandment:[52]

You show kindness to the thousandth generation, but visit the guilt of the fathers upon their children after them.	עשה חסד לאלפים ומשלם עון אבות אל־חיק בניהם אחריהם.

Two changes should be noted. The first is one of style: the prophet switches the order of the two epithets, thereby opens with a statement of divine benevolence but ends with the weight of the sentence upon retribution (note also the semantic change of פקד עון into משלם עון, which brings Jer 32:18 closer to Deut 7:10).[53] The second change is one of substance: the prophet disconnects the meting out of punishment from the four-generation limit given in the Decalogue (likewise Exod 34:7; Num 14:18). Here, judgment is still transgenerational but has no chronological limitations. This transformation of the Decalogue's conception of retribution, then, forms the basis for the prophet's contention that the present sinful generation (the sons) within the sixth century is under judgment for a long period of transgression, from the time of the settlement in the land until their own day.[54]

52. The allusion to the divine epithet within the Decalogue (Exod 20:5–6; Deut 5:9–10) is pointed out by interpreters, oftentimes to substantiate the DtrJ character of this prayer; see Thiel, *Jeremia 26–52*, 32. But the literary dependencies and the exegetical traits should be understood in a much broader perspective; see Fishbane, *Biblical Interpretation*, 335–45, esp. 341–45.

53. See §11.1. A similar chiastic transposition occurs between Exod 20:5–6 and 34:7; see Weiss, *Scriptures in Their Own Light*, 492–93. The lexical difference between פקד עון and משלם עון may be explained as a paraphrastic attraction of שלם as a substitute for פקד. The verb שילם commonly occurs in Jeremiah in contexts describing retribution (eight times): in the phrases שילם עון (16:18; 32:18), שילם כפעלה/ם (25:14; 50:29), and שילם גמול/רעה (51:6, 24, 56 [2x]). It likewise occurs elsewhere in the Hebrew Bible in retribution contexts, denoting both reward and punishment (Gen 44:4: Deut 7:10; 32:41; Judg 1:7; Ps 7:5; Ruth 2:12), with שילם עון also in Isa 65:6–7. Compare פקד עון, which occurs twice in Jeremiah (25:12; 36:31). This change is one of the indicators for the use of an original Jeremianic idiom even within the conventional expressions of this prayer.

54. A similar transformation of divine epithets occurs in Deut 7:9–10. The chronological pattern is interpreted differently there, so that "kindness" lasts לאלף דור (which suggests an accurate interpretation of לאלפים), but judgment is immediate within the lifetime of the transgressor, אל־פניו; there is no mention of transgenerational retribution (7:10). Compare Weiss (*Scriptures in Their Own Light*, 501–2), who explains על־

c. The day Jerusalem is established

One passage, Jer 32:26–35, invokes this moment as the beginning of the period of transgression, specifically 32:30–31:[55]

[30] For the people of Israel and Judah have done nothing but evil in My sight since their youth; the people of Israel have done nothing but vex Me by their conduct—declares the LORD. [31] This city has aroused My anger and My wrath from the day it was built until this day; so that it must be removed from My sight.	כי־היו בני־ישראל ובני יהודה [30] אך עשים הרע בעיני מנערתיהם[56] כי בני־ישראל אך מכעסים אתי במעשה ידיהם נאם־יהוה. [31] כי על־אפי ועל־חמתי היתה לי העיר הזאת למן־היום אשר בנו אותה ועד היום הזה להסירה מעל פני.

Disobedience to God (32:33) is expressed in terms of cultic iniquities per-petrated in YHWH's temple, on roofs of private houses within the city, and in the Valley of the Son of Hinnom (32:29, 34, 35). A long list of po-litical and religious leaders, as well as the entire population of Jerusalem, participates in these denigrated cults (32:30, 32). But what seems to be of special interest is the reference to the history of Jerusalem. The people's youth (מנערתיהם, 32:30) is defined as the time of the establishment of Jerusalem; thus their transgressions have accumulated throughout the monarchic period, the Davidic regime.[57]

The common denominator in Jeremiah's use of these three times to

---

שלשים ועל־רבעים in the Decalogue as undefined and unlimited, thus equal to לאלפים. Weiss is followed by Weinfeld, *Deuteronomy 1–11*, 296–97.

55. Duhm (*Jeremia*, 266–70), Mowinckel (*Zur Komposition des Buches Jeremia*, 31), Thiel (*Jeremia 26–52*, 34–37), and others consider Jer 32:26–44 to be from the DtrJ sermons. The significant difference between the units 32:26–35 and 32:36–44 in artic-ulating the beginning of transgression is but one of the distinctions that substantiate the argument that the passages within Jer 32 are clearly not of one prophetic hand.

56. מנערתיהם (Jer 32:30) is a *hapax*; compare the use of the more frequent noun נעורים. Jer 32:30a and 32:30b MT present a doublet; the Septuagint does not have 32:30b; see Holladay, *Jeremiah*, 2.205.

57. References to the people's iniquity together with their royal leaders during the monarchic period may also be traced in Jer 19:4; 44:9, 17, 21. In Jer 44, the sinners themselves understand their actions to constitute a legitimate continuation of their long tradition of cultic practices to מלכת השמים (44:17, 21). In Jer 7:18, this cult is further said to be handled by whole families and thus led by several proximate generations within families, who share the guilt for its conduct. But note that 32:26–35 remains

characterize the people's transgressions seems to be the great chronological gap between these historical events or epochs and his hearers' present. Hundreds of years are brought together in close proximity to illustrate the heavy burden of sins carried by the people and now subject to divine judgment. Merismatic phrasing and chronological constriction construct a close connection of continuity between fathers and sons, so that the history of transgression becomes a part of the present burden of sin carried by Jerusalem and Judah. To correspond with this long-term period of iniquity, the prophet transforms the Decalogue's traditional divine epithet פקד עון אב על־בנים על־שלשים ועל־רבעים to characterize God as the one who "visit[s] the guilt of the fathers upon their children after them" (Jer 32:18)—for an unlimited period of time. God acts severely against Jerusalem, but he is certainly not a capricious God; he acts as one could expect, as a judge who metes out justice against a people that continuously violates his covenant (11:1–14; 32:20–23, 30–31).

11.2.2.2. Ezekiel and Transgenerational Retribution Conception

The idea that the generation of the destruction add their own sins to a long tradition of iniquity is clearly held by Ezekiel as well. Since Ezekiel is acclaimed as the innovator of the conception of individual and immediate retribution, it seems useful to examine those prophecies where the prophet emphasizes that a long history of transgression by the people and their ancestors culminates in the divine judgment of the deportations to Babylon and the total annihilation of Jerusalem.

Ezekiel's commissioning prophecy in 1:1–3:15 presents the destruction generation as another bead in a long chain of national sinners. In this introductory prophecy, the prophet does not differentiate between the Jehoiachin exiles now in Babylon and those who still remained in Jerusalem after 597.[58] The prophecy accentuates the people as a whole as ongoing rebellious in three ways.

(a) The prophet locates his contemporaries within the transgenerational chain of transgression. Ezekiel 2:3–5 uses בני ישראל, which is the

---

with *bamot* and rooftop worship for the Baal, pouring libations to other gods, and Molech worship (32:29, 35).

58. The commission prophecy is the only passage in Ezekiel that takes this harsh position against Ezekiel's immediate audience. On Ezekiel's general attitude toward his fellow-Jehoiachin exiles versus those who still remain in Jerusalem, see Rom-Shiloni, *Exclusive Inclusivity*, 140–85.

general national label, but less common in Ezekiel.[59] Under this rubric, three phrases further characterize this people: they rebel against God (גוים המורדים אשר מרדו־בי ["those nations of rebels, who have rebelled against Me"], 2:3a);[60] they and their ancestors rebel from of old until the present (המה ואבותם פשעו בי עד־עצם היום הזה ["they as well as their fathers have defied Me to this very day"], 2:3b); and "the sons"—the present generation to whom Ezekiel is sent—are tougher and even more rebellious than their predecessors (והבנים קשי פנים וחזקי־לב אני שולח אותך אליהם ["for the sons are brazen of face and stubborn of heart. I send you to them"], 2:4a; see §11.4.1.1). This gradual zooming in on the sons and the explicit reference to המה ואבותם are implicit references to the divine epithet פקד עון אבת על בנים in the Decalogue.

(b) Rebellion appears to be an innate character of the people, who rebelled for generations and therefore are called by Ezekiel בית המרי ("house of rebellion," 2:5, 6, 8; but only מרי in 2:7). This designation is an elaborated borrowing of בני־מרי (Num 17:25), the denigrating designation by which God calls בני ישראל (17:27) at the close of the Korahite rebellion (Num 16–17). Adapting מרי, Ezekiel applies this designation to his audience, thus giving special force to the severity of the problem with the people's behavior. Both בני and בית emphasize distinctively that the present generation's rebellion represents the transgenerational continuation of the earlier generation's sin. Yet, Ezekiel seems to cling to בית מרי following his more common reference to his audience as בית ישראל (e.g., 3:4, 7 [2x]; and throughout the book).[61]

(c) Rebellious behavior is a continuing phenomenon. The use of *yiqtol*

59. Greenberg ("Use of the Ancient Versions") convincingly suggests a literary and contextual explanation for the use of בני ישראל here and thus validates the Masoretic Text reading. See also Zimmerli, *Ezekiel*, 2.563–65.

60. Commentators struggle with the use of the plural expression גוים המורדים; see Rashi and Qimhi; the Septuagint omits the phrase אל־גוים in a wish to ease the difficulty. A distinctive designation of the exiles as descendants of the two nations and use of the term גוים as a unifying name for the two kingdoms (Israel and Judah) occur explicitly in Ezek 37:22 and implicitly in 35:10 and 36:12–15. This might be explainable as an intentional omission due to the exegetical problem. See also Zimmerli (*Ezekiel*, 1.133), who (following the Septuagint) accepts אל־גוים as a secondary addition referring to the prophet's mission to the nations (influenced by Jer 1:5, 10). Compare NJPS, which translates this phrase in the singular.

61. So Greenberg, *Ezekiel 1–20*, 65–66. Sixteen of twenty-three occurrences of מרי in the Hebrew Bible are within Ezekiel; fourteen of them are in the phrase בית (ה)מרי,

and participial verbal forms (2:5; 3:7–9), alongside with the portrayal of the qualities of the people through such attributes as קשי פנים וחזקי־לב (2:4; 3:7), contributes to the understanding that rebellion is a steady, constant, ongoing stance of the people toward their God (3:7). Nevertheless, Ezekiel puts special stress on the independent status of the sons, in comparison with their fathers (see §11.4.1.1).

The transgenerational retribution conception also stands in the background of the second of the symbolic acts in Ezek 4–5. The symbolic act divides into separate pictures by content and geographical places. Four of the units refer to Jerusalem under siege and build a gradual story of its suffering (4:1–3, 9–11, 16–17), which then culminates in the representation of its fall and annihilation in 5:1–4 (see §9.1.1). In this sequence, 4:4–8 opens up a different issue, the issue of divine justice, with emphasis on the people's iniquity (a topic that closes the chapter in 4:16–17). Yet this new topic seems to be part of the basic narrative flow of the unit, since 4:9–11 refers to preparation of food while the prophet is lying on his left side (compare 4:9b and 4:4).[62] Ezekiel 4:12–15, on the other hand, seems to be out of place in this sequence, differing in both geographical target and content; these verses treat the question of defiled food in exile and confront the tragedy of dislocation.[63] The concluding statement in 4:16–17 (borrowed from Lev 26:39)—ונשמו איש ואחיו ונמקו בעונם ("they shall stare at each other, heartsick over their iniquity")—is used to justify the harsh judgment: sinners suffer because of their own iniquities:[64]

---

and two appear with מרי alone (2:7; 44:6). See עם מרי in Isa 30:9. מרי as a description of the people's behavior and deeds is also found in Deut 31:27 and Neh 9:17.

62. Compare Zimmerli (*Ezekiel*, 1.163–64), who takes 4:4–8 as a secondary insertion by the Ezekiel school (perhaps even in several phases), which may explain the seeming contradictory attitude to Israel and Judah in these verses in comparison to Ezek 23. But see Joyce (*Ezekiel*, 85–86), who aptly points out the interchangeability of Israel and Judah when these terms are placed together in Ezekiel (8:6, 17) and the specific, *different* terms the prophet uses when addressing the North.

63. Ezek 4:12–15 refers to existence in exile, and I therefore consider this passage to be an expansion focused on exile in a context that otherwise focuses on Jerusalem and its fate. See Rom-Shiloni, *Exclusive Inclusivity*, 173–78, esp. 176–77.

64. So translated by Greenberg, *Ezekiel 1–20*, 99. נמקק/(מקק) בעון occurs only in Lev 26:39 and twice in Ezekiel (4:17; 24:23); see מוך בעון in Ps 106:43. For this style of closing the prophecy by announcing a calamitous verdict upon the sinner, see Ezek 3:18, 19; 7:13, 16, 19; 18:17–20; 21:30, 34; 24:23; 33:6, 8, 9; 35:5; 44:10.

Ezekiel 4:4–8 illustrates in the most figurative way the phrase נשא עון, as the prophet is to literally bear the people's burden of iniquity lying on each of his two sides for long periods of time:

<table>
<tr>
<td>

[4] "Then lie on your left side, and let it bear the punishment of the House of Israel; for as many days as you lie on it you shall bear their punishment. [5] For I impose upon you three hundred and ninety days, corresponding to the number of the years of their punishment; and so you shall bear the punishment for the House of Israel. [6] When you have completed these, you shall lie another forty days on your right side, and bear the punishment of the House of Judah. I impose on you one day for each year. [7] Then, with bared arm, set your face toward besieged Jerusalem and prophesy against it. [8] Now I put cords upon you, so that you cannot turn from side to side until you complete your days of siege."

</td>
<td>

‫⁴ואתה שכב על־צדך השמאלי‬
‫ושמת את־עון בית־ישראל‬
‫עליו מספר הימים אשר תשכב‬
‫עליו תשא את־עונם. ⁵ואני‬
‫נתתי לך את־שני עונם למספר‬
‫ימים שלש־מאות ותשעים יום‬
‫ונשאת עון בית־ישראל. ⁶וכלית‬
‫את־אלה ושכבת על־צדך‬
‫הימוני (ק: הימני) שנית ונשאת‬
‫את־עון בית־יהודה ארבעים יום‬
‫יום לשנה יום לשנה נתתיו לך.‬
‫⁷ואל מצור ירושלים תכין פניך‬
‫וזרעך חשופה ונבאת עליה.‬
‫⁸והנה נתתי עליך עבותים ולא‬
‫תהפך מצדך אל־צדך עד־‬
‫כלותך ימי מצורך.‬

</td>
</tr>
</table>

While at face value, several of the diverse, and at times even opposite, meanings of נשא עון may be playing simultaneously in this context, the audience (or the listener/reader) perceives only one of them in the current context.[65]

---

65. See Greenberg, *Ezekiel 1–20*, 104, 123–25; and see references to the reception of this symbolic act in early rabbinic sources (*Leviticus Rabbah* 21:9) and medieval interpreters, who seem to have understood the repetition of שם עון על and נשא עונם in 4:4 to convey two meanings. Rashi and Qara suggest that the phrasing means "suffer for their sins" and, by that, atone for them; and Qimhi explains the first phrase as both "bear and suffer for their sins."

נשא עון stands for the process of atonement in which a priest bears the burden of iniquity and thus cleanses the sinner of his sin (Lev 10:17; 16:21–34; Exod 28:38); this sense is used metaphorically in the divine epithet נשא עון (Exod 34:7).[66] But נשא עון stands just as easily for "bearing the burden of guilt," thus liable to judgment (Lev 5:1, 17; 7:18; Num 14:33–38).[67] Ezekiel certainly draws on his priestly background and knowledge in using this pun in this symbolic act; but in this context, bearing the people's burden does not symbolize any relief or atonement. Rather, it illustrates the long period of transgression committed over many generations by the house of Israel and the house of Judah, and the suffering that may be expected as a result of the coming siege.

A remaining aspect of this passage is the much studied issue of the differing time frames used to measure the people's iniquity: 390 days to symbolize the years of iniquity of the house of Israel and 40 days for the years of the house of Judah.[68] Based on the thematic analysis presented here, this long period of 390/40 years stands for the iniquity of multiple generations, reaching back through the history of Israel (illustrated in-

---

66. See also the phrase העביר עון/חטאת (2 Sam 12:13; 24:10; Zech 3:4; Job 7:21) in contexts of forgiveness (or lack thereof).

67. נשא עון in the meaning "bear iniquity" occurs in Ezek 14:10; 18:19, 20; 44:12; see Cooke, *Ezekiel*, 52; Zimmerli, *Ezekiel*, 1.164–65; and Joyce, *Ezekiel*, 85. For the different meanings of נשא עון, see Schwartz, "Bearing of Sin." Following Schwartz, Anderson (*Sin*, 15–26) explains נשא עון as "bear (the weight of one's) sin" and emphasizes that it stands for the culpability of the offender for his/her crime (24–25, regarding Lev 5:1). Another such metaphor of burden/block of sins that cause downfall is מכשול עון (7:19; 14:3, 4, 7; 18:30; 44:12) translated as "stumbling-block of iniquity" by Greenberg, *Ezekiel 1–20*, 152–53.

68. It is not necessary to revisit the full discussion of the time frames mentioned in this verse. Briefly, see Eliezer of Beaugency (on 4:4–5) for an attempt to map the Masoretic Text's 390 days as standing for those years of iniquity. The Septuagint records different numbers of days: 150 and 40. These numbers correspond to the projected period of judgment, of exile, and thus reflect the understanding of נשא עון as "bear its judgment." This interpretive possibility is suggested by Qimhi (4:4) and embraced by Cooke, *Ezekiel*, 51–54; Zimmerli, *Ezekiel*, 1.167–68; and Greenberg (*Ezekiel 1–20*, 105–6), who suggests that the 40 years of Judah are meant to correspond with the span of its exile according to Ezek 29:11–13. From this perspective, Greenberg suggests that the Septuagint reading of 150 years is an interpretive gloss to draw back as far as circa 700. It is even more troubling to accommodate the 40 years of the house of Judah. The distinction between the sins of Samaria and those of Judah repeats in the metaphoric stories in 16:44–58 and 23:1–35, but in both the iniquities of Judah are said to be more severe than those of its sister(s).

terchangeably by the two kingdoms) and now brought to an end by the destruction and exile.[69]

A third use of the transgenerational conception of retribution is found in three distinctive passages that suggest historical retrospectives on the God-people relationship. Those retrospectives take their places in the disputation speech of Ezek 20:1–38 and in the five familial metaphoric stories (formulated into judgment prophecies) in Ezek 16 and 23. These passages differ both in genre and in their perspectives on the legitimacy of the two Judean communities in Babylon and Jerusalem, but they nevertheless share the same long-term concept of sin and retribution.[70] The retrospectives each begin by dating the people's iniquity to the very early years of their existence. According to 20:1–38 and 23:1–35, the people's iniquity began in Egypt (20:7; 23:3, 19) very soon after God's initial choice of the people (20:5; 23:4).[71] In Ezek 16 and 23 the early years of the relationship between God and Jerusalem are portrayed in terms of the marital metaphor, as the immature period of נעורים, "youth." According to 16:1–14, this youthful period takes place in Canaan and is characterized by God's great care toward the abandoned infant, who then becomes his bride. Yet soon after her marriage, Jerusalem reveals her ingratitude through sinful behavior (16:15–34), resulting in part from having forgotten her youth (16:22, 43). Ezekiel 23:1–35 reinforces the Egyptian connection through repeated references to Oholibah's wild, adulterous youth there (23:3, 8, 19, 21 [2x]).[72]

Beyond these differences between the prophecies (and many more), they all share the conception that the people's disloyalty stems from of old; they behave continuously in this way, from that distant historical point

---

69. In במספר הימים יום לשנה (Ezek 4:5–6) the prophet draws on Num 14:34: אשר־תרתם את־הארץ ארבעים יום יום לשנה יום לשנה תשאו את עונתיכם ארבעים שנה ("You shall bear your punishment for forty years, corresponding to the number of days—forty days—that you scouted the land: a year for each day"); but Ezekiel reverses the direction from the year to the day.

70. On the differences between Ezek 20:1–38 and Ezek 16 and 23 in terms of their perspectives on the opposing claims of the Jehoiachin exiles and those who remain in Jerusalem over the identity of the true people of Judah, see Rom-Shiloni, *Exclusive Inclusivity*, 156–71.

71. Ezek 16:44–58 brings Jerusalem with her two sisters, Samaria and Sodom; thus in ahistoric fashion the passage suggests the long-term iniquity of these two cities(/kingdoms) as well. See Galambush, *Jerusalem in the Book of Ezekiel*, 109–17, esp. 110 and nn54–55.

72. See Galambush, *Jerusalem in the Book of Ezekiel*, 110 and n56.

till present-day Jerusalem (16:36–43, 51–58; 23:22–35, 46–49) or Babylon (20:30–31).[73]

Ezekiel draws on two of the historical starting points for the people's transgression used by Jeremiah: the sojourn in Egypt (Ezek 23:1–4) and the exodus (20:5–9); he also refers to the monarchic period and the long history of the two kingdoms (4:4–11). This prophetic line of justification is meticulously constructed using formal devices that emphasize that God's severe actions against Jerusalem and Judah are in line with the people's iniquity. Great emphasis is given to the principle of measure for measure— that is, God's actions as judge are in accord with the severity of people's transgressions. This principle also stands behind the retrospective construction of the people's iniquity as reaching back to ancient times: the lengthy timespan of sinfulness matches the severity of God's judgment.

Both prophets, then, emphasize that the people's disloyalty existed of old, manifested as continuous, sinful behavior with which God is patient for a very long time; by the early sixth century, God finally decides to act against his people. Turning to this long history of iniquity illustrates the prophets' acceptance of the severity of the current judgment; but at the same time, it implies their recognition of an imbalance between the sins of the current generation and the judgment meted out against them. The concept of transgenerational retribution functions as a major argument of justification exactly because it accumulates human responsibility in proportion to the disaster. This line of argumentation clears God of moral responsibility for overkill, while preserving his roles of just judge and warrior. If we map this prophetic argument onto Green's trilemma of theodicy, we see that it maintains God's roles as both all-powerful warrior and just judge, whose actions are appropriate to the level of human iniquity (see fig. 11.2). But from the moral point of view, responsibility for the distress is laid squarely upon the people who suffer the calamity. Whereas God is proactive in his role as warrior, when it comes to his role as judge, he is at the stage of only reacting to human iniquities. In this justifying configuration, the aspect of divine justice is reconciled with God's roles in causing the distress, as the punishment so absolutely fits the crime(s).

---

73. Ezekiel repeatedly refers to "the fathers" in 20:4, 18, 24, 36 in addition to his direct question in 20:30–31, which is addressed at the current generation of the Jehoiachin exiles (see 20:42, where the promise of the land is to "your fathers"). Such general references to "the fathers" characterize consolation prophecies in 36:28; 37:25 (Jacob); 47:14.

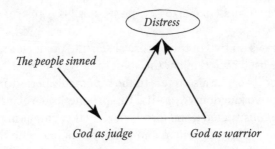

Fig. 11.2. The people's responsibility solves the trilemma of theodicy

While historiographers and prophets frequently use this argument, laying responsibility for the destruction squarely upon the people while justifying God's actions as powerful warrior *and* just judge, it is also evident, though to a lesser extent, from the people's side; that is, this line of justification may also be heard within communal laments in Psalms and Lamentations.

11.2.3. Communal Laments Sporadically Choose Confession of Sins

According to Claus Westermann, confession of sins is not specified as a formal feature of communal laments, and for apt reasons. Confessions of sins rarely appear in the communal laments, or are totally absent from those texts, and there are even several counterclaims of innocence in them (Pss 44:18–23; 80:19).[74] Of the seventeen psalms that presumably reflect on the destruction and its aftermath, confession of sins occurs in only four (79:8; 90:7–9; 103:10–14; 106:6); similarly, within the five laments of Lamentations only thirteen verses constitute such confessions.[75]

74. In his studies on the communal laments, Westermann suggests a five-element structure: address (including introductory petition), lament, turning to God (confession of trust), petition, and vow of praise. See Westermann, *Praise and Lament*, 52–64; and *Lamentations*, 95–98; Westermann bases his work on Mowinckel, *Psalms in Israel's Worship*, 1.195–204; see also Broyles, *Conflict of Faith and Experience*, 220–21; and the discussion at §3.4.3.

75. Individual verses in Lam 1, 3, 4, and 5 substantially enlarge our database (1:5, 8, 9, 14, 18, 20, 22; 3:39, 42; 4:6, 22; 5:16). Lam 2:14 has at most only an implicit confession, and 5:7 is an example of protest. Confession of sins is a useful marker of generic distinction between communal laments and penitential prayers; see Rom-Shiloni, "Socio-Ideological Setting."

At face value, these confessions are clear markers of justification of God, as they presumably clear God of any unjustified or precipitate action that has caused suffering (צדיק הוא יהוה כי פיהו מריתי ["the LORD is in the right, for I have disobeyed Him"], Lam 1:18).[76] These confessions constitute acceptance of responsibility by the current generation for both their own (3:42) and their predecessors' (Pss 79:8; 106:6) actions, thereby portraying God as reacting against current (and previous) intolerable iniquities. But there are several restrictions that nevertheless call these justificatory statements into question.

(a) These psalmodic compositions are clearly not cut of one cloth. Most importantly, they differ on the roles given to God in causing the distress. Psalm 79:1, for example, follows the (A' → C) conception of war and pleads for divine help in the ongoing suffering (79:5-13); whereas 90:7-9 accentuates the divine wrath and conceals any involvement of human enemies in causing the distress and, hence, is closer to the (C') approach. The poems of Lamentations differ in and within themselves on this issue; Lam 1 uses the (B') conception (1:5) and the (C') conceptions (1:20-22); Lam 2 to a greater extent highlights God as the sole enemy of his city and people, in keeping with the (C') conception (2:1-9a); human foes do appear in Lam 2 as summoned by God, hence the (B') conception, but their roles are minimized (2:7b, 16, 17c), and most importantly for the present discussion, Lam 2 has no confession of sins; Lam 3:40-48 confesses profoundly (3:40-42), takes God as the main afflicter (3:43), the (C') conception, and yet the poet still recognizes the involvement of human enemies devouring the people (3:46), in the (B') conception, and further challenges God for not showing pardon to his devoted people (3:40-45; see §1.2.2). It is remarkable that though these compositions differ in conceptualizing the role of God as warrior, they oftentimes (with the exception of Lam 2 and several others) nonetheless find quite similar ways to justify God as judge, by taking upon themselves responsibility for their own distress. Psalm 103:10-14 uses extreme justification to suggest that the punishment is less harsh than expected. Like a father to sons, God is benevolent and compassionate (103:11-13), even while afflicting his people (103:10)![77] This would have been hard even for the author of Lam 1 to accept.

---

76. מרי designates rebellion against God in Lam 1:20 and 3:42; it is used in prophetic accusations against Samaria (Hos 14:1) and Jerusalem (Isa 1:20; 30:9; Jer 4:17); and abundantly in Ezekiel in the phrase בית (ה)מרי; see §11.2.2 (b).

77. For the play between חסד and רחמים in Ps 103:4, 8, 11-13, 17, see §12.1.

(b) Expressions of confession are usually recognized as conventional formulations that treat iniquity on only a very general level—חטא (Lam 1:8; 3:39; 4:13; 5:16), פשע (1:5, 14, 22; 3:42), or עון (2:14; 4:13, 22)[78]—or that make use of the metaphor of Jerusalem as an adulterous wife (1:8, 9).[79]

(c) These confessions of sins give limited indications of a perception of transgenerational responsibility. Using first-person verbs (or pronouns), mostly in the plural ("us" in 4:17–20 and Lam 5; but first-person singular for Jerusalem in 1:11c–16, 18–22 or for the anonymous poet in 3:1–21, 52–66), they all assert the current generation's responsibility (3:42; 4:13). But the few references to the issue of diachronic shared responsibility are again scarce (e.g., the protest in 5:7). The fathers' iniquities are mentioned only in Pss 79:8 and 106:6, but in Ps 106, where iniquities are detailed and capture the greater part of the lament, the psalmist goes back to the very distant periods of the desert wanderings and the settlement, implying that the sins of those times are borne by the people down to the very destruction (106:34–42). Even so, a gap of time implied between the activity is expressed in third-person plural forms ("they" up to 106:46) and the one and only verse of pleading (106:47), which returns to the first-person plural with הושיענו וקבצנו and thus forms an *inclusio* with the confession of sins in 106:6. This gap leaves open the question of what blame (if any) the current generation (now possibly in exile) accepts upon itself. Or, is this implication of shared guilt merely a matter of literary convention?

(d) Confessions of sins, or recognition of the people's iniquities, in Lamentations is characterized by two features. First, such statements fall in close proximity to phrases that accuse God of causing the distress, that is, using the (B′) and (C′) conceptions of war. Second, they occur in contexts that elaborate on already long-lasting, ongoing, and painful suffering, for instance: תבא כל־רעתם לפניך ועולל למו כאשר עוללת לי על כל־פשעי כי־

78. חטא (and its many derivatives) is the most common and general term for iniquity, and yet to a large extent it serves to designate cultic transgressions against God, as in Exod 32:31; 1 Kgs 14:16; Hos 8:11. For חטא in the human arena, see 1 Sam 19:4; 20:1. Jeremiah 33:8 presents פשע, חטא, and עון as synonymous. פשע (Lam 1:5, 14, 22) designates crimes against God (see Josh 24:19); a similar use is found in describing the political relationships between countries (Amos 1:3, 6, 9) and between the subject/vassal and his lord (1 Sam 24:11). Compare Hillers, *Lamentations*, 84. Lam 1:9 mentions טמאתה בשוליה ("her uncleanness clings to her skirts"), bringing cultic issues to the fore or simply working with the metaphor of the adulterous wife who suffers sexual abuse as her judgment; see Berlin, *Lamentations*, 63–65.

79. Sins are further mentioned as having been committed by specific groups within the people; see 2:14; 4:13.

רבות אנחתי ולבי דוי ("Let all their wrongdoing come before You, and deal with them as You have dealt with me for all my transgressions. For my sighs are many, and my heart is sick," 1:22).[80] These characteristics lead Frederick Dobbs-Allsopp (among others) to recognize that confessions of sins in Lamentations do not actually justify God or the suffering caused by him. Suffering still captures the largest place in each of the five laments (including Lam 1, which includes seven verses of confession of sins). Hence, this tactic of bringing together confession and suffering, according to Dobbs-Allsopp, has a practical goal—it is meant to arouse God to take notice of the people's distress and to take action on behalf of them.[81]

(e) Finally, these confessions of sins are still a minority within the communal laments, and even within their contexts do not try to cover over or convey relief from the grief and the suffering that God is persistently held responsible for. Justification is but one alternative, and a problematic one, for the poets of the communal laments.

11.3. PROTEST: THE CURRENT GENERATION IS CLEAN OF SIN

Another response, found within some communal laments and quoted words in the prophets, is to contest the transgenerational conception itself. This opposition may be seen in both explicit and implicit refutations of blame for the sins of the fathers and the status of the current generation. The former, explicit refutations of blame occur in Lam 5:7 and are quoted twice in Jeremiah and Ezekiel (Jer 31:29; Ezek 18:2); the implicit refutations are seen in assertions of the people's innocence quotations in Jer 2; Pss 44:18–23; 80:19).

11.3.1. Why Should "We Bear Their Guilt"? (Lamentations 5:7)

The tactic of distinguishing the fathers from the sons and referring back to the fathers' iniquities characterizes one phrase in Lamentations and a saying quoted in Jeremiah and Ezekiel. These sayings clearly confront the traditional retribution conception and suggest that the present suffering

---

80. עלל means "harm, treat with cruelty" and otherwise refers to God's treatment of the Egyptians (Exod 10:2); in relation to human behavior, see Jer 38:19; Ps 141:4; 1 Chr 10:4; Judg 19:25.

81. See Dobbs-Allsopp, *Lamentations*, 60–61; and Berlin, *Lamentations*, 64–65.

represents, not divine justice, but divine *injustice* against the destruction generation, as seen in Lam 5:7:

Our fathers sinned and are no more;	אֲבֹתֵינוּ חָטְאוּ אֵינָם (ק: וְאֵינָם)
And we must bear their guilt.	אֲנַחְנוּ (ק: וַאֲנַחְנוּ) עֲוֹנֹתֵיהֶם סָבָלְנוּ.

This is the only explicit protest against the exercise of divine justice in Lamentations.[82] The saying may be identified as an intrusion because it breaks the flow in the surrounding verses that specify the collective distress caused by subjugation—defeat and hunger (5:2–6 and 5:7–15).[83] Furthermore, 5:7 contradicts the confession of sins in 5:16b that reflects a recognition of the immediate conceptions of retribution. Lamentations 5:7 protests that the fathers are not held responsible for their iniquities within their own lifetimes; that is, it opposes the very principle of transgenerational (vicarious) retribution.[84] Thus, it reveals the contemporary idea that the "sons," those of the generation of the destruction, should not be accused of religious misbehavior; the current generation is unjustly suffering a divine judgment that should have been laid upon its ancestors. By distinguishing between "we" and "they," this verse argues that this current generation themselves did not sin; they do *not* share in their fathers' iniquities (עֲוֹנֹתֵיהֶם)![85]

82. Contrast this single occurrence to the thirteen verses of confession of sins in Lam 1, 3, 4; 5; see §11.2.3.

83. Hillers (*Lamentations*, 163) considers 5:6–7 as "interrupting" the depiction of trouble, although he minimizes the tone of protest in 5:7 (164). Westermann (*Lamentations*, 213–14) notes that 5:2–18 presents the lengthiest description of the people's prolonged distress, which draws back on both the destruction and the misery thereafter with no way to specify more the particular circumstances.

84. Compare Frevel (*Die Klagelieder*, 334), who evaluates the protest of 5:7 in light of 5:16: "The speaker generation of Lamentations 5 is wrongly burdened with the consequences of the mistakes of the fathers, even though they formulated in 5:16 quite a confession of sins for such" (my translation). I find the evaluative tone surprising and prefer to leave the contradiction unexplained.

85. Compare the harmonistic way Westermann (*Lamentations*, 215) tries to reconcile the significantly contradictory perspectives of 5:7 and 5:16b, arguing that "both attitudes are appropriate for the lamenters" and that 5:7 attests to a "transformation of attitude" among the survivors of the catastrophe, whereas the confession in 5:16b illustrates that both conceptions continue to be held. Dobbs-Allsopp (*Lamentations*, 146–47) starts his discussion by saying the two conceptions are but "slightly different notions of sin" (146) but then warns (aptly) against harmonizing them (147). Berlin (*Lamentations*, 120) leaves open the question concerning the relationship between

This same sense of the blamelessness of the current generation is expressed in proverbial terms in two almost identical quotations in Jeremiah and Ezekiel.[86]

[1] The word of the LORD came to me: [2] What do you mean by quoting this proverb upon the soil of Israel, "Parents eat sour grapes and their children's teeth are blunted"? (Ezek 18:1–2)	¹וַיְהִי דְבַר־יהוה אֵלַי לֵאמֹר. ²מַה־לָּכֶם אַתֶּם מֹשְׁלִים אֶת־הַמָּשָׁל הַזֶּה עַל־אַדְמַת יִשְׂרָאֵל לֵאמֹר אָבוֹת יֹאכְלוּ בֹסֶר וְשִׁנֵּי הַבָּנִים תִּקְהֶינָה.
In those days, they shall no longer say, "Parents have eaten sour grapes and children's teeth are blunted." (Jer 31:29)	בַּיָּמִים הָהֵם לֹא יֹאמְרוּ עוֹד אָבוֹת אָכְלוּ בֹסֶר וְשִׁנֵּי בָנִים תִּקְהֶינָה.

That both prophets cite this saying, along with its location on the "soil of Israel" in Ezekiel, attests to the authenticity of this perception as current in Jerusalem during this period. On the lexical level, the use of קהה in this context causes difficulties.[87] But on the thematic level, the proverb is nevertheless clear. Eating unripe fruit causes in the eater an immediate

---

previous generations and the current one, but having both perspectives in Lam 5 leads her to say that 5:7 "is not rejecting accepted theology" (120). Hillers (*Lamentations*, 164) even finds a way to reconcile the two. I am afraid that these suggestions minimize or even completely lose the harsh protest of 5:7.

86. For the minor grammatical differences between the two passages, see Greenberg (*Ezekiel 1–20*, 327), who concludes that "the variations . . . are such as are to be expected in oral transmission." For the prophetic responses that refute these sayings, see §11.4.

87. קהה otherwise occurs only in Eccl 10:10, in reference to sharpness of iron (a knife?); Rashi probably follows this Ecclesiastes meaning and suggests the French equivalent *sont agacées* to transcribe איגצט, meaning "set on edge" (Banith, *Le Glossarire de Bale*, no. 5378; see also no. 5377 for אכל בסר); I thank Dr. Ronela Merdler for this reference. See Koehler, Baumgartner, and Stamm, *Hebrew and Aramaic Lexicon*, 1078: "become blunt, dull." Jer 38:29 LXX (= 31:29 MT) reads οἱ πατέρες ἔφαγον ὄμφακα, καὶ οἱ ὀδόντες τῶν τέκνων ᾑμωδίασαν ("fathers eat unripe grapes, and the sons' teeth are set on edge"; i.e., the teeth are affected by an acid food, which Accordance translates "speechless"), whereas Ezek 18:2 LXX translates תקהינה by ἐγομφίασαν, thus "the sons' teeth are ground" (the verbal form γομφιάζω meaning "grind" [and γομφίος meaning "a grinder tooth"] occurs otherwise only in Ben Sira 30:10). The Targum chooses to move away from the figurative image and translates the phrase by its results, retaining (or re-creating) rhythm and rhyme: אבהתא חטן ובניא לקן ("fathers sin and sons are punished"). See Lundbom, *Jeremiah 21–36*, 461–63.

reaction of unease (even if this unease is difficult to specify). While this proverb focuses on the teeth, unease is felt through the entire organ of eating, the lips, the teeth, the tongue, and the mouth in general.[88] The beauty of this proverb is in the paradox it expresses, in moving between the casual experience of an immediate effect, so familiar in daily life, and the observation it wishes to convey, concerning the retribution conception in these current circumstances of destruction. What could never happen when eating unripe fruit happened in Jerusalem and Judah—those who ate the fruit, that is, the previous generations, are not punished for their actions; instead, the current generation suffers the consequences. The sense of injustice is blatant, and the complaint is addressed to God, who is held solely responsible for the disastrous events.[89]

These three passages indicate the contours of the Judean theological debate on the question of the current generation's responsibility for their fate. The opposition between fathers and sons constructed here explicitly challenges the divine epithet from the Decalogue, פקד עון אבת על־בנים, presenting the sons as innocent.

11.3.2. "We Have Not Sinned" (Quotations in Jeremiah 2 and Psalm 44)

These three passages suggest another intriguing possibility—that at least some Judeans of the early sixth century persisted in a perception of innocence, of blamelessness, or even righteousness, in their religious loyalty to God, hence facing the concomitant sense (expressed often only implicitly) that the destruction is unjust. The prophets repeatedly fought against this perception, insistently accusing the people in Jerusalem, in Egypt, and to some extent in Babylon of various and severe sins against God (such that clearly justified the harsh judgment). But, if we attend to quotations within

---

88. Prov 10:26 similarly uses the teeth as a metonym for the mouth, in conveying the effect of the taste of vinegar; see Greenberg, *Ezekiel 1–20*, 328. For discussion of the content, taking the meaning of this expression for granted, see McKane, *Jeremiah 26–52*, 815–16.

89. I therefore understand this objection to be framed in terms of the opposition between transgenerational and immediate retributions; compare Greenberg (*Ezekiel 1–20*, 328), who quotes a private communication from David N. Freedman, in which he argues that "it does not matter to God who suffers so long as the balance of sin and punishment is kept."

Jeremiah and read them together with communal laments, we get a much more complex picture of the issues at stake.[90]

Jeremiah 2 in its many subunits focuses on issues of loyalty and disloyalty to God and rhetorically constructs a lively, at times furious, dialogue between God, the prophet, and the people. No less than nine quotations are found in the various units; all are vehemently refuted by the prophet.[91] Among them, 2:20–25 and 2:35 raise the people's repeated claim that לא חטאתי ("I have not sinned," 2:35b) or נקיתי ("I have been acquitted," 2:35a);[92] 2:23 sets the quotation in a rhetorical question that ridicules the claim of blamelessness: איך תאמרי לא נטמאתי אחרי הבעלים לא הלכתי ("How can you say, 'I am not defiled, I have not gone after the Baalim'?"). None of these quotations seem to be authentic in terms of their verbal-literal forms. Rather, the prophet uses formulas for proclaiming innocence to express what he considers to be Jerusalem's hypocritical attitude toward God.[93] Yet, when these statements are set alongside other quoted passages—such as the questions cited in 5:19 and 16:10, the proverbial protest of Jer 31:29 and Ezek 18:2, and the lament of Lam 5:7, in conjunction with the strong expressions of loyalty in some communal laments (e.g., Pss 44:18–23; 80:19)—they emerge as more than artificial, formulaic constructions. Taking together all these passages, it is reasonable to argue that voices in Jerusalem during the times of destruction and in its aftermath argue that the catastrophe God initiates in Jerusalem is unjustified at that specific time. One such prominent voice may be heard in Ps 44.

Psalm 44 is an example of a tough protest against God in his role as the warrior who summons enemies against his own people and hands his people over to them, the (B') conception of war (see §8.2). In the context

90. See §10.2 on the questions quoted in Jeremiah and their points of similarity with the communal laments.

91. Quotations may be identified in Jer 2:6, 8, 20, 23, 25, 27, 31, 35 (2x). Their predominance leads Overholt ("Jeremiah 2") to focus on this chapter in his study of the general phenomenon of quotations in Jeremiah.

92. נקה in Jer 2:35 might stand for the complete phrase נקה מעון, as in Num 5:31: "be clear of guilt." נקה also may imply God's remission of punishment, as stated in the negative (Exod 34:7; 20:7; Deut 5:11) and invoked in the prophets (Jer 30:11; 46:28; PAN Jer 49:12; Nah 1:3). נקה further occurs in civil-legal contexts (Exod 21:19; 1 Sam 26:9).

93. So I argue in reference to Jer 2:20–25, where the prophetic accusation and the people's refutation are portrayed through an allusion to the trial of the *sotah* in Num 5:11–31 and its major focus on נטמאה/לא נטמאה, on the question whether the woman has or has not behaved as an adulterous woman; see Rom-Shiloni, "How Can You Say." The use of נקיתי and לא חטאתי in Jer 2:35 is similarly formulaic.

of this discussion of God as a just judge, two additional issues deserve attention: Ps 44's polemics against certain conceptions in both prophetic and wisdom literature, and the psalmist's self-imposed limitations in moderating his direct accusations against God.

Examination of 44:18–23 through its intertextual relationship to Deuteronomistic literature, prophetic exhortation, and wisdom/psalmodic literature shows that in addition to a clear protest against God, these verses mount two covert polemics against contemporary views on the theological meaning of the present calamity.

> a. *Who is responsible for breaching the covenant relationship?*

A polemical protest opens each of the two subsections of this passage, 44:18–20 and 44:21–23:

[18] All this has come upon us,	כל־זאת באתנו
yet we have not forgotten you,	ולא שכחנוך
or been false to Your covenant....	ולא־שקרנו בבריתך.
[21] If we forgot the name of our God	[21] אם־שכחנו שם אלהינו
and spread forth our hands to a foreign god,	ונפרש כפינו לאל זר.
[22] God would surely search it out,	[22] הלא אלהים יחקר־זאת
for He knows the secrets of the heart.	כי־הוא ידע תעלמות לב.

In the arena of the God-people relationship, the verb שכח ("forget") commonly occurs in the Hebrew Bible in phrases that reverse subject and object: העם שכח את־יהוה אלהיו ("the people forgot the LORD God") and יהוה שכח את־עמו ("the LORD forgot His people"). In Deuteronomy, in the Deuteronomistic historiographical writings,[94] and in the prophets

---

94. Gross considers Ps 44 to be a refutation of the Deuteronomistic theology of guilt that predominates in this period. According to Gross, Ps 44 suggests a correction of the prevailing conception of God that is closer to the mystery of the divine in Job ("Geschichtserfahrung," 213–16). Gerstenberger (*Psalms, Part 1*, 182–86) notes the resemblances to Deuteronomistic phraseology and themes in 44:2–3 and accepts the resemblance to Job's "protestation of innocence" (184–85); see also Kraus, *Psalms 1–59*, 447–47. Finally, Berlin ("Psalms and the Literature of Exile," 71–74) recognizes the Deuteronomic phrases and themes, but considers them examples not of polemic, but

(especially Jeremiah)[95] the accusation of forgetting God plays a central role in the justification of God's punishment of his people. Psalm 44's repeated use of שכח, first in the negative (44:18) and then in an oath (44:21), refutes this accusation, declaring it impossible.

Deuteronomy uses העם שכח את־יהוה as part of its covenant terminology, exhorting the people not to forget God—the creator of the nation (32:18), the lord of Israel (8:11), the savior of the people from Egypt (6:12; 8:14), and therefore the one who demands obedience and obliges Israel to follow his commandments (4:9, 23; 6:12–13; 8:11–19). The Deuteronomists pursue this theme as part of a history of sin and judgment, in which forgetting God is exemplified by worship of other gods. Thus, human forgetting brings about divine judgment, experienced as being handed over to the enemy, defeat, and subjugation (Judg 3:7; 1 Sam 12:9).[96]

Jeremiah continues this line of thought in his exhortations of judgment against the people, using Deuteronomic phraseology and themes to lay the blame for the present distress on their disobedience (Jer 3:21; 13:25; 23:27 [2x]). In two series of rhetorical questions and answers, the prophet uses the verb to express the inexplicable behavior of Israel. First, 2:32 asks: הת־ שכח בתולה עדיה כלה קשריה ועמי שכחוני ימים אין מספר ("Can a maiden forget her jewels, a bride her adornments? Yet My people have forgotten Me—days without number"). Subsequently, in 18:13–17, the prophet designates the people's behavior as unheard of (18:13–15) and horrible in their inevitable consequences (18:16–17):

[13] Assuredly, thus said YHWH:	לכן כה אמר יהוה [13]
Inquire among the nations:	שאלו נא בגוים
Who has heard anything like this?	מי שמע כאלה
Maiden Israel has done	שעררת עשתה מאד
A most horrible thing.	בתולת ישראל.

---

rather of an exilic perspective that adapted Deuteronomic and prophetic approaches to demonstrate that the exile should end.

95. While Hosea invokes the retributive power of שכח (4:6; 8:14; 13:6), Jeremiah uses this verb the most: six times in pronouncements of judgment (2:32; 3:21; 13:25; 18:15; 23:27 [2x]) and once to indicate obedience in the future (50:5). Close to this use are Hos 2:15; Ezek 22:12; 23:35 (with the imagery of Israel/Jerusalem as God's wife). Compare this frequency to the single reference in Isaiah son of Amoz (Isa 17:10) and the two occurrences in Second Isaiah (51:13; 49:14–15 [disputation speech]).

96. Preuss, "שָׁכַח šākaḥ."

[14] Does one forsake Lebanon snow	היעזב מצור שדי
From the mountainous rocks?	שלג לבנון
Does one abandon cool water	אם ינתשו מים זרים
Flowing from afar?	קרים נוזלים
[15] Yet My people have forgotten Me;	[15] כי שכחני עמי
They sacrifice to a delusion:	לשוא יקטרו
They are made to stumble in their ways—	ויכשלום בדרכיהם
The ancient paths—	שבילי עולם
And to walk instead on byways,	ללכת נתיבות
On a road not built up.	דרך לא סלולה.

Three points of similarity connect Ps 44:18–23 with Jer 18:1–17. First, the use of the verb שכח denotes, for the prophet, the people's violation of the covenant: כי־שכחני עמי לשוא יקטרו ("yet My people have forgotten Me: they sacrifice to a delusion," Jer 18:15; also 23:27); the psalmist fiercely negates this accusation: ולא שכחנוך ("yet we have not forgotten You," Ps 44:18). Second, the image of transgression as straying off the road, implying the worship of other gods (Jer 18:15; also 3:19–22, esp. 3:21) is contravened in Ps 44:19: "Our hearts have not gone astray, nor have our feet swerved from Your path."[97] Finally, both texts portray God's active role in the coming judgment. Cast in the first-person, Jeremiah's prophecy threatens that God's active judgment will cause military defeat (18:17) and total destruction (18:16). Psalm 44 presents this same conception as the core of its protest in 44:10–17.

Hence, Ps 44 stands explicitly against these and other similar Deuteronomic/Deuteronomistic and prophetic conventions, opposing the explanation that places all responsibility for the current situation upon the people's violation of the covenant. In refuting these conventions, Ps 44 joins proclamations heard in other communal laments (Pss 42:10; 74:19; 77:10; Lam 5:20) or communal laments that forcefully negate the possibility that God may forget his people (Pss 9:13, 19; 10:11–12). Yet, like Ps 44, all of these texts give precedence to the people's feelings of desertion and neglect by God. They call upon God not to forget his obedient servants/people and not to withdraw from the long-standing covenant relationship (74:20; 89:50; and the communal lament in Jer 14:19–22).[98]

97. For the geographical background of Jeremiah's imagery, see Hareuveni, *Desert and Shepherd*, 118–27.

98. Second Isaiah (49:14–21) provides further evidence dating from the second half

Through its direct accusation of God, then, Ps 44 elucidates the contradiction between the actions of a God who seems to have forgotten his people, and the people's constant piety and loyalty to him. For this the psalmist coins a *hapax*—ולא־שקרנו בבריתך ("we were not false to Your covenant," 44:18b)[99]—and declares the people's innocence (44:18–19). Thus this section protests against the injustice of God's actions (44:18–20), rephrases the protest in an oath (44:21–22), and concludes with an additional description of the people's distress (44:23).

b. Does God act according to the measure of justice?

In both subsections of Ps 44:18–23, the psalmist examines the ideology of retribution through allusions to 37:30–31, where the conception of retribution is set forth in the most conventional way to describe the "righteous one":[100]

---

of the sixth century, when it quotes and refutes the statement of protest that blames God for forgetting Jerusalem. Such promises occur in the exilic passage of Deut 4:31. שכח further illustrates feelings of divine desertion and neglect in individual lament (Ps 13:2) and is one of the pleas in Hannah's prayer and vow (1 Sam 1:11).

99. Two phrases in the communal laments are close to this *hapax*: (1) Isa 63:8: אך־עמי המה בנים לא ישקרו ("surely they are My people, children who will not play false"); both Ps 44 and Isa 63:7–64:11 share the basic idea that the people's obedience to the covenant promises salvation, and their disobedience promises defeat (63:8–10); and (2) Ps 89:34b: ולא־אשקר באמונתי ("and I will not betray My faithfulness") contrasts with Ps 44 in its statement of God's loyalty to his covenant with David. This divine oath, however, breaks down in 89:39 and is explicitly challenged in 89:50: איה חסדיך הראשנים אדני נשבעת לדוד באמונתך ("O Lord, where is Your steadfast love of old which You swore to David in Your faithfulness?"). Thus, 89:39–46 shares abandonment themes and languages with Ps 44 (שסה, היה חרפה לשכניו, and זנח). The two examples are not in any literary intertextual connection with Ps 44, yet they do enlighten the thematic value of this *hapax*.

100. Weiser (*Psalms*, 315–16) considers Ps 37 to be "a collection of proverbs" similar to those in the book of Proverbs; they are drawn from "the treasure of the popular maxims of the Wisdom writers" and brought together for the practical didactic purpose of expressing "the calm serenity and assuredness of a firm faith." Compare Brueggemann ("Psalm 37"), who sets out two different readings of Ps 37. According to the first, ideological reading, the psalm is a social manifesto speaking for landowners, based on a confident, coherent, and unambiguous view of moral conduct and reward that functions as "'structure legitimating' and serves to sustain a socio-theological 'orientation'" (238–45 at 245). In a second, utopian reading (which may be influenced by the New Testament's Sermon on the Mount), Ps 37 gains an eschatological significance of hope

³⁰ The mouth of the righteous utters wisdom,   30 פי צדיק יהגה חכמה
and his tongue speaks what is right.   ולשונו תדבר משפט.
³¹ The teaching of his God is <u>in his heart</u>;   31 תורת אלהיו בלבו
<u>his feet</u> do not slip.   לא תמעד אשריו.

The sequence of לב ("heart") and אשרים ("feet") in close parallelism is unique to Ps 37 and 44:19: "Our hearts [לבנו] have not gone astray, nor have our feet [אשרנו] swerved from Your path." This pairing thus serves as a marker of the intertextual connection between these two psalms, through which 44:19 alludes to the description of the righteous in Ps 37. In both contexts the term לב indicates a thoughtful attitude of piety and obedience, whereas אשרים metaphorically denotes following God.[101] Through this linguistic allusion to Ps 37, the poet of Ps 44 makes an analogy between the people and Ps 37's "righteous one." As the righteous one does not stray from God's path, so the people neither stray from the covenant nor disobey God.[102]

The linguistic connection between the two psalms draws attention to the author evoking other verses from the earlier psalm as covert hints that his own lament is in dialogue with this psalm.[103] In the explanatory clauses of 44:22b, the author makes yet a second allusion to Ps 37: "God would

---

for the landless, which reflects a sociotheological dispute close to Job and suggests a revision of the old ideology (245–54).

101. אשורים ("feet") in parallel to רגלים and פעמים occurs in contexts of obedience to God with נטה (Ps 73:2; Job 23:11; also Ps 17:5). Compare Briggs (*Psalms*, 330); following the Septuagint and Peshitta, he reads ולא in 37:31b and thus interprets this verse as indicating the reward of the pious, drawing on 37:23–24 as well. מעד indeed appears with this meaning in 2 Sam 22:37 and Ps 18:37; but to indicate obedience, see 26:1 (with the verbs הלך and מעד in a similar context, though without any of the nouns).

102. In military contexts, נסוג אחור means "turn back, withdraw, flee" (2 Sam 1:22; Jer 38:22). In the religious sphere, standing in *parallelismus membrorum* to פשע, מרי, בגד, etc., this phrase denotes disloyalty to God and rebellion against him (Isa 59:13; Zeph 1:6; Mic 2:6; Ps 78:57). In the mouth of the pious one, the phrase conveys denial of any disloyalty: ואנכי לא מריתי אחור לא נסוגותי ("and I did not disobey, I did not run away," Isa 50:5); a similar assertion is made by the poet of Ps 80:19, reflecting the crisis of the destruction: ולא־נסוג ממך תחינו ובשמך נקרא ("we will not turn away from You; preserve our life that we may invoke Your name").

103. For the concept of an "intertextual pattern" gained through the interaction of these two texts, see Tanner, *Book of Psalms*, 73. For Ps 37's influence on Second Temple period literature (*1 Enoch* and the Qumran *Pesher on Psalm 37* [4Q171]), see Clements, "Let the Wicked Vanish."

surely search it out, for He knows the secrets of the heart [כִּי־הוּא יֹדֵעַ תַּעֲלֻמוֹת לֵב]." This statement echoes 37:3–4: "Trust in the Lord and do good, abide in the land and remain loyal. Seek the favor of the Lord, and He will grant you the desires of your heart [וְיִתֶּן־לְךָ מִשְׁאֲלֹת לִבֶּךָ]." Yet in this context, this echo raises a grievous outcry: God certainly knows the secrets of the heart (44:22), but seems to have ignored this knowledge (and betrayed the people's trust) in visiting disaster upon his people, whom he must know are innocent of wrongdoing.

A third thematic connection between the two psalms rests on the association between land and righteousness. Walter Brueggemann points out Ps 37's emphasis on the land as the reward of the righteous (37:3, 9, 11, 18, 22, 34)[104] and on the divine presence and help guaranteed to the pious. The two are exemplified Ps 37:27–29:

[27] Shun evil and do good,	²⁷ סוּר מֵרָע וַעֲשֵׂה־טוֹב
and you shall abide forever.	וּשְׁכֹן־לְעוֹלָם.
[28] For the Lord loves what is right,	²⁸ כִּי יְהוָה אֹהֵב מִשְׁפָּט
He does not abandon His faithful ones.	וְלֹא־יַעֲזֹב אֶת־חֲסִידָיו
They are preserved forever,	לְעוֹלָם נִשְׁמָרוּ
while the children of the wicked will be cut off.	וְזֶרַע רְשָׁעִים נִכְרָת.
[29] The righteous shall inherit the land,	²⁹ צַדִּיקִים יִירְשׁוּ־אָרֶץ
and abide forever in it.	וְיִשְׁכְּנוּ לָעַד עָלֶיהָ.

While, except for לֵב and אשרים, there is no literal similarity (thus no direct echo or allusions), Ps 44 seems to stand in thematic opposition to Ps 37's conventions of reward and retribution.[105] Psalm 44 accentuates the tension between the people's piety and the distressing reality of dislocation that they face (44:12–15). Contrary to Ps 37's assertion, "He does not abandon His faithful ones" (37:28), God indeed deserted his faithful people ("yet You have rejected and disgraced us," 44:10); thus the psalmist requests "do not reject us forever" (44:24).[106] Their suffering as they are

---

104. Brueggemann ("Psalm 37," 234) argues that the psalm widens its perspective to the communal-social-ethical context and reflects "the voice of a self-assured property-owning class which believes 'the system works.'"

105. Compare לְעוֹלָם and לָעַד (Ps 37:27, 28, 29) to לָנֶצַח (44:24); and עֹזַב (37:28) to זנח (44:24). Note the absence of the verbs שכן and ירש in Ps 44.

106. Although Ps 44 does not use the more common verb עֹזַב (as in 37:28), both עֹזַב and זנח indicate desertion and have God as the subject; cf. the use of זנח in 74:1;

scattered among the peoples (44:12–17) can hardly illustrate the promise (or the convention) that the faithful "shall abide forever" and "are preserved forever" in the land (37:27b, 28b; see 44:23). The direct accusation in 44:20—"though You cast us, crushed, to where jackals[107] reside, and covered us over with deepest darkness"—indicates the loss of the inherited land and the loss of life, that is, the fate opposite to that of the righteous one, so emphasized in 37:27–29.

Nevertheless, protest has its limits. In making use of the conception of retribution, the psalmist takes upon himself two restrictions. First, only covertly, through these echoes to Ps 37, does he identify himself and his contemporaries not only as loyal and pious, but as righteous.[108] The psalmist seems deliberately to refrain from directly using the terminology typical of the wisdom psalms (צדיק, רשע, etc.).[109]

88:15; 89:39; and in military circumstances in 60:12; 108:12. Compare Yaron's discussion of זנח as indicating God's anger ("Meaning of *Zanah*"). Although Yaron's suggestion is intriguing, I consider the context of זנח in Ps 44 to emphasize the lack of God's presence and involvement, and thus rejection, not anger. For זנח in the semantic field of divine desertion and neglect, and its consequences in military defeat, see Melanchthon, *Rejection by God*, 75–80.

107. NJPS's "sea monster" follows תנים of Ezek 29:3 and 32:2. However, מקום תנים in this context may better suit a place "where jackals reside"; see Briggs, *Psalms*, 381, 382; Weiser, *Psalms*, 355; and Kraus, *Psalms 1–59*, 448.

108. This then may be the reason for the absence of terms connoting righteousness and wickedness in Ps 44—ideas that are so prominent in Ps 37. Compare Ps 7, which petitions God to act as a judge in favor of the innocent psalmist, who is called צדיק (7:10). His enemy is first designated צוררי, רדפי, and אויב ("my pursuers, my foe, enemy," 7:2–6); the singular is transformed to the plural in the national sphere: צוררי, לאמים, and עמים ("my foes, peoples, peoples," 7:7–9); finally, in opposition to the צדיק, the enemies are labeled רשעים ("wicked ones," 7:10). Gerstenberger (*Psalms, Part 1*, 65) defines the genre of Ps 7 as "protestations of innocence." Kraus's reference (*Psalms 1–59*, 448) to the implied צדיק theme in Ps 44 suggests a similar direction of interpretation. But Kraus does not suggest an intentional avoidance of wisdom terminology.

109. The opposition between righteous and wicked is transformed in the communal laments as part of the conception of God as judge; see Ps 74:18–21 and also Pss 9–10, which use the terms גוים ("nations") and רשע ("wicked") alternatively in 9:16–18, 20–21 to designate the opponents, whereas the people are indicated by expressions such as דך ("oppressed"), יתום ("orphan"), and עני/ענוים ("lowly, downtrodden") in 9:10; 10:2, 9, 18; by חלכאים ("the hapless") in 10:10; and by יודעי שמך and דרשיך ("those who know Your name . . . those who seek You") in 9:11, set in opposition to כל־גוים שכחי אלהים ("all the nations who forget God," 9:18). This last contrast draws a national and religious distinction between the two groups. On the contrary, Ps 44 does not employ

Second, the author treats cautiously the tripartite relationship of God, the righteous, and the wicked. The conventional scheme presented clearly in 37:32–33 (and likewise in 37:12) guarantees God's involvement on behalf of the righteous one against his evil enemy:

[32] The wicked watches for the righteous,	³²צוֹפֶה רָשָׁע לַצַּדִּיק
seeking to put him to death;	וּמְבַקֵּשׁ לַהֲמִיתוֹ.
[33] YHWH will not abandon him to his powers;	³³יְהוָה לֹא־יַעַזְבֶנּוּ בְיָדוֹ
He will not let him be condemned in judgment.	וְלֹא יַרְשִׁיעֶנּוּ בְּהִשָּׁפְטוֹ.

In contrast, the human enemies are not at the core of the distress in Ps 44. They do appear in 44:10–17, but only as those who benefit from *God's* actions against his people (44:11, 12, 15); whereas God, conventionally the source of confidence and salvation to the righteous (Ps 37), is here the source of distress, directly responsible for the defeat, the destruction, and the exile. Still, this reversal of roles is not spelled out openly; it is only implied through these echoes of Ps 37 evoked by the author of Ps 44.

Psalm 44 fully accepts the conventional traditions of obedience to the covenant and divine justice. Protest reaches its height *because* of the unresolved dissonance between the circumstances of crisis and accepted theological conventions,[110] that is, the collective historical memory and heritage of God's salvation in the past (44:2–4) and the people's complete and continuing loyalty to God and to his covenant in the present (44:18–23). Through the implicit allusions to Ps 37, the people's loyalty in their agony is set in even starker opposition to traditional conceptions of judgment, retribution, and reward. Protest against God thus responds to those conventional voices that aim to justify God at all costs. As suggested by Erhard Gerstenberger, Ps 44 indeed remains on Job's side in preferring the believer's faithful struggle to the acceptance of the conventional abso-

---

this terminology and is directed only to the national distress, drawing primarily on the imagery of God as warrior and only implicitly on the image of God as judge.

110. Brueggemann (*Psalms*, 16–25) writes about "the collapse of convention" (21) as motivating theological questions and disorientation in the lament. This notion, however, does not seem to contradict the sense of the psalmist's staunch piety. Compare Heschel, who quotes Ps 44 in full as an example of "the guidance of faith" (*Man Is Not Alone*, 155–56). I thank Rabbi Dr. Michael Marmur for referring me to Heschel's observations.

lute justification of God.[111] Further, in his pious protest, the poet clings to the just people over the justification of God.

In closing the discussion on "we have not sinned," one further component needs to be taken into account, that is, the diverse attitudes toward the confession of sins found in communal laments. Psalm 44 and 80:19 are the two places where explicit (and implicit) claims of innocence are proclaimed. More common, however, among our target group of communal laments is the choice of silence in this area, that is, the lack of any reference to the people's iniquity and the absence of a confession of sins (see §11.2.3). This suggests that a fundamental element of this group of compositions is a conviction of the people's piety, faithfulness, and innocence of any accusations of wrongdoing that would have made them confess over their responsibility for the catastrophe. While this is largely an *argumentum ex silencio*, it is a telling one, as it concerns Pss 9–10, 42–43, and 74, where the role of God as judge is explicit, yet there is no recognition that the people have sinned against God (9:8–9; 43:1; 74:18–23), and Pss 77, 102, 123, 137, where the role of God as judge is not addressed at all. In terms of our literary historical project of mapping the range of responses to the catastrophe, these poems mount a vigorous challenge to the prophetic and Deuteronomic conceptions of national and/or intergenerational guilt as the causative factor.

Referring again to Green's model of the trilemma of theodicy, this conviction of innocence comprises a significant point of difference between these communal laments and prophetic justifications of God (see fig. 11.3). On behalf of their contemporaries (in both nonprophetic and nonhistoriographic circles), the poets refuse to accept responsibility for the present political distress—but the consequence is that they are unable to resolve the trilemma. The protesting voices discussed here share the recognition of God's power and knowledge as lord of history, and they hold God responsible for his people's distress (though they describe that in different ways; compare Lam 2 to Ps 44). Yet, these protests challenge the workings of divine justice, as they confront the inadequacy of traditional conceptions of divine goodness and compassion in the face of the current (and ongoing) distress.

---

111. So Gerstenberger, *Psalms, Part 1*, 185. In contrast to Gross ("Geschichtserfahrung," 218–21), who emphasizes the resemblance to Job in the theological *resolution* of the crisis, I accentuate Ps 44's *unresolved* cry of protest.

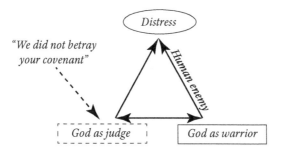

Fig. 11.3. Psalm 44 and the trilemma of theodicy

11.4. RESPONDING TO DOUBT AND PROTEST IN EZEKIEL AND JEREMIAH

Prophetic proclamations respond explicitly, and even more often implicitly, to such expressions of protest as seen in Ps 44 and other communal laments. According to the major prophetic viewpoint, the current generation is the last in a long line of sinners. The present afflictions, however, cause a theological crisis for *all* parties in relation to the traditional transgenerational retribution conception, as reflected in the Decalogue's divine epithet פקד עון אבת על־בנים. Three independent reworkings of this conception are seen in Ezekiel and Jeremiah, with a fourth response of Jeremiah to quoted words of protest. These prophetic responses occur in rhetorical contexts that reveal their polemic nature and may thus participate in the theodical discourse gradually revealed in this study.

11.4.1. Ezekiel Reworks Transgenerational Retribution

11.4.1.1. The Destruction Generation Has Sinned beyond Its Fathers

This conception deviates from the traditional transgenerational conception by placing the heaviest burden of guilt on the destruction generation itself. It occurs only once in Ezekiel and in two prophecies in Jeremiah (see §11.4.2.1) and is not found in quotations or poetic passages.

Defining the prophet's mission in the commission prophecy, Ezek 2:3–4 sets a distinction between fathers and sons, with special emphasis on the latter (see §11.2.2.2). The sons participate in the rebellious behavior of the fathers, yet surpass them, singled out as being קשי פנים וחזקי־לב. These phrases, which are *hapax* expressions in Ezekiel, are accumulative in nature. קשי פנים suggests the familiar phrase קשה ערף, but substitutes the expected ערף with the term פנים ("the face"), which is the place of emotions, including religious ones (Exod 20:20). The heart, however, is the center of knowledge and thought (Gen 6:5), hence חזקי לב indicates stubbornness and persistence in evil thoughts and actions (Exod 4:21; 9:12, 35). Moreover, in Ezek 3:7 the phrase חזקי־מצח וקשי־לב changes the order of components. Switching the attributes that accompany the face/forehead and the heart illustrates an interior and exterior combination of negative qualities of inner stubbornness and outward insolence.[112] Thus here, too, the prophet uses a combination of familiar terms in unfamiliar ways to draw attention to the sins of the present generation having surpassed those of its predecessors.

11.4.1.2. Shrinking the Gap between Transgenerational and Immediate Communal Retribution (Ezekiel 18 and 14)

The sharpest alternative to the transgenerational retribution conception is its opposite, that is, the portrayal of the present calamity as direct and immediate retribution against the generation that sinned. In many of the judgment prophecies constructed according to the measure-for-measure principle, Ezekiel indeed lays responsibility for the destruction on the current generation (see §11.2.1 and §11.2.2.2). Repeating phrases like ושפ־ טתיך כדרכיך (7:3, 9) or איש בעונו (7:13, 16), these prophecies emphasize contemporary sins committed in Jerusalem with no hint of misconduct by previous generations or of any shared transgenerational responsibility of fathers and sons.[113] The cultic abominations practiced in the temple (Ezek 8), as a further example, take place in front of the prophet's eyes as he is led through the temple courts, and there is no indication that these abominations are part of Jerusalem's sins for generations over time.[114]

In Ezek 18 and Ezek 14, the prophet fully disconnects conceptions of retribution, whether reward or punishment, from the diachronic sphere of transgenerational iniquity. According to these particular passages, retribu-

---

112. חזק לב draws on the hardening of the pharaoh's heart (Exod 7:22–23); see Greenberg, *Ezekiel 1–20*, 63–64. Another expression of the people's infidelity is "hardening the face" in Jer 5:3: חזקו פניהם מסלע ("they made their faces harder than rock").

113. So Kasher, *Ezekiel 1–24*, 116.

114. Kaufmann (*Toldot Ha-'Emunah*, 3.369–76) argues that Ezekiel and Jeremiah exaggerate in their extreme descriptions of the sins in Jerusalem during the time of Manasseh, precisely in order to justify God; also Moshe Greenberg's "Prolegomenon" to Torrey, *Pseudo-Ezekiel*, xi–xxix, esp. xviii–xxv.

tion is constructed as an immediate and synchronic connection between sin and punishment on the one hand and righteousness and salvation on the other. Yet, in 18:1–20 and 14:12–23, retribution remains communal (see §11.1).

The disputation speech of 18:1–20 portrays God's role as a just judge of his people, using pentateuchal legal phraseology to refute the protest quoted in 18:2, which is designated as having been said in the land of Israel (see §11.3.1):

[1] The word of the LORD came to me:	¹וַיְהִי דְבַר־יהוה אֵלַי לֵאמֹר.
[2] What do you mean by quoting this proverb upon the soil of Israel, "Parents eat sour grapes and their children's teeth are blunted"?	²מַה־לָּכֶם אַתֶּם מֹשְׁלִים אֶת־הַמָּשָׁל הַזֶּה עַל־אַדְמַת יִשְׂרָאֵל לֵאמֹר אָבוֹת יֹאכְלוּ בֹסֶר וְשִׁנֵּי הַבָּנִים תִּקְהֶינָה.
[3] As I live—declares the Lord GOD—this proverb shall no longer be current among you in Israel.	³חַי־אָנִי נְאֻם אֲדֹנָי יהוה אִם־יִהְיֶה לָכֶם עוֹד מְשֹׁל הַמָּשָׁל הַזֶּה בְּיִשְׂרָאֵל. ⁴הֵן
[4] Consider, all lives are Mine; the life of the parent and the life of the child are both Mine. The person who sins, only he shall die.	כָּל־הַנְּפָשׁוֹת לִי הֵנָּה כְּנֶפֶשׁ הָאָב וּכְנֶפֶשׁ הַבֵּן לִי־הֵנָּה הַנֶּפֶשׁ הַחֹטֵאת הִיא תָמוּת.
[5] Thus, if a man is righteous and does what is just and right: [6] If he has not eaten on the mountains or raised his eyes to the fetishes of the House of Israel; if he has not defiled another man's wife or approached a menstruous woman; [7] if he has not wronged anyone; if he has returned the debtor's pledge to him and has taken nothing by robbery; if he has given bread to the hungry and clothed the naked; [8] if he has not lent at advance interest or exacted accrued interest; if he has abstained from wrongdoing and executed true justice between man and man; [9] if he has followed My laws and kept My rules and acted honestly—he is righteous. Such a man shall live—declares the Lord GOD.	⁵וְאִישׁ כִּי־יִהְיֶה צַדִּיק וְעָשָׂה מִשְׁפָּט וּצְדָקָה. ⁶אֶל־הֶהָרִים לֹא אָכָל וְעֵינָיו לֹא נָשָׂא אֶל־גִּלּוּלֵי בֵּית יִשְׂרָאֵל וְאֶת־אֵשֶׁת רֵעֵהוּ לֹא טִמֵּא וְאֶל־אִשָּׁה נִדָּה לֹא יִקְרָב. ⁷וְאִישׁ לֹא יוֹנֶה חֲבֹלָתוֹ חוֹב יָשִׁיב גְּזֵלָה לֹא יִגְזֹל לַחְמוֹ לְרָעֵב יִתֵּן וְעֵירֹם יְכַסֶּה־בָּגֶד. ⁸בַּנֶּשֶׁךְ לֹא־יִתֵּן וְתַרְבִּית לֹא יִקָּח מֵעָוֶל יָשִׁיב יָדוֹ מִשְׁפַּט אֱמֶת יַעֲשֶׂה בֵּין אִישׁ לְאִישׁ. ⁹בְּחֻקּוֹתַי יְהַלֵּךְ וּמִשְׁפָּטַי שָׁמַר לַעֲשׂוֹת אֱמֶת צַדִּיק הוּא חָיֹה יִחְיֶה נְאֻם אֲדֹנָי יהוה.

In this passage Ezekiel sets guidelines for punishment (18:4, 20), compiles lists of sins that bring together cultic and moral-social spheres, and constructs these lists as legal precedents in the third-person singular (18:5–19).[115] The prophet uses a schematic framework of three generations—the righteous person, his wicked son, and the grandson who does not follow in his father's ways—to drive home the point that each member of the chain will be punished or rewarded on his own (de)merits. This threefold model does not easily fit the prophet's usual depiction of Jerusalem's (or the people's) history of iniquity. In the historical retrospectives of Ezek 16, 23, 20, the people's sins begin with the initiation of the covenant relationship; hence, there is no parallel to the period of the righteous father (18:5–9).

On the other hand, there is of course no difficulty in matching up the character of the בֶּן־פָּרִיץ שֹׁפֵךְ דָּם ("a son who is a ruffian, a shedder of blood," 18:10–13) with the generations that sinned in Jerusalem. But the focus of this typological scheme is the third generation, the son of the wicked one who nevertheless follows his righteous grandfather (18:14–18). Indeed, the exilic audience expresses its astonishment over the good fate foreseen for the third generation (18:19), for they identify themselves with it;[116] and the prophet refutes their word proclaiming a further "legal" ruling (18:20):

115. Priestly legal style may be further recognized in the language of Ezek 18:4, with its use of נֶפֶשׁ (see Lev 7:20, 21; 23:30), in the combination of נֶפֶשׁ with חֹטֵא (as in Lev 4:2, 27; 5:1, 17, 21; Num 15:27), and in constructions of נֶפֶשׁ with an adjective or a participle (as in Lev 7:18; Num 19:22). On the repeated lists of the things done/not done by the three generations, see Greenberg (*Ezekiel 1–20*, 328–32, 342–47), who points out the selective nature of these lists and the use of both Priestly and Deuteronomic legal allusions.

116. While the speakers behind the quotation in 18:19 are anonymous, I assume they are members of the immediate audience that heard Ezekiel in exile. Their question differs in tone from the protest of 18:2, which is designated as a rebellious statement from "the land of Israel" and thus is fiercely refuted. For this constant distinction between rebellious sayings marked as said in the land of Israel by those who remained and the exiles' desperate and pleading words, which are treated with empathy by the prophet, see Rom-Shiloni, *Exclusive Inclusivity*, 141–42. The speakers of 18:19 accept the transgenerational retribution conception; so much so that the prophet's words seem too innovative to their ears. In addition, the prophet answers calmly to their inquiry (18:19b–20), with a hopeful message. Compare this reading to that of Greenberg (*Ezekiel 1–20*, 332), who argues that 18:19a is but a provocative rhetorical statement made by the prophet himself. Block (*Ezekiel 1–24*, 561) argues that both quotations (18:2 and 18:19) are from the exiles; he thus needs to explain the contradiction between them.

¹⁹ And now you ask, "Why has not the son shared the burden of his father's guilt?" But the son has done what is right and just, and has carefully kept all My laws: he shall live! ²⁰ The person who sins, he alone shall die. A child shall not share the burden of a parent's guilt, nor shall a parent share the burden of a child's guilt; the righteousness of the righteous shall be accounted to him alone, and the wickedness of the wicked shall be accounted to him alone.

19ואמרתם מדע לא־נשא
הבן בעון האב
והבן משפט וצדקה עשה
את כל־חקותי שמר ויעשה
אתם חיה יחיה. 20 הנפש
החטאת היא תמות בן לא־
ישא בעון האב ואב לא
ישא בעון הבן צדקת הצדיק
עליו תהיה ורשעת רשע (ק)
הרשע) עליו תהיה.

In his response, Ezekiel invokes and transforms the Deuteronomic criminal law expressed in Deut 24:16, which stands against transgenerational punishment:[117]

Parents shall not be put to death for children, nor children be put to death for parents: a person shall be put to death only for his own crime.

לא־יומתו אבות על־בנים
ובנים לא־יומתו על־אבות
איש בחטאו יומתו.

Ezekiel treats this law quite freely in regard to both style and content. First, the prophet retains the symmetrical pattern between fathers and sons, although this is clearly not part of his agenda in Ezek 18; he could clearly do well with just the second component: ובנים לא־יומתו על־אבות. Second, Ezekiel transforms the Deuteronomic law's plural language into the singular, in accordance with the general style of the presentation in Ezek 18. Similarly, the prophet changes the order of the components to fit the needs of his prophecy, in order to accentuate the status of the son in relation to his father's sins. Finally, the prophet transfers this law from its criminal legal context to a theological one.[118]

By closing his argument in this refutation speech with the *inclusio* (18:20) that returns us to 18:4, Ezekiel criticizes (even if implicitly) his fellow exiles in Babylon, who might also have considered themselves in-

---

117. For the role of this law within Hebrew Bible criminal law, see Greenberg, "Some Postulates."

118. See Greenberg, *Ezekiel 1–20*, 332–33. Deut 24:16 is quoted in 2 Kgs 14:6 and also reflected in 9:26; see Joyce, *Divine Initiative*, 49, 141 and n57.

nocent. In contradistinction to their self-identification as the third generation, using this criminal law, Ezekiel draws the parallel between the destruction generation and the second generation in this scheme, that of the wicked son. This is the kernel of Ezekiel's response to both the words of protest from "the soil of Israel" (עַל־אַדְמַת יִשְׂרָאֵל, 18:2) and to the doubt raised by his immediate audience (18:19). The prophet justifies God for the destruction: it is the proper divine punishment at that time. Nevertheless, this scheme of three generations leaves hope for the Jehoiachin exiles, the prophet's immediate audience, for they have the possibility of correcting their ways and gaining life, as is done by the righteous grandson.[119] This wish to put hope in the exiles' hearts characterizes the second part of this chapter, 18:21–32, where the prophet expresses the possibility that even the individual may transform his ways within his own lifetime.

The conception of immediate retribution also stands in the background of 14:12–23, where the prophet expresses an implicit counterposition to the second part of the divine epithet: וְעֹשֶׂה חֶסֶד לַאֲלָפִים לְאֹהֲבַי וּלְשֹׁמְרֵי מִצְוֹתָי ("but showing kindness to the thousandth generation of those who love Me and keep My commandments," Exod 20:6; Deut 5:10).[120]

The repeated emphasis in this passage on the personal righteousness of the three ancient, non-Israelite figures, Noah, Dan'el (qere: Daniel), and Job, and their inability, righteousness notwithstanding, to protect their own descendants, seems to be a polemical response against the traditional transgenerational conception of retribution, according to which one might argue that the merit of the fathers should protect their descendants, just as the sons are punished for their fathers' iniquities. Countering this idea, Ezekiel sets out two basic premises in 14:13–14: First, the general disaster is a divine judgment for מַעַל, which designates a sin within the sphere of obedience to God.[121] Second, the

119. On the prophet's intention to give hope to the exiles in Ezek 18:21–32, see Block, *Ezekiel 1–24*, 557–89.

120. Since there is no phraseological or allusive connection between this prophecy and the divine epithet of the Decalogue, scholars have not noted the reversal of the Decalogue's עֹשֶׂה חֶסֶד לַאֲלָפִים in Ezek 14:12–23. But, based on the larger theological context, I suggest this.

121. Almost all occurrences of מַעַל in the Hebrew Bible designate a sin against God; Num 5:12 is an exception. The sin falls within the sphere of holiness and cult (as in Josh 7:1; 1 Chr 10:13; 2 Chr 26:16–18). Milgrom ("Concept of Ma'al," 240–47) argues that

righteous ones will be saved from the catastrophe, a promise of salvation that stands in clear contradiction to the all-inclusive formula that repeats in this passage: והכרתי ממנה אדם ובהמה ("and cut off man and beast from it," 14:13, 17, 19, 21).[122] This seeming contradiction allows Ezekiel to distinguish between the communal judgment and the fate of righteous individuals.[123]

But in addition, this picture of total judgment, with nevertheless a few survivors, raises another very disturbing issue. The fate of the anonymous land that sins (ארץ כי תחטא) along with its inhabitants (14:12–20) is expressed in general terms, yet it is of genuine significance to the national-social reality of the postdestruction era, as described in 14:21–23. While 14:12–20 predicts total destruction of the land, the final verbs in 14:21–23 express the tension between the prospect of total annihilation and the reality of a remnant (פלטה), that is, those few survivors (called בנים ובנות in 14:22) who are destined for Babylon and might already have reached the Judean Jehoiachin exiles' community there.[124] Ezekiel's prophecy (14:21–23) echoes voices among the Babylonian exiles who wonder whether those survivors of the destruction are saved on account of their own merit or rather because of the merit of their parents. In response, Ezekiel suggests (14:22b–23) an entirely different reason for their survival, an educational one—they are to serve as a constant lesson to the Jehoiachin exiles. When they look at this remnant from Jerusalem, the 597 exiles will always be able to justify God for his deeds against Jerusalem in 586 (14:23). The prophet thus calls for a continuing attitude of exclusivity toward the second wave of deportees and separation from them.[125] It is their own ways and iniquities, not those of previous generations, that

---

the basic meaning of מעל is an assault against God's name and against the covenant oaths (see the parallelism between מעל and מרד in Josh 22:22); therefore, מעל may be expressed as worship of other gods (as in 2 Chr 28:22–25).

122. והכרתי ממנה אדם ובהמה is one of the formulas that designate total annihilation of humans, animals, and the entire ecological system in the course of a destruction; see §9.1.3.

123. See Joyce, *Divine Initiative*, 70–73.

124. Greenberg (*Ezekiel 1–20*, 261–63) emphasizes the thematic and lexical connections between 14:12–20 and 14:21–23; in the same vein, see Block, *Ezekiel 1–24*, 441; and Kasher, *Ezekiel 1–24*, 362. But often, 14:21–23 is counted as a secondary appendix to this prophecy; see, e.g., Zimmerli, *Ezekiel*, 1.312.

125. For this position of extreme exclusivity, see Rom-Shiloni, *Exclusive Inclusivity*, 179–80.

caused God to initiate his fierce judgment against Jerusalem. Thus, in this polemic against the Judean exiles of 586, we may detect another response to the attitude from "the land of Israel" quoted in 18:2 (and Jer 31:29): the Jerusalem survivors are not righteous in the eyes of the prophet; even if they are sons and daughters of acclaimed righteous persons, the merits of their fathers cannot help them.

Ezekiel 14:12–23 forms a mirror image of 18:1–20. Together, the two prophecies illustrate that Ezekiel's conception of immediate retribution is consistent and applicable to both judgment (Ezek 18) and reward (Ezek 14). Yet, as elsewhere, retribution is communal—affecting the generation as a whole and divided between the Jehoiachin exiles and those who remain in Jerusalem/Judah.[126]

11.4.1.3. Immediate and Individual Retribution in Ezekiel

Within this general picture of conceptions of retribution in Ezekiel, there are only a few explicit references to a distinction between the fate of the individual and that of the community. Ezekiel 14:12–20 is an example of the hypothetical possibility that three righteous typological heroes would be saved in circumstances of total calamity inflicted on an anonymous land, and yet even they could not save their own sons and daughters. In two other passages, 9:4–11 and 21:6–10, Ezekiel accentuates the lack of any distinction between individuals in circumstances of destruction.

The order in 9:4–11 to mark those "men who moan and groan because of all the abominations that are committed in" the city (האנשים הנאנחים והנאנקים על כל־התועבות הנעשות בתוכה) is exceptional in Ezekiel's treatments of the question of retribution:

---

126. Throughout Ezek 1–24, Ezekiel categorizes those who remained in Jerusalem as sinners who deserve the calamity they faced, but the question of whether the Jehoiachin exiles deserved deportation is not explicitly discussed; see Rom-Shiloni, *Exclusive Inclusivity*, 169–73.

⁴ And the Lord said to him, "Pass through the city, through Jerusalem, and <u>put a mark on the foreheads of the men who moan and groan because of all the abominations that are committed in it."</u> ⁵ To the others He said in my hearing, "Follow him through the city and strike; show no pity or compassion. ⁶ Kill off graybeard, youth and maiden, women and children; <u>but do not touch any person who bears the mark.</u> Begin here at My Sanctuary." So they began with the elders who were in front of the House. ⁷ And He said to them, "Defile the House and fill the courts with the slain. Then go forth." So they went forth and began to kill in the city. ⁸ When they were out killing, and I remained alone, I flung myself on my face and cried out, "Ah, Lord God! Are you going to annihilate all that is left of Israel, pouring out Your fury upon Jerusalem?" ⁹ He answered me, "The iniquity of the Houses of Judah and Israel is very, very great, the land is full of crime and the city is full of corruption. For they say, 'The Lord has forsaken the land, and the Lord does not see.' ¹⁰ I, in turn, will show no pity or compassion; I will give them their deserts." ¹¹ And then the man clothed in linen with the writing case at his waist brought back word, saying, "I have done as You commanded me."

⁴ויאמר יהוה אלו (ק: אליו)
עבר בתוך העיר בתוך ירושלים
<u>והתוית תו על־מצחות האנשים</u>
<u>הנאנחים והנאנקים על כל־</u>
<u>התועבות הנעשות בתוכה.</u>
⁵ולאלה אמר באזני עברו בעיר
אחריו והכו על (ק: אל)־תחס
עינכם (ק: עיניכם) ואל־תחמלו.
⁶זקן בחור ובתולה וטף ונשים
תהרגו למשחית <u>ועל־כל־איש</u>
<u>אשר־עליו התו אל־תגשו</u>
וממקדשי תחלו ויחלו באנשים
הזקנים אשר לפני הבית.
⁷ויאמר אליהם טמאו את־הבית
ומלאו את־החצרות חללים צאו
ויצאו והכו בעיר. ⁸ויהי כהכותם
ונאשאר אני ואפלה על־פני
ואזעק ואמר אהה אדני יהוה
המשחית אתה את כל־שארית
ישראל בשפכך את־חמתך
על־ירושלים. ⁹ויאמר אלי עון
בית־ישראל ויהודה גדול במאד
מאד ותמלא הארץ דמים והעיר
מלאה מטה כי אמרו עזב יהוה
את־הארץ ואין יהוה ראה.
¹⁰וגם־אני לא־תחוס עיני ולא
אחמל דרכם בראשם נתתי.
¹¹והנה האיש לבש הבדים
אשר הקסת במתניו משיב דבר
לאמר עשיתי כאשר צויתני.

Interestingly, the men marked are not designated as "righteous" (the term the prophet uses in four other passages), but by their ad hoc reactions to the abominations conducted in Jerusalem (9:4, referring to the actions described in Ezek 8).¹²⁷ The men marked are said to be excluded from the

---

127. See Greenberg (*Ezekiel 1–20*, 177) for this exceptional presentation of a group

mass killing that takes place in Jerusalem starting at the very temple; they will survive the affliction (9:5–7). However, the prophet's cry (9:8) and God's response (9:9–10) do not refer any further to the fate of this marked group; rather the prophecy focuses on only the total annihilation brought upon the city, with no survivors (9:11).[128] Hence, this passage leaves no clear answer as to the fate of any individuals marked for survival. The prophecy is rather focused on the massive general killing with no mercy (9:5–7).[129]

Moreover, the common pictures of Jerusalem's destruction illustrate the total annihilation of the city, conveyed through the lack of any distinction between the fates meted out to the righteous and the wicked, as explicitly expressed in Ezek 21:8–10:[130]

[8] Say to the land of Israel: Thus said the LORD: I am going to deal with you! I will draw My sword from its sheath, <u>and I will wipe out from you both the righteous and the wicked</u>. [9] <u>In order to wipe out from you both the righteous and the wicked</u>, My sword shall assuredly be unsheathed against all flesh from south to north; [10] and all flesh shall know that I the LORD have drawn My sword from its sheath, not to be sheathed again.	⁸ואמרת לאדמת ישראל כה אמר יהוה הנני אליך והוצאתי חרבי מתערה <u>והכרתי ממך צדיק ורשע.</u> ⁹<u>יען אשר הכרתי ממך</u> <u>צדיק ורשע</u> לכן תצא חרבי מתערה אל־כל־בשר מנגב צפון. ¹⁰וידעו כל־בשר כי אני יהוה הוצאתי חרבי מתערה לא תשוב עוד.

When it comes to Jerusalem itself, Ezekiel seems to tolerate outright injustice, presented as the unavoidable consequences of the total calamity God brings over the city and its inhabitants.

The indiscriminate character of the sword in this passage, killing righteous and wicked together, contrasts with four other passages in Ezekiel that present pictures of individual and immediate retribution. In two calls to repentance (18:21–32; 33:10–20) and in two passages that articulate the

---

of "righteous Jerusalemites" in contrast to the usual emphasis on the sinful behavior in Jerusalem in Ezek 6:9; 7:16; 12:16; 14:22–23.

128. See Joyce, *Divine Initiative*, 63–65. This is probably behind the talmudic reference to possible reasons for their subsequent annihilation; see b. Shabbat 55a, Rashi, and Greenberg, *Ezekiel 1–20*, 177.

129. See Bodi (*Erra and Ezekiel*, 95–110) for the extreme and total judgment presented in Ezek 9.

130. See §11.2.1. Compare other passages of judgment in Ezekiel, all of which argue for a total annihilation in Jerusalem that leaves no survivors at all (5:12; 7:10–27; 9:5–10; 11:7–12; 16:1–43).

prophet's responsibility as a warning watchman (3:16–21; 33:1–9), Ezekiel refers to the opportunities given to a person (or rather to the generation?) to change the fate within one's (or the generation's) life span.[131]

In 18:21–32 (also 33:10–20), the prophet continues to speak in the singular about a single wicked or a righteous individual who changes his or her manners (18:21–27); he continues to refute his immediate audience's words that challenge God's ways (18:25, 29 following 18:19); and he closes with another principle of retribution (18:30; also 18:4, 20).[132] The major perspective that these verses contribute to the structuring of the retribution conception in the first part of the chapter is the further closure of the chronological gap between human deeds and their fitting retaliation. With this constrict of time, it seems that the prophet attends to individual and immediate retribution:[133]

[21] Moreover, if the wicked one repents of all the sins that he committed and keeps all My laws and does what is just and right, he shall live; he shall not die. [22] None of the transgressions he committed shall be remembered against him; because of the righteousness he has practiced, he shall live. [23] Is it my desire that a wicked person shall die?—says the Lord GOD. It is rather that he shall turn back from his ways and live. [24] So, too, if a righteous person turns away from his righteousness and does wrong, practicing the very abominations that the wicked person practiced, shall he live? None of the righteous deeds that he did shall be remembered; because of the treachery he has practiced and the sins he has committed—because of these, he shall die.	[21] והרשע כי ישוב מכל־חטאתו (ק: חטאתיו) אשר עשה ושמר את־כל־חקותי ועשה משפט וצדקה חיה יחיה לא ימות. [22] כל־פשעיו אשר עשה לא יזכרו לו בצדקתו אשר־עשה יחיה. [23] החפץ אחפץ מות רשע נאם אדני יהוה הלוא בשובו מדרכיו וחיה. [24] ובשוב צדיק מצדקתו ועשה עול ככל התועבות אשר־עשה הרשע יעשה וחי כל־צדקתו (ק: צדקתיו) אשר־עשה לא תזכרנה במעלו אשר־מעל ובחטאתו אשר־חטא בם ימות.

---

131. For Ezek 3:16–21 and 33:1–9 as part of the prophet's mission and his role as a "watchman," see Kasher, "Dumbness in the Book of Ezekiel."

132. Based on these three characteristics of Ezek 18:21–32, Joyce (*Divine Initiative*, 50–55) considers this passage to follow the same communal approach that focuses on the communal human responsibility (18:1–20) and still sees the repentance as collective by that generation. Yet, Joyce recognizes that the option of addressing individuals cannot be overruled (53–54).

133. See Greenberg, *Ezekiel 1–20*, 334, 340.

²⁵ Yet you say, "The way of the LORD is im-
possible." Listen, O House of Israel: Is My
way unfair? It is your ways that are unfair!
²⁶ When a righteous person turns away from
his righteousness and does wrong, he shall
die for it; he shall die for the wrong he has
done. ²⁷ And if a wicked person turns back
from the wickedness that he practiced and
does what is just and right, such a person
shall save his life. ²⁸ Because he took heed
and turned back from all the transgressions
that he committed, he shall live; he shall
not die.

²⁹ Yet the House of Israel say, "The way of
the Lord is impossible." Are My ways unfair,
O House of Israel? It is your ways that are
unfair! ³⁰ Be assured, O House of Israel,
I will judge each one of you according to
his ways—declares the Lord GOD. Repent
and turn back from your transgressions; let
them not be a stumbling block of guilt for
you. ³¹ Cast away all the transgressions by
which you have offended, and get your-
selves a new heart and a new spirit, that
you may not die, O House of Israel. ³² For
it is not My desire that anyone shall die—
declares the Lord GOD. Repent, therefore,
and live!

25 וַאֲמַרְתֶּם לֹא יִתָּכֵן דֶּרֶךְ אֲדֹנָי
שִׁמְעוּ־נָא בֵּית יִשְׂרָאֵל הֲדַרְכִּי
לֹא יִתָּכֵן הֲלֹא דַרְכֵיכֶם לֹא
יִתָּכֵנוּ. 26 בְּשׁוּב־צַדִּיק מִצִּדְקָתוֹ
וְעָשָׂה עָוֶל וּמֵת עֲלֵיהֶם בְּעַוְלוֹ
אֲשֶׁר־עָשָׂה יָמוּת. 27 וּבְשׁוּב
רָשָׁע מֵרִשְׁעָתוֹ אֲשֶׁר עָשָׂה
וַיַּעַשׂ מִשְׁפָּט וּצְדָקָה הוּא אֶת־
נַפְשׁוֹ יְחַיֶּה. 28 וַיִּרְאֶה וַיָּשׁוב
(ק: וַיָּשָׁב) מִכָּל־פְּשָׁעָיו אֲשֶׁר
עָשָׂה חָיוֹ יִחְיֶה לֹא יָמוּת.

29 וְאָמְרוּ בֵּית יִשְׂרָאֵל לֹא יִתָּכֵן
דֶּרֶךְ אֲדֹנָי הֲדַרְכִּי לֹא יִתָּכֵנוּ
בֵּית יִשְׂרָאֵל הֲלֹא דַרְכֵיכֶם
לֹא יִתָּכֵן. 30 לָכֵן אִישׁ כִּדְרָכָיו
אֶשְׁפֹּט אֶתְכֶם בֵּית יִשְׂרָאֵל
נְאֻם אֲדֹנָי יהוה שׁוּבוּ וְהָשִׁיבוּ
מִכָּל־פִּשְׁעֵיכֶם וְלֹא־יִהְיֶה
לָכֶם לְמִכְשׁוֹל עָוֹן. 31 הַשְׁלִיכוּ
מֵעֲלֵיכֶם אֶת־כָּל־פִּשְׁעֵיכֶם אֲשֶׁר
פְּשַׁעְתֶּם בָּם וַעֲשׂוּ לָכֶם לֵב
חָדָשׁ וְרוּחַ חֲדָשָׁה וְלָמָּה תָמֻתוּ
בֵּית יִשְׂרָאֵל. 32 כִּי לֹא אֶחְפֹּץ
בְּמוֹת הַמֵּת נְאֻם אֲדֹנָי יהוה
וְהָשִׁיבוּ וִחְיוּ.

Using the categories צדיק and רשע, the prophet argues that the person's last behavior will be the determinative one for life or death (18:21b,
22b, 24b, 26, 27b, 28b; and 33:12–16). Both passages, 18:21–32 and 33:10–20,
quote the same reaction by the exiles, those of the prophet's immediate
audience, who say לֹא יִתָּכֵן דֶּרֶךְ אֲדֹנָי ("the way of the LORD is impossible
[NJPS: unfair]").¹³⁴ Ezekiel's very clear and schematic presentations on

134. לֹא יִתָּכֵן (Ezek 18:25, 29; 33:17, 20) challenges the ways of God as not in or-

individual and immediate repentance are rejected as unacceptable innovation to a well-known retribution tradition.

The concluding rule the prophet proclaims: לכן איש כדרכיו אשפט
אתכם בית ישראל ("be assured, O House of Israel, I will judge each one of
you according to his ways," 18:30a) clearly expresses retribution directed
at the individual.[135] Yet, it is quite remarkable that at this crucial point,
the prophet addresses the exilic community as a whole. Ezekiel 18:30–32
refers to בית ישראל in the second-person plural, thus mentioning the
entire community, composed of the many individuals.[136] Joyce concludes
that "it is no part of the purpose of Ezekiel here to argue for the repentance of individuals in isolation from the corporate people of God."[137] Yet,
there is no need to diminish the individual and immediate retribution
conception that those verses suggest. Following 18:1–20, 18:21–32 supplies
hope to the Jehoiachin exiles, both in the communal and in the individual
spheres.[138] The proximity of the two passages in Ezek 18 as two parts of
a long essay, and 18:21–32 in itself, show that Ezekiel integrates the individual perspective within the collective address to "the house of Israel,"
to the Jehoiachin exiles.

The two conceptions are not mutually exclusive and certainly not polemical; the debate Ezekiel handles with his Babylonian contemporaries
is over time: Who is the generation responsible for the disaster? Is punishment transgenerational or immediate? and even, How immediate is it?
In the two units, Ezekiel holds a coherent answer—the present generation
is responsible for its own suffering (18:1–20), and this same generation
may even change its own fortune as only the last deeds of a person (or the
community) count (18:21–32).[139] Hence, while the Jehoiachin exiles are a

der, as incorrect; see תכן in Koehler, Baumgartner, and Stamm, *Hebrew and Aramaic
Lexicon*, 1733.

135. Compare Joyce (*Divine Initiative*, 50–55), who suggests the following paraphrase for 18:30: "Therefore I will judge you, O house of Israel, by analogy to the legal
principle whereby each individual is punished for his own crime" (53).

136. See Zimmerli, *Ezekiel*, 1.386. Joyce (*Divine Initiative*, 54–55) takes those
corporate addresses to confirm the communal address of this passage, and thus the
entire chapter.

137. Joyce, *Divine Initiative*, 55.

138. For a combination of individual and communal responsibility for sin and for
the subsequent punishment and the tensions between the individual and the group,
see Joyce, *Divine Initiative*, 79–87; and Kaufmann, *Toldot Ha-'Emunah*, 3.595–600.

139. Zimmerli (*Ezekiel*, 1.387) notes the emphasis on the present in this passage.

part of the destruction generation and are responsible for their own fate, they have the possibility of repairing their own ways (individually and collectively) and gaining deliverance.

11.4.2. Jeremiah Challenges the Retribution Traditions

11.4.2.1. The Current Generation Sins beyond Its Fathers

Ezekiel places the heaviest responsibility for the present events upon the destruction generation itself only once, in the commission prophecy (2:2–3), rather than on any previous generation. Jeremiah conveys this same idea in two oracles through the phrase הרע(ו) (לעשות) מאבותם ("they/you have acted worse than their/your fathers," Jer 7:26; 16:12).

Jeremiah 7:21–28[140] starts by making a demand for loyalty and full obedience to God as a higher priority than cultic worship:[141]

---

140. While Jer 7:21–22 is often considered one of Jeremiah's calls for the importance of moral-social behavior over cult, note that the opposition is not between moral-social and cultic demands, but between obedience and cult, and this is altogether a different issue; see McKane, *Jeremiah 1–25*, 173–74, and the second interpretation of Lundbom (*Jeremiah 1–20*, 482), which I find more probable. In addition, 7:22 is interpreted, according to the Deuteronomic conception of the Sinai/Horeb covenant, as referring exclusively to the Decalogue, thus in conformity with this prophetic proclamation that emphasizes that no cultic orders are given in Sinai (Thiel, *Jeremia 1–25*, 122–23; and Lundbom, *Jeremiah 1–20*, 481–82, 486–89). But the expression "on the day" of the exodus follows a Priestly formula and conception; see Rom-Shiloni, "On the Day," 634–44; and §11.2.2.1.

141. Weinfeld ("Jeremiah and the Spiritual Metamorphosis," 52–53) argues that this passage presents a thesis and antithesis structure. Weinfeld finds Jeremiah's innovative message to be "a slap in the face of the Priestly Code with all its details, for according to it the law of the burnt-offering and the sacrifice was given to Moses at Sinai as stated in Num 28:6" (53).

²¹ Thus said the LORD of Hosts, the God of Israel: Add your burnt offerings to your other sacrifices and eat the meat! ²² For on the day I freed your fathers from the land of Egypt, I did not speak with them or command them concerning burnt offerings or sacrifice. ²³ But this is what I commanded them: Do My bidding, that I may be your God and you may be My people; walk only in the way that I enjoin upon you, that it may go well with you. ²⁴ Yet they did not listen or give ear; they followed their own counsels, the willfulness of their evil hearts. They have gone backward, not forward, ²⁵ from the day your fathers left the land of Egypt until today. And though I kept sending all My servants, the prophets, to them daily and persistently, ²⁶ they would not listen to Me or give ear. They stiffened their necks, they acted worse than their fathers. ²⁷ You shall say all these things to them, but they will not listen to you; you shall call to them, but they will not respond to you. ²⁸ Then say to them: This is the nation that would not obey the LORD their God, that would not accept rebuke. Faithfulness has perished, vanished from their mouths.

²¹ כה אמר יהוה צבאות אלהי ישראל עלותיכם ספו על־זבחיכם ואכלו בשר. ²²כי לא־דברתי את־אבותיכם ולא צויתים ביום הוציא (ק: הוציאי) אותם מארץ מצרים על־דברי עולה וזבח. ²³ כי אם־את־הדבר הזה צויתי אותם לאמר שמעו בקולי והייתי לכם לאלהים ואתם תהיו־לי לעם והלכתם בכל הדרך אשר אצוה אתכם למען ייטב לכם. ²⁴ ולא־שמעו ולא־הטו את־אזנם וילכו במעצות בשררות לבם הרע ויהיו לאחור ולא לפנים. ²⁵ למן־היום אשר יצאו אבותיכם מארץ מצרים עד היום הזה ואשלח אליכם את־כל־עבדי הנביאים יום השכם ושלח. ²⁶ ולוא שמעו אלי ולא הטו את־אזנם ויקשו את־ערפם הרעו מאבותם. ²⁷ ודברת אליהם את־כל־הדברים האלה ולא ישמעו אליך וקראת אליהם ולא יענוכה. ²⁸ ואמרת אליהם זה הגוי אשר לוא־ שמעו בקול יהוה אלהיו ולא לקחו מוסר אבדה האמונה ונכרתה מפיהם.

Obedience gains this higher status because it is commanded at the initial event that constituted the covenant relationship with the people: "On the day I freed your fathers from the land of Egypt" (7:22).[142] Disobedience,

---

142. The borders of this unit and its contents are under scholarly debate. Rudolph (*Jeremia*, 56–59) finds 7:21–28 to be one integral unit; McKane (*Jeremiah 1–25*, 172–73) includes the poetic 7:29 in this unit; and Carroll (*Jeremiah* 214, 218) separates 7:21–26 from 7:27–28 and 7:29 as distinct additions. The connections between 7:27–28 and the rest of the passage are not straightforward, which leads Lundbom (*Jeremiah 1–20*, 480) to suggest that these verses constitute directions to Jeremiah (similar to the way

however, characterized the people's behavior since that very event and throughout its history and gradually became the major issue for which prophets are sent (again, from the exodus event until the present; 7:23); but all these efforts have been in vain, as is repeated in 7:24 and 7:26.

This unit shows constant alteration between second-person plural and third-person plural verbal phrases and pronouns. In keeping with these rhetorical alterations, the demand for obedience is cast in second-person plural verbal forms (7:22–23, 25) whereas disobedience is described using third-person plurals (7:24, 26 and thus 7:27–28).[143] The shifts between this demand and the accusations of disobedience give additional force to the prophetic message—there is continuing disobedience throughout the generations. While formally, the references to the present generation's iniquities remain in the third-person plural (7:26–28), the prophecy treats the generation that suffers the destruction as the one that sinned far worse than its predecessors. Jeremiah 7:24 and 7:26 convey this message:[144]

וילכו במעצות בשררות לבם הרע ²⁴ולא שמעו ולא־הטו את־אזנם
ויהיו לאחור ולא לפנים.

ויקשו את־ערפם ²⁶ולא שמעו אלי ולא הטו את־אזנם
הרעו מאבותם.

Jeremiah 7:24 and 7:26 begin with the same two components but continue differently and thus adjoin four additional accusations to illustrate the people's ongoing transgression. Jeremiah 7:24 collates two phrases: וילכו במעצות בשררות לבם הרע ("they followed their own counsels, the willfulness of their evil hearts"). The former is of wisdom origin, and the latter is a typically Jeremianic phrase;[145] these two are paired with the

---

Lundbom understands 7:16–18). I understand 7:21–28 to be an integral unit, and 7:28 is an important component of Jeremiah's accusations against his contemporaries.

143. The use of the second-person plural here follows the legal style of Deuteronomy, which regularly uses second-person, in either singular or plural (e.g., 5:1–4; Deut 32–33). Therefore, there is no reason to prefer the Septuagint, Peshitta, and Vulgate readings for 7:25, which feature the third-person plural. McKane (*Jeremiah 1–25*, 173, 175) argues that the reading found in the versions does not ease the difficulty; and he suggests that these transitions are rhetorical markers, showing God's address to the prophet.

144. See Lundbom (*Jeremiah 1–20*, 480) for the suggestion that the repetition forms an *inclusio*.

145. מועצות are "(bed) counsels or ways" according to Prov 1:31; 22:20; Ps 5:11; and thus Hos 11:6. Is it a coincidence that מועצה/מועצות is formed as תועבה/תוע־

hapax expression ויהיו לאחור ולא לפנים ("they have gone backward, not forward") to designate a turning away from God.[146] In a similar fashion, 7:26 first continues with a more familiar phrase to designate stubborn disobedience—ויקשו את־ערפם ("they stiffened their necks")[147]—and then concludes with the *nearly hapax* accusation: הרעו מאבותם ("they acted worse than their fathers"). But the prophet does not give any evidence as to how they have become worse than their predecessors, but 7:27–28, which instructs the prophet to attend his contemporary audience, adds crucial points. The destruction generation makes the iniquity worse in two respects. First, they did not learn from the history of their ancestors' disobedience and from past events of affliction, ולא לקחו מוסר (7:28a).[148] Second, the lamenting cry אבדה האמונה ונכרתה מפיהם ("faithfulness has perished, vanished from their mouths," 7:28b) refers to their current iniquity. Using the verbs אבד and כרת, the prophet illustrates the severity of their disobedience: it destroys the basis of their connection with God.[149]

The second passage, Jer 16:10–13, constitutes the prophet's refutation of a quoted question concerning the reasons for the harsh divine judgment on

---

בות? Jeremiah seems to coin the phrase הלך במועצות in 7:24 (probably attracted to הלך בשררות לב), and this is reflected in Mic 6:16 and Ps 81:13. הלך (איש) בשררות לבו occurs eight times in Jeremiah (3:17; 7:24; 9:13; 11:8; 13:10; 16:12; 18:12; 23:17) and otherwise only in Deut 29:18 and Ps 81:13. Jer 7:24 shows an elaborated formula with במעצות, possibly influenced by Ps 81:13.

146. For ויהיו לאחור ולא לפנים, see Lundbom, *Jeremiah 1–20*, 483–84.

147. עם־קשה־עורף is a recognized designation of the people of Israel in pentateuchal sources (Exod 32:9; 33:3, 5; 34:9; Deut 9:6, 13; 31:27); it otherwise occurs once in the historiography (2 Kgs 17:14), three times in Jeremiah (7:26; 17:23; 19:15), and once in Second Isaiah (48:4).

148. לקח מוסר occurs six times in Jeremiah, in both poetry and prose (2:30; 5:3; 7:28; 17:23; 32:33; 35:13; with a closely similar phrase in 30:14). Four of these occurrences are side by side with שמע (לא) (the two phrases are similarly conjoined in Zeph 3:2). This is another one of the wisdom phrases found in Jeremiah (see Prov 1:3; 8:10; 24:32) and thus cannot be taken as a Deuteronomic influence (the only occurrence of מוסר in Deuteronomy is 11:2, where it refers to God's diverse actions as a warrior against Egypt and during the desert wanderings).

149. אבד and כרת occur in reference to God's deeds of judgment, and they designate total annihilation. Note אבד in the causative *piel* or *hiphil* (Jer 1:10; 12:17; 15:7). כרת usually denotes a divine action against the nations (Deut 12:29; Josh 23:4) or against Israel (Isa 9:13; Zeph 1:3, 4). Their use to denote human activity, with the object אמונה, is exceptional. אמונה is the opposite of שקר in Jer 9:2 and has the meaning of loyalty to God in Hab 2:4: וצדיק באמונתו יחיה. Carroll (*Jeremiah*, 218–19) prefers the first meaning and translates: "truth has perished."

"us" (16:10; see §10.2), while 16:12 forms the climax of the refutation. The refutation uses the second-person plural to mount an explicit and direct accusation against the destruction generation. In answer to the people's inquiry concerning the reason for the distress (16:10), the prophet draws a clear distinction between fathers and sons. The iniquity of the earlier generations (16:11) is expressed as a string of evil deeds;[150] the current generation, however, is not paying for that long history of disobedience, but rather commits its own special iniquities, including the hardness of heart that characterizes disobedience in Jeremiah.

Thus, both passages in Jeremiah frame their radical revisions of the transgenerational retribution conception in familiar language that may deflect attention from the radicalness of the change.

11.4.2.2. Immediate and Communal Retribution: The Destruction Generation Pays for Itself Alone

The idea that the destruction represents immediate retribution for the sins of the current generation appears both implicitly and explicitly in Jeremiah. In the first category, the supposition that the people have the possibility of changing their own fate stands at the background of the prophet's repeated calls for repentance. Other passages explicitly challenge the notion of transgenerational or long-term retribution by articulating, first, the disconnection from the sins of the forefathers and, second, the disjunction from earlier sinful behaviors of the current generation itself. All passages stress present behavior as the cause of the (imminent) disaster and hold out the hope that the people's fortunes might change for the better, depending on their behavior.

Calls for a change—such as שובה משבה ישראל ("turn back, O Rebel Israel," Jer 3:12) and שובו בנים שובבים ("turn back, rebellious children," 3:14, 22)—and the unattended hope—אולי ישמעו וישבו איש מדרכו הרעה ("perhaps they will listen and turn back, each from his evil way," 26:3)[151]— may be taken together with other calls for a religious transformation, for

---

150. A similar catalogue of misdeeds is found in other passages that draw straightforwardly on the transgenerational concept (e.g., Jer 1:6); the passages under discussion here (7:26; 16:12) use similar literary techniques but step out of the traditional framework.

151. Calls to "turn back" appear also in Jer 18:11; 25:5; 35:15; but they appear only three times in Ezekiel (14:6; 18:30; 33:11) and infrequently in other prophetic books (Hos 14:3; Joel 2:12; Zech 1:3, 4; Mal 3:7).

example, המלו ליהוה והסרו ערלות לבבכם ("open your hearts to the LORD, remove the thickening about your hearts," 4:4) or the call (ו דרכיכם) היטיבו מעלליכם ("mend your ways and your actions"), which repeats four times in Jeremiah (7:3, 5; 18:11; 35:15). Led by the presupposition that conceptions of repentance must be exilic or postexilic, developed and held by Babylonian exiles or repatriates of the Persian period, scholars often categorize these passages as part of the DtrJ layer of the book.[152] However, William Holladay shows that the frequent use of שוב in Jeremiah, as well as the nouns משבה and שובבה, are genuinely Jeremian.[153] John Bright, and more elaborately Helga Weippert, similarly demonstrate the Jeremian character of the calls to "mend your ways."[154] Through those different phrases, those prophecies demand a change from the destruction generation, in which the fate of the current addressees is independent of that of their fathers. Those calls for repentance that require significant changes are restricted to the prophet's addressees' own previous sinful ways. The retributive conception that stands behind those calls is, therefore, the immediate retribution, arguing that the change from a sinful past to an obedient behavior in the present is both necessary and sufficient to mitigate the current distress. This Jeremian conception corresponds, therefore, to the repentance passages in Ezekiel (18:21–32; 33:10–20) that are shaped in more schematic language.

Jeremiah's judgment prophecies reflect the view that the destruction generation is punished for its own sins. The pattern of action and consequence, so emphasized by the rhetorical structure of measure for mea-

152. Thiel (*Jeremia 1–25*, 87–102) considers those calls for change in Jer 2–6 to be markers of Deuteronomistic intervention.

153. Holladay (*Root Šûbh*, 6–9) presents the statistical data for the root שוב, its meaning, and its thematic use within the covenant conception, where he locates differences of use and function between poetic passages (Jeremian, according to Mowinckel) and prose passages considered to be DtrJ (128–39, 149–54). Holladay thus argues against the exilic and postexilic dating of this conception and emphasizes Jeremiah's special place in constructing this conception (156–57). For attention to the language "(re)turn to YHWH," see Lambert, *How Repentance Became Biblical*, 71–118.

154. The root יטב in the *hiphil* appears in Jeremiah in four contexts. The first two are unique to Jeremiah and therefore could be considered Jeremian: (1) demands that the people mend their ways (7:3, 5; 18:11; 26:13; 35:15); and (2) exhortations concerning sins that stand in opposition to changing for the better (2:33; 4:22; 10:5; 13:23). The next two contexts are shared by Deuteronomy and Jeremiah: (3) the formula למען ייטב לך, repeated eight times in Deuteronomy (e.g., 4:40; 5:16) and twice in Jeremiah (7:23; 42:6); and (4) statements of God's benefit to the people (Deut 8:16; 28:63; Jer 18:10; 32:40–41). See Bright, "Prose Sermons of Jeremiah," 30; and Weippert, *Die Prosareden des Jeremiabuches*, 137–48.

sure, describes the sins as taking place in the present; and in most of these prophecies there is no reference to the share of past generations in the transgression.[155] Where the fathers' sins are mentioned, a clear distinction is made between past sins and present sins, along with a declaration that the present judgment comes upon those who sinned in their own lifetime (Jer 34:17–21; 44:7–11, 22–23).[156]

In addition, two of the covenant speeches (11:1–14; 17:19–27) and the exhortation against breaking the covenant (34:8–22) express a clear distinction between the sins and fate of the forefathers and the sins and fate of the current generation. Both the fathers and the destruction generation sinned by disobeying God (11:7–8; 17:23; 34:14); but the latter have the option to change their fates, by changing their behavior.[157] This generational distinction is given special emphasis in 34:8–22, which reports on an "independent" sin committed by the destruction generation: they subjugate anew their male and female slaves (34:11, 16). In this passage, which presents a retrospective view of the national history, the prophet on the one hand emphasizes the continuity of sinful behavior throughout the generations and on the other hand distinguishes between the history of transgenerational sin and the behavior of the contemporary generation. Zedekiah's generation sins because they violate the covenant that the king, his officials, and the entire people recently made before God (34:18–19). Thus, that the king, the officials, and the people are now given into the hands of the Babylonians constitutes a judgment against their own violation of the covenant *in the present* (34:20–22) and has no connection with the prior history of transgenerational sins.

This disconnection of the contemporary deeds of the destruction generation from any ancestral history of transgression is given a schematic con-

155. The following prophecies make no mention of forefathers' sins: Jer 4:4, 15–18; 5:1–6, 7–9, 12–14, 16–21 (at 5:19); 9:6–8; 14:10; 16:16–18; 26:3; 30:12–15 (at 30:14–15); 33:5; 36:30–31 (but note: "and I will punish him and his offspring and his courtiers for their iniquity"); 42:15–17, 21–22. Neglect of forefathers' sins also occurs in reference to the prophet's enemies (11:21–23) and to other contemporaneous prophets who sinned (29:23, 25, 31–32). On measure for measure, see §11.2.1.

156. Compare 44:17–19 MT, where those who descended to Egypt are quoted emphasizing the partnership of both parents and children in the worship of מלכת השמים (this transgenerational guilt occurs in 44:2–6, 9–10). The reference to multiple generations has two different goals depending on the speakers. The community in Egypt presents this as a long and positive tradition they are carrying on now in exile, whereas in the prophetic words this ancestral tradition clearly enhances their guilt.

157. The call to the current generation to change their ways occurs also in the other covenant speeches, but without reference to the forefathers' sins; see Jer 7:3, 5; 22:1–5.

struction in Jeremiah only in the symbolic act in the potter's house (18:1–12). The potter's work on the wheel represents God's freedom of action in his customary relationships with the peoples under his national and universal sovereignty, and thus the retribution conception is clearly not the core of discussion.[158] But God's relationship to the people(s) may suddenly change (רגע, 18:7, 9), as a result of the people's and the kingdom's disobedience (18:8, 10).[159] This possibility of divine change is to encourage the people to change their own behavior, with the expectation that God will respond in kind (18:7–10). This scenario leads to the call addressed to "the men of Judah and the inhabitants of Jerusalem," to each mend their ways, which despairingly is answered with a further rebellious statement (18:11–12):

[11] And now, say to the men of Judah and the inhabitants of Jerusalem: Thus said the LORD: I am devising disaster for you and laying plans against you. <u>Turn back, each of you, from your wicked ways</u>, and mend your ways and your actions! [12] But they will say, "It is no use. We will keep on following our own plans; <u>each of us will act in the willfulness of his evil heart</u>."	[11] ועתה אמר־נא אל־איש־יהודה ועל־יושבי ירושלים לאמר כה אמר יהוה הנה אנכי יוצר עליכם רעה וחשב עליכם מחשבה <u>שובו נא איש מדרכו הרעה והיטיבו</u> דרכיכם ומעלליכם. [12] ואמרו נואש כי־אחרי מחשבותינו נלך ואיש <u>שררות לבו־הרע נעשה.</u>

While this address to individuals within the Judean community may tempt us to locate individual conceptual threads in this passage, there is no ground to understand the partitive reference to איש־יהודה (18:11a) or the individual call for a personal return from sinful ways (שובו נא איש מדרכו הרעה, 18:11b) as referring to a conception of an individual retribution. In both cases, the partitive meaning of איש designates an entire community or a people.[160] Furthermore, the symbolic act focuses on the communal sphere, that is, the nation is בית ישראל (18:6); the schematic generalization, while using the singular, addresses nations as גוי and ממלכה (18:7–10); and 18:11–12 closes

---

158. Compare the division often made of 18:1–12 into two parts: 18:1–6 describes the symbolic act, and 18:7–11 is then considered a DtrJ elaboration. See, for instance, McKane, *Jeremiah 1–25*, 420–23.

159. רגע designates a sudden change in Jer 4:20 (where it occurs in parallel to פתאם); Ps 73:19; Job 34:20; Lam 4:6; see Holladay, *Jeremiah*, 1.516.

160. The phrase איש יהודה וישבי ירושלים occurs also in Jer 4:4; 11:2, 9; 17:25; 32:32; 35:13; 36:31; otherwise in Dan 9:7; 2 Kgs 23:2; 2 Chr 34:30. Thus throughout, this construct shows an incongruence of number between its two phrases. There is only one exception to this: יושב ירושלים ואיש יהודה in Isa 5:3.

with direct address to the entire community in verbal forms and pronouns all in the second-person plural. Thus, this passage validates the combination of the communal and the immediate perceptions in the retribution conception, changeable constantly according to the divine judgment.

11.4.2.3. Immediate and Individual Retribution in Jeremiah

References to the fate of the individual do occur in Jeremiah. In a number of passages, the prophet focuses on the fates of specific individuals within the general community. Judgment prophecies against the "House of the king of Judah" (21:11–23:8), that is, Josiah's descendants, make specific references to the individual fates of Shallum-Jehoachaz, Jehoiakim, Jehoia-chin, and possibly also Zedekiah (23:5–6 in a positive prophecy; compare his judgment in 32:1–5); and consolation prophecies note Ebed-melech the Kushite (39:15–18) and Baruch son of Neriah (45:1–5). The singling out of individuals in the judgment prophecies further accentuates the prophet's view that the destruction generation as a collective is punished justifiably for its own sins (see §11.2.1, §11.4.2.1, §11.4.2.2).

A seemingly exceptional reference to an individual conception of retribution is found in 17:9–10, one of the wisdomlike short prophetic sayings within 17:5–18:

[9] Most devious is the heart;	עקב הלב מכל[161] [9]
It is perverse—who can fathom it?	ואנש הוא מי ידענו.
[10] I the LORD probe the heart,	אני יהוה חקר לב [10]
Search the mind—	בחן כליות
To repay every man according to his ways,	ולתת לאיש כדרכו
With the proper fruit of his deeds.	(ק: כדרכיו)[162] כפרי מעלליו.

161. The Septuagint reads βαθεῖα ἡ καρδία παρὰ πάντα ("deep is the heart beyond all"), reflecting עמק, thus serving more closely the metaphor of 17:10 with the divine knowledge of the interior hidden human motivations. See McKane (Jeremiah 1–25, 397–98) for three "different exegetical orientations" he identifies in the versions and in the history of interpretation. The Masoretic Text's עקב goes well with Jer 9:3 (invoking Gen 27:36) and the sinful heart of Jer 17:1.

162. 4QJerª reads the ketiv's singular דרכו, whereas the plural form is reflected by the Masoretic Text's qere, Septuagint, Peshitta, and Targum and is also attested in Jer 32:19b MT. The discrepancy singular דרך and plural מעללים occurs also in 4:18 MT; 17:10 (the Masoretic Text's qere and the Septuagint's plural); 23:22; 25:5; 26:3; 35:15; as also Judg 2:19. Compare the more common congruence of number in the Masoretic Text of Jer 7:3, 5; 18:11; 26:13; 32:19; also Hos 12:3; Ezek 36:31; Zech 1:4, 6.

Jeremiah 17:5–18 is recognized as a cluster of independent passages (or rather fragments) within the collection of individual prayers in Jer 11–20.[163] Rhetorically, 17:9–10 is crafted as a dialogue between the prophet's words (closing with the rhetorical question מי ידענו in 17:9; see Prov 24:12) and God's response: אני יהוה חקר (17:10).[164] These two parts of the dialogue are connected through the shared object of knowing, that is, the heart.[165] Each of the two verses bears wisdom characteristics and phrases.[166] Jeremiah 17:9 reflects in a melancholy vein on the deceitful nature of the human heart, while 17:10 responds with a general statement on how God "handles" the heart as omniscient, employing his role as a just judge (Pss 7:10; 17:3).

The programmatic phrasing ולתת לאיש כדרכו (ק: כדרכיו) כפרי מעלליו ("to repay every man according to his ways, with the proper fruit of his deeds") occurs elsewhere in Jer 32:19b (although פרי מעלליו is not represented in Septuagint) and serves in judgment prophecies in 21:14 (also Isa 3:10; Mic 7:13).[167] The "wisdom" cast of this interchange in Jer 17:9–10 may explain why the focus remains squarely on the individual in this passage[168] and how this same phrase serves just as well in Jeremiah's prayer, where this individual perspective is embedded into a national context (32:19b within 32:16–25). For the current discussion, the major point is that the prophet is well aware of the individual conception of retribution, which he seems to borrow from the wisdom arena, but then this conception is well implemented to suit his prophetic messages in several different contexts.

---

163. See Holladay, *Jeremiah*, 1.494–96; McKane, *Jeremiah 1–25*, 394–98; Lundbom, *Jeremiah 1–20*, 786–88; and Hoffman, *Jeremiah 1–25*, 393–95.

164. Lundbom (*Jeremiah 1–20*, 786) points out such a dialogue in Jer 10:23–24 and possibly in 17:1–4. Holladay (*Jeremiah*, 1.495) designates it "a dialogue of the deaf."

165. The heart (as also the fruit, פרי) may also explain the editorial sequence of 17:9–10 following 17:5–8; thus McKane, *Jeremiah 1–25*, 395, 397. Although the passage is structured as dialogue, see Holladay (*Jeremiah*, 1.494–96) on the differences in mood between the two verses, to the point that Holladay designates the passage "a dialogue of the deaf," similar to that between Job and his friends (495).

166. See Holladay, *Jeremiah*, 1.494.

167. See also פרי מחשבותם (Jer 6:19). McKane (*Jeremiah 1–25*, 396–97) aptly emphasizes that Isa 3:10 and Jer 17:10 share the interest in the individual.

168. Holladay (*Jeremiah*, 1.495) mentions that the words in Jer 17:9–10 are "stripped of all particularity: not the heart of Judah, not the heart today, but the heart, the mind, anywhere, anytime: devious above all else, of any sort."

11.4.2.4. *The Future Holds a Change in the Workings of Divine Justice*

Jeremiah 31:29–30 takes the form of a thesis and antithesis, "they shall no more say this . . . , but this. . . ."[169] Jeremiah's rejection of contemporary thought on retribution is remarkable:

[29] In those days, they shall no longer say, "Parents have eaten sour grapes and children's teeth are blunted." [30] But every one shall die for his own sins: whosoever eats sour grapes, his teeth shall be blunted.	29 בימים ההם לא־יאמרו עוד אבות אכלו בסר ושני בנים תקהינה. 30 כי אם־איש בעונו ימות כל־האדם האכל הבסר תקהינה שניו.

It appears that the prophet himself feels that the notion of transgenerational retribution is inadequate and requires revision, one that would reconceptualize the status of the sons, independently of their predecessors' iniquities. In contradistinction to Ezekiel, who refutes a similar protest as invalid for contemporary circumstances (18:1–20), Jeremiah rather foresees a *future* transformation of transgenerational retribution into immediate and delimited punishment. With the phrase איש בעונו ימות, the prophet establishes the concept that in the future, judgment will be implemented within the lifetime of the person who sins, for the sins that he (and he alone) committed.[170] In framing such a future transformation in

---

169. Six such passages are identified in Jeremiah; they are all designated by Weinfeld ("Jeremiah and the Spiritual Metamorphosis") as highly significant to Jeremiah's revolutionary religious thinking. A similar formula is "not like this . . . but like this . . ." (Jer 31:32–33, 34). The passages constructed in this way display a variety of literary forms— oaths (16:14–15; 23:7–8), religious declarations (3:16–17), or popular sayings (31:29–30, which focuses on reward and punishment). The other passages evoke other significant traditions and values drawn from the national history: the ark of the covenant (3:16–17), the tablets of the covenant (31:33–34), the tradition of the exodus from Egypt (23:7–8; 16:14–15), and according to Weinfeld, also the realm of sacrifices (7:21–23). Weinfeld considers these antitheses to articulate no less than a "spiritual rebirth of Israel."

170. For איש בעונו ימות, see Deut 24:16 and Lundbom, *Jeremiah 21–36*, 461–63. Compare Weinfeld ("Jeremiah and the Spiritual Metamorphosis," 35–39), who finds Jeremiah to be influenced here, as elsewhere, by Deuteronomy, and yet does not emphasize the distinctions between Jeremiah and Ezekiel. Weiss (*Scriptures in Their Own Light*, 482–85) compares the two and argues that Jeremiah's vision of the future emphasizes a change in the people's appreciation of God's actions and not a transformation in the concept of divine retribution itself.

a consolation prophecy, the prophet indirectly admits the problems with the contemporary conception.[171]

11.5. SUMMARY

The four diverse perspectives on the destruction generation's responsibility for their fate are expressed by different speakers, but they all share the same theological conception as their point of departure. This shared conception is that God is a just judge who judges his people (and other nations) according to principles of justice, as illustrated by the measure-for-measure concept. All speakers struggle in different ways with the divine epithet פקד עון אבת על בנים ("visiting the guilt of the parents upon the children") and with traditional conceptions of retribution. These conceptions fall into four categories: transgenerational retribution, immediate retribution, communal retribution, and individual retribution. Although these four conceptions might be classed as two pairs of opposites, each component may be paired with any of the others.

This study has identified four general perspectives on the role of God as judge in the face of the destruction in relation to retribution conceptions. Three of them accept in some way (in justification or in protest) the conception of the destruction as a retribution for transgenerational iniquity; the fourth explains the destruction as an immediate judgment upon the current generation. Although all four perspectives work from a basic sense of divine retribution as collective in its force, the fourth also opens the way to an awareness of individual culpability and punishment. Placing them in the framework of the theodical discourse, one of the four represents protest, and the rest struggle with different forms of justification of God in his severe judgment:

a.   Protest—challenges to divine justice, arguing that the destruction generation itself did not sin but is suffering gratuitously for the sins of others, may be heard within quotations in Jeremiah (31:29) and Ezekiel (18:2) as well as Lam 5:7. These passages take פקד עון אבת על

---

171. For the place of 31:29–30 within this consolation prophecy (31:27–30), see Lundbom (*Jeremiah 21–36*, 459); he concurs with scholars who argue that the prophecy is Jeremian (or a Jeremian tradition, not DtrJ) and dates the prophecy to shortly past 586, because it foresees the change as taking place at a distant future point.

בנים to mean that God afflicts innocent sons for their fathers' iniquities; thus they see themselves as victims of unjust divine punishment. This line of challenge to a fault in the transgenerational conception of retribution is also hinted at in Jeremiah's refutation of the quoted words (31:29–30).

b. Justification—the destruction generation is accused of continuing its predecessors' traditions of iniquity. Continuity creates shared responsibility between fathers and sons; thus, this perspective understands the divine epithet as "visiting the guilt of the parents upon [sinning] children." This justifying perspective characterizes the historiography of 2 Kings, the prophecies of Jeremiah and Ezekiel, and the confession of sins in several communal laments within Psalms and Lamentations.

c. Justification—the idea that the destruction generation sins more severely than their predecessors is an extreme view within the spectrum of views that accept the notion of transgenerational retribution. Twice in Jeremiah and only once in Ezekiel, the prophets argue that the current generation deserves this severe judgment on its own account. By placing a much heavier responsibility upon this last generation—"visiting the guilt of the parents upon the [tremendously sinning] children"—this perception minimizes the burden of iniquity accumulated over time and holds the current generation responsible for their own fate.

d. Justification—the idea that the destruction constitutes immediate retribution meted out to the present generation for their own deeds may be seen in both prophetic books and once in a desperate quotation of the Jehoiachin exiles: כי־פשעינו וחטאתינו עלינו ובם אנחנו נמקים ואיך נחיה ("our transgressions and our sins weigh heavily upon us; we are sick at heart about them. How can we survive?," Ezek 33:10). This principle stands in clear opposition to the transgenerational conception in two significant ways. First, the notion of immediate retribution disconnects the fate of the destruction generation from their predecessors, either for better (Ezek 14:12–23) or, more often, for worse (Ezek 18:1–20; Jer 11:1–8; 17:19–27; 34:8–22). Second, it shrinks the chronological gap between deed and retaliation, implying that the generation's fate (including the individuals therein) is determined only by its most recent history (Ezek 18:21–32; 33:10–20; Jer 18:1–12; 7:3, 5).

The severity of the circumstances surrounding the destruction causes a theological crisis across the board in terms of traditional perceptions of the workings of divine justice, which are dealt with in different ways. While anonymous quotations and communal laments raise doubts and protest against divine injustice, only Jeremiah and Ezekiel, of the contemporary voices we considered, actually take steps to move out of the traditional framework toward notions of individual and immediate retribution, by which they can justify God as judge. Jeremiah's rhetoric in this respect seems to be shaped by the dynamics of the genre of judgment prophecies, by wisdom conceptions, and by pentateuchal legal phraseology and traditions; Ezekiel is also very much influenced by the judgment prophecy framework and by the abundant legal pentateuchal traditions that illustrate the people's guilt.

These diverse arguments of justification, used mainly by both Jeremiah and Ezekiel, seem to be polemic responses to the challenging question: Why has God initiated the catastrophe at this time, over this specific generation? The impression one gets from the plethora of prophetic answers is that of great difficulty to indeed supply satisfactory explanations, and even quite an embarrassment on the side of the prophets facing the atrocities of the destruction and dislocation. The need to reconcile God's roles as omnipotent warrior *and* as just judge demands creative justifying arguments, which include the virtuosic stretching of the traditional retributive conceptions.

Based on this general picture it is useful to revisit the scholarly assumptions articulated at the beginning of this chapter concerning Ezekiel's position within these different contemporary approaches to divine justice. First, Ezekiel is neither the first nor the only sixth-century speaker to articulate a conception of immediate retribution (§11.4.1.3 and §11.4.2.3). Second, the idea of individual retribution does not capture a central place in Ezekiel's message; its impact is relatively minor in comparison to the other approaches taken by the prophet to divine retribution and divine justice. Furthermore, references to individual responsibility and retaliation are clearly embedded in the collective conception of retribution, and this combination in itself stands in line with the long heritage of retribution conceptions that Ezekiel embraces. Finally, Ezekiel is indeed unique in his exceptional rhetorical skills, in his ability to phrase his message in abstract and schematic ways. But it seems that the theological discussion of the role of God as judge, and his punishment of the destruction generation, is an ongoing dialogue between multiple parties. It encompasses the two prophets—Jeremiah and Ezekiel—and their different contemporary audiences. While there is no direct or implicit connection between the two prophets themselves, it is of interest that three of the perceptions are used by both prophets.[172]

This is the place to reconsider the scholarship on Jeremiah and Ezekiel that emerges from this diverse theological picture. Cooke, Eichrodt, Zimmerli, and others accept Ezekiel's diverse perceptions of retribution as a proof that Ezekiel did not write a coherent "systematic theology" of retribution. Rather, the prophet supplies ad hoc answers, shaped according to the acute needs of this and that prophecy and rhetorical situation. Ezekiel's prophecy is recognized as having a base in the crises of the pre-destruction and postdestruction eras, and therefore, there is no room to expect a uniformity of message in the prophecies of this single prophet.[173] Another explanation, suggested by Rimon Kasher, is that the "internal contradictions" typify the personality of Ezekiel.[174]

It is thus remarkable to note that, by contrast, in scholarship on the book of Jeremiah diversity and contradicting prophetic messages concerning retribution are taken unfailingly as distinguishing markers for *literary* layers in the book, as differentiating the prophet from his DtrJ editors and possibly from his post-DtrJ tradents.

As I have argued, the theological debate is diverse and lively. These different perceptions of the workings of divine justice, and specifically on the question of the responsibility of the destruction generation for its fate (or not), cannot be taken as distinctive criteria for differentiating between those many hands involved in the evolution of the book of Jeremiah.

172. This implicit (silent) agreement, with some divergences, is another arena where the noncommunication between Jeremiah and Ezekiel (or vice versa, and their books) is intriguing. See Rom-Shiloni, "Ezekiel and Jeremiah."

173. These scholars of Ezekiel do not overlook the literary history of the book, but nevertheless are ready to speak of a historical prophet behind significant parts of the book and reflected in the prophetic message. For instance, Cooke (*Ezekiel*, 195) explains the contradicting prophetic proclamations by suggesting that ideas concerning divine justice arose with the prophet himself (as in Ezek 9:4; 14:6, 11, 14, 16, 18, 20), but that popular-saying attitudes cause him to further develop his own thoughts on this subject. See Eichrodt, *Ezekiel*, 237, 246–48; Zimmerli, *Ezekiel*, 1.66–67; *Ezekiel*, 2.386–87; and Joyce, *Divine Initiative*, 21–31.

174. See Rimon Kasher, *Ezekiel 1–24*, 120. Fishbane ("Sin and Judgment," 148) explains the different approaches in Ezekiel as a response to the changing psychological and religious situation of the Judean exiles, who synchronically hold different perceptions.

Rather, I reiterate Meir Weiss's observations concerning the great diversity of approaches to retribution in the Hebrew Bible, in both the synchronic and the diachronic spheres. Weiss argues that the search for an ordered, constant, even unified conception of retribution in the Hebrew Bible, and the search for a developmental line from communal to individual retribution, are equally in vain. The multiplicity of voices, and even what seem to be internal contradictions, in each of the prophets constitute the *genuine character* of prophecy:

> The interest of prophecy is not with the factual truth, nor with the realistic truth, and not with the theological truth, but with the truth that calls to a human being at this (specific) hour. The major interest of prophecy is not with the traits of God, but with human traits, and when prophecy speaks on the traits of God it does not mean to teach how to know God, but to guide human beings. The exposition of the divine traits in prophecy is not the goal but the vehicle. We should, therefore, be more precise, and argue that only the theologian or the philosopher finds a contradiction between the communal retribution and the individual retribution conceptions. The straightforward religious person does not see in these two contradictory conceptions but an antonymy. This is the way all those whose words were preserved in the Hebrew Bible saw these conceptions, and first and foremost those outstanding figures who felt in direct contact with God, the prophets.[175]

The exploration of expressions of doubt and protest and prophetic attempts to grapple with these bring into focus the question of divine mercy: How does (or should) God exercise the attribute of mercy in the critical period of disaster? How do (or should) the people respond if that mercy seems to be withheld? What does this imply about the covenant relationship?

---

175. Weiss, *Scriptures in Their Own Light*, 484–89 at 485–86 (my translation).

12

GOD AND THE ATTRIBUTE OF MERCY

No discussion of God's role as judge would be complete without consideration of the attribute of divine mercy. This divine characteristic is rarely mentioned in the passages under discussion here; when it appears, it often struggles with the "other side" of God. The attribute of mercy suggests the reversal of the active role God plays in executing judgment upon the people by bringing on the destruction.

The characteristic of divine mercy brings us back again to the courtroom metaphor and to God who serves as a just judge (see §10.1). The expectation that God the judge will be attentive to his people's suffering appears in two of the major components of communal laments: in descriptions of the suffering (Ps 79:1–4) and/or in the petition part of the laments (79:11–13).[1] While there may not be explicit use of mercy language, such references request or expect that God (as judge and king) will act with compassion on behalf of those in oppressed situations (9:2–12; 10:12–18; 43:1–2; 94:1–7, 14–15, 22–23). God is called to be vigilant on behalf of the one(/those) imprisoned, to release him(/them) from bondage: תבוא לפניך אנקת אסיר כגדל זרועך הותר בני תמותה ("let the groans of the prisoners reach You; reprieve those condemned to death, as befits Your great strength," 79:11); and לשמע אנקת אסיר לפתח בני תמותה ("to hear the groans of the prisoner, to release those condemned to death," 102:21). The communal lament petitions are formed using verbal phrases drawn from judicial proceedings (e.g., עשה משפט in 9:5 and רב ריב in 74:22 and PAN Jer 25:31). The poets call upon God to take note of the misery caused by the enemies of his people (ראה יהוה את־עניי כי הגדיל אויב ["see, O LORD, my misery; how the enemy jeers!]," Lam 1:9c) and to execute judgment

---

1. Similar expressions also occur within verses of praise, as in Ps 103:3–6; see §12.1.

upon them (נקם and נקמה in Ps 79:10 and PAN Jer 51:36; שילם גמול in Ps 137:8 and PAN Jer 51:6, 56).

Less frequently, poets address God using explicit verbal phrases drawn from the semantic field of mercy, such as חנן and רחם, as in אל־תזכר־לנו עונת ראשנים מהר יקדמונו רחמיך כי דלונו מאד ("do not hold our former iniquities against us; let Your compassion come swiftly toward us, for we have sunk very low," Ps 79:8); and חנני יהוה ראה עניי משנאי ("have mercy on me, O LORD; see my affliction at the hands of my foes," 9:14).

All these descriptions and pleas are set in contexts where the suffering is presented as having been caused by human enemies—the (A' → C) framework (see chap. 7). In these contexts, God is requested to pursue justice by defending and saving his loyal people from these human enemies. Yet these sources also convey the absence of any immediate divine salvation. They illustrate the poets' intensive but seemingly ineffective efforts to awaken God to action on behalf of his suffering people.

Should these texts be classified as protests? I argue that implicit and explicit references to divine mercy in these descriptions of distress and in the petition sections of the communal laments oftentimes set the peaks of protest. The poets simultaneously show their firm belief in God's role as a just judge, their recognition of his power to act for his people in the present situation and, not least, their own internal struggles against the loss of hope that God will save his people. In terms of a theological framework, protest arises from precisely this sense of piety, from the turmoil that results when the biblical authors cannot reconcile their strong beliefs with the absence of divine salvation.

Challenges to God's seeming refusal to act with mercy appear most fiercely in passages where God is pictured as causing the distress—that is, in passages using the (B') or (C') conceptions of war, where God is portrayed as either summoning the human enemies or as the sole foe of his people (see chaps. 8–9). Such passages are predominantly found in Jeremiah and Ezekiel, where they present God's power and control of the events concerning his people's destruction, thus forming a line of justification. Quotations within the prophetic books and communal laments in Psalms and Lamentations use the (B') or (C') conceptions mostly to express doubt and protest against God the warrior. When it comes to the attribute of divine mercy, it seems that the prophets are not free of the theological turmoil that their contemporaries go through. Rather, the two prophetic books often challenge God's perceived roles as good and compassionate. Hence, authors across the board recognize that the eras of destruction and the exiles are not times of divine mercy. They must therefore explain this absence of mercy using diverse arguments that employ different theological strategies. Poets react to this lack of divine mercy with expressions of doubt and protest, whereas prophets are called to explain (thus, justify) God for *not* showing mercy in the current situation.

The theological deliberations over divine mercy in the face of the people's suffering are characterized by three shared features. First, there are relatively few verbal references to mercy in the sources under discussion. The primary roots used are חנן, חמל, חוס, and ריחם; the noun forms חנות/ רחמים, חנינה, and חסד; and expressions of atonement: סלח, מחה חטאת, and (עוון/חטאת) כיפר.[2] Second, when it *is* mentioned, God's mercy is referred to in one of two ways: either in a very stereotyped manner or within expressions that negate the possibility of an active divine mercy. Third, expressions of mercy (positive or negative) use clear functional distinctions between past, present, and future. Discussion should focus on these three features as they appear in both doubt and protest, on the one hand, and within two different contexts of justification, on the other. Psalm 103 is a justification text and incorporates some conventional expressions, thus serving as a point of departure.

12.1. JUSTIFICATION: "SO GREAT IS HIS STEADFAST LOVE TOWARD THOSE WHO FEAR HIM" (PSALM 103)

References to divine mercy occur in only four of our seventeen target psalms (Pss 9, 89, 103, 106) and in three chapters of Lamentations (chs. 1–3). These references appear mostly in clearly stereotyped formulas, residing on the divine mercy as recalled in the national-historical memory of Israel (see §12.2). Thus the term חסד occurs in different phrases that emphasize its enduring eternity: חסד(י) יהוה עולם אשירה ("I will sing of the LORD's steadfast love forever," Ps 89:2) and וחסד יהוה מעולם ועד־עולם על־יראיו ("but the LORD's steadfast love is for all eternity toward those who fear Him," 103:17). In a similar vein, note וינחם כרב חסדיו ("and in His great faithfulness relented," 106:45; and the slight variation in Lam 3:32).[3] The repeated epithet צדיק הוא יהוה ("righteous is the LORD"),

---

2. For a lexical discussion of these expressions, see Rom-Shiloni, *God in Times of Destruction*, 461–69.

3. See Zobel, "חֶסֶד *hesed*," who translates חסד "kindness" in its religious use; and Sakenfeld, *Meaning of Hesed*, 147–50.

which occurs in individual and communal laments (Lam 1:18) and in the second-person צדיק אתה יהוה ("You, O Lᴏʀᴅ, are righteous," Jer 12:1), falls in this category of conventional formulas.[4] A cluster of conciliatory formulas is found in Lam 3, with the declaration that חסדי יהוה כי לא־תמנו כי לא־כלו רחמיו ("the kindness of the Lᴏʀᴅ has not ended, His mercies are not spent," 3:22)[5] and כי לא יזנח לעולם אדני. כי אם־הוגה ורחם כרב חסדו (ק: חסדיו) ("for the Lord does not reject forever, but first afflicts, then pardons in His abundant kindness," 3:31–32). The insistence on God's qualities as righteous and merciful emphasizes the pious and painful struggle of the writers with ongoing divine judgment.

A question quoted in Jer 3:5a and fairly similarly phrased in Ps 103:9 illustrates two different approaches to the relevance of, or to the activation of, conceptions of divine mercy in times of distress, understood as times of divine judgment.[6] The prophet quotes the people as asking: "Does one hate for all time [הינטר לעולם]? Does one rage forever [אם־ישמר לנצח]?" (Jer 3:5a). The prophecy then quite rudely refutes those questions in a disputation speech that spells out the termination of the covenant relationship between God and his people on account of the people's infidelity, described as adulterous behavior within the metaphoric framework of marriage.[7]

---

4. See a similar phrasing in Ps 119:137. The attribute צדיק for God occurs also in Zeph 3:5; Pss 11:7; 129:4; 145:17. Compare Dan 9:14 and Neh 9:33, where the epithet צדיק goes well with God's acts of judgment, which in these contexts are justified as retaliation for the people's sins. NJPS translates Lam 1:18: "The Lord is in the right."

5. The verbal form תמנו in Lam 3:22 raises an interpretive difficulty in terms of the lexical use of תמם, which usually appears to describe death from famine and sword (Num 14:35; 17:28; Jer 44:12, 18), and a formal difficulty in the first-person plural that refers to the people rather than to the divine kindness. Lam 3:22–24 is not in the Septuagint; the Peshitta (גמרין) and Targum (פסקו) connect the verb with חסדי יהוה as agent and thus read לא־תמו (by analogy with לא־כלו in the second half of the verse); and NJPS seems to follow them. See Albrektson, *Text and Theology*, 145–46; and Hillers, *Lamentations*, 115.

6. The issue of the duration of divine judgment and wrath is also found in Isa 57:16–21. The literary relationships between Ps 103:9 and Isa 57:16 lead scholars to date the psalm late, presuming its dependence on the prophecy. But, could not Ps 103:9 be the evoked phrase for both prophecies? Or would it not be plausible that all three compositions struggle with the same issue, using the same well-known expression?

7. For the genre, structure, and intertextual aspects of Jer 3:1–5, see Rom-Shiloni, "Actualization of Pentateuchal Legal Traditions," 262–67; and "Compositional Harmonization," 928–33. The subsequent prophetic passages in Jer 3 try to minimize the harsh message of 3:1–5; see, for instance, 3:12–13. See §10.2 at n. 21.

Psalm 103, on the other hand, contextualizes this question of judgment versus divine mercy in the broader context of God's role as judge (103:6–18) and, quite surprisingly, turns doubt into a justificatory statement (103:9) within a broader proclamation of praise:

[6] The LORD executes righteous acts and judgments for all who are wronged.	עֹשֵׂה צְדָקוֹת יְהוָה [6] וּמִשְׁפָּטִים לְכָל־עֲשׁוּקִים.
[7] He made known His ways to Moses, His deeds to the children of Israel.	יוֹדִיעַ דְּרָכָיו לְמֹשֶׁה [7] לִבְנֵי יִשְׂרָאֵל עֲלִילוֹתָיו.
[8] The LORD is compassionate and gracious, slow to anger, abounding in steadfast love.	רַחוּם וְחַנּוּן יְהוָה [8] אֶרֶךְ אַפַּיִם וְרַב־חָסֶד.
[9] He will not contend forever, or nurse His anger for all time.	לֹא־לָנֶצַח יָרִיב [9] וְלֹא לְעוֹלָם יִטּוֹר.
[10] He has not dealt with us according to our sins, nor has He requited us according to our iniquities.	לֹא כַחֲטָאֵינוּ עָשָׂה לָנוּ [10] וְלֹא כַעֲוֹנֹתֵינוּ גָּמַל עָלֵינוּ.
[11] For as the heavens are high above the earth, so great is His steadfast love toward those who fear Him.	כִּי כִגְבֹהַּ שָׁמַיִם עַל־הָאָרֶץ [11] גָּבַר חַסְדּוֹ עַל־יְרֵאָיו.
[12] As east is far from west, so far has He removed our sins from us.	כִּרְחֹק מִזְרָח מִמַּעֲרָב [12] הִרְחִיק מִמֶּנּוּ אֶת־פְּשָׁעֵינוּ.
[13] As a father has compassion for his children, so the Lord has compassion for those who fear Him.	כְּרַחֵם אָב עַל־בָּנִים [13] רִחַם יְהוָה עַל־יְרֵאָיו.
[14] For He knows how we are formed; He is mindful that we are dust.	כִּי־הוּא יָדַע יִצְרֵנוּ [14] זָכוּר כִּי־עָפָר אֲנָחְנוּ.
[15] Man, his days are like those of grass; he blooms like a flower of the field;	אֱנוֹשׁ כֶּחָצִיר יָמָיו [15] כְּצִיץ הַשָּׂדֶה כֵּן יָצִיץ.
[16] a wind passes by and it is no more, its own place no longer knows it.	כִּי רוּחַ עָבְרָה־בּוֹ וְאֵינֶנּוּ [16] וְלֹא־יַכִּירֶנּוּ עוֹד מְקוֹמוֹ.
[17] But the LORD's steadfast love is for all eternity toward those who fear Him, and His beneficence is for the children's children	וְחֶסֶד יְהוָה [17] מֵעוֹלָם וְעַד־עוֹלָם עַל־יְרֵאָיו וְצִדְקָתוֹ לִבְנֵי בָנִים.
[18] of those who keep His covenant and remember to observe His precepts.	לְשֹׁמְרֵי בְרִיתוֹ [18] וּלְזֹכְרֵי פִקֻּדָיו לַעֲשׂוֹתָם.

Psalm 103 is the only psalm of praise (or thanksgiving) among our seventeen psalms that reflect theologically on the destruction of Judah and its aftermath.[8] While it is difficult to decipher the suffering primarily targeted in this psalm—is it sickness (103:3–5) or the national catastrophe (103:6–18)?[9]—the emphasis on God's חסד and רחמים is evident (103:4, 8, 11, 13, 17). In its central section (103:6–18), the psalmist fashions a well-structured, didactic sermon, praising God for his love and care. This sermon is comprised of three main arguments:

a.   Divine justice is defined (only) by the gracious epithets of mercy and care (Ps 103:6–9).[10] Alluding to Exod 34:6, the psalmist quotes accurately the positive epithets from that passage: רחום וחנון יהוה ארך אפים ורב־חסד. In place of the epithets of threat and judgment that follow in Exod 34:7, however, he proclaims that God's anger and judgment are temporally bound and short lived: לא־לנצח יריב ולא

8. See §3.4.3. In genre, Ps 103 is categorized as an individual thanksgiving psalm by Allen (*Psalms 101–150*, 19–20); but Goldingay prefers to categorize it as a testimony psalm or praise psalm (*Psalms*, 3.164–65). The arguments for postexilic dating are persuasive, relying on linguistic features such as Aramaisms, Late Biblical Hebrew terms (such as מלכות, 103:19), as well as the potential intertextual relationship of 103:9 to either Jer 3:12 and/or Isa 57:16.

9. The imagery of healing in reference to national catastrophe, along with the metaphor of God as a healer, is repeated in Jeremiah. See Jer 8:15, 21–23; 14:19; and note the reversal of this metaphor in a consolation prophecy (33:6), where God returns to be his people's healer.

10. Ps 103:6 starts with the well-known judicial phrase and terms עשה צדקות and עשה משפטים (note also the use of צדקתו in 103:17). This particular way of ordering terms (צדקות / משפטים) is fairly unique in the Hebrew Bible (9 times, e.g., Gen 18:19; Ps 33:5); compare to the 37 occurrences of the hendiadys substantives in the order משפט וצדקה (e.g., 2 Sam 8:15; Isa 33:5). The phrase עשה משפטים otherwise occurs in two contexts in the Hebrew Bible. In most cases it designates judicial support for the people and thus for their salvation (e.g., עשה משפט in Deut 10:18; 1 Kgs 8:45, 49, 59; Jer 9:23; Mic 7:9 [ועשה משפטי . . . אראה בצדקתו]; Pss 9:5; 140:13; 146:7); see also the use of צדקה to denote deliverance (Isa 46:13; 51:6, 8; Pss 31:2; 36:7; 71:15; 143:11), which goes together with inflicting judgment on the enemies (Isa 45:24; Jer 51:10; Ps 98:2). But forms of משפט are also used to proclaim judgment upon Israel (e.g., עשה משפטים, Ezek 5:8, or ויסרתיך למשפט ["I will discipline you according to judgment"], Jer 30:11; 46:28; Ps 51:6). The phrase עשה משפט וצדקה serves also as the main epithet of the human (Davidic) kings (2 Sam 8:15; 1 Kgs 3:28; 10:9; Jer 22:3, 15; 23:5; 33:15; Ezek 45:9) and, in a broader sense, as a general code of behavior (Jer 5:1; Ezek 18:5, 19, 21, 27; 33:16, 19; Isa 56:1; Ps 119:121; Prov 21:3, 15).

לעולם ינטור (Ps 103:9). Thus, 103:9 seems implicitly to override the assurance of punitive judgment found in Exod 34:7 with a declaration of hope. This rewriting of Exod 34:6–7 suggests an awareness of an already long and enduring period of national suffering, perceived as judgment, which the psalmist nevertheless guarantees will come to an end before long: God will not be wrathful "forever."

b. God's gracious love overpowers his judgment (Ps 103:10–14). This section illustrates in a different way those epithets set out in 103:8. God is "compassionate and gracious, slow to anger, abounding in steadfast love" insofar as he never afflicts his devotees according to the principle of measure for measure (103:10)—his compassion by far exceeds his judgment![11] In five comparative phrases (103:10–13) the psalmist presents different images to illustrate the qualities of God's חסד and רחמים, images that come on the one hand, from the cosmic control of God in his world and, on the other, from the intimate imagery of God as a father. God's immeasurable love, which is saved for those who are pious and obedient to him (יראיו; see 103:11, 13, 17), is measured against the vertical axis of heaven and earth; God's act of distancing his people from their sins is set against the horizontal axis of east and west (103:12); and, finally, God's parental compassion demonstrates that he is conscious of the human failings of his devotees (103:13–14). This second segment thus implicitly acknowledges that the people (the devotees) sinned and suffered, although to a lesser degree than they deserve.

c. Divine compassion is eternal, placed in diametric opposition to temporally bound human existence (Ps 103:15–18). This final argument, which contrasts between temporal and insignificant humanity and the eternal compassion of humanity's creator, appears to follow upon the closing verse of the earlier passage (103:14).[12] Here, as before, for the third time, the exercise of God's compassion is limited to those who fear him (103:17–18). Psalm 103:17 provides yet another "completion" of Exod 34:7, which entirely replaces God's attributes of anger

11. Such phrasing otherwise occurs only in Ezra 9:13: כי אתה אלהינו חשכת למטה מעוננו ("though You, our God, have been forbearing, [punishing us] less than our iniquity [deserves]").

12. Compare the common mode of praise that focuses on God himself in Pss 90:2 (ומעולם עד־עולם אתה אל); 106:48; Neh 9:5; 1 Chr 16:36; 29:10. A similar, more limited comparison may be seen in Isa 40:6–8, where human temporality is compared to the eternal *word* of God (see Goldingay, *Psalms*, 3.174).

and vengefulness with love and beneficence. The determined stress on God's qualities of love and compassion, to the exclusion of harsh attributes associated with judgment, seems, again implicitly, to hint at the people's all too familiar experience of this harsher side of God in the present distress.

These three arguments, which constitute the bulk of Ps 103, are thus a remarkable illustration of one pious poet's effort to justify God. The psalmist clings to God's gracious qualities and eliminates any hint of other aspects of God. Praise in this psalm arises from circumstances of ongoing distress, and it is structured by close adherence to traditional conceptions of divine benevolence (as expressed, e.g., in Exod 34:6). This reading, then, sees Ps 103 as a remarkable representation of a struggle with the need to justify God in an enduring situation of distress (which the poet implicitly admits is caused by God); the poet repeatedly encourages himself (103:1–2) and then others (103:20–22) to bless God, clinging to pious truths that seem contradicted by present circumstances and thus severely challenged. But, these justificatory words of Ps 103 are clearly exceptional in their apologetic tone. More frequently do we find that poets struggle with the seeming absence of mercy, as they raise questions of doubt and express strong protest.

12.2. Doubt and Protest: "Where Is Your Steadfast Love of Old?" (Psalms 77 and 89; Lamentations 2 and 3)

In Ps 89 the phrase חסדי יהוה opens and closes the psalm. The term חסד may be variously nuanced in this psalm (as in its other occurrences) as divine benevolence, steadfast love, or faithfulness.[13] In a situation where imminent and enduring suffering raises doubts about the workings of God's חסד, the psalm begins from the understanding that this attribute is the foundation of divine activity. But, the imminent and enduring suffering raises doubts about the continued working of divine benevolence, love, and fidelity.

13. חסד is central to the various segments of Ps 89, and it occurs in specific repeated pairs, as follows: חסד/אמונה, 89:2, 3, 25, 34, 50 (this pair also occurs in 36:6; 88:12; 92:3; 98:3; 100:5 and as part of a longer list of epithets in 40:11); חסד ואמת, 89:15; חסד/ברית, 89:29; and חסידיך, 89:20. All these pairs connect חסד with the semantic field and theological theme of covenant; see Ward, "Literary Form," 331–32. On the possible translations for חסד, see §12.1.

חסד is the "device" by means of which God established heaven (earth) and the entire world (89:2–3); and the psalmist sets the covenant with God's chosen one, his servant David, on the same eternal level (89:4–5). Using *yiqtol* verbal forms (89:6–9, 16–17), the poet proclaims his present and continuing commitment to praising God, as king (89:18–19), for his past and eternal legacies, which are described in conventional celebratory phrases (89:14–19). These two targets of praise—creation and the Davidic covenant—are elaborately introduced in the central segments of this psalm (89:6–19, 20–38).[14] But praise collapses from 89:39 and forward, when the poet protests God's rejection of his anointed one. In second-person verbs, the poet accuses God of himself acting against the king (89:39–41) by supporting his enemies in their war against him (89:42–44), to the point of holding God (rather than any human enemies) responsible for removing the king from his position (89:45–46). The psalm closes with a series of painful questions (89:47–50), followed by petitions (89:51–52).[15] The last of those questions, 89:50, closes by way of an *inclusio* with 89:1–5 and calls into question God's historical commitment to David: איה חסדיך הראשנים אדני נשבעת לדוד באמונתך ("O Lord, where is Your steadfast love of old which You swore to David in Your faithfulness?"). This final question remains as an open and powerful cry. Much shorter than the long and magnificent verses of praise in 89:6–38, this cry is answered negatively by the

14. On both literary and thematic grounds (see §3.4.3), I take Ps 89 as a typical communal lament and an organic literary composition. The literary integrity of this psalm is thoroughly argued by Ward, "Literary Form"; and see also the plausible comments of Tate (in criticism of Ward) that the psalm might have achieved its unity through the interweaving of preexisting materials (*Psalms 51–100*, 415–16). On the basis of Tate's comments, I argue that the poem is intentionally composed as a communal lament in the aftermath of early-sixth-century events, that is, either the Jehoiachin exile of 597 or the final destruction in the time of Zedekiah in 586. See further Tate (416–17), but contrast also Ward (336–39), who suggests a much earlier occasion for the composition, which I find untenable.

15. Compare this holistic reading to other scholarly studies of this psalm. Literary-historical approaches are influenced by Gunkel (*Psalms*, 386–94), who argues for the collation of two independent psalmodic segments—a hymn (89:2, 3, 6–19) and a lament (89:39–52)—with the possible addition of other segments, e.g., an oracle (89:20–38) and petitions (89:47–52). Tradition-historical approaches are taken by, e.g., Kraus (*Psalms 60–150*, 202–3), who suggests that elements of lament are added to an earlier hymn in reaction to Josiah's death at Megiddo; or Goldingay (*Psalms*, 2.660–92), who suggests a "staged process" (666). For additional literary-historical and tradition-historical studies of this psalm, see Clifford, "Psalm 89"; and Tate, *Psalms 51–100*, 413–18.

reality of suffering described in 89:39–46. Hence, doubt is conveyed by emphasizing the significant difference between experienced reality and the expectation that God will act with steadfast love, expressed in benevolence or fidelity to his eternal commitments. Psalm 89 painfully challenges the seeming absence of these positive qualities of God at this critical point.[16]

Additional expressions of doubt concerning the workings of divine care and compassion are found in the course of Ps 77. This psalm is unique among the communal laments in that it contains only two of this genre's characteristic features: a lament over the present distress (77:2–10) and praise addressed to God for his wonders on behalf of his people in the past (77:11–21).[17] As Meir Weiss notes, the lament section focuses on the poet and his emotional deterioration, as he recognizes that his cries to God in his day of distress have been in vain.[18]

A comparison of the first two subunits of this psalm reveals the poet's theological agony, which reaches its peak in 77:8–10. Psalm 77:2–4 and 77:5–7 reflect on the remembered past (see the use of זכר in 77:4, 7). The first unit speaks of God directly in the third-person (אלהים repeats three times in 77:2–4, אדני once), but there is no such address in 77:5–7, although a second-person verbal form is used at the very beginning of the passage. In 77:2–4, the poet addresses God in a loud, clear voice—קולי אל־אלהים ואצעקה ("I cry aloud to God," 77:2)—in the explicit hope that God will listen: והאזין אלי ("that He may give ear to me," 77:2b). This call deteriorates in volume to one of moaning and complaint (ואהמיה אשיחה ["I moan, I complain, my spirit fails"], 77:4); and then in 77:5–7 the poet completely loses the faculty of speech—נפעמתי ולא אדבר ("I am overwrought, I cannot speak," 77:5)—to the point that his conversation is solely internal: עם־לבבי אשיחה ("I commune with myself," 77:7). The poet's steep descent is further expressed by the references to the spirit that close

16. See Ward ("Literary Form," 333–36 at 336), who cautiously locates the unique message of Ps 89 within the royal psalms; or Tate (*Psalms 51–100*, 429), who encourages his readers to consider Ps 89, with Ps 74 (and Ps 80), as struggling with the theological dilemma of God's seeming abandonment of earlier covenant commitments to either the people or the Davidic dynasty.

17. The literary integrity of Ps 77 is questioned by scholars. I accept Weiss's reading of the psalm as an organic composition; see Weiss, *Ideas and Beliefs*, 109–25; Tate, *Psalms 51–100*, 268–76, esp. 271; and Goldingay, *Psalms*, 2.458–73, esp. 460. The discussion here does not address issues frequently considered in reference to 77:17–21, with its references to the exodus, or rather the theomachy, traditions; see Day, *God's Conflict with the Dragon*, 88–140; and Mettinger, "Fighting the Powers of Chaos."

18. Weiss, *Ideas and Beliefs*, 109–17.

each of these two subunits; the gloomy mood or spirit of וֹתתעטף רוחי ("my spirit fails," 77:4) transforms into the lost spirit of ויחפש רוחי ("my spirit inquires [better: *seeks*]," 77:7b). All these phrases portray theological turmoil, the feeling of losing contact with God, as the poet emotionally closes within himself and looks there for the comfort he had hoped to receive from God.[19]

Psalm 77:8–10 thus expresses the low theological point the poet is at and the height of his doubts:

[8] Will the Lord reject forever	הלעולמים יזנח אדני [8]
and never again show favor?[20]	ולא־יסיף לרצות עוד.
[9] Has His faithfulness disappeared forever?	האפס לנצח חסדו [9]
Will His promise be unfulfilled for all time?	גמר אמר לדר ודר.
[10] Has God forgotten how to pity?	השכח חנות אל [10]
Has He in anger stifled His compassion?	אם־קפץ באף רחמיו
Selah.	סלה.

The psalmist formulates six rhetorical questions, by which he asks whether God's rejection of his people is eternal (זנח and לא רצה in 77:8).[21]

---

19. Weiss (*Ideas and Beliefs*, 115–17) argues for yet another transformation in the poet's mood, as he discovers within himself the wonders of God (77:11–13); this discovery allows him to praise God for his past deeds, this time addressing God in the second-person (77:12–21). An inner transformation that eases the personal distress is similarly suggested by Weiser, *Psalms*, 532; and Brueggemann, *Israel's Praise*, 136–40. I part ways here with Weiss (and others), however; to me, the poet's reflections on God's deeds as cosmic ruler and warrior suggest not a change in attitude but rather a continuing clash between the glorious deeds of salvation remembered from the distant past and the present profoundly unrelieved distress (note the double mention of זכר in 77:12; and the similar theme in Ps 74). See further Tate (*Psalms 51–100*, 271), who mentions working with the tenses and modes of the verbs in order to decipher whether the psalm is a lament or a thanksgiving; he eventually concludes that "the psalm seems to indicate a situation of present distress existing for the speaker, a prayer which awaits for an answer" (271); and then he contends that there is no change of mood in the psalm and that all of its questions are left open (273; also 274–75). I find this to be a much more plausible reading.

20. רצה *qal* with God as agent designates divine favor toward the individual or the people, which is demonstrated by means of divine presence and assistance; see 2 Sam 24:23; Hos 8:13; Isa 42:1; Pss 40:14; 85:2; 119:108; 147:11; 149:4; Job 33:26; Prov 3:12; 16:7; Eccl 9:7; 2 Chr 10:7; likewise Jer 14:10; Ezek 20:41; Ps 44:4.

21. זנח occurs with modifiers indicating eternity (לעולמים or לנצח) in Pss 44:24 (see 44:10); 74:1; Lam 2:7. It is fiercely negated in Lam 3:31; see also Pss 43:2; 60:3, 12;

He then takes us to the divine qualities of Exod 34:6, asking first whether the divine trait of חסד has ceased forever (לנצח);[22] and in Ps 77:10, he further challenges God's qualities of חנון ורחום.[23] Each of the two stitches of this verse sets great paradoxes against those well-known divine qualities. While the poet accentuates his own remembrance of God (זכר repeats four times before and after this part of the psalm in 77:4, 7, 12 [2x]), he asks if God could have forgotten his basic quality of mercy: השכח חנות אל?[24] Finally, the last question, אם־קפץ באף רחמיו ("has He in anger stifled His compassion?"), brings the opposition between the antonyms of compassion and anger into a single phrase. The divine wrath, which enflames God's actions against his people, is often referred to as situated in the nose; mercy does not seem to belong in that facial area at all, and the proximity of אף and רחמים in this verse is exceptional.[25] Furthermore, קפץ (ב־) is used to designate "closing up on," as in reference to the hand (Deut 15:7) or the mouth (Ps 107:42; Job 5:16). Psalm 77:10 is the only reference to such a divine action; and closing up mercy within the nose is the opposite action of the divine wrath raging out of God's nose, as in חרון אף (see §9.1.5). Therefore, it might be suggested that the poet purposefully establishes this impossible linguistic connection and thus expresses his own doubt by raising this option that closes down on compassion. Could it be that God's compassion is held off, is prevented from the people, as if it is situated in the place of wrath?

89:39; 108:12. Compare, on the one hand, the prophetic accusation of Hos 8:3 that it is the people who desert God and, on the other, the consolation words of Zech 10:6, which collates לא־זנח ענה, and ריחם as God's redemptive deeds.

22. In Ps 103 the divine חסד is celebrated in the liturgy as eternal (see Pss 118 and 136; also 100:5; 103:17; 107:1); this liturgical use is echoed in 89:2; Jer 33:11; Ezra 3:11; 1 Chr 16:34, 41; 2 Chr 5:13; 7:6; 20:21. The pairing of חסד and עולם is repeated further in reference to God's commitments either to David (2 Sam 22:51; Pss 18:51; 89:29; and transformed to the people in Isa 55:3) or to the people (Isa 54:8). Among the individual laments, see Ps 52:10 and 25:6, which brings חסדים and רחמים as of eternity כי מעולם המה.

23. For the allusions to Exod 34:6 (and the exodus tradition more broadly) in this psalm, see Kselman, "Psalm 77."

24. חנות is the infinitive construct of חנן; see Gesenius, Kautzsch, and Cowley, *Gesenius' Hebrew Grammar*, §67r.

25. Etymologically, רחמים is explained as connected to the womb, thus to that feminine feeling of love and care; see Simian-Yofre, "רחם *rḥm*"; and Loeland, *Silent or Salient Gender?* 148–58, 190–92. According to Jer 31:19, the internal organs (in parallel to בטן)—the intestines and possibly the womb and the birth canal—are the physical locations of mercy.

Clearer and stronger proclamations of protest occur within Lamentations, with four occurrences of the phrase (לא חמל(ת, three in Lam 2 and one in Lam 3:

2:2   The Lord has laid waste without pity [בלע ... ולא חמל]
All the habitations of Jacob;
He has razed in His anger
Bat-Judah's strongholds.
He has brought low in dishonor
The kingdom and its leaders.

2:17   The Lord has done what He purposed,
Has carried out the decree
That He ordained long ago;
He has torn down without pity [הרס ולא חמל].
He has let the foe rejoice over you,
Has exalted the might of your enemies.

2:21   Prostrate in the streets lie
Both young and old.
My maidens and youths
Are fallen by the sword;
You slew them on Your day of wrath,
You slaughtered without pity [טבחת לא חמלת].

3:43   You have clothed Yourself in anger and pursued us,
You have slain without pity [הרגת לא חמלת].

חמל means to "spare the life (of man or beast)"; within the human sphere, it occurs in reference to events of war (1 Sam 15:3, 9, 15; Isa 30:14).[26] The three occurrences of לא חמל in Lam 2 constitute a fierce protest against God's refusal to spare his own people (see §1.2.2).

Lamentations 3:40–48 presents the theological turmoil brought on by the Judean defeat in its full complexity. Set at the center of the book,

---

26. Occurrences of the verb with God as agent come from a similar context of war. God orders Babylon's enemies not to spare her (PAN Jer 50:14; 51:3); consolation prophecies present God as the agent of חמל (Joel 2:18; Mal 3:17); God's חמל is negated in PAN (Hab 1:17; Zech 11:5–6 [in retaliation for the faults of Israel's leaders]).

Lam 3 garners scholarly attention due to its exceptional character within Lamentations itself, as a mixture of the features of individual and communal laments, with wisdom characteristics as well.[27] The wisdom passages found in 3:22–39 include proclamations that refer to God's mercy as eternal truth; these statements are seen by scholars as highly conventional or stereotypical (3:22, 31–32; see §12.1).[28] These conventional sayings seem to drop out of consideration already by the following segment of this specific lament (3:40–48):

[40] Let us search and examine our ways,	נחפשה דרכינו ונחקרה [40]
And turn back to the LORD;	ונשובה עד־יהוה.
[41] Let us lift up our hearts with our hands	נשא לבבנו אל־כפים [41]
To God in heaven:	אל־אל בשמים.
[42] We have transgressed and rebelled,	נחנו פשענו ומרינו [42]
And You have not forgiven.	אתה לא סלחת.
[43] You have clothed Yourself in anger and pursued us,	סכתה באף [43] ותרדפנו
You have slain without pity.	הרגת לא חמלת.
[44] You have screened Yourself off with a cloud,	סכותה בענן לך [44]
That no prayer may pass through.	מעבור תפלה.
[45] You have made us filth and refuse	סחי ומאוס תשימנו [45]
In the midst of the peoples.	בקרב העמים.
[46] All our enemies loudly	פצו עלינו [46]
Rail against us.	פיהם כל־איבינו.
[47] Panic and pitfall are our lot,	פחד ופחת היה לנו [47]

27. For a discussion of the position, the mixed literary character, and the unique themes of Lam 3, see commentaries, which make a number of interesting suggestions to identify the author with historical or literary figures. Hillers (*Lamentations*, 61–65 at 64) considers the poem to be an individual lament, composed by "a typical sufferer" and invoking a different "I" in 3:52–66. Berlin (*Lamentations*, 84–86) suggests that the voice of the speaker in Lam 3 is "the personified voice of the exile" (84) and sees similarities to Job in the wisdomlike verses (92–95). Dobbs-Allsopp (*Lamentations*, 106–9) holds that a single speaking voice is heard throughout this lament and represents a full merger between the individual and the community; he thus suggests that this voice is an archetype of the king (108). See also Renkema, *Lamentations*, 344–45, 430–31.

28. On the conventional, stereotyped, language, see Dobbs-Allsopp, *Lamentations*, 114–16; he suggests that the wisdom style of 3:25–39 presents a traditional view on "how to cope with suffering" (119–22). Berlin (*Lamentations*, 92–93) finds this passage to be "an intellectual essay about God" or "a kind of theodicy," composed by the author in a wisdom-literature style.

Death and destruction.	הַשֵּׁאת וְהַשָּׁבֶר.
[48] My eyes shed streams of water	[48] פַּלְגֵי־מַיִם תֵּרַד עֵינִי
Over the ruin of my poor people.	עַל־שֶׁבֶר בַּת־עַמִּי.

Lamentations 3:40–41 constitutes the poet's call for his people to return to God in prayer. As Adele Berlin suggests, these verses mark a four-phase transition in this chapter: (1) from the individual voice (3:1–39) to first-person plural speech (3:42–47); (2) from references to God in the third-person (3:1–39) to direct address of God in the second-person (3:42–66); (3) "from [the genre of] wisdom discourse to [that of] lament or penitential psalm";[29] and most importantly, (4) from a view of God as good and merciful to a view of God as one who will not forgive his people, even though they confess and repent of their sins.[30]

This sudden theological shift at 3:40 is indeed remarkable—whether these later verses are composed by the author of the earlier part of the chapter or constitute a segment of an independent communal lament, combined with the earlier verses.[31] The dissonance created in 3:42, where a confession of sins is followed by a direct accusation against God, becomes even stronger in 3:43–45. Three intertwined issues are raised in this part of the lament.

First, confession, as a liturgical expression of repentance, does not automatically guarantee divine forgiveness.[32] With נַחְנוּ פָשַׁעְנוּ וּמָרִינוּ (3:42a),

29. Berlin, *Lamentations*, 95.

30. Berlin, *Lamentations*, 95–96; compare Dobbs-Allsopp (*Lamentations*, 123), who considers these verses to follow up on the previous section. I prefer Berlin's perspective here.

31. According to Berlin (*Lamentations*, 95) the change of tone and content is part of the theological stressful state the poet is in, as in 3:42–47 he speaks in the name of the people: "Despite the valiant attempt at theodicy, reason cannot conquer all. The poem is not an intellectual exercise but a national lament . . . [the poet's] forbearance and hope turn to anger and despair; and the language of wisdom is overwhelmed by the language of lament." Compare Hillers (*Lamentations*, 64–65, 72–74), who accepts 3:42–66 as "a collective prayer," composed of "disparate elements" (72). In this view, the differences between 3:40–42 and 3:43–47 may be due to the different "voices"/authors brought together in the new composition; it is then plausible that 3:43–47 represents a fragment of a communal lament brought into this context of confession. In any event, in 3:48–51 the poet reverts to a first-person account, and as of 3:52 the lament goes back to an individual lament; though it is different in tone from 3:1–39, as suggested by Hillers (*Lamentations*, 73–74).

32. Berlin (*Lamentations*, 96) understands this realization, that "there is no direct

the people admit their own responsibility in the present situation; the expected divine response to such a formulaic liturgical confession would have
been pardon, as expressed by סלח (Dan 9:19; cf. Num 14:19–20) or כיפר
(Ps 65:4).[33] Against these expectations that God would accept the people's
confession and employ his חסד and רחמים (Lam 3:22, 32), God does *not*
forgive his people: אתה לא סלחת (3:42b).[34]

Second, God's responses are entirely motivated by the wrath engendered by their sins: סכתה באף ותרדפנו (3:43a); he ignores the people's
confession and refuses them forgiveness. The first occurrence of סכך ב־
introduces an imagery within the context of God as warrior, who covers
himself with wrath as with a garment and pursues his people to death with
no pity (הרגת לא חמלת in 3:43b; compare 2:21).[35]

---

relationship between repentance and forgiveness," to be the major issue at stake in
these verses.

33. Compare the opening verses of various penitential prayers: Dan 9:5 (חטאנו
ועוינו והרשענו ומרדנו; and see 9:15–19); Ezra 9:6; Neh 1:7. For the close connections
between a leader's, or the people's, prayer or confession of sins and its divine acceptance, signified by God's forgiveness (with סלח) see Dan 9:19 and, among the individual
laments, Pss 25:11; 32:5; 86:1–7. For ריחם and סלח, see Isa 55:7; note also God's immediate reaction to Moses's petition in the narrative of Num 14:19–20. כיפר and סלח occur
together as an almost automatic outcome of ritual procedures of atonement conducted
by the priest on behalf of the individual; see Lev 4:20, 26, 31, 35; 5:10, 13, 16, 18, 26;
19:22; Num 15:25–26, 28; also 30:6, 9, 13. In its basic meaning, כפר denotes "cover"
(Gen 6:14); in reference to sin the verb means cover over it, annul its substance, and
thus allow forgiveness. This ritual term occurs once in Jer 18:23 and five times in Ezekiel
(four times in cultic contexts 43:20, 26; 45:17, 20; and once in 16:63). This procedure
of annulment (and covering) of sin also stands behind the phrasing מחה (עון/חטאת)
in Isa 43:25; 44:22; Jer 18:23; Ps 109:14; Neh 3:37.

34. Dobbs-Allsopp (*Lamentations*, 123) notes that the use of the independent personal pronouns "we" and "you" in 3:42 accentuates the adverse relationship between
God and the people. The possibility that God would not be willing to forgive a sinner occurs in Deut 29:18–20, as an exception in a situation of extreme disobedience.
A similar categorical statement that God is not willing to forgive his people occurs in
2 Kgs 24:4. Circumstances under which forgiving is impossible are named in Jer 5:1,
7. Prophecies of consolation (31:34; 33:8; 50:20) transform this divine approach and
accentuate that God forgives the people for their past iniquities (presented as a hypothetical option in 36:3).

35. Compare Lam 3:66, where the enemies are the object of God's pursuit (רדף).
This sequence, in which the people sin and God pursues them in wrath to the point of
total destruction, without pity, is well attested; see, for instance, Hos 14:1 and Isa 1:20
and within the communal laments: והמה מרו ועצבו את־רוח קדשו ויהפך להם לאויב
הוא נלחם־בם ("but they rebelled, and grieved His holy spirit; then He became their
enemy, and Himself made war against them," Isa 63:10); as well as Jer 5:22–29; Ezek

Third, the second occurrence of סכך ב־ in this context invokes different imagery altogether: סכותה בענן לך מעבור תפלה (3:44) configures a cloud as a barrier between God and the people (as in Exod 13:21–22; see Ps 105:39). In this accusation, the cloud that is the symbol of theophany, of divine presence with and assistance to the people (e.g., Num 14:14), serves as a barrier, purposefully set by God between himself and his people, to stop the voices of their prayers from reaching him in their time of distress (מעבור תפלה).[36] This figurative portrayal of God as actively blocking himself above the cloud contradicts the basic essence of prayer as a venue of communication between man and God. In particular, this imagery seems to speak against the Deuteronomistic conception that portrays God as attentive to his people's prayers and readily forgiving them from his heavenly abode (see ושמעת וסלחת in 1 Kgs 8:30, 34, 36, 39; note the connection between hearing the prayers and a specific act of mercy in 8:50).[37]

Lamentations 3:42–44 thus presents a shocking protest, which witnesses to God's refusal to exercise the attribute of mercy, in three respects:

20:8, 13, 21 and many other judgment prophecies in the two books. This same imagery is further attested at the background of Lam 1:18, 20 (see §9.1.5). Yet, this presentation of the strict logical progression of sin and judgment is refuted in the penitential prayers (e.g., Neh 9:6–37), where time and again God is said to have employed his "many mercies," overcoming the great sins of the people (9:16–19, 26–31; also Ezra 9:13).

36. The two occurrences of סכך ב־ in 3:43–44 thus each emerge from quite distinctive contexts of imagery; see Hillers, *Lamentations*, 61 (on the stylistic device of repeating initial words to serve the acrostic schema in Lam 3) and 59 (on possible meanings of this repeated phrase)—although I cannot accept Hillers's interpretation of סכך as transitive in 3:43 and intransitive (or reflexive) only in 3:44 (with לך). By their theological contents both verbs need to be intransitive, thus "you covered yourself with (anger/a cloud)" (so NJPS and, for instance, Renkema, *Lamentations*, 433–35). As presented by Berlin (*Lamentations*, 96) both meanings stand in diametric opposition to the meaning of סכך as conveying protection, throughout the wilderness journey (connected with the tabernacle; see Ps 140:8; Job 1:10) and through the cloud in other occurrences. She understands these verses as "a masterfully ironic allusion . . . ; rather than sheltering them, . . . the cloud 'protects' God from the people" (96).

37. See also the pleas for God to hear Nehemiah's and the people's prayers, which contain clear allusions to Deut 4 and Deut 30. Berlin (*Lamentations*, 96) considers the description in Lam 3:44 to be a purposeful strategy of the lamenter to come to grips with the contradiction between repentance and forgiveness as confined by the conception of divine immanence. However, this verse does not show a change in the conception of presence, nor a deficiency in God's abilities to overcome the cloud barrier. Rather, this metaphor presents a purposeful divine deed that stands as a counter-conception of God's attentiveness to prayer and confession.

(a) God does not respond favorably to, and even totally neglects, his people's confession of sins; (b) he is passionate in acting as his people's fierce and pitiless enemy; and (c) he actively blocks himself away, to keep the people's prayers from reaching him in his heavenly abode. In this framework, God does not allow himself to hear the people's cries of distress or to attend the horrendous sight of their suffering (see 3:48–51, with the emphasis on the poet's waiting, hoping that God will observe and see: עַד־יַשְׁקִיף וְיֵרֶא יְהוָה מִשָּׁמָיִם, 3:50); most significantly, God refuses to attend to expressions of confession, repentance, and pleas for help. Rather than taking action on behalf of his people, and thus implementing his attribute of mercy, God continues with actions of war against them, to the point that he makes them into סְחִי וּמָאוֹס תְּשִׂימֵנוּ בְּקֶרֶב הָעַמִּים ("You have made us filth and refuse," 3:45), and the pressure of suffering is not relieved (3:46–51).[38]

12.3. Justification: No Current Divine Mercy in Ezekiel and in Jeremiah

Jeremiah and Ezekiel inherited the same traditional presumptions as their contemporaries about the workings of divine mercy, but they have clearly different conceptions of the place of this divine attribute in the present situation. Neither book mentions it often (and Ezekiel substantially less so than Jeremiah); in both books mercy language is mostly cast negatively, and those conventional sayings and thoughts appear only in Jeremiah. Both prophets follow a very different path from the other sources presented above (§12.2), using various strategies to justify God's lack of mercy toward his suffering people in their present situation.

The book of Ezekiel features only very restricted expressions of mercy. These references appear exclusively in judgment prophecies against Jerusalem, and always in the negative. Seven times the prophet uses the phrase לֹא חָסָה עֵינִי: once on its own (5:11); five other times along with the phrase וְלֹא חָמַל (7:4, 9; 8:18; 9:5, 10); and once in a triple string: לֹא־אֶפְרַע וְלֹא־אָחוּס וְלֹא אֶנָּחֵם ("I will not refrain or spare or relent," 24:14).[39] Hence, the

---

38. The phrase סְחִי וּמָאוֹס is a *hapax* and in this context seems to represent actions of scorn, shame, and disgrace; see Renkema, *Lamentations*, 435–36.

39. The Septuagint and Peshitta do not reflect a translation of וְלֹא אֶנָּחֵם. See Allen,

refusal to exercise mercy is generally directed against those who remained in Jerusalem, against whom God decrees total destruction.[40]

There are only three exceptions to this use, and each of them underscores in different ways this refusal of divine mercy in the present. חמל occurs positively only once in Ezekiel: ואחמל על שם קדשי ("therefore I am concerned for My holy name," 36:21). This statement, made in the context of a prophecy of restoration, shows that even in relation to the exiles, there is no intention of mercy toward the people; God will act to restore his people from exile only in order to guarantee that his name not be profaned in the eyes of the foreign nations.[41] חוס occurs positively in Ezekiel one time—referring to God's deeds in favor of his people in the distant past: ותחס עיני עליהם משחתם ("but I had pity on them and did not destroy them," 20:17).[42] The verb ריחם appears once in a positive sense in Ezekiel within a consolation prophecy addressed to the Babylonian exiles (39:25); and yet 39:23–29 is aptly suspected as a late non-Ezekielian passage.[43]

In addition, there are no formulaic, conventional references to the attribute of mercy in Ezekiel, and thus no mention of חסד or of phrases of forgiveness such as מחה, כיפר, חנן, or סלח. Ezekiel rarely uses mercy language, and then only in ways that differ markedly from the use of this language in other contemporary sources. We find either the denial of

---

Ezekiel 20–48, 57, who defends the Masoretic Text of 24:14b and takes 24:10–14 as "Ezekiel's elaboration" of the previous passages (24:3b–5 and 24:9–10).

40. See Rom-Shiloni, *Exclusive Inclusivity*, 139–85.

41. This concern for God's name is repeated in a retrospective review of the distant past (Ezek 20:9, 14, 22) or in forecasts for the future (20:44; 36:22).

42. Within the narrative context of the prophecy, Ezek 20:17 designates a change in God's repeated actions against the sinning people (see 20:8, 13, 21). Nevertheless, Cooke (*Ezekiel*, 217) argues that the verse is essential to the context. Greenberg (*Ezekiel 1–20*, 367) does not consider this phrase to convey a change in divine motivation; he suggests rather that "*ḥûs 'al* here means no more than to spare, i.e., not to inflict destruction upon" and is followed by Block, *Ezekiel 1–24*, 633.

43. See Zimmerli (*Ezekiel*, 2.319–21, 323–24), who considers Ezek 39:23–29 to have been added by the prophet's disciples to the original core of the Gog prophecies, functioning as a summary by the editor(s) of the book (further argued by many subsequent commentators; see Allen, *Ezekiel 20–48*, 208–9). This passage indeed features a preponderance of unique language and themes, which on the one hand have nothing to do with the previous Gog prophecies and on the other introduce for the first and only time in the book the concept of divine compassion and hiddenness of the divine face (הסתר פנים). Furthermore, the linkage of restoration and compassion in 39:25 is close to the language of Jer 33:26 (similarly 12:15 and 31:20), although the phrasing in Ezekiel shows a complete two-stich parallelism.

mercy toward the people, in judgment prophecies against Jerusalem, or the positive use of mercy language only in reference to God's own name, to the distant past, and (possibly) to the eschatological future (if this last is authentic)—and we find in addition an absence of any ritual language evoking the arena of divine mercy. These unusual features confirm the notion that Ezekiel virtually eliminates the possibility of mercy toward the people from the repertoire of God's deeds in the destruction.

It is particularly significant that except for 39:25, which is probably not the prophet's own utterance, the attribute of mercy is not even part of this prophet's portrayal of *future* consolation. Scholars emphasize Ezekiel's unique picture of the future, in which God's wrath and tendency to warlike activity continue to govern even redemption and restoration (e.g., 20:32).[44] Compassion and mercy are clearly not motives for deliverance in Ezekiel. Rather, the people's eventual deliverance will occur solely to reconfirm God's kingship and universal sovereignty (20:33) or to resanctify God's name in the eyes of the nations (36:22–23).[45]

The book of Jeremiah features the largest number of expressions of divine mercy in comparison with any other source studied in this book. Six roots from the semantic field of mercy occur in the book—נחם, ריחם, חמל, חנן, חסד, and חוס—in addition to various expressions of forgiveness or atonement: סלח, מחה חטאת (לא), כיפר (לא). Yet, most of these expressions occur only once in the book; all are found in negative phrases within judgment prophecies; and the total number of occurrences of such phrases does not go beyond twenty, limited to but a few prophetic passages. Positive expressions that promise the exercise of divine mercy are found only in consolation proclamations (using סלח and ריחם). Hence, the prophet distinguishes his uses of the attribute of mercy according to categories of genre and theme.

In distinction from Ezekiel, prophecies in Jeremiah do evoke conventional formulas. In three prophecies, Jeremiah uses חסד and עשה חסד in ways that intentionally evoke stylistic and thematic conventions concerning divine mercy and benevolence (9:22–23; 32:18; 33:10–11). While the

---

44. See Greenberg, *Ezekiel 1–20*, 371–72; and Schwartz, "Ezekiel's Dim View."

45. Compare Ganzel ("Descriptions of the Restoration," 209), who argues that the "optimistic" verses are Ezekielian; she holds that these sporadic allusions to atonement, return, compassion, and deliverance within Ezekiel reflect Ezekiel's postfall restoration expectations (200). I do not find her discussion persuasive, at least when it comes to the attribute of mercy; the data presented here contradict any possibility of the development of optimism toward the future or a sense of theological transformation.

three passages are of different genres (wisdom saying, prayer, consolation prophecy), in all three the prophet (or his tradents) alludes to passages in pentateuchal, psalmodic, or wisdom literature that treat divine benevolence as an eternal quality of God.

In Jeremiah's prayer (32:18), עשה חסד alludes to the divine epithet found in the second commandment (Exod 20:5–6; Deut 5:9–10; compare נצר חסד in in Exod 34:7; see also 2 Sam 22:51; Ps 18:51; see §12.1 and §12.2). In Jer 33:10–11, one of the consolation prophecies of restoration in the land, the liturgical formula is quoted: הודו את־יהוה צבאות כי־טוב יהוה כי־לעולם חסדו ("give thanks to the LORD of Hosts, for the LORD is good, for His kindness is everlasting!"), which echoes similar prescripts in Pss 106:1; 107:1; 118:1; 136:1.[46] Paraphrased with minor changes in Jeremiah, this liturgical quotation conveys the joy that will result from the restoration of cultic life back in the land.

Finally, Jer 9:22–23 brings a cluster of wisdom sayings in prophetic costume:[47]

[22] Thus said the LORD:	[22] כה אמר יהוה
Let not the wise man glory in his wisdom;	אל־יתהלל חכם בחכמתו
Let not the strong man glory in his strength;	ואל־יתהלל הגבור בגבורתו
Let not the rich man glory in his riches.	אל־יתהלל עשיר בעשרו.
[23] But only in this should one glory:	[23] כי אם בזאת יתהלל המתהלל

46. Jer 33:10–11 overturns the portrayal of the destruction in 7:34; 9:9; 16:9; 25:10. Duhm (*Jeremia*, 273) further suggests that the repeated phrases on the total destruction of both man and beast in 33:10 are a reversal of 4:23–26 and 9:9. Such a transformation of judgment into deliverance occurs in 33:1–9, esp. 33:6, which reverses 8:22; see Holladay, *Jeremiah*, 2.224. This transformation is differently treated by scholars. It is common to categorize this change from a redaction-critical viewpoint as a marker of a later layer of tradents; see, e.g., Schmid, *Buchgestalten des Jeremiahbuches*, 355–75. Jer 33 (with all its diverse passages) should be seen as repatriate ideology (Rom-Shiloni, "Group-Identities in Jeremiah," 35–43).

47. Commentators struggle with the place of this unique passage in Jeremiah. Holladay (*Jeremiah*, 1.316–18), for instance, suggests that these verses should be taken as a piece of "folk wisdom" that mounts a critique of royal ideology (317). Craigie (in Craigie, Kelley, and Drinkard, *Jeremiah 1–25*, 152–53) points out the uniqueness of these wisdom-style proclamations in their present location within Jer 8–9 (connected by the catchwords ידע and חכם) as well as in comparison to wisdom tradition generally (which otherwise avoids the constellation of wise, mighty, and rich as well as the negative attitude to wealth).

In his earnest devotion to Me.	הַשְׂכֵּל וְיָדֹעַ אוֹתִי
For I the LORD act with kindness,	כִּי אֲנִי יְהוָה עֹשֶׂה חֶסֶד
Justice, and equity in the world;	מִשְׁפָּט וּצְדָקָה בָּאָרֶץ
For in these I delight	כִּי־בְאֵלֶּה חָפַצְתִּי
declares the LORD.	נְאֻם־יְהוָה.

God's qualities of benevolence, justice, and equity are contrasted with three sources of human power: wisdom, might, and wealth (similar, in a way, to Mic 6:8). This schematic presentation of the triplet עשה חסד משפט וצדקה constitutes an exceptional cluster, which conflates the otherwise well-attested expressions: עשה חסד and עשה משפט (וצדקה) (Ps 99:4).[48]

The formulaic nature of each of these three passages illustrates how detached they are from the descriptive language that the prophet (and possibly also his tradents) generally use to portray God's activity during the destruction and in its aftermath. Unlike those formulaic references, expressions in Jeremiah that address divine mercy and consider its actual activation (or nonactivation) feature distinctive markers of genre and time, differentiating past, present, and future. Referring to the present (or predicting imminent events of destruction), expressions of mercy occur only in the negative. Such is the triple string: לא־אחמול ולא־אחוס ולא ארחם מהשחיתם ("I will have no pity, I will have no compassion, and I will have no mercy that will stop Me from destroying them," 13:14)[49] or לא־אתן לכם חנינה ("for I will show you no mercy," 16:13).

The proclamation כי־אספתי את־שלומי מאת העם־הזה נאם־יהוה את־ החסד ואת־הרחמים ("for I have withdrawn My favor from that people— declares the LORD—My kindness and compassion," 16:5) uses the imagery of the harvest. God gathers in his care for his people, his שלום, which includes חסד and רחמים, taking those away from his people so that death and great agony, with no proper chance for mourning, will control the streets of Jerusalem (16:6–8).[50] This metaphor of ingathering creates a

---

48. The nouns צדקה ומשפט and חסד occur otherwise together in Ps 33:5: אהב צדקה ומשפט חסד יהוה מלאה הארץ ("He loves what is right and just; the earth is full of the Lord's faithful care"). See §12.2.

49. Compare NJPS Jer 13:14: "No pity, compassion, or mercy will stop Me from destroying them." The first-person verbs in the Hebrew accentuate God's active role. This triplet also occurs in Jer 21:7 as the human reaction of the Babylonian king; see §1.1.2.

50. The Septuagint does not represent these components here and misses the words from נאם־יהוה in 16:5b to לא יקברו in 16:6a. McKane (*Jeremiah 1–25*, 365) seems to accept Janzen's suggestion (*Studies in the Text of Jeremiah*, 98) that the Septuagint text shows "an accidental omission from the Hebrew *Vorlage*."

powerful distinction in time—divine mercy is a recognized quality of God, it had its day with the people, but now it is a matter of the past.[51] Against expectations of continuing שלום (as promised by the peace prophets in 6:14; 14:13), the destruction era is a time when God actively withdraws those aspects of his from which stem his deeds of favor toward his people.[52] Contrary to such expectations, then, God intentionally establishes this critical time as a period of no mercy for his own people.[53]

In forward-looking passages, that is, in restoration prophecies within Jeremiah, the only two positive expressions of mercy are סלח and רחם. Each occurrence of these terms shows the reliance of the prophetic passages on earlier authoritative pentateuchal traditions concerning divine mercy. סלח occurs in three prophecies of consolation:[54]

No longer will they need to teach one another	ולא ילמדו עוד איש את־
and say to one another, "Heed the LORD";	רעהו ואיש את־אחיו לאמר
for all of them, from the least of them to the	דעו את־יהוה כי־כולם ידעו
greatest, shall heed Me—	אותי למקטנם ועד־גדולם
declares the LORD.	נאם־יהוה
<u>For I will forgive their iniquities,</u>	<u>כי אסלח לעונם</u>
<u>and remember their sins no more.</u> (31:34)	<u>ולחטאתם לא אזכר־עוד.</u>

51. For אסף as an agricultural operation, see Exod 23:10; Lev 25:3; Deut 11:14; 16:13. Agriculture scenes with אסף serve in presenting vast scenes of disaster as well (Isa 16:10; 17:5–6), but this passage in Jeremiah takes the imagery a significant step further by associating it with the withdrawal of mercy. In addition, following the context within Jer 16:1–9 of the vast death of parents and children together, the prophecy may be punning on אסף and using it also in its other meaning (mostly in the *niphal*): נאסף אל־עמיו/אל־אבתיו ("be gathered into the family graveyard," thus "die," as in Gen 25:8; 2 Kgs 22:20).

52. Holladay (*Jeremiah*, 1.471) suggests that taking away the שלום in this prophecy is a counter-response to the peace prophets. He also proposes that Isa 54:10 in turn constitutes a corrective to and reversal of Jeremiah's judgment prophecy, since it features the three components ברית שלומי, and חסד and the epithet מרחמך ("[the one] who has mercy on you").

53. In this phenomenological discussion, I do not enter into questions of the actual authorship of Jer 16:1–9. See McKane (*Jeremiah 1–25*, 366–68) for the different considerations; McKane finally accepts this passage (and specifically the reference to שלום) as "an exilic view of Jeremiah" (368). If this view is accepted as plausible, the theological difference between Jer 16:5 and Isa 54:10 should then find a synchronic (rather than a diachronic) solution.

54. Two additional occurrences of סלח in Jer 5:1, 7 designate the impossibility of forgiveness. The exhortation in this chapter is also built on an earlier tradition, the narrative of Sodom.

And I will purge them of all the sins which they committed against Me, <u>and I will pardon all the sins which they committed against Me</u>, by which they rebelled against Me. (33:8)

וטהרתים מכל־עונם אשר
חטאו־לי וסלחתי לכול
(ק: לכל)־עונתיהם אשר
חטאו־לי ואשר פשעו בי.

In those days and at that time
—declares the Lord—
<u>The iniquity of Israel</u> shall be sought,
And there shall be none;
<u>The sins of Judah</u>,
And none shall be found;
<u>For I will pardon</u> those I allow to survive. (50:20)

בימים ההם ובעת ההיא
נאם־יהוה
<u>יבקש את־עון ישראל</u>
ואיננו
<u>ואת־חטאת יהודה</u>
ולא תמצאינה
<u>כי אסלח לאשר אשאיר.</u>

Jeremiah 36:3 couches the same promise in hypothetical language:

Perhaps when the House of Judah hear of all the disasters I intend to bring upon them, they will turn back from their wicked ways, <u>and I will pardon their iniquity and their sin.</u>

אולי ישמעו בית יהודה את כל
הרעה אשר אנכי חשב לעשות
להם למען ישובו איש מדרכו
הרעה וסלחתי לעונם ולחטאתם.

While each prophecy differs from the others, they share a common literary denominator that sets the terms for the theological conceptions of forgiveness that each develops.[55] The constellation of סלח with עון and

---

55. Without discussing each of these passages separately, I note several factors that mitigate against deriving some shared, uniform theological conception. Two unsolved questions seem to trouble the authors, be they the prophet and/or his followers and tradents; subsequently, these questions are answered fairly differently across these four passages. First, does divine forgiveness come as a result of human repentance, or is it independent of human behavior? Second, is forgiveness connected with any ritual procedures, and who activates those? I do not see a convincing way of distinguishing between authorial voices through the answers to these questions: (1) Jer 36:3 sets forgiveness in the context of, and as conditional on, repentance. This conception is well documented in 1 Kgs 8:34, and thus Jer 36:3 is often added to the list of Deuteronomistic phrases in Jer 36; but the same idea also appears in Isa 55:7, and it is clearly not mandatory for Jeremiah. (2) In regard to Jer 31:34, commentators point out the unclear connection between 31:34b and 31:34a; is forgiveness connected to or detached from repentance? (see McKane, *Jeremiah 26–52*, 822–23). (3) Jer 33:8 uses clearly cultic phraseology, which is otherwise not present in Jeremiah's prophecies of consolation.

חטאת is unique to these references and otherwise appears only in Moses's prayer in Exod 34:9: וסלחת לעוננו ולחטאתנו ("pardon our iniquity and our sin").[56] It seems that Jeremiah and possibly also his tradents formulate their conceptions of forgiveness by drawing on that inherited prayer formula. Thus, the proclamation of past forgiveness is transformed into a promise for the future, when God will indeed be attentive to the people's prayers and forgive them.[57] This promise may be taken as a prophetic corrective to expressions of doubt or protest, such as those in Lam 3:42–44, to counter that (only) in the future will God's lack of attention (or negative attention) be transformed into forgiveness and restoration.

ריחם occurs four times in four Jeremian consolation prophecies. Although quite different from one another, these passages make a clear connection between restoration and mercy in their portrayals of the way God will treat his people (and in one case the nations) in the future:

Then, after I have uprooted them, <u>I will take them back into favor</u>, and restore them each to his own inheritance and his own land. (12:15)[58]	והיה אחרי נתשי אותם <u>אשוב ורחמתים</u> והשבתים איש לנחלתו ואיש לארצו.

טהר occurs otherwise only in 13:27; in 33:8, however, טהר *piel* is a divine action, such as might be a response to Lev 16:30 (טהר מחטאת) and also close to that of Ezek 36:25 (טהר מטמאה), 36:33 (טהר מעון), and 37:23; cf. Lundbom (*Jeremiah 21–36*, 532), who much too easily draws the connection between Jer 33:8 and 31:34 and 50:20. (4) Jer 50:20 closes the passage 50:17–20. If it is integral to the earlier verses, it configures forgiveness as following restoration to the land. A new element by comparison with the other passages is the notion that forgiveness marks the end of exile (as in Isa 40:2); see McKane, *Jeremiah 26–52*, 1270–71. Lundbom (*Jeremiah 37–50*, 397) explains Jer 50:20 as "a happy reversal" of 2:22 and 30:14–15.

56. סלח ל־ is elsewhere paired with either עון (Num 14:19; Pss 25:11; 103:3) or חטאת (1 Kgs 8:34, 36, 50; 2 Chr 6:25, 27, 39; 7:14); but in only these four Jeremian passages, along with Exod 34:9, do both nouns occur together with this verb. Therefore, I connect this phrasing to Exod 34:9 rather than to 34:6–7 (compare Lundbom, *Jeremiah 21–36*, 470–71).

57. It is possible that the context of Exod 34 plays even more of a role in these Jeremian passages. I suggest considering the narrative of the reinstitution of the covenant relationship with the people (Exod 34:10–16), a subject that is at the core of Jer 31:31–34.

58. Jer 12:14–17 is one of the more controversial passages in the book. Jer 12:15–17 portrays a universal restoration of God's "bad neighbors" of different lands and religious affiliations, along with the recognition of Judean groups of deportees settled in the surrounding territories. It is thus remarkable that the language of mercy and

Thus said the Lord:
I will restore the fortunes of Jacob's tents,
And [I will] have compassion upon his dwell-
ings. (30:18)

כה אמר יהוה
הנני־שב שבות אהלי יעקוב
ומשכנתיו ארחם.

Indeed, I will restore their fortunes and take
them back, <u>and I will have compassion upon
them.</u> (33:26)[59]

כי־אשוב (ק: אשיב) את־
שבותם ורחמתים.

<u>I will dispose him to be merciful to you: he
shall show you mercy</u> and bring you back to
your own land. (42:12)[60]

ואתן לכם רחמים ורחם
אתכם והשיב אתכם
אל־אדמתכם.

Once again, two components of deliverance, שב שבות and רחם, unite
those different prophetic passages, recalling the Deuteronomic promise
in Deut 30:3: ושב יהוה אלהיך את שבותך ורחמך ושב וקבצך מכל העמים
אשר הפיצך יהוה אלהיך שמה ("Then the Lord your God will restore your
fortunes and take you back in love. He will bring you together again from
all the peoples where the Lord your God has scattered you").[61] In line
with the Deuteronomic perspective, these prophecies in Jeremiah consider
mercy to be an active part only of future deliverance.

---

restoration (especially with the notion of inheritance) is applied, even in relation to
these presumed outsiders. See Holladay (*Jeremiah*, 1.390–92), who suggests that the
passage is authentic but is composed in two stages, 12:14 following the 598 defeat and
12:15–17 as a proclamation to the exiles in Babylon around 594. McKane, on the contrary (*Jeremiah 1–25*, 279–84, esp. 283), considers this passage to be "a late, artificial
prophetic composition (vv. 14–15)" with even later additions (12:16–17) addressed to
the "post-exilic Jerusalem community" (284).

59. NJPS translates ורחמתים as an adverb: "in love"; my translation reflects more
clearly the first-person verbal form.

60. Jer 42:10–12 is unique because it directs God's benevolence (through the actions
of the Babylonian king) to the remnant of Judah (as opposed to the exiles). This promise of restoration is founded on their obedience to God's command to remain in the
land. In the phrase ניחם אל־הרעה (42:10; see similar uses in 18:8, 10; 26:3, 13, 19; and
compare passages where ניחם is cast in the negative: 4:28; 15:6; 20:16), the exercise of
divine mercy is not just a future possibility, but may (at least, theoretically) be active
in the present; in this case the phrase signifies the possibility that God will relent, will
step back from his original plan of punishment, conditional (again) on the people's
obedience. See Rom-Shiloni, *Exclusive Inclusivity*, 198–252, esp. 228–33.

61. These same two components repeat also in Ezek 39:25.

Taken together, סלח and ריחם in Jeremiah illustrate how the attribute of mercy continues to function in its traditional (almost clichéd) conventional forms, in constructing prophecies of future deliverance. The prophet or his tradents draw on earlier traditions and promises concerning divine benevolence, to set the parameters for his (or their) contemporary message of future restoration.

12.4. SUMMARY

For the most part, sixth-century prophets and poets draw on the attribute of divine mercy (מידת הרחמים) only in order to highlight the intensity of the exercise of divine judgment (מידת הדין). With the exception of Ps 103, the communal laments in Psalms and Lamentations, as well as Jeremiah and Ezekiel, share the notion that the destruction and the exiles illustrate such an intense stance of divine judgment, that not even a small amount of divine benevolence and mercy may be found to mitigate the present catastrophe.

Mapping this diversity of painful reactions to the trilemma of theodicy, the distinctions between justification and protest present the same pattern as seen in the roles of God as warrior (see §9.4). Communal laments use conventional, even clichéd, proclamations of eternal divine care and mercy, and these serve to justify God's delayed, or rather apparently nonexistent, response to contemporary suffering. As Ps 103 shows, justification of God requires strenuous efforts to subdue voices of doubt and protest as completely as possible on the one hand and to repeat, emphasize, and even exaggerate proclamations of eternal mercy in a variety of guises on the other. But more prevalent is the use of expressions of mercy, especially cast in negative terms, to present fierce protests against the God who did not spare his people, as seen in relation to Lam 2 and Lam 3.

Jeremiah and Ezekiel show a very different strategy in their efforts to justify God in the face of his lack of mercy. They completely avoid alluding to this quality of God when it comes to presenting the disastrous events. Accordingly, judgment prophecies in both Jeremiah and Ezekiel emphasize the absence of any current of divine mercy in contemporary events; this emphasis goes along with the presentation of God as a fully active, all-powerful agent in causing the distress. This pole of the trilemma of theodicy—acknowledgment of God's goodness and compassion—is thus entirely left out of consideration by both Jeremiah and Ezekiel.

Beyond this important shared point of reference, there are clear differences between Jeremiah and Ezekiel in the ways in which they struggle with the need to justify the lack of divine mercy. Ezekiel gives barely any room to this quality of God in either judgment or consolation prophecies, and he emphasizes the suppression of this divine quality in God's actions against Jerusalem. Furthermore, mercy is completely absent from Ezekiel's picture of the future (with the exception of 39:25); and the human experience of this aspect of God may belong only with the past (20:17).

Jeremiah shows a much more complicated struggle with the concept of divine mercy. Side by side with the notion of a lack of mercy in the present, which characterizes the judgment prophecies in the book, conventional traditions of divine mercy do sporadically occur; they are explicitly used in prophecies of future consolation. Thus, the prophet and his followers/ tradents use chronological distinctions to map God's exercise of mercy onto the past and the future, leaving the present devoid of divine mercy.

13

Summary and Conclusions

This book explores selected Hebrew Bible sources that come directly out of and offer theological reflections on the sixth-century crises under the subjugation of the Neo-Babylonian Empire. Presumed to have been composed either during the dramatic decades of deportation and destruction or shortly thereafter (i.e., up to the early Persian period), these Hebrew Bible compositions allow us to collect, categorize, and then describe the diverse theological perspectives on the crisis, stemming from both Judah and the Babylonian diaspora. The multifaceted and at times multilayered interplay of voices reflects the many roles God is understood to have played, either by actively causing and bringing on the distress or by passively allowing it, through not defending his people.

The diverse threads explored here draw a broad map of the theological perspectives found among the sixth-century sources. The theodical discourse that emerges from this collection of sources shows the interrelationships between the perspectives of justification of, doubt concerning, and protest against God's perceived roles in the disaster. A descriptive Hebrew Bible theology must, therefore, present a literarily and historically focused, rather than faith-driven, portrait of Hebrew Bible religious thought.

13.1. Descriptive Hebrew Bible Theology: Concluding Observations

The motivation for this experiment and great challenge—the project of writing a descriptive Hebrew Bible theology—came from the recognition that traditional Hebrew Bible theologies, Christian or Jewish, are generally driven by concerns and frameworks external to the Hebrew Bible texts themselves. While the resulting Christian theology and Jewish philosophy may be serviceable for the person of faith, it oftentimes does not represent the historical and theological contexts with which Hebrew Bible texts grapple.

The notion of a *descriptive* theology is aimed, first and foremost, at trying to let the sources speak for themselves, that is, by using the tools of philological, historical, literary, and redaction criticism to tease out the theological concerns implied in specific passages, by particular speakers, using particular expressions. Not surprisingly, the result of such explorations is the articulation of a range of diverse theological perspectives, as diverse as the speakers (and the authors) themselves in both synchronic and diachronic dimensions. The phenomenology of the theological deliberation—the different topics and the diverse perspectives upon them—is set at the core of this investigation.

This descriptive and phenomenological investigation oftentimes challenges the long-accepted diachronic distinctions between literary layers within biblical compositions, most often in reference to the prophetic literature. Extending the discussion to a wide spectrum of literary compositions (historiography, prophecy, and psalmodic literature) opened my eyes to the synchronic interrelations between them. Each theological conception seems to appear in texts that scholars date as either preexilic or exilic/postexilic.[1] The reconstruction of the theological map thus suggests a much more synchronic or contemporaneous period of deliberation that stretches over the early sixth century, that is, the Neo-Babylonian period down to the early Persian era, thus through the first two or three generations facing the destruction, the exiles, and their aftermath. Although I am interested in establishing more refined nuances of difference within this time frame, the Hebrew Bible texts examined usually do not lend themselves to such distinctions.

Almost, by definition, then, the goal of such a descriptive theology cannot be synthetic, that is, the writing of a comprehensive theology of the Hebrew Bible in its entirety. On the contrary, I chose to focus on one fairly limited period of time and only on those sources that directly address the political crises of the Babylonian destruction of Judah, arguing that they participate in a theological enterprise that addresses that specific historical situation. In methodological terms this descriptive enterprise may, however, be fruitfully brought to bear on quite different subcorpora among the literature of the Hebrew Bible.

---

1. This could be argued in relation to the portrayals of God as warrior and for the (C') conception of war, which both von Rad and Seeligmann consider to be late; and similarly for the idea of individual and immediate retribution within the description of God as judge, suggested to be Ezekiel's innovation.

13.2. THE THEOLOGICAL MAP: SHARED CONCEPTIONS AND POLEMICS OVER THE ROLES OF GOD AS KING

The leading descriptive questions of this monograph are: What did the ancient voices/authors say about their God? How did they define God's roles in the crisis? How did they perceive their own share in the events? Through seeking the answers to these descriptive questions, I have identified both the formative theological conception of God as king and the theological framework of theodicy as discourse as inherent in the material. These two conceptual matrices thus serve to articulate the theological deliberations and to track transformations and polemics in the different statements.

The metaphor of God as king and the conceptions that shape that metaphor demonstrate the inherited, shared conceptual framework and linguistic universe used by all biblical speakers in their portrayal of God. This metaphor and its related conceptions form the scaffolding for a hierarchy of themes, identifiable by (rare) occurrences of the root מלך in relation to God, by symbols of sovereignty, and most frequently by descriptions of God's roles. This last technique is used by poets, prophets, and historiographers alike. This study has shown the extent to which the prophetic books of Jeremiah and Ezekiel make use of this anthropomorphic metaphor in all of its facets—using physical imagery, mental qualities, and human roles and customs of life and deeds to characterize and describe God's actions—serves to emphasize God's strength, his exercise of justice, and his sovereignty over his people, even in the present crisis with temple and city in ruins, with the people defeated and dislocated. Accordingly, the theological description was constructed by following the portrayals of God as warrior, judge, and (combining those roles) lord of the covenant.

In addition, this shared conception of God as king was set within a theological framework comprised of three distinct theological approaches recorded in varying tones in the various sources: justification, doubt, and protest. These three theological approaches to God's actions in terms of both forms and themes—and the interaction between the three approaches to the theodical discourse—were illustrated by mapping these approaches onto the trilemma of theodicy as described by Ronald Green.

The identification of the diverse voices participating in this theological discourse suggested an additional descriptive question: How does each statement about God differ from the others? Thus, the dynamic of theological pluralism is a genuine characteristic of Hebrew Bible theology.

One of the most remarkable common threads that runs through the examined sources is the constant tension between the perceived actions of God as king, in his specific roles as warrior and judge, and the human share in the catastrophe. Human responsibility in turn is variously assigned to human enemies or to the people of Judah themselves. The entire theological map is structured by way of this tension between divine and human roles or responsibility.

13.2.1. *God as Warrior in the Destruction and Exiles*

God's role as lord of universal and national history, on the one hand, and the actions of human enemy forces that fought against the people of God, on the other, serve as building blocks for the biblical portrayals of divine and human roles in the political and military defeat. Theological reflections on the defeat can be described as mirror images of three biblical conceptions of divine and human roles in events of victory in war, as set out by Gerhard von Rad and Isaac Seeligmann (see §6.2):

> (A)　*The victorious human agent acts alone (rare).*
> (B)　*God summons and assists the human agent.*
> (C)　*God fights alone (without human assistance)*
> 　　　*for his people.*

In descriptions of defeat, the biblical authors invert these traditional conceptions:

> (A′)　*The human agent (the enemy) acts alone.*
> (B′)　*God summons the enemy against his people.*
> (C′)　*God himself fights (alone) against his people.*

The traditional framework for thinking about God's roles in the context of national distress naturally brings together two of these conceptions:

> (A′ → C)　*If God is by definition the people's king and sav-*
> 　　　　*ior, the human enemy must be acting on his own*
> 　　　　*initiative; conversely, God can be expected to act*
> 　　　　*singlehandedly to save his people.*

The contrast between these outlooks is explicitly brought to the fore in the conflict between Zedekiah's officials and Jeremiah (Jer 21:1–7). The officials ask Jeremiah to call upon God to save his people from the Babylonian threat—the (A′ → C) conception. The prophet, in response, suggests a different theological perspective: God himself is bringing about the crisis. Jeremiah minimizes the role of the human tyrant, proclaiming fiercely that *God*, not Babylon, is the ultimate foe of Jerusalem. God's omnipotence and omniscience, which *saved* his people in the past, are now turned against them—the (C') conception. But this extreme portrayal of the role of God as *the* true and sole enemy fuels protest in its turn (e.g., Lam 2).

Chapters 6–9 developed this complex picture in detail (see §9.4). The governing conceptions (B') and (C') function in the words of prophets to justify God as the powerful warrior and king of his people; God himself brings about the crisis, *either* by means of his agent, the king of Babylon, or singlehandedly through his own arsenal; the (B') conception serves a similar function in the historiographers' reports in 2 Kings. That is, these disastrous events do not show that God loses his omnipotence, but rather precisely show that God, and God alone, orchestrates these events, with the intent to destroy and thereby chastise his temple, city, and people. But the prophets' contemporaries—poets, officials, and anonymous speakers quoted by the prophets—draw on these same theological explanations to express their own doubts about God (e.g., Jer 8:19–20) or even to protest against God's lack of assistance, suggesting that the crisis events call into question both God's presence and his ability to save (e.g., Jer 14:7–9; Pss 74; 77:8–10). The (B') conception is most frequently drawn on by all sides of the argument, either to justify God (as in the historiography of 2 Kings and in both Jeremiah and Ezekiel) or to protest against his current handling of his people (as in Ps 44:10–17). Even so, the traditional (A' → C) conception continues to operate as the basic theological assumption of many groups in addition to Zedekiah's officials—including some poets (Ps 79:1–4) and most importantly the peace prophets, who continue to hold out a confident promise of divine salvation even within the critical years of decline (Jer 28:2–4).

This broad mapping of sixth-century theological reflection allows us to recognize the conceptions shared by all these contemporary speakers.

1. Apart from one anonymous statement of denial (Jer 5:12–13), all share the conviction that God is involved in the atrocities that his people experienced during the first quarter of the sixth century. These same voices quite profoundly disagree, however, on the nature of the role played by God in these events.
2. All voices take for granted the portrayal of God as king and warrior; both prophets and poets use this anthropomorphic metaphor to the utmost possible ends of the spectrum.

3. None of the speaking voices are really ready to give up the theological premise that God is committed to saving his people. The polemic between them concerns when this salvation is to occur, not the theological principle itself. Even Jeremiah and Ezekiel believe in this commitment, but they understand that it will be realized only in the future; thus, it forms a feature of their consolation prophecies. For the contemporary present, the two prophets independently portray God as the wrathful and powerful enemy of his own people.

The major distinction between these various speakers is the individual place they each occupy along the broad spectrum of the theodical discourse.

13.2.2. The Role of God as Judge and the Exercise of Divine Justice

The metaphorical arena of God as king features additional shared conceptions:

1. God is portrayed as judge by all voices alike (historiographers, prophets, poets, officials, and laypeople).
2. All speakers take for granted the idea that God acts (or should act) according to categories of justice, informed by a principle of retribution (i.e., of clear connections between [mis]deeds and retaliation); thus, the political-military events are taken as divine judgments in retaliation for Jerusalem's and Judah's sins against God, mostly sins of religious disobedience.
3. The conceptual frameworks used by the different speakers combine four distinct notions of retribution: immediate (i.e., close in time to the target transgression), transgenerational (i.e., deferred to the future and cumulative), individual, and communal. While there is a tendency to present these four components as two pairs of antonyms, their use in our sources shows more fluid and complex uses of these components, in a variety of combinations.
4. All speakers are aware of all four components, and by the early sixth century they are used synchronically by all; that is, historiographers, prophets, and poets use these contradictory pairs (immediate and transgenerational retribution; individual and communal retribution) according to the needs of their own messages. An important corollary of this observation is the recognition that Ezekiel is not the exclusive

initiator of either the notion of individual retribution or of immediate retribution.

5. All speakers seem to be cognizant of the divine epithet פֹּקֵד עֲוֹן אָבוֹת עַל־בָּנִים ("visiting the guilt of the parents upon the children"). This epithet stands in the background of efforts to frame the destruction and exiles in terms of God's justice and divine retribution: the biblical speakers either accept or struggle against it, particularly in trying to articulate the degree of responsibility of the destruction generation for its own fate.

Notwithstanding these shared premises, disagreements and at times explicit polemics arise in connection with three main topics: (a) divine justice, with specific attention to the severity of the disaster as punishment, in relation to the severity of the people's sins; (b) the question of timing and the extent of the current generation's responsibility for their fate; and (c) the question of whether the measure of divine mercy is at all in action during that distressing period. These questions are met by diverse expressions of justification, doubt, and protest that together constitute the theodical discourse.

(a) The Nature of Divine Justice. All the sources wrestle with the question of *how* divine justice may be seen to operate in this crisis. (1) The historiographers combine transgenerational and communal retribution conceptions (e.g., 2 Kgs 24:20) with a repeated focus on the proximity of events that relates the kings' religious-cultic sins of disobedience to an immediate judgment—the political-military distress inflicted upon both the kings and the nation. This construction thus draws on the components of immediate and communal retribution (2 Kgs 23:36–24:4; 24:8–17; 24:18–25:2). (2) In even sharper fashion, the prophets accentuate the congruence between sins and retaliation, to the extent that divine retaliation is often presented as a matter of measure for measure (Jer 5:19; Ezek 7:27). However, (3) only a small number of passages express acknowledgment of the people's guilt through confessions of sins—a few quotations in Jeremiah, four of the seventeen communal laments in Psalms, and only thirteen verses in Lam 1, 3, and 5. These mostly very formulaic constructions (Jer 8:14; 14:7; Ezek 33:10; Ps 79:8–9; Lam 1:8) may be taken as implying acquaintance with conventional modes of prayer. (4) Some quotations in Jeremiah express yet another perspective, proclaiming the people's innocence (2:35; 3:4–5). Jeremiah intends these quotations to illustrate the people's sins, as may be seen in his easy dismissals of such claims (5:19; 9:11; 13:22; 16:10); or as a

testimony to the grave disaster, put in the mouth of foreigners passing by the ruined city (22:8). (5) The communal laments testify, however, that such claims are real contemporary arguments raised in confronting the disaster and in its aftermath (Pss 44:18–23; 80:19).

Hence, taken together, these examples indicate that the issue of divine justice is *the* epicenter of controversy. Although the historiographers' and the prophets' voices are well represented, they are by no means the only participants in the lively polemics that characterize the theological deliberation over divine justice.

(b) The Question of Timing. Another acute theological challenge is represented by the question of why the catastrophe is visited upon this specific generation. This question centers upon the divine epithet פקד עון אבות על־בנים ("visiting the guilt of the parents upon the children"), which is given no less than five different interpretations. Three of these accept the notion of transgenerational retribution: (1) The prophets tend to present a transgenerational history of sin as uniting fathers and sons from the distant past to the present (Jer 2:4–9; 11:6–8; 32:30–31; Ezek 2:3–4). A similar recognition of a long and enduring period of sin appears in communal laments and in confessions of sins quoted in Jeremiah (Ps 79:8; Jer 3:24–25). (2) The exilic historiographers of 2 Kings focus more specifically, explaining that the destruction comes upon Zedekiah as retaliation for the sins of Manasseh, his predecessor of four generations earlier (2 Kgs 21:10–15; 23:26–27; 24:3; the same argument appears once in Jer 15:4). This explanation reads the divine epithet quite literally. (3) Very rarely, Jeremiah and Ezekiel explicitly accuse the destruction generation of sinning *beyond* their predecessors (Jer 7:25–26; 16:10–13; Ezek 2:3–4) and thus of bringing retribution for the history of sins crashing justifiably about their own heads.

Two other positions concerning retribution reject the transgenerational connection: (4) Both Ezekiel and Jeremiah assert in various contexts that the destruction and exiles constitute immediate and communal retribution against the generation that sinned (Ezek 14:12–23; 18:1–20; Jer 11:1–8; 17:19–27; 32:19; 34:8–22). A similar conception of immediate and communal retribution is regularly expressed by historiographers in Kings, where it is furthermore not seen to contradict the notion of an ongoing, transgenerational accumulation of sins (2 Kgs 24:19–25:2). Finally, this idea of immediate retribution is found in one quotation, Ezek 33:10, where it reflects the Babylonian exiles' great agony and despair. (5) In contexts of calls for a change (repentance), both Ezekiel and Jeremiah take the notion of immediacy to another level, shrinking the chronological gap between deed and retaliation even more by arguing that only the most recent deeds are counted in determining the fate of individuals as part of the entire generation (Ezek 18:21–32; 33:10–20; Jer 18:1–12; 32:19).

(c) The Attribute of Mercy. All speakers recognize the lack of divine mercy and benevolence during this devastating period (the only exception is Ps 103).[2] But this profound agreement functions quite differently for the different speakers. (1) Both Jeremiah and Ezekiel, who for the most part portray God as orchestrating the atrocities—the (B') and (C') conceptions of war—understand God's refusal to act with mercy as a component in their justifications of God's measures against Jerusalem and Judah. They both use negative expressions concerning the lack of compassion, to emphasize the grief (Jer 4:28; Ezek 8:18). But here they part ways: (2) Jeremiah retains stereotypical expressions of divine mercy (Jer 9:22–23; 32:18) and expects the reinstitution of divine mercy as part of his consolation prophecies (31:20; 33:10–11). (3) Ezekiel does not look forward to any reinstatement of divine mercy at any future point of consolation (20:33–34). The communal laments struggle in different ways with this issue. (4) Those of the (A' → C) approach plead with God to (re)activate his attribute of mercy; the poets express the wish that God awaken to act on his people's behalf (Ps 79:5–9). (5) In other contexts, the lack of mercy gives rise to doubt (77:10; 89:50) or to protest against God (44:18–27; Lam 2:2, 17, 21; 3:42–47).

13.2.3. Theological Implications:
Deliberations on the Role of God as Lord of His People

The dual portrayals of God as warrior and judge shed light upon a third and not less polemical arena of discourse: that is, the question of the overall relationship between God and his people in the face of (and following) the early sixth-century catastrophes. The role of God as sovereign in the covenant relationship with his people surely deserves independent discussion, but I content myself here with a summary of aspects of this important topic, for the sake of completing this mapping of sixth-century theological deliberations.[3]

Sixth-century writings exhibit both shared and divergent conceptions of the covenant relationship between God and his people. By the early

2. There is one exception to this general deliberation over the attribute of mercy; the historiographers of 2 Kgs 21–25 do not refer to this divine quality at all.

3. For general discussion, see Rom-Shiloni, *God in Times of Destruction*, 320–418. I discuss conceptions of the God-people covenant in Jeremiah in "Covenant in the Book of Jeremiah" and "On the Day" and the divine presence in Jeremiah in "Challenging the Notion." On covenant in Ezekiel, see my *Exclusive Inclusivity*, 139–85.

sixth century, three shared metaphoric systems are in use: the political metaphor on the one hand, and the marital and adoption metaphors on the other. The political metaphor portrays God as king and the people as his subjects, whereas family metaphors present God as father or husband. Each of these metaphoric worlds functions as a complete and independent system that includes five parameters: institution of the covenant, commitments of the two participating sides, parameters of violation of the covenant, judgment upon evildoers, and the possibility of ultimately either reinstituting or completely annulling the covenant relationship between God and his people.

An interesting distinction, however, cuts across the sources discussed in this study, in terms of portrayals of the covenant relationship. (1) Both historiographers and the two prophets use covenantal language as the main means of describing the relationship between God and his people, drawing on all three of these independent political and familial (marital and adoption) metaphoric frameworks.[4] Yet only a relatively small number of psalmodic and other nonprophetic sources (quotations) use covenant language from these metaphoric frameworks (Pss 44, 74, 80, 89, 106). (2) For the most part, poets avoid the language of covenant and portray the God-people relationship by describing two other aspects of divine action: presence and involvement.

The major difference between these two sets of reflections seems to be one of directionality. The use of covenant metaphors, political *or* familial, denotes a stance that focuses on the people's obligations toward God (and their lack of fulfillment in the past and/or present). The avoidance of covenant language in the quotations and most communal laments, on the contrary, denotes a concern with God's commitments to his people (and to individuals) in terms of presence and involvement and of divine care (and the perceived absence of such care in the present crisis).

(3) Quotations and communal laments either protest against God's seeming absence and lack of actual involvement or they raise doubts concerning God's presence and involvement (Jer 14:7–9). These two elements are taken for granted in traditional frameworks as the basis of hope for God's salvation of his people (8:19–20). In keeping with the anthropomor-

---

4. The historiographic perspective on the God-people relationship may only implicitly be inferred. Nevertheless, these sources appear to draw on the political metaphoric framework, repeating accusations of disobedience against God (as sovereign) by the kings (as his vassals, e.g., 2 Kgs 24:2–3, 19–20) and juxtaposing this disobedience with the political distress, thus portrayed as a divine judgment, first upon the kings themselves; cf. the second concept of transgenerational retribution.

phic metaphors, desertion and neglect are portrayed by verbal phrases with God as agent, such as נטש, עזב, and זנח (Pss 44:10, 24; 77:8; 89:39; Lam 1:9; 2:7; 5:20); by a lack in the activities of the senses of sight (quotations in Ezek 8:12; 9:9) or hearing (Pss 10:17; 80:2; 102:3); and/or by a seeming lack of divine sympathy (42:10–11; 43:1–2). Among the fiercest complaints (and petitions) are those that assert that God hid his face (הסתיר פניו in 10:11; 44:25; 102:3). Conceptually, this metaphor illustrates that although God is present, he purposefully closes his eyes, his ears, his mouth, and abstains from turning his face in favor. Thus, according to this complaint, God closes all those organs that would allow his favorable involvement in the events and in so doing brings disaster upon his people. This imagery, then, constitutes an antonym to divine involvement on behalf of an individual or the people. But it is dependent on the conception of presence, that is, God is clearly present when he chooses to hide his face and be uninvolved in his people's long-enduring agony.[5]

(4) Jeremiah and Ezekiel, separately and independently, refute such complaints, arguing that God is both present and involved in the catastrophic events. The prophets justify God by either accentuating his presence and sole involvement as the foe in the catastrophic events (Jer 21:5; Ezek 5:8–17) or by distinguishing between presence and involvement—that is, God may be present, but he may choose, nevertheless, *not* to be involved on behalf of his people but to deliver them into the hands of their human foes (Jer 21:10). Thus, the prophets cut the long-accepted ties between divine presence and salvation, arguing that during the destruction God is/was present in Jerusalem to execute the atrocities himself or to summon others to the annihilation of the city and its residents (Ezek 8–11 at 11:23).[6] According to Jeremiah, God is both present and omniscient (Jer 23:23–24). Not surprisingly, the phrase הסתר פנים occurs in only two prophecies of consolation (Jer 33:5; Ezek 39:23, 24, 29), as part of a prophetic promise that in the future, God will no longer hide his face.[7]

(5) In other consolation prophecies, both Jeremiah and Ezekiel empha-

---

5. For הסתר פנים in national contexts, see Deut 31:16–18; Isa 54:7–8; 57:17; 64:6–7; in individual laments, see Pss 13:2; 27:9; 143:7 (and note the request for God to hide his face from the psalmist's sins in 51:11). A related image of hiddenness that prevents favorable involvement is found in Lam 3:44 (see §12.2).

6. The perception of God's insistence on continuing to pursue his plan to destroy Jerusalem is precisely the basis of the protests within the communal laments, as, for instance, in Lam 2:8, 17.

7. Ezek 39:23–29 is tagged as inauthentic (Joyce, *Ezekiel*, 217–18). For the current discussion, this question is not crucial; while *not* from the prophet himself, this passage

size the transformation in this very aspect: God will again show his face, and thus his favor, to his people (Jer 51:5; Ezek 36:9; more elaborately in 34:17–31; also the non-Jeremian passage in Jer 24:6). All these promises of future salvation, then, indirectly witness to the perception on the part of both prophets (and their books) that during this period of destruction, although God is present, his care and favor are in abeyance.

From the standpoint of directionality, two issues capture the most attention in the theological deliberations. First is the question of who is ultimately responsible for the annulment of the covenant, the break that brought about the catastrophe—God or the people. Did God back away from his commitments as king? or did the people first default on their covenant obligations? Second is the issue of the present and the future status of these relationships—does the destruction symbolize the end of the God-people relationship? If the answer is, alas, positive, then can there be any future hope for the people? But if, however, the answer is negative, how can the relationship be reestablished? These two broad issues are addressed by the sources in various ways.

13.2.3.1. Who Is Responsible for the Annulment of the Covenant Relationship?

(1) From the prophets' point of view, the covenant is initiated by God and betrayed by the people (Jer 11:1–14; Ezek 16:1–43; 20:1–38). Thus, the justification of God's actions in the present circumstances (as in the discussion of God as judge) lays responsibility (or actual blame) for the distress on the people alone. However, (2) quotations in Jeremiah argue for an opposing perspective; that is, it is God who defaults on his covenantal commitments (8:19–22; 14:7–9, 19–22). This perspective, furthermore, is the source of doubt and protest in four communal laments that explicitly proclaim that God dissolves the covenant and/or should be reminded of his covenantal commitments (Pss 44:18–23; 74:20; 80:19; 89:39, 50). These psalms portray the people as obedient and persisting in their piety, trapped in an unexplainable distress that thus fuels their protest (also Jer 33:23–26).

As a further indicator of this aspect of directionality, one may follow the use of זנח, עזב, and נטש, the major verbal roots from the semantic field of desertion. Apart from minor semantic differences between them, the three verbs share the function of identifying which covenant partner initiates the

---

likely reflects close followers of the prophet later on within the sixth century (Joyce, *Ezekiel*, 217).

rupture by deserting the other—is it God or the people? זנח ("detest, reject") does not appear in either Jeremiah or Ezekiel, but it is fairly common in communal laments (Pss 42–43, 44, 74, 77, 89; Lam 2–3). Besides Lam 2:7, where it designates God's rejection of the temple, it expresses complaints against God for detesting the people (or the king in Ps 89:39), for distancing himself from the people (or the individual in 43:2), and therefore for acting as though he is not involved in their fate (44:10, 24; 74:1; 77:8).

נטש ("give something up") with God as agent occurs twice in Jeremiah, where it designates judgment inflicted upon the destruction generation (דור עברתו in parallel to מאס: "the brood that provoked His wrath," 7:29 NJPS) and desertion of the people to their fate in the hands of their enemies, in a parallelism of עזב and נטש: "I have abandoned My House [עזבתי את־ביתי], I have deserted My possession [נטשתי את־נחלתי], I have given over My dearly beloved into the hands of her enemies [נתתי את־ידדות נפשי בכף איביה]" (12:7); the phrasing brings together the themes of desertion, wrath, rejection, and even hatred (על־כן שנאתיה, 12:8).

נטש is also used by the prophet to accuse the people of "giving up" God (15:6; see Deut 32:15). But most significant in this group is עזב ("leave, abandon"), which is used with God as agent only six times in the Hebrew Bible. Four of these instances occur in quoted complaints against God, pertaining to the destruction and its aftermath. God is accused of abandoning his people (Lam 5:20), the land (Ezek 8:12; 9:9), and the city of Jerusalem in sources of the second half of the sixth century (Isa 49:14).[8]

Both Jeremiah and Ezekiel respond to such complaints (and protests). In Jeremiah, only two instances portray God as having left his people in hatred and anger (12:7; 25:38). Instead, Jeremiah primarily uses עזב with the people as agents; they are the ones who abandon God—that is their major sin (1:16; 2:13, 17; 5:7, 19; 9:12; 16:11 [2x]; 17:13 [2x]; 18:14; 19:4)—or leave his Torah (9:12) or his covenant (22:9). In Ezekiel's refutation of the quoted complaint (characterized as coming from Jerusalem, 8:12), the prophet describes God's exit (יצא or עלה מעל, 10:18; 11:23) from the city proper as a consequence of the people's sins, but then God stands on the mountain east of the city. Ezekiel seems to intentionally refrain from using עזב or otherwise conveying the idea of abandonment. According to Ezekiel, God is present and thus can monitor and certainly see the atrocities taking place in his temple and city.

---

8. These relatively rare complaints may be compared to the more common proclamations that emphasize that God did not leave his people (1 Kgs 6:13; Ps 94:14).

The events of destruction and dislocation underscore significant differences between the historiographers and prophets, on the one hand, and the poets and the anonymous voices quoted in the prophecies, on the other. Heterogeneous groups as they each are, all speakers seem cognizant of an idea of abandonment by God, but they configure this in different ways, with different consequences. They all use the same expressions of neglect and desertion to place the blame on either the people or on God; but both positions convey the realization that at that critical time of distress the covenant relationship came to a breaking point.

13.2.3.2. Does the Destruction Symbolize the End of the God-People Relationship?

Is there hope for a future reinstitution of this relationship? (1) These troubling questions seem to underlie the various petitions for immediate help; they appear to be motivated by the fear that the delay in divine assistance (or the persistence of suffering) signifies the end of God's commitment to his people: אל־תנחנו ("do not forsake us!," Jer 14:9), המאס מאסת את־יהודה אם־בציון געלה נפשך ("Have You, then, rejected Judah? Have You spurned Zion?," 14:19), זכר אל־תפר בריתך אתנו ("remember, do not annul Your covenant with us," 14:21), and the questions closing Lam 5 (5:20, 22).

The prophets distinguish between the catastrophic present and the future to articulate hopes for the reinstitution of the covenant relationship. The books of Jeremiah and Ezekiel exhibit significantly different perspectives on the future of the God-people covenant relationship, using the political and marital metaphors in distinctive ways. While according to both metaphorical frameworks, the people are responsible for their current distress, the metaphors part company in the ways they portray God's reactions to the people's behavior and thus in the ways that they suggest possibilities for restoration.

(2) Jeremiah uses the marital metaphor to portray God as the one who brought the covenant relationship with the people to an end. In his disputation speech (3:1–5; also 7:29; 12:7–8; see ידדות נפשי and שנאתיה), the prophet draws on Deuteronomic and Priestly legal traditions to present the termination of the relationship.[9] However, the prophet uses political metaphors to portray the future reinstitution of the covenant relationship.

9. See Rom-Shiloni, "Covenant in the Book of Jeremiah," 161–69. The five prophetic passages that follow Jer 3:1–5 in this chapter (3:6–11, 12–13, 14–18, 19–25; 4:1–2) each

Prophecies in Jeremiah are innovative in the ways they employ the two political formats, the covenant of grant and the treaty. The metaphor of the treaty has a great importance within Jeremiah's arguments of justification, both those of the prophet himself and those of the book as a whole. The prophecies maintain that throughout the current crisis of destruction and exiles, God's role is circumscribed to that of a sovereign who carries out punishment against his rebellious people. Yet, in both judgment prophecies and consolations, God in no respect withdraws from the covenant and thus retains his royal prerogative to reinstitute the covenant relationship in the future. The consolation prophecies (both those of the prophet and those of his followers and tradents) portray the enduring covenant using the pattern of the covenant of grant (31:35–37; 33:17–26), but they never give up the treaty format by which God obligates the people to obey him (31:31–34).

In contrast, (3) Ezekiel manipulates these metaphoric worlds to convey different attitudes toward the two Judahite communities. The Jehoiachin exiles, on the one hand, are the community with which God *will* reestablish his covenant (11:14–21; 20:1–38); on the other hand, those who remained in Jerusalem under Zedekiah are doomed to total annihilation, in accordance with "the punishment of women who commit adultery and murder" (16:1–43 at 16:38; also Ezek 23).[10] The political metaphor is used to build future hope for the Jehoiachin exiles, while the marital metaphor cancels any future hope for those who remained and portrays Jerusalem's total annihilation.[11]

Despite their very different national and community perspectives, the two prophets agree in principle on the way in which the two metaphors operate. Each of them (independently and differently) use the marriage metaphor to close off all future hopes for the reestablishment of the God-people relationship, representing either the people as a whole (Jeremiah) or Jerusalem and the remnant in Judah (Ezekiel) as an adulterous woman sentenced to death. In contrast, they each use the political metaphor to portray the future reinstitution of the (covenant) relationship, stemming from a divine initiative of future transformation.

Once these prophetic strategies concerning the covenant relationship

---

respond in different ways to this extreme prophetic proclamation; they may come from the prophet himself or some of his followers/tradents.

10. See Rom-Shiloni, *Exclusive Inclusivity*, 156–69.

11. This sociological differentiation leaves traces within the book of Jeremiah as well, yet only in non-Jeremian prophecies (Jer 24; 32:36–41). For the complete discussion, see Rom-Shiloni, "Prophecy for 'Everlasting Covenant'"; *Exclusive Inclusivity*, 220–52; and "Covenant in the Book of Jeremiah," 159–60.

are compared to those adopted by other sources of the sixth century, it becomes clear that both Jeremiah and Ezekiel intentionally avoid any mention of God's abandonment of the *political* covenant relationship (see §8.2). This principle governs their distinctive approaches to the state of the covenant relationship during the events of the destruction, characterized by their accusations that the people—not God—betray the covenant. The corollary that God's covenant commitment remains steadfast if presently in abeyance forms the basis for the perceived future in their prophecies of consolation, as so powerfully portrayed by Ezek 20:33–38.

13.2.4. Conclusions

This mapping of the theological world of thought allows for some sociological and theological observations. The very rich data indicate that the Hebrew Bible sources of the sixth century attest to a dynamic theological deliberation, both in Judah and in the Babylonian exile. This leads me to the following conclusions:

1. Agreements and disagreements between the diverse sources tell of a vast, lively, and at times polemical interaction. The theological perspectives on each divine role (God as warrior, judge, and lord of his people) suggest that the members of the diverse social-literary circles active within the Judean societies of the sixth century (but prior to 538) share a set of inherited theological imagery and conceptions, which are a subject of debate between them. Overall, we may discern closer agreements between prophets and historiographers, on the one hand, than between prophets and poetic laments, on the other. Furthermore, while there is a clear diversity within poetic compositions (communal laments), there are many correspondences between the quotations of laypeople in the prophetic books and these poetic laments.[12] The interplay between shared themes or questions—and divergent answers—points to both explicit and implicit connections between the different literary-authorial circles behind these sources.[13]

12. See also §8.1, which notes theological correspondences between the historiographers of the last chapters of 2 Kings (Dtr2, the exilic Deuteronomistic source) and the two prophetic books and traces specific thematic similarities that tie them together.

13. This observation has far-reaching implications, as it contradicts the scholarly assumption of the isolation of various circles in preexilic (or postexilic) Jerusalem (or Babylon). One major arena for which this observation is relevant is the discussion of the

2. The three main portrayals of God—as warrior in the destruction, as judge, and as lord of his people—are derived from the imagery used by the Hebrew Bible to describe God's roles in these critical events. All the authorial circles reflected in the sixth-century sources that are discussed in this book agree on two points of departure: (a) the foundational anthropomorphic imagery and conception of God as king and (b) the genuine urge to find a theological explanation for the defeat, destruction, and subsequent dislocation. They thus share a passion to justify God's actions in the events, although not all parties are able to arrive at that goal. Their theological deliberations together construct the theodical discourse.

3. The ideological and theological basis of the proclamations of doubt and protest that characterize quotations in the prophetic books and the lament literature is well contextualized in relation to established, predestruction Judahite religious conceptions:

   a. The role of God as warrior, and particularly God's role as savior of his people in times of need—the (A' → C) conception of war—is a foreground conception within the Deuteronomistic History, psalmodic literature, and prophecy. This conception is intertwined with conceptions of the theology of Zion, that is, the idea that the inviolability of Jerusalem is guaranteed by the presence of God and secured by his temple (quoted and refuted in Jer 7:4; see also the Zion psalms [Pss 46, 48] and the prophecies of Isaiah son of Amoz in Isa 8:18; 37:35).

   b. The idea of God as the just judge, executing justice tempered with mercy, is likewise well known from different Hebrew Bible compositions.

   c. The contemporary sixth-century discussion of the responsibility of the destruction generation for their fate revolves around the divine epithets taken from the Decalogue, particularly the concept that divine retribution is transgenerational, directed against the descendants of sinners (as well as against the sinners themselves). This conceptual basis is shared alike by historiographers, prophets, poets, and laypeople. Protests against the perceived workings

---

presumed isolation of the authorial circles responsible for the pentateuchal literature. I find this entire assumption completely unsound. Compare the isolation (or near isolation) advocated by neo-documentarian descriptions, such as that of Baden, *J, E, and the Redaction of the Pentateuch*, 255–86, esp. 258–60. See Rom-Shiloni, "Introduction: Rethinking the Relationship," 836–39.

of divine justice in the framework of the disaster (Ezek 18:2, 19; implicitly in Ps 44:18–23) are based on this shared concept of retribution.

d. The concept of covenant continues to undergird the proclamations of Jeremiah and Ezekiel. Covenant concepts also underlie some protests, which accuse God of rejecting his own covenant with his people; one such protest (Jer 14:19–22) uses the covenant formulas of the Holiness Legislation (Lev 26).

4. Both the prophets and their dialogue partners allude to specific pentateuchal traditions to shape or to authorize their arguments. The despair that captures the elders of Israel (e.g., Ezek 20:32) is based on the Deuteronomic conception of exile (Deut 4:25–28). The prophet's response (Ezek 20:5–38) draws explicitly on the language of the exodus traditions to counter their despair and articulate hope for redemption.

This list, of course, is not exhaustive, and yet it suffices to establish that *not only* the prophets, but a substantial group of other speakers, rely on, allude to, struggle with, and at times reverse pentateuchal traditions. These same nonprophetic speakers may be seen to struggle with earlier (and contemporary) prophetic formulations, wisdom conventions, and established poetic formulas. The evidence of our sources indicates a broad-based knowledge of the national cultural Judahite heritage and religion that clearly goes beyond the boundaries of what have usually been considered the intellectual, social, and literary elites of ancient Israel. This realization leads to the reconception of the sixth-century theological debate as taking place among diverse, well-informed partners whose stances are based on respectable understandings of the inherited religious tradition.

These observations also furnish some answers to questions posed in §3.1 concerning the internal relationships and interconnections between different social and literary circles in the early sixth century. In their use of traditional conceptions of God, including their arguments of justification, the prophetic voices show obvious similarities to the Deuteronomistic historiographers. Therefore, counter to Rainer Albertz's perspective, the prophets should not be seen as belonging to anti-establishment groups, placing themselves in opposition to "nationalist religious circles" or to "official Yahwistic religion." The wide spectrum of theological perspectives studied here shows that the two prophetic books (as these comprise the work of the prophets and their immediate followers and later tradents) represent mainstream and thus official Yahwistic-Judahite religious voices of the era. Neither should the nonprophetic voices reflected in quotations or in psalmodic literature be seen as representing popular, peripheral, or spiritually insensitive positions of arrogance or hubris that would have offended mainstream representatives of Israelite/Judahite religious thought (counter James Crenshaw and Walter Brueggemann).

The theological study of those diverse perspectives demonstrates that there are no real grounds to draw hierarchical distinctions between popular perceptions and more developed or refined prophetic conceptions, nor is there evidence for a dichotomy between pious and heretical expressions of belief (counter Abraham Kuenen). All the examined biblical speakers draw on a store of shared religious traditions; they all speak from stances of piety toward YHWH, their God, and show similar theological sophistication. Beyond the explicit and implicit polemics, many points of agreement sharpen the disputations still further, at times to the point of life-and-death struggles. The prophetic literature, by virtue of its literary character, quotes other positions and responds to them by reformulating the religious thought to comprehend the ever-new theological challenges. But once we locate the prophetic proclamations along the wider spectrum suggested here, we are able to see the theological disputations as more of a polemical interchange within a single, shared theological thought-world or a deliberation among equals.

13.3. Interrelationships within the Elements of Theodical Discourse: Justification, Doubt, and Protest

Theodicy is the theological framework within which the sixth-century theological deliberation on the crisis of the destruction takes place. Although both Christian and Jewish scholarship distinguishes between theodicy and protest, the Hebrew Bible evidence calls for a rethinking of these nonbiblical categories and their interaction. The framework of theodicy includes God's activity, not only in his role as a just judge, but also in his other roles.[14] The sixth-century sources indicate that theodicy and protest were not mutually exclusive modes of theological engagement. Rather, protest and doubt occur along with arguments of justification as essential elements of the ongoing ne-

14. I thus concur with Crenshaw ("Theodicy," 444; "Introduction") that theodicy is not restricted to God's role as a just judge; see §1.1.1 and §1.3.

gotiation, in the words of diverse sixth-century social/authorial groups. Each group supplies theological explanations for the disaster that can reconcile current circumstances with traditional perceptions of God as lord of history, warrior-sovereign, just judge, and compassionate and benevolent deity.

The broadly inclusive framework of theodical discourse proves to be a rubric that can incorporate the different theological perspectives discerned in chapters 6–12. Throughout the discussions of God's roles as warrior and as judge, as well as the shared theological perceptions (of covenant, divine retribution, etc.) undergirding those roles, Green's definition of the trilemma of theodicy emerges as a valuable tool by which to recognize points of congruence and difference between the participants in the theodical discourse revealed by the Hebrew Bible texts.

These three types of theological engagement—justification, doubt, and protest—arise from the same basic point of departure; that is, they are motivated by a desire to justify God. Poets, like prophets, make sincere efforts to find explanations for the current distress that will preserve traditional conceptions of divine omnipotence and divine justice. Yet, doubt and protest enter the picture when these authors realize that, as the crisis continues and worsens (without relief in sight), the trilemma of theodicy cannot be resolved. Because of their piety, these authors refuse to give up any of God's qualities. Against the reality of their continuous distress, protest and doubt convey the conviction that God should be depended upon to awaken and act from benevolence. Justification, on the other hand, is built upon the understanding that in the face of the distress, only two of the poles of the trilemma may stand up to theological reflection and that one of the poles needs to be given up.

Beyond giving up one of the poles of the trilemma of theodicy, these texts use two additional techniques of justification. The most common justificatory solution is to lay heavy responsibility upon the people: their own sins cause God to execute a fitting judgment upon them. The second strategy plots God's deeds as warrior, judge, and sovereign along a chronological axis. In justifying God, both prophets and poets move between God's past deeds of salvation and prospects for future deliverance. The catastrophic present, however, is left without explanation or prospect of immediate deliverance, even by the prophets.

By way of an answer to my initial questions—What did *ancient authors* say about *their* God? How did *they* define God's roles in the crisis? How did *they* perceive their own share in the events?—I offer the following overall observation. The explicit and implicit theological deliberations in the face of Judah's destruction seem to reveal that historiographers, prophets (and their followers and tradents), poets, and laypeople, shared the conceptions of God as king, warrior, judge, and sovereign. Their piety brings each and every one of them to an inner theological struggle, in which they anxiously search for ways to justify God in a period when the historical reality of distress threatens to uproot all of their long-accepted religious concepts.

Justification of God in those times of distress is a great challenge to all, a costly challenge in theological terms. In order to cope with the distressful present, all speakers choose between giving up one of God's attributes, putting the blame for the disaster on the people, or clinging to either past national memories or future hopes. The voices of protest seem unable to accept any of these solutions and thus are not able to justify God, but are left in a theological turmoil of doubt and protest.

If we read with care and empathy these diverse reflections on the distress—reflections involving justification, doubt, and protest—we may recognize that all of these sixth-century speakers are struggling with the trilemma of theodicy. We are left with the clues to their often desperate search for a theological resolution to the seemingly unresolvable contradiction between the incomprehensible reality of suffering and the two fundamental conceptions of God as good and benevolent *and* as lord of history, omnipotent and omniscient.

Aaron, David H. *Biblical Ambiguities: Metaphor, Semantics, and Divine Imagery.* Leiden: Brill, 2002.

Ackroyd, Peter R. *Exile and Restoration: A Study of Hebrew Thought of the Sixth Century B.C.* Philadelphia: Westminster, 1972.

Ahituv, Shmuel. *Echoes from the Past: Hebrew and Cognate Inscriptions from the Biblical Period.* Jerusalem: Carta, 2008.

———. *Ha-Ketav VeHa-Miktav: Handbook of Ancient Inscriptions from the Land of Israel and the Kingdoms beyond the Jordan.* 2nd ed. Biblical Encyclopedia Library 21. Jerusalem: Bialik, 2012 (Hebrew).

Albertz, Rainer. *A History of Israelite Religion in the Old Testament Period.* Translated by J. Bowden. 2 vols. Old Testament Library. Louisville: Westminster John Knox, 1994.

———. "In Search of the Deuteronomist: A First Solution to a Historical Riddle." Pages 1–17 in *The Future of the Deuteronomistic History.* Edited by T. Römer. Leuven: Leuven University Press, 2000.

———. *Israel in Exile: The History and Literature of the Sixth Century B.C.E.* Translated by D. E. Green. Studies in Biblical Literature 3. Atlanta: Society of Biblical Literature, 2004.

Albrektson, Bertil. *History and the Gods: An Essay on the Idea of Historical Events as Divine Manifestations in the Ancient Near East and in Israel.* Lund: Gleerup, 1967.

———. *Studies in the Text and Theology of the Book of Lamentations.* Studia Theologica Lundensia 21. Lund: Gleerup, 1963.

Allen, Leslie C. *Ezekiel 20–48.* Word Biblical Commentary 29. Waco: Word, 1990.

———. *Psalms 101–150.* Word Biblical Commentary 21. Waco: Word, 1983.

Alt, Albrecht. "Gedanken über das Königtum Jahwes." Pages 345–57 in volume 1 of *Kleine Schriften zur Geschichte des Volkes Israel.* Munich: Beck, 1953.

Anderson, Bernhard W. "Response to Mattityahu Tsevat 'Theology of the Old Testament—A Jewish View.'" *Horizons in Biblical Theology* 8 (1986): 51–59.

Anderson, Gary A. *Sin: A History*. New Haven: Yale University Press, 2009.

Andre, Gunnel. *Determining the Destiny: PQD in the Old Testament*. Oudtestamentische Studiën 16. Lund: Gleerup, 1980.

Aster, Shawn Z. *The Unbeatable Light: Melammu and Its Biblical Parallels*. Alter Orient und Altes Testament 384. Münster: Ugarit-Verlag, 2012.

Avioz, Michael. "The Historical Setting of Jeremiah 21:1–10." *Andrews University Seminary Studies* 44 (2006): 213–19.

Avishur, Isaac. "Patterns of Double and Triple Interrogative Clauses in the Bible and Ugaritic and Their Divergences." Pages 421–64 in *Zer Li-Gevurot: The Zalman Shazar Jubilee Volume: A Collection of Studies in Bible, Eretz Yisrael, Hebrew Language, and Talmudic Literature*. Edited by B. Z. Luria. Jerusalem: Kiryat Sefer, 1973 (Hebrew).

Bach, Robert. *Die Aufforderungen zur Flucht und zum Kampf im Alttestamentlichen Prophetenspruch*. Neukirchen-Vluyn: Neukirchener Verlag, 1962.

Baden, Joel S. *J, E, and the Redaction of the Pentateuch*. Tübingen: Mohr Siebeck, 2009.

Balentine, Samuel E. *Prayer in the Hebrew Bible: The Drama of Divine-Human Dialogue*. Overtures to Biblical Theology. Minneapolis: Fortress, 1993.

———. "Prayers for Justice in the Old Testament: Theodicy and Theology." *Catholic Biblical Quarterly* 51 (1989): 597–616.

———. "Traumatizing Job." *Review and Expositor* 105 (2008): 213–28.

Banith, Menahem. *Le Glossaire de Bale*. Jerusalem: Académie Nationale des Sciences et des Lettres d'Israël, 1972.

Barr, James. *The Concept of Biblical Theology: An Old Testament Perspective*. Minneapolis: Fortress, 1999.

———. "The Synchronic, the Diachronic, and the Historical: A Triangular Relationship?" Pages 1–14 in *Synchronic or Diachronic? A Debate on Method in Old Testament Exegesis*. Edited by J. de Moor. Old Testament Studies 34. Leiden: Brill, 1995.

———. "The Theological Case against Biblical Theology." Pages 3–19 in *Canon, Theology, and Old Testament Interpretation: Essays in Honor of B. S. Childs*. Edited by G. M. Tucker et al. Philadelphia: Fortress, 1988.

———. "Theophany and Anthropomorphism in the Old Testament." Pages 31–38 in *Congress Volume: Oxford*. Edited by G. R. Driver. Vetus Testamentum Supplement 7. Leiden: Brill, 1960.

————. "Why? in Biblical Hebrew." *Journal of Theological Studies* 36 (1985): 1–33.

Barrett, Justin L., and Frank C. Keil. "Conceptualizing a Nonnatural Entity: Anthropomorphism in God Concepts." *Cognitive Psychology* 31 (1996): 219–47.

Barstad, Hans M. *The Myth of the Empty Land: A Study in the History and Archaeology of Judah during the "Exilic" Period*. Symbolae Osloenses Supplement 28. Oslo: Scandinavian University Press, 1996.

Batto, Bernard F. "The Sleeping God: An Ancient Near Eastern Motif of Divine Sovereignty." *Biblica* 68 (1987): 153–77.

Bautch, Richard. *Developments in Genre between Post-Exilic Penitential Prayers and the Psalms of Communal Lament*. Academia Biblica 7. Atlanta: Society of Biblical Literature, 2003.

Becking, Bob. *Between Fear and Freedom: Essays on the Interpretation of Jeremiah 30–31*. Leiden: Brill, 2004.

————. "Jehojachin's Amnesty, Salvation for Israel? Notes on Kings 25,27–30." Pages 283–93 in *Pentateuchal and Deuteronomistic Studies: Papers Read at the XIIIth IOSOT Congress*. Edited by C. Brekelmans and J. Lust. Leuven: Leuven University Press, 1990.

Begg, Christopher T. "Yahweh's 'Visitation' of Zedekiah (Jer 32,5)." *Ephemerides Theologicae Lovanienses* 63 (1987): 113–17.

Benavides, Gustavo. "Cognitive and Ideological Aspects of Divine Anthropomorphism." *Religion* 25 (1995): 9–22.

Berlin, Adele. *Lamentations: A Commentary*. Old Testament Library. Louisville: Westminster John Knox, 2002.

————. *Poetics and Interpretation of Biblical Narrative*. Winona Lake: Eisenbrauns, 1994.

————. "Psalms and the Literature of Exile: Psalms 137, 44, 69, and 78." Pages 64–86 in *The Book of Psalms: Composition and Reception*. Edited by P. W. Flint et al. Vetus Testamentum Supplement 99. Leiden: Boston, 2005.

————. "Speakers and Scenarios: Imagining the First Temple in Second Temple Psalms (Psalms 122 and 137)." Pages 341–55 in *Functions of Psalms and Prayers in the Late Second Temple Period*. Edited by M. S. Pajunen and J. Penner. Beihefte zur Zeitschrift für die alttestamentliche Wissenschaft 486. Berlin: de Gruyter, 2017.

————. *Zephaniah*. Anchor Bible 25A. New York: Doubleday, 1994.

Berridge, John M. *Prophet, People, and the Word of Yahweh: An Examination of Form and Content in the Proclamation of the Prophet Jeremiah*. Basel Studies of Theology 4. Zürich: EVZ, 1970.

Biddle, Mark E. *Polyphony and Symphony in Prophetic Literature: Rereading Jeremiah 7–20*. Macon: Mercer University Press, 1996.

Black, Max. *Models and Metaphors*. Ithaca: Cornell University Press, 1962.

Blenkinsopp, Joseph. *Ezekiel*. Interpretation. Louisville: John Knox, 1990.

———. *Isaiah 1–39*. Anchor Bible 19. New York: Doubleday, 2000.

Block, Daniel I. *Ezekiel 1–24*. New International Commentary on the Old Testament. Grand Rapids: Eerdmans, 1997.

Boase, Elizabeth. "Constructing Meaning in the Face of Suffering: Theodicy in Lamentations." *Vetus Testamentum* 58 (2008): 449–68.

———. *The Fulfilment of Doom? The Dialogic Interaction between the Book of Lamentations and the Pre-Exilic/Early Exilic Prophetic Literature*. Library of Hebrew Bible/Old Testament Studies 437. New York: T&T Clark, 2006.

Boda, Mark J. "From Complaint to Contrition: Peering through the Liturgical Window of Jer 14,1–15,4." *Zeitschrift für die alttestamentliche Wissenschaft* 113 (2001): 186–97.

———. *Praying the Tradition: The Origin and Use of Tradition in Nehemiah 9*. Beihefte zur Zeitschrift für die alttestamentliche Wissenschaft 277. Berlin: de Gruyter, 1999.

———. "The Priceless Gain of Penitence: From Communal Lament to Penitential Prayer in the 'Exilic' Liturgy of Israel." *Horizons in Biblical Theology* 25 (2003): 51–75.

Boda, Mark J., Daniel K. Falk, and Rodney A. Werline. *Seeking the Favor of God*, vol. 1: *The Origins of Penitential Prayer in Second Temple Judaism*; vol. 2: *The Development of Penitential Prayer in Second Temple Judaism*; vol. 3: *The Impact of Penitential Prayer beyond Second Temple Judaism*. Early Judaism and Its Literature 21. Atlanta: Society of Biblical Literature, 2006–2008.

Bodi, Daniel. *The Book of Ezekiel and the Poem of Erra*. OBO 104. Freiburg: Universitätverlag Freiburg/Göttingen Vandenhoeck & Ruprecht, 1991.

Breiterman, Zachary. *(God) after Auschwitz: Tradition and Change in Post-Holocaust Jewish Thought*. Princeton: Princeton University Press, 1998.

Brettler, Marc Z. "Biblical History and Jewish Biblical Theology." *Journal of Religion* 77 (1997): 563–83.

———. *God Is King: Understanding an Israelite Metaphor*. Journal for the Study of the Old Testament Supplement 76. Sheffield: Sheffield Academic Press, 1989.

———. *How to Read the Bible*. Philadelphia: Jewish Publication Society, 2005.

———. "Ideology, History, and Theology in 2 Kings xvii 7–23." *Vetus Testamentum* 39 (1989): 262–82.

———. "Images of YHWH the Warrior in Psalms." Pages 135–65 in *Women, War, and Metaphor: Language and Society in the Study of the Hebrew Bible*. Edited by C. R. Fontaine and C. V. Camp. Semeia 61. Atlanta: Scholars Press, 1993.

———. "The Metaphorical Mapping of God in the Hebrew Bible." Pages 219–32 in *Metaphor, Canon, and Community: Jewish, Christian, and Islamic Approaches*. Edited by R. Bisschops and J. Francis. Bern: Peter Lang, 1999.

———. "Psalms and Jewish Biblical Theology." Pages 187–98 in *Jewish Bible Theology: Perspectives and Case Studies*. Edited by I. Kalimi. Winona Lake: Eisenbrauns, 2012.

Bright, John. "The Date of the Prose Sermons of Jeremiah." *Journal of Biblical Literature* 70 (1951): 15–35.

———. *Jeremiah*. Anchor Bible 21. New York: Doubleday, 1965.

Brin, Gershon. *A Prophet in His Struggle: Studies in Four Biographical Narratives in the Prophetic Literature*. Tel Aviv: Tel Aviv University Press, 1983 (Hebrew).

———. *Studies in the Book of Ezekiel*. Tel Aviv: HaKibutz HaMeuhad, 1975 (Hebrew).

Brown, Francis, Samuel Rolles Driver, and Charles A. Briggs. *A Hebrew and English Lexicon of the Old Testament*. Oxford: Clarendon, 1907.

Broyles, Craig C. *The Conflict of Faith and Experience in the Psalms: A Form-Critical and Theological Study*. Journal for the Study of the Old Testament Supplement 52. Sheffield: Sheffield Academic Press, 1989.

Brueggemann, Walter. "Biblical Theology Appropriately Postmodern." Pages 97–108 in *Jews, Christians, and the Theology of the Hebrew Scriptures*. Edited by A. Ogden Bellis and J. S. Kaminsky. Atlanta: Society of Biblical Literature, 2000.

———. "The Costly Loss of Lament." *Journal for the Study of the Old Testament* 36 (1986): 57–71.

———. "The Crisis and Promise of Presence in Israel." *Horizons in Biblical Theology* 1 (1979): 47–86.

———. "Crisis-Evoked, Crisis-Resolving Speech." *Biblical Theology Bulletin* 24 (1994): 95–105.

———. *Israel's Praise: Doxology against Idolatry and Ideology*. Philadelphia: Fortress, 1988.

———. "Psalm 37: Conflict of Interpretation." Pages 229–56 in *Of Prophets' Visions and the Wisdom of Sages: Essays in Honour of R. Norman*

Whybray. Edited by H. A. McKay and D. J. A. Clines. Journal for the Study of the Old Testament Supplement 162. Sheffield: Sheffield Academic Press, 1993.

———. *The Psalms: The Life of Faith*. Edited by P. D. Miller. Minneapolis: Fortress, 1995.

———. "Some Aspects of Theodicy in Old Testament Faith." *Perspectives in Religious Studies* 26 (1999): 253–68.

———. "Theodicy in a Social Dimension." *Journal for the Study of the Old Testament* 33 (1985): 3–25.

———. *Theology of the Old Testament: Testimony, Dispute, Advocacy*. Minneapolis: Fortress, 1997.

———. *An Unsettling God: The Heart of the Hebrew Bible*. Minneapolis: Augsburg Fortress, 2009.

———. "Weariness, Exile, and Chaos (A Motif in Royal Theology)." *Catholic Biblical Quarterly* 34 (1972): 19–38.

Buber, Martin. *Kingship of God*. Translated by Richard Scheimann. 3d ed. London: Allen & Unwin, 1967.

———. *The Prophetic Faith*. Translated by C. Witton-Davies. New York: Macmillan, 1949.

Carr, David M. *Holy Resilience: The Bible's Traumatic Origins*. New Haven: Yale University Press, 2014.

———. "Reading into the Gap: Refractions of Trauma in Israelite Prophecy." Pages 295–308 in *Interpreting Exile: Displacement and Deportation in Biblical and Modern Contexts*. Edited by B. E. Kelle, F. R. Ames, and J. L. Wright. Atlanta: Society of Biblical Literature, 2011.

Carroll, Robert P. "The Aniconic God and the Cult of Images." *Studia Theologica* 31 (1977): 51–64.

———. *From Chaos to Covenant*. London: SCM, 1981.

———. *Jeremiah*. Old Testament Library. Philadelphia: Westminster, 1986.

———. "The Myth of the Empty Land." *Semeia* 59 (1992): 79–93.

Caruth, Cathy, ed. *Trauma: Explorations in Memory*. Baltimore: Johns Hopkins University Press, 1995.

———. *Unclaimed Experience: Trauma, Narrative, and History*. Baltimore: Johns Hopkins University Press, 1996.

Cassuto, Moshe D. *Biblical Literature and Canaanite Literature*. Jerusalem: Magnes, 1979 (Hebrew).

Charney, Davida H. *Persuading God: Rhetorical Studies of First Person Psalms*. Sheffield: Sheffield Phoenix, 2015.

Chicago Assyrian Dictionary. Edited by Erica Reiner et al. Chicago: Oriental Institute, 1956–2006.

Childs, Brevard S. *Biblical Theology in Crisis*. Philadelphia: Westminster, 1970.

———. "The Enemy from the North and the Chaos Tradition." *Journal of Biblical Literature* 78 (1959): 187–98.

———. *Isaiah*. Old Testament Library. Louisville: Westminster John Knox, 2001.

Clark, Douglas R. "The Citations in the Book of Ezekiel." PhD diss., Vanderbilt University, 1984.

Clements, Ruth. "Let the Wicked Vanish Like Smoke: Psalm 37 and the Conception of 'Us' vs. 'Them' in Early Jewish and Christian Interpretation." Paper presented at the Society of Biblical Literature Annual Meeting, San Antonio, TX, November 2004.

Clifford, Richard J. "Psalm 89: A Lament over the Davidic Ruler's Continued Failure." *Harvard Theological Review* 73 (1980): 35–47.

Coats, George W. "The King's Loyal Opposition: Obedience and Authority in Exodus 32–34." Pages 91–109 in *Canon and Authority*. Edited by G. Coats and B. O. Long. Philadelphia: Fortress, 1977.

Cogan, Mordechai (Morton). *Imperialism and Religion: Assyria, Judah, and Israel in the Eighth and Seventh Centuries B.C.E.* Society of Biblical Literature Monograph 19. Missoula, MT: Scholars Press, 1974.

Cogan, Mordechai, and Hayim Tadmor. *II Kings*. Anchor Bible 11. New York: Doubleday, 1988.

Cohen, Mark E. *The Canonical Lamentations of Ancient Mesopotamia*. 2 vols. Potomac, MD: Capital Decisions, 1988.

———. *Sumerian Hymnology: The Ershemma*. Hebrew Union College Annual Supplement 2. Cincinnati: Hebrew Union College Press, 1981.

Collins, John J. "Is a Critical Biblical Theology Possible?" Pages 1–17 in *The Hebrew Bible and Its Interpreters*. Edited by H. Propp, B. Halpern, and D. N. Freedman. Winona Lake: Eisenbrauns, 1990.

Cooke, G. A. *The Book of Ezekiel*. International Critical Commentary. Edinburgh: T&T Clark, 1936.

Cooper, Jerrold S. *The Curse of Agade*. Baltimore: Johns Hopkins University Press, 1983.

Craigie, Peter C. *The Problem of War in the Old Testament*. Grand Rapids: Eerdmans, 1981.

Craigie, Peter C., Page H. Kelley, and Joel F. Drinkard. *Jeremiah 1–25*. Word Biblical Commentary 26. Dallas: Word, 1991.

Cranfield, Charles E. B. *The Epistle to the Romans*. 2 vols. International Critical Commentary. Edinburgh: T&T Clark, 1975–90.

Crenshaw, James L. "Introduction." Pages 1–17 in *Theodicy in the Old Testament*. Edited by James L. Crenshaw. Issues in Religion and Theology 4. Philadelphia: Fortress/London: SPCK, 1983.

———. "Popular Questioning of the Justice of God in Ancient Israel." *Zeitschrift für die alttestamentliche Wissenschaft* 82 (1970): 380–95.

———. *Prophetic Conflict*. Beihefte zur Zeitschrift für die alttestamentliche Wissenschaft 124. Berlin: de Gruyter, 1971.

———. "Theodicy." Pages 444–47 in volume 6 of *Anchor Bible Dictionary*. Edited by David Noel Freedman et al. New York: Doubleday, 1992.

———. "YHWH *Seba'ot Šemo*: A Form-Critical Analysis." *Zeitschrift für die alttestamentliche Wissenschaft* 81 (1969): 156–75.

Cross, Frank M. *Canaanite Myth and Hebrew Epic: Essays in the History of the Religion of Israel*. Cambridge: Harvard University Press, 1973.

Crow, Loren D. "The Rhetoric of Psalm 44." *Zeitschrift für die alttestamentliche Wissenschaft* 104 (1992): 394–401.

Crüsemann, Frank. *Studien zur Formgeschichte von Hymnus und Danklied in Israel*. Wissenschaftliche Monographien zum Alten und Neuen Testament 32. Neukirchen-Vluyn: Neukirchener Verlag, 1969.

Dahood, Mitchell. *Psalms 1–50*. Anchor Bible 16. New York: Doubleday, 1968.

———. *Psalms 51–100*. Anchor Bible 16B. New York: Doubleday, 1968.

Darshan, Guy. "The Meaning of ברא (Ez 21,24) and the Prophecy concerning Nebuchadnezzar at the Crossroads (Ez 21,23–39 [18–24])." *Zeitschrift für die alttestamentliche Wissenschaft* 128 (2016): 83–95.

Davidson, Richard M. "Some Aspects of the Theological Significance of Doubt in the Old Testament." *Annual of the Swedish Theological Institute* 7 (1970): 41–52.

Davidson, Robert. *The Courage to Doubt*. London: SCM, 1983.

Davis, Ellen F. *Swallowing the Scroll: Textuality and the Dynamics of Discourse in Ezekiel's Prophecy*. Journal for the Study of the Old Testament Supplement 78. Sheffield: Sheffield Academic Press, 1989.

Day, John. *God's Conflict with the Dragon and the Sea: Echoes of a Canaanite Myth in the Old Testament*. Cambridge: Cambridge University Press, 1985.

Day, Peggy L. "The Bitch Had It Coming to Her: Rhetoric and Interpretation in Ezekiel 16." *Biblical Interpretation* 8 (2000): 231–54.

Diamond, James A. "The Buried, Raging Sermons of the Warsaw Ghetto Rabbi." *Mosaic: Advancing Jewish Thought*. April 5, 2018. mosaic

magazine.com/observation/2018/04/the-buried-raging-sermons-of
-the-warsaw-ghettorabbi/.

———. "The Warsaw Ghetto Rebbe: Diverting God's Gaze from a Utopian End to an Anguished Now." *Modern Judaism* 30 (2010): 299–331.

Dietrich, Manfried, and Oswald Loretz. *"Jahwe und seine Aschera": Anthropomorphes Kultbild in Mesopotamien, Ugarit und Israel—Das biblische Bilderverbort.* Ugaritisch-biblische Literatur 9. Darmstadt: Ugarit-Verlag, 1992.

Dille, Sarah J. *Mixing Metaphors: God as Mother and Father in Deutero-Isaiah.* London: T&T Clark Continuum, 2004.

Dobbs-Allsopp, Frederick W. *Lamentations: A Biblical Commentary for Teaching and Preaching.* Interpretation. Louisville: John Knox, 2002.

———. "Linguistic Evidence for the Date of Lamentations." *Journal of the Ancient Near Eastern Society* 26 (1998): 1–36.

———. "Tragedy, Tradition, and Theology in the Book of Lamentations." *Journal for the Study of the Old Testament* 74 (1997): 29–60.

———. *Weep, O Daughter of Zion: A Study of the City-Lament Genre in the Hebrew Bible.* Biblica et orientalia 44. Rome: Pontifical Biblical Institute, 1993.

Duhm, Bernard. *Das Buch Jeremia.* Kurzer Hand-Commentar zum Alten Testament 11. Tübingen: Mohr, 1901.

———. *Die Theologie der Propheten als Grundlage für die innere Entwicklungsgeschichte der israelitischen Religion.* Bonn: Marcus, 1875.

Ehrlich, Arnold B. *Randglossen zur hebräischen Bible: Textkritisches, Sprachliches und Sachliches.* Hildesheim: Olms, 1968 (originally 1914).

Eichrodt, Walther. *Ezekiel.* Translated by C. Quin. Old Testament Library. Philadelphia: Westminster, 1970. German original: *Die Prophet Hezekiel.* Das Alte Testament Deutsch 22. Göttingen: Vandenhoeck & Ruprecht, 1959.

———. "Faith in Providence and Theodicy in the Old Testament." Pages 17–41 in *Theodicy in the Old Testament.* Edited by J. L. Crenshaw. Issues in Religion and Theology 4. Philadelphia/London: Fortress, 1983. German original: "Vorsehungsglaube und Theodizee im Alten Testaments." Pages 45–70 in *Festschrift Otto Procksch.* Edited by A. Alt et al. Leipzig: Hinrichs, 1934.

———. *Theology of the Old Testament.* Translated by J. A. Baker. 2 vols. London: SCM, 1961–67. German original: *Theologie des Alten Testaments.* 3 vols. 5th/6th ed. Stuttgart: Klotz, 1933–59.

Eissfeldt, Otto. "Jahwe als König." *Zeitschrift für die alttestamentliche Wis-*

senschaft 46 (1928): 81–105. Reprinted as pages 172–93 in volume 1 of *Kleine Schriften*. Edited by R. Sellheim and F. Maass. 5 vols. Tübingen: Mohr, 1962.

Eph'al, Israel. *The City Besieged: Siege and Its Manifestations in the Ancient Near East*. Leiden: Brill, 2009.

Eppstein, Victor. "The Day of Yahweh in Jer 4:23–28." *Journal of Biblical Literature* 87 (1968): 93–97.

Erikson, Kai. "Notes on Trauma and Community." Pages 183–99 in *Trauma: Explorations in Memory*. Edited by Cathy Caruth. Baltimore: Johns Hopkins University Press, 1995.

Ewald, Georg H. A. *The Prophets of the Old Testament*. Translated by J. F. Smith. 5 vols. Edinburgh: Williams & Norgate, 1875–81. German original: *Die Propheten des Alten Bundes*. 2nd ed. Göttingen: Vandenhoeck & Ruprecht, 1867–68.

Fackenheim, Emil L. *The Jewish Bible after the Holocaust: A Re-reading*. Manchester: Manchester University Press, 1990.

Fenton, Terry. "Differing Approaches to the Theomachy Myth in Old Testament Writers." Pages 337–81 in *Studies in Bible and the Ancient Near East Presented to Samuel E. Loewenstamm on His Seventieth Birthday*. Edited by Y. Avishur and Y. Blau. Jerusalem: Rubinstein, 1978 (Hebrew).

Fischer, Georg. "Is There Shalom, or Not? Jeremiah, a Prophet for South Africa." *Old Testament Essays* 28 (2015): 351–70.

———. *Jeremia 1–25*. Herders Theologischer Kommentar zum Alten Testament. Freiburg: Herder, 2005.

———. *Jeremia 26–52*. Herders Theologischer Kommentar zum Alten Testament. Freiburg: Herder, 2005.

———. *Theologien des Alten Testaments*. Neuer Stuttgarter Kommentar, Altes Testament 31. Stuttgart: Katholisches Bibelwerk, 2012.

Fishbane, Michael A. *Biblical Interpretation in Ancient Israel*. New York: Oxford University Press, 1985.

———. "Ethics and Sacred Attunement." *Journal of Religion* 93 (2013): 421–33, 495–97.

———. "Jeremiah iv 23–26 and Job iii 3–13: A Recovered Use of the Creation Pattern." *Vetus Testamentum* 21 (1971): 151–67.

———. *Sacred Attunement: A Jewish Theology*. Chicago: University of Chicago Press, 2008.

———. "Sin and Judgment in the Prophecies of Ezekiel." *Interpretation* 38 (1984): 131–50.

Fogelin, Robert J. *Figuratively Speaking*. Rev. ed. Oxford: Oxford University Press, 2011 (originally 1988).

Fohrer, Georg. *History of Israelite Religion*. Translated by D. E. Green. Nashville: Abingdon, 1972.

Frank, Daniel. "The Limits of Karaite Scripturalism: Problems in Narrative Exegesis." Pages 41–82 in *A Word Fitly Spoken: Studies in Medieval Exegesis of the Hebrew Bible and the Qur'an Presented to Haggai Ben-Shammai*. Edited by M. M. Bar-Asher, S. Hopkins, S. Stroumsa, and B. Chiesa. Jerusalem: Ben Zvi Institute, 2007.

Frankel, David. *The Land of Canaan and the Destiny of Israel: Theologies of Territory in the Hebrew Bible*. Siphrut 4. Winona Lake: Eisenbrauns, 2011.

Frankfort, Henri. *Ancient Egyptian Religion*. 2nd ed. New York: Harper & Row, 1961 (originally 1948).

Fredriksson, Hennig. *Jahwe als Krieger: Studien zum alttestamentlichen Gottesbild*. Lund: Gleerup, 1945.

Fretheim, Terence E. *The Suffering of God: An Old Testament Perspective*. Philadelphia: Fortress, 1985.

Frevel, Christian. *Die Klagelieder*. Neuer Stuttgarter Kommentar, Altes Testament 20/1. Stuttgart: Verlag Katholisches Bibelwerk, 2017.

Friebel, Kelvin G. *Jeremiah's and Ezekiel's Sign-Acts*. Journal for the Study of the Old Testament Supplement 283. Sheffield: Sheffield Academic Press, 1999.

Frymer-Kensky, Tikvah. "The Emergence of Jewish Biblical Theologies." Pages 109–22 in *Jews, Christians, and the Theology of the Hebrew Scriptures*. Edited by A. O. Bellis and J. S. Kaminsky. Society of Biblical Literature Symposium 8. Atlanta: Society of Biblical Literature, 2000.

Fuhs, Hans. "נַעַר *naʿar*." Pages 474–85 in volume 9 of *Theological Dictionary of the Old Testament*. Edited by G. J. Botterweck, H. Ringgren, and H.-J. Fabry. Translated by D. E. Green. Grand Rapids: Eerdmans, 1998.

Gabbay, Uri. *Pacifying the Hearts of the Gods: Sumerian Emesal Prayers of the First Millennium BC*. Heidelberger Emesal-Studien 1. Wiesbaden: Harrassowitz, 2014.

———. "The Performance of Emesal Prayers within the Regular Temple Cult: Content and Ritual Setting." Pages 103–22 in *Temple im Alten Orient*. Edited by K. Kaniuth et al. Colloquien der Deutschen Orient-Gesellschaft 7. Wiesbaden: Harrassowitz, 2013.

Gabler, Johan P. "An Oration on the Proper Distinction between Biblical and Dogmatic Theology and the Specific Objectives of Each." Pages 492–506 in *The Flowering of Old Testament Theology: A Reader in Twentieth-Century Old Testament Theology, 1930–1990*. Edited by B. C. Ollenburger, E. A. Martens, and G. F. Hasel. Winona Lake: Eisenbrauns, 1992.

Gadd, Cyril J. "An Inscribed Barrel Cylinder of Marduk-Apla-Iddina II." *Iraq* 15 (1953): 123–34.

Galambush, Julie. *Jerusalem in the Book of Ezekiel: The City as Yahweh's Wife.* Society of Biblical Literature Dissertation Series 130. Atlanta: Scholars Press, 1992.

Galil, Gershon. "The Babylonian Calendar and the Chronology of the Last Kings of Judah." *Biblica* 72 (1991): 367–78.

Ganzel, Tova. "The Descriptions of the Restoration of Israel in Ezekiel." *Vetus Testamentum* 60 (2010): 197–211.

Garber, David G., Jr. "Trauma, History, and Survival in Ezekiel 1–24." PhD diss., Emory University, 2005.

———. "Trauma Studies." Pages 421–28 in *The Oxford Encyclopedia of Biblical Interpretation.* Edited by S. L. McKenzie. Oxford: Oxford University Press, 2013.

———. "Trauma Theory and Biblical Studies." *Currents in Biblical Research* 15 (2015): 24–44.

———. "Traumatizing Ezekiel: Psychoanalytic Approaches to the Biblical Prophet." Pages 215–35 in *Psychology and the Bible: A New Way to Read the Scriptures.* Edited by J. H. Ellens and W. G. Rollins. Westport, CT: Praeger, 2004.

———. "A Vocabulary of Trauma in the Exilic Writings." Pages 309–22 in *Interpreting Exile: Displacement and Deportation in Biblical and Modern Contexts.* Edited by B. E. Kelle, F. R. Ames, and J. L. Wright. Atlanta: Society of Biblical Literature, 2011.

Gelston, Anthony. "A Note on Psalm lxxiv,8." *Vetus Testamentum* 34 (1984): 82–87.

Gerstenberger, Erhard S. *Israel in the Persian Period: The Fifth and Fourth Centuries BCE.* Translated by S. S. Schatzmann. Biblical Encyclopedia 8. Atlanta: Society of Biblical Literature, 2011.

———. *Psalms, Part 1: With an Introduction to Cultic Poetry.* Forms of the Old Testament Literature 14. Grand Rapids: Eerdmans, 2001.

———. *Psalms, Part 2, and Lamentations.* Forms of the Old Testament Literature 15. Grand Rapids: Eerdmans, 2001.

———. *Theologies in the Old Testament.* Translated by J. Bowden. New York: T&T Clark Continuum, 2002.

Gertz, Jan C. "Noah und die Propheten: Rezeption und Reformulierung eines altorientalischen Mythos." *Deutsche Vierteljahrsschrift für Literaturwissenschaft und Geistesgeschichte* 81 (2007): 503–22.

Gesenius, Wilhelm. *Gesenius' Hebrew Grammar*. Edited by Emil Kautzsch. Translated by A. E. Cowley. 2nd edition. Oxford: Clarendon, 1910.

Gibson, John C. L. *Textbook of Syrian Semitic Inscriptions*, vol. 2: *Aramaic Inscriptions*. Oxford: Clarendon, 1975.

Goldingay, John. *Psalms*. 3 vols. Grand Rapids: Baker, 2006–2008.

Goldstein, Roni. *The Life of Jeremiah: Traditions about the Prophet and Their Evolution in Biblical Times*. Biblical Encyclopedia Library 30. Jerusalem: Bialik, 2013 (Hebrew).

Gordis, Robert. "The Asseverative *Kaph* in Ugaritic and Hebrew." *Journal of the American Oriental Society* 63 (1943): 176–78.

Goshen-Gottstein, Alon. "The Body as Image of God in Rabbinic Literature." *Harvard Theological Review* 87 (1994): 171–95.

Goshen-Gottstein, Moshe. "Jewish Biblical Theology and the Study of Biblical Religion." *Tarbiz* 50 (1981): 37–64 (Hebrew).

———. "Tanakh Theology: The Religion of the Old Testament and the Place of Jewish Biblical Theology." Pages 617–44 in *Ancient Israelite Religion: Essays in Honor of Frank Moore Cross*. Edited by P. D. Miller, P. D. Hanson, and S. D. McBride. Philadelphia: Fortress, 1987.

Gottwald, Norman K. *Studies in the Book of Lamentations*. Studies in Biblical Theology 14. London: SCM, 1954.

———. *The Tribes of Yahweh: A Sociology of the Religion of Liberated Israel, 1250–1050 B.C.* New York: Orbis, 1979.

Gray, John. *The Biblical Doctrine of the Reign of God*. Edinburgh: T&T Clark, 1979.

———. "The Hebrew Conception of the Kingship of God: Its Origin and Development." *Vetus Testamentum* 6 (1956): 268–85.

———. *I and II Kings*. Revised edition. Old Testament Library. Louisville: Westminster John Knox, 1971.

———. "The Kingship of God in the Prophets and Psalms." *Vetus Testamentum* 11 (1961): 1–29.

Grayson, Albert K. *Assyrian and Babylonian Chronicles*. Locust Valley, NY: Augustin, 1970.

Green, Margaret W. "The Eridu Lament." *Journal of Cuneiform Studies* 30.3 (1978): 127–67.

Green, Ronald M. "Theodicy." Pages 430–41 in volume 14 of *Encyclopedia of Religion*. Edited by M. Eliade. New York: Macmillan, 1987.

Greenberg, Moshe. "Anthropopathism in Ezekiel." Pages 1–10 in *Perspectives in Jewish Learning*. Edited by M. Harris. Chicago: College of Jewish Studies Press, 1965.

———. *Biblical Prose Prayers as a Window to the Popular Religion of Ancient Israel*. Berkeley: University of California Press, 1983.

———. *Ezekiel 1–20*. Anchor Bible 22. New York: Doubleday, 1983.

———. *Ezekiel 21–37*. Anchor Bible 22A. New York: Doubleday, 1995.

———. "Quotations in the Book of Ezekiel as Background to the Prophecies." *Beit Mikra* 17 (1972): 273–78 (Hebrew).

———. "Some Postulates of Biblical Criminal Law." Pages 5–29 in *Yehezkel Kaufmann Jubilee Volume: Studies in Bible and Jewish Religion Dedicated to Yehezkel Kaufmann on the Occasion of His Seventieth Birthday*. Edited by M. Haran. Jerusalem: Magnes, 1960.

———. "The Use of the Ancient Versions for Understanding the Hebrew Text: A Sampling from Ezek. ii.1–iii.11." Pages 131–48 in *Congress Volume: Göttingen, 1977*. Edited by J. A. Emerton. Vetus Testamentum Supplement 29. Leiden: Brill, 1978.

Gross, Heinrich. "Geschichtserfahrung in den Psalmen 44 und 77." *Trierer Theologische Zeitschrift* 80 (1971): 207–21.

Gunkel, Hermann. "Klagelieder Jeremia." Pages 1049–52 in volume 3 of *Die Religion in Geschichte und Gegenwart*. Edited by Friedrich Michael Schiele and Leopold Zscharnack. Tübingen: Mohr, 1912.

———. *The Psalms: A Form-Critical Introduction*. Translated by T. M. Horner. Philadelphia: Fortress, 1967.

Gunkel, Hermann, and Joachim Begrich. *Introduction to the Psalms: The Genres of the Religious Lyric of Israel*. Translated by J. D. Nogalski. Macon: Mercer University Press, 1998. German original: *Einleitung in die Psalmen: Die Gattungen der religiösen Lyrik Israels*. 4th ed. Göttingen: Vandenhoeck & Ruprecht, 1985.

Guthrie, Stewart E. *Faces in the Clouds: A New Theory of Religion*. New York: Oxford University Press, 1993.

Gwaltney, William C. "The Biblical Book of Lamentations in the Context of Near Eastern Lament Literature." Pages 191–211 in *Scripture in Context*, vol. 2: *More Essays on the Comparative Method*. Edited by W. Hallo, J. Moyer, and L. Perdue. Winona Lake: Eisenbrauns, 1983.

Haar, Murray J. "The God-Israel Relationship in the Community Lament Psalms." PhD diss., Union Theological Seminary (Richmond), 1985.

Hacham, Amos. *Psalms*. Jerusalem: Kook, 1990.

Halpern, Baruch. *The First Historians: The Hebrew Bible and History*. San Francisco: Harper & Row, 1988.

Hamori, Esther J. *"When Gods Were Men": The Embodied God in Biblical and

Near Eastern Literature. Beihefte zur Zeitschrift für die alttestamentliche Wissenschaft 384. Berlin: de Gruyter, 2008.

Hanson, Paul D. "Israelite Religion in the Early Postexilic Period." Pages 485–508 in *Ancient Israelite Religion: Essays in Honor of F. M. Cross.* Edited by P. D. Miller, P. D. Hanson, and S. D. McBride. Philadelphia: Fortress, 1987.

Haran, Menahem. "The Ark and the *Kerubim*: Their Symbolic Meaning and Their Shape—The Problem of Archaeological Parallels." *Eretz-Israel* 5 (1958): 83–90 (Hebrew).

———. "The Divine Presence in the Israelite Cult and the Cultic Institutions." *Biblica* 50 (1969): 251–67.

Hareuveni, Nogah. *Desert and Shepherd in Our Biblical Heritage.* Neot Kedumim: Neot Kedumim Press, 1991 (Hebrew).

———. *New Light on the Book of Jeremiah.* 3rd ed. Jerusalem: Kiryat Sefer, 1968 (originally 1950) (Hebrew).

Hasel, Gerhard F. "The Nature of Biblical Theology: Recent Trends and Issues." *Andrews University Seminary Studies* 32 (1994): 203–15.

———. *Old Testament Theology: Basic Issues in the Current Debate.* Grand Rapids: Eerdmans, 1972.

———. "The Problem of the Center in the OT Theology Debate." *Zeitschrift für die alttestamentliche Wissenschaft* 86 (1974): 65–82.

———. "Recent Models of Biblical Theology: Three Major Perspectives." *Andrews University Seminary Studies* 33 (1995): 55–75.

Hayes, John H., and Frederick C. Prussner. *Old Testament Theology: Its History and Development.* Atlanta: John Knox, 1985.

Heim, Knut M. "The Personification of Jerusalem and the Drama of Her Bereavement in Lamentations." Pages 129–69 in *Zion, City of Our God.* Edited by R. S. Hess and G. J. Wenham. Grand Rapids: Eerdmans, 1999.

Held, Moshe. "Rhetorical Questions in Ugaritic and Biblical Hebrew." *Eretz-Israel* 9 (1969): 71*–79* (Hebrew).

Hendel, Ronald. "Aniconism and Anthropomorphism in Ancient Israel." Pages 205–28 in *The Image and the Book: Iconic Cults, Aniconism, and the Rise of Book Religion in Israel and the Ancient Near East.* Edited by Karel van der Toorn. Contributions to Biblical Exegesis and Theology 21. Leuven: Peeters, 1997.

Hertzberg, Hans W. *I and II Samuel.* Translated by J. S. Bowden. Old Testament Library. London: SCM, 1964.

Heschel, Abraham J. *Man Is Not Alone.* Philadelphia: Jewish Publication Society, 1951.

———. *Prophets*. 2 vols. San Francisco: Harper, 1962.

Hillers, Delbert R. *Lamentations*. 2d rev. ed. Anchor Bible 7A. New York: Doubleday, 1992.

———. *Treaty Curses and the Old Testament Prophets*. 2nd ed. Biblica et orientalia 16. Rome: Pontifical Biblical Institute, 1964.

Hobbs, Trevor R. *2 Kings*. Word Biblical Commentary. Waco: Word, 1985.

Hoffman, Yair. "The Creativity of Theodicy." Pages 117–30 in *Justice and Righteousness: Biblical Themes and Their Influence*. Edited by H. G. Reventlow and Y. Hoffman. Journal for the Study of the Old Testament Supplement 137. Sheffield: Sheffield Academic Press, 1992.

———. "The Deuteronomist and the Exile." Pages 659–75 in *Pomegranates and Golden Bells: Studies in Biblical, Jewish, and Near Eastern Ritual, Law, and Literature in Honor of Jacob Milgrom*. Edited by D. P. Wright, D. N. Freedman, and A. Hurvitz. Winona Lake: Eisenbrauns, 1995.

———. *The Doctrine of the Exodus in the Bible*. Tel Aviv: Tel Aviv University Publishing Projects, 1983.

———. "'Isn't the Bride Too Beautiful?' The Case of Jeremiah 6:16–21." *Journal for the Study of the Old Testament* 64 (94): 103–20.

———. *Jeremiah 1–25*. Mikra LeIsrael. Tel Aviv/Jerusalem, 2001 (Hebrew).

———. *Jeremiah 26–52*. Mikra LeIsrael. Tel Aviv/Jerusalem, 2001 (Hebrew).

———. *The Prophecies against the Nations in the Bible*. Tel Aviv: Tel Aviv University/HaKibbutz HaMeuchad, 1977 (Hebrew).

———. "Reflections on the Relationship between Theopolitics, Prophecy, and Historiography." Pages 85–99 in *Politics and Theopolitics in the Bible and Postbiblical Literature*. Edited by H. G. Reventlow, Y. Hoffman, and B. Uffenheimer. Journal for the Study of the Old Testament Supplement 171. Sheffield: JSOT Press, 1994.

Hoffner, Harry A. "Theodicy in the Hittite Texts." Pages 57–89 in *Theodicy in the World of the Bible*. Edited by A. Laato and J. C. de Moor. Leiden: Brill, 2003.

Holladay, William L. *Jeremiah*. 2 vols. Hermeneia. Philadelphia: Fortress, 1986–89.

———. "Jeremiah and Moses: Further Observations." *Journal of Biblical Literature* 85 (1966): 17–27.

———. *The Root Šûbh in the Old Testament, with Practical Reference to Its Usage in Covenantal Contexts*. Leiden: Brill, 1958.

———. "The So-called 'Deuteronomic Gloss' in Jer. viii 19b." *Vetus Testamentum* 12 (1962): 494–98.

Holtz, Shalom E. *Neo-Babylonian Court Procedure.* Cuneiform Monographs 38. Leiden: Brill, 2009.

———. "Praying as a Plaintiff." *Vetus Testamentum* 61 (2011): 258–79.

Hornkohl, Aaron D. *Ancient Hebrew Periodization and the Language of the Book of Jeremiah: The Case for a Sixth-Century Date of Composition.* Leiden: Brill, 2014.

Hornung, Erik. *Conceptions of God in Ancient Egypt: The One and the Many.* Translated by J. Baines. London: Routledge & Kegan Paul, 1983.

Hossfeld, Frank L., and Erich Zenger. *Psalms,* vol. 2. Translated by L. M. Maloney. Hermeneia. Minneapolis: Fortress, 2005.

Huffmon, Herbert B. "The Covenant Lawsuit in the Prophets." *Journal of Biblical Literature* 78 (1959): 285–95.

Hurowitz, Victor A. *I Have Built You an Exalted House: Temple Building in the Bible in Light of Mesopotamian and Northwest Semitic Writings.* Journal for the Study of the Old Testament Supplement 115. Sheffield: Sheffield Academic Press, 1992.

———. "Make Yourself an Idol." *Beit Mikra* 40 (1995): 337–47 (Hebrew).

Jacobsen, Thorkild. "The Graven Image." Pages 15–32 in *Ancient Israelite Religion: Essays in Honor of F. M. Cross.* Edited by P. D. Miller, P. D. Hanson, S. D. McBride. Philadelphia: Fortress, 1987.

———. "Pictures and Pictorial Language (The Burney Relief)." Pages 1–12 in *Figurative Language in the Ancient Near East.* Edited by M. Mindlin, M. J. Geller, and J. E. Wansbrough. London: School of Oriental and African Studies, 1987.

———. *Toward the Image of Tamuz and Other Essays on Mesopotamian History and Culture.* Harvard Semitic Studies 21. Cambridge: Harvard University Press, 1970.

———. *The Treasure of Darkness: A History of Mesopotamian Religion.* New Haven: Yale University Press, 1976.

Janowski, Bernd. *Arguing with God: A Theological Anthropology of the Psalms.* Translated by Ermin Siedlecki. Louisville: Westminster John Knox, 2013.

Janssen, Enno. *Juda in der Exilzeit: Ein Beitrag zur Frage der Entstehung des Judentums.* Forschungen zur Religion und Literatur des Alten und Neuen Testaments 51. Göttingen: Vandenhoeck & Ruprecht, 1956.

Janzen, David. *The Violent Gift: Trauma's Subversion of the Deuteronomistic History's Narrative.* Library of Hebrew Bible/Old Testament Studies 561. New York: T&T Clark, 2012.

Janzen, Gerald J. *Studies in the Text of Jeremiah*. Harvard Semitic Monograph
6. Cambridge: Harvard University Press, 1973.

Japhet, Sara. "The Establishment and the Early History of the Bible Depart-
ment (1925–1949)." Pages 283–303 in volume 1 of *The History of the
Hebrew University: Establishment and Development*. Edited by Hagit
Lavski. 3 vols. Jerusalem: Magnes, 1995 (Hebrew).

———. *I and II Chronicles*. Old Testament Library. Louisville: Westminster
John Knox, 1993.

———. *The Ideology of the Book of Chronicles and Its Place in Biblical Thought*.
Translated by Anna Barber. 2nd ed. Beiträge zur Erforschung des Alten
Testaments und des Antiken Judentums 9. Frankfurt am Main: Peter
Lang, 1997.

Jepsen, Alfred. "Warum? Eine lexikalische und theologische Studie." Pages
106–13 in *Das ferne und nahe Wort: Festschrift Leonhard Rost zur Vollend-
ung seines 70. Lebensjahres am 30. November 1966 gewidmet*. Edited by
F. Maass and L. Rost. Beihefte zur Zeitschrift für die alttestamentliche
Wissenschaft 105. Berlin: de Gruyter, 1967.

Jevons, Frank B. "Anthropomorphism." Pages 573–78 in volume 1 of *Encyclopedia of Religion and Ethics*. Edited by J. Hastings. Edinburgh: T&T
Clark, 1908.

Johnson, Aubrey R. *Sacral Kingship in Ancient Israel*. Cardiff: University of
Wales Press, 1967.

Johnson, Elsie. "אָנַף *'ānaph*." Pages 348–60 in volume 1 of *Theological Dictionary of the Old Testament*. Edited by G. J. Botterweck and H. Ringgren. Translated by J. T. Willis. Revised edition. Grand Rapids: Eerdmans, 1977.

Joyce, Paul M. "Dislocation and Adaptation in the Exilic Age and After." Pages
45–58 in *After the Exile: Essays in Honor of Rex Mason*. Edited by J. Bar-
ton and D. J. Reimer. Macon: Mercer University Press, 1996.

———. *Divine Initiative and Human Response in Ezekiel*. Journal for the Study
of the Old Testament Supplement 51. Sheffield: Sheffield Academic
Press, 1989.

———. *Ezekiel: A Commentary*. Library of Hebrew Bible/Old Testament Studies 482. New York/London: T&T Clark, 2007.

———. "Individual Responsibility in Ezekiel 18?" *Studia Biblica* 1 (1978): 185–
96.

———. "Lamentations and the Grief Process: A Psychological Reading." *Biblical Interpretation* 1 (1993): 304–20.

———. "Synchronic and Diachronic Perspectives on Ezekiel." Pages 115–28 in *Synchronic or Diachronic? A Debate on Method in Old Testament Exegesis*. Edited by J. C. de Moor. Oudtestamentische Studiën 34. Leiden: Brill, 1995.

Kahn, Dan'el. "Some Remarks on the Foreign Policy of Psammetichus II in the Levant (595–589 BCE)." *Journal of Egyptian History* 1 (2008): 139–57.

Kaiser, Otto. *Isaiah 1–12*. Translated by R. A. Wilson. Old Testament Library. Philadelphia: Westminster, 1972.

Kalimi, Isaac. *Early Jewish Exegesis and Theological Controversy: Studies in Scriptures in the Shadow of Internal and External Controversies*. Jewish and Christian Heritage Series 2. Assen: Van Gorcum, 2002.

———. "History of Israelite Religion or Hebrew Bible/Old Testament Theology? Jewish Interest in Biblical Theology." *Journal for the Study of the Old Testament* 11 (1997): 100–123.

Kang, Sa-Moon. *Divine War in the Old Testament and in the Ancient Near East*. Beihefte zur Zeitschrift für die alttestamentliche Wissenschaft 177. Berlin: de Gruyter, 1989.

Kasher, Rimon. "Anthropomorphism, Holiness, and Cult: A New Look at Ezekiel 40–48." *Zeitschrift für die alttestamentliche Wissenschaft* 110 (1998): 192–208.

———. "The Dumbness in the Book of Ezekiel (Ezek 3:22–27)." *Beit Mikra* 43 (1998): 227–44 (Hebrew).

———. *Ezekiel 1–24*. Mikra Le-Israel. Jerusalem: Magnes/Tel Aviv: Am Oved, 2004.

Katz, Dina. "Reconstructing Babylon: Recycling Traditions toward a New Theology." Pages 123–34 in *Babylon: Wissenskultur in Orient und Okzident*. Topoi 1: Berlin Studies in the Ancient World. Berlin: de Gruyter, 2011.

Katz, Moshe. *The Book of Rabbi Judah Ibn Kuraish*. Tel Aviv: Dvir, 1952 (Hebrew).

Kaufmann, Yehezkel. *Toldot Ha-'Emunah Ha-Yisre'elit* (*The Religion of Israel, from Its Beginnings to the Babylonian Exile*). 4 vols. Jerusalem: Bialik, 1952–76 (Hebrew).

Keel, Othmar, and Christoph Uehlinger. *Gods, Goddesses, and Images of God in Ancient Israel*. Translated by T. H. Trapp. Minneapolis: Fortress, 1998.

Kessler, Martin. "From Drought to Exile: A Morphological Study of Jer. 14:1–15:4." *Amsterdamse cahiers voor exegese en Bijbelse theologie* 2 (1981): 65–85.

———. "Psalm 44." Pages 193–204 in *Unless Some One Guide Me . . . : Festschrift for Karel A. Deurloo*. Edited by Janet W. Dyk et al. Maastricht: Shaker, 2001.

Klawans, Jonathan. "Josephus, the Rabbis, and Responses to Catastrophes Ancient and Modern." *Jewish Quarterly Review* 100 (2010): 278–309.

Klein, Ralph W. *Israel in Exile: A Theological Interpretation.* Overtures to Biblical Theology 6. Philadelphia: Fortress, 1979.

Knierim, Rolf P. *The Task of Old Testament Theology: Substance, Method, and Cases.* Grand Rapids: Eerdmans, 1995.

Knohl, Israel. *Biblical Beliefs: The Borders of Biblical Revolution.* Jerusalem: Magnes, 2007 (Hebrew).

———. *The Sanctuary of Silence: A Study of the Priestly Strata in the Pentateuch.* Jerusalem: Magnes, 1992 (Hebrew).

Knoppers, Gary N. *Two Nations under God: The Deuteronomistic History of Solomon and the Dual Monarchies,* vol. 2: *The Reign of Jeroboam, the Fall of Israel, and the Reign of Josiah.* Harvard Semitic Monograph 53. Atlanta: Scholars, 1994.

Koch, Klaus. "Is There a Doctrine of Retribution in the Old Testament?" Translated by T. H. Trapp. Pages 57–87 in *Theodicy in the Old Testament.* Edited by J. L. Crenshaw. Issues in Religion and Theology 4. Philadelphia: Fortress, 1983. German original: "Gibt es ein Vergeltungsdogma im Alten Testament?" *Zeitschrift für Theologie und Kirche* 52 (1955): 1–42.

Koehler, Ludwig, and Walter Baumgartner. *Lexicon in Veteris Testamenti Libros.* 2nd ed. Leiden: Brill, 1958.

Koehler, Ludwig, Walter Baumgartner, and Johann J. Stamm, eds. *The Hebrew and Aramaic Lexicon of the Old Testament.* Translated by M. E. J. Richardson et al. 4 vols. Leiden: Brill, 1994–99.

Kramer, Samuel N. *Lamentation over the Destruction of Ur.* Assyriological Studies 12. Chicago: Oriental Institute, 1940.

Kratz, Reinhard G. *The Prophets of Israel.* Translated by A. C. Hagedorn and N. MacDonald. Critical Studies in the Hebrew Bible 2. Winona Lake: Eisenbrauns, 2015.

Kraus, Hans J. *Klagelieder.* 3rd ed. Biblischer Kommentar, Altes Testament 20. Neukirchen-Vluyn: Neukirchener Verlag, 1968.

———. *Psalms 1–59: A Commentary.* Translated by H. C. Oswald. Continental Commentary. Minneapolis: Fortress, 1988.

———. *Psalms 60–150: A Commentary.* Translated by H. C. Oswald. Continental Commentary. Minneapolis: Fortress, 1988.

Kselman, John S. "Psalm 77 and the Book of Exodus." *Journal of the Ancient Near Eastern Society* 15 (1983): 51–58.

Kübler-Ross, Elisabeth. *On Death and Dying.* London/Toronto: Collier-Macmillan, 1969.

Kuenen, Abraham. *National Religions and Universal Religions.* Hibbert Lectures 1882. London: Williams & Norgate, 1882.

———. *The Prophets and Prophecy in Israel: An Historical and Critical Enquiry.* Translated by A. Milroy. London: Longmans, Green, 1877. Dutch original: Leiden: Engels, 1875.

Kutsko, John F. *Between Heaven and Earth: Divine Presence and Absence in the Book of Ezekiel.* Biblical and Judaic Studies 7. Winona Lake: Eisenbrauns, 2000.

Laato, Antti. "Assyrian Propaganda and the Falsification of History in the Royal Inscriptions of Sennacherib." *Vetus Testamentum* 45 (1995): 198–226.

Laato, Antti, and Johannes C. de Moor, eds. *Theodicy in the World of the Bible.* Leiden: Brill, 2003.

Lakoff, George. *Women, Fire, and Dangerous Things.* Chicago: University of Chicago Press, 1987.

Lakoff, George, and Mark Johnson. *Metaphors We Live By.* 2nd ed. Chicago: University of Chicago Press, 2003 (originally 1980).

Lakoff, George, and Mark Turner. *More Than Cool Reason: A Field Guide to Poetic Metaphor.* Chicago: University of Chicago Press, 1989.

Lambert, David A. *How Repentance Became Biblical: Judaism, Christianity, and the Interpretation of Scripture.* New York: Oxford University Press, 2016.

Lambert, Wilfred G. "Mesopotamian Creation Stories." Pages 15–59 in *Imagining Creation.* Edited by M. J. Geller and M. Schipper. Leiden: Brill, 2008.

Lane, Belden C. "Arguing with God: Blasphemy and the Prayer of Lament in Judaism and Other Faith Traditions." Pages 2543–51 in *Remembering for the Future: Working Papers and Addenda*, vol. 3: *The Impact of the Holocaust and Genocide on Christians and Jews.* Edited by Y. Bauer et al. Oxford: Pergamon, 1989.

Langer, Susanne K. *Philosophy in a New Key: A Study in the Symbolism of Reason, Rite, and Art.* 3d ed. Cambridge: Harvard University Press, 1979 (originally 1942).

Lanser, Susan S. *The Narrative Act: Point of View in Prose Fiction.* Princeton: Princeton University Press, 1981.

Leibniz, Gottfried W. *Theodicy: Essays on the Goodness of God, the Freedom of Man, and the Origin of Evil.* Translated by E. M. Huggard. London: Routledge & Kegan Paul, 1951.

Lemaire, André. "Toward a Redactional History of the Book of Kings." Pages 446–61 in *Reconsidering Israel and Judah: Recent Studies on the Deuteronomistic History.* Edited by G. N. Knoppers and J. G. McConville. Winona Lake: Eisenbrauns, 2000.

Leshem, Yossi, and Yoram Yom-Tov. "Routes of Migrating Soaring Birds." *Ibis* 140 (1998): 41–52.

Leuchter, Mark. *Josiah's Reform and Jeremiah's Scroll: Historical Calamity and Prophetic Response*. Hebrew Bible Monographs 6. Sheffield: Sheffield Phoenix, 2006.

———. *The Polemics of Exile in Jeremiah 26–45*. Cambridge: Cambridge University Press, 2008.

Levenson, Jon D. *Sinai and Zion: An Entry into the Jewish Bible*. Minneapolis: Winston, 1985.

———. "Theological Consensus or Historical Evasion? Jews and Christians in Biblical Studies." Pages 82–105 in *Hebrew Bible or Old Testament? Studying the Bible in Judaism and Christianity*. Edited by J. J. Collins and R. Brooks. Notre Dame: University of Notre Dame Press, 1990.

———. "Why Jews Are Not Interested in Biblical Theology." Pages 281–307 in *Judaic Perspectives on Ancient Israel*. Edited by J. Neusner, B. A. Levine, and E. S. Frerichs. Philadelphia: Fortress, 1987. Reprinted in *The Hebrew Bible, the Old Testament, and Historical Criticism: Jews and Christians in Biblical Studies*, pages 33–61. Louisville: Westminster John Knox, 1993.

Levin, Christoph. "The Empty Land in Kings." Pages 61–89 in *The Concept of Exile in Ancient Israel and Its Historical Contexts*. Edited by E. Ben Zvi and C. Levin. Beihefte zur Zeitschrift für die alttestamentliche Wissenschaft 404. Berlin: de Gruyter, 2010.

Levinson, Bernard M. "Review: Michael Fishbane, *Sacred Attunement: A Jewish Theology* (2008)." *Interpretation* 64 (2010): 294–300.

Levitt-Kohn, Risa. *A New Heart and a New Soul: Ezekiel, the Exile and the Torah*. Journal for the Study of the Old Testament Supplement 358. Sheffield: Sheffield Academic Press, 2002.

Liddell, Henry George, Robert Scott, and Henry Scott Jones, eds. *A Greek-English Lexicon*. 9th ed. with revised supplement. Oxford: Clarendon, 1996.

Limburg, James. "The Root ריב and the Prophetic Lawsuit Speeches." *Journal of Biblical Literature* 88 (1969): 291–304.

Linafelt, Tod. *Surviving Lamentations: Catastrophe, Lament, and Protest in the Afterlife of a Biblical Book*. Chicago: University of Chicago Press, 2000.

Lind, Millard C. *Yahweh Is a Warrior: The Theology of Warfare in Ancient Israel*. Scottsdale, PA: Herald, 1980.

Lindars, Barnabas. "Ezekiel and Individual Responsibility." *Vetus Testamentum* 15 (1965): 452–67.

Lipschits, Oded. *The Fall and Rise of Jerusalem*. Winona Lake: Eisenbrauns, 2005.

Lipschitz, Ora. "The 'Beit David' Polemic: Following the Tel Dan Inscription." Pages 9–68 in *David King of Israel Alive and Enduring?* Edited by H. Baron and O. Lipschitz. Jerusalem: Simor, 1997 (Hebrew).

Loeland (Levinson), Hanne. *Silent or Salient Gender? The Interpretation of Gendered God-Language in the Hebrew Bible, Exemplified in Isaiah 42, 46, and 49*. Tübingen: Mohr Siebeck, 2009.

Loewenstamm, Samuel A. "The Shiver of Nature in the Appearance of God." Pages 508–20 in *Oz Le-David: Studies in the Bible Presented to David Ben-Gurion on His Seventy-Seventh Birthday*. Edited by Y. Kaufmann et al. Jerusalem: Kiryat Sefer, 1964 (Hebrew).

———. *The Tradition of the Exodus in Its Development*. Jerusalem: Magnes, 1987 (Hebrew).

Lohfink, Norbert F. "Was There a Deuteronomistic Movement?" Pages 36–66 in *Those Elusive Deuteronomists: The Phenomenon of Pan-Deuteronomism*. Edited by L. S. Schearing and S. L. McKenzie. Journal for the Study of the Old Testament Supplement 268. Sheffield: Sheffield Academic Press, 1999.

Löhr, Max. "Alphabetische und alphabetisierende Lieder im Alten Testament." *Zeitschrift für die alttestamentliche Wissenschaft* 25 (1905): 173–98.

———. "Threni III. und die jeremianische Authorschaft des Buches der Klagelieder." *Zeitschrift für die alttestamentliche Wissenschaft* 24 (1904): 1–16.

Long, Burke O. "Two Question and Answer Schemata in the Prophets." *Journal of Biblical Literature* 90 (1971): 129–39.

Loprieno, Antonio. "Theodicy in Ancient Egyptian Texts." Pages 27–56 in *Theodicy in the World of the Bible*. Edited by A. Laato and J. C. de Moor. Leiden: Brill, 2003.

Lorberbaum, Yair. *The Image of God: Halakhah and Aggadah*. Tel Aviv: Schocken, 2004 (Hebrew).

Lundbom, Jack R. *Jeremiah 1–20*. Anchor Bible 21A. New Haven: Yale University Press, 1999.

———. *Jeremiah 21–36*. Anchor Bible 21B. New Haven: Yale University Press, 2004.

———. *Jeremiah 37–52*. Anchor Bible 21C. New Haven: Yale University Press, 2004.

Luzzatto, Samuel D. *Isaiah*. Tel Aviv: Dvir, 1970. Hebrew original: Padua, 1856–97.

Lyons, John. *Semantics*. 2 vols. Cambridge: Cambridge University Press, 1977.

MacGregor, Geddes. "Doubt and Belief." Pages 2423–29 in volume 4 of *Encyclopedia of Religion*. Edited by L. Jones. 2nd ed. Detroit: Macmillan, 2005.

Machinist, Peter. "Anthropomorphism in Mesopotamian Religion." Pages 67–99 in *Göttliche Körper—Göttliche Gefühle: Was leisten anthropomorphe und anthropopathische Götterkonzepte im Alten Orient und im Alten Testament?* Edited by A. Wagner. Orbis Biblicus Orientalis 270. Fribourg: Academic Press/Göttingen: Vandenhoeck & Ruprecht, 2014.

———. "Assyria and Its Image in the First Isaiah." *Journal of the American Oriental Society* 103 (1983): 719–37.

Malamat, Abraham. "The Last Kings of Judah and the Fall of Jerusalem." *Israel Exploration Journal* 18 (1968): 137–56.

———. "The Twilight of Judah: In the Egyptian-Babylonian Maelstrom." Pages 123–45 in *Congress Volume: Edinburgh, 1974*. Edited by G. W. Anderson et al. Vetus Testamentum Supplement 28. Leiden: Brill, 1975.

Mandolfo, Carleen. *God in the Dock: Dialogic Tension in the Psalms of Lament*. Journal for the Study of the Old Testament Supplement 357. Sheffield: Sheffield Academic Press, 2002.

Margaliot, Meshullam. "Jeremiah x 1–16: A Re-Examination." *Vetus Testamentum* 30 (1980): 295–308.

Matties, Gordon H. *Ezekiel 18 and the Rhetoric of Moral Discourse*. Society of Biblical Literature Dissertation Series 126. Atlanta: Society of Biblical Literature, 1990.

Mauser, Ulrich. "Historical Criticism: Liberator or Foe of Biblical Theology?" Pages 99–113 in *The Promise and Practice of Biblical Theology*. Edited by J. Reumann. Minneapolis: Fortress, 1991.

McDonough, Sheila. "Orthodoxy and Heterodoxy." Page 124 in volume 11 of *The Encyclopedia of Religion*. Edited by M. Eliade et al. 16 vols. New York/London: Macmillan, 1987.

McKane, William. *Jeremiah 1–25*. International Critical Commentary. Edinburgh: T&T Clark, 1986.

———. *Jeremiah 26–52*. International Critical Commentary. Edinburgh: T&T Clark, 2000.

———. *A Late Harvest: Reflections on the Old Testament*. London: T&T Clark, 1995.

————. "Prophet and Institution." *Zeitschrift für die alttestamentliche Wissenschaft* 94 (1982): 251–66.

McKay, John W. *Religion in Judah under the Assyrians, 732–609 B.C.* London: SCM, 1973.

McKenzie, Steven L. *The Trouble with Kings.* Vetus Testamentum Supplement 42. Leiden: Brill, 1991.

Meier, Samuel A. *Speaking of Speaking: Marking Direct Discourse in the Hebrew Bible.* Leiden: Brill, 1992.

Melanchthon, Monica J. *Rejection by God: The History and Significance of the Rejection Motif in the Hebrew Bible.* Studies in Biblical Literature 22. New York: Peter Lang, 2001.

Mettinger, Tryggve N. D. *The Dethronement of Sabaoth: Studies in the Shem and Kabod Theologies.* Coniectanea Biblica: Old Testament Series 18. Lund: Gleerup, 1982.

————. "Fighting the Powers of Chaos and Hell—Towards the Biblical Portrait of God." *Studia Theologica* 39 (1985): 21–38.

————. "Gudsbildens gestaltning: Literäre kategorier och religiös tro." *Svensk Religionsgustoris Aersskkrift* 1 (1985): 42–63.

————. *In Search of God: The Meaning and Message of the Everlasting Names.* Translated by F. H. Cryer. Philadelphia: Fortress, 1987.

————. *No Graven Image? Israelite Aniconism in Its Ancient Near Eastern Context.* Coniectanea Biblica: Old Testament Series 42. Stockholm: Almqvist & Wiksell, 1995.

————. "The Study of the *Gottesbild*—Problems and Suggestions." *Svensk Exegetisk Åarsbok* 54 (1989): 135–45.

————. "The Veto on Images and the Aniconic God in Ancient Israel." Pages 15–20 in *Religious Symbols and Their Functions.* Edited by H. Biezals. Scripta Instituti Donneriani Aboensis 10. Stockholm: Almqvist & Wiksell, 1979.

Meyers, Eric M. "The Babylonian Exile Revisited: Demographics and the Emergence of the Canon of Scriptures." Pages 61–73 in *Judaism and Crisis: Crisis as a Catalyst in Jewish Cultural History.* Edited by A. Lange, D. K. F. Römeld, and M. Weigold. Schriften des Institutum Judaicum Delitzschianum 9. Göttingen: Vandenhoeck & Ruprecht, 2011.

Michalowski, Piotr. *The Lamentation over the Destruction of Sumer and Ur.* Winona Lake: Eisenbrauns, 1989.

————. "Presence at the Creation." Pages 381–96 in *Lingering over Words: Studies in Ancient Near Eastern Literature in Honor of W. Moran.* Edited by

T. Abusch, J. Huehnergard, and P. Steinkeller. Harvard Semitic Studies 37. Cambridge: Harvard University Press, 1990.

Middlemas, Jill. *The Templeless Age: An Introduction to the History, Literature, and Theology of the "Exile."* Louisville: Westminster John Knox, 2007.

———. *The Troubles of Templeless Judah.* New York: Oxford University Press, 2005.

Milgrom, Jacob. "The Alleged 'Demythologization and Secularization' in Deuteronomy." *Israel Exploration Journal* 23 (1973): 156–61.

———. "The Concept of Ma'al in the Bible and the Ancient Near East." *Journal of the American Oriental Society* 96 (1976): 236–47.

Miller, Patrick D. *The Divine Warrior in Early Israel.* Cambridge: Harvard University Press, 1973.

———. "God the Warrior: A Problem in Biblical Interpretation and Apologetics." *Interpretation* 19 (1965): 39–46.

———. *They Cried to the Lord: The Form and Theology of Biblical Prayer.* Minneapolis: Fortress, 1994.

Moberly, Robert W. L. *The Old Testament of the Old Testament: Patriarchal Narratives and Mosaic Yahwism.* Minneapolis: Fortress, 1992.

Moor, Johannes C. de. *Synchronic or Diachronic? A Debate on Method in Old Testament Exegesis.* Oudtestamentische Studiën 34. Leiden: Brill, 1995.

———. "Theodicy in the Texts of Ugarit." Pages 108–50 in *Theodicy in the World of the Bible.* Edited by A. Laato and J. C. de Moor. Leiden: Brill, 2003.

Morgenstern, Julian. "The Cultic Setting of the 'Enthronement Psalms.'" *Hebrew Union College Annual* 35 (1964): 1–42.

Morrow, William S. *Protest against God: The Eclipse of a Biblical Tradition.* Hebrew Bible Monographs 4. Sheffield: Sheffield Phoenix Press, 2006.

———. "Tribute from Judah and the Transmission of Assyrian Propaganda." Pages 183–92 in *"My Spirit at Rest in the North Country" (Zechariah 6:8): IOSOT XX Congress, Helsinki 2010.* Edited by H. M. Niemann and M. Augustin. Frankfurt am Main: Peter Lang, 2011.

Mowinckel, Sigmund. *Psalmenstudien,* vol. 2: *Das Thronbesteigungsfest Jahwäs und der Ursprung der Eschatologie.* 2nd ed. Amsterdam: Schippers, 1966 (originally 1922).

———. *The Psalms in Israel's Worship.* Translated by D. R. Ap-Thomas. 2 vols. Oxford: Blackwell, 1962. German original: 1951.

———. *Zur Komposition des Buches Jeremia.* Kristiania: Dybwad, 1914.

Mrozek, Andrzej, and Silvano Votto. "The Motif of the Sleeping Divinity." *Biblica* 80 (1999): 415–19.

Muffs, Yochanan. *The Personhood of God: Biblical Theology, Human Faith, and the Divine Image*. Woodstock, VT: Jewish Lights, 2005.

Murphy, Roland E. "A Response to 'The Task of Old Testament Theology.'" Pages 28–32 in R. P. Knierim's *The Task of Old Testament Theology: Substance, Method, and Cases*. Grand Rapids: Eerdmans, 1995.

Na'aman, Nadav. "Criticism over Willful Subjugation to Foreign Rulers: Historiographic Study in the Book of Kings." Pages 63–70 in *Proceedings of the Eleventh World Congress of Jewish Studies: Division A: Bible and Its World*. Edited by D. Assaf. Jerusalem: Magnes, 1993.

Nelson, Richard D. *The Double Redaction of the Deuteronomistic History*. Journal for the Study of the Old Testament Supplement 18. Sheffield: Sheffield Academic Press, 1981.

Nicholson, Ernest W. *Preaching to the Exiles: A Study of the Prose Tradition in the Book of Jeremiah*. Oxford: Blackwell, 1970.

Niditch, Susan. *War in the Hebrew Bible: A Study in the Ethics of Violence*. New York: Oxford University Press, 1993.

Nielsen, Kirsten. "Metaphors and Biblical Theology." Pages 263–73 in *Metaphor in the Hebrew Bible*. Edited by P. van Hecke. Bibliotheca Ephemeridum Theologicarum Lovaniensium 187. Leuven: Leuven University Press/Peeters, 2005.

———. *Yahweh as Prosecutor and Judge: An Investigation of the Prophetic Lawsuit (Rib-Pattern)*. Journal for the Study of the Old Testament Supplement 9. Sheffield: Sheffield Academic Press, 1978.

Noth, Martin. *The Deuteronomistic History*. Journal for the Study of the Old Testament Supplement 15. Sheffield: Sheffield Academic Press, 1981. German original: 1957 (2nd ed.).

———. "The Jerusalem Catastrophe of 587 B.C. and Its Significance for Israel." Pages 260–80 in Noth's *The Laws in the Pentateuch and Other Studies*. Translated by D. R. Ap-Thomas. Edinburgh: Oliver & Boyd, 1966.

Obeyesekere, Gananath. "Theodicy, Sin, and Salvation in a Sociology of Buddhism." Pages 7–40 in *Dialectic in Practical Religion*. Edited by E. R. Leach. Cambridge: Cambridge University Press, 1968.

O'Brien, Mark A. *The Deuteronomistic History Hypothesis: A Reassessment*. Göttingen: Vandenhoeck & Ruprecht, 1989.

O'Connor, Kathleen. *Jeremiah: Pain and Promise*. Minneapolis: Fortress, 2011.

———. *Lamentations and the Tears of the World*. Maryknoll, NY: Orbis, 2002.

Oded, Bustenai. "The Historical Background of the Syro-Ephraimite War Reconsidered." *Catholic Biblical Quarterly* 34 (1972): 153–65.

———. *War, Peace, and Empire: Justifications for War in Assyrian Royal Inscriptions*. Wiesbaden: Reichert, 1992.

———. "When Was the Kingdom of Judah Subjugated to Babylon?" *Tarbiz* 35 (1965): 103–7 (Hebrew).

———. "Where Is the 'Myth of the Empty Land' to Be Found?—History versus Myth." Pages 55–74 in *Judah and the Judeans in the Neo-Babylonian Period*. Edited by O. Lipschits and J. Blenkinsopp. Winona Lake: Eisenbrauns, 2003.

Oeming, Manfred. *Gesamt biblische Theologien der Gegenwart: Das Verhältnis von AT und NT in der hermeneutischen Diskussion seit Gerhard von Rad*. 2nd ed. Stuttgart: Kohlhammer, 1987.

Ollenburger, B. C., E. A. Martens, and G. F. Hasel, eds. *Flowering of Old Testament Theology: A Reader in Twentieth-Century Old Testament Theology, 1930–1990*. Winona Lake: Eisenbrauns, 1992.

Olsson, Tord. "Gudsbild: Talsituation och literature genre." Pages 91–109 in *Aersbok 1983 för Föreningen Lärare i Religionskunskap*. Klippan, 1983.

Ornan, Tallay. "Idols and Symbols: Divine Representation in First Millennium Mesopotamian Art and Its Bearing on the Second Commandment." *Tel Aviv* 31 (2004): 90–121.

———. "In the Likeness of Man: Reflections on the Anthropomorphic Perception of the Divine in Mesopotamian Art." Pages 93–151 in *What Is a God? Anthropomorphic and Non-Anthropomorphic Aspects of Deity in Ancient Mesopotamia*. Edited by B. N. Porter. Winona Lake: Eisenbrauns, 2009.

———. *The Triumph of the Symbol: Pictorial Representation of Deities in Mesopotamia and the Biblical Image Ban*. Orbis Biblicus Orientalis 213. Fribourg: Academic Press/Göttingen: Vandenhoeck & Ruprecht, 2005.

Osswald, Eva. *Falsche Prophetie in Alten Testament*. Tübingen: Mohr, 1962.

Overholt, Thomas W. *Channels of Prophecy: The Social Dynamics of Prophetic Activity*. Minneapolis: Fortress, 1989.

———. "Jeremiah 2 and the Problem of 'Audience Reaction.'" *Catholic Biblical Quarterly* 41 (1979): 262–73.

———. "Jeremiah 27–29: The Question of False Prophecy." *Journal of the American Academy of Religion* 35 (1967): 241–49.

Pannenberg, Wolfhart. "Problems in a Theology of (Only) the Old Testament." Pages 275–80 in *Problems in Biblical Theology: Essays in Honor of Rolf Knierim*. Edited by H. T. C. Sun and K. L. Eades. Grand Rapids: Eerdmans, 1997.

Parpola, Simo. *Assyrian Prophecies.* State Archives of Assyria 9. Helsinki: Helsinki University Press, 1997.

Paul, Shalom M. *Isaiah 40–66.* Eerdmans Critical Commentary. Grand Rapids: Eerdmans, 2012.

Peake, Arthur S. *The Problem of Suffering in the Old Testament.* London: Epworth, 1904.

Peled, Ilan. "A New Manuscript of the Lament for Eridu." *Journal of Cuneiform Studies* 67 (2015): 39–43.

Pepper, Stephen C. *World Hypotheses: A Study of Evidence.* Berkeley: University of California Press, 1972 (originally 1942).

Perdue, Leo G. *Biblical Theology: Introducing the Conversation.* Edited by L. G. Perdue, R. Morgan, and B. D. Sommer. Library of Biblical Theology. Nashville: Abingdon, 2009.

———. *Wisdom in Revolt: Metaphorical Theology in the Book of Job.* Journal for the Study of the Old Testament Supplement 112. Sheffield: Sheffield Academic Press, 1991.

Person, Raymond F. *The Deuteronomic School: History, Social Setting, and Literature.* Studies in Biblical Literature 2. Leiden: Brill, 2002.

Pohlmann, Karl-Friedrich. *Studien zum Jeremiabuches.* Forschungen zur Religion und Literatur des Alten und Neuen Testaments 118. Göttingen: Vandenhoeck & Ruprecht, 1978.

Polliack, Meirah. "The Karaite Inversion of 'Written' and 'Oral' Torah in Relation to the Islamic Arch-Models of Qur'an and Hadith." *Jewish Studies Quarterly* 22 (2015): 243–302.

Porter, Barbara N. "Blessings from a Crown, Offerings to the Drum: Were There Non-Anthropomorphic Deities in Ancient Mesopotamia?" Pages 153–94 in *What Is a God? Anthropomorphic and Non-Anthropomorphic Aspects of Deity in Ancient Mesopotamia.* Edited by B. N. Porter. Winona Lake: Eisenbrauns, 2009.

Porter, Barbara N., ed. *What Is a God? Anthropomorphic and Non-Anthropomorphic Aspects of Deity in Ancient Mesopotamia.* Winona Lake: Eisenbrauns, 2009.

Preminger, Alex, and Terry V. F. Brogan. *The New Princeton Encyclopedia of Poetry and Poetics.* Princeton: Princeton University Press, 1993.

Preuss, Horst. "שָׁכַח *šākaḥ.*" Pages 671–77 in volume 14 of *Theological Dictionary of the Old Testament.* Edited by G. J. Botterweck, H. Ringgren, and H.-J. Fabry. Translated by D. W. Stott. Grand Rapids: Eerdmans, 2004.

Provan, Iain. *Lamentations.* New Century Bible Commentary. Grand Rapids: Eerdmans, 1991.

Quell, Gottfried. *Wahre und falsche Propheten*. Gütersloh: Bertelsmann, 1952.

Raabe, Paul. "Why Prophetic Oracles against the Nations?" Pages 236–57 in *Fortunate the Eyes That See: Essays in Honor of D. N. Freedman in Celebration of His Seventieth Birthday*. Edited by A. B. Beck et al. Grand Rapids: Eerdmans, 1995.

Rad, Gerhard von. "The Deuteronomic Theology of History in I and II Kings." Pages 205–21 in von Rad's *The Problem of the Hexateuch and Other Essays*. Translated by E. W. Trueman Dicken. Edinburgh: Oliver & Boyd, 1966.

———. *Holy War in Ancient Israel*. Translated by M. J. Dawn. Grand Rapids: Eerdmans, 1991. German original: 1951.

———. *Old Testament Theology*. Translated by D. M. G. Stalker. 2 vols. Edinburgh: Harper Collins, 1962. German original: *Theologie des Alten Testament*. 2 vols. 4th ed. Munich: Kaiser, 1958–60.

———. *Studies in Deuteronomy*. Translated by D. M. G. Stalker. London: SCM, 1953.

Raitt, Thomas M. *A Theology of Exile: Judgment/Deliverance in Jeremiah and Ezekiel*. Philadelphia: Fortress, 1977.

Re'emi, S. Paul. *God's People in Crisis: Lamentations*. Edinburgh: Handsel, 1984.

Reimer, David. "Good Grief? A Psychological Reading of Lamentations." *Zeitschrift für die alttestamentliche Wissenschaft* 114 (2002): 542–59.

Reiser, Daniel. *Rabbi Kalonymus Kalman Shapira, Sermons from the Years of Rage: The Sermons of the Piaseczno Rebbe from the Warsaw Ghetto, 1939–1942*. 2 vols. Jerusalem: Herzog Academic College, World Union of Jewish Studies and Yad Vashem, 2017.

Rendtorff, Rolf. *Canon and Theology: Overtures to an Old Testament Theology*. Translated and edited by M. Kohl. Edinburgh: T&T Clark, 1994.

———. "A Christian Approach to the Theology of Hebrew Scriptures." Pages 137–51 in *Jews, Christians, and the Theology of the Hebrew Scriptures*. Edited by A. Ogden Bellis and J. S. Kaminsky. Atlanta: Society of Biblical Literature, 2000.

Renkema, Johan. *Lamentations*. Historical Commentary on the Old Testament. Leuven: Peeters, 1998.

———. "Theodicy in Lamentations?" Pages 410–28 in *Theodicy in the World of the Bible*. Edited by A. Laato and J. C. de Moor. Leiden: Brill, 2003.

Reumann, John. "Whither Biblical Theology?" Pages 1–31 in *The Promise and Practice of Biblical Theology*. Edited by J. Reumann. Minneapolis: Fortress, 1991.

Reumann, John, ed. *The Promise and Practice of Biblical Theology*. Minneapolis: Fortress, 1991.

Reventlow, Henning Graf. *Liturgie und prophetisches Ich bei Jeremia*. Gütersloh: Mohn, 1963.

———. *Problems of Old Testament Theology in the Twentieth Century*. Philadelphia: Fortress, 1985.

Richards, Ivor A. *The Philosophy of Rhetoric*. New York: Oxford University Press, 1965 (originally 1936).

Rofé, Alexander. "The Name YHWH *Ṣĕbā'ôt* and the Shorter Recension of Jeremiah." Pages 307–15 in *Prophetie und geschichtliche Wirklichkeit im alten Israel: Festschrift für Siegfried Herrmann zum 65. Geburtstag*. Edited by R. Liwak und S. Wagner. Stuttgart: Kohlhammer, 1991.

———. *The Prophetical Stories: The Narratives about the Prophets in the Hebrew Bible, Their Literary Types and History*. Translated by D. Levy. Jerusalem: Magnes, 1988.

———. "Studies on the Composition of the Book of Jeremiah." *Tarbiz* 44 (1974–75): 1–29 (Hebrew).

Rom-Shiloni, Dalit. "Actualization of Pentateuchal Legal Traditions in Jeremiah: More on the Riddle of Authorship." *Zeitschrift für altorientalische und biblische Rechtsgeschichte* 15 (2009): 254–81.

———. "Challenging the Notion of 'Spiritual Metamorphosis': Conceptions of Divine Presence and Anthropomorphic Language in Jeremiah." *Hebrew Bible and Ancient Israel* (2021).

———. "Compositional Harmonization: Priestly and Deuteronomic References in Jeremiah—An Earlier Stage of a Recognized Interpretive Technique." Pages 913–42 in *The Formation of the Pentateuch: Bridging the Academic Cultures of Europe, Israel, and North America*. Edited by J. C. Gertz et al. Forschungen zum Alten Testament 111. Tübingen: Mohr Siebeck, 2016.

———. "The Covenant in the Book of Jeremiah: On the Employment of Marital and Political Metaphors." Pages 153–74 in *Covenant in the Persian Period: From Genesis to Chronicles*. Edited by R. J. Bautch and G. N. Knoppers. Winona Lake: Eisenbrauns, 2015.

———. *Exclusive Inclusivity: Identity Conflicts between the Exiles and the People Who Remained (6th–5th Centuries BCE)*. Library of Hebrew Bible/Old Testament Studies 543. New York: Bloomsbury, 2013.

———. "Ezekiel among the Exiles." In *Oxford Handbook of the Book of Ezekiel*. Edited by C. Carvalho. New York: Oxford University Press, 2021.

———. "Ezekiel and Jeremiah: What Might Stand behind the Silence?" *Hebrew Bible and Ancient Israel* 2 (2012): 203–30.

———. "Ezekiel as Voice of the Exiles and Constructor of Exilic Ideology." *Hebrew Union College Annual* 76 (2005): 1–45.

———. "Facing Destruction and Exile: Inner-Biblical Exegesis in Jeremiah and Ezekiel." *Zeitschrift für die alttestamentliche Wissenschaft* 117 (2005): 189–205.

———. "The Forest and the Trees: The Place of Pentateuchal Materials in Prophecy as of the Late Seventh/Early Sixth Centuries BCE." Pages 56–92 in *IOSOT XXII Congress, Stellenbosch, South Africa, 2016*. Edited by C. Maier and L. Jonker. Leiden: Brill, 2017.

———. "From Prophetic Words to Prophetic Literature: Challenging Paradigms That Control Our Academic Thought." *Journal of Biblical Literature* 138.3 (2019): 565–86.

———. *God in Times of Destruction and Exiles: Tanakh (Hebrew Bible) Theology*. Jerusalem: Magnes, 2009 (Hebrew).

———. "Group-Identities in Jeremiah: Is It the Persian Period Conflict?" Pages 11–46 in *A Palimpsest: Rhetoric, Stylistics, and Language in Biblical Texts from the Persian and Hellenistic Periods*. Edited by E. Ben-Zvi, D. Edelman, and F. Polak. Perspectives on Hebrew Scriptures and Its Contexts 5. Piscataway, NJ: Gorgias, 2009.

———. "Hebrew Bible Theology: A Jewish Descriptive Approach." *Journal of Religion* 96 (2016): 165–84.

———. "How Can You Say, 'I Am Not Defiled'" (Jer 2:20–25): Allusions to Priestly Legal Traditions in the Poetry of Jeremiah." *Journal of Biblical Literature* 133 (2014): 757–75.

———. "Introduction: Rethinking the Relationship between the Law and the Prophets." Pages 831–40 in *The Formation of the Pentateuch: Bridging the Academic Cultures of Europe, Israel, and North America*. Edited by J. C. Gertz et al. Forschungen zum Alten Testament 111. Tübingen: Mohr Siebeck, 2016.

———. "'On the Day I Freed Them from the Land of Egypt': A Non-Deuteronomic Phrase within Jeremiah's Covenant Conception." *Vetus Testamentum* 65 (2015): 621–47.

———. "The Prophecy for 'Everlasting Covenant' (Jeremiah 32:36–41): An Exilic Addition or a Deuteronomistic Redaction?" *Vetus Testamentum* 53 (2003): 201–23.

———. "Psalm 44: The Powers of Protest." *Catholic Biblical Quarterly* 70 (2008): 683–98.

———. "Socio-Ideological Setting or Settings for Penitential Prayers?" Pages 51–68 in *Seeking the Favor of God*: vol. 1: *The Origins of Penitential Prayer in Second Temple Judaism*. Edited by M. Boda, D. K. Falk, and R. A. Werline. Early Judaism and Its Literature 21. Atlanta: Society of Biblical Literature, 2006.

———. "Theodical Discourse: Theodicy and Protest in Sixth Century BCE Hebrew Bible Theology." Pages 53–72 in *Theodicy and Protest: Jewish and Christian Perspectives*. Edited by B. Ego et al. Kirche und Israel. Leipzig: Evangelische Verlagsanstalt, 2018.

Rom-Shiloni, Dalit, and Corry L. Carvalho, eds. "The Book of Ezekiel in Its Babylonian Context." Special issue of *Die Welt des Orients* 45.1 (2015).

Römer, Thomas. "The Invention of History in Ancient Judah and the Formation of the Hebrew Bible." *Die Welt des Orients* 45 (2015): 255–72.

Roskies, David G. *Against the Apocalypse: Responses to Catastrophe in Modern Jewish Culture*. Cambridge: Harvard University Press, 1984.

———. *The Literature of Destruction: Jewish Responses to Catastrophe*. Philadelphia: Jewish Publication Society, 1988.

Rudolph, Wilhelm. *Jeremia, Die Klagelieder*. 2nd ed. Kommentar zum Alten Testament 17. Gütersloh: Mohn, 1939, 1962.

Saggs, Henry W. F. *The Encounter with the Divine in Mesopotamia and Israel*. London: Athlone, 1978.

Sakenfeld, Katharine D. *The Meaning of Hesed in the Hebrew Bible: A New Inquiry*. Harvard Semitic Museum. Missoula, MT: Scholars Press, 1978.

Salters, Robert B. "Scepticism in the Old Testament." *Old Testament Essays* 2 (1989): 96–105.

Samet, Nili. *The Lamentation over the Destruction of Ur*. Mesopotamian Civilizations 18. Winona Lake: Eisenbrauns, 2014.

———. "Sumerian City Laments and the Book of Lamentations: Toward a Comparative Theological Study." *Shnaton* 21 (2012): 95–110 (Hebrew).

Sandys-Wunsch, John, and L. Eldredge. "J. P. Gabler and the Distinction between Biblical and Dogmatic Theology: Translation, Commentary, and Discussion of His Originality." *Scottish Journal of Theology* 33 (1980): 133–58.

Sarna, Nahum M. "The Abortive Insurrection in Zedekiah's Day (Jer. 27–29)." *Eretz-Israel* 14 (1978): *79–*96.

———. "Psalm 89: A Study in Inner Biblical Exegesis." Pages 29–46 in *Biblical and Other Studies*. Edited by A. Altman. Cambridge: Harvard University Press, 1963.

Sarot, M. "Theodicy and Modernity." Pages 1–26 in *Theodicy in the World of the Bible*. Edited by A. Laato and J. C. de Moor. Leiden: Brill, 2003.

Schmid, Konrad. *Buchgestalten des Jeremiahbuches: Untersuchungen zur Redaktions- und Rezeptionsgeschichte vor Jer 30–33 im Kontext des Buches*. Wissenschaftliche Monographien zum Alten und Neuen Testament 72. Neukirchen-Vluyn: Neukirchener Verlag, 1996.

———. "The Conquests of Jerusalem 597 BCE and 587 BCE in History and in Biblical Interpretation (2 Kings 24–25)." Pages 81–97 in *Story and History: The Kings of Israel and Judah in Context*. Edited by J. U. Ro. Tübingen: Mohr Siebeck, 2019.

———. *A Historical Theology of the Hebrew Bible*. Translated by P. Altmann. Grand Rapids: Eerdmans, 2019. German original: *Theologie des Alten Testaments*. Tübingen: Mohr Siebeck, 2018.

———. "How to Date the Book of Jeremiah: Combining and Modifying Linguistic- and Profile-Based Approaches." *Vetus Testamentum* 68 (2018): 1–30.

———. *Is There Theology in the Hebrew Bible?* Translated by P. Altmann. Critical Studies in the Hebrew Bible 4. Winona Lake: Eisenbrauns, 2015. German original: *Gibt es Theologie im Alten Testament? Zum Theologiebegriff in der alttestamentlichen Wissenschaft*. Zurich: Theologischer Verlag, 2013.

———. "Jeremiah." Pages 431–50 in *T&T Clark Handbook of the Old Testament: An Introduction to the Literature, Religion, and History of the Old Testament*. Edited by J. C. Gertz et al. Translated by J. Adams-Massmann. London: T&T Clark, 2012.

Schunck, Klaus. "כָּחַשׁ *kāḥaš*." Pages 132–35 in volume 7 of *Theological Dictionary of the Old Testament*. Edited by G. J. Botterweck, H. Ringgren, and H.-J. Fabry. Translated by D. E. Green. Grand Rapids: Eerdmans, 1995.

Schwally, Friedrich. *Der heilige Krieg im alten Israel*. Semitische Kriegsaltertümer 1. Leipzig: Dietrich, 1901.

Schwartz, Baruch J. "The Bearing of Sin in the Priestly Literature." Pages 3–21 in *Pomegranates and Golden Bells: Studies in Biblical, Jewish, and Near Eastern Ritual, Law, and Literature in Honor of Jacob Milgrom*. Edited by D. P. Wright, D. N. Freedman, and A. Hurvitz. Winona Lake: Eisenbrauns, 1995.

———. "Ezekiel's Dim View of Israel's Restoration." Pages 43–68 in *The Book of Ezekiel: Theological and Anthropological Perspectives*. Edited by M. S. Odell and J. T. Strong. Society of Biblical Literature Symposium 9. Atlanta: Society of Biblical Literature, 2000.

Schweid, Eliezer. *To Declare That God Is Upright: Theodicy in Jewish Thought.* Bat Yam: Tag, 1994 (Hebrew).

Seebass, Horst. "נֶפֶשׁ *nepeš.*" Pages 497–518 in volume 9 of *Theological Dictionary of the Old Testament.* Edited by G. J. Botterweck, H. Ringgren, and H.-J. Fabry. Translated by D. E. Green. Grand Rapids: Eerdmans, 1998.

Seeligmann, Isaac L. "Human Heroism and Divine Salvation—Double Causality in Biblical Historiography." Pages 62–81 In Seeligmann's *Studies in Biblical Literature.* Translated by R. Blum. Jerusalem: Magnes, 1992 (Hebrew). German original: 1963.

Seitz, Christopher R. *Isaiah 1–39.* Interpretation. Louisville: John Knox, 1993.

———. *Theology in Conflict: Reactions to the Exile in the Book of Jeremiah.* Beihefte zur Zeitschrift für die alttestamentliche Wissenschaft 176. Berlin: de Gruyter, 1989.

Sellin, Ernst. *Introduction to the Old Testament.* Revised by G. Fohrer. Translated by D. E. Green. New York: Abingdon, 1968.

Selms, Adrianus van. "Motivated Interrogative Sentences in Biblical Hebrew." *Semitics* 2 (1971–72): 143–49.

Seybold, Klaus. "מֶלֶךְ *melek.*" Pages 346–75 in volume 8 of *Theological Dictionary of the Old Testament.* Edited by G. J. Botterweck, H. Ringgren, and H.-J. Fabry. Translated by D. W. Stott. Grand Rapids: Eerdmans, 1997.

Sharp, Carolyn J. *Prophecy and Ideology in Jeremiah: Struggles for Authority in the Deutero-Jeremianic Prose.* Old Testament Studies. London: T&T Clark, 2003.

Simian-Yofre, H. "רחם *rḥm.*" Pages 437–54 in volume 13 of *Theological Dictionary of the Old Testament.* Edited by G. J. Botterweck, H. Ringgren, and H.-J. Fabry. Translated by D. E. Green. Grand Rapids: Eerdmans, 2004.

Sisson, Jonathan P. "Jeremiah and the Jerusalem Conception of Peace." *Journal of Biblical Literature* 105 (1986): 429–42.

Skinner, John. *Prophecy and Religion: Studies in the Life of Jeremiah.* Cambridge: Cambridge University Press, 1922.

Smend, Rudolf. "Das Gesetz und die Völker: Ein Beitrag zur deuteronomistischen Redaktiongeschichte." Pages 494–509 in *Probleme biblischer Theologie: Gerhard von Rad zum 70. Geburtstag.* Edited by H. W. Wolff. Munich: Kaiser, 1971.

———. *From Astruc to Zimmerli: Old Testament Scholarship in Three Centuries.* Translated by M. Kohl. Tübingen: Mohr Siebeck, 2007.

———. *Yahweh War and Tribal Confederation: Reflections upon Israel's Earliest History.* Translated by M. G. Rogers. Nashville: Abingdon, 1970. German original: 1963.

Smith, John M. P. *Micah, Zephaniah, and Nahum.* International Critical Commentary. Edinburgh: T&T Clark, 1911.

Smith, Mark S. *The Origins of Biblical Monotheism: Israel's Polytheistic Background and the Ugaritic Texts.* New York: Oxford University Press, 2001.

———. "Ugaritic Anthropomorphism, Theomorphism, Theriomorphism." Pages 117–40 in *Göttliche Körper—Göttliche Gefühle. Was leisten anthropomorphe und anthropopathische Götterkonzepte im Alten Orient und Alten Testament.* Edited by A. Wagner. Orbis Biblicus Orientalis 270. Fribourg: Academic Press/Göttingen: Vandenhoeck & Ruprecht, 2014.

Smith, Ralph L. *Old Testament Theology: Its History, Method, and Message.* Nashville: Broadman & Holman, 1993.

Smith-Christopher, David L. *A Biblical Theology of Exile.* Overtures to Biblical Theology. Minneapolis: Augsburg Fortress, 2002.

———. "Reading War and Trauma: Suggestions toward a Social-Psychological Exegesis of Exile and War in Biblical Texts." Pages 253–74 in *Interpreting Exile: Displacement and Deportation in Biblical and Modern Contexts.* Edited by B. Kelle, F. R. Ames, and J. L. Wright. Ancient Israel and Its Literature 10. Atlanta: Society of Biblical Literature, 2011.

———. *The Religion of the Landless: The Social Context of the Babylonian Exile.* Bloomington: Meyer Stone, 1989.

Soden, Wolfram von. *Akkadisches Handwörterbuch.* 3 vols. Wiesbaden: Harrassowitz, 1965–81.

Sommer, Benjamin D. *The Bodies of God and the World of Ancient Israel.* Cambridge: Cambridge University Press, 2009.

———. "Dialogical Biblical Theology: A Jewish Approach to Reading Scripture Theologically." Pages 1–53 in *Biblical Theology: Introducing the Conversation.* By Leo G. Perdue, Robert Morgan, Benjamin D. Sommer. Library of Biblical Theology. New York: Abingdon, 2009.

———. *A Prophet Reads Scripture: Allusion in Isaiah 40–66.* Contraversions. Stanford: Stanford University Press, 1998.

———. "Revelation at Sinai in the Hebrew Bible and in Jewish Theology." *Journal of Religion* 79 (1999): 422–51.

Soskice, Janet M. *Metaphor and Religious Language.* Oxford: Clarendon, 1985.

Steck, Odil Hannes. *The Prophetic Books and Their Theological Witness.* Translated by J. Nogalski. St. Louis: Chalice, 2000.

Stendahl, Krister. "Biblical Theology, Contemporary." Pages 418–32 in volume 1 of *The Interpreter's Dictionary of the Bible.* Edited by G. A. Buttrick. New York: Abingdon, 1962.

Stipp, Hermann J. "'But into the Water You Must Not Dip It' (Jeremiah 13:1): Methodological Reflections on How to Identify the Work of Deuteronomistic Redaction in the Book of Jeremiah." Pages 167–95 in *Thinking of Water in the Early Second Temple Period*. Edited by E. Ben Zvi and C. Levin. Berlin: de Gruyter, 2014.

———. "The Concept of the Empty Land in Jeremiah 37–43." Pages 103–54 in *The Concept of Exile*. Edited by E. Ben Zvi and C. Levin. Berlin: de Gruyter, 2010.

———. "Das judäische und das babylonische Jeremiabuch: Zur Frage der Heimat der deuteronomischen Redaktionen des Jeremiabuchs." Pages 239–64 in *IOSOT XIX Congress Volume Ljubljana, 2007*. Edited by A. Lemaire. Vetus Testamentum Supplement 133. Leiden: Brill, 2010. Reprinted as pages 325–49 in Stipp's *Studien sum Jeremiabuch: Text und Redaktion*. Forschungen zum Alten Testament 96. Tübingen: Mohr Siebeck, 2015.

———. "Offene Fragen zur Übersetzungskritik des antiken griechischen Jeremiabuches." *Journal of Northwest Semitic Languages* 17 (1991): 117–28.

———. "Probleme des redaktionsgeschichtlichen Modells der Entstehung des Jeremiabuches." Pages 225–62 in *Jeremia und die "deuteronomistische Bewegung."* Edited by Walter Gross. Weinheim: Beltz Athenäum, 1995.

———. "Sprachliche Kennzeichen jeremianischer Autorschaft." Pages 148–86 in *Prophecy in the Book of Jeremiah*. Edited by H. M. Barstad and R. G. Kratz. Beihefte zur Zeitschrift für die alttestamentliche Wissenschaft 388. Berlin: de Gruyter, 2009.

Stolz, Fritz. *Jahwes und Israels Kriege: Kriegstheorien und Kriegserfahrungen im Glauben des alten Israels*. Abhandlungen zur Theologie des Alten und Neuen Testaments 60. Zürich: Theologischer Verlag, 1972.

Strawn, Brent A. *What Is Stronger than a Lion? Leonine Image and Metaphor in the Hebrew Bible and the Ancient Near East*. Orbis Biblicus Orientalis 212. Göttingen: Academic Press/Fribourg: Vandenhoeck & Ruprecht, 2005.

Strong, John. "God's *Kabod*: The Presence of Yahweh in the Book of Ezekiel." Pages 69–95 in *The Book of Ezekiel: Theological and Anthropological Perspectives*. Edited by M. S. Odell and J. T. Strong. Atlanta: Society of Biblical Literature, 2000.

Sutcliffe, Edmund F. "A Note on לא הוא Jer 5,12." *Biblica* 41 (1960): 287–90.

Sweeney, Marvin A. "King Manasseh of Judah and the Problem of Theodicy in the Deuteronomistic History." Pages 264–78 in *Good Kings and Bad Kings*. Edited by L. L. Grabbe. Library of Hebrew Bible/Old Testament Studies 393. London: T&T Clark, 2005.

———. *Reading the Hebrew Bible after the Shoah: Engaging Holocaust Theology*. Minneapolis: Fortress, 2008.

———. *Tanak: A Theological and Critical Introduction to the Jewish Bible*. Minneapolis: Fortress, 2012.

———. "Tanakh versus Old Testament: Concerning the Foundation for a Jewish Theology of the Bible." Pages 353–72 in *Problems in Biblical Theology*. Edited by H. Sun and K. L. Eades. Grand Rapids: Eerdmans, 1997.

———. "Why Jews Should Be Interested in Biblical Theology." *Central Conference of American Rabbis Journal* 44 (1997): 67–75.

———. *Zephaniah*. Hermeneia. Minneapolis: Fortress, 2003.

Tadmor, Hayim. "Ahaz and Tiglath-Pileser in the Book of Kings: Historiographic Considerations." *Biblica* 60 (1979): 491–508.

———. "Sennacherib's Campaign to Judah: Historical and Historiographical Considerations." *Zion* 50 (1986): 65–80 (Hebrew).

———. *"With My Many Chariots I Have Gone up the Heights of the Mountains": Historical and Literary Studies on Ancient Mesopotamia and Israel*. Edited by M. Cogan. Translated by M. Feinberg-Vamosh. Jerusalem: Israel Exploration Society, 2011.

Talmon, Shemaryahu. "YHWH's Wars." Pages 1064–65 in *Encyclopedia Mikra'it*. Jerusalem: Bialik, 1963 (Hebrew).

Talshir, Zipora. "The Three Deaths of Josiah and the Strata of Biblical Historiography (2 Kings xxiii 29–30: 2 Chronicles xxxv 20–5; 1 Esdras i 23–31)." *Vetus Testamentum* 46 (1996): 213–36.

Tanner, Beth L. *The Book of Psalms through the Lens of Intertextuality*. Studies in Biblical Literature 26. New York: Peter Lang, 2001.

Tate, Marvin E. *Psalms 51–100*. Word Biblical Commentary 20. Waco: Nelson, 1990.

Thiel, Winfried. *Die deuteronomistische Redaktion von Jeremia 1–25*. Wissenschaftliche Monographien zum Alten und Neuen Testament 41. Neukirchen-Vluyn: Neukirchener Verlag, 1973.

———. *Die deuteronomistische Redaktion von Jeremia 26–52: Mit einer Gesamtbeurteilung der deuteronomistischen Redaktion des Buches Jeremia*. Wissenschaftliche Monographien zum Alten und Neuen Testament 52. Neukirchen-Vluyn: Neukirchener Verlag, 1981.

Thompson, Michael E. W. *Situation and Theology: Old Testament Interpretations of the Syro-Ephraimite War*. Sheffield: Almond, 1982.

Tinney, Steve. *The Nippur Lament: Royal Rhetoric and Divine Legitimation in the Reign of Ishme-Dagan of Isin (1953–1935 B.C.)*. Occasional Publications of the Samuel Noah Kramer Fund 16. Philadelphia: University Museum, 1996.

Toorn, Karel van der. *Scribal Culture and the Making of the Hebrew Bible.* Cambridge: Harvard University Press, 2007.

———. "Theodicy in Akkadian Literature." Pages 57–89 in *Theodicy in the World of the Bible.* Edited by A. Laato and J. C. de Moor. Leiden: Brill, 2003.

Toorn, Karel van der, ed. *The Image and the Book: Iconic Cults, Aniconism, and the Rise of Book Religion in Israel and the Ancient Near East.* Contributions to Biblical Exegesis and Theology 21. Leuven: Peeters, 1997.

Torrey, Charles, C. *Pseudo-Ezekiel and the Original Prophecy, and Critical Articles.* New York: Ktav, 1970.

Tov, Emanuel. "The Jeremiah Scrolls from Qumran." *Revue de Qumran* 14 (1989): 189–206.

Tsevat, Matitiahu. "God and the Gods in Assembly." *Hebrew Union College Annual* 40–41 (1969–70): 123–37.

———. "Theology of the Old Testament: A Jewish View." *Horizons in Biblical Theology* 8.2 (1986): 33–50.

Uffenheimer, Benjamin. "Biblical Theology and Monotheistic Mythology." Pages 79–94 in *Proceedings of the Eighth World Congress of Jewish Studies, Panel Sessions: Bible Studies and Hebrew Language.* Jerusalem: World Union of Jewish Studies, 1981.

———. "On Drought [Jeremiah 14:1–15:1]." Pages 33–51 in volume 5 of *Hagut BaMikra.* Tel Aviv: Am Oved, 1978 (Hebrew).

Van Seters, John. "In the Babylonian Exile with J: Between Judgment in Ezekiel and Salvation in Second Isaiah." Pages 71–89 in *The Crisis of Israelite Religion: Transformation of Religious Tradition in Exilic and Post-Exilic Times.* Edited by B. Becking and M. C. A. Korpel. Old Testament Studies 42. Leiden: Brill, 1999.

Vanderhooft, David S. "Ezekiel in and on Babylon." Pages 99–119 in *Bible et Proche-Orient: Mélanges André Lemaire.* Edited by J. M. Durand and J. Elayi. Transeuphratene 46. Paris: Gabalda, 2014.

———. *The Neo-Babylonian Empire and Babylon in the Latter Prophets.* Harvard Semitic Monograph 59. Atlanta: Scholars Press, 1999.

Volz, Paul. *Der Prophet Jeremia.* 2nd ed. Kommentar zum Alten Testament 10. Leipzig: Scholl, 1928.

Waltke, Bruce K., and Charles Yu. *An Old Testament Theology: An Exegetical, Canonical, and Thematic Approach.* Grand Rapids: Eerdmans, 2007.

Wanke, Gunther. *Untersuchungen zur sogenannten Baruchschrift.* Beihefte zur Zeitschrift für die alttestamentliche Wissenschaft 122. Berlin: de Gruyter, 1971.

Ward, James M. "The Literary Form and Liturgical Background of Psalm lxxxix." *Vetus Testamentum* 11 (1961): 321–29.

Watts, John D. W. *Isaiah 1–33*. Word Biblical Commentary 24. Waco: Word, 1985.

Weinfeld, Moshe. *Deuteronomy 1–11*. Anchor Bible 5. Garden City, NY: Doubleday, 1991.

———. *Deuteronomy and the Deuteronomic School*. 2nd ed. Winona Lake: Eisenbrauns, 1992 (originally 1972).

———. "Jeremiah and the Spiritual Metamorphosis in Israel." *Zeitschrift für die alttestamentliche Wissenschaft* 88 (1976): 17–56.

———. *Justice and Righteousness in Israel and the Nations*. Jerusalem: Magnes, 1985 (Hebrew).

———. "כָּבוֹד *kābôd*." Pages 22–38 in volume 7 of *Theological Dictionary of the Old Testament*. Edited by G. J. Botterweck, H. Ringgren, and H.-J. Fabry. Translated by D. E. Green. Grand Rapids: Eerdmans, 1995.

Weippert, Helga. *Die Prosareden des Jeremiabuches*. Beihefte zur Zeitschrift für die alttestamentliche Wissenschaft 132. Berlin: de Gruyter, 1973.

Weippert, Manfred. "'Heiliger Krieg' in Israel und Assyrien." *Zeitschrift für die alttestamentliche Wissenschaft* 84 (1972): 460–93.

Weiser, Artur. *The Psalms*. Translated by H. Hartwell. Old Testament Library. Philadelphia: Westminster, 1962. German original: *Die Psalmen*. 5th ed. Göttingen: Vandenhoeck & Ruprecht, 1959.

Weiss, Meir. *The Bible from Within: The Method of Total Interpretation*. Translated by B. J. Schwartz. Jerusalem: Magnes: 1984.

———. *Ideas and Beliefs in the Book of Psalms*. Jerusalem: Bialik, 2001 (Hebrew).

———. *Scriptures in Their Own Light: Collected Essays*. Jerusalem: Bialik, 1988 (Hebrew).

Wellhausen, Julius. *Prolegomena to the History of Israel*. Translated by J. S. Black and A. Menzies. Edinburgh: A&C Black, 1885. Reprinted 1994.

Werblowsky, Raphael J. Z. "Anthropomorphism." Pages 316–20 in volume 1 of *The Encyclopedia of Religion*. Edited by M. Eliade. 14 vols. London: Macmillan, 1987.

Werline, Rodney A. *Penitential Prayer in Second Temple Judaism: The Development of a Religious Institution*. Early Judaism and Its Literature 13. Atlanta: Scholars Press, 1998.

Wessels, Wilhelm J. "Zion, Beautiful City of God—Zion Theology in the Book of Jeremiah." *Verbum et Ecclesia* 27 (2006): 729–40.

Westermann, Claus. *Basic Forms of Prophetic Speech*. Translated by H. C. White. Philadelphia: Westminster, 1967. German original: 1960.

———. *Lamentations: Issues and Interpretation*. Translated by C. Muenchow. Minneapolis: Fortress, 1994. German original: 1990.

———. *Praise and Lament in the Psalms*. Translated by K. R. Crim and R. N. Soulen. Atlanta: John Knox, 1981.

———. "The Role of the Lament in the Theology of the Old Testament." *Interpretation* 28 (1974): 20–38.

———. *What Does the Old Testament Say about God?* London: SPCK, 1979.

Whitley, Charles F. *The Exilic Age*. Westport, CT: Greenwood, 1975 (originally 1957).

Wilson, Robert R. *Prophecy and Society in Ancient Israel*. Philadelphia: Fortress, 1980.

Winitzer, Avraham. "Assyriology and Jewish Studies in Tel Aviv: Ezekiel among the Babylonian Literati." Pages 163–216 in *Encounters by the Rivers of Babylon: Scholarly Conversations between Jews, Iranians, and Babylonians in Antiquity*. Edited by U. Gabbay and S. Secunda. Texte und Studien zum antiken Judentum 160. Tübingen: Mohr Siebeck, 2014.

Winton Thomas, David. "The Sixth Century BC: A Creative Epoch in the History of Israel." *Journal of Semitic Studies* 6 (1961): 33–46.

Wolde, Ellen J. van. "The God Ezekiel Envisions." Pages 87–106 in *The God Ezekiel Creates*. Edited by P. M. Joyce and D. Rom-Shiloni. Library of Hebrew Bible/Old Testament Studies 607. London: Bloomsbury, 2015.

Wolff, Hans W. *Das Zitat im Prophetenspruch: Eine Studie zur prophetischen Verkündigungsweise*. Beiheft zur evangelischen Theologie 4. Munich: Kaiser, 1937. Reprinted in Wolff's *Gesammelte Studien zum Alten Testament*. Theologische Bücherei 22. Munich: Kaiser, 1964.

Yaron, Reuven. "The Meaning of *Zanah*." *Vetus Testamentum* 13 (1963): 237–39.

Zakovitz, Yair. *Song of Songs*. Mikra Le-Israel. Jerusalem: Magnes/Tel Aviv: Am Oved, 1992 (Hebrew).

Zevit, Zioni. "Jewish Biblical Theology: Whence? Why? Whither?" *Hebrew Union College Annual* 76 (2005): 289–340.

Zimmerli, Walther. *Ezekiel*. 2 vols. Translated by R. E. Clements and J. D. Martin. Hermeneia. Philadelphia: Fortress, 1979–83.

———. *Old Testament Theology in Outline*. Translated by D. E. Green. Atlanta: John Knox, 1978.

———. "Visionary Experience in Jeremiah." Pages 95–118 in *Israel's Prophetic Tradition: Essays in Honour of Peter R. Ackroyd*. Edited by R. Coggins, A. Phillips, and M. Knibb. Cambridge: Cambridge University Press, 1982.

Zobel, Hans. "חֶסֶד ḥesed." Pages 44–64 in volume 5 of *Theological Dictionary of the Old Testament*. Edited by G. J. Botterweck and H. Ringgren. Translated by D. E. Green. Grand Rapids: Eerdmans, 1986.

Index of Modern Authors

513

Index of Subjects

Ahaz, king, 105n80, 184, 185
Ammonites, 284, 309, 311
ancient Near East, 214; gods, 18n31, 130–32, 135, 146n61, 239, 291–92, 300–301, 309–11, 324n137; judgment, 288–92, 298, 335n3
aniconism, 136; ancient Near Eastern religions, 132–33, 138n36; Hebrew Bible, 134, 135–36, 137
anthropomorphisms, 123; ancient Near Eastern gods, 130–33, 135, 136–37, 146n61; body of God, 134–36, 152–55, 433, 460–61; conception of God, 123, 138, 452; definitions, 131n7, 146n51, 150; God as king, 158–64; in the Hebrew Bible, 133–38, 139–40, 149–52; as metaphor, 4, 82–83, 146–52, 452; monotheistic belief, 145–46; in prophetic books, 139–44, 146, 152–55, 156–58; religious thought development, 138–44, 149n73
appeals to God, 92, 103–4, 106–7, 155–56, 199–200, 220–21, 294n55
Assyria, Assyrian, 18n31, 177n4, 335n6, 345n1. *See also* Neo-Assyrian Empire
atonement, 373, 424, 441
authorial settings, 85–87

Babylonian Empire. *See* Neo-Babylonian Empire
Babylonian exile. *See* exile, Babylonian; Jehoiachin exiles
Babylonian gods, 178–79, 310–11. *See also* Mesopotamian religion

benevolence, 17, 154, 156, 300, 335–36, 342–43, 365–67; eternal commitment, 424–27, 428–29, 430–32, 442–43
Bible. *See* Hebrew Bible/Old Testament
biblical theology, 42–46, 49–50, 52, 56–61; Christian, 43–47, 48–49, 56–58, 60, 68–69, 73–75, 151, 450–51; descriptive, 56–58, 62–63, 65–66, 73–76, 122–23, 451; dialogical, 52–53, 56, 58
birds, 286, 294–95
body of God, 134–36, 152–55, 433, 460–61; face, 153–55, 433, 460–61; hand, arm, 152–53

Canaan, Canaanites, 132, 202n17; king, God as metaphor, 161–63, 164, 165, 167
Carmel, the, 296–98
Catholic biblical theology, 44
Christian, Christianity, 38; biblical theology, 43–47, 48–49, 56–58, 60, 68–69, 73–75, 151, 450–51; Catholic, 44, 68n88, 71; Judaism and, 70–72; lament, 20–23; Protestant, 42, 44, 50n30, 53, 66, 68, 71, 78; supersessionism, 46n14, 49, 57n53, 68, 74
communal laments, 213, 457; appeals to God, 92, 103–4, 106–7, 155–56, 199–200, 220–21, 294n55; confession of sin, 27–28, 33, 37, 216, 328–29, 332, 352–53, 364, 376–79, 392; destruction of Judah, 165–68, 201–2, 215–18, 265–66, 288, 314; doubt, 430–33; God as enemy, 317–19, 338; God as judge, 339–42, 343, 423; in Lamentations, 376–77, 378–79;

Index of Scripture and Other Ancient Texts